THE COMPLETE HISTORY OF
GRAND PRIX

MOTOR RACING

Adriano Cimarosti

CRESCENT BOOKS
New York

Editor: David McKinney

Dedicated to my wife Donotella and our son Arrigo

Frontispiece
The start of the 100-mile race
on the new brick track in
Indianapolis in 1909. Two years
later this was the venue for the
first of the famous 500-mile
races. No. 34, a Buick, won in
1909.

Previous double page photo
The Williams FW11-Honda, as
driven by Nigel Mansell and
Nelson Piquet, won the 1986
Formula One Manufacturers'
Trophy.

Cover picture
The Camel Lotus at Monaco.

This United States edition published in 1990 by
Crescent Books, distributed by Crown Publishers,
Inc., 225 Park Avenue South, New York 10003, in
association with David Bateman, Auckland, New
Zealand and Hallwag AG, Bern, Switzerland.

© 1986 Hallwag AG, Bern
© English translation, David Bateman Ltd

Printed and bound in Singapore
Production: Paul Bateman
Jacket design: Errol McLeary
ISBN 0-517-69709-2

hgfedcba

Contents

Contents

Start of the 1963 Dutch Grand Prix.

MY THANKS

go to the following people who have
helped me with pictures, drawings,
technical data and other relevant material:

Giovanni Cavara, Carignano
Cesare De Agostini, Mantova
Ing. Dott. h. c. Enzo Ferrari, Maranello
Georges Gédovius, St-Denis-d'Oléron
Carl Imber, Laufen
Conte Ing. Dott. Giovanni Lurani, Cernusco
Giorgio Piola, Santa Margherita
Franco Villani, Villanova di Castenaso
Franco Zagari, Budrio

All Photographs

and pictures which are not from the
Automobil Revue archives have been supplied
by the following photographers and
agencies:

Jesse Alexander, Santa Barbara
Werner Bernet, Zürich
Bernard Cahier, Evian
DPPI, Levallois-Perret
Werner Eisele, Stuttgart
Carl Imber, Laufen
International Press Agency, Geneva
Federico B. Kirbus, Buenos Aires
Rodolfo Mailander, Turin
Günther Molter, Stuttgart
Joseph and Daniel Reinhard, Sachseln
Kurt Wörner, Bernbach
Franco Zagari, Budrio
David Phipps, Norfolk

Archive Pictures

Cesare De Agostini, Mantova
Indianapolis Motor Speedway, Indianapolis
Charles G. Proche, Long Beach
Franco Zagari, Budrio

Pictures from Automobile Factories

Alfa Romeo, BMW, Daimler-Benz, Fiat,
Ford, Matra, Peugeot, Porsche and Renault

Drawings

Anglia Art, London
Etienne-Bernard Becker, Marseille
Giovanni Cavara, Carignano
Georges Gédovius, St-Denis-d'Oléron
Christian Hoefer, Fellbach
London Art Tech, London
Theo Page, Beckenried
Giorgio Piola, Santa Margherita

Drawings from Automobile Factories

Alfa Romeo, BMW, Daimler-Benz, Fiat,
Ford, March, Matra, Porsche and Renault

Foreword

Numerous books have been written on motor racing and they all bear witness to its great popularity as a sport. This work deserves special mention because it gives both an all encompassing chronological overview of the historical and technological development of motor racing and because it is written by a professional journalist who is recognised as an expert in his field. The author is a connoisseur of the sport in all its ramifications. I have known Adriano Cimarosti personally for years; he has often visited my home country, Argentina, to attend different international races. I have often had the opportunity to have interesting and fruitful discussions with "Cima", as his friends call him, on the most varied aspects of the sport which is so dear to us both. He has impressed me with his excellent knowledge of his subject and his serious professional involvement.

I have therefore followed the development of this book with great interest. It contains everything that characterises motor racing: not only does it describe the great events but also goes behind the scenes and describes many small peripheral happenings. This book reflects everything that has happened in motor racing since 1894 right up to the present. The author presents a clear and precise report which will first of all be of particular interest to all those who have viewed racing only from the outside and have not had any direct contact with the complex and fascinating world of this sport which is the highest and clearest expression of our epoch — the age of the motorcar.

Juan Manuel Fangio, World Champion in 1951, 1954, 1955, 1956, and 1957.

Introduction

Every year, from all over the world, hundreds of thousands of spectators are attracted to the Grand Prix circuits and many millions more follow the action on their television sets. Formula One motor racing has the widest public following of any sport and it is no wonder that for the past 20 years and more it has been a focal point for the advertising industry. It was never a cheap sport, but today it is immensely expensive and it has to attract huge sums of money from sponsors in order to support its high-technology infrastructure.

But some things never change, and as always it is the performance of the driver and his car on the track which provides the attraction — the battle, from the moment the green starting light is switched on until eventually the chequered flag is waved, to prove which is the winning combination of man and machine and who will take the top place on the victory rostrum.

I saw my first race on June 8th 1947. It was the Swiss Grand Prix on the Bremgarten circuit in Berne. Since that eventful day I have been obsessed not only by contemporary motor racing but also by the history of this exciting sport. Studying the many magazines, books and documents from earlier eras can give you the feeling that somehow you have missed out. How wonderful it must have been to have witnessed events such as the Paris-Rouen run for "horseless carriages" in 1894 when those fragile machines with their tall wheels and, by later standards, feeble performance fought for the prize offered by *Le Petit Journal*; or to have been at Le Mans in 1906 when that first Grand Prix was run by the *Automobile Club de France* and to have seen Szisz and his amazing Renault cross the finishing line after a two-day ordeal totalling 1236km with blood all over his hands. Those were heroic times!

If only one could have been at the ACF Grand Prix near Lyons on July 5th 1914, when Lautenschlager in a Mercedes and Boillot in a Peugeot fought their exciting duel; or watched the 1920s races between Fiat and Sunbeam, Alfa Romeo and Delage, or Bugatti and Maserati, races which created such intense interest and excitement. Perhaps those where the best times? Or was it the second half of the 1930s, the era of the all-powerful Mercedes-Benz and Auto Union teams?

Some contemporary racing enthusiasts feel that the days of the 2.5-litre formula from 1954 to 1960 were the best. In those days the cars, still mostly front-engined, were painted in national colours rather than the colours of their sponsors as is the case today. Those people will tell you that the cars

from that period represented the ultimate in classic design. But enthusiasts for the present era far outnumber them. Today's racing cars, with their sophisticated carbon-fibre chassis and body structures and 3.5-litre engines delivering between 600 and 700bhp, are brimful of technical interest and in their way as difficult to drive as any of their predecessors.

It is impossible to say who has been the best driver of all time because one cannot make true comparisons from different epochs. Each driver had his own aura and each car revealed a certain stage of technical advancement relevant to its era. But no period of Grand Prix racing lacked its star performers who did so much to swell the crowds.

Most motor racing books are limited to a certain period of time, sometimes just one season, or to an individual driver or make of car, but in this book I have striven to provide the entire history of Grand Prix racing in chronological order from the turn of the century to today. In doing so I have singled out for special mention all the races and cars which played a major role in that history as well as the people — drivers as well as those behind the scenes — who made a significant contribution to the progress of the sport.

My researches drew me towards numerous publications, supporting information and documents, but in particular to the articles printed in *Automobile Revue*, which has been in existence since 1906 (making it as long-established as Grand Prix racing itself) and is published today by Hallwag Verlag in Berne. Throughout the book I have stressed the importance of the technical side of the history of the sport and I hope that this will give the reader a clearer understanding of the spectacular technological advances which have been made through Grand Prix racing, many of which have filtered through to the design and construction of more efficient and safer road cars for the benefit of all drivers and their passengers.

Many manufacturers consider motor racing to be an integral part of their research and development programmes, while for others the sport is used primarily to promote the sale of their products. Although governments are applying ever stricter standards around the world to ensure that cars pollute the atmosphere as little as possible, the privately owned car remains surely the greatest toy of the century, while the racing car will continue to represent the epitome of achievement by the latest in automobile technology.

Motor racing, of course, also has its darker side,

and many drivers have died during their pursuit of the sport; I knew of a number of them personally including some who were good friends. Thankfully, safety standards have improved dramatically over the years and will continue to do so, although unfortunately the fatal accident can never be eliminated altogether.

Because Grand Prix racing is the pinnacle of the sport it tends to attract the best people, both on and off the track. Throughout the years covered by this book there have been some mighty achievers, people who set new standards and then went on to improve on them time and time again. They are part of motor racing's heritage, and no-one stands higher in the memory of most racing enthusiasts than the sport's illustrious patriarch, Enzo Ferrari, who died in Modena during 1988 as I was preparing the late pages of this book. He was a legend many years before his long life drew to an end, whose name, black prancing horse emblem and distinctive scarlet cars became the ultimate symbols of Italian engineering excellence, style, craftsmanship and performance. His association with motor racing spanned more than 60 years and involved three notable eras — first as racing driver, then as team manager and finally as a car constructor in his own right — in a remarkable lifetime of immense dedication, strong passion, uncompromising ideals and great achievement... qualities which epitomize all that is best in Grand Prix racing.

Adriano Cimarosti

The cockpit of the
1956 Maserati 250F

**Double page
overleaf**
In the years between
the wars the Targa
Florio was held in
Sicily. Pictured here is
Achille Varzi driving an
Alfa Romeo P2 to
victory in the 1930
race.

The First Motor Races

The first races for horseless carriages are held in France, where an active and enthusiastic motorsport movement develops. Paris is its centre. The races are mostly run from one town to another.

The motor car was born towards the end of the last century following a number of inventions patented in a variety of European countries. France celebrated the motor car's centenary in 1984, England in 1985 and Germany in 1986, and these three, together with the United States, must share the credit for making the car a viable commercial proposition, and for creating a substantial industry to back it.

But although the German products built by Daimler and Benz led the way technically, it was in France alone that the sport of motor racing began.

What is traditionally regarded as the world's first motoring competition was not a race, but the type of event which

Pierre Giffard

would later come to be termed a reliability trial. The event was announced on December 19th 1893 by Pierre Giffard, publisher of the Paris newspaper *Le Petit Journal*, and its rules required competitors to cover the 126km between Paris and Rouen on the day specified, July 22nd 1894, within eight and a half hours. The first prize (5000 francs) would be awarded to the entrant whose "horseless carriage" was considered to have displayed the best combination of safety, economy and ease of handling. By the time entries closed, no fewer than 102 competitors had submitted their names. That petrol engines had by no means gained universal acceptance by this time can be judged by the fact that among the entries were cars powered by steam, electricity and kerosene as well as petrol.

A large proportion of the vehicles originally entered did not even pass the inspection test, after which only 25 in fact remained. Another four machines were eliminated in a preliminary test held on July 19th.

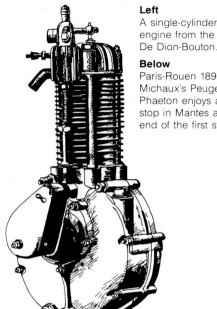

Left
A single-cylinder engine from the 1898 De Dion-Bouton.

Below
Paris-Rouen 1894. Michaux's Peugeot Phaeton enjoys a short stop in Mantes at the end of the first stage.

On July 22nd, the day of the competition, the 21 competitors were sent off from Paris at intervals of 30 seconds with Bouton, in a De Dion-Bouton steam car, quickly taking a commanding lead over his rivals. Most of the field reached Mantes at the end of the first leg with time to spare and, after a pause for refreshment, resumed their journey at 1.30pm. All 13 Peugeots and Panhard-Levassors duly arrived in Rouen, and 12 of them covered the distance within the stipulated time. The only Benz entered also covered the route in the prescribed time, but of the seven steam engines that had started, only three reached Rouen. After a panel of judges had examined the cars, they awarded the first prize donated by *Le Petit Journal* jointly to the Panhard-Levassors and Peugeots, all of which were powered by Daimler motors of between 3 and 4 horsepower. The De Dion steam cars, which had actually taken less time for the journey, were considered too cumbersome, their top speed being 20km/h and their average speed assessed at 17km/h.

An article in the journal of the Institute of French Engineers shortly after the historic event stated that the competition was probably the answer to the problem of promoting cars to the man in the street.

The 1894 Paris–Rouen trial set the first cornerstone for the building of motor racing, and in the years that followed many races took place between various European centres. The dominant makes in the early years were Panhard-Levassor, Peugeot, De Dion-Bouton, Renault, Benz, Daimler and, later, Fiat.

The event usually regarded as the first actual motor race in history was run from Paris to Bordeaux and back, a distance of about 1200km, in 1895. The event was organised by a group of Paris newspaper publishers who would later join the French Touring Club in forming the *Automobile Club de France*, still responsible for racing in France today. Competitors in the Paris–Bordeaux race were expected to cover the distance in 100 hours, but the winner, Levassor in a Panhard-Levassor, took 48 hours and 48 minutes, an average speed of 24.14km/h. He was followed by three Peugeot drivers, Rigoulot, Koechlin and Doriot, with Thum in a Benz further back. A further point of historical interest concerning the Paris–Bordeaux–Paris race is that it marked the first occasion on which a vehicle with pneumatic tyres was seen in competition. The typical wheel of that time was the same design as those used on horse-drawn carts, with iron or solid rubber rims. André Michelin wanted to test his pneumatic tyres in this difficult race, though he knew the stony, unsealed roads of the day would be very hard on them. He accordingly set up a number of service points along the route but even so had to stop and change tyres so often that his Peugeot in fact failed to finish within the prescribed time. At first the "air tyre" was ridiculed, but within a short time this ingenious invention greatly increased driving comfort and the pneumatic tyre soon dominated the market.

The first Italian race took place on May 18th 1895, over the 93km route from Turin to Asti and back. Five competitors set out at 7.30am, and three returned to Turin. The winner was Simone Federmann in a Daimler Omnibus with a seating capacity of four. He outpaced two motorcycles and averaged 15.5km/h.

The ACF was formed in Paris in November 1895. On the second of that month the *Chicago Times Herald* sponsored the first automobile race in the United States. Only two competitors took part —

Muller in a Benz and Duryea in a Duryea — and only the Benz reached the finishing line, taking 8 hours and 44 minutes for the 150km.

The following year's New York Cosmopolitan Race had only six competitors. In France, the Bordeaux–Agen–Bordeaux race was run over 276km, but the longest race of the year was the Paris–Marseilles–Paris, organised by the ACF in the autumn over a distance of 1710km. Designed as a true test of vehicles, the competition was divided into ten stages of about the same length, and lasted from September 24th to October 3rd. The 32 entries included 24 cars with petrol engines and three powered by steam; there were also three three-wheelers. The race was won by Mayade from Merkel, both driving Panhards, ahead of a De Dion-Bouton tricycle driven by Viet. Panhards continued to dominate these long-distance races until the turn of the century. In 1898 they were victorious in the 230km Marseilles–Nice race, as well as the Paris–Bordeaux of 574km and several smaller events.

The most important event in 1898 was the Paris–Amsterdam–Paris race, run from July 7th to 13th over a distance of 1431km. Again, the winner was Panhard, Charron and Girardot taking the first two places. Charron's time was 33 hours 4 minutes and 34 seconds, and the average speed worked out at 43.31km/h. The first place-getters were all French-built cars.

The first Tour de France automobile race took place the following year. Run from July 16th to 24th, this was not the reliability event the Tour later became, but a pure 2291km race. Nineteen vehicles took part, starting at 30-second intervals, and after several days of racing it became clear that Panhards would win yet again. Winner was de Knyff ahead of Girardot, de Chasseloup-Laubat and Voigt.

Also in 1899, a race was sponsored by the magazine *Le Velo* and run between Paris and Bordeaux. Seventy-four competitors were registered to take part, and on the day, May 24th, there were 24 cars — all of them French — and 37 motorcycles at the starting line ready to begin the race of 564.7km. Charron, the winner, covered the distance in 11 hours 43 minutes and 20 seconds, ahead of four more Panhards.

The most important racing car designs between 1895 and 1905

Year	Make & model	Cylinders	Capacity	Bore	Stroke	bhp	Max. revs
1895	Panhard	2	1 257	80	120	4	800
1896	Panhard	4	2 514	80	120	8	800
1899	Panhard	4	3 306	90	130	12	950
1899	Panhard	4	4 396	100	140	16	950
1900	Winton	1	3 788	165,1	177,8	16	1100
1900	Panhard	4	5 322	110	140	24	950
1900	Snoeck Bolide	4	10 603	150	150	30	900
1901	Panhard	4	7 433	130	140	40	1050
1901	Mors	4	10 087	130	190	60	950
1901	Napier	4	17 157	165,1	190,5	103	800
1902	Panhard	4	13 672	160	170	70	1200
1902	Mors	4	9 236	140	150	60	900
1902	C.G.V.	4	9 852	140	160	40	900
1902	Napier	4	6 435	127	127	44,5	950
1902	Wolseley 30	4	6 435	127	127	30	800
1902	Wolseley 45	3	8 312	152,4	152,4	45	800
1903	Panhard	4	13 672	160	170	80	1200
1903	Mors	4	11 559	145	175	70	1100
1903	Mercedes 60HP	4	9 293	140	151	65	1050
1903	Napier	4	7 708	139,7	127	45	1200
1903	Napier	4	13 726	166,1	152,4	80	1200
1903	Wolseley	4	11 082	152,4	152,4	70	900
1903	Star	4	11 082	152,4	152,4	70	1500
1903	Winton	4	8 513	133,4	152,4	40	800
1903	Winton	8	17 016	133,4	152,4	80	1000
1903	Peerless	4	11 082	152,4	152,4	80	1300
1903	Spyker 60PK (4 × 4)	6	8 817	120	130		
1904	Richard-Brasier	4	9 896	150	140	80	1300
1904	Hotchkiss	4	17 813	180	175	108	1250
1904	Darracq	4	11 259	160	140	100	1200
1904	Panhard	4	15 435	170	170	100	1400
1904	Clement-Bayard	4	11 309	150	160	80	1200
1904	Clement-Bayard	4	16 286	180	160	100	1250
1904	Mors	4	13 619	170	150	100	1450
1904	Gobron Brillié	4	13 596	140	220	110	1250
1904	De Dietrich	4	12 831	155	170	100	1300
1904	Mercedes	4	11 974	165	140	98	1150
1904	Fiat 75HP	4	14 112	165	165	76	1200
1904	Napier	4	13 726	165,1	152,4	100	2000
1904	Wolseley 72	4	11 896	152,4	165,1	72	1150
1904	Wolseley 96	4	11 896	152,4	165,1	96	1300
1904	Pipe	4	13 469	175	140	60	1000
1904	Dufaux	8	12 761	125	130	80	1300
1905	Mercedes	4	14 040	175	146	115	1200
1905	Fiat 100HP	4	16 286	180	160	110	1100
1905	Napier 4	4	13 726	165,1	152,4	80	1200
1905	Napier 6	6	15 083	158,7	127	90	1150
1905	Wolseley	4	11 896	152,4	165,1	90	1000
1905	Star	4	10 108	139,7	165,1	90	1300
1905	Siddeley	4	15 685	181	152,4	100	1400
1905	Weir	4	11 259	160	140	90	1600
1905	Pope-Toledo	4	8 564	139,7	139,7	60	1300
1905	Locomobile	4	17 657	177,8	177,8	90	1050
1905	Dufaux	4	26 400	225	166	150	1200
1905	Brasier	4	11 259	160	140	96	1200
1905	De Dietrich	4	17 012	190	150	130	1250
1905	Renault 90HP	4	12 970	166	150	90	1300
1905	Panhard	4	15 435	170	170	120	1200
1905	Hotchkiss	4	18 816	185	175	125	1050
1905	Clement-Bayard	4	12 868	160	160	120	1200
1905	C.G.V.	4	12 868	160	160	100	1050
1905	Automoto	4	13 619	170	150	90	1200
1905	Darracq	4	9 896	150	140	85	1250

The Gordon Bennett Races

At the beginning of the new century, a new racing formula is introduced, and the sport becomes truly international. French makes continue to be most successful. Closed racing circuits are used for the first time.

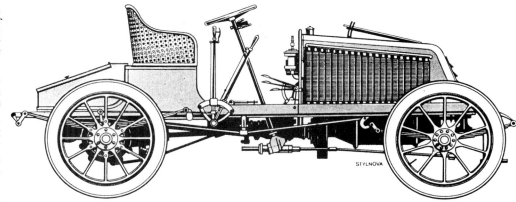

The first race of 1900 took place on February 25th outside the town of Pau in southern France. Panhard achieved another 1-2 in this event, the 335km Circuit du Sud-Ouest.

The famous Gordon Bennett races, which played such an important part in the history of motor sport, began in 1900 and continued till 1905. This competition, which saw the introduction of the first motor-racing formula, was financed by the American newspaper tycoon James Gordon Bennett, who also donated the trophy.

The Gordon Bennett formula stipulated that competing vehicles must weigh between 400 and 1000kg, without driver, fuel, oil, water, battery, tools, spares, luggage, clothing or foodstuffs. The car had to carry a driver and a co-driver weighing at least 60kg each, differences in weight having to be made up by ballast. Competitors had to be registered by a national automobile club, which was responsible for selecting the entrants, and each country's application

was limited to three cars. All parts of the vehicle had to be manufactured in the country of origin, and each race had to take place on roads over a distance of between 550 and 650km. (The minimum distance was not always adhered to.) The automobile club of the winning car had to take responsibility for the organisation of the following year's race: if there was not a suitable road in the winner's country, the race would be held in France. The first race in the series was organised by the ACF, who chose the 570km Paris-Lyons route. As well as the host country, teams were entered by Belgium, Germany and the United States, but on the starting day, June 14th 1900, only five vehicles left Paris. Charron in

a Panhard was declared the winner, reaching the finishing line in 9 hours and 9 minutes, and clocking an average speed of 62.1km/h.

There was a race from Paris to Toulouse the same year, covering a distance of 1348km, which Levegh in a Mors won at an average speed of 64.7km/h. In Italy Vincenzo Lancia, who later founded the famous Turin make that bears his name, won the 220km Venice-Bassano-Treviso-Padua race in a Fiat with a two-cylinder motor of 1082cc capacity. Third place went to Felice Nazzaro, who in time would become one of the most famous racing drivers of his day.

The second Gordon Bennett race was run in 1901, and once again the ACF took

Above
The much-coveted Gordon Bennett Trophy (17kg silver) which is now held in trust by the FIA in Paris.

Right
Marcel Renault arrives in Vienna on June 29th 1902, winning the race from Paris in his Renault.

Top right
Marcel Renault's Renault Type K, in which he won the 1902 Paris-Vienna race. Its four-cylinder engine (100 x 120mm, 3770cc capacity) developed 26hp, giving the car a top speed of about 120km/h.

Overleaf
The fourth Gordon Bennett race was held in Ireland on July 2nd 1903. The winner, Camille Jenatzy in a 60hp Mercedes, at the end of a long straight.

Right
The Athy circuit in
Ireland, used for the
1903 Gordon Bennett
race. This was the first
major circuit race in
history. The first,
second and fifth laps
had to be driven on
the 65km track (right),
and the second,
fourth, sixth and
seventh laps on the
83km circuit. Total race
distance was 527km.

Far right
The Kaiser's Cup for
the winner of the 1904
Gordon Bennett race,
held in Germany.

over the organisation. Although Fournier
in a Mors won the first leg, from Paris to
Bordeaux, Girardot in a Panhard was the
eventual winner.

The 1902 Gordon Bennett Trophy was
contested over a distance of 565km from
Paris to Innsbruck, in conjunction with
the Paris-Vienna race. There was no
restriction on the number of starters in
the longer race but, as before, only three
entries from each country could start the
Gordon Bennett race, and France chose
Fournier, de Knyff and Girardot. Special
permission had to be obtained from the
Swiss Government to allow the
competition to pass through that country
as racing was not normally permitted on
Swiss roads. The stretch from Basle to
Bregenz was covered at a crawl.

Fournier and Girardot had to
withdraw in the early stages because of
transmission and engine trouble. The
Arlberg Pass took further toll, and then
de Knyff's Panhard broke down 48km
from Innsbruck. The Frenchman Marcel
Renault, driving a car of his own
manufacture, won the Paris-Vienna race
at an average speed of 62.59km/h, but it
was the Englishman Edge, in a Napier,
who won the Gordon Bennett Trophy.
He reached Innsbruck after covering the
distance in 11 hours, 2 minutes and 52.6
seconds. This was Britain's first significant
success in international motoring
competition. With this win, the Gordon
Bennett Trophy went to Britain, and that
meant the next race had to be run in that
country.

As well as the big classic races held
around the turn of the century there were
also races for smaller cars, known as
"voiturettes". The rules which applied for
this class between 1901 and 1905

Above
Opel driver Carl Jörns
gets in some practice
on a horse racing track
near Frankfurt in 1903.
The car is the Opel
12/24.

Left
Madame Camille du
Gast driving a 5.7-litre
30hp De Dietrich on
the disastrous trip from
Paris to Madrid in
1903. Much acclaimed
by feminists, this all-
round sportswoman
reached Chatellerault
in fifth place (ahead of
Jenatzy in a Mercedes)
but lost her advantage
by stopping to help a
team-mate who had
had an accident. This
delay put her back to
45th place.

Right
The 1904 Vanderbilt
Cup race at Long
Island, New York. Ed
Hawley's Mercedes
waits on the start-line.
The race was won by
Heath in a Panhard.

stipulated a weight of between 250 and 400kg.

The last classic town-to-town race was held in 1903. Scheduled to run between Paris and Madrid, it started in controversy when the ACF refused to accept the De Dietrich designed by Italian-born Ettore Bugatti. The scrutineers ruled before the event that the radical car had too little ground clearance.

The race was a disaster, and following a number of serious accidents was stopped at Bordeaux, after 552km. Two drivers (including the designer Marcel Renault), two riding mechanics, two spectators and two soldiers lost their lives in what was the biggest catastrophe in the early history of the automobile. Gabriel in a Mors was declared winner at Bordeaux, ahead of Louis Renault, who now retired from racing after his brother's accident. But after this inter-city racing was banned, and the first chapter of the long history of motor racing came to an end.

The first Gordon Bennett race to be held on a racing circuit (as distinct from a town-to-town route) took place in Ireland in 1903. Competitors were required to complete a total of seven laps of two adjacent circuits, one of 65km and the other 83km. The first, third and fifth laps were run on the shorter loop, and the second, fourth, sixth and seventh on the longer course, making up a total distance of 527km.

It was here that Mercedes celebrated the first big international success of their long racing history. The victor was Jenatzy in a four-cylinder Mercedes, ahead of Panhard drivers de Knyff and

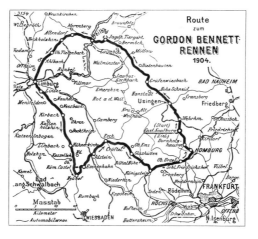

Marcel Renault

Camille Jenatzy

Farman. With this win, Germany became the organiser of the race for the first time the following year.

Around the turn of the century only two- and four-cylinder engines were in existence. The first eight-cylinder car appeared in 1903 in the United States, a straight-eight of 17,016cc capacity built by

Left
The 1904 Gordon Bennett race took place on a 127.25km circuit near Frankfurt which had to be lapped four times.

Below
Before the 1903 Paris-Madrid race. Louis Renault and co-driver Ferenc Szisz in their Renault 30CV wait at Versailles.

Above
The famous Charles Stewart Rolls in 1904, at the wheel of an 80hp Dufaux built in Geneva.

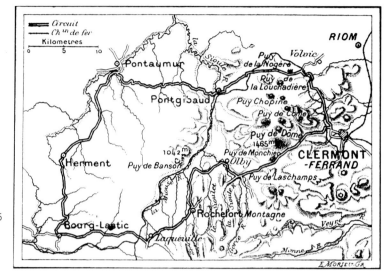

The sixth, and last, of the Gordon Bennett races was held in 1905 on a 137km circuit in the Auvergne. The winner was Théry in a Brasier.

Winton. In the following year, another eight-cylinder racing car was built in Switzerland by the brothers Charles and Frederic Dufaux. A later eight from the creative Dufaux had a capacity of 12,756cc and developed 90 horsepower at 1200rpm.

1903 saw the world's first four-wheel-drive racing car, built by the Dutch brothers, Jacobus and Hendrik Jan Spyker. The 4 x 4 Spyker was also the world's first six-cylinder car. The cylinder dimensions of the 60PK Racer were 120 x 130mm, giving a capacity of 8817cc. This Dutch-built car (with the chassis of a touring car) won a 1906 Birmingham Motor Club hillclimb.

The Swiss Automobile Club, founded in Parc-des-Eaux-Vives near Geneva in 1898, became more and more active in motor sport events. The first significant event in Switzerland was a Flying Kilometre sprint near Geneva in 1903, won by G. Perrot in a Rochet-Schneider at an average speed of 90.0km/h. The Eaumorte Flying Kilometre was famous for several decades.

Entries for the fifth Gordon Bennett race reached Germany from Britain, France, Switzerland, Italy, Austria and the United States. The race was held over a total distance of 512km on June 17th 1904, on a difficult track with many curves, situated in the Taunus mountains.

After a gruelling battle between Théry in a Richard-Brasier and Jenatzy in a Mercedes, the Richard-Brasier finished first in 5 hours 50 minutes and 14 seconds, an average speed of 87.245km/h. Jenatzy took second place; Vincenzo Lancia in a

Fiat was eighth.

Also in 1904 the Belgian Automobile Club held the first of their Ardennes circuit races. Heath in a Panhard, with an average speed of 90.75km/h, won from his team-mate Teste.

Vincenzo Lancia in a Fiat won the Coppa Florio race in Italy — Brescia-Cremona-Mantua-Brescia — ahead of Teste's Panhard and Florio's Mercedes. (This race should not be confused with the Targa Florio, first run in 1906.) The winning Fiat had a four-cylinder 165 x 165mm engine of 14,112cc, which developed 76bhp at 1200rpm, and weighed 800kg.

Motor racing competitions had not so far attracted much support in the United States, but in 1904, in an attempt to promote the sport, multi-millionaire William K. Vanderbilt donated the Vanderbilt Cup and advertised a race on Long Island. It was run over a distance of 458km, and Panhard driver Heath came first, ahead of Clément in a Clément-Bayard.

The last of the Gordon Bennett races was held in 1905, when the ACF chose a 137km circuit in the Auvergne. The following countries (with their drivers and cars) were represented in this event: England with Rolls (Wolseley), Bianchi (Wolseley) and Earp (Napier); United States with Lytle (Pope Toledo), Tracy (Locomobile) and Dingley (Pope Toledo); Austria with Braun, Burton and Hieronymus (all Mercedes); Italy with Lancia, Nazzaro and Cagno (all Fiat) and France with Théry (Brasier), Caillois (Brasier) and Duray (De Dietrich). Fiat driver Lancia proved to be the fastest competitor but had to give up on the third lap with a radiator fault, and the Frenchman Théry took his Brasier to victory ahead of the Italians Nazzaro and Cagno in their Fiats.

The Gordon Bennett Trophy had been the first racing series in history, from 1900 to 1905. After four French victories the much-acclaimed trophy found its resting place in the Automobile Club de France in Paris, where it remains to this day.

The Gordon Bennett rule stipulating that no country could enter more than three cars in any race had come under a lot of criticism, especially in France, where there were a great many makers of racing cars vying with one another.

In 1905, Britain staged the first of its famous Tourist Trophy races. Only touring cars complying with a strict fuel-consumption limit were admitted to the race, held on the Isle of Man over a distance of 323.13km. The winner was Napier in an Arrol-Johnston, with an average speed of 54.192km/h, ahead of Northey in a Rolls-Royce.

The Gordon Bennett Cup winners 1900 to 1905

Year	Country	Route & distance	Winner	Car	km/hr
1900	F	Paris—Lyon 570 km	Charron (F)	Panhard 24HP	62,12
1901	F	Paris—Bordeaux 527 km	Girardot (F)	Panhard 40HP	59,53
1902	F	Paris-Innsbruck, 565km	Edge (GB)	Napier 40HP	51,18
1903	GB	Athy Circuit (Ireland), 527km	Jenatzy (B)	Mercedes 60HP	79,16
1904	D	Taunus Circuit, 512km	Théry (F)	Richard-Brasier 80HP	87,71
1905	F	Auvergne Circuit, 548km	Théry (F)	Brasier 96HP	77,87

The ACF stages the first Grand Prix, on a circuit near Le Mans. Szisz wins for Renault. The first Targa Florio race takes place in Sicily.

The Vanderbilt Cup at Long Island was contested again in 1906, but there were other events this year too, which had even longer-lasting fame. After France had won the Gordon Bennett Trophy outright, another award had to be found, and the ACF decided to create a Grand Prix. The first race was organised by the Automobile Club de l'Ouest, later famous for the 24-hour Le Mans race, on a 103km road circuit near the same town. The organisers stipulated that the length of the Grand Prix should be 1236km, and that it should take place over a two-day period. A new formula was devised, specifying a maximum weight of 1000kg (with an additional 7kg permitted for a magneto), excluding wings, lights, light fittings,

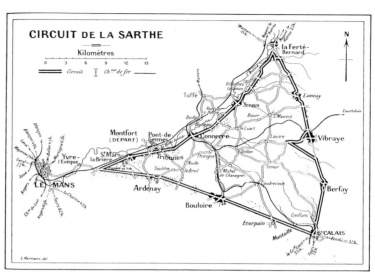

CIRCUIT DE LA SARTHE

Left
The Circuit de la Sarthe on which the first ACF Grand Prix was held in 1906. It was 103km long. The race covered 1236km and was held over two days.

Below
Francois (Ferenc) Szisz from Hungary with his co-driver Marteau at the wheel of the Renault Type AK 90CV (4 cylinder, 166 x 150mm = 12,986cc, 90HP at 1200rpm, maximum 165km/h). Szisz won the first ACF Grand Prix in 1906 driving this car.

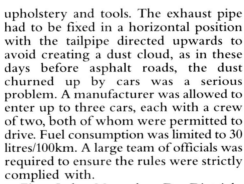

Above
The 1906 Renault AK 90CV already had a driveshaft with fixed rear axle drive (no differential), while most of the cars at that time were still fitted with a chain drive.

upholstery and tools. The exhaust pipe had to be fixed in a horizontal position with the tailpipe directed upwards to avoid creating a dust cloud, as in these days before asphalt roads, the dust churned up by cars was a serious problem. A manufacturer was allowed to enter up to three cars, each with a crew of two, both of whom were permitted to drive. Fuel consumption was limited to 30 litres/100km. A large team of officials was required to ensure the rules were strictly complied with.

Fiat, Itala, Mercedes, De Dietrich, Renault, Darracq, Brasier, Gobron-Brillé, Panhard, Hotchkiss, Clément-Bayard and Grégoire were all represented in the race. The Renault, Fiat and Clément-Bayard entries had detachable wheel rims, the first time they had been seen in a race. These rims, which were made by Michelin, reduced enormously the time taken to change punctured tyres. Ferenc Szisz in a Renault covered the first day's distance in 5 hours 45 minutes and 30.4 seconds, an average speed of 107.5km/h. Clément in a Clément-Bayard came in second ahead of Nazzaro in a Fiat and

Feri
Ferencz Szisz

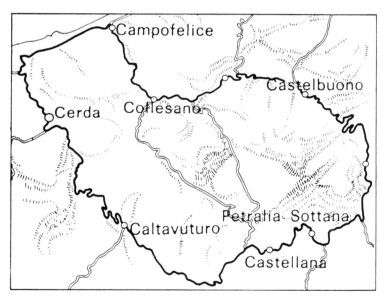

Above
Scrutineering the cars before the 1906 ACF Grand Prix. Car 6C is the Mercedes of Vincenzo Florio, who organised the first Targa Florio race in Sicily in the same year.

Centre
The first Targa Florio was run on the 148km Long Madonie circuit, which was used from 1906 to 1911 and again in 1931.

Below
Civelli de Bosch driving his imposing Grégoire to scrutineering, shortly before the 1906 ACF Grand Prix. The four-cylinder engine had a capacity of 7433cc.

Shepard in a Hotchkiss. The Renault had a four-cylinder engine of 166 x 150mm (12,986cc), three-speed transmission with a leather cone clutch, a track of 1350mm, 2900mm wheelbase and weighed 990kg. The Clément-Bayard was also a four, but of 160 x 160mm (12,868cc) and had a four-speed gearbox with metal disc clutch, a 1350mm track, 2900mm wheelbase and weighed 1004kg. The four-cylinder 180 x 160mm (16,286cc) Fiat engine also had a four-speed gearbox with spiral spring clutch; its track was 1350mm, wheelbase 2840mm and weight 1006kg. The four-cylinder Hotchkiss (180 x 160mm, 16,286cc) had four-speed gearbox, leather cone clutch, 1450mm track and 2650mm wheelbase, and weighed 1007kg. Seventeen competitors were still running at the end of the first day. Szisz was able to maintain his position on the second day but Nazzaro pushed his way into second place ahead of Clément. Fourth went to Barillier in a Brasier (four-cylinder engine, 165 x 140mm, 11,974cc, three-speed gearbox, leather cone clutch, 1350mm track, 2750mm wheelbase, weight 1000kg) and Lancia in a Fiat was fifth. The winner of this first Grand Prix in racing history covered the total distance in 12 hours 14 minutes and 7 seconds at an average speed of 101.195km/h.

The second important event of 1906 was the first Targa Florio race, which continued to be run in Sicily each year till the 1970s. These races were financed by the wealthy Sicilian Vincenzo Florio. The Targa of 1906 was run on the Big Madonie circuit of 148.832km (part of this track was still in use in 1972) and the circuit had to be lapped three times, for a total distance of 446.496km. The first race was for cars under 1300kg and was dominated by Itala cars, Alessandro Cagno winning and Graziani taking second place; Bablot in a Berliet was third. Cagno set fastest lap at 52.45 km/h; the winner's average speed was 46.82km/h. Ten competitors took part.

Another important event on the 1906 racing calendar was the Tourist Trophy race, which took place on the Isle of Man on September 27th. This second race of the series was won by the constructor C S Rolls in a Rolls-Royce, which covered the 259km distance in 4 hours and 6 minutes, achieving an average speed of 63.5km/h. He finished ahead of Bablot's Berliet, Lee Guinness in a Darracq and Brand in a Clément.

Left
Vincenzo Florio had a richly decorated grandstand built in Petralia Sottana for VIP members of Sicilian society. From here, there was a good view over the Targa Florio route.

Below
Felice Nazzaro at the wheel of the four-cylinder Fiat (180 x 160mm, 16,286cc, 110bhp at 1200rpm; top speed 160km/h) in the 1906 ACF Grand Prix. The car had been built for the 1905 Gordon Bennett race.

Below
In the first Targa Florio races, the starting and finishing line was on the straight running parallel to the beach at Bonfornello (about 50km from Palermo). Later, in 1911, the starting point was moved to Cerda. This picture was taken in 1906.

Year of the Italians

Fiat driver Felice Nazzaro wins the ACF Grand Prix, the Targa Florio and the Kaiserpreis. An Itala wins the mammoth race from Peking to Paris by a margin of two months!

The year 1907 was the year of the Italians, with cars such as Fiat, Isotta-Fraschini and Itala winning the most important races, and breaking the sequence of successes by France and Germany.

For this year's ACF Grand Prix the 1000kg weight formula was replaced by a formula based on consumption, under which engines were measured for fuel consumption per 100km and were not allowed to use more than 30 litres. With the introduction of this rule, the Automobile Club put a stop to the quest for larger and larger engines, and narrowed the gap between racing cars and touring cars. This new rule did not

cause an immediate reduction in the size of motors however, as most of the engineers used the previous year's four-cylinder engines of between 12 and 17 litres.

In November 1906 Fiat driver Vincenzo Lancia had founded his own automobile manufacturing company, unfortunately destroyed several months later by fire. Undaunted, Lancia immediately rebuilt it, so that in September 1907 the first Lancia car left the new factory. Despite that, Lancia continued to drive Fiats in competition.

Felice Nazzaro from Turin appeared to be unbeatable with his relaxed driving style, and his racing career lasted for three

decades. (He also established his own car manufacturing plant.) Nazzaro won the 450km Targa Florio at an average speed of 53.19km/h in a smaller 28/40hp Fiat, with a 7363cc (125 x 150mm) four-cylinder engine which developed 60bhp at 1200rpm. Team-mate Lancia in a similar car was second.

In Germany the famous Kaiserpreis was awarded on a race in the Taunus mountains. No racing cars were permitted, only touring cars of under eight litres and weighing less than 1165kg. The Kaiserpreis generated great excitement and a large number of entries were received. The German Automobile Club (ADAC) in fact had so many entries

Felice Nazzaro

Above
Felice Nazzaro was Italy's first great racing driver. Here he is pictured with co-driver Fagnano in 1907, the year he won the Targa Florio, the ACF Grand Prix and the Kaiserpreis. He later founded his own manufacturing company, which produced Nazzaro cars from 1911 till 1923 (apart from war years).

Right
The 117.4km Taunus circuit devised for the 1907 Kaiserpreis was part of the circuit used for the 1904 Gordon Bennett race.

Left
Cars competing in the Targa Florio had to be lifted onto ships to be transported to Palermo.

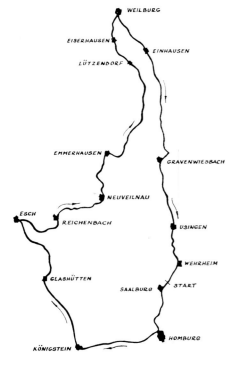

Vincenzo Lancia

Above
The Fiat team with the Kaiserpreis they won in 1907. From left: Vincenzo Lancia, Giovanni Agnelli, Felice Nazzaro (winner) and Louis Wagner.

Top
Nazzaro in a 130hp Fiat, winner of the 1907 ACF Grand Prix at Dieppe, here driving under the railway bridge.

that two 236km elimination heats had to be held to select the finalists for the actual race, the first 20 to finish each heat qualifying for the final which was run over four laps, a distance of 472km.

The Fiats (140 x 130mm, capacity 8004cc, developing 72bhp at 1200rpm) dominated the meeting, Lancia winning the first heat and Nazzaro the second. Nazzaro went on to win the final as well, covering the course in 5 hours 34 minutes and 28.2 seconds, an average speed of 84.68km/h. Hautvast in a Pipe came second, ahead of Carl Jörns in an Opel, Michel in another Opel and the two remaining Fiat drivers, Wagner and Lancia. Among those who failed to make it through to the final had been Alfieri Maserati in a Bianchi: almost two decades later, in 1926, Maserati and his brothers founded the famous firm of Maserati in their home town of Bologna.

The four-cylinder Kaiserpreis engines were almost all "oversquare" (bore greater than stroke). This sort of bore/stroke ratio was used to reduce the mean piston speed and thus reduce wear on the moving parts of the motor. When later formulae limited bore diameters, engineers had to design engines with longer strokes to achieve the same horsepower ratings for a given size.

The highlight of 1907 was the second running of the ACF Grand Prix. Held this time on a 76.98km circuit near Dieppe, the race ran for 10 laps. A Fiat (four-cylinder, 180 x 160mm, 16,286cc, 130bhp at 1600rpm, weight 830kg), again driven by Felice Nazzaro, was the winner, covering the 769.8km distance in 6 hours 46 minutes and 33 seconds, at an average of 113.637km/h. Ferenc Szisz, winner of the previous year's race, took second

place in a Renault (four-cylinder, 165 x 150mm, 12,830cc) ahead of Paul Baras in a Brasier (four-cylinder, 165 x 140mm, 11,974cc) and Fernand Gabriel in a Lorraine-Dietrich (four-cylinder, 180 x 170mm, 17,304cc). Mercedes had to be satisfied with a victory later in 1907 in the Ardennes race in Belgium (de Caters). The Coppa Florio near Brescia was a touring-car race based on the Kaiserpreis formula and won by Ferdinando Minoia in an Isotta-Fraschini. Twenty years later, in 1927, Minoia won the first Mille Miglia, which also started and finished in Brescia. Another Italian car, the Itala, made a name for itself at the same meeting when Alessandro Cagno won the Coppa Velocità.

An important and classic competition the same year was the race from Peking to Paris, which was sponsored by the Paris newspaper *Le Matin*. The distance was 15,000km and led through extremely difficult terrain in Asia (the desert) and Europe. The four-cylinder Itala, with Prince Scipione Borghese, journalist Luigi Barzini and mechanic Ettore Guizzardi, completed the distance in exactly two months (from June 10th to August 10th 1907) to win this gruelling race. Two months after the Itala's triumph, the De Dion-Bouton arrived in Paris; the Dutch Spyker and the three-wheeled Contal never finished. The Peking-Paris was not only a great achievement for Italy but also for the general acceptance of the motor car by the public. The Itala can be found today in the Turin Automobile Museum, an intriguing object because of its three huge spare tanks, two of them mounted on the side of the central back seat. The engine has two blocks (130 x 140mm, capacity 7433cc, developing 45 horsepower at 1250rpm).

Above
Vincenzo Lancia at scrutineering before the 1907 ACF Grand Prix at Dieppe, with his Fiat (180 x 160mm, 16,286cc, 130bhp).

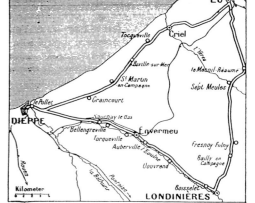

Left
Peking-Paris 1907: arrival of the victorious Itala in the Bois de Boulogne. The crew consisted of Prince Scipione Borghese, journalist Luigi Barzini and mechanic Ettore Guizzardi. The Itala won the 15,000km event by two months!

Above
The 76.98km Dieppe circuit, venue of the ACF Grand Prix in 1907, 1908 and 1912.

Mercedes Victory at Dieppe

Lautenschlager wins the ACF Grand Prix. Thomas wins the New York-Paris race. Twenty-four-hour long-distance races are held on turf horse-tracks in the United States.

Left
ACF Grand Prix in Dieppe in 1908. An Opel and a Motobloc in front of the pits.

Below
Nando Minoia in a 13,586cc Lorraine-Dietrich before the 1908 Grand Prix. In 1927 Minoia would be winner of the first Mille Miglia, in an OM.

German as well as Italian makes shared the spoils in the 1908 season; the French, whose cars had been dominant from the turn of the century till 1906, hardly received a mention.

The racing season opened with the Targa Florio on May 18th. The Fiats of Lancia and Nazzaro led at the start but soon fell back, and Trucco in an Isotta-Fraschini won in 7 hours 49 minutes and 26 seconds, averaging 57.07km/h for the 446.5km, with Lancia second. Nazzaro made fastest lap at 58.25km/h.

At the same time, the first important motor race in Russia took place. The route was from St Petersburg to Moscow (705km), and Hémery in a Benz covered the distance in 8 hours 33 minutes 48 seconds, to win at an average of 82.71km/h.

The ACF Grand Prix rules were changed again this year. Minimum weight was now 1100kg, without water, petrol, tools, spare parts or spare tyres. There was also a maximum bore size of 155mm for four-cylinder engines, less for multi-cylinder engines; there was no limitation on the stroke. The intention of these regulations was to prevent engines getting bigger and bigger, and to encourage the construction of lighter cars. The change of formula led to a different type of engine, which was now

designed to attain higher piston speeds. An example of this development was the single-cylinder Sizaire-Naudin of 1908. The Sizaire actually ran in the voiturette class rather than Grands Prix, but as the formula for the smaller cars was also based on limiting bore size, it provides a perfect illustration. The Sizaire's bore of 100mm was offset by a stroke of 250mm, which gave a capacity of 1963cc. The height of the engine, which developed 42 horsepower at 2400rpm, required an absurdly tall bonnet, though the car was capable of speeds well in excess of 100km/h.

The Sizaire-Naudin had independent front suspension as early as 1908, but it was the 1930s before independent front suspension became common to the majority of racing cars.

The first ACF Grand Prix under the new formula took place on the 76.98km Dieppe circuit, and ended in a clear victory for Germany. At the end of the first lap factory engineer Salzer in a Mercedes was leading. Nazzaro in a Fiat then overtook him but the Italian had to drop out of the race on the third lap because of defective wheel bearings, leaving his team-mate, the Frenchman Wagner, to take the lead in an identical car. But Wagner also had to retire, which enabled Hémery in a Benz to take the lead, with Lautenschlager in a Mercedes second. At half-distance, Christian Lautenschlager overtook Hémery and carried on to win the race, covering the 769.8km in 6 hours 55 minutes and 43.4 seconds, for an average of 111.29km/h. The final order was: 1st — Christian Lautenschlager in a Mercedes (four-cylinder, 154.7 x 180mm, 13,533cc, 135bhp at 1400rpm, four-speed gearbox, chain drive, 1410mm track, 2690mm wheelbase); 2nd — Victor Hémery in a Benz (four-cylinder, 154.9 x 165mm, 12,443cc, leather cone clutch, chain drive); 3rd — René Hanriot in another Benz; and 4th — Victor Rigal in a Clément-Bayard (four-cylinder, 155 x 185mm, 13,963cc, four-speed gearbox, metal disc clutch). Carl Jörns in an Opel (four-cylinder, 154.8 x 160mm, 12,045cc, leather cone clutch, shaft drive) was 6th and Dmitriewitch, the best Renault (four-cylinder, 155 x 160mm, 12,076cc, leather cone clutch, shaft drive) driver, was 8th.

Felice Nazzaro made up for his previous losses when he won the 528km Targa Bologna for Fiat.

The Tourist Trophy was won by an Englishman, Watson, in a Hutton. This four-cylinder car had been built by the

Napier company especially for this race, the regulations for which called for a maximum bore of 4 inches (101.6mm).

In the United States the famous Vanderbilt Cup race took place on Long Island, but only Americans took part this year (the winner was Robertson in a Locomobile). Nearly all the leading Europeans were however at Savannah in Georgia on November 7th for the inaugural American Grand Prize. The Fiats dominated the 658km race, Louis Wagner winning at an average speed of 104.92km/h, from Hémery in a Benz.

After the epic race from Peking to Paris in 1907, there was a similar but even more demanding test in 1908. Again, it was the French newspaper *Le Matin* which staged the race, the route this time taking competitors around the world from New York to Paris, via Alaska, Japan, Moscow and Berlin. Six crews entered: three French (in De Dion-Bouton, Motobloc and Sizaire-Naudin cars), an Italian (in a Zust), a German (in a Protos), and an American (in a Thomas). The starting point was Times Square in New York on February 12th, and the cars then headed east. After traversing the North American continent, the Thomas led the Zust into San Francisco, the American factory having been able to provide the best service along the way. It was rumoured that the Americans had transported their car part of the way by rail, but what had actually happened was that the crew,

finding the road blocked by snow, had driven along 72km of the railway from Carter in Wyoming to Evanston. It was however found that the German Protos had been taken by train for part of its journey and it was promptly given a penalty of 30 days' travelling time.

Because racing across the icy wastes of Alaska was considered too risky, the cars were loaded onto ships for transport to Japan. After crossing Japan, they were again loaded onto a ship, this time bound for Vladivostok. The route from Peking via St Petersburg and Berlin was almost identical to that covered in the Peking-Paris the year before. At this point Count de Dion ordered the withdrawal of the De Dion-Bouton team, apparently because of the controversy surrounding the American and German entries, though there is some question about the real reason.

The remaining competitors kept going, and the Protos arrived at the *Le Matin* offices in Paris on July 28th. Four days later, the Thomas followed and the Zust two weeks after that. Each of the three teams considered themselves the winners. The Americans were of the opinion that the Germans had to add 30 days to their travelling time as part of their penalty, and were therefore far behind the Thomas. The Germans still alleged that the Thomas crew had used the railways for transporting their car. The crew of the Zust considered the victory was theirs. The organisers and the

public were disgusted at the lack of control on the way.

Finally, after much controversy, the victory was awarded to the American crew of Schuster, Montague Roberts and Williams, in the Thomas. Today, the Thomas is in the famous Harrah Auto Museum in Reno, Nevada. George Schuster died in Springvale in 1972, at the age of 99.

From 1905 to 1910, a whole series of largely-forgotten 24-hour races took place in the United States of America. The only 24-hour races which survive today are those at Le Mans, Spa and Daytona, but in the time under review more than that number took place in America each year. The first of them were held on disused horse-racing tracks which often became dust bowls after a couple of laps as the cars churned through the grass surface. The first recorded 24-hour competition actually dates back to 1904, when a Packard raced against the clock in a demonstration of its safety.

The first actual 24-hour race followed in 1905, some half-dozen cars facing the starter at Columbus, Ohio. The brothers Soules in a 30hp Pope-Toledo won, covering a total distance of 828.5 miles. The same year Guy Vaughan established a solo 1000-mile record in a 40bhp Decauville, covering the route in 23 hours 33 minutes and 20 seconds, though this time was beaten on a small track at Indianapolis later in 1905. The next

200

Above
A Renault of the kind used shortly after the turn of the century; it was most successful in races where the course was from one town to another.

Below
A drawing of the impressive Fiat S 76, by the Swiss designer Werner Bührer

1911 S 76 FIAT

BÜHRER-MUNOT '66.

Diagram of a typical Grand Prix car between 1906 and 1910.

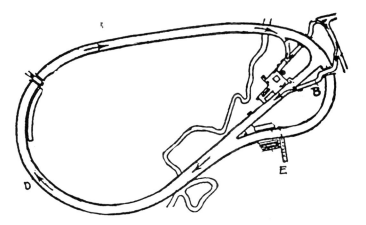

The banked Brooklands track near London, the world's first permanent autodrome, opened in 1907. Racing was held there till 1939 on a variety of configurations, but the track then fell into disrepair.

24-hour race took place in 1907 at Point Breeze (Philadelphia), the winner this time covering 781 miles.

In England meanwhile Selwyn Francis Edge (winner of the 1902 Gordon Bennett race) drove a Napier continuously for 24 hours on the famous Brooklands track on June 17th 1907. (The track today is derelict, but at that time one lap measured 2.75 miles.) He averaged 60mph on this course with its two banked curves.

No fewer than seven 24-hour races took place in the United States in 1907: at Brighton Beach, in Brooklyn, at Morris Park, in the Bronx, in Milwaukee, at Point Breeze and in Detroit. The winners were Ford, Lozier, Locomobile, Jackson, Thomas, Renault and Fiat cars. A year later there were 24-hour races at Brighton Beach (won by Lozier and Simplex cars) and in Milwaukee (Locomobile) as well as at Ascot Park in Los Angeles (Locomobile), though in

another event at Birmingham (Alabama) the Swiss driver Emile Stricker in a Renault was killed in an accident. In 1909 a series of three "twice around the clock" races took place at Brighton Beach, where the winners were Simplex, Renault and Lozier; a Hudson meanwhile won at Seattle.

The last of these 24-hour racecourse events took place at Brighton Beach in 1910 (the winners were Simplex and Stearns), but after this there were no American 24-hour races until 1965, when NASCAR president Bill France organised an international 24-hour World Championship sportscar race at Daytona. He intended this event to outshine the traditional 12-hour race at Sebring, but success remained somewhat elusive.

Racing commenced on the famous Brooklands track near Byfleet, about 20 miles from the centre of London, in 1907. The track was officially opened on June 17th, and was a boon to a country where racing on public roads was prohibited. The Brooklands track consisted of two elevated curves, the Byfleet Banking with a large radius and the slightly sharper Members' Banking, together with the Railway Straight and Finishing Straight. In later years the track was modified (usually by the liberal application of straw-bales) to approximate a genuine road circuit. Brooklands became famous for the very high speeds attainable there, mainly due to the steep bankings, but in time it wore out and by the time it closed in 1939 it was full of pot-holes.

The Italian Felice Nazzaro set a track record on April 18th 1908 in his Fiat SB4 with an 18.1-litre four-cylinder engine developing 175hp at 1200rpm. Competing in a match race with a Napier he set a controversial lap record of 195.7km/h which was not bettered until 1922, when Lee Guinness created a new record in a V12 Sunbeam.

Left
Start of the New York-Paris race in 1908. From left: the Thomas (the winning car), the Zust, the De Dion and the Sizaire-Naudin.

Overleaf
Two American Locomobiles in the 1908 Vanderbilt Cup race on Long Island. The winner was Robertson in a 16,850cc version. This was the first time an American car had beaten its European rivals in a major event.

Fewer Races Run

The crisis years. A general falling off in racing activity brings technical development to a standstill. Renault withdraws. The "Blitzen Benz" creates a furore in the US.

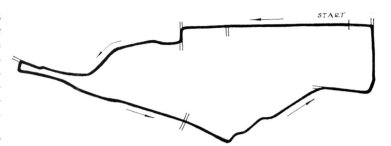

The American Grand Prize races between 1908 and 1916 were the most prestigious in North America. Races were run on this 17-mile Savannah road circuit in 1910 and 1911.

A marked decrease in racing activities set in at the start of 1909 in the wake of an economic depression which seriously affected the European motor industry. Renault withdrew from Grand Prix racing and did not rejoin until 1977–85. A new formula had been devised for the 1909 ACF Grand Prix (maximum bore 130mm, minimum weight 900kg), but the race was boycotted. The first to take this action (or lack of it) were the French manufacturers, who had been suffering defeat after defeat in the past few races. Panhard-Levassor, Brasier, Clément-Bayard, Lorraine-Dietrich, Darracq, Motobloc, Peugeot and Berliet all joined Renault in withdrawing from the race. Later, the foreign firms — Benz, Mercedes, Pipe, Fiat, Isotta-Fraschini and Minerva — followed suit, and the ACF had little choice but to cancel their race.

Over the next few years only the Targa Florio and, in America, the Vanderbilt Cup and the American Grand Prize, were run on a regular basis.

The French Grands Prix had had a stimulating effect on the motor industry, and played a major part in furthering automobile technology. But between the cancellation of the 1909 race and the revival of the Grand Prix in 1912, technical development was at a virtual standstill.

A new German racing car, developed by Dr Hans Nibel, attracted much attention in these lean years. Known as the "Blitzen Benz", this famous car was built at the Benz factory in Mannheim in 1909, a development of the four-cylinder Benz car which had come second to Lautenschlager's victorious Mercedes in the 1908 ACF Grand Prix at Dieppe.

That result had inspired Benz to develop a new engine with a 154.9mm bore and 165mm stroke, giving a capacity

of 12,443cc and developing 150bhp at 1500rpm. The cylinders were cast in pairs, with valves operated by the conventional system of pushrods and rockers. The carburettor was a Benz design with adjustable jets. Like the Grand Prix Mercedes, the 150hp Benz had twin-plug ignition, the spark-plugs mounted opposite each other to optimise timing. The cooling system, designed to match the engine size and performance, had a geared water-pump and the usual Benz Lamellen radiator. The chassis was based on the conventional touring design, though chain-drive was utilised in place of the usual prop-shaft. The rear-wheel brakes were operated by cable, but there was also a transmission brake, which could be activated independently by either a right or left pedal. The gearbox had four forward gears and one reverse, driving through a leather cone clutch mounted on the flywheel.

The most successful development of this 150hp car was the 200hp "Blitzen Benz" which held the world speed record from 1909 to 1922. This motor had a bore of 185mm and a stroke of 200mm, giving a capacity of 21,504cc, and developed its 200hp at 1600rpm. The front axle was forked and the rear axle fixed while the car had a track of 1320mm and a wheelbase of 2775mm, and weighed 1200kg. The car can be seen today in the

Daimler-Benz factory museum in Stuttgart.

The unveiling of the "Blitzen Benz" immediately gave rise to all sorts of speculation about its performance. The Frenchman Victor Hémery established a record of 202.691km/h with it at Brooklands on November 8th 1909, beating the old mark for one kilometre, and then on March 16th 1910 American Barney Oldfield raced the German car on a flat stretch of sand at Daytona Beach in Florida, and achieved a new mark of 211.977km/h, though this was not recognised as a world record. A few weeks later, with the same car, Bob Burman bettered that speed when he clocked 227.510km/h on April 23rd 1910. This record was not officially recognised either, as Burman covered the measured distance in one direction only, and world records have to be set by an average of runs in opposite directions — though it should be pointed out that this rule was not established until December 1910.

Disregarding these runs, Hémery's 202.691km/h stood as the official record from 1909 until May 17th 1922, when Kenelm Lee Guinness in a Sunbeam officially established a new world speed of 215.244km/h. The Sunbeam used an 18,322cc (120 x 135mm) aero engine which developed 355bhp at 2300rpm.

Left
A race between car and aeroplane on the sand at Daytona Beach, Florida in 1909. The famous Bob Burman is driving a stripped Buick. In 1911, on the same beach, Burman broke the world speed record in the "Blitzen Benz".

Right
Racing formulae that weren't well thought out led to peculiar car shapes. The 1906-09 voiturette formula specified a maximum bore of 80mm for two-cylinder motors, but there was no limitation on stroke. This led to the tower-like cylinders (80 x 280mm) of the 2813cc Lion-Peugeot shown here.

The First Indianapolis 500

A Marmon wins the first 500-mile race on the Indianapolis track, built two years before. The winning car has motoring's first rear view mirror. Fiat chases the records with a monster new car.

In 1911 another racing classic was added to those already established — the 500-mile race at Indianapolis. Over the course of years, this circuit has stood the test of time and earned a reputation which is unequalled to this day. From their inception, the 500-mile races have seen the most famous cars and drivers, and have received more publicity than any other race — certainly in America. Its fame was built on very high speeds, huge crowds of spectators and enormous sums paid to the prize-winners. "Indy" can look back on a long tradition of races interrupted only by the two world wars.

The track was first laid down on February 19th 1909 by Carl G. Fisher, one of the owners of the Prest-O-Lite Company and the Indianapolis Motor Speedway Corporation, at a cost of $250,000. The two-and-a-half-mile circuit was built with four sweeping right-angled curves, each a quarter of a mile long and slightly cambered, forming a rectangle with rounded-off corners. Later

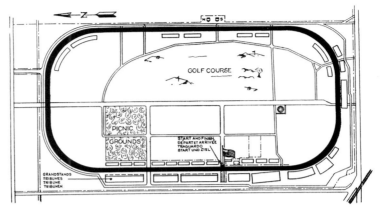

The Indianapolis circuit, built in 1909, has been the venue of the famous 500-mile race since 1911. The layout of the 2.5-mile (4.024km) course with its four slightly banked bends has not been changed since its opening.

nicknamed the Brickyard, after a resurfacing operation, the Indianapolis Motor Speedway was officially opened on June 5th 1909 with a ballooning competition and, in August of the same year, racing began. Louis Schwitzer won the first race, over five miles, and Bob Burman the 250-mile feature event.

The surface of the track was originally constructed of natural rock which had been steamrollered. This, however,

proved to be too dangerous and it was decided to pave the whole track with bricks. Approximately three million bricks were ordered and laid. The track retained this surface until 1935 when, with the exception of the straight near the start/finish line, it was asphalted. The last of the brick paving disappeared in 1961 when the entire course, apart from a symbolic brick strip at the finish-line, was asphalted.

Left
The start of the first Indianapolis 500 in 1911. The winner was Ray Harroun in a Marmon Wasp at an average speed of 120km/h.

Above right
The famous American driver David Bruce-Brown in a Fiat S74, at the start of the 1911 American Grand Prize at Savannah. Bruce-Brown won the 651.4km race at an average speed of 120.3km/h. The Fiat's four-cylinder 14,137cc engine developed 190bhp at 1600rpm.

Only short races were run in 1909 and 1910, but on May 30th 1911 the first Indianapolis 500 took place. The date chosen was Memorial Day, the day each year America commemorates those who have fallen in battle. For over half a century this important event always took place on Memorial Day until, in 1971, USAC decided on a slight departure from tradition and altered it to the last Sunday in May.

Rules for the 1911 race restricted engines to 600 cubic inches (9832cc) and

the winner was Ray Harroun with a six-cylinder (114.3 x 127mm, 7820cc, three-speed gearbox) car he had designed for the Marmon company. The Marmon Wasp had a top speed of 140km/h, and won the 500-mile (804km) race in 6 hours 42 minutes and 8 seconds, at an average of 120km/h. Harroun, uniquely in the field, did not have a mechanic on board to keep an eye on the opposition during the race, and to attend to minor tasks such as working the fuel-pressure pump and lubricating various engine and chassis parts. Instead he mounted a 20 x 7cm mirror on top of the windscreen which enabled him to tell at a glance what was going on behind. Thus was born the rear-view mirror.

Second place went to Ralph Mulford in a Lozier, followed by David Bruce-Brown in a Fiat; a year later Bruce-Brown would take part in the ACF Grand Prix at Dieppe and lead Europe's best for virtually the whole race. The development of the huge German "Blitzen Benz" engine was immediately challenged in size by Fiat with their 300hp S76 record car. This two-seater had an unusually high bonnet-line, the four-cylinder overhead-camshaft engine having a bore of 190mm and a stroke of 250mm, giving a capacity of 28,338cc. To fire this immense device, three spark plugs were used for each cylinder,

actuated by a magneto ignition system. At 1900rpm, it developed 290bhp. Drive was transmitted by chain to the wheels, which had dimensions of 895 x 135mm but were dwarfed by the high bonnet and large pear-shaped radiator demanded by the huge engine. Track was 2750mm, wheelbase 1300mm, and total weight 1650kg.

Pietro Bordino took this car to England in 1911 and, after an unsuccessful bid at Brooklands, topped 200km/h on the beach at Saltburn. The highest speed the

car achieved was on December 8th 1913, when the Belgian Arthur Duray achieved 213.023km/h at Ostend, but this was not officially recognised because no run was made in the opposite direction.

The first Monte Carlo Rally was held in January 1911. Competing drivers set off from various European capitals and all met up in the Alps overlooking Monte Carlo. These events, held under severe winter conditions, contributed much to the development of improved car safety standards.

Racing cars 1906 to 1911

Year	Make & model	Cylinders	Capacity	Bore	Stroke	bhp	rpm	Gears	Max speed km/h
1906	Lorraine-Dietrich	4	18 146	190	160	130	1100	4	157
1906	Fiat 110HP	4	16 286	180	160	110	1100	4	160
1906	Renault 90HP	4	12 975	166	150	90	1200	3	148
1906	Darracq	4	12 711	170	140	120	1400	3	150
1906	Brasier	4	11 974	165	140	105	1400	3	153
1906	Mercedes 120HP	6	16 119	185	150	120	1200	4	152
1906	Gobron Brillié	4	13 547	140	220	90	1100	3	140
1906	Itala 100HP	4	16 666	185	155	100	1500	3	155
1906	Gregoire	4	7 433	130	140	65	1200	3	140
1906	Panhard-Levassor	4	18 279	185	170	120	1300	4	158
1906	Hotchkiss	4	16 286	180	160	115	1250	4	155
1906	Bayard-Clément	4	12 868	160	160	95	1300	4	155
1907	Christie	4	19 891	185	185	115	1200	2	150
1907	Corre	4	10 603	150	150	90	1300	3	147
1907	Darracq	4	15 268	180	150	125	1400	3	155
1907	Dufaux Marchand	8	14 726	125	150	110	1200	3	158
1907	Fiat 130HP	4	16 286	180	160	130	1600	4	160
1907	Germain	4	5 123	112	130	60	1150	3	140
1907	Lorraine-Dietrich	4	17 304	180	170	120	1250	4	152
1907	Minerva	4	7 900	145	120	90	2200	3	145
1907	Mercedes	4	11 974	165	140	100	1300	4	160
1907	Motobloc	4	11 974	180	150	95	1200	4	150
1907	Panhard-Levassor	4	15 435	170	170	100	1200	4	155
1907	Porthos	8	9 123	110	120	85	1150	4	152
1907	Renault	4	12 830	165	150	105	1200	3	150
1907	Weigel	8	14 866	130	140	100	1250	2	153
1908	Austin	6	9 635	126,9	127	95	1350	4	155
1908	Itala 120HP	4	12 076	155	160	120	1800	4	160
1908	Mercedes	4	12 780	154,7	170	135	1600	4	158
1908	Motobloc	4	12 831	155	170	95	1400	4	150
1908	Renault	4	12 076	155	160	105	1800	3	155
1908	Lorraine-Dietrich	4	13 586	155	180	100	1250	4	150
1908	Benz	4	12 443	154,9	165	100	1500	4	160
1908	Fiat S61	4	10 087	130	190	115	1800	4	150
1908	Brasier	4	12 045	154,8	160	100	1700	3	157
1908	Porthos	6	9 121	127	120	85	1350	3	148
1908	Opel	4	12 045	154,8	160	95	1300	4	150
1908	Bayard-Clément	4	13 963	155	185	105	1450	4	155
1908	Weigel	4	12 781	154,7	170	100	1500	3	155
1908	Mors	4	12 798	154,8	170	95	1400	3	150
1908	Thomas	4	11 176	154	150	90	1350	4	150
1908	Panhard-Levassor	4	12 831	155	170	95	1450	4	155
1908	Germain	4	12 443	154,9	165	90	1400	4	150
1909	Blitzen Benz	4	21 500	185	200	200	1650	2	225
1911	Lorraine-Dietrich	4	15 095	155	200	130	1500	4	160
1911	Peugeot	4	7 603	110	200	95	1400	4	155
1911	Fiat S74	4	14 137	150	200	190	1600	4	165
1911	Marmon	6	7 820	114,3	127	105	1700	3	165

Peugeot Leads the Way

The four-cylinder Peugeot, designed by Ernest Henry, has two camshafts, a desmodromic system for opening and closing valves, of which there are four per cylinder. The ACF Grand Prix revived and run again at Dieppe.

New technical developments in 1912 resulted in more attention being paid to the aerodynamic efficiency of racing cars. Bodies began to be shaped like torpedoes, with fuel-tanks and spare wheels covered by streamlined tail sections. The six-cylinder engine enjoyed something of a comeback this year, the Belgian Excelsior company entering cars in the ACF Grand Prix (held for the first time since 1908) with two blocks of three cylinders (110 x 160mm, total capacity 9138cc) and a five-speed gearbox.

This was still the era of the long-stroke motor, which provided better cooling, but they now sported four valves per cylinder and twin overhead camshafts.

The organisers of the ACF Grand Prix decided not to use a fixed formula, except for cockpit width, which was supposed to be 175mm. They also admitted cars running in the concurrent Coupe des Voiturettes, with engines under 3000cc, and the venue was the famous Dieppe circuit. The race took place over a period of two days, distance being 1540km (10 laps), and favourites were the Italian Fiats, the British Sunbeams and Vauxhalls, and the French Lorraine-Dietrichs and Peugeot cars.

The American David Bruce-Brown in a Fiat (four-cylinder, 150 x 200mm, developing 190bhp at 1600rpm, and weighing 1250kg) crossed the finishing line in first place at the end of day one; his time was 6 hours, 36 minutes and 37.3 seconds, having averaged 116.2km/h. In second place was the Frenchman Georges Boillot in a Peugeot 76 (four-cylinder, 110 x 200mm) ahead of Louis Wagner in a Fiat and Dario Resta in a Sunbeam (four-cylinder, 80 x 149mm). It

Right
Cutaway of the valve operation of a Peugeot engine.

Far right
The brilliant four-cylinder Peugeot engine with twin overhead camshafts, designed by the Swiss engineer Ernest Henry.

Below
Italian-born American Ralph De Palma in a Fiat S74 at the start of the 1912 ACF Grand Prix at Dieppe.

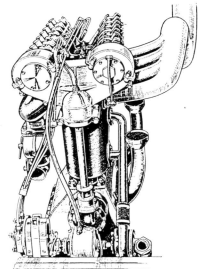

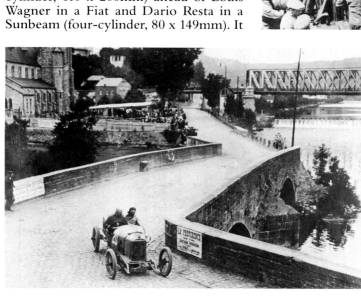

Above
Georges Boillot wins the 1912 ACF Grand Prix at Dieppe in one of the famous 7598cc Peugeots.

Left
Zuccarelli in a 3-litre Peugeot L3 during the Ardennes Circuit. His team-mate Thomas, driving a second Peugeot, was winner.

rained on the second day and Bruce-Brown in his huge Fiat had the misfortune to collide with a dog. His fuel-tank was ruptured and the American had to refuel en route, but as refuelling was permitted only at the pits, the Fiat was disqualified.

The French celebrated their victory with Boillot in the Peugeot, clocking the best time of 13 hours 58 minutes and 2.3 seconds, an average of 110.256km/h, ahead of Wagner's Fiat and the three Sunbeams driven by Rigal, Resta and Médinger. The Sunbeams were actually running in the 3-litre voiturette class.

The 7.6-litre Peugeot's defeat of the 14.1-litre Fiat was justification for the French company's faith in the new philsophy of small engine and light construction. The four-cylinder engine developed 148bhp at 2200rpm and had two inlet and two exhaust valves per cylinder, driven by twin overhead camshafts.

Peugeot was outstandingly successful during 1912. Jules Goux won the Grand Prix de France (not to be confused with the ACF Grand Prix), and Zuccarelli the Sarthe Cup.

The Targa Florio was won by Snipe/Pardini in an Italian SCAP, and the second 500-mile race at Indianapolis went to Dawson in an American National ahead of Tetzlaff in a Fiat. There was also a Mercedes victory by De Palma in the Vanderbilt Cup race at Milwaukee. (David Bruce-Brown was killed during practice at this circuit.)

The American Grand Prize, also held at Milwaukee, was won by Bragg in a Fiat. Motor racing at last seemed to have picked up after its decline in the years since 1909. With more events being run, it appeared that a bright new future was developing for the sport.

Robert Peugeot

A group photograph of the drivers taking part in the 1912 Indianapolis 500. Joe Dawson in a National won at an average of 127.49 km/h.

Power Reaches 20bhp/litre

The ACF's new Grand Prix formula stipulates weight limits and fuel economy. With their modern motors, Peugeot continue their successes. Smaller engines conquer the giants.

1913 was another successful year for the French. Jules Goux in a Peugeot won the Indianapolis 500, and then Peugeot took a double victory in the ACF Grand Prix at Amiens, Boillot taking first place and Goux second. The Grand Prix de France at Le Mans meanwhile was won by Bablot in a Delage from team-mate Guyot; Pilette in a Mercedes was third. The Voiturette Grand Prix at Boulogne was also won by Peugeot, though the Targa Florio went to Italy, when the great driver Felice Nazzaro — a long-standing Fiat man — drove a car of his own manufacture to victory.

The ACF chose the 31km Amiens circuit in Picardy for their 1913 Grand Prix, the 917km race being run over 29 laps. In an effort to reverse any trend towards bigger engines and heavier cars, this year's rules required competing cars to weigh between 800 and 1100kg, and to use no more than 20 litres of fuel each 100km. There were fewer total entries than the previous year, but manufacturers such as Sunbeam, Delage, Opel, Mathis, Excelsior, Schneider, Itala and Peugeot all promised to take part.

In the absence of both Mercedes and Fiat (Nazzaro drove an 8325cc Itala), interest was centred on the innovative

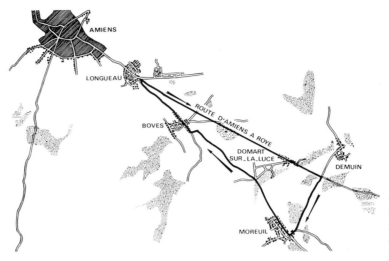

The 1913 ACF Grand Prix was held on a 31.63km circuit near Amiens in Picardy. The race was run over 29 laps (917km).

new Peugeots. Indeed, after the first few laps Boillot had one of the French cars in the lead, and his compatriot Goux in another Peugeot soon took over. After the 16th lap however Guyot in a Delage Type Y was in front, but then disaster struck when the Delage punctured a tyre. His mechanic jumped out of the moving car, stumbled, and fell with his legs under the wheels. He suffered serious injuries, and Guyot helped his friend off the

circuit and assisted with first aid. Only then did he return to the race, but Boillot and Goux in the Peugeots were now too far ahead for him to make up the lost time.

The winner was Georges Boillot, who covered the distance in 7 hours 53 minutes and 56.4 seconds, averaging 116.063km/h. The winning Peugeot had a four-cylinder engine with twin overhead camshafts and four valves per

Scrutineering for the 1912 ACF Grand Prix at Amiens.

Left
Bablot in a four-cylinder Delage Type Y designed by Arthur Michelat (110 x 185mm, 7032cc). He was fourth across the finishing line at Amiens.

Below
Another success for Peugeot. The driver, Georges Boillot, receives an enthusiastic and tumultuous welcome on finishing.

Right
Carl Jörns in a four-cylinder Opel (90 x 156mm, 3970cc) prior to the Amiens race.

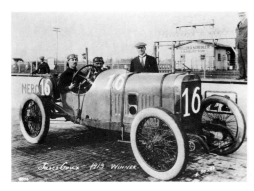

Top
With Jules Goux at the wheel, Peugeot won the 1913 Indianapolis 500. The car, a Peugeot Type L76, with a 7.6-litre engine, covered the 804km at an average speed of 122.155km/h.

Above
The four-cylinder engine of the Peugeot was reduced from 7.6 litres to 5.6 litres to comply with the regulations for the 1913 ACF Grand Prix. Boillot's winning car (pictured here) had a fuel consumption of 17 litres/100km.

cylinder. Capacity was 5655cc (100 x 180mm) and the engine developed 115bhp at 2200rpm. The car had a four-speed gear box with leather cone clutch and was capable of speeds up to 168km/h. Fuel economy proved well inside the allowance, Boillot's using 17 litres per 100km and Goux's 18. Third place behind the two Peugeots went to Jean Chassagne in a six-cylinder 4479cc (80 x 148.5mm) Sunbeam.

The Peugeot was without doubt the most technically advanced car of the time, with twin camshafts, hemispherical combustion chambers and two pairs of valves per cylinder, inclined at 45 degrees and desmodromically operated. These features are still found in high-performance engines to this day. The increased efficiency of the racing engine of the day can be illustrated by comparing the 1913 Peugeot with the 130hp Fiat of the type used by Nazzaro to win the 1907 ACF Grand Prix. The Italian car developed eight horsepower per litre, its French successor 20.4bhp/litre. The Peugeot Grand Prix car of 1913 was the first to use dry-sump lubrication, a system which later became a standard concept,

and vital as car designs called for engines to be placed lower in the chassis in the interests of reducing the centre of gravity and improving aerodynamic efficiency. Racing engine design underwent tremendous technical change in the 1912–13 period, much of it pioneered by Peugeot.

In an article in *Auto-Jahr* the English motor engineer and journalist Harry Mundy wrote:-

"The three promoters, Boillot, Goux and Zuccarelli, submitted an interesting plan to Robert Peugeot which, showing considerable foresight, he enthusiastically supported. According to this plan a number of cars were to be designed and built in preparation for races without involving the main Peugeot factory. The budgetted production cost per car was estimated to be 45,000 marks and the design was planned to be a combination of the successful French Grand Prix car of 1912 and two 3-litre vehicles which had participated in the Coupe de l'Auto.

"None of these three gentlemen had any qualifications in racing engine design but they were able to contribute valuable first-hand driving experience. Zuccarelli was the man with the ideas. He had an extraordinary conceptual ability and had had an invaluable training period with Birkigt at Hispano-Suiza.

"As none of them was a designer, they looked around for someone with the necessary technical expertise, and found their man in Swiss engineer Ernest Henry, at that time working for the Labor-Picker motor company. Henry's achievements have, in many ways, been somewhat exaggerated by historians. After the War he would be responsible for the eight-cylinder Ballot engine, and was then lured by Louis Coatalen to Sunbeam in England, but he ended his professional life as a draughtsman with Citroën in Paris. His reputation was built on his extraordinary ability to convert ideas into accurate detailed drawings on paper from which, without any difficulty, the parts could be manufactured. The concept of an overhead camshaft had been used earlier by Mercedes and Clément-Bayard. Similarly, the parallel line of overhead valves had also been seen before, in Benz and Pipe designs, and Benz had used four valves per cylinder. But Peugeot pioneered the use of hemispherical combustion chambers, four valves per cylinder driven by twin overhead camshafts and one central spark plug. It was Zuccarelli who furthered this design, the concept of a compact combustion chamber and large valve seats to minimise wear of the valve assembly.

"The cylinder head was cast in one piece and screwed on to a two-part crankcase. The slightly bow-shaped pushrods had bearings at each end of their own return springs. Each unit was totally enclosed and individually lubricated. The valves and valve springs were exposed to maximise cooling.

"The Grand Prix motor of 1912 had a bore of 110mm and a stroke of 200mm (7598cc). Although no precise performance data is now available, it is believed that the engine generated 140bhp at 2200rpm.

"The 1912 ACF Grand Prix was held at Dieppe and the favourites were the Fiats, which had huge (14,143cc) four-cylinder engines. The French did not consider these large engines as serious competition for their, as yet unproven, motors which were miniatures by comparison.

Above
Dario Resta in the 3-litre Sunbeam at the 1913 Coupe de l'Auto in Boulogne.

Middle
Rear view of Chassagne's Sunbeam in front of the pits at Boulogne.

Above right
Felix Magone, the Fiat driver, and his mechanic set an unofficial world record on the track at Bakersfield in California: 25 seconds for a tyre change!

Above
The brilliant Swiss designer, Ernest Henry. He was responsible for the Peugeot's success.

Left
In 1913 the Grand Prix de l'ACF was held in Dieppe, but a Grand Prix de France was also held at Le Mans (picture). Jules Goux in a Peugeot was the winner of this non-formula race.

"Boillot passed all the other competitors and won with an overwhelming margin of 13 minutes at an average speed of 110.25km/h, the car having been clocked at 163.58km/h on the straight. This victory significantly influenced design for the following decade. The Peugeot valve-gear design was the most copied item in future racing motors and many of the principles embodied in it are still valid today."

Other historians maintain that Zuccarelli got his twin-OHC idea from Marc Birkigt, with whom he had worked at Hispano-Suiza, then passed the concept on through Henry to Peugeot. There is even evidence to suggest that Birkigt had patented the design, and that he later took action to protect his interests; the results of any such action are not known. Henry also had connections with the Swiss Pic-Pic company, which made cars under licence for Hispano-Suiza.

Racing cars 1912 to 1913

Year	Make & model	Cylinders	Capacity	Bore	Stroke	bhp	rpm	Gears	Max speed km/h	Dry weight
1912	Sunbeam	4	2 986	80	149	85	2200	4	135	908
1912	Alcyon	4	2 986	85	132	85	2200	4	130	1022
1912	Sizaire-Naudin	4	2 982	78	156	95	2100	4	140	1082
1912	Vinot-Deguingand	4	2 996	89	120	90	2300	3	135	1012
1912	Schneider	4	2 993	80	149	78	2000	4	140	970
1912	Gregoire	4	2 974	80	149	85	2300	6	140	827
1912	Lorraine-Dietrich	4	15 095	155	200	115	2400	4	150	1600
1912	Mathis	4	1 849	70	120	60	2000	4	148	550
1912	Peugeot L76	4	7 598	110	200	148	2200	4	160	1400
1912	Calthorpe	4	2 971	80	149	70	1900	4	145	950
1912	Fiat S74	4	14 137	150	200	190	1600	4	165	1500
1912	Singer	4	2 986	85	132	82	2200	4	150	1120
1912	Arrol-Johnston	4	2 974	80	149	77	2100	5	160	965
1912	Côte	4	2 986	85	132	80	2300	4	145	1045
1912	Rolland-Pilain	4	6 272	110	165	120	2200	4	170	1350
1912	Vauxhall	4	2 991	90	118	89	2400	4	155	877
1912	Lion-Peugeot	4	2 982	78	156	90	2900	4	153	860
1912	Excelsior	6	9 138	110	160	125	2000	5	160	1600
1912	Duesenberg	4	5 750	109	152	135	2400	4	165	1045
1913	Sunbeam	6	4 479	80	148	95	2300	4	165	1072
1913	Delage	4	7 032	110	185	110	2200	5	170	1036
1913	Opel	4	3 970	90	156	88	2300	3	165	842
1913	Mathis	4	1 460	70	140	65	2000	3	150	820
1913	Excelsior	6	6 107	90	160	120	2100	4	160	1008
1913	Schneider	4	5 501	96	190	110	2300	4	158	1096
1913	Itala GP	4	8 345	125	170	120	2000	4	165	1100
1913	Peugeot	4	5 655	100	180	115	2200	4	168	1040
1913	Delage	4	6 200	105	180	105	2300	5	160	1370
1913	Isotta Fraschini	4	10 620	130	200	125	2300	4	150	1065

A Memorable Grand Prix

A great race is run at Lyons. Lautenschlager in a Mercedes wins after a battle against Boillot in a Peugeot. An epoch ends.

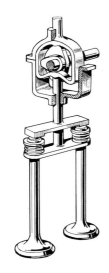

Right
Illustration of the double-valve operation used on the 1914 Delage Grand Prix motor.

Centre
Louis Delage (right) and Arthur Michelat (left) who designed the Type S. Driver Arthur Duray is in the background behind the engine. This photo was taken just before the 1914 Grand Prix.

Below
Dario Resta and mechanic Tommy Harrison at Lyons in 1914. The car is a four-cylinder 4441cc 16-valve Sunbeam.

The 1914 ACF Grand Prix was a high point in motor racing history as shortly afterwards the First World War broke out and the roar of racing engines was silenced for some five years. Ceirano driving a SCAT won the Targa Florio which was run over more than 1000km around Sicily. Felice Nazzaro once again won the Coppa Florio, which was held in Palermo over a distance of 446.5km, this time in one of his own Nazzaro cars. Another make which sprang to fame for the first time here and was to be associated with racing for decades to come was Alfa Romeo.

The French took the first four places in the Indianapolis 500. Thomas was first in a Delage, then Duray in a Peugeot, Guyot in a Delage, and Goux in a Peugeot. A new formula had been introduced for this race, specifying that the engine capacity should be no greater than 450 cubic inches (7274cc).

The ACF Grand Prix, held this time over 752.62km (20 laps of a 37.631km circuit) near Lyons on July 5th, was eagerly anticipated. The 1914 formula restricted engine capacity to 4500cc and weight to 1100kg and there was a sensational number of entries: three French Aldas, three Opels, two Belgian Nagants, three Vauxhalls, three Peugeots, three French Schneiders, three Nazzaros, three Delages, three Sunbeams, two Piccard-Pictets from Switzerland, one Aquila from Italy, three Fiats and a German team of five Mercedes.

The race was an exciting head-on clash between Mercedes and Peugeot. Max Sailer (a Mercedes director) had the task of heading off the French opposition. He led for the first few laps, with Boillot in a Peugeot hanging on grimly behind. Perhaps not surprisingly in view of the political tension in Europe at that time, the race seemed almost to assume political overtones.

Louis Delage

Right
The 1914 ACF. Grand Prix was held on this 37.631km circuit near Lyons. The 1924 Grand Prix was run on the northern half of the track.

Left
Two of these Picard-Pictet cars competed in the 1914 Lyons race. The cars were built in Geneva and had 150hp Schieber engines. The driver is Paul Tournier who had to pull out of the race after 612km.

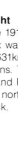
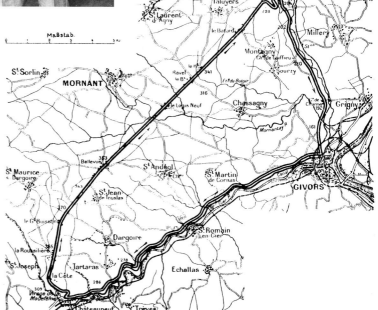

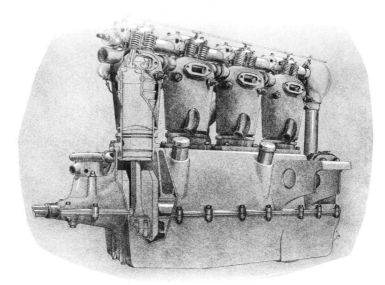

Bottom
The victorious Mercedes team at Lyons poses for a photograph in front of the Mercedes company's administration building in Stuttgart. From left: Lautenschlager (first), Salzer (third) and Wagner (second). Sailer, who had to retire from the race, is also in Wagner's car.

Below
Georges Boillot in a 4494cc Peugeot. He fought bravely but had to give up due to an engine defect.

In this race the Peugeot and Delage Type S cars were fitted for the first time with four-wheel brakes. Mercedes still had a two-wheel braking system, but the German cars had the edge on their competitors as they handled the fast corners much better under the dusty conditions. The aerodynamically shaped tail of the Peugeots, in which the two spare tyres were stowed vertically, proved to be a major drawback under cornering.

Then the leading Mercedes developed a con-rod defect and on the sixth lap Boillot in his Peugeot took the lead. Meanwhile on the 11th lap Wagner in a second Mercedes overtook Goux in the other Peugeot and then also passed Mercedes team-mate Lautenschlager, who was tailing Boillot's Peugeot. Before long Goux had to quit the race when his engine overheated and that left Boillot alone to fight off the aggressive Germans.

On the 15th lap the Peugeot was still 2 minutes and 28 seconds ahead of Wagner, but soon afterwards Lautenschlager got back to second place

For the second time since 1908 Christian Lautenschlager wins the ACF Grand Prix in a Mercedes. He is directed to the grandstand after the victory.

The winning Mercedes had four separate cylinders with measurements of 93 x 164mm, giving a total capacity of 4456cc. The steel cylinders had water-jackets welded on to cool the engine, and two overhead inlet and two exhaust valves per cylinder. The valves were driven by an overhead camshaft and rocker gear. The engine developed 115bhp at 3200rpm (output per litre reached 25.8bhp with a mean piston speed of 17.5 m/sec). Lautenschlager's car weighed in at 1080kg at the inspection station.

This ACF Grand Prix was the last major race in Europe before the outbreak of the First World War, though three more classic races were run in the United States in 1915 and 1916 (the Indianapolis 500, the Vanderbilt Cup and the American Grand Prize).

The Lyons Grand Prix heralded the end of an epoch. The first chapter of a long, varied and fascinating history finished that day. It was the era of the first inter-city races, of races on very long improvised road circuits with all the danger to competitors and spectators that might be imagined, the age of heroic drivers who, under the most difficult conditions, covered murderous distances

and started to reduce the gap between himself and the leading Frenchman. He succeeded in taking the lead, and on the 18th lap the Mercedes was 33 seconds ahead of the Peugeot, increasing that to 1 minute and 7 seconds on the next lap. And then the worst happened.

On the last lap the Peugeot's motor overheated, and it retired with a broken valve. That gave the first three places to Mercedes, Lautenschlager, Wagner and

Salzer finishing in that order. But there was no applause for the winners, only a hesitant acknowledgement of Goux's arrival at the finish in fourth place ahead of Resta in the Sunbeam. Lautenschlager covered the 752.62km in 7 hours 8 minutes and 18.4 seconds (which included stops for petrol and tyres), an average speed of 105.515km/h. With his prize money of 25,000 gold francs, Lautenschlager built himself a house.

Photo taken before the start of the 1914 Tourist Trophy race on the Isle of Man.

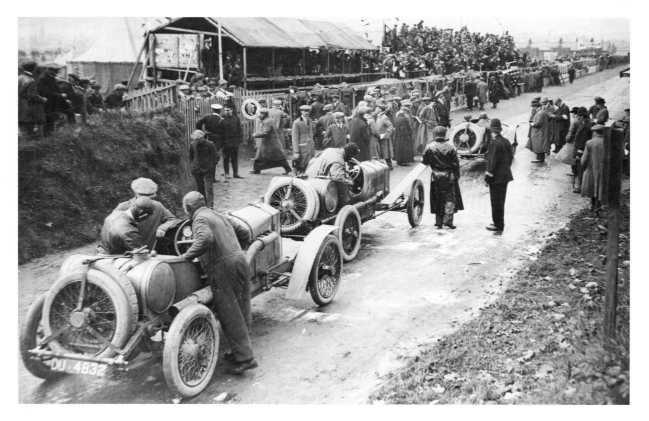

A contemporary Peugeot poster between 1912 and 1914.

PRIMO GRAN PREMIO D'EUROPA
CIRCUITO DI MILANO: R.° PARCO DI: MONZA
8-9 SETTEMBRE 1923

Poster of the 1923 European Grand Prix at Monza.

without either driving comfort or relief. It was the era of strong men who clung to huge steering wheels, with their rudimentary steering linkages, travelling over rough tracks until their hands were bruised and bloody from the continuously jerking steering wheels. The speeds, compared with those of today's racing cars, were not high, but one must not overlook the rubble roads, and the inadequate suspension on the cars. There was no protection against the elements, nor against the dust and stones thrown up by the cars ahead.

The names of the men of these early racing days, names which are closely linked with the technical advancement of the automobile, will always have their place in history and be remembered as pioneers of motor-racing. Some of these names are: Marcel Renault, Camille Jenatzy, Vincenzo Lancia, Felice Nazzaro, Christian Lautenschlager, Jules Goux, Carl Jörns, Ferenc Szisz, Georges Boillot, Alessandro Cagno, Paul Bablot, Louis Wagner, Arthur Duray, Victor Hémery, Dario Resta, Max Sailer, Barney Oldfield, Otto Salzer, Théodore Pilette, David Bruce-Brown and Ralph De Palma.

Top
A 3.3-litre Vauxhall in the 1914 Tourist Trophy race.

Above
In 1915 Ralph De Palma won the Indianapolis 500 in the same car which had won the 1914 Lyons race, a 4.5-litre Mercedes.

Racing cars 1914 to 1916

Year	Make & model	Cylinders	Capacity	Bore	Stroke	bhp	rpm	Gears	Max. speed km/h	Dry weight
1914	Sunbeam	4	3300	81	160	92	2800	4	160	850
1914	Peugeot	4	4491	92	169	112	2800	5	180	910
1914	Peugeot L25	4	2472	75	140	80	3000	4	150	880
1914	Alda	4	4441	94	160	100	2700	4	155	1010
1914	Opel	4	4441	94	160	105	2700	4	160	935
1914	Nagant	4	4443	94,5	158	108	2600	5	150	1055
1914	Vauxhall	4	4487	101	140	130	3300	4	160	1070
1914	Peugeot	4	4494	92	169	112	2800	4	185	1060
1914	Schneider	4	4441	94	160	110	2800	4	150	1085
1914	Nazzaro	4	4441	94	160	100	2700	4	155	1095
1914	Delage S	4	4441	94	160	113	2800	5	160	1098
1914	Sunbeam	4	4441	94	160	115	2900	4	165	1095
1914	Piccard-Pictet	4	4431	97	150	107	2600	4	145	1095
1914	Aquila Italiana	6	4494	85	132	118	2800	4	150	1095
1914	Fiat S57/14B	4	4492	100	143	135	3000	4	145	1025
1914	Alfa	4	4490	100	143	88	2950	4	150	1050
1914	Humber	4	3288	82	156	90	2600	4	160	1045
1914	Mercedes	4	4483	93	165	115	3200	4	180	1092
1914	Duesenberg	4	5920	111	152	95	2600	4	165	1020
1914	Maxwell	4	4885	95	171	130	3200	4	175	1010
1915	Stutz	4	4839	94	164	120	2700	4	160	1070
1916	Duesenberg	4	4900	99	152	100	2800	4	180	1000
1916	Duesenberg	4	4890	95	171	125	3000	4	180	970
1916	Frontenac	4	4900	98	162	140	3100	4	185	1045
1916	Miller	4	4740	92	178	125	2950	4	185	990
1916	Premier	4	4500	93	168	135	3200	4	180	1030

Again the Engines Roar

After the war, the era of the eight-cylinder engine begins. Ballot builds racers for Indianapolis in record time. Designers apply lessons learned in the aero industry.

Racing continued in the United States — on a restricted basis — throughout the war. The Indianapolis 500 was held twice: in 1915 (when Ralph De Palma won in the same Mercedes that Lautenschlager had driven to victory in the 1914 ACF Grand Prix) and in 1916 (Dario Resta in a Peugeot). 1916 was the year of the unbeatable Henry-designed Peugeots, which won the American Grand Prize and the Vanderbilt Cup as well as Indianapolis.

November 11th 1918 came, and after the terrible years of the war the world started to breathe again; the global conflict was over. But no racing took place in Europe yet: people were more concerned with rebuilding their homes and cities.

The first postwar Indianapolis 500 however took place on May 30th 1919. This and subsequent races at the track were of considerable historical significance because they marked the rise of the eight-cylinder engine. Design and engineering knowledge, particularly in the field of aeronautics, had progressed enormously in the war years, far faster than would have been achieved in peacetime, and new discoveries in metallurgical research enabled lighter and more powerful engines to be built. The technological advancements achieved during the war, particularly in the area of materials, were immediately applied to motor racing.

By now all racing cars had twin camshafts, and chain drive had given way to shafts. Vehicle shapes followed the laws of aerodynamics and car bodies became more and more streamlined, the centre of gravity lowered. At the same time the four-cylinder engines of the prewar years, with their long stroke and large capacity, disappeared, and newly developed eight-cylinder motors took their place. The lighter materials now used for moving parts enabled engines to run at higher revolutions, which in turn resulted in more power for given engine size.

The 1919 Indianapolis race was run to the 300 cubic inch (4916cc) engine capacity formula in force since 1915. For the event, Peugeot sold their four-cylinder OHC 4.5-litre cars, built for the 1914 ACF Grand Prix, to an American team, and dispatched a team of engineers and observers to Indianapolis for the first big international race of the postwar era.

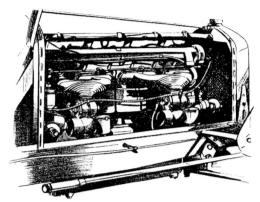

But there had been a major development in France. Between the end of the war on November 11th 1918 and the running of the Indianapolis 500 on May 30th 1919, racing driver René Thomas had persuaded Edouard Ballot to build a new eight-cylinder car. To design the new engine Ballot immediately hired Ernest Henry, who had left Peugeot during the war and become involved in the design of the famous Bugatti aero engine, which consisted of two blocks of eight cylinders each. In record time four 5-litre racing cars were built at Ballot's factory, with the engine made up of two

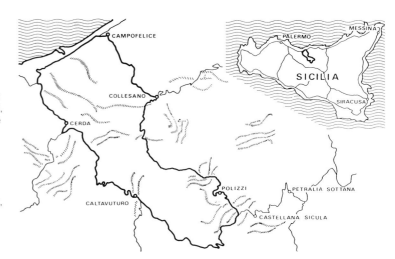

four-cylinder blocks. Cylinder dimensions were 74 x 140mm (4817cc) and the engines, fitted with two Claudel carburettors, developed 140bhp at 3000rpm — which represents 46.7bhp/litre. The weight of the car was 1246kg, which means the power-to-weight ratio was 98bhp/tonne. The strong technical influence of Peugeot and Bugatti was apparent in the Ballot, each of whose cylinders had four valves set at 60 degrees, driven by twin overhead camshafts. The new French car had a top speed of 190km/h.

After exactly 101 days the four vehicles were ready and left Le Havre on April 26th 1919, with drivers Thomas, Guyot, Wagner and Bablot. Testing at Indianapolis showed the gear ratios to be too low, which caused very high tyre wear, but there wasn't time for major modification before the race.

The American Duesenberg brothers had also developed a new eight-cylinder car, with three valves per cylinder which were driven by push rods and an overhead camshaft. In order to minimise surface friction as much as possible the camshaft was supported in only three places. This modern vehicle had cylinder dimensions of 76 x 133mm and a capacity of 4850cc, and developed 120bhp at 4000rpm. The performance at mean piston speed of 18.2m/second was 24.8bhp/litre. The Duesenberg brothers

had built Bugatti aero engines during the war and their design revealed a strong Bugatti influence. Duesenberg became a celebrated name in later years in the world of luxury passenger-car manufacture.

Ralph De Palma in a new 12-cylinder Packard led the race for quite some time, but fell back to sixth place with mechanical problems. The Ballot, the most technically advanced vehicle in the field, had set fastest time in qualifying, but Guyot's was the only one to make it to the finishing line; it took fourth place. The Duesenbergs did not make it either (Allen was fifth). The winner was a four-cylinder Peugeot driven by the American Wilcox. He covered the distance of 804km in 5 hours 40 minutes and 42.8 seconds, averaging 141.68km/h. The advanced prewar Peugeot designs engineered by Ernest Henry provided formidable opposition for many years.

Peugeot had another victory the same year, in the first important postwar race in Europe, the Targa Florio in Sicily. The winning car was a smaller (75 x 140mm, 2472cc) four-cylinder car which developed 80bhp at 3000rpm (26.7bhp/litre). Winning driver was André Boillot, younger brother of the famous prewar driver Georges Boillot, who had been shot down and killed over the English Channel during the war. Behind him came Moriondo in an Itala, Gamboni in a Diatto, Masetti in a Fiat and Negro in a Nazzaro.

The Indianapolis formula was changed in 1920 from a 300 cubic-inch maximum to 183 cubic inches (3000cc), and this year Peugeot and Ballot both sent teams of new cars to the race. The Peugeot was the last true racing car made by that

illustrious firm, a four-cylinder (80 x 149mm, 2996cc) model with three camshafts, five valves per cylinder and twin ignition. Drivers were 1913 Indianapolis winner Goux, 1919 winner Wilcox and André Boillot. There were also new eight-cylinder cars from Duesenberg as well as Ballot (65 x 112mm, 107bhp at 3800rpm). In one of the Ballots De Palma led for 186 of the 200 laps but had to slow with a magneto malfunction, a bitter disappointment for the enormously successful Italo-American.

Winner was Swiss-born Gaston Chevrolet in a four-cylinder Monroe (79 x 152mm, 92bhp at 3200rpm). In spite of the much smaller engine limit in force, Chevrolet's winning average of 142.43km/h was only marginally slower than the record of 144.55km/h set by De Palma in the 4.5-litre Mercedes in 1914. Thomas finished second in another Ballot, followed by Duesenberg drivers Milton and Murphy, then De Palma in his Ballot.

After an interval of six years international racing returned to France with a 410.4km voiturette race at Le Mans. Cars in this race had to weigh between 350 and 500kg and have engines smaller than 1400cc. Friderich in a Bugatti won the race at an average speed of 92.134km/h.

Only Italians entered the next race, the 432km Targa Florio, and Meregalli in a Nazzaro crossed the finishing line first, with Enzo Ferrari, then aged 22, second in an Alfa Romeo. In the 1930s Ferrari would use Alfa Romeos in his Scuderia Ferrari; after the Second World War, he became world-famous as manufacturer of the cars that bear his name.

The First Italian Grand Prix

Italy runs her first Grand Prix, near Brescia, along the lines of the ACF race, revived this year at Le Mans. Hydraulic four-wheel brakes are fitted to the Duesenberg which Murphy takes to victory at the Sarthe.

PONTLIEUE

START

HIPPODROME CAFÉ

ARNAGE

MULSANNE

1921 saw the revival of the French Grand Prix, run as ever by the ACF, and the first Italian Grand Prix. The 3-litre Indianapolis formula, with a minimum weight of 800kg, was adopted for both these races. The French Grand Prix took place on the 17.26km Le Mans circuit which, from 1923 onwards, would be home of the famous 24-hour sportscar race. For the 1921 Grand Prix the circuit was lapped 30 times for a total distance of 517.86km. On the starting line were Duesenberg, Ballot, Talbot, Mathis and Talbot-Darracq.

The Duesenberg was admired not only for its immaculate finish but also for its brakes, for it was the first car ever to start a Grand Prix equipped with a hydraulic four-wheel system — another technical milestone. The American car had an eight-cylinder 2964cc (63.5 x 117mm) engine which delivered 115bhp at 4225rpm. The race became a neck and neck duel between Duesenberg and Ballot, and at the end it was American Jimmy Murphy who won for Duesenberg, with his countryman De Palma second for Ballot. Murphy's average was 125.69km/h, achieved in spite of the bumpy track, which was not sealed and deteriorated rapidly as the race progressed. Ballot also entered a 2-litre

car (69.6 x 130mm, 1986cc, 90bhp at 5000rpm), which Goux brought home in third place.

The 1921 Indianapolis race had gone to Milton in an eight-cylinder Frontenac (67 x 107mm, 2980cc, 125bhp at 4300rpm, 1020kg) ahead of Sarles in a Duesenberg. In the Targa Florio, the Italian teams of Fiat, Alfa Romeo, Itala, Ceirano, SCAT, Diatto, Aquila and Chiribiri met fierce competition from the German Mercedes. Giulio Masetti won in a Fiat Type S57A/14B (four-cylinder, 104 x 143mm, 4859cc, 150bhp at 3500rpm), a model originally built in 1916 but incorporating the latest technology. Second across the line was Sailer in a Mercedes 28/95, followed by a pair of 20/30ES Alfa Romeos (102 x 143mm, 4250cc, 67bhp at 2600rpm) driven by Giuseppe Campari and Ugo Sivocci.

Until now the ACF Grand Prix had been the only race of its kind, but this year the Italians joined in with a similar race of their own. The inaugural Italian Grand Prix took place on September 4th, on a 17.3km triangular road circuit based on Montichiari near Brescia. There were only six starters, three 3-litre Ballots driven by Goux, Chassagne and De Palma, and a trio of new eight-cylinder Fiats driven by Pietro Bordino (a former Fiat riding mechanic), Louis Wagner and Ugo Sivocci. Fiat's new contender, the 801-402, had a 2973cc (65 x 112mm) engine developing 120bhp at 4400rpm (40.2bhp/litre); mean piston speed was 16.4m/second, power/weight ratio 130bhp/tonne. In one of these Bordino led for much of the race but was then forced to abandon. Goux in a Ballot took over, and had the privilege of making the first entry in the list of winners of the Italian Grand Prix.

After a successful racing programme spanning three years, Ballot now withdrew from the circuits to concentrate on building passenger cars. They continued in this business until 1931, when they were taken over by Hispano-Suiza. Their chief design engineer, Ernest Henry, meanwhile left the firm to work on the development of the racing Sunbeams.

The 3-litre formula was abandoned at the end of 1921 and with its passing, another era ended. From now on European cars raced less and less in the United States and, conversely, the Americans did not appear so often in Europe: the Duesenberg team competed in Europe on one further occasion, at

Above left
In 1921 the ACF Grand Prix was held at Le Mans on its 17,262 km circuit. Later, the 24-hour races were held over this same stretch.

Centre extreme left
Jimmy Murphy, who won at Le Mans in 1921 in a Duesenberg, pointing out the hydraulic brakes.

Centre left
Henry Segrave in the 1921 16-valve Talbot with 1.5-litre engine.

Below left
In 1921 Tommy Milton won the Indianapolis 500 in a Frontenac.

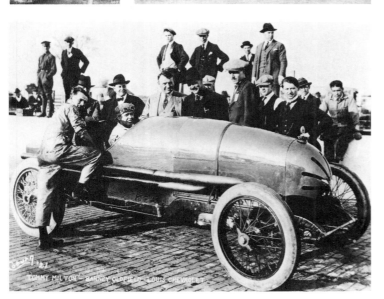

Monza in 1925, but many more years would pass before Transatlantic competitors returned in strength. Indeed, there was little American influence in Europe until the mid 1960s, when Ford and Chaparral sportscars were able to compete on even terms against the top European makes in such events as the Le Mans 24-hour races. Trade the other way had resumed in 1939 and 1940, when an Italian Maserati driven by the American Wilbur Shaw twice won at Indianapolis, but the old tradition of the 1910s was not revived until the 1960s when the British Lotus, Brabham, Lola and — later — McLaren designs started winning at Indianapolis and in similar races in North America. A few European drivers were on the starting line in the first Indianapolis races after the Second World War, and Alberto Ascari in a Ferrari attracted a lot of attention in 1952. There was a different sort of clash between American and European racing traditions in 1957 and 1958 when a 500-mile race was staged on the high-speed banked track at Monza, the Milan Automobile Club inviting the top drivers from Indianapolis as well as European teams. But the two races run received little support from the Europeans — or the paying public — and the experiment was not repeated.

The 3-litre formula was replaced by one for engines two-thirds that size, bringing to an end the era of long-stroke motors. These had delivered high power at low engine speeds, which kept piston speed to an acceptable level. The eight-cylinder Ballot with which Jules Goux won the first Italian Grand Prix, for example, had a stroke 1.8 times the bore, and its mean piston speed at engine speeds between 4000 and 4500rpm was between 15 and 19m/sec. But now an increasing amount of research was directed towards reducing engine weight which led to the use of lighter metals and alloys.

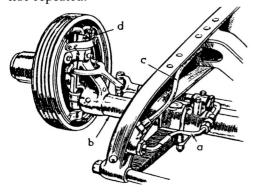

Above
The four-wheel hydraulic brake system of the Duesenberg which won the ACF Grand Prix at Le Mans in 1921.

Right
Valve-gear arrangement of the 3-litre Ballot of 1921.

Racing cars 1919 to 1921

Year	Make & model	Cylinders	Capacity	Bore	Stroke	bhp	rpm	Gears	Max. speed km/h	Dry weight
1919	Ballot Indianapolis	8	4817	74	140	140	3000	4	189	1246
1919	Ballot 3L	8	2973	65	112	108	3800	4	180	920
1919	Duesenberg	8	4260	73	127	100	3000	3	185	1130
1919	Duesenberg	8	4850	76	133	120	4100	3	180	1150
1919	Miller	4	2980	79	152	118	4000	3	185	970
1920	Peugeot	4	2996	80	149	105	3800	4	165	1000
1920	Duesenberg GP	8	2980	63	117	115	4250	3	183	1160
1920	Frontenac	4	2980	79	151	120	4200	3	185	1020
1920	Monroe	4	3000	79	152	98	3200	3	165	1060
1921	Alfa Romeo 40/60	4	6082	110	160	82	2400	4	160	1100
1921	Alfa Romeo 20/30ES	4	4250	102	130	67	2600	4	155	830
1921	Mercedes 28/95	6	7274	105	140	150	4200	4	185	980
1921	Ceirano CS/24	4	2968	85	130	95	3950	3	155	850
1921	Sunbeam GP	8	2973	65	112	108	4000	4	176	1014
1921	Diatto GP	4	2950	90	116	105	3700	4	155	960
1921	Peugeot Indianapolis	4	2976	80	148	108	4000	4	176	1050
1921	Peugeot Indianapolis	4	2950	85	130	110	4200	4	180	1050
1921	Fiat 801-401	4	2973	85	131	112	4000	4	160	810
1921	Fiat 801-402	8	2973	65	112	120	4400	4	170	920
1921	Frontenac	8	2980	67	107	125	4300	3	180	1020
1921	Miller	8	2980	68	104	125	4000	3	185	990
1921	Austro-Daimler	6	2992	74	116	109	4500	4	176	1130
1922	Duesenberg	8	2980	63	117	125	4000	3	185	1170
1922	Frontenac	4	2980	79	151	120	4200	3	185	1030
1922	Bentley	4	2994	80	149	90	3900	4	160	1250

A New 2-Litre Formula

Fiat wins both the ACF Grand Prix at Strasbourg and the Italian Grand Prix at Monza, on a circuit built in 100 days. New eight-cylinder engine for Bugatti.

In 1922 the Grand Prix formula was replaced by a 2-litre formula and the vehicle weight specified at 650kg minimum, though Indianapolis did not make the switch until 1923. The new formula remained in force till 1925.

New racing circuits were being built too. A privately owned course, regarded as one of the best of its time, was constructed in Berlin. This was known as the AVUS, an abbreviation of the German words for Automobile Traffic and Practice Road. First mooted before the First World War, work on the track was started by thousands of prisoners during the war but then came to a standstill. The construction work was completed only shortly before the track's official opening on September 24th and 25th 1921. The Avus was 19.7km long but, after the Second World War, only 8.25km of this was used. It reached the height of its popularity in the thirties when specially prepared Mercedes and Auto Union streamliners raced before crowds of 300,000, clocking speeds of 300km/h. The circuit consisted of two long straights and two bends. The original North Curve was a fairly gradual bend but it was remodelled in 1936 and banked at 43 degrees. The Avus was used in its altered state till 1967, but for some unknown reason the banked corner was subsequently demolished and, since 1971, has been a flat and gradual sweep.

Another new complex opened this year became even more of a household word, and a mecca for racing enthusiasts from all over the world. This was the Monza Autodrome just outside Milan in

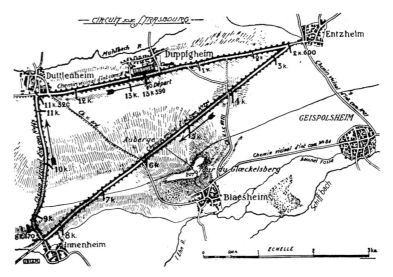

The 1922 ACF Grand Prix took place on a 13.39km triangular circuit at Strasbourg. The Bugatti factory was nearby.

Italy. Built in a former royal park, on land donated to the Club by the local Milan and Monza communities, the project was publicly announced in February 1922. Work began on May 15th, Felice Nazzaro and Vincenzo Lancia turning the first sods. The first race was scheduled to take place on September 3rd and work had to be finished by August 15th, so the track had to be built in exactly 100 days. The day after the official ceremony, 3500 workers started with 200 horse-drawn carts, 30 trucks and two small steam-engines. A small railway was laid alongside the planned 5km circuit on which 80 wagons moved the soil from excavations. The job was finished on August 15th, a 5.5km road circuit and a 4.5km banked oval having been built in exactly 100 days. Today the oval is no

longer in use, the soft underlying terrain having made it increasingly uneven over the years.

Although the 5.5km track is nearly 80 years old and has undergone several modifications, it is still being used, and, since the 1939 demise of the Brooklands

Above
Biagio Nazzaro (nephew of Felice Nazzaro) in his Fiat 804 before the Strasbourg Grand Prix. The younger man died in an accident during the race.

Left
The broad start/finish straight of the Strasbourg circuit. The cars are being lined up for the race.

Top
The victor Felice Nazzaro, in his fast six-cylinder 1991cc Fiat 804-404. Nazzaro was also winner of the 1907 ACF Grand Prix.

Centre
De Vizcaya in a streamlined 1991cc eight-cylinder Bugatti Type 29. The exhaust was centrally located at the rear of the car.

Below
Clive Gallop in his twin-cam four-cylinder 1487cc Aston-Martin. A second Aston-Martin was driven at Strasbourg by Count Zborowski.

Top
A 1975cc four-cylinder Sunbeam, with Segrave driving. He had to give up while in fifth position, when his car developed tappet trouble. For 1923 Sunbeam built a six-cylinder engine.

Centre
The former Peugeot driver Jules Goux raced a very streamlined four-cylinder Ballot at Strasbourg. Ballot's designer Henry had redesigned the earlier eight-cylinder engine as a four.

Below
Louis Wagner in an eight-cylinder Rolland-Pilain, which had left-hand steering.

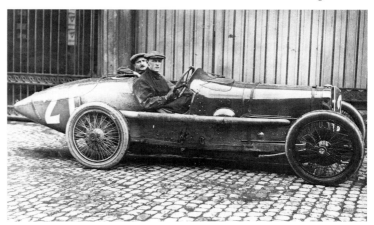

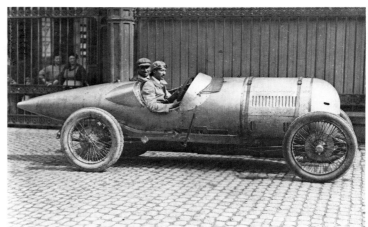

track in England (built in 1907), is the oldest purpose-built motor racing circuit in Europe.

Indianapolis, built in 1909, remains the world's oldest circuit still in use.

Fiat's successful 1922 season started with the ACF Grand Prix, held this year on a 13km circuit near Strasbourg. The beautifully-built six-cylinder Fiat 804–404 had a twin overhead-camshaft engine of 1991cc (65 x 100mm) and, with a 7:1 compression ratio, developed 112bhp at 5000rpm. Drivers were Felice Nazzaro, his nephew Biagio Nazzaro and Pietro Bordino. Among the other makes, Bugatti introduced its new eight-cylinder Type 29, Sunbeam started with a four-cylinder car designed by the former Peugeot and Ballot engineer Ernest Henry, Aston Martin was represented by a four-cylinder 1.5-litre machine and Rolland-Pilain fielded an eight-cylinder car. Other firms participating were Mathis, Slim-Pilain and Ballot.

For the first time in Europe competitors were sent off in this race from a massed start (as was the practice at Indianapolis) rather than being dispatched singly or in pairs, and the Fiats led all the way. The old battler Felice Nazzaro, winner of the 1907 ACF Grand Prix at Dieppe, took the lead from the start but was overtaken on the fifth lap by his team-mate Bordino. On the last lap Biagio Nazzaro was killed in an accident caused by a fault in the rear axle. Bordino retired through the same cause, though fortunately survived the experience, and Felice Nazzaro won the ill-fated race in which his nephew had died. It was his last

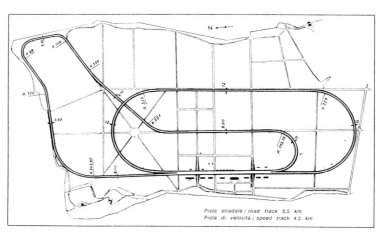

The Monza circuit was built in 100 days. It consisted of a 5.5km road course and a 4.5km high-speed oval. Felice Nazzaro and Vincenzo Lancia turned the first sods.

Pista stradale / road track 5,5 km
Pista di velocità / speed track 4,5 km

major victory. Only three cars rolled across the finishing line. Nazzaro covered the 802km distance in 6 hours 17 minutes and 17 seconds, at an average speed of 127.67km/h. De Vizcaya was second in a Bugatti, one hour beind the winner, followed by Marco in another Bugatti.

Fiat was also successful in the second Italian Grand Prix, held on the newly completed Monza track on September 10th. (The track was then known as the

Paul de Vizcaya

Circuito di Milano.) Once again the Fiat 804–404 won, this time with Pietro Bordino at the wheel. The circuit had been inaugurated a week earlier with a Voiturette Grand Prix for 1500cc cars, when some 100,000 spectators lined the track in teeming rain to witness Bordino take a four-cylinder Fiat 803–403 (65 x 112mm, 1486cc, 63bhp at 5000rpm) to victory.

In other races this year Giulio Masetti won the Targa Florio for Mercedes, Chassagne took the Tourist Trophy, the first held since 1914, in a Sunbeam, and Jimmy Murphy won the Indianapolis 500, the last run under the 3-litre formula, in a Murphy Special, which was a Duesenberg powered by a powerful new Miller engine.

Above
Alfieri Maserati in a Diatto 20S during a stop in the 1922 Italian Grand Prix at Monza. It was a rainy day and Maserati careered off the track.

Right
Some 100,000 spectators lined the track, despite the teeming rain, to watch the first Monza race in 1922.

The supercharged eight-cylinder Fiats win the third Italian Grand Prix. Segrave in a Sunbeam is first over the line in the ACF Grand Prix. The first 24-hour race is run at Le Mans.

1923 was significant for a number of reasons. Single-seater racing cars appeared at Indianapolis for the first time and, also for the first time, a supercharged car (the Fiat 805–405) won a Grand Prix. In addition, a mid-engined car appeared — years before its time. This was the Benz, in which the engine was mounted just forward of the rear axle, and which also employed independent suspension on all four wheels, another first for a Grand Prix car. The trend towards improved streamlining continued, with torpedo shapes, circular in cross-section, appearing on Bugatti, Ballot and Benz cars. There was no

Right
The 1923 ACF Grand Prix was run on this 22.83km circuit at Tours.

Below
The Bugatti team took part at Tours with these four rather tank-like Type 32 cars, using the 1991cc eight-cylinder engine.

Above
Victor Hémery in an eight-cylinder Rolland-Pilain.

Left
There was no fire-wall between cockpit and engine in the Bugatti Type 32.

shortage of originality in other designs. *Société Anonyme des Aeroplanes Gabriel Voisin* built a special machine with all-enclosed bodywork, its sharp lines appearing very odd to modern eyes. Voisin, inspired by his experience in the aero industry, constructed the cars on a semi-monocoque principle, but their six-cylinder 1978cc motors were lacking in power compared with the opposition. The Voisin team took part in both the ACF and Italian Grands Prix without success.

Right
Henry Segrave after his win at Tours. His Sunbeam was a copy of the previous year's six-cylinder Fiat, and had been designed by the former Fiat engineer Bertarione, who now worked for Sunbeam.

Above
Voisin called on his experience in aviation construction to build a monocoque chassis out of timber reinforced with small steel tubes and plated with aluminium. The motor was however underpowered.

Following Fiat's lead, Sunbeam and Alfa Romeo both introduced six-cylinder models in 1923, but Fiat switched to a new eight-cylinder (60 x 87, 1979cc) car, to which a supercharger had been fitted. This gave it some 130bhp at 5500rpm and the cars led the ACF Grand Prix at Tours until falling back and ultimately retiring because of damage inflicted on the superchargers by dirt and stones drawn into them. Englishman Henry Segrave won in a Sunbeam, whose six-cylinder engine was a copy of the

The first Grand Prix win by a supercharged car was achieved by Fiat in 1923 with the eight-cylinder Type 405 (60 x 87.5mm, 1975cc). A front-mounted Wittig unit of American design was used.

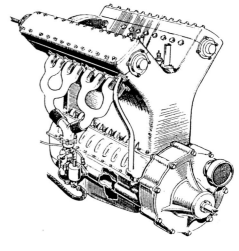

Carlo Salamano

successful Fiat 804–404 with which Nazzaro had won at Strasbourg in 1922. The British car (67 x 94mm, 1988cc) developed 108bhp at 5000rpm, weighed 675kg and had a top speed of 180km/h. Cynics said that the former Fiat engineer Vincenzo Bertarione, who was actively involved with the Fiat 804 design and who was now with Sunbeam, had built a Fiat-Sunbeam. Contemporary publications were equally critical in their references to the "English Fiat" and the "British Racing Green Fiat". With this victory, Henry Segrave became the first British driver ever to win a Grand Prix, whilst for Sunbeam, the win was the most significant event in its history.

Alfa Romeo built their six-cylinder P1 model for the 1923 season but it was never raced. Tragically, driver Ugo Sivocci was killed during a practice run the day before the Italian Grand Prix at Monza, and the car was destroyed. The accident happened on the Vialone Curve, where Alberto Ascari would meet with a similar fate in 1955.

The first 24-hour race at Le Mans took place in 1923, open to touring cars, though most entries were of the type that would later be called sportscars. The Frenchmen Lagache and Léonard drove a Chenard-Walcker for 2209.53km in the 24 hours to win the race at an average speed of 92.064km/h.

The European Grand Prix was held at Monza and Fiat, now with a new type of supercharger, took first place, Carlo Salamano being the successful driver and Felice Nazzaro taking second in another Fiat 805. Salamano stayed with Fiat till the 1960s, as test driver responsible for prototype vehicles, and probably covered millions of kilometres during his test-driving career. His Monza success in the eight-cylinder 805, designed by the three-man team of Zerbi, Fornaca and Cavelli, was the first time a car with a supercharged engine had won a Grand Prix.

Right
Final preparations at
the start of the 1923
Indianapolis 500. Three
eight-cylinder Bugatti
Type 30s are in the
second row.

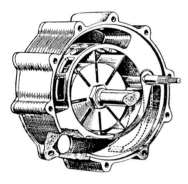

The European 2-litre formula was adopted by Indianapolis in 1923. Milton in an HCS Special won the race at an average speed of 146.3km/h.

The Swiss motorcycle Grand Prix meeting was held on June 9th and 10th 1923 and, for the first time, included a Swiss car Grand Prix.

The first permanent racing track in Spain was built in 1923, at Sitges, near Barcelona. It was a high-speed two-kilometre circuit in the Brooklands style, with steeply banked curves, and was opened on October 28th by King Alfonso, a great racing enthusiast. The first race was for voiturettes, but the big event, run over 300 laps (600km), went to Albert Divo in a Grand Prix Sunbeam. A week after this race another voiturette race was held at Sitges, and won by Dario Resta in a Talbot. Also taking part at this meeting, in a 1.5-litre Chiribiri, was Tazio Nuvolari, yet to achieve the international reputation he was to enjoy in the future.

But Sitges was a complete failure. It was obvious from the start that serious errors had been made in the design of the corners, and the circuit was not used again. The track still exists, but has fallen into disrepair. All major Spanish races between' 1925 and the beginning of the Second World War were held either at San Sebastian or on the Pedralbes circuit in Barcelona. (In some racing records the 1923 Sitges races are referred to as the Spanish Grand Prix.)

A two-kilometre high-speed oval was opened at Sitges near Barcelona in October 1923. The track was abandoned after very few races however as the bankings had been poorly designed.

Alfa Romeo versus Delage

Jano introduces the supercharged eight-cylinder P2 Alfa Romeo. Delage campaigns a V12. Porsche designs an eight-cylinder Mercedes.

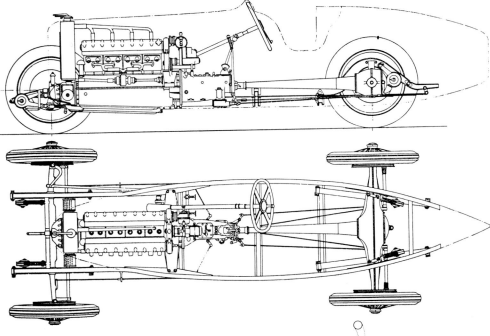

The Grands Prix of 1924 and 1925 were dominated by a new Italian model, the supercharged eight-cylinder P2 Alfa Romeo. At the end of 1923 Alfa Romeo had hired the young technician Vittorio Jano (who, as late as 1954, was responsible for the design of the Formula One Lancia D50). Starting with the six-cylinder P1 Alfa in which Ugo Sivocci had been killed at Monza, Jano designed a new twin-camshaft straight-eight engine of 61 x 85mm (1987cc), fitted with a Roots supercharger. This gave 145bhp at 5500rpm in the first year, at a mean piston speed of 15.6m/sec. The chassis was built in the traditional fashion with two large metal rails on either side of the car, across which were rigid axles supported by leaf springs front and rear. Together with the 12-cylinder Delage, the Alfa Romeo P2 became the best known and most successful car in 1924 and 1925.

The red two-seater, with its clover-leaf emblem on the scuttle, appeared in public for the first time at Cremona, where it won, and then took the ACF and European Grand Prix, held this year on a 23km circuit near Lyons, and also the Italian Grand Prix at Monza. Bugatti's reputation dates from that Lyons race, where the famous eight-cylinder Type 35, which would become the most successful model in the history of the marque, made its appearance. Alfa Romeo took part in the ACF race with a trio of P2s driven by Antonio Ascari, Giuseppe Campari and Louis Wagner. Their strongest rivals were Sunbeam, Delage, Fiat and Bugatti. Segrave in a Sunbeam led at the start but was soon overtaken by Bordino in a Fiat. By the ninth lap the Alfa Romeo driven

by Ascari was in the lead but had to drop out in the 32nd lap due to engine trouble. This let Giuseppe Campari into the lead and his Alfa duly carried on to win the European Grand Prix. Delage 2LCV V12s driven by Divo and Benoist were second and third, followed by Wagner in his Alfa Romeo and Segrave in his Sunbeam.

The Delages, the only 12-cylinder Grand Prix cars built for the 2-litre formula, had been developed from the 1923 design of engineer Charles Planchon, a cousin of Louis Delage. The engine, whose cylinder dimensions were 51.4 x 80mm (1985cc), had four overhead camshafts and two carburettors, and

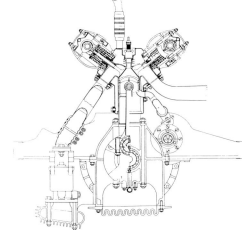

Left
The three Delage 2LCs with two-litre V12 engines at the French and European Grand Prix at Lyons in 1924. These machines were originally designed by Planchon in 1923, but redesigned by Albert Lory.

Top
The successful supercharged Alfa Romeo P2 was designed by Vittorio Jano after he left Fiat to join Alfa Romeo in 1923.

Above
The eight-cylinder Alfa Romeo Type P2 had cylinder dimensions of 61 x 85mm and a capacity of 1987cc. In 1924 it developed 140bhp at 5500rpm, but by 1930 that had risen to 175bhp at 5500rpm.

developed 120bhp at 6000rpm. This 12-cylinder 2LCV from Courbevoie (the town where Louis Delage had built his factory) was the first successful V12 in Grand Prix history. It was raced from 1923 to 1925, being continually developed by Planchon and his young assistant Albert Lory.

Ascari made up for his Lyons disappointment by taking a P2 Alfa Romeo to victory in the Italian Grand Prix at Monza. In fact, four red Alfas crossed the finish line in the first four places, Ascari being followed by Wagner, Campari and Minoia, and Alfa Romeo became a household word.

The 1924 Spanish Grand Prix was run at San Sebastian and, in the absence of the Italian teams, Alfa Romeo and Fiat, was won by Segrave in a Sunbeam. He was followed over the line by an eight-cylinder Bugatti and a 12-cylinder Delage. The Delage was considered at this time to suffer from chassis deficiencies, and Albert Lory, the young Delage engineer, was given the task of modifying the car for 1925. At the start of the Spanish race the lead had been

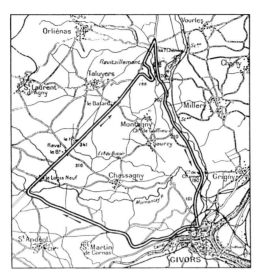

taken by a four-cylinder Mercedes driven by Guilio Masetti, but he subsequently left the road and had to retire. But earlier in the year Mercedes had once again won the Targa Florio, Christian Werner leading the field home with a supercharged four-cylinder car developing 120bhp.

Only Americans took part in the Indianapolis race, the Europeans appearing to have lost interest in these long 500-mile battles.

Vittorio Jano was not the only brilliant new designer to appear on the 1924 racing scene with a new Grand Prix model: there was also Ferdinand Porsche.

Then aged 48, Ferdinand Porsche had joined the Daimler company in Stuttgart from Austro-Daimler in Vienna, where he had been responsible for the design of the little "Sascha" models which had distinguished themselves in the 1922 Targa Florio. Under his direction the four-cylinder 2-litre Mercedes was fitted with a supercharger, and it was with one of these M7294 cars that Christian Werner won the Targa Florio on April 27th 1924. It was the first victory for a supercharged Mercedes. Also on the 1924 Mercedes team was Alfred Neubauer, later famous as team manager; he had moved from Austro-Daimler to Stuttgart with Porsche. It was in this year that the technical department of the University of Stuttgart conferred an honorary doctorate on the genial Ferdinand

Antonio Ascari

Giuseppe Campari

Above
The 1924 European Grand Prix was held on a 23.145km circuit south of Lyons.

Left
Last-minute briefing for drivers before the Lyons race.

Right
The famous Bugatti Type 35 (two-litre eight-cylinder) made its debut at the European Grand Prix at Lyons. Ettore Bugatti is at the wheel.

Left below
Victory celebration in the Alfa Romeo camp at Lyons in 1924. On the right, winner Giuseppe Campari (with racing goggles and Alfa pullover); Ascari is next to him.

Porsche. He meanwhile designed and developed a new supercharged eight-cylinder 2-litre car for the Italian Grand Prix, originally set down for September 7th. However Fiat withdrew their entries and when Mercedes encountered technical problems with the new engine, the Italian Grand Prix organisers postponed the race until October 19th.

The supercharged Alfa Romeo P2, with Antonio Ascari driving, crossed the finishing line first. This victory was convincing evidence of the genius of the young engineer Jano, who was a leading member of the P2 design crew.

The Mercedes team at Monza in the eight-cylinder M218s included Werner, Masetti, Neubauer, Merz, Zborowski and

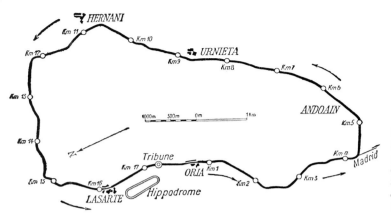

a young man by the name of Rudolf Caracciola. But in spite of the entry of four cars and the M218s' extremely powerful eight-cylinder motors they were unable to defeat Alfa Romeo. Optimum performance of the Mercedes could only be achieved at peak revolutions and problems also arose with the cars' roadholding.

But the most tragic event was the death of Zborowski when his Mercedes left the track on the Lesmo Curve. Following this accident the M218 was never used again as a Grand Prix car, though the M214 was later rebuilt into a sportscar with which Rudolf Caracciola won the 1926 German Grand Prix on the Avus track in Berlin.

The Alfa Romeo P2 was the first successful Grand Prix model built by the Milan company. Vittorio Jano, responsible for the P2, had been with Fiat in Turin since 1911 and had been closely involved with the building of the Fiat which raced in the 1914 ACF Grand Prix at Lyons. He was hired by Nicola Romeo in September 1923 and joined Alfa Romeo in Milan. The fact that, again and again, leading designers were enticed away from Fiat was partly responsible for the Turin car maker withdrawing from Grand Prix

racing. During 1923 Jano fitted the GPR/P1 model with a supercharger for testing purposes, the car never being raced after Ugo Sivocci's fatal accident in practice at Monza. Jano then designed the P2, which was a winner.

Jano was joined in January 7th 1924 by Gioachino Colombo, then in his 20s, in the capacity of technical draftsman. Colombo became Jano's personal assistant and worked with him till 1937. During 1937 and 1938 Colombo designed the Alfetta 158 and was responsible after the war for the first Ferrari V12 motor.

In 1924 a new racing car appeared. It was a Swiss-French Schmid design with a six-cylinder sleeve-valve engine with cylinder measurements of 64.8 x 100mm and a capacity of 1980cc, which was

installed in a 1922 French Rolland-Pilain chassis. It first appeared in the ACF Grand Prix and also raced in Spain and Italy. Drivers were Goux and Foresti but the sleeve-valve engine had a poor performance and it soon vanished from sight.

In 1924, the first Spanish Grand Prix was run on a 17.315km circuit at Lasarte near San Sebastian. This circuit was used till 1935.

Left
In 1924, Mercedes won the Targa Florio with a supercharged 2-litre four-cylinder car. The M-7294 motor was designed by Ferdinand Porsche (to the right). At the wheel is Alfred Neubauer, later team manager.

Left below
Mercedes introduced its new eight-cylinder supercharged M218 car at Monza in 1924. The car proved to be poorly designed and was modified in 1926, when it won the German sportscar Grand Prix on the Avus circuit in Berlin.

Top
Winner Antonio Ascari (left) and mechanic Giulio Ramponi pose for the photographer before the 1924 Italian Grand Prix at Monza. The driver's six-year-old son Alberto Ascari (at the wheel of the P2) would be World Champion in 1952 and 1953.

Above
Any driver lapping Monza at over 100km/h in the twenties was made a member of the Club dei Cento all 'Ora and awarded a diploma; Antonio Ascari, pictured, was one of the first.

Alfa Romeo is World Champion

After succeeding in two Grand Prix races Alfa Romeo of Milan wins the first World Championship. Delage wins at Montlhéry and San Sebastian. Motors are now developing more than 90bhp/litre.

The four most important Grand Prix races in the 1925 season resulted in two victories each for Alfa Romeo and Delage. The 1923 V12 Delage 2LCV was fitted with a Roots supercharger which increased performance to an incredible 180bhp at 7000rpm. This represented a figure of 90bhp/litre, and the dream of achieving the magic figure of 100bhp/litre began to look more than possible. But in spite of the power available it was not possible to use this engine to its maximum as the chassis was incapable of handling such power.

The output of the Milan Alfa Romeo P2 was increased from 145 to 155bhp this year, still at 5500rpm. These two cars, the P2 Alfa Romeo and the Delage 2LCV, were in a class of their own in 1925.

Antonio Ascari won the first Belgian Grand Prix at Spa-Francorchamps in an Alfa Romeo ahead of the similar car of his team-mate Giuseppe Campari. The Alfa Romeos were the only cars left running after the Delages all retired. A famous story is told about this race. The spectators were, understandably, not particularly thrilled by the spectacle of two red Alfas circulating alone on the long track, and started booing the Alfa team. Apparently in response to this, the

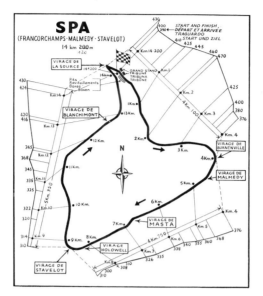

Alfa team manager set out some food on the pit-corner and the drivers stopped, enjoyed a relaxed meal, and then continued with the race.

The next event of the 1925 season was the ACF Grand Prix, which took place this year on a newly built circuit at Montlhéry, near Paris. On the starting line were teams from Alfa Romeo, Delage, Sunbeam and Bugatti. There was

now open rivalry between the Alfa Romeo drivers Giuseppe Campari and Antonio Ascari, both eager to demonstrate their driving skills, and at flagfall they shot into the lead and got straight down to a neck-and-neck duel. But Antonio Ascari lost control of his car, ran off the track and was killed instantly. (Ascari's son, then seven years old, followed in his father's footsteps, winning many races in 1952–53, but sadly suffered the same fate in 1955 during a test-drive in a Ferrari.) As a mark of respect, Alfa Romeo withdrew from the Montlhéry race.

The winner was Delage, the car shared by Benoist and Divo taking first place ahead of Wagner and Torchy in a second car. Masetti was third in a Sunbeam, followed by the eight-cylinder Bugattis of Costantini and Goux.

Bugatti later developed these famous Type 35 models into the most successful racing cars ever produced. Ettore Bugatti, born in Milan in 1881, built his first cars in Molsheim in Alsace and designed the Type 35 in 1924. This eight-cylinder vehicle (61 x 85mm, 1991cc) had a single overhead camshaft and three valves per cylinder. The chassis was built in the typical Bugatti fashion and the car was

Albert Divo

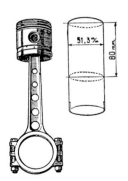

Top
The first Belgian (and European) Grand Prix took place on the 14.2km Spa-Francorchamps circuit in the Ardennes in 1925.

Above
This drawing of the con-rod and piston of the Delage 2LCV demonstrates the bore/stroke ratio of the long-stroke engines of the day.

Right
Albert Divo at Spa. All three V12 Delages had to withdraw, and only two cars, both P2 Alfa Romeos, finished the race.

fitted with lightweight spoked alloy wheels with integral brake drums. The Type 35 was produced in several outwardly identical variations. A detuned version went on sale in 1926 as the Type 35A, while the following year a supercharged version, the Type 35C, was added. At the same time two 2.3-litre versions for non-formula races were introduced, the unsupercharged Type 35T and the supercharged 35B.

Alfa Romeo was not represented at the 1925 Spanish Grand Prix at San Sebastian, and Delage took the first three places, Divo winning from Benoist and Thomas. But the French team withdrew from the Italian Grand Prix at Monza, where the P2 Alfa Romeos of Count Gastone Brilli-Peri and Giuseppe Campari filled the first two places, ahead of Bugatti. In the same year Bugatti, with Costantini driving, took the arduous Targa Florio race in Sicily for the first time.

Most followers of motor racing know that the World Championship has been running since 1950, but few are aware that there was an earlier attempt at a global series for manufacturers, 25 years before. In the 1925 contest, the winning car was awarded a single point, second two, third three and fourth four. A car retiring during the race was given five points, and six were awarded if it withdrew at the start. Another peculiarity was that participation in the Italian Grand Prix was mandatory. Points were awarded on the Indianapolis 500 (won by De Paolo in a Duesenberg), the Belgian and European Grand Prix at Spa, and the

Above
Jules Goux in the 1925 San Sebastian Grand Prix. The Bugatti 35 was still unsupercharged.

Right
Start of 1925 ACF Grand Prix in Montlhéry. De Vizcaya in a Bugatti 35 leads Antonio Ascari in a P2 Alfa Romeo and Count Giulio Masetti in a Sunbeam.

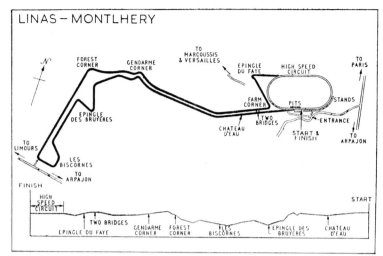

LINAS – MONTLHERY

Following these remarkable successes Alfa Romeo decided to change their logo. The emblem which contained the Coat of Arms of Milan on the left and the Coat of Arms of the Visconti to the right, was from now on surrounded with a laurel wreath.

1925 marked the end of the 2-litre formula that had been introduced in 1922. It was a formula well suited to super-charged engines. Engine performances climbed rapidly from 50bhp/litre for a typical 3-litre car in 1921 to 90bhp/litre for the best 1925 2-litre cars. Engine speeds went up at the same time, especially after the introduction of the supercharger, increasing from 4000/4500rpm to 6000/7000.

ACF Grand Prix at Montlhéry, as well as the Monza race. The Spanish Grand Prix was not however included, apparently at the request of the Italian Automobile Club.

Alfa Romeo won both the European Grand Prix at Spa and the Italian Grand Prix at Monza, though they withdrew from the ACF Grand Prix at Montlhéry following the death of their driver, Antonio Ascari, and Delage won the race. Alfa thus won the inaugural World Championship with 13 points, followed by Duesenberg with 17 and Bugatti with 19 points.

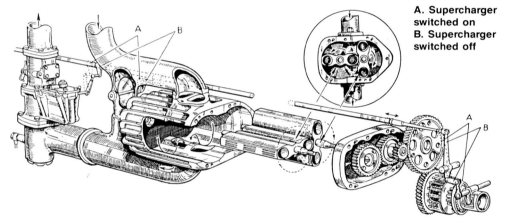

**A. Supercharger switched on
B. Supercharger switched off**

Bartolomeo Costantini

The design concept devised by Swiss engineer Ernest Henry for the 1912 Peugeot, with two overhead camshafts and hemispherical combustion chambers, was almost universally adopted after the First World War, nearly all racing engine designers copying the principle which is still highly regarded. It would not have been possible to develop such powerful engines with the push-rod and rocker-arm system in use before then; the invention of overhead camshafts enabled much closer synchronisation of valve movement with firing sequence at high revolutions.

The new high performance overhead-camshaft system had fewer and lighter components. Valve opening and closing times were more precise and, as a result, a shorter spark could be used for ignition. The system was therefore more effective and, at the same time, tappet noise was eliminated.

Above
In 1925 Pete De Paolo, a nephew of Ralph de Palma, was the first driver at Indianapolis to cover the 500 miles in less than 5 hours. He set the 100mph record in a Duesenberg.

Above right
A Delage 2LCV with a V12 motor at Montlhéry. To the right, Louis Delage.

Above
The cup for the first World Championship (1925) went to Alfa Romeo. From this time the Alfa logo has been encircled by a laurel wreath.

Grand Prix cars of the 2-litre formula era 1922 to 1925

Year	Make & model	Cylinders	Capacity	Bore	Stroke	bhp	rpm	Gears	Max speed km/h	Dry weight
1922	Ballot	4	1994	69,9	130	90	5000	4	165	786
1922	Austro-Daimler	4	1996	74	116	90	5000	4	160	990
1922	Bugatti 29	8	1991	60	88	90	5000	4	185	750
1922	Fiat 804-404	6	1991	65	100	112	5000	4	175	660
1922	Diatto 20 S	4	1997	79,7	100	75	4500	4	155	697
1922	Sunbeam	4	1975	68	136	88	4500	4	160	680
1923	Alfa Romeo P1	6	1990	65	100	95	5000	4	180	850
1923	Alfa Romeo P1 s/c	6	1990	65	100	118	5000	4	205	870
1923	Benz-Tropfenwagen	6	1998	65	100	95	5000	4	185	745
1923	Fiat 805-405	8	1979	60	87,5	130	5500	4	220	680
1923	Rolland-Pilain	8	1968	53	90	100	5300	4	180	820
1923	Miller	8	1978	59,5	89	120	5000	3	186	850
1923	Sunbeam	6	1988	67	94	108	5000	3	180	675
1923	Voisin	8	1978	62	110	90	4400	4	175	710
1924	Alfa Romeo P2	8	1987	61	85	140	5500	4	225	750
1924	Bugatti 35GP	8	1991	60	88	90	6000	4	180	750
1924	Mercedes M7294	4	1989	70	129	150	4800	4	185	870
1924	Mercedes M218	8	1980	61,7	82,8	170	7000	3	210	660
1924	OM	6	1991	65	100	130	5600	4	195	720
1924	Sunbeam	6	1988	67	94	138	5500	3	200	680
1924	Schmid	6	1980	65	100					
1925	Alfa Romeo P2	8	1987	61	85	155	5500	4	240	750
1925	Bugatti 35A	8	1991	60	88	80	4300	4	175	750
1925	Delage 2 LCV	12	1983	51,3	80	190	7000	4	215	1066
1925	Diatto	8	1982	62	82	130	5600	4	175	698
1925	Guyot	6	1984	70	86	125	5500	4	193	690
1925	Miller 122	8	1977	59,6	88,9	200	5800	4		
1925	Duesenberg	8	1984	60,3	86,9	150	6000	4		

French Teams Dominate

Bugatti, Delage and Talbot dispute the new 1.5-litre formula. Most Grand Prix victories in 1926 go to Bugatti and in 1927 to Delage. The 100bhp/litre figure is reached for the first time.

Alfa Romeo, Fiat and Sunbeam all withdrew from Grand Prix racing at the end of the 2-litre era, though the previous season's successful P2 Alfa Romeo was frequently seen in modified form in Formule Libre races with private owners, right up until 1930.

The 1926 and 1927 World Championship Grand Prix seasons favoured the French Delage and Bugatti cars, but a new name, Talbot, also became well known. This Anglo-French marque had been very successful in the 1500cc voiturette class, the size that was being adopted for the new Grand Prix formula. The minimum weight under the new regulations was 600kg, rising to 700kg in 1927. Although cars no longer had to be two-seaters (from now on only the driver had to be carried) most in fact remained in this form.

The two racing seasons of 1926 and 1927 were marked by further advances in engine design and construction.

Below
The design of the eight-cylinder Delage was the best of its time. The 1496cc (55.8 x 76mm) engine was the first in Grand Prix racing to develop more than 100bhp/litre.

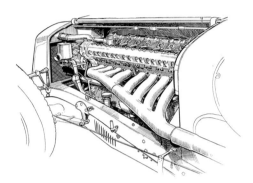

Right
Albert Lory, responsible for the design of the Delage 15-S-8, gained his experience in the aero industry. After the Second World War he designed the CTA-Arsenal and, in the fifties, the Renault turbine car.

Right
Jules Goux is congratulated by Ettore Bugatti after winning the 1926 European Grand Prix at San Sebastian.

Left
Drivers of the Delage 15-S-8 in 1926 suffered extreme physical discomfort due to the location of the exhaust pipes. At the European Grand Prix at San Sebastian the car illustrated had to have five drivers as they were overcome one by one by heat and fumes. All needed medical attention. For the next season Lory turned the cylinder-head around to move the exhaust pipes away from the driver's side.

Because of the formula's restrictions, designers were forced to extract as much power as possible from their newly developed engines if the cars were to be anywhere near as fast as before. By reducing the stroke of their supercharged overhead-camshaft engines they were able to increase engine speeds to 7000 and even 8000rpm, and the magic figure of 100bhp/litre became a reality. In later years, when no limitations on engine size were laid down, performance dropped back to between 70 and 80bhp/litre, and the figures from the 1500cc formula were not in fact bettered until the 750kg weight formula forced designers once again to concentrate on extracting the maximum power within limitations imposed by regulation.

For the 1926 racing season Albert Lory designed the eight-cylinder Type 15-S-8 Delage which, together with the Bugatti 39A, was the most successful car in the

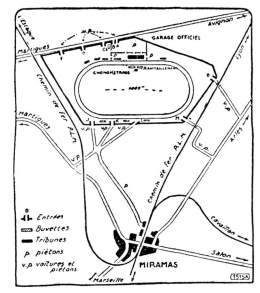

1.5-litre formula. The Delage drivers however suffered great physical discomfort due to the high temperatures around their feet and legs caused by the location of the exhaust system, which made it impossible for them to complete a race without a "cooling off" stop. The design also caused a vacuum to develop and this sucked exhaust fumes into the cockpits. The Delage management accordingly withdrew the car from further competition so that it could be redesigned.

Bugatti, with its well-proven and conventional Type 39 engine, was the success of the racing season. Driven by Jules Goux, the car won the ACF Grand Prix on the fast track at Miramas near Marseilles, though as only Bugattis competed, this was not much of a test. (Goux retired from racing after this event, ending a long career.) Bugatti also won the Spanish Grand Prix and the

Targa Florio with the Italian Costantini driving, and the Italian Grand Prix at Monza, where Jean Charavel, who raced under the pseudonym of "Sapiba", was the winner. In a brochure published by Bugatti in 1926 it was stated that the Molsheim company had won 503 competitions in a single year between January 24th and September 19th 1926, which worked out to more than two victories per day! Included in this total must have been many national as well as international events, as well as numerous class successes.

The 15-S-8 eight-cylinder Delage, despite all Albert Lory's progressive ideas and technical innovations, was able to achieve only one victory, in the British Grand Prix on the high-speed Brooklands circuit, where Robert Sénéchal and Louis Wagner shared the driving of the winning car.

Another car on the racing scene in 1926 was the Type 26 Maserati. Driven by its designer Alfieri Maserati and Guerino Bertocchi, it won the 1.5-litre class of the Targa Florio.

The reason so many leading manufacturers had withdrawn from Grand Prix racing was the enormous research and development costs involved in the

continual design and construction of new cars to meet each formula change.

The Type 15-S-8 Delage was a case in point. Its straight-eight iron block was cast in unit with the cylinder head, used two superchargers and employed no fewer than 60 bearings, making it a very intricate and expensive design. The 55.8 x 76mm (1496cc) engine had twin overhead camshafts and twin carburettors, and developed 165bhp at the unusually high (for those times) engine speed of 6500rpm. That power translates to 110bhp/litre, the first time the magic 100bhp/litre figure had been exceeded. Its rivals, by comparison, produced per-litre figures of 93 (for the 140bhp Talbot) and 80bhp (the 120bhp Bugatti 39A). When the Delage's exhaust system was modified for 1927 in the interests of driver comfort, power went up to 170bhp at 8000rpm (at a mean piston speed of 20.3m/sec). The whole car was very low-slung by comparison with its contemporaries, and had very little ground clearance.

Albert Lory, the car's distinguished designer, had been hired by Louis Delage in 1921 after working as a design engineer for Panhard, Salmson and SCAP. He worked first under the direction of Charles Planchon, a relative of Delage, who had been responsible for the 1923 V12 Delage Type 2LCV. Lory soon took over as head of the racing division and the 15-S-8 Grand Prix car was his first individual project; his second was its successor, which would sweep all before it in 1927. Lory left Delage in 1930 to join SNCM, the aircraft manufacturer, and did not reappear on the motor racing scene until 1947, as designer of the CTA-Arsenal. This car, hailed as France's postwar Grand Prix challenger, was not however a success.

Delage's main rival in 1926, the Bugatti 39A, was the supercharged 1.5-litre version of the 1924 2-litre Type 35. Ettore Bugatti's approach to engine design was a conventional one, allowing only very careful movement along the path of progress. The 39A's supercharged engine (60 x 66mm, 1492cc) with its eight cylinders and overhead camshaft had three vertically positioned valves per cylinder and developed 120bhp at 5500rpm. Bugatti rapidly gained a reputation in this era for producing sturdy and very reliable cars with perhaps less power than some, but compensation in the form of excellent driving qualities and superb roadholding.

The Talbot, designed by the former Fiat and Sunbeam engineer Vincenzo Bertarione, was another new eight-cylinder design. With its low-slung chassis

Ferdinando Minoia

it proved very fast, but was far from reliable. This 1496cc (56 x 75.5mm) car used a Solex carburettor and developed 140bhp at 7000rpm.

The Maserati Type 26 was yet another eight, with twin overhead camshafts and equipped with a Roots supercharger. Its 1491cc (60 x 66mm) engine developed 120bhp at 5500rpm. The Type 26, the first-ever Maserati racing car, was first seen in public at the Targa Florio.

It was obvious at this time that Grand Prix races were attracting fewer spectators and fewer competitors. Only two Bugatti drivers completed the Italian Grand Prix, Charavel and Costantini. In the European Grand Prix at San Sebastian only three drivers crossed the finish line, Goux in a Bugatti, Bourlier in a Delage and Meo Costantini in another Bugatti (Costantini later became manager of the Bugatti factory team). In Spain only Bugatti, Delage and OM were represented.

Above
In 1926 the first British Grand Prix was held at Brooklands. Earth banks were used to incorporate artificial corners into the circuit. Segrave in an eight-cylinder Talbot (making its first public appearance) is seen leading Benoist's Delage.

Left
Sénéchal and Wagner in a Delage 15-S-8 after their victory in the British Grand Prix at Brooklands. The famous "hot exhaust" is visible on the right-hand side of the car. Sénéchal died in 1985 at the age of 95.

Above
Bertarione and Becchia built the 1.5-litre Grand Prix Talbot at Suresnes, Paris. The car had a supercharged eight-cylinder engine but, in spite of its modern design, was not a success. Williams is at the wheel in this photograph.

Robert Sénéchal

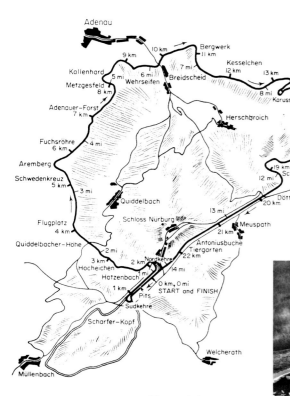

Nürburg-Ring: Start und Ziel mit Nordkehre. Original-Fliegeraufnahme

Above
The Nürburgring, consisting of a 22.835km northern circuit and a 7.747km southern loop, opened in 1927. The circuit was built during the 1920s German slump as a community project to ease unemployment. It had 88 left-hand bends and 84 to the right. The start/finish straight was 2.238km long.

Above right
Three Mercedes-Benz 680s on the start-line for the inaugural Nürburgring race on June 19th 1927. Winner was Rudolf Caracciola in one of these big six-cylinder cars.

Right
A postcard of the Nürburgring shortly after its completion, showing the starting grid and garages.

As previously mentioned the Delage drivers suffered very much from the heat of the exhausts in this race, the location of the pipes causing exhaust fumes to be drawn into the cockpits and temperatures to soar to unbearable levels. Morel was half delirious after ten laps and rolled into the pits. Wagner took over the car but could manage only five laps before he too had to give up. Benoist in another of the Delages also stopped, almost overcome by the heat and fumes, and after 15 laps, only one Delage was still in the race — the two others were parked in front of the pits.

Then a very heart-warming and sportsmanlike event occurred when the despondent Delage management found

the Bugatti driver Sénéchal among the spectators, and he agreed to take one of the stationary Delages back into the race. He wasn't able to last more than five laps either. Goux won the race in a Bugatti.

The second German Grand Prix was run this year on the Avus circuit near Berlin, and won by Rudolf Caracciola in a 1923 Mercedes M218. The M218 had a supercharged 2-litre eight-cylinder engine developing 150bhp at 7000rpm. The first German Grand Prix in 1925 had been raced not on the Avus track but on a 31.3km circuit in the Taunus region, part of the course used for the 1904 Gordon Bennett race and the 1907 Kaiserpreis. Otto Merz won the 1925 race in a Mercedes sportscar, but for some reason this earlier race came to be forgotten, and the official list of German Grands Prix starts with the 1926 Avus

race won by Caracciola.

The 1926 European 1.5-litre Grand Prix formula was also used for the Indianapolis races and, for the first time, the famous name of Miller appears as winner, with a new car driven by Lockhart. Miller cars would dominate Indianapolis racing for many years.

The second World Championship in history was easily won by Bugatti with his supercharged eight-cylinder 1.5-litre Type 39A cars. The Championship events were the Indianapolis 500, the ACF Grand Prix at Miramas, the European Grand Prix at San Sebastian, the British Grand Prix at Brooklands and the Italian Grand Prix at Monza. Bugatti had won at Miramas (a race in which only three Bugattis participated as no other teams had lodged entries), San Sebastian and Monza, Delage took first place at

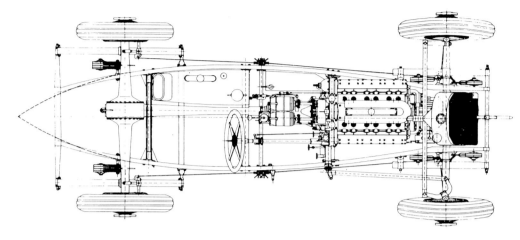

Below
The 1927 Fiat Type 806, whose 1.5-litre 12-cylinder engine was made up of two blocks of six cylinders set in a vee, with two crankshafts. The valves were driven by three overhead camshafts. The cylinder dimensions were 50 x 63mm, giving a capacity of 1483cc, and the engine developed 185bhp at 8500rpm, making it the most powerful Grand Prix engine of its day.

Right
Engine of the Fiat 806 was offset slightly to the left, the driver sitting on the right. The fuel tank was located next to the driver.

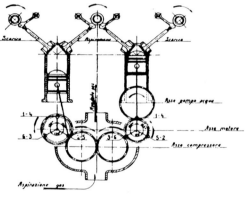

Brooklands, and Miller won the Indianapolis 500. In the final analysis Bugatti, with 11 points, became World Champion, ahead of Delage with 23.

On June 28th and 29th 1926 the two German manufacturers Daimler and Benz had amalgamated to become Daimler-Benz AG, and from now on their products were called Mercedes-Benz. At that time, incidentally, there were no fewer than 86 motor companies in Germany, producing a total of 144 different models.

The 1927 racing season was an especially successful year for Delage. After its winter modifications, the eight-cylinder 15-S-8 proved to be unbeatable. Robert Benoist won the ACF Grand Prix at Montlhéry in one of the Courbevoie (near Paris) cars, and also the Spanish Grand Prix at San Sebastian, the British

Grand Prix at Brooklands and the Italian Grand Prix at Monza. The Targa Florio meanwhile fell to Emilio Materassi in a Bugatti.

The German Grand Prix was held for the first time on the newly-constructed Nürburgring course in 1927 and won by Otto Merz in a supercharged six-cylinder (98 x 150mm, 6789cc) Mercedes-Benz Type S sportscar. The Nürburgring, with a 22.8km northern loop and a 7.8 southern circuit, was built in the mountainous Eifel region in the hope that racing events would attract visitors and tourists — and their cash — to the remote area. The circuit was built over a two-year period and provided much-needed work for the area's unemployed.

The first major event in 1927 had been the Mille Miglia (1000-mile race) in Italy. This was a road race between the towns

On September 4th 1927 Pietro Bordino won the Milan Grand Prix at Monza in the Fiat 806. It was Fiat's last race.

Il «mantovano volante»
e il bolide rosso

Print of a hand-coloured black and white photo of Tazio Nuvolari in the Alfa Romeo P 3 after it made its successful debut at Monza.

A contemporary painting of the 1927 Fiat 806.

A poster of the 1934 Swiss Grand Prix

Right
The first Maserati, the 1.5-litre eight-cylinder Type 26, is readied in Bologna for the Targa Florio. On the right is the car's designer, Alfieri Maserati, who drove the car in Sicily, and next to him is Emilio Materassi. Fourth from the right is the legendary Maserati mechanic Guerino Bertocchi.

of Brescia and Rome and back and was won by Nando Minoia in a 2-litre eight-cylinder OM sportscar. He covered the 1628km distance in 21 hours, 4 minutes and 48.2 seconds at an average speed of 77.238km/h.

Fiat appeared in one race in 1927 with a remarkable new design, which caused a sensation in racing circles. This was the 12-cylinder Type 806 whose motor had two blocks of six cylinders in parallel in a common crankshaft housing, though each set of cylinders had its own crankshaft. The four rows of valves were driven by three overhead camshafts. The supercharged engine had a power output of 185bhp/litre. (The American eight-cylinder Miller, a competitor in the Indianapolis races, was even more powerful.) The Fiat's cylinder dimensions were 50 x 63mm which gave a capacity of 1483cc, and it was capable of speeds up to 250km/h. Its only race was the Milan Grand Prix at Monza where Pietro Bordino drove it to victory. After that successful event, Fiat vanished forever from the racing tracks. The 804, 805 and 806 models were destroyed under instructions from Fiat's board, an order which met with disbelief at the time and which is no easier to understand today. But the famous Turin auto manufacturer was never again represented in Grand Prix racing — apart from its later association with Ferrari.

The 1.5-litre Grand Prix formula ended at the close of the 1927 season, after which cars of this size appeared only in voiturette races, where they had a great public following. Towards the end of 1927, Delage and Talbot followed Fiat and retired from Grand Prix racing.

The most powerful racing car in the

1.5-litre class in the late twenties was the American Miller Type 91 with front-wheel drive. The motor was an eight-cylinder (55.5 x 76.2mm, 1468cc) unit with two overhead camshafts and a centrifugal supercharger. Running on alcohol fuel, it was able to use a compression ratio of 9:1 which gave it 200bhp at 8000rpm. The car was tailored for the Indianapolis track and proved rather less suitable on road circuits. The Miller 91 was used for racing in Indianapolis till 1929 and won the 500-mile event twice, in 1926 and 1928.

Now and again Delage racing cars appeared on various tracks driven by private racing teams and they were still seen in the thirties driven by the British drivers Earl Howe and Richard Seaman in 1.5-litre voiturette races. In 1929, even

the Bugatti works racing driver Louis Chiron could be seen on the start-line for the Indianapolis 500 in a Delage. The car was clocked at 172.72 km/h and Chiron took seventh place in the race.

The third World Championship, held in 1927, was won by Delage with their vastly superior eight-cylinder cars. All four European rounds, at Montlhéry, San Sebastian, Brooklands and Monza, were won by Robert Benoist in a Delage. The Indianapolis 500, won by Souders in a Duesenberg, was once again included in the World Championship but since Americans predominated the points had no bearing on the outcome of the Championship. At the end of the season Delage, with 10 points, was first, followed by Miller with 23 and Duesenberg and Bugatti with 24 points each.

Grand Prix cars of the 1.5-litre formula era 1926 to 1927

Year	Make & model	Cylinders	Capacity	Bore	Stroke	bhp	rpm	Gears	Max speed km/h	Dry weight
1926	Alvis	8	1498	55	78.75	95	5400	4	190	750
1926	Aston Martin	4	1486	65	112	54	4500	4	160	660
1926	Bugatti 39A	8	1492	60	66	120	5500	4	190	740
1926	Delage 15-S-8	8	1487	55,8	76	170	8000	5	209	748
1926	Eldridge	4	1496	69	100	112	5500	4	195	720
1926	Guyot	6	1481	60	86	120	6000	4	190	630
1926	Halford	6	1496	63	80	96	5300	4	190	680
1926	Maserati 26	8	1491	60	66	120	5500	4	200	720
1926	OM	8	1496	56	76	118	5700	4	195	715
1926	Talbot-Darracq	8	1489	56	75.5	140	7000	4	210	700
1927	Bugatti 37A	4	1496	69	100	90	5000	4	180	720
1927	Fiat 806	12	1484	50	63	187	8500	4	250	700

The Formula Changes

Several firms withdraw from racing due to the world-wide economic crisis. Bugatti goes from success to success. Louis Chiron makes a name for himself.

Left
Emilio Materassi in a 1.5-litre eight-cylinder Talbot at Mugello in 1928. Later in the year he was killed at Monza in a similar car.
Below
The Boulogne Trophy race was still being run on unmade roads. Shortly after the start of the 1928 race, Malcolm Campbell leads in a Delage 15-S-8.

Formulae based on engine size had been used to govern Grand Prix racing since 1914: first 4.5 litres, then 3, 2 and finally 1.5 litres, but between 1928 and 1933 there were no such restrictions at the top level, though engine-size limitations remained for the smaller voiturette and "cyclecar" classes. The basis of the Grand Prix formula now was weight and fuel consumption. From 1931 an unrestricted formula was introduced with no limitations for the vehicles but a duration minimum for Grand Prix events.

The official Grand Prix regulations were in fact all but ignored in this period as organisers ran their races under "Formule Libre", a free formula without weight, fuel consumption or distance limitations. The relaxation of the strict Grand Prix rules resulted in a great deal of success for Bugatti, Alfa Romeo and Maserati. Most victories went to Louis Chiron, Grover-Williams, Tazio Nuvolari, Giuseppe Campari, Achille Varzi, Luigi Fagioli and Rudolf Caracciola.

In the 1928 Grand Prix formula the following rules were laid down: minimum weight 500kg, maximum 750kg and minimum race distance 600km.

This was a Bugatti year, the supercharged eight-cylinder Type 35B (60 x 100mm, 2270cc) dominating the major races throughout Europe. Considering that a supercharged car had achieved its first success in the 1923 Italian Grand Prix, Bugatti's adoption of this development was a long time coming. Although the Molsheim manufacturer was now offering a large number of engine variations, each model looked the same — not only the same as each other, but the same as earlier models in the range. Ettore Bugatti had never seen the need to divert from his basic chassis/body configuration.

A handicap formula for sportscars was introduced for the ACF Grand Prix which took place at Comminges and was won by Williams in a Bugatti.

The rising star amongst the racing drivers was Louis Chiron from Monaco who won both the Spanish and Italian Grands Prix this year in a Bugatti 35B.

In a number of biographies of Louis Chiron he is described as the 1928 World Champion, though it has never been discovered whether these World Championships ever took place and if so whether they were recognised as such.

Elisabeth Junek

Louis Chiron

Right
Louis Chiron won the 1928 Spanish Grand Prix at San Sebastian and also the European Grand Prix at Monza.

There were six races towards the end of the year of which three were Grand Prix events. Towards the end of the twenties Grand Prix racing activity tapered off.

The German Grand Prix was once again run for sportscars on the Nürburgring and Rudolf Caracciola repeated his 1926 victory, this time in the new six-cylinder 7.1-litre Mercedes SS. Caracciola, also called "Caratsch", shared the driving with his fellow countryman Christian Werner in this race.

Bugatti had shown well earlier in the season when Albert Divo won the Targa Florio. But there was considerable surprise when it became known that the leader for the first few laps, in a Type 35B, was a lady, the Czechoslovakian Elisabeth Junek. In the German Grand Prix she shared the driving with her husband Vincenz Junek, owner of one of Prague's banking houses. Vincenz Junek had a fatal accident in this event however and as a consequence his wife withdrew from racing.

The 1.5-litre formula was used for the Indianapolis 500 till 1929. Lou Meyer won the 1928 race in a Miller Special with an eight-cylinder twin-overhead-camshaft engine. The meticulously built Miller (it was claimed that it took 6500 working hours to build each car) had the highest horsepower rating of any car built during that time. Lou Meyer also won the 500-mile race in 1933 and 1936, then retired from driving and joined up with Drake to build the four-cylinder Meyer-Drake engine which was to become so well-known in later years. Drake ran the business on his own in the sixties, while Meyer built and prepared the Ford V8 4-OHC engines which were successful in the Indianapolis 500.

Another Bugatti Year

Sixteen-cylinder engines are tried. Bugatti obtains two eight-cylinder Miller engines at the end of the racing season, to study their twin-camshaft design.

1929 was a great year for Bugatti and their drivers, Williams and Chiron, who emerged as joint winners of the most Grand Prix races. Victories in the less important races mainly went to the Alfa Romeo P2, originally built for the 1924–25 2-litre formula.

The official Grand Prix formula for 1929 stipulated a minimum weight of 900kg and a maximum fuel consumption of 14 litres/100km. This formula was however applied to only two Grands Prix, the Spanish race at San Sebastian and the French at Le Mans, most other races being run under unrestricted Formule Libre regulations.

These races reintroduced the trend towards larger capacity engines. Maserati developed a new design, the Type V4, which in effect used two engines, with parallel eight-cylinder Type 26B blocks mounted on a common crankcase, which housed two crankshafts linked by gears. The 3958cc (62 x 82mm) V4 was fitted with two Roots superchargers and developed 300bhp at 5500rpm.

In the German Grand Prix, which was run to sportscar regulations, Louis Chiron in a Bugatti crossed the finishing line first.

The second Grand Prix of 1929 took place on the Monte Carlo street circuit which is still in use, albeit in modified form, today. This first Monaco race was a double victory for Bugatti with Williams and Bouriano in Type 35Bs

taking the first two places. Rudolf Caracciola with his mighty Mercedes SSK (supercharged 7.1-litre engine developing 225bhp) was third. Caracciola and the white Mercedes also won the Tourist Trophy sportscar race. Giuseppe Campari won the Mille Miglia in an Alfa Romeo for the second year in succession, this time at the wheel of a GC Super Sport model with supercharged six-cylinder 1487cc engine.

Léon Duray was the first American to tackle the European season for some time when he took part in a number of 1929 races with a pair of eight-cylinder front-wheel-drive Millers, called Packard Cable Specials, with which he set several speed records at Montlhéry. At the end of the year Duray, who had something of a playboy reputation, swapped his two cars with Bugatti for three Bugatti Type 43 sportscars with 2.3-litre eight-cylinder engines. The supercharged twin-overhead-camshaft Miller engines were the most advanced of the time, and were capable of outstanding performance, but it apparently took Jean Bugatti to persuade his father to enter into the arrangement with Duray. The direct result of the deal was the appearance of the Type 51 Bugatti, a supercharged 2.3-litre eight which was identical to the Type 35B except for its use of double overhead camshafts. All Bugattis from this time would have this feature.

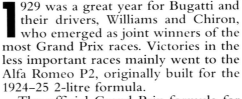

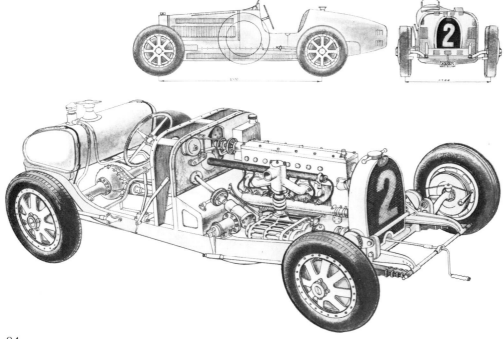

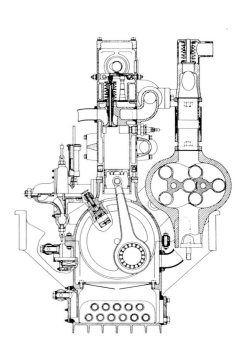

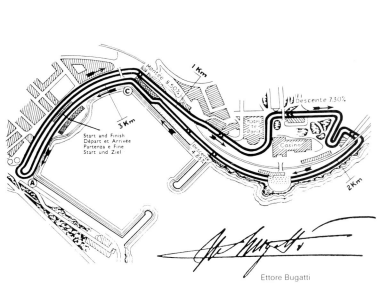

Ettore Bugatti

Above left

The 3.14km Monte Carlo circuit remained unchanged from 1929 until the 1970s, and is still in use in only slightly modified form today.

Above

Williams won the first Monaco Grand Prix in a Bugatti, ahead of an Alfa Romeo 6C-1750 and Caracciola who was third in a mighty Mercedes-Benz SSK.

Left

In the years between the wars most of the major British races were run at Brooklands. The track was best known for its short handicap races, but hosted the British Grand Prix in 1926 and 1927. Brooklands was not used after the Second World War. This picture was taken during the 500 Miles Race in 1929.

Maserati's First GP Victories

Bugatti still dominates the racing scene, but the eight-cylinder Maseratis from Bologna win at San Sebastian and Monza. Indianapolis finally departs from the Grand Prix formula.

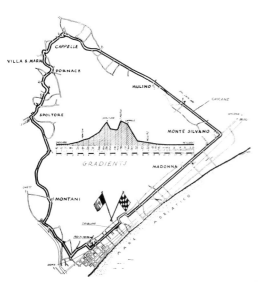

The official Grand Prix formula was being changed more frequently now, with alterations every year. At the end of 1929 it was decided to modify the fuel consumption ruling, and at the same time the weight limit was increased to 900kg. The result was that 30% more fuel was required to compensate for the additional weight.

Alfa Romeo's old P2 was modernised once again, incorporating features from the successful 1930 sportscar. Bugatti built his Type 45, a car with two eight-cylinder engines on the Maserati V4 principle except that the blocks were mated to a common crankshaft. The 16-cylinder 3801cc (60 x 84mm) engine developed 250bhp at 5700rpm. The car was not however a success and the Type 35B remained Bugatti's primary contender. The twin-engined monsters were in fact singularly unsuccessful, for although engine performance was impressive they handled badly, were hard to steer, and suffered from excessive tyre wear.

1930 was another successful Bugatti year. They won the ACF Grand Prix, the Belgian Grand Prix and the Monaco Grand Prix.

Top
The 25.579km Pescara circuit where races where held from 1923 to 1961.

Above
Achille Varzi after his 1930 San Sebastian victory. Standing behind him is the mechanic Parenti.

Above right
Start of the 1930 Spanish Grand Prix at San Sebastian, with Maserati, Peugeot and Bugatti in the front row. Varzi's winning Maserati 26M (No. 8) is on the second row. His wins here and at Monza were Maserati's first.

Left
The Scuderia Ferrari workshops at Modena, with one of the team's Alfa Romeos being prepared for a race.

Above
The Bugatti Type 45 had two parallel eight-cylinder 60 x 84mm blocks. The 16-cylinder 3801cc engine was fitted with two Roots superchargers.

Another excellent performer was the Maserati Type 8C-2500, whose 2495cc (65 x 94mm) engine with Roots supercharger developed 175bhp at 6000rpm. With one of these Achille Varzi won the San Sebastian Grand Prix in Spain and the Monza GP in Italy.

A milestone in the history of the Mille Miglia was Tazio Nuvolari's victory in an Alfa Romeo 6C-1750, when he was the first to average over 100km/h for the course.

In America, meanwhile, the European racing formula was abandoned, and the rules for Indianapolis modified to suit specific local requirements. The engine limit was increased to 366 cubic inches (6000cc) with a minimum weight equivalent to 207kg per litre. Supercharged engines were banned, except for two-stroke engines. This new formula was aimed to encourage designers to bring racing cars more into line with stock production vehicles and at the same time to encourage the industry to produce new vehicles.

Baconin Borzacchini

Vittorio Jano

Vittorio Jano, the man responsible for Alfa Romeo design from 1924 to 1937.

Above
Baconin Borzacchini at the start of the 1930 Brno race. The car is a 1930 version of the P2 Alfa Romeo, with suspension, steering and brakes adapted from the 6C-1750 and a flat radiator fitted. The eight-cylinder 1987cc motor was fitted with a new supercharger and developed 175bhp at 5500rpm.

Racing cars 1920 to 1930

Year	Make & model	Cylinders	Capacity	Bore	Stroke	bhp	rpm	Gears	Max. speed km/h	Dry weight
1920	Ceirano CS24	4	2 968	85	130	105	4600	4	180	820
1920	Gregoire	4	2 855	78	156	100	3500	4	170	870
1920	Sunbeam	6	4 914	81,5	157	150	3000	4	185	1010
1920	Sunbeam	12	18 322	120	135	350	2000	4	215	1490
1921	Fiat 801-401	4	2 971	85	131	112	4000	4	160	810
1921	Alfa Romeo 20/30ES	4	4 250	102	130	67	2600	4	150	890
1921	Austro-Daimler	6	2 992	74	116	109	4500	4	175	990
1921	Benz 10/30 PS	4	2 610	84	119	60	2800	4	150	850
1921	Chitty-Chitty-Bang-Bang	6	23 092	165	180	270	1400	4	190	1250
1921	Diatto	4	2 950	90	116	108	5500	4	170	910
1921	Sunbeam	8	2 973	65	112	108	4000	4	190	1060
1921	Wolseley	12	11 762	120	130	160	2200	4	195	1150
1922	Chitty-Chitty-Bang-Bang	6	18 815	145	190	240	1400	4	185	1220
1922	Delage	6	5 136	85	150	195	5600	4	195	1060
1922	Eldridge	6	20 392	160	170	200	1400	4	180	1170
1922	Elizalde 5181	8	3 384	70	110	110	5200	4	160	950
1922	Hispano Suiza Monza	6	6 860	102	140	150	3500	4	175	940
1922	Mercedes 28/95 PS	6	7 274	105	140	100	1800	4	150	990
1922	Peugeot 174S	4	3 828	95	135	130	4200	4	175	980
1922	Thomas	8	7 266	89	146	220	3000	4	220	1230
1922	Vauxhall	4	2 996	85	132	110	4500	4	190	1080
1922	Wolseley	4	2 778	80	130	105	4000	4	170	990
1923	Alfa Romeo RL Targa Florio	6	2 994	76	110	88	3600	4	145	980
1923	Alfa Romeo RL Targa Florio	6	3 154	78	110	95	3800	4	157	980
1923	Delage	12	10 600	90	140	280	3200	4	230	1110
1923	Itala 41SS	4	2 831	83	130	98	3900	4	155	810
1923	Mercedes M7294	4	1 990	70	129	120	4500	4	180	920
1923	Mercedes White	6	14 778	140	160	174	1400	4	185	1200
1923	Steyr	6	3 325	80	110	90	3000	4	160	890
1924	Alfa Romeo RL Targa Florio	6	3 620	80	120	125	3800	4	180	1000
1924	D'Aoust	8	9 420	100	150	170	4900	4	190	970
1924	Hispano Suiza Boulogne	6	7 983	110	140	165	4100	4	195	1500
1924	Mercedes	4	4 483	93	165	230	5200	4	200	980
1924	Steyr	6	4 014	88	110	100	4000	4	190	920
1925	Peugeot 174S	4	3 990	97	135	100	4200	4	190	960
1925	Vauxhall OE	4	4 224	98	140	108	3300	4	190	1060
1926	Bugatti 35T	8	2 261	60	100	110	5000	4	185	760
1926	Steyr	6	4 890	88	134	155	4100	4	195	940
1926	Sunbeam	12	3 976	67	94	305	5300	4	250	990
1926	Thomas	8	8 468	95	140	230	3300	4	225	1230
1926	Thomas Babs	12	27 059	127	178	550	2000	4	290	1640
1927	Bugatti 35B	8	2 261	60	100	140	5200	4	210	770
1927	Montier	4	2 780	87	120	98	4900	4	185	1025
1927	Peugeot	4	2 491	80	124	70	4200	4	180	830
1928	Alfa Romeo 6C-1500SS	6	1 487	62	82	84	5000	4	155	860
1929	Alfa Romeo 6C-1750GS	6	1 752	65	88	95	4800	4	165	860
1929	Austro-Daimler	6	2 992	76	110	120	4200	4	195	1020
1929	Bentley	4	4 398	100	140	240	4900	4	225	1030
1929	Maserati V4	16	3 958	62	82	300	5200	4	255	1050
1930	Bugatti 45	16	3 801	60	84	250	5700	4	225	910
1930	Itala 4.7	4	4 722	100	150	160	4900	4	165	880
1930	Talbot (GB)	6	2 276	69,5	100	103	4300	4	185	890

Formule Libre is adopted for Grand Prix races. The first twin-camshaft Bugatti appears. Alfa Romeo introduces new Grand Prix models.

1931 saw the change from the poorly supported consumption formulae of the past to an unrestricted formula where the only stipulation was the duration of a race — Grands Prix had to run a minimum of ten hours. That meant that a team of two drivers per vehicle was required. The ten-hour requirement was adopted by the ACF Grand Prix and the Belgian and Italian races.

The Monaco Grand Prix was however run over 100 laps totalling 318km, and won by Louis Chiron in a Bugatti Type 51, the twin-overhead-camshaft version of the familiar supercharged straight-eight.

Apart from its new engine, the T51 looked no different from its successful predecessors. Cylinder measurements remained the same as before (60 x 100mm, 2261cc) and it had only two valves per cylinder, and a single Zenith

Left
The Czechoslovakian Elisabeth Junek, who attracted so much attention in the 1928 Targa Florio, seen here with Achille Varzi during a break in practice at Brno.

Below
The difficult Masaryk circuit at Brno, which hosted important races in the early thirties. In its original form the track was 29.142km long.

Above
Alfa Romeo introduced its new Type A Monoposto, with two six-cylinder engines mounted in parallel, in 1931. Campari's car (above) suffered overheating problems at Pescara, though the cup of water in Enzo Ferrari's hand is presumably for the driver.

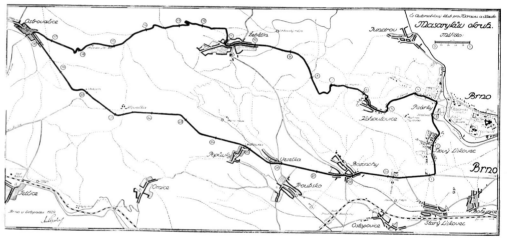

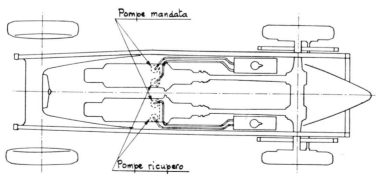

The basic layout of the Alfa Romeo Type A is shown in this drawing. The two 6C-1750 (56 x 80mm) engines gave a total capacity of 3504cc, and produced 230bhp. A central lever controlled both gearboxes. Oil tanks were located on either side of the driver.

carburettor. Power output however was now increased to 180bhp at 5500rpm.

As well as the T51, Bugatti also introduced the larger Type 54 this year, with eight-cylinder 4972cc (86 x 107mm) engine developing 300bhp at 4500rpm. This motor was taken from the Type T50 sportscar. A third Molsheim car seen this year was the Type 53, of which only two were built. They had the large Type 54 motor in a four-wheel-drive chassis with independent front suspension. It proved unsuitable for racing, but ideal for hillclimbs.

Alfa Romeo unveiled two new models at the Italian ten-hour Grand Prix, the Monza and the twin-engined Type A. The Monza was a racing version of the very successful 2.3-litre sportscar which was in production between 1931 and 1933 and which won several 24-hour races at Le Mans and Spa. The supercharged eight-cylinder engine comprised two

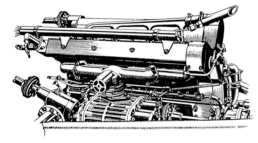

Top

Drivers Divo (cleaning the windscreen) and Bouriat (in the background) and their Type 51 Bugatti during a stop in the ten-hour ACF Grand Prix at Montlhéry in 1931. They were later forced out of the race when mechanical troubles developed.

Above

The supercharged Bugatti T51 was the twin-camshaft development of the 35B. The cylinder measurements remained 60 x 100mm (2261cc) and there were only two valves per cylinder; the engine block and head were cast in one piece.

single blocks of four 65 x 88mm cylinders with steel liners, giving a total capacity of 2336cc. The camshafts were driven by a central gear train between the blocks. In Grand Prix specification the engine developed 165bhp at 5400rpm though later modifications increased that to 178bhp, still at 5400rpm. With the new car Tazio Nuvolari and Giuseppe Campari broke Bugatti's stranglehold on Grand Prix victories by winning the Italian race.

But Chiron and Varzi in the French cars won the ten-hour races at Montlhéry and Spa, to add to their earlier Monaco success. Rudolf Caracciola in his Mercedes SSK sportscar meanwhile won the German Grand Prix at the Nürburgring.

Bugatti had hoped to win the Italian Grand Prix with their 5-litre T54, appearing for the first time, but Achille Varzi, who drove Molsheim's latest product, was third behind two Alfa Romeos.

It was during this period that private racing organisations were first established, to carry on racing the products of manufacturers who had withdrawn from direct participation. instead of the manufacturers sponsoring works racing teams, the organisations hired the drivers. The most famous of these organisations was formed in December 1929 by the former Alfa Romeo driver Enzo Ferrari. Scuderia Ferrari, based at Modena, would be very successful with Alfa Romeos when that factory withdrew from racing a few years later.

In addition to the 16-cylinder Maserati V4 and Bugatti T54, the Italian Grand Prix also saw the debut of an Alfa Romeo model of similar concept, also intended for use on the faster circuits. There were however two major differences. The first was that the basis for the engine was the company's six-cylinder, 1750cc sportscar engine, rather than an eight. And secondly, instead of mating the parallel blocks to a common crankcase, as both the Bugatti and the Maserati did, the Type A Alfa duplicated the entire power train: it not only had two crankshafts, but also two gearboxes (controlled by a single lever) and twin driveshafts operating twin differentials. The seat was located between the driveshafts which made the Type A the first single-seat Alfa Romeo. The Type A was basically a sound design but was in fact used very little and soon became known at the factory as *il Capriccio*, the temperamental. It was replaced the following year by the Type B, or P3 as it is better known.

Much interest was created by the sensational 1931 Mille Miglia win by Rudolf Caracciola and his co-driver Sebastian in a Mercedes SSK, for this was the first time that anyone other than an Italian had won this race. The local drivers, with an intimate knowledge of

Luigi Arcangeli

the roads and conditions, were always considered to have an unbeatable advantage in this race. The only other foreigners to win the Mille Miglia, also in a Mercedes, were Stirling Moss and the journalist Denis Jenkinson, with a 300SLR in 1955, though the German drivers von Hanstein and Bäumer won the substitute 1940 race in a 2-litre BMW

328. After the war, the Mille Miglia was once again run on its historic route. In addition to its domination of this race, Alfa Romeo also scored a string of victories in the Le Mans 24-hour race from 1931 to 1934.

The new 8C Alfa Romeos, with 2.3-litre eight-cylinder engines similar to the Monza racers, had led the early stages of the 1931 Mille Miglia, the drivers of the two cars being Nuvolari/Borzacchini and Arcangeli/Campari, but they soon fell back.

The first major international race meeting held in Switzerland, the Geneva Grand Prix on the 9.3km Meyrin circuit, took place on June 7th 1931. The race was won by the Bugatti works driver Lehoux at an average speed of 139.5km/h.

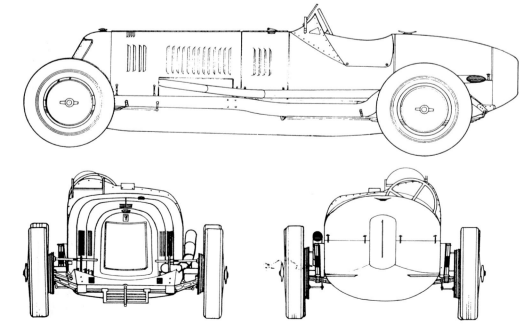

Left
The Maserati 26M, built between 1930 and 1932. The supercharged eight-cylinder engine (65 x 94mm, 2495cc) developed 185bhp at 5600rpm.

Above
The 8C-2300 Alfa Romeo Monza achieved its first big win in the 1931 Italian Grand Prix, driven by Tazio Nuvolari and Giuseppe Campari. Designer Vittorio Jano is on the right.

Debut of the P3 Alfa Romeo

Alfa introduces its new wonder car, the P3, at the Italian Grand Prix. But in general the Formule Libre years have made very little impact on technical development.

The new Alfa Romeo Type B from Milan, better known as the P3, was the talk of the tracks during the 1932 season.

The only restriction this year was again one of duration: now, however, the minimum was five hours, and the maximum ten.

Daimler-Benz had now withdrawn from racing so their top driver, Rudolf Caracciola, was free to drive Alfa Romeos, and duly joined the company for 1932. His first races were in eight-cylinder Monza models, but from the Italian Grand Prix he drove the famous P3 model, which had made its debut on June 5th 1932.

Vittorio Jano, its designer, had built the eight-cylinder engine in two blocks of four, each fed by its own Roots supercharger. The cylinders measured 65 x 100mm, which gave a capacity of 2654cc, and in this form the engine developed 215bhp at 5600rpm. Later the

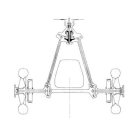

The 1932 P3 Alfa Romeo was fitted with a fixed axle, but in 1935 this was replaced by a Dubonnet independent system (illustrated). The size of the eight-cylinder engine was steadily increased each year. Power was transmitted through twin driveshafts

Pierre Veyron

Below
The victorious Alfa Romeo Type B, or P3, with driver Tazio Nuvolari at the 1932 Italian Grand Prix.

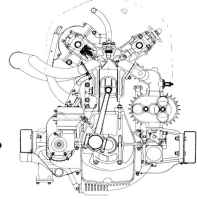

Left
The streamlined Mercedes SSK with which Manfred von Brauchitsch won the 1932 Avus race.

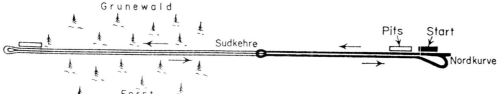

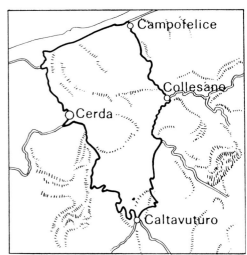

Above right
The Targa Florio circuit was reduced once again in 1932, this time to its final length of 72km.

Above
The Avus track in Berlin was part of an Autobahn with a corner at either end. The original corners were flat, but the famous North Curve near the finishing line, was banked in 1937. At the same time the track was shortened slightly, to 19.363km. After the war, only the stretch nearest the North Curve (dark outline) was used, giving a circuit length of 6.31km. Only two German Grands Prix were held here, one in 1926 and the other in 1959.

Left
Aerial photo of the South Curve, used until 1939.

capacity was enlarged first by increasing the bore to 68mm, which gave 2905cc, and then in 1935 to 71mm, giving 3165cc; the 2.9-litre version developed 255bhp at 5400rpm and the 3.2 another 10bhp at the same engine revolutions. The car employed a unique transmission system, whereby the differential was coupled direct to the four-speed gearbox and engine, and power transmitted to the rear wheels by two driveshafts. This enabled the driver's seat to be located lower in the frame, between the two driveshafts, thereby ensuring that the centre of gravity could be kept as low as possible. Suspension was initially by semi-elliptic leaf springs but in 1935 an independent front suspension system of the Dubonnet type was substituted.

Six examples of the first version of the P3, clothed in a very pleasing body, were built, and in their first year they won six major races for Alfa Romeo, including the ACF Grand Prix at Rheims (driver Nuvolari), the German Grand Prix at the Nürburgring (Caracciola) and the Italian Grand Prix at Monza (Nuvolari). Earlier in the year Nuvolari had won the Monaco Grand Prix in the previous model Alfa Romeo, the two-seater Monza.

The Formule Libre years in fact contributed little to technical development in engine design, for when there is no limit to cubic capacity, the easiest and cheapest road to increased power is to build bigger engines. But they were no more productive in terms of a ratio of power to size. For example the P3 Alfa Romeo of 1932, with 215bhp available from its 2654cc engine, produced only 81bhp per litre. Five years earlier the eight-cylinder Delage from the

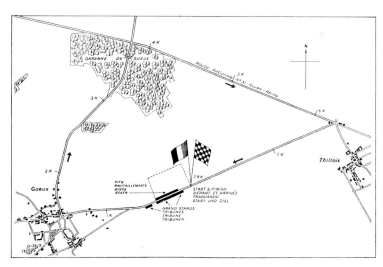

The Rheims circuit, used for national events since 1925, hosted its first ACF Grand Prix in 1932. Until the early 1950s the circuit passed through the village of Gueux. The original track was 7.815km long, though 8.347km and 8.301km versions were used later.

The 16-cylinder 4905cc Maserati V5, built with two eight-cylinder motors, on the start-line at Monza in 1932. Luigi Fagioli (picture) won his heat.

1.5-litre formula had developed 110bhp/litre and the 12-cylinder Fiat 806 from the same era 123bhp/litre. But at the same time, the new wave of larger-capacity engines were, thanks to lower engine speeds, more reliable.

Bugatti again relied on its two basic eight-cylinder models, the 2.3-litre Type 51 and the 4.9-litre Type 54, in 1932. The Bugattis of this time still all looked very much the same. The major difference between the newer cars and the earlier models was that one-piece tubular front axles were not employed.

To compete with the new Alfas, Maserati modified its eight-cylinder engine by increasing the size to 2795cc (68 x 94mm) so that it now developed 198bhp at 6000rpm. This version was known as the Type 8C-2800. A similar development increased the size of the 16-cylinder car to 4905cc (69 x 82mm), and it developed 330bhp at 5200rpm.

In addition to the very successful Alfa Romeo operation from Milan, Scuderia Ferrari of Modena competed in all this year's Grands Prix with 2.3-litre Monza models. And when at the end of its hugely successful year, Alfa Romeo unexpectedly decided to retire from racing, Scuderia Ferrari and its Monzas were left as sole representatives of the marque in Grand Prix racing. The Modena firm bored the Monza engines out to 2556cc, in which form they developed 180bhp at 5600rpm. But at 920kg, they were about 200kg heavier than the more modern P3, considered to be the leading Grand Prix design of the time.

While the Type 51 Bugatti was built for commercial sale as well as factory use, the Type 54 (here with Varzi at Monza) was developed for the exclusive use of the works team. It had a supercharged eight-cylinder 4972cc (86 x 107mm) engine, but still used cable-operated brakes. The forged axle on the Type 54 consisted of two parts joined in the middle with a rubber boot.

Private Entrants to the Fore

Nuvolari leaves Alfa Romeo and joins Maserati. Alfa Romeo's P3 is finally handed over to the Scuderia Ferrari. September 10th tragedy on the Monza track.

The 1933 racing season was the last held under Formule Libre regulations: the only stipulation this year was that Grands Prix had to be run over a minimum distance of 500km. The season opened with the Tripoli Grand Prix, held on a fast, palm-lined circuit, with prize-money raised by a special lottery. But individual events no longer held the appeal they had in the previous decade. Only two major Grands Prix, the ACF and Italian races, remained, and they continued to be the high points of the season.

Bugatti, Alfa Romeo and Maserati were again the principal competitors in the 1933 season. For the French company, Varzi won at Tripoli, at Monaco and on the Avus track in Germany. At the suggestion of the well-known French racing journalist Charles Faroux, competitors for the Monte Carlo race were positioned on the starting line in order of the times achieved in their practice runs rather than by ballot, a practice since adopted universally by race organisers but at the time a novelty. Before this team managers had been able to place their best drivers in the cars which drew the most advantageous positions.

Highlight of the Monte Carlo race was

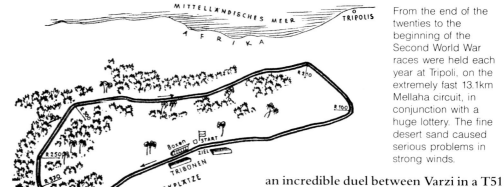

Achille Varzi

Tazio Nuvolari

From the end of the twenties to the beginning of the Second World War races were held each year at Tripoli, on the extremely fast 13.1km Mellaha circuit, in conjunction with a huge lottery. The fine desert sand caused serious problems in strong winds.

an incredible duel between Varzi in a T51 Bugatti and Nuvolari in a Monza Alfa Romeo. For 99 of the 100 laps they raced wheel to wheel, each lap seeming to be faster than the one before until, on the very last lap, Nuvolari had to drop out with engine trouble, and Varzi rolled over the finishing line first. During practice Rudolf Caracciola had had a bad accident in an Alfa Romeo and withdrew from racing for the season. After the Alfa Romeo company had left Grand Prix racing at the end of 1932, Caracciola had formed a racing partnership with Chiron which now had to be dissolved.

The ACF Grand Prix at Montlhéry was won by the jovial Giuseppe Campari in an old two-seater Maserati 8C-2800. But the Scuderia Ferrari Monza Alfas all developed faults, and Tazio Nuvolari

Tazio Nuvolari pushing his Monza Alfa Romeo to the finish line in the 1933 Monaco Grand Prix. It blew its engine on the last lap after an epic battle, which lasted for 99 of the 100 laps, with Achille Varzi's T51 Bugatti. Varzi carried on to win.

The start of the ill-fated Monza race in 1933. The third car, the Maserati driven by Borzacchini, and the last, an Alfa Romeo driven by Campari, both crashed during the race, and both drivers were killed.

decided to leave the Modena firm and race for Maserati instead. Maserati had just built the new single-seater 8CM model with a supercharged eight-cylinder 2991cc (69 x 100mm) engine developing 220bhp at 5500rpm, and weighing 865kg, the car having been raced for the first time at Monaco. With a similar car Nuvolari won the Belgian Grand Prix at Spa and alarm bells immediately started ringing at Alfa Romeo. The Milan company decided that, to meet the new Maserati challenge, it would make its P3s available to Scuderia Ferrari for the rest of 1932. And so at the Italian Grand Prix at Monza the most famous name in racing was back in action. In the race Nuvolari and Taruffi in 8CM Maseratis were matched against Fagioli and Chiron in the P3s and at the end of a very exciting race, after Nuvolari had fallen back with tyre problems, Fagioli in a P3 was the winner.

September 10th 1933 was a black day in the history of motor racing; it actually became known as the Black Day of Monza. In the afternoon, following the Italian Grand Prix, the Monza Grand Prix was held. In the first heat an American Duesenberg driven by Count Felice Trossi lost its oil on one of the steeply banked curves of the high speed oval. The

oil spill was never cleaned up properly and on the first lap of the second heat Giuseppe Campari in an Alfa Romeo and Baconin Borzacchini in a Maserati lost control of their vehicles at the very spot. The cars skidded and overturned and both drivers were killed.

Then later, in the final, Count Czaykowski in his 5-litre Bugatti was also killed on the same bend.

The 1933 racing season ended with the Czechoslovakian Grand Prix at Brno and the Spanish Grand Prix at San Sebastian and Chiron and Fagioli in P3 Alfas filled the first two places in both.

With their running, the Formule Libre regulations and various fuel-consumption formulae came to an end. The distances which had to be raced then were never repeated again. During the Libre era Italian, British, French and American designers had concentrated little on improving engine performance, continuing a trend which had begun in the late 1920s and ended only with the introduction of the 750kg formula at the beginning of 1934. What improvement in engine performance there was had been achieved principally by the use of superchargers. Little attention had been paid either to chassis or suspension design in that period, or to more efficient body styling. This neglect is exemplified by Bugatti who used exactly the same design for all their models, the only differences being in the size of the brake drums, the width of the horseshoe-shaped radiator and the tyre section.

Racing cars of the Formule Libre era 1930 to 1933

Year	Make & model	Cylinders	Capacity	Bore	Stroke	bhp	rpm	Gears	Max. speed km/hr	Dry weight
1930	Alfa Romeo P2 Targa Florio	8	1987	61	85	175	5500	4	225	780
1931	Alfa Romeo 8C-2300 Monza	8	2336	65	88	165	5400	4	210	920
1931	Alfa Romeo Tipo A	12	3504	56	88	230	5200	3	240	930
1931	Bugatti 51	8	2261	60	100	180	5500	4	230	750
1931	Bugatti 54	8	4972	86	107	300	4500	4	240	930
1931	Bugatti 51A	8	1492	60	66	135	5500	4	200	750
1931	Maserati 8C-2800	8	2812	69	94	205	5500	4	225	820
1931	Mercedes SSKL	6	7069	100	150	295	3500	4	230	1400
1931	Nacional Pescara	8	2947	72	90	120	5000	4	195	850
1932	Alfa Romeo Type B (P3)	8	2654	65	100	215	5600	4	232	700
1932	Bugatti 53 (4 × 4)	8	4972	86	107	300	4500	4	240	940
1932	Maserati V5	16	4905	69	82	330	5200	4	250	1050
1933	Alfa Romeo 8C-2600 Monza	8	2556	68	88	180	5600	4	225	920
1933	Bugatti 59	8	2819	67	100	250	5700	4	250	760
1933	Maserati 8C-3000	8	2991	69	100	220	5500	4	240	850
1933	Maserati 8CM	8	2991	69	100	240	5500	4	250	750
1933	Maserati 4C-2000	4	1969	80	98	165	5500	4	215	580
1933	Maserati 4C-2500	4	2483	84	112	195	5300	4	225	700

The 750kg Formula

Revolutionary designs from Mercedes-Benz and Auto Union generate new technical advances. Clear domination of Grand Prix racing by the two German manufacturers.

In the whole of Grand Prix history there had never been an era so dominated by the designs of one particular country as the period between 1934 and 1939. These years were referred to as the "Golden Years" of the German manufacturers Mercedes-Benz and Auto Union, whose unchallenged superiority in that period extended over two different formulae, the 750kg formula between 1934 and 1937 and the 3-litre formula of 1938–39. Only on rare occasions was a red Italian Alfa Romeo able to defeat the silver German monopostos. No longer were there strings of major victories for the cars which had been so successful before. As the German cars continued to be unbeatable in the years before the war, many famous manufacturers withdrew from Grand Prix racing, turning their efforts instead to the 1.5-litre voiturette class, where they could enjoy more success.

Chassis and suspension designs changed significantly during the period from 1934 to 1939. The German firms led the field and their designs were soon imitated by manufacturers in other countries. Both Mercedes and Auto Union started off with independent suspension of all four wheels, but the drivers did not much like these systems as the cars tended to be unstable on bumpy surfaces and difficult to handle in high-speed corners. In 1937 therefore Mercedes reverted to a De Dion system at the rear, and Auto Union followed suit

in 1938. The system employed by both constructors kept the driving wheels parallel to each other, which resulted in an immediate improvement in roadholding characteristics. The De Dion rear axle would remain in general use in Grand Prix design until the end of the 1950s. But in spite of the increased power and higher speeds brought about by the structural and design changes of cars between 1934 and 1939, very few drivers lost their lives in racing accidents in that period.

In the years between 1928 and 1933 the fastest cars such as Bugatti, Maserati and Alfa Romeo were considered to have become simply too fast, and it was this view which had led to the new formula.

Manfred von Brauchitsch

Left
The independent front suspension of the Mercedes W25 with its horizontally mounted coil spring.

Right
Pictured standing next to the Type A Auto Union at Montlhéry, from left: team manager Willy Walb, driver Hans Stuck and designer Ferdinand Porsche.

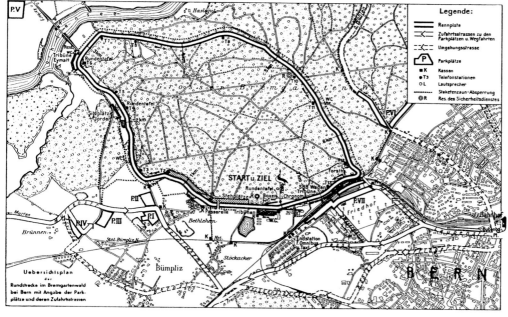

Left
The Swiss Grand Prix took place at Berne between 1934 and 1954 on the 7.28km Bremgarten circuit, a road course which demanded great skill and bravery.

Below
The V16 Auto Union
engine had a central
overhead camshaft
which operated the
inlet valves for both
banks of cylinders.

Centre
The complex
crankshaft of the Auto
Union V16 was made
up of a multitude of
parts.

Centre right
The A-Type Auto Union
during a stop in the
1934 Coppa Acerbo at
Pescara. Note crank-
handle at the rear.

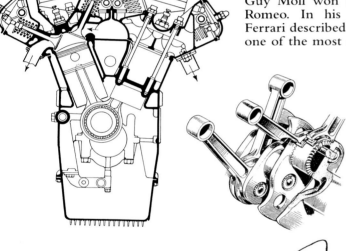

Hans Stuck

Dr. Ferdinand Porsche

Under its rules the maximum weight without fuel, oil, water or tyres was to be 750kg; a minimum width of 850mm was also specified but choice of fuel was free. Race distances remained at the 500km minimum.

All the successful manufacturers already had cars around this weight classification — the P3 Alfa weighed 700kg, the T59 Bugatti 760kg and the Maserati 4C-2500 800kg — and bringing them into line was not difficult.

A new talent emerged at Monte Carlo this year when Scuderia Ferrari recruit Guy Moll won the race in a P3 Alfa Romeo. In his autobiography, Enzo Ferrari described the young Algerian as one of the most capable drivers he had ever met. Moll went on to win the Avusrennen in Berlin later in the year and also took a number of major placings but his successful run was a short-lived one: on August 15th he was killed when his car left the road at 250km/h on one of the Pescara circuit's kilometre-long straights. He was 24.

The arrival on the scene of the recently announced German teams was awaited with considerable interest, but their entries for the first races were withdrawn as the cars were not yet ready to race.

The first of the new generation of German cars appeared in the Avusrennen on May 27th. Daimler-Benz withdrew their entries at the last minute but Auto Union made the start, with Hans Stuck

and August Momberger as drivers. Stuck led convincingly for the first few laps, but fell back and Guy Moll won the race in a P3 Alfa Romeo with streamlined body designed specially for the event, at an average speed of 205.29km/h.

The Mercedes-Benz W25s were finally ready for the Eifelrennen at the Nürburgring on June 3rd, and one of them, driven by von Brauchitsch, battled for first place with Stuck in the Auto Union and Chiron in an Alfa Romeo. Von Brauchitsch came through to give the car victory at its first appearance.

The Italian and French designers immediately realised their cars were inferior in every respect to the Auto Union and Mercedes. This conclusion prevailed even after the ACF Grand Prix at Montlhéry where Alfa Romeo's P3s took the first three places, Chiron winning from Varzi and a car shared by Moll and Trossi. All the German cars had

Right
Jean-Pierre Wimille at
Monaco in 1934 in an
eight-cylinder Type 59
Bugatti. The motor had
a capacity of 3257cc
(72 x 100mm) and
developed 240bhp, but
Bugatti's dominance of
Grand Prix racing was
now coming to an end.

Right
Jean-Pierre Wimille at
Monaco in 1934 in an
eight-cylinder Type 59
Bugatti. The motor had
a capacity of 3257cc
(72 x 100mm) and
developed 240bhp, but
Bugatti's dominance of
Grand Prix racing was
now coming to an end.

Below
The 1934 T59 Bugatti
was still equipped with
cable brakes, though
hydraulic brakes had
appeared on the
winning Duesenberg in
the ACF Grand Prix 13
years before.

developed mechanical faults during the
race and had been forced to abandon.

Daimler-Benz and Auto Union both
received government subsidies to support
the cost of their research and
development programmes. Since Adolf
Hitler's coming to power in 1933, his
ambitious government wanted victories
to boost the prestige of their country and
to demonstrate German superiority to the
world. The subsidies in fact offset only a
small proportion of the total expenses for
the companies' motorsport activities. In
March 1933 Mercedes estimated its
budget to be about one million
Reichsmarks, and thanks to good government connections, the company was able
to obtain the promise of an annual grant
of 450,000 Reichsmarks, with bonuses to
be paid for victories. However, as Auto
Union was also planning a Grand Prix
programme, the Ministry of Transport
insisted that the annual subsidy should be
divided equally between Mercedes and
Auto Union, each firm receiving 225,000
Reichsmarks.

In reality, of course, costs were much
higher: it was estimated that Daimler-
Benz needed an annual amount of some
four million Reichsmarks to support their
motor racing.

The situation was similar in Italy,
where racing victories, as in Germany,
were used for political propaganda
purposes. Benito Mussolini was an
enthusiastic follower of motor racing
and, eager to support the Alfa Romeo
marque, brought the Milan manufacturer
under the wing of the state-owned IRI
(*Instituto di Riconstruzione Industriale*).
Between 1935 and 1940 Alfa Romeo
turned out a multitude of racing models
and engines, perhaps more than any other
manufacturer in racing history. Eight-,
12- and even 16-cylinder engines were
built in quite complicated combinations
and variations. It was partly at least due
to these frequent design changes that Alfa
Romeo was unable to compete successfully against their German counterparts.

In contrast to the Italian approach, the
German constructors concentrated on
one car and engine design for a particular
formula and then developed and
improved it progressively throughout its
life.

In the early 1930s the German car
industry had been through a crisis which
sent several manufacturers to the wall.

Right
Start of the Masaryk
Grand Prix at Brno in
1934. Achille Varzi
leads in a P3 Alfa
Romeo entered by
Scuderia Ferrari, from
the A-Type Auto Union
driven by Hans Stuck
and another Ferrari
Alfa Romeo, driven by
Louis Chiron. The race
was won by Stuck.

Four such firms — Horch, Audi, Wanderer and DKW — had amalgamated to form Auto Union. The combine's revolutionary 16-cylinder Grand Prix cars were designed by the former Mercedes engineer, Professor Ferdinand Porsche, with engines located behind the driver. Although this concept is usually referred to as rear-engined, it is more accurate to describe it as mid-engined. Porsche's design was not the first mid-engined Grand Prix car: that honour belongs to the Benz *Tropfenwagen*, developed by Nibel in 1922 and 1923, with its radiator positioned over the tail (on the Auto Union the radiator was at the front). The Porsche design was however the first mid-engined car to win a Grand Prix.

Motor racing enthusiasts had believed that the 750kg weight limit would force manufacturers to build smaller engines with less power, but found to their astonishment that the Germans had come up with an answer to this problem. Using extremely light materials and a compact design it was possible to construct engines with an increased power output.

Auto Union's Type A model had a 4360cc (68 x 75mm) motor which initially developed 295bhp at 4500rpm, though later in the season its bore was increased to 82.5mm which gave a capacity of 4950cc, boosting power to 375bhp at

Above
Guy Moll during a pit-stop at Pescara. The 23-year-old Algerian was considered one of the most promising drivers, having already won the Monaco Grand Prix and the Avusrennen this year. Here, he takes the Scuderia Ferrari P3 Alfa Romeo out of the pits shortly before his fatal accident.

Top right
Tazio Nuvolari left Alfa Romeo in 1933 and drove for Maserati. Here, he is at the wheel of the eight-cylinder supercharged 8CM Maserati (69 x 100mm, 2991cc) in the Coppa Acerbo at Pescara.

4700rpm. Once again increased performance had been obtained from an engine with greater bore than stroke.

The supercharged motors ran on special fuels mixed to very secret formulae by engineers from the oil companies and the chemical industry working together. The exhaust fumes poured out by engines running in the pits were so strong that bystanders complained of nausea, headaches, and eye and respiratory problems.

The secret of the German cars' specification lay in the use of lightweight tubular frames and independent suspension of all four wheels, both unknown concepts before this time. The outmoded approach of the opposition still incorporated flexible chassis design and very firm suspension by rigid axles at both ends, a concept little changed over the previous ten or 15 years. Chassis and suspension design had been virtually neglected in the 1920s and '30s as constructors directed their resources towards extracting more and more power, first from small engines, then larger units, and applied improved supercharger technology to boost the power of these engines. In this particular regard technical advancement had come to a complete standstill. The softer suspension systems and rigid frames favoured by both German contenders resulted in improved traction and superior cornering.

The origins of the single-seater Auto Union go back to November 15th 1932 when the idea of a new Grand Prix car was discussed at a meeting Professor Porsche, then aged 57, had with his chief designer, Karl Rabe, and his finance partner Adolf Rosenberger. After the

meeting Porsche, without the knowledge or consent of the other two participants, completed the designs of a new car. His idea was that the car should be constructed by his own company, which would also campaign it in Grands Prix. When however he was approached by the new Auto Union company and commissioned to design a new Grand Prix car for them, he admitted to already having plans drawn up. These plans for the "P-Wagen", as the car was at first known, were immediately taken over by Auto Union and the car built in the Horch factory in Zwickau.

At the same time, unknown to Porsche, Daimler-Benz were working on their own prototype for the 750kg formula. Ferdinand Porsche Junior, then aged 23, who later became head of the Porsche enterprise, was instrumental in the development of this model, particularly regarding the design of the supercharger.

Professor Porsche's Auto Union was fitted with the famous torsion-bar suspension by which each wheel was independently sprung by leaf springs linked by a control arm. Power from the rear-mounted engine was transmitted through a ZF differential to half-shafts which drove large diameter wheels. The rather simple frame consisted of two large tubes running the length of the car, joined by a number of cross-members. The impressive supercharged light-alloy V16 motor was located immediately behind the cockpit. This layout of engine immediately behind the driver, but forward of the rear axle, was revived by the British Cooper company with considerable success in the 1950s, and since the early 1960s has been in universal use by all manufacturers of single-seater cars from Grand Prix machinery down.

Many light alloy parts were used in the construction of the Auto Union chassis and, whenever possible, components were drilled out and lightened to save every available gram of weight. Even the upright metal bars of the radiator grille, and the windscreen frame, were drilled to reduce weight. And yet, compared with the designs of later eras (even to this day), very few material defects were encountered.

Porsche's idea on engine design was to have a large motor with a moderate compression ratio to provide optimum torque at low engine speeds. The 16-cylinder engine had its two cylinder blocks inclined at an angle of 45 degrees to each other which required an unusual system to operate the valves. A single overhead camshaft actuated all 32 valves. The inlet valves were opened and closed with the aid of very short finger-like cam-followers while the exhaust valves, positioned on the outside, required rocker arms as well as cam-followers. The combustion chambers were conically shaped, in contrast to the more common hemispherical design.

The result of all this was an engine whose performance could best be described as moderate, compared with the smaller motors produced by Delage, Miller or Fiat in the second half of the 1920s, and was still far short of the magic 100bhp/litre figure. The first 4.4-litre model delivered 67.7bhp/litre and the subsequent 4.9-litre version 75.7bhp/litre.

The body of the Auto Union received a lot of attention, too. Subjected to strenuous testing in the wind tunnels of the German Institute for Aerodynamics, its shape was altered and redesigned to provide a strength never known before. But the entire Auto Union package proved rather tricky to handle throughout its life, and very few drivers were able to master it completely.

In 1934 and 1935 Mercedes-Benz was able to boast more significant victories than Auto Union, most of whose achievements came the following year, 1936, thanks to the extraordinary talents of their ace driver Bernd Rosemeyer.

The Mercedes W25, designed by Dr. - Ing Hans Nibel, was a front-engined car with a light chassis made from square tubing. Apart from the supercharged 2-litre M218 model designed in 1924, and which Rudolf Caracciola had taken to

Scuderia Ferrari built a streamlined version of the P3 Alfa Romeo for the 1934 Avus race. The body was designed by Pallavicino, an engineer from the Breda Institute of Aerodynamics. Guy Moll, here testing the car on an Italian Autostrada, succeeded in winning the Avusrennen with this car. Standing in the centre, beside the car, is Enzo Ferrari.

victory in the 1926 German Grand Prix at the Avus, Mercedes had not built any pure racing vehicles, concentrating instead on its sportscar designs. The W25 had independent front suspension and a swing-axle rear end.

The eight-cylinder 3360cc (78 x 88mm) motor had steel cylinders, two overhead camshafts and four valves per cylinder, and developed 345bhp at 5800rpm. This gave it a per-litre output of 105.34bhp. The supercharger was positioned in front of the engine, from which two pressure carburettors each supplied fuel to four of the cylinders.

The chassis of the Mercedes Grand Prix car directly influenced the design of the company's passenger cars, the independent front suspension system proving so successful for example that it was adopted for all models manufactured for sale to the public. Although the principle of independent suspension was not new, this was one of its first successful applications. In 1934 Rudolf Caracciola was timed over one kilometre at 317.5km/h in a W25 with a closed cockpit.

In the course of the following year the engine of the successful eight-cylinder Mercedes was increased from 3360cc through 3990cc to 4310cc and ultimately 4740cc. The famous W125 Mercedes-Benz of 1937 had a 5660cc engine.

During this period the Italian teams, too, increased the size of their engines. Scuderia Ferrari enlarged the P3 Alfa Romeo to 2905cc (68 x 100mm, developing 255bhp at 5400rpm) and Maserati their Type 34 to 3322cc (84 x 100mm, developing 260bhp at 5000rpm) but even this was not enough to put them

in the same class as the German cars. The Bugatti Type 59 had a 3257cc engine (72 x 100mm, developing 240bhp at 5400rpm) but was let down by its outmoded chassis design, rigid axles and cable brakes.

The German cars won most of the major races of 1934. Hans Stuck in an Auto Union won the German and Swiss Grands Prix, Caracciola in a Mercedes the Italian and Fagioli, also in a Mercedes, the Spanish. The P3 Alfa Romeo took the Monaco and Avus events driven by Moll and the ACF Grand Prix at Montlhéry with Chiron.

This year, with the construction of the Bremgarten circuit in Berne, Switzerland joined the circle of nations hosting Grand Prix races. Three motorsport events of international importance were in fact held in Switzerland in 1934, bringing to that country in the space of a few weeks a series of significant events unparalleled in its motorsport history. On June 3rd the first (and only) Montreux Grand Prix was run on a new street circuit and won by Count Carlo Felice Trossi, president of the Scuderia Ferrari, in a P3 Alfa Romeo. On August 5th the last of the famous Klausen "mountain races" (hillclimbs) took place and Grand Prix cars dominated the results, Rudolf Caracciola establishing the best time in his Mercedes W25 ahead of his arch-rival Hans Stuck in the V16 Auto Union. The third, and most prestigious, event was held at Berne on August 26th and was the first international Swiss Grand Prix on the 7.28km Bremgarten circuit. (Races called the Swiss Grand Prix had occasionally been run in the past on the Meyrin circuit at Geneva.)

Mercedes drivers are the most successful. A talented new Auto Union driver emerges in Bernd Rosemeyer. Nuvolari wins on the Nürburgring in the 'old' P3 Alfa.

Mercedes and Auto Union both updated their cars for the 1935 season. Ferdinand Porsche fitted torsion-bar suspension to the rear of his design (now known as the Type B) in place of the leaf springs used until then. He also increased the engine capacity to 4950cc (72.5 x 75mm) in which form it developed 375bhp at 4800rpm (76bhp/litre) at a mean piston speed of 12m/sec. The Mercedes W25 was meanwhile bored out to 3990cc (82 x 94.5mm) which gave it 430bhp at 5800rpm (107.8bhp/litre).

Among the opposition Bugatti increased the Type 59 engine to 3.8 litres and Scuderia Ferrari the P3 Alfa Romeo's to 3165cc (71 x 100mm, developing

265bhp at 5400rpm). At the same time the P3s were fitted with Dubonnet independent front suspension.

The new Mercedes was definitely superior on paper and Caracciola duly

Luigi Fagioli

won the newly introduced European Championship with victories in the Belgian, Swiss and Spanish Grands Prix. In another Mercedes, Fagioli was first at Monaco while Stuck won the Italian Grand Prix for Auto Union. The surprise of the 1935 season however was the performance of that great survivor Tazio Nuvolari who, quite unexpectedly, won the German Grand Prix at the Nürburgring with his inferior, old-fashioned P3 Alfa Romeo. Most of the Germans had to withdraw due to breakdowns but Nuvolari put up a typically remarkable fight. His courage and enormous driving skill more than

compensated for the technically inferior Alfa and he eventually overtook the Mercedes-Benz driven by von Brauchitsch. Contrary to the advice of his mechanics, von Brauchitsch had decided not to change tyres at his last pit stop but on the last lap, when still in the lead, one rear tyre burst and a second followed suit soon afterwards.

The engine on Nuvolari's car had been bored out to 3822cc for this race and it developed about 330bhp, but the model's marvellous career came to an end with this victory on the Nürburgring. The Alfa P3 had participated in about 70 events between 1932 and 1935 and had won about two dozen of them. This success rate was bettered only by one other Grand Prix car, the eight-cylinder

Top right
A sketch of the French SEFAC, a supercharged eight-cylinder car which appeared in practice for the 1935 ACF Grand Prix, driven by Lehoux, but then disappeared. It was designed by Emile Petit, the former Salmson designer.

Above
Rudolf Caracciola on his way to winning the 1935 Swiss Grand Prix in a Mercedes-Benz W25.

Right
Photo taken in the Mercedes-Benz pits after the Swiss Grand Prix on the Bremgarten circuit in Berne.

From top to bottom
Tazio Nuvolari in conversation with the charming Alice Caracciola in the pits at Berne.

René Dreyfus (left)
Louis Chiron (right)

Luigi Fagioli (left)
Hans Stuck (right)

Rudolf Caracciola after his 1935 Berne victory.

Right
An Auto Union with fully-enclosed wheels and streamlined bodywork, specially prepared for record-breaking, pictured in a wind-tunnel in Berlin.

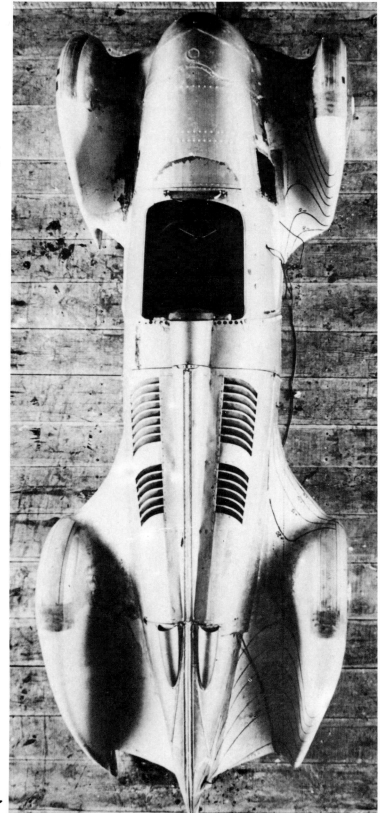

Rudolf Caracciola

Malcolm Campbell

1.5-litre Alfa Romeo Type 158/159 "Alfetta", which raced from 1938 to 1951. In later years racing designs had much shorter lives due to the rapid technical advances and continual developments that took place.

The brilliant driver Bernd Rosemeyer first appeared on the racing scene in 1935. In spite of (or because of) having raced only motorcyles before, he adapted quickly to the rear-engined Auto Union, a car which most drivers found difficult to manage, and was soon driving it as fast as its more experienced drivers. In his short but successful career, Rosemeyer drove Auto Unions exclusively. In his first season, 1935, he won the Masaryk race at Brno; it was here that he met the famous pilot Elly Beinhorn, who shortly afterwards became his wife.

With the blessing of Alfa Romeo,

Below
The gearbox of the "Bimotore" Alfa Romeo positioned between two engines. Twin driveshafts transmitted the power to the rear wheels.

Centre
The "Bimotore" had one supercharged engine in front of the driver, the other behind.

Below right
Tazio Nuvolari with Luigi Bazzi, who built the "Bimotore". This car, built for ultra-fast circuits, was powered by two P3 motors giving a total of 6330cc.

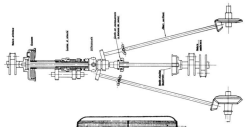

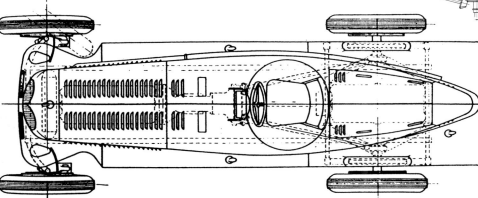

differential were located between the two engines, and two driveshafts transmitted power to the rear wheels in a fashion similar to the P3. The *Bimotore* had a total capacity of 6330cc and developed 540bhp, and first appeared on May 12th at Tripoli, where one example took fourth place and another fifth, Caracciola winning the race in a Mercedes. The *Bimotore* appeared again in the Avusrennen where Chiron finished second behind Fagioli in a Mercedes, while later in the year Tazio Nuvolari set a new world kilometre record of 321km/h on the Florence Autostrada. The *Bimotore* however proved to be a very difficult machine to handle, on top of which tyre wear was extraordinarily high and fuel consumption defied imagination.

Between 1934 and 1939 Auto Union and Daimler-Benz both took part in a number of speed-record attempts, which took place during the winter months on various stretches of the new German Autobahnen, where Stuck, Caracciola and Rosemeyer, driving eight-, 12- and 16-cylinder cars, reached speeds of up to 400km/h. The world land speed record was regularly broken in this period by the Englishmen Campbell, Eyston and Cobb with their huge aero-engined cars and rose from 408.7km/h (Campbell in 1932) to 594.9km/h (Cobb 1939). The site of these record attempts moved in 1935 from their traditional home at Daytona Beach in Florida to the Bonneville salt flats in Utah.

Scuderia Ferrari in Modena built a new twin-engined single-seater in 1935. Known as the *Bimotore,* the new car was intended for fast tracks such as Tripoli, Tunis and the Avus, where Ferrari hoped it would defeat the Auto Union and Mercedes opposition. A replica of the *Bimotore* can still be seen today in the Alfa Romeo factory museum at Arese.

A long-time Ferrari employee, Luigi Bazzi, was responsible for the car's unusual design. A special chassis was devised to carry the two eight-cylinder P3 motors, one of which was mounted in front of the cockpit and the other behind the driver. The clutch was adjacent to the front engine whilst the gearbox and

Luigi Bazzi

Bernd Rosemeyer's Year

The young Auto Union driver goes from success to success and is idolised in Germany. The Mercedes is clearly inferior. Alfa Romeo builds the Type C.

Alfred Neubauer

1936 was the year of the Type C Auto Union — and the year of Rosemeyer, the young star and his modern 16-cylinder car proving virtually unbeatable. The C-Type had a bigger engine than its forebears, a 6006cc (75 x 85mm) unit which developed 520bhp at 5000rpm, a rate of 85bhp/litre. In addition, a lot of work had been carried out to improve its handling.

The new, shorter, Mercedes W25 had a 4740cc (86 x 102mm) engine developing 494bhp at 5800rpm (104bhp/litre). By increasing engine capacity and output within the constraints of the 750kg formula the Germans had done it again, and were able to maintain their superiority over the Italian cars.

Alfa Romeo had introduced their bulbous eight-cylinder Type C with four-wheel independent suspension at the end of 1935. This model's supercharged eight-cylinder 3822cc (78 x 100mm) engine developed 330bhp at 5400rpm (86bhp/litre) but for 1936 a 12-cylinder 4060cc (70 x 88mm) unit which produced 370bhp at 5800rpm (91bhp/litre) was also available. In Nuvolari's hands the Type C Alfa won at Budapest, Milan and Leghorn in 1936, but these were all minor races. In Grands Prix the car could not match Bernd Rosemeyer's record with Auto Union: he won the German, Italian and Swiss events. Rosemeyer also won

lesser races at the Nürburgring (the Eifelrennen) and Pescara (the Coppa Acerbo). With these successes the 27-year-old idol of Germany became European Champion of 1936.

The Swiss Grand Prix, held at Berne on August 23rd, developed into a straight fight between Rudolf Caracciola in the Mercedes and Rosemeyer in the Auto Union. Caracciola took the lead at the start but his rival stuck like glue to the tail of the Mercedes. Caracciola had to call on all his vast experience to stay ahead of Rosemeyer, who several times shook his fist at the car in front. In the pits harsh words were exchanged, and eventually the Clerk of the Course was called in and signalled Caracciola in no uncertain terms that he should let Rosemeyer past. The Mercedes driver finally relented on the ninth lap but the drivers were still arguing with each other at the prize-giving ceremony and it was many months before they shook hands.

Later, the legendary Mercedes team manager Alfred Neubauer remarked, "If a driver should ever feel he is being prevented from overtaking, ambition and tenacity will be the deciding factor." Bernd Rosemeyer was very ambitious but so was Rudi Caracciola who was ten years his senior. One wanted to take the champion's crown which the other did not want to give up. But it is difficult to

Bernd Rosemeyer

Left
Bernd Rosemeyer on the way to his convincing win in the 1936 Swiss Grand Prix in a C-Type Auto Union.

Top left
Alfred Neubauer, the legendary Daimler-Benz team manager, on the pit road at Berne in 1936.

Above
Bernd Rosemeyer with the laurels after his Swiss victory.

Poster of the 1935 Monaco Grand Prix.

A contemporary painting (c. 1935) of the German Grand Prix on the Nürburgring.

An Auto Union advertisement following Rosemeyer's victory in the 1936 Swiss Grand Prix. Rosemeyer joined Auto Union the year before, having previously raced only motorcycles. Usually said to be the only driver ever to master Porsche's difficult mid-engined GP car, he had an incredibly successful year in 1936.

Großer Preis der Schweiz 23. 8. 1936

Wieder dreifacher Sieg der AUTO UNION

- **SIEGER:** *Bernd Rosemeyer* auf AUTO UNION
  Neuer Streckenrekord in 3:09:01.6 std. — 161.57 km/std.
  Neuer Rundenrekord in 3:34.5 Minuten — 169.633 km/std.
- **ZWEITER:** *Achille Varzi* auf AUTO UNION
  in 3:09:54.2 std.
- **DRITTER:** *Hans Stuck* auf AUTO UNION
  in 3:10:41.0 std.
- **FÜNFTER:** *Rudolf Hasse* auf AUTO UNION
  in 3:11:03.8 std.

Ein grandioser Beweis für die überragende Qualität deutscher Arbeit! Von 17 gestarteten Wagen erreichen nur 5 das Ziel, davon alle 4 gestarteten AUTO UNION-Wagen

Erkämpft mit CONTINENTAL-Reifen, BOSCH-Zündung und BOSCH-Kerzen

AUTO UNION

Below
From 1934 to 1937 the maximum weight of Grand Prix cars, excluding fuel, oil, water and tyres, was 750kg. The 1936 Mercedes-Benz, not a particularly successful car, is shown on the weighbridge.

Right
The Maserati V8RI of 1935–36 had a V8 motor (84 x 108mm, 4788cc) which developed 320bhp but performance on the track was indifferent.

see how Rosemeyer could have got past without Caracciola's co-operation. The 1936 Auto Union handled better than the Mercedes so Rosemeyer was faster on the corners. There was not much difference between the two on the straights however, and the few straights at Bremgarten were not long enough to let Rosemeyer past without upsetting his braking for the next corner, and nobody could have realistically expected him to take such a risk. When Caracciola saw the Clerk of the Course waving the blue flag he had to let his rival pass, for he knew he would have been disqualified had he failed to do so. Bernd was undoubtedly the better driver of the two in the 1936 racing season.

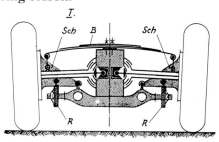

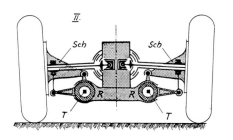

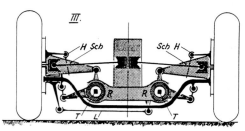

Left
The Spanish Grand Prix was first run on the 3.79km Montjuich circuit in Barcelona in 1936. Previous races had been run at San Sebastian.

Above
The different rear suspension designs of the Auto Union racing cars are pictured here:
I the swing axle and transverse leaf used on the 1934 Type A.
II the swing axle with torsion bars on the 1936-37 Type C.
III the De Dion layout on the 1938–39 Type D.

Above right
The supercharged eight-cylinder Alfa Romeo Type 8C engine of 1935–36 was more complicated than earlier Alfa designs. The twin-supercharged engine was in two blocks of four cylinders with dimensions of 78 x 100mm (3822cc), and developed 330bhp at 5400rpm.

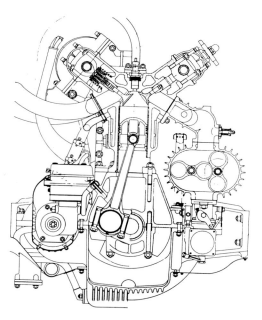

Right
Tazio Nuvolari in a 12C Alfa Romeo beat the German opposition in the 1936 street race at Budapest.

Below
The Earl Howe in a Bugatti Type 59 at Monaco in 1936.

1936 was in fact a poor year for Mercedes. Caracciola could clock up only two wins, one at Monte Carlo and the other at Tunis. In addition to his other successes, meanwhile, Nuvolari, driving an Alfa Romeo Type C, won a new event, or rather a long-forgotten one that had been revived: the Vanderbilt Cup, famous at the turn of the century, was held again, on Long Island, New York. The Germans did not take part in this race but many of the cars seen at Indianapolis were there, though they were not at all suited to this road circuit. A young Frenchman, Jean-Pierre Wimille, took second place in the 1936 Vanderbilt Cup with a new Bugatti, the Type 59/50B, with eight-cylinder 4741cc (84 x 107mm) engine developing 370bhp at 5700rpm, but, remarkably, still clinging to its old-fashioned suspension layout.

Daimler-Benz had built a new V12 motor for Grand Prix racing in 1935 but it proved to be far too heavy, and was never raced. At the same time the company established an independent racing department under the direction of 30-year-old engineer Rudolf Uhlenhaut, comprising team manager Alfred Neubauer and various engineers who had formerly worked in the design department.

The 1936 Mercedes Grand Prix car was not a successful design, and the company in fact withdrew from racing partway through the year to devote its energies to an intensive test programme in an effort to iron out design or construction deficiencies. Their absence from the circuits did no harm to the campaign of Auto Union and Bernd Rosemeyer.

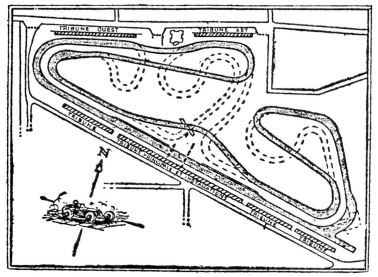

Above
This Lincoln was given to Tazio Nuvolari during his 1936 visit to the USA, when he won the Vanderbilt Cup race on Long Island in an Alfa Romeo.

Left
The Roosevelt Raceway on Long Island, New York, was used for the Vanderbilt Cup in 1936 and 1937, when the race was revived after a lapse of many years. A 6.437km layout was used the first year, 5.364km in 1937.

The W125 is Unbeatable

After its losses in 1936, Daimler-Benz once again produces a successful model. Caracciola is European Champion in the new car. Streamlined cars race at the Avus.

After the poor season they had experienced in 1936, Mercedes bounced back in 1937, the last year of the 750kg formula, with their legendary Type W125. Stuttgart had done it again, for the W125 was the most technically advanced design built in this period. Its supercharged eight-cylinder 5660cc (94 x 102mm) engine developed 646bhp at 5800rpm. That represented 114bhp per litre, which was an extremely impressive performance for such a large engine, and the car's power-to-weight ratio was more than 850bhp/tonne. The designers had developed a machine whose performance would not be surpassed for decades, indeed not until 1965, when 775bhp (at 9800rpm) was produced from the supercharged 2.8-litre V8 engine of the four-wheel-drive Novi-Ferguson which Bobby Unser drove at Indianapolis that year.

One of the engineers responsible for the design of the W125 was Rudolf Uhlenhaut, who would work on all the Grand Prix models built by Mercedes up till 1955. As well as being a leading

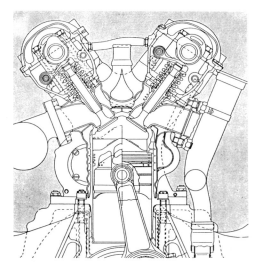

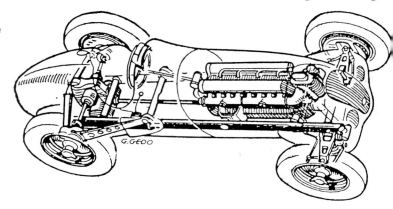

Top
Rudolf Caracciola in a Mercedes-Benz W125 during the 1937 Swiss Grand Prix, which he won.

Above
The W125 motor was the ultimate in Mercedes engineering and delivered more power than any eight-cylinder car before.

Right
Rear suspension of the Mercedes-Benz W125 was on the De Dion principle, while double wishbones were employed at the front. The chassis was made from oval-section steel tubing. Gearbox and differential were mounted in unit on the rear axle.

designer, he was also a first-class driver, and never hesitated to test-drive new models, invariably turning in very impressive times.

The Mercedes W125 was very similar in design and appearance to its less successful predecessor, with a frame made from specially hardened oval steel tubing. With normal ratios in its transmission system (four-speed gearbox and ZF limited-slip differential) it could be driven at 120km/h in first gear, 185 in second, 215 in third and 270 in fourth gear. It could, with special gear ratios, achieve 300km/h and, with the aerodynamically developed streamlined bodywork used for record attempts and for racing at Avus, was capable of 400km/h. The independent front suspension consisted of double wishbones with coil springs, a forerunner of the systems in general use today, while at the rear a De Dion axle was fitted, with Lockheed brakes and two brake shoes per drum. Acceleration and braking forces on the De Dion tube were absorbed by a torsion bar bolted to the chassis. Power was transmitted to the rear axle through a double-universal-jointed driveshaft.

Mercedes once again took the limelight in 1937, with Hermann Lang driving the W125 to victory in the German, Swiss, Italian and Czechoslovakian Grands Prix. Mercedes-Benz also established several world speed records in the different classes with modified versions of their Grand Prix cars. Their rival Auto Union did too, but in the face of the rejuvenated Mercedes campaign on the circuits the rear-engined cars could not match their 1936 success in the major races.

The 16-cylinder C-Type Auto Union had not been updated beyond a slight power increase (to 545bhp), and the only successes it achieved were Bernd Rosemeyer's victories in the Vanderbilt Cup race on Long Island and at Donington Park in England.

The Alfa Romeo Type C took several leading places but late in the year a new 12-cylinder model appeared. Powered by a 4495cc (72 x 92mm) engine which developed 430bhp at 5800rpm, the new 12C/37 was a smaller and lower car than the older Type 8C from the 1935-36 period. The new 12C Alfa raced for the first time at Pescara on August 15th 1937, and then on September 12th in the Italian Grand Prix which this year took place not at Monza but on the Montenero circuit at Leghorn. Guidotti drove the car at Monza but it developed a number of faults and didn't finish the race. Back at the factory the chassis design was found to be insufficiently strong and in the internal recriminations that ensued Vittorio Jano, the engineer responsible for

Below
Two streamlined Mercedes-Benz cars await the start of the 1937 Avus race. In one of them Lang won the event at an average speed of 261.64km/h, but von Delius in an Auto Union was only 1.6 seconds behind at the end.

Overleaf
Rosemeyer's streamlined Auto Union is pushed out for practice at the Avus. The race was divided into two qualifying heats and a relatively short final, as the tyres would not stand up to sustained high speeds.

Left
The famous banked North Curve on the Avus circuit in Berlin. The track was opened in 1922 but the banking was not added until 1936. Its inauguration in this form the following year resulted in what was then the fastest race of all time. This circuit, with its steeply banked curves, was in use until 1967, after which it was considered too dangerous, especially after rain.

the design, resigned from Alfa Romeo and went to Lancia. The 12C chassis was subsequently strengthened and formed the basis of the new 3-litre model in 1938.

Maserati played a relatively minor role in 1937, their new cars being insufficiently robust and the small Bologna firm suffering constant liquidity problems. Bugatti's reputation had faded over the last couple of years and their cars now appeared only infrequently and then with little success. The French company's reluctance to modernize their cars, to abandon long-superseded design and production methods, had left their cars inferior to the competition, and consequently unable to achieve very much in the way of results.

One event of 1937 worth special mention is the Avusrennen, held on the Berlin circuit on May 30th. The Avus track, consisting of two long straights and two 180° corners, had never been considered particularly challenging, but in 1936, apparently at the suggestion of Adolf Hitler, the North Curve was steeply banked and repaved with cobblestones. This alteration reduced the length of the track slightly, from 19.6 to 19.363km, but made for much higher average speeds.

Daimler-Benz and Auto Union both showed off their new streamliners for the big 1937 race in front of a large crowd drawn by the promise of unusually high speeds. There were two qualifying heats and a final which Hermann Lang won in a Mercedes, beating Auto Union driver Ernst von Delius by just 1.6 seconds. Rosemeyer returned the fastest lap at 276.4km/h, a time never recorded at Tripoli or, at that time, Indianapolis. The winning Avus Mercedes was a modified 1936 car with M125 motor.

The 750kg formula finished at the end of 1937. During its lifetime there had been considerable technical development, in stark contrast to the period immediately before, 1928 to 1933, when the regulations in force had done little to encourage progress. It had been expected before its introduction that the 750kg formula would lead to less powerful engines, but instead more powerful motors than ever were built in the period it was in operation.

This formula, which had a marked influence on design for many years to come, had seen the introduction of many important technical innovations. Hardened lightweight materials were used for frames, independent suspension was introduced, De Dion axles were used

Left
Bernd Rosemeyer in a C-Type Auto Union during the Czechoslovakian Grand Prix on the Masaryk circuit at Brno. The photographs on this page were all taken from the same position.

Antonio Brivio

Centre left
Manfred von Brauchitsch in a Mercedes-Benz W125.

Centre right
Count Antonio Brivio in a Scuderia Ferrari 12C Alfa Romeo.

Right
Emanuel de Graffenried in a Maserati 4CM-1500 of the Swiss-American Racing Team.

Below
Nuvolari preparing to test the 1937 Alfa Romeo 12C on an Italian Autostrada. This was the fastest Alfa that Vittorio Jano

designed before he left the Milan firm and went to Lancia. The 12C had a twin-supercharged 4495cc V12 engine which delivered 430bhp.

Richard Seaman

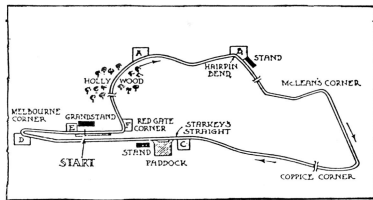

Left
The Donington circuit in Britain in its pre-war 5.028km configuration. Auto Unions raced there twice and won twice, with Rosemeyer in 1937 and Nuvolari in 1938.

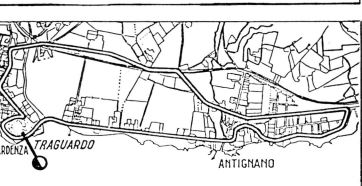

Centre
The 1937 Italian Grand Prix was held on the 7.218km Montenero circuit near Leghorn, venue of the Coppa Ciano, rather than its usual Monza home. Winner was Caracciola in a Mercedes-Benz.

again, limited-slip differentials appeared, coil and torsion-bar suspension, twin-shoe drum brakes, hydraulic shock absorbers, different tyre sizes on front and rear wheels, different tyre profiles and high temperature coolants — all were devised or improved in this period. So too were special fuels, highly volatile mixtures of benzol, alcohol, acetone and ether which led to vast power increases — at huge costs in fuel consumption: the Mercedes consumed 160 litres per 100km.

The drivers of these unbelievably powerful vehicles faced two major problems: brakes and tyres. If they were to last the length of a Grand Prix, brakes could not be jumped on at the last moment before a corner, and indeed a safe margin between cars was usually maintained in the interests of minimising braking. At the same time drivers had to compromise between optimum cornering speeds and the risk of blow-outs, for tyre technology was one area that had not kept pace with the rapid technical development in other areas. Even using 19-, 20- and even 21-inch diameter wheels, tyres rarely lasted more than 100km at racing speeds.

The winner of races in this era was not

the driver who was fastest into the corners, applying his brakes at the last moment, but the one whose experience or instinct allowed him to throttle back sufficiently to take the curves with minimum use of brakes and tyres, and thus extend the time on the circuit between pit-stops.

Grand Prix cars of the 750kg formula era 1934 to 1937

Year	Make & model	Cylinders	Capacity	Bore	Stroke	bhp	rpm	Gears	Max. speed km/h
1934	Alfa Romeo Tipo B (P3)	8	2905	68	100	255	5400	4	262
1934	Auto Union A	16	4358	68	75	295	4500	5	270
1934	Auto Union B	16	4951	72,5	75	375	4800	5	290
1934	Bugatti 59	8	3251	72	100	240	5400	4	245
1934	Maserati 6C-34	6	3724	84	112	260	5300	4	250
1934	Mercedes W25A	8	3360	78	80	354	5800	4	280
1934	Mercedes M25AB	8	3720	87	88	398	5800	4	295
1934	Mercedes M25B	8	3990	82	94,5	430	5800	4	310
1934	SEFAC	8	2770	70	90	250	6500	4	240
1935	Alfa Romeo Tipo B	8	3165	71	100	265	5400	4	275
1935	Alfa Romeo 8C	8	3822	78	100	330	5400	4	275
1935	Maserati V8-R1	8	4785	84	108	320	5300	4	270
1935	Mercedes M25C	8	4310	82	102	462	5800	4	315
1935	Trossi Monaco	16	3982	65	75	250	6000	4	295
1936	Alfa Romeo 12C	12	4064	70	88	370	5800	4	290
1936	Auto Union C	16	6005	75	85	520	5000	5	300
1936	Bugatti 50B	8	4744	84	107	370	5700	4	260
1936	Mercedes W25E	8	4740	86	102	480	5800	4	315
1937	Alfa Romeo 12C	12	4495	72	92	430	5800	4	310
1937	Mercedes W125	8	5660	94	102	610	5800	4	320

The New 3-Litre Formula

Rosemeyer dies in an accident at the end of January. The Germans dominate in spite of a change of formula. Alfa Romeo introduces the Type 158.

The 750kg formula had been devised in an attempt to reduce speeds, for the rule-makers could not have foreseen the metallurgical advances which would enable even more powerful cars to be built within the weight limit. For 1938 therefore the formula was replaced by one which called for an increase in weight and at the same time returned to the concept of limiting engine size. Grand Prix regulations at that time were determined by the *Association Internationale des Automobile Clubs Reconnus* (AIACR) which, after the war, became the *Federation Internationale de l'Automobile* (FIA). At the same time the FIA's *Commission Sportive Internationale* (CSI) was given responsibility for devising international rules.

The new Grand Prix rules for 1938 laid down a sliding scale of minimum weights between 400 and 850kg according to engine size. Included in the calculations for weight were gearbox and differential oil and tyres but not engine oil, fuel or coolants. At the same time the size of competing cars' engines was limited to a maximum of 3000cc (and a minimum of 666cc) though larger engines, between 1000cc and 4500cc, were admitted if superchargers were not used. The ratio between supercharged and unsupercharged engines was thus 1:1.5. No restrictions were placed on the type of fuel, and would not be until 1958 when avgas was specified; later cars were required to use commercially available petrol.

The formula attempted, for the first time, to establish a relationship between supercharged and unsupercharged engines, but in practice the ratio proved unfair on the unsupercharged units: they put out around 250bhp compared with figures of between 350 and 490bhp achieved by the supercharged engines.

Before the 1938 season began, motor racing suffered a sad loss when on January 28th Bernd Rosemeyer, one of the greatest drivers of the time, was killed during a record attempt on the Frankfurt–Darmstadt autobahn when his streamlined Auto Union was hit by a gust of wind while travelling at approximately 400km/h and swept off the road. Germany's darling, the idol of the people, was killed instantly. The accident was probably caused by a combination of the wind and the car's aerodynamics, for it is believed the car may have become airborne just before the accident. Less was known about the science of

aerodynamics those days than now.

Mercedes-Benz, Auto Union, Alfa Romeo, Maserati and Bugatti all built 3-litre supercharged engines for the new formula while the French Delahaye and Talbot concerns fielded 4.5-litre cars. Mercedes made a comeback in 1938 and 1939 but Auto Union only managed to record a few minor successes with Tazio Nuvolari and HP(Hermann)Müller who were under contract to them at the time.

The new 3-litre Mercedes-Benz W154 was based on the previous model, but with a new low-slung chassis and, of course, all-new engine. The Stuttgart firm departed from the eight-cylinder philosophy that had guided its 750kg exploits and settled on a V12 motor (67 x 70mm, 2962cc) which developed 468bhp at 7800rpm at a mean piston speed 18.2m/sec. The new model represented a giant leap forward in power output per litre compared with its predecessor, returning 158bhp/litre compared with the 114 of the 1937 W125.

The new motor was arranged in two rows of six cylinders at a 60° angle, with fixed cylinder-heads and water-jackets welded onto the cylinders to provide cooling. The crankshaft had needle main and big-end bearings, and no fewer than nine oil pumps supplied lubrication for the engine. The two Roots superchargers

Prof. Robert Eberan von Eberhorst

were located up front, feeding two down-draught carburettors. The superchargers required 150bhp at maximum revolutions and provided boost at a pressure of 1.26kg/cc. The compression ratio was 6.5:1, not very high for a 12-cylinder engine. Four overhead camshafts drove the 48 overhead valves.

Auto Union introduced their new Type D for which Director Werner, Chief Engineer Siebler and the engineers Jakob, Eberan von Eberhorst and Werner Strobel were responsible. Professor Ferdinand Porsche had by this time

Left top to bottom
The supercharged V12 Mercedes-Benz W154 (2962cc).

The unsupercharged V12 Delahaye Type 155 single-seater (4490cc).

The supercharged eight-cylinder Auto Union Type D (2990cc).

Bugatti's "3 Litre" with supercharged eight-cylinder engine (2980cc).

Right
The Mercedes-Benz W154 team cars in front of the pits at Berne. Dietrich, the tyre engineer from Continental, has his back to the camera.

Below right
Manfred von Brauchitsch climbs out of his W154 which started to smoke after a few practice laps on the Bremgarten circuit in Berne. Next to the his car is a special short-chassis W154.

accepted a new commission, the development of the Volkswagen, but the new team remained faithful to his original concept of rear engine placement, though they abandoned the swing-axle suspension.

The new car used a 60 V12 2990cc (65 x 75mm) motor with Roots superchargers, developing 420bhp at 7000rpm on a compression ratio of 10:1, at a mean piston speed of 10.5m/sec. The superchargers ran at a boost of 1.19kg/cc though in 1939 this was increased to 1.61kg with a corresponding increase in power, to 485bhp. Light-alloy cylinder heads were used, with three overhead camshafts. The driver's seat was placed further back in this model than in the V16 of the 750kg formula. Front suspension was by the Porsche torsion-bar system and rear by the De Dion principle, which had by now become almost universal in Grand Prix usage and would remain so until the end of the 1950s. More attention than before had been paid to

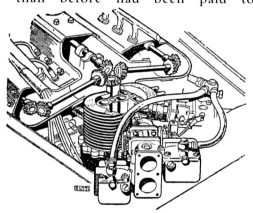

Left
A D-Type Auto Union of the type Nuvolari used to win the Italian and Donington Grands Prix of 1938. The horizontal tail-fins were a feature of this model.

Far left
The cam drive of the V12 C-Type Auto Union. The earlier V16 had only one central overhead camshaft, but the V12, as illustrated, had three. Also visible are the Roots supercharger and the carburettors. The cylinders measured 65 x 75mm (2990cc).

aerodynamic efficiency, and the body was of a much smoother design, complete with trim-fins at the rear. The car weighed exactly 850kg dry, or in race trim, complete with fuel, oil and driver, 1220kg.

Alfa Romeo had signified their intention of returning to direct participation in racing in 1938 by setting up a new department within the factory at the end of the previous year. This new section, called Alfa Corse, took over the functions previously handled by Scuderia Ferrari, and took on Enzo Ferrari in an advisory capacity.

Their new car used the chassis seen at the end of 1937, with all-independent suspension, but with a choice of no fewer than three supercharged 3-litre engines, an eight-cylinder, a 12 and a 16. Many

supporters, even within Alfa Corse, considered the factory should have concentrated on one project.

The first of these, the Type 308, had its 69 x 100mm cylinders placed in parallel blocks of four, each with its own supercharger, and developed 295bhp at 6000rpm from its 2991cc. This gave it less than 100bhp/litre, considerably short of the 158bhp/litre of the Mercedes-Benz W125. Dry weight was 880kg.

The V12 Type 312 had cylinders measuring 66 x 73mm (2995cc) and developed 350bhp at 6500rpm, a considerable improvement on the Type 308 but still no match for the German competition.

The twin-supercharged Type 316 engine was even more powerful, developing 440bhp at 7500rpm. That put

it very close to Mercedes and Auto Union figures, for on a ratio of power to size, the 16-cylinder (58 x 70mm, 2958cc) Alfa engine developed 149bhp/litre. Instead of building a conventional V16, Alfa's engine consisted of two blocks of eight cylinders bolted together at a 60° angle, with two crankshafts positioned next to each other in a wide crankcase. Each bank of cylinders had its own supercharger running at 0.8kg/cc pressure. It was half a Type 316 engine which, later in the year, provided the basis for the Type 158 Alfa Romeo which was campaigned in the 1500cc voiturette class. This car, the famous "Alfetta", was the forerunner of the car which took Giuseppe Farina and Juan Manuel Fangio to their World Championship successes in 1950 and 1951.

d'Automobile de Course. This had originally been built for the 750kg formula but appeared only rarely and never finished a race. It now reappeared in modified form to comply with the new formula with a supercharged motor of rather unusual twin-block construction and cylinder dimensions of 70 x 90mm (capacity 2770cc) but developing only 250bhp. After a few events in which it failed to gain a place the SEFAC disappeared forever.

The only teams making use of the "unsupercharged" provisions of the regulations were the French Talbots and Delahayes, whose engines of between 4 and 4.5 litres still used the old system of operating the valves by push rods and rocker gear. But in spite of this René Dreyfus in one of the big Delahaye Type 145s won the first race run under the new Formula, at Pau on April 10th 1938. A major factor in his success was that he did not have to make a refuelling stop whereas the Mercedes W154, driven first by Caracciola and then by Lang, lost time with a fuel stop, and later with clutch trouble.

Bugatti's contender was the supercharged eight-cylinder Type 59/50 B111 (78 x 78mm, 2980cc) but it still retained the traditional Bugatti chassis layout without independent suspension.

Another French 3-litre car on the books this year was the SEFAC, built by the *Société des Études et de la Fabrication*

The V12 Delahaye, designed by the chief engineer Jean Francois, had a capacity of 4490cc (75 x 84.7mm) and developed 245bhp at 5000rpm. The Delahayes were campaigned by a private team called Ecurie Bleu. The stable's name was subsequently changed to Ecurie Lucy O'Reilly Schell in honour of its owner, whose son Harry Schell would achieve international note as a driver after the war. During 1938 a lighter single-seater version of V12 Delahaye was built, but it in fact did not appear in more than a handful of races.

Although uncompetitive in Grand Prix events, the Type 145 Delahaye was also adapted to sportscar use, in which category it was a serious contender. Indeed one of these, in the hands of Chaboud and Trémoulet, won the 24-hour race at Le Mans on June 18–19th 1938, at an average speed of 132.53km/h.

The Talbot, designed by Walter Becchia, used a six-cylinder 4464cc (92 x 112mm) engine which developed 245bhp at 5000rpm, and the famous Wilson preselector gearbox. Like the Delahaye, it too could be adapted for sportscar use, by little more than the addition of wings and lamps. A single-seater version was however built in 1939, and this was the forerunner of the famous Talbot-Lago Type T26C models which achieved many successes after the war, often in the hands of French private entrants, through their ability to complete entire race distances without refuelling, when the supercharged opposition had to stop.

Maserati's new Grand Prix challenger, the Type 8CTF, used a twin-supercharged eight-cylinder 2992cc (69 x 100mm) engine which developed 350bhp at 6300rpm. Its high piston speed (21.0m/sec) however made it susceptible to mechanical failure. But while they lasted the 8CTFs proved very fast. Driven by Carlo-Felice Trossi, Achille Varzi and Gigi Villoresi, the red cars left the German competition standing as often as not. The highlight of the car's Grand Prix career came in 1939 when Paul Pietsch, later publisher of the *Auto Motor und Sport* magazine, led the entire Mercedes-Benz and Auto Union teams in the German Grand Prix, and finally finished third.

Tazio Nuvolari ended his long association with Alfa Romeo when a fuel leak developed in his Type 308 during practice for the Pau Grand Prix. The car caught fire and Nuvolari, who suffered burns in the incident, swore he would never race an Alfa again. Much to the disappointment of his Italian fans he kept his word, and in the middle of the year signed to drive for Auto Union, making his debut for them on July 24th 1938 in the German Grand Prix at the Nürburgring.

Nuvolari initially had some difficulty in adapting to the rear-engined car but was soon at home with it and Auto Union came to regard him as their replacement for Bernd Rosemeyer. The wiry little Italian won the Italian Grand Prix at Monza as well as the Donington Grand Prix in England, but this was another Mercedes year, the new W154s notching up most of the successes of the 1938 season. Caracciola won the Swiss Grand Prix at Berne, Hermann Lang the Tripoli Grand Prix, von Brauchitsch the ACF Grand Prix, run for a second time at Rheims, and the young Englishman Dick Seaman the German Grand Prix at the Nürburgring. In addition to these results Lang won the Coppa Ciano at Leghorn and Caracciola the Coppa Acerbo at Pescara, Caracciola's success bringing him the European Championship title for the third time (1935, 1937 and 1938).

The 1938 3-litre Grand Prix formula was used with only minor modifications for the major American race, the Indianapolis 500. Indeed the rules laid down for the 1938 Indianapolis race form the basis for the regulations still in use. The major changes made were in the 1960s, when a large number of differing engine sizes had to be incorporated.

René Dreyfus

Above

Wilbur Shaw finished second in the 1938 Indianapolis 500 in this Shaw Special, which had a four-cylinder Offenhauser engine in his own chassis. He had won with this car in 1937, and was victorious again in 1939 and 1940, with an eight-cylinder Maserati 8CTF.

Success for Hermann Lang

Mercedes-Benz are clearly the leading cars — Lang becomes European Champion. Surprise appearance of the 1.5-litre Mercedes at Tripoli. An eight-cylinder Maserati wins at Indianapolis.

There were few changes for 1939. Mercedes saw little reason for radical change to their elegantly designed W154, but did give it an updated motor. This was the Type M163, a twin-supercharged 12-cylinder unit which developed 485bhp at 8000rpm, at a rate of 162bhp/litre. The Daimler-Benz engineers also experimented with fuel injection, though this would not appear in serious competition until the 1950s.

Auto Union meanwhile carried out a winter development programme on their 12-cylinder engines, also using two-stage superchargers, which resulted in their obtaining the same power as their Mercedes counterparts.

Alfa Romeo's modifications to the 16-cylinder twin-crankshaft Type 316 were mainly cosmetic, the car appearing this year with a body-style based on the beautiful lines of the Alfetta 158. The 316 appeared in this form only once however, in the Belgian Grand Prix at Spa, where Giuseppe Farina, after a promising start, had to retire with a mechanical problem.

But this car was intended only as a stopgap, for Alfa Romeo was at the time working on plans for its replacement, the Type 162. This model had a "square" (62 x 62mm) 16-cylinder 2995cc motor which was probably one of the most complicated engines ever built. Two three-stage superchargers were employed for each bank of cylinders, coupled to a centrifugal blower mounted between the cylinders, the combined result of which was 3kg/cc boost. The fuel/air mixture was regulated by two triple-choke carburettors. This engine was tested in 1940 and, running with a compression ratio of 6.8:1, developed 490bhp at 7800rpm, which was still not as much as that of the German engines from the previous racing season. The motor's design, however, was a typical example of the versatility and creativity of Alfa Romeo. Parts for six cars were completed, though only one car was ever assembled and it never raced, due to the outbreak of the war.

It was believed in Alfa Romeo circles that further development of this 16-cylinder engine could have brought a minimum output of 560bhp at 8200rpm.

Another experimental Alfa Romeo which never saw the light of day because of Italy's entry into the war was the rear-engined 512. This had a twin-supercharged 12-cylinder 1490cc (54 x 54mm) "Boxer" motor located in front of the rear axle in a chassis built from oval-section tubing. Under test the 12-cylinder engine developed 335bhp at 8600rpm but in spite of its advanced specification, the 512 was considered inferior to the Type 158 Alfetta, especially with regard to its chassis design. As an experiment the Boxer motor was also fitted in the front of a 158. After the war the classic front-engined eight-cylinder Alfetta design proved to be so far ahead of its competition that no further development of the 512 motor was undertaken.

Leading Alfa Romeo designer in this period was the Spanish engineer Wilfredo Ricart who would later be responsible for the V8-engined Pegaso sportscar built in Spain in the 1950s. Enzo Ferrari, still working as a consultant for Alfa Corse, did not get on at all well with Ricart and at the end of 1938 left Alfa Corse, and returned to his own operation at Modena. During the war the Ferrari company was diverted to the manufacture of machine tools.

1939 was yet another successful season for Mercedes. Hermann Lang won the Belgian Grand Prix at Spa, a race marred by a fatal accident involving Richard

Hermann Lang

Above
Maserati built a streamlined four-cylinder 1.5-litre voiturette for the fast 1939 Tripoli race, run that year for the smaller machinery rather than to Grand Prix regulations.

Right
Hermann Lang was European Champion in 1939. The former racing mechanic won numerous races in his fast Mercedes-Benz W154.

Far right
Daimler-Benz secretly developed a voiturette — the W165 — with a supercharged 1493cc V8 engine for the Tripoli race. With these cars Lang and Caracciola took the first two places.

Right
Start of the 1939 Swiss Grand Prix. The M163-engined W154 Mercedes-Benz cars of (from left) Lang, von Brauchitsch and Caracciola fill the front row, with the Auto Unions behind.

Centre
Engineer Rudolf Uhlenhaut tests his latest brainchild at Monza in March 1939.

Below
The 1939 Mercedes-Benz used the V12 M163 engine. The gear-driven camshafts were inclined at 60 degrees. Cylinder dimensions were 67 x 70mm (2960cc) and the engine developed 485bhp.

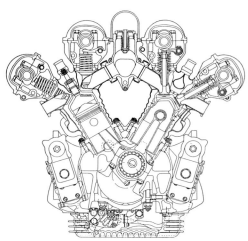

R.E. Uhlenhaut.
Rudolf Uhlenhaut

Seaman. Unable to undo the lock which would have enabled him to release the steering wheel (necessary for getting in and out of the car), he died in his burning Mercedes. Caracciola won the German Grand Prix at the Nürburgring again while, in addition to his Spa success, Lang also won the Swiss Grand Prix. In addition Lang also won the Pau Grand Prix, the Eifelrennen and at Rio so that at the end of the season the former Mercedes-Benz racing mechanic was declared European Champion for 1939.

Auto Union's first race win of 1939 was in the ACF Grand Prix at Rheims where, after all the Mercedes had broken down, Auto Union junior driver Hermann Paul Müller celebrated a surprise victory.

There was, however, only one other European race, the first (and last) Yugoslavian Grand Prix at Belgrade,

Hermann Paul Müller

before the shadow of war fell across the world. Nuvolari won this last competition, on September 3rd 1939, in an Auto Union.

International tension resulted in the cancellation of all Grand Prix events from the beginning of September. A second Grand Prix in Switzerland, planned to coincide with a big inter-Canton festival, had been planned for the Schwamendingen road circuit at Zurich, but had to be cancelled after the Mercedes-Benz, Auto Union, Alfa Romeo and Maserati teams one by one withdrew their entries.

The 1939 3-litre Mercedes Grand Prix cars survived the war and were used again 12 years later when, in the winter of 1951, a trio of cars driven by Juan Manuel Fangio, Karl Kling and Hermann Lang raced in two Formule Libre events in Argentina. But the W163s were unable to make full use of their 500bhp on the twisting makeshift circuits, and they had also been unable to obtain suitable fuels. They were defeated in both races by the fearless Froilan Gonzales in a supercharged 2-litre V12 Ferrari.

Maserati did achieve one major victory in 1939 when Wilbur Shaw took an 8CTF to victory in the Indianapolis 500, defeating a high-quality field of American

Cover of the English magazine "Speed", August 1937 edition. Subject: the AVUS race in Berlin.

Poster of the 1937 Swiss Grand Prix.

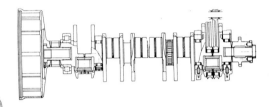

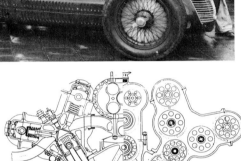

cars and drivers. He repeated this success in the same car one year later.

Bugatti, a marque that had been so famous in racing circles in the 1920s and early 1930s, celebrated one final major victory in 1939 when Wimille/Veyron crossed the finishing line first in the **24-hour race at Le Mans. The last prewar racing season had provided one other surprise**, in the Tripoli Grand Prix. The Italian organisers had unexpectedly switched this from Grand Prix to voiturette regulations, hoping no doubt for an Italian victory, as the smaller class was dominated at the time by the Alfa Type 158 and the four-cylinder Maserati Type 4CL. But in the six months before the event Mercedes designed and built their own voiturette from scratch. The W165, to all intents and purposes a scaled-down W163, was powered by a new V8 1493cc (64 x 58mm) engine which with four overhead camshafts and two-stage supercharging gave 254bhp at 8250rpm. The Alfa Romeo 158 developed 225bhp at 7200rpm and the Maserati 4CL 220 at 8000, neither approaching the German car's performance of 170bhp/litre. The appearance of the small Mercedes at Tripoli caused a sensation and resulted in it taking the first two places. Hermann

Lang was winner with Rudolf Caracciola second, followed by Emilio Villoresi (brother of Gigi Villoresi) in an Alfa Romeo and Piero Taruffi in a Maserati.

There were no more races for the fabulous W165 after the Tripoli event, though in 1951 the factory announced its intention of reviving it for Grand Prix racing, as the formula at that time was for

1.5-litre supercharged engines. Shortly afterwards however the International Sports Commission announced that World Championship Grand Prix races from then on would be restricted to 2-litre unsupercharged cars, and this put paid to any further development in the design and construction of a second series of W165s.

Grand Prix cars of the 3-litre formula era 1938 to 1939

Year	Make & model	Cylinders	Capacity	Bore	Stroke	bhp	rpm	Gears	Max. speed km/h	Dry weight
1938	Alfa Romeo 308	8	2991	69	100	295	6000	4	260	870
1938	Alfa Romeo 312	12	2995	66	73	350	6500	4	285	880
1938	Alfa Romeo 316	16	2958	58	70	440	7500	4	300	920
1938	Auto Union D	12	2984	65	75	485	7000	5	310	890
1938	Bugatti T59/50B	8	2980	78	78	270	6000	4	280	800
1938	Delahaye 145	12	4490	75	84,7	225	5000	4	225	1065
1938	Delahaye 155	12	4490	75	84,7	235	5000	4	250	860
1938	Maserati 8CTF	8	2992	69	100	350	6300	4	290	870
1938	Mercedes W154	12	2962	67	70	468	7800	5	300	890
1938	Sefac Type B	8	2960	72,5	90	250	6000	4	260	880
1938	Talbot (2str) T150	6	4464	92	112	245	5000	4	230	860
1939	Talbot (Istr)	6	4483	93	110	255	5100	4	240	850
1939	Auto Union D	12	2990	65	75	485	7000	5	320	890
1939	Alfa Romeo 162	16	2995	62	62	490	7800	4		1075
1939	Mercedes W154-M163	12	2962	67	70	485	7800	5	310	900

Racing Ceases in Europe

Many countries are already at war. The roar of racing engines has died, though some racing events are still run in Italy.

Few races were run in 1940. There were two races for 1500cc voiturettes, the Targa Florio (on a circuit in Favorita Park in Palermo) and the Tripoli Grand Prix, and there was also an important sportscar race. Although this event was called the Mille Miglia, it was run on a shorter triangular circuit in the Po Valley.

And the Indianapolis 500 took place too, America not yet being involved in the conflict. Indeed, the 1941 Indianapolis was also run before America joined the war, this race being won by Mauri Rose in a Miller. Then all racing stopped.

Enzo Ferrari meanwhile built his first car, the Type 815 sportscar with an eight-cylinder 1.5-litre engine, in 1940. Two examples started in the Mille Miglia but as Ferrari's agreement with Alfa Romeo meant he was not allowed to use his own name, the cars were raced under the name of Auto-Avio Costruzioni.

Wilbur Shaw

Above
It is wartime (October 1941) and fuel is rationed. The roar of racing engines has ceased. Ernesto, Bindo and Ettore Maserati cycle through the town of Modena.

Above right
Wilbur Shaw in an 8CTF won great acclaim for Maserati in the 1939 and 1940 Indianapolis 500s. The supercharged 2991cc eight-cylinder motor developed 366bhp at 6300rpm and was mounted in a chassis suspended by torsion bars at the front and quarter-elliptic leaf springs at the rear.

The racing cars in the Voiturettes category (to 1500cc) 1930 to 1940

Year	Make & model	Cylinders	Capacity	Bore	Stroke	bhp	rpm	Gears	Max. speed km/h	Dry weight
1931	Austin Yellow Canary	4	747	56	76	56	6000	4	160	470
1931	Maserati 4CTR	4	1088	65	82	105	5500	4	150	690
1931	MG C-Type Midget	4	746	57	73	44	6400	4	205	670
1931	MG C comp.	4	746	57	73	52	6500	4	140	680
1932	Maserati 4CM-1500	4	1496	69	100	135	5600	4	155	680
1932	MG J4	4	746	57	73	72	6000	4	210	710
1933	MG K3	6	1087	57	71	120	6500	4	190	790
1933	Riley	6	1486	57,2	95,2	96	5600	4	190	890
1934	MG EX135	6	1087	57	71	120	6500	4	185	780
1935	Alta	4	1486	68,7	100	140	5800	4	200	680
1935	ERA B	6	1488	57,5	95,2	150	6500	4	200	780
1936	Austin Seven	4	744	60,3	65	116	6200	4	195	520
1936	Maserati 6CM	6	1493	65	75	155	6200	4	215	650
1937	Alta	4	1486	68,7	100	200	6200	4	210	670
1937	Maserati 4CM-1500	4	1496	69	100	150	5600	4	215	690
1937	Maserati 4CM-1100	4	1088	65	82	125	6000	4	200	580
1938	Alfa Romeo 158	8	1479	58	70	195	7200	4	232	620
1939	Alfa Romeo 158	8	1479	58	70	225	7500	4	240	620
1939	ERA E	6	1487	63	80	270	7500	4	275	720
1939	Maserati 4CL	4	1489	78	78	220	8000	4	250	630
1939	Mercedes W165	8	1493	64	58	278	8250	5	285	720

Open Exhausts Again

Prewar racing cars reappear in spite of the shortage of materials. Wimille in a Bugatti wins the first postwar race in the Bois de Boulogne. Italian cars and drivers dominate.

The Second World War ended in Europe in May 1945, and the first postwar race meeting was held on September 9th, the French staging three races on a circuit in the Bois de Boulogne in Paris for vehicles which had survived the war. First race was the Robert Benoist Trophy, a memorial to the former Delage and Bugatti driver who had been shot by the Gestapo during the war. Restricted to cars under 1500cc, this race was won by Amédée Gordini in a car based on Simca-Fiat parts. Gordini would soon become famous throughout the racing world, but as a constructor rather than as a driver. The second race, the Liberation Trophy for 2-litre cars, went to Henri Louveau in a Maserati, while the Coupe des Prisonniers was won by Jean-Pierre Wimille in a 4.7-litre Bugatti Type 59/50B.

Meanwhile in Italy, during the summer of 1945, Enzo Ferrari had got in touch with Alfa Romeo designer Gioachino Colombo, the man responsible for the very successful prewar Alfa Romeo 158. During their first meeting

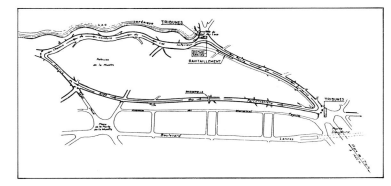

they agreed to build a new racing Ferrari. Colombo designed an engine in his Milan home and this became the basis for a long and successful run of V12 Ferrari engines.

The red Italian cars, the Alfa Romeos, Maseratis and Ferraris, were the most successful in the early postwar racing years. The Maseratis and Ferraris starred for a good decade, and their run of successes was interrupted only by Mercedes-Benz in 1954 and 1955 with their unbeatable eight-cylinder Type

The first postwar race meeting in Europe took place on a 2.779km circuit in the Bois de Boulogne in Paris on September 9th 1945, when three races were held.

Most cars in the Coupe du Salon race on the Bois de Boulogne circuit in October 1946 were prewar sports-based machinery with unsupercharged engines, or supercharged 1.5-litre monopostos of the old voiturettes class. France was represented by Delage, Delahaye and Talbot, but they were unable to keep up with the supercharged Maserati 4CLs or the English ERAs.

Right
The first postwar race in 1945 was Bugatti's last significant victory. Jean-Pierre Wimille (third from left) won the Coupe des Prisonniers at the Bois de Boulogne in a prewar car with 4.7-litre eight-cylinder motor. Ettore Bugatti (light suit) was present at the race; born in Milan, he died in Paris in 1947.

Clemente Biondetti

W196, and that car was the result of the type of research and development that could be undertaken only by a large organisation with considerable expertise and skilled staff. After 1957 Britain also became a challenge to the Italian supremacy.

More events were held in 1946, many of them run on improvised street circuits in places such as Nice, Marseilles, Geneva, Milan, Turin and Paris. Maserati and Alfa Romeo with their prewar 1.5-litre supercharged cars won most of these, though Eugène Chaboud won the Belgian Grand Prix at Spa in an unsupercharged 4.5-litre V12 Delahaye.

The Alfa Romeo 158 made its first postwar appearance in the St Cloud race in Paris on June 9th 1946, with Giuseppe Farina and Jean-Pierre Wimille as drivers. But the sleek Alfettas, which had been hidden in a hay-shed during the war, were less than perfectly prepared and failed to finish, leaving Raymond Sommer to win the race in a 4CL Maserati.

The peak years in the racing history of the eight-cylinder Alfas followed from that race, and lasted until 1951. After the 1946 St Cloud debacle the Alfettas started in 26 races and won 26 in a row before they were next defeated.

The Alfetta Type 158 (it was changed to the 159 at the peak of its development in 1951) deserves all the praise it has been given as the most successful vehicle in Grand Prix racing at that time. Originally designed and built at Scuderia Ferrari in Modena in 1937, under the direction of the immensely competent Alfa Romeo engineer Gioachino Colombo, the 158 was of classic concept, with a chassis of tubular steel construction to which was

Luigi Villoresi

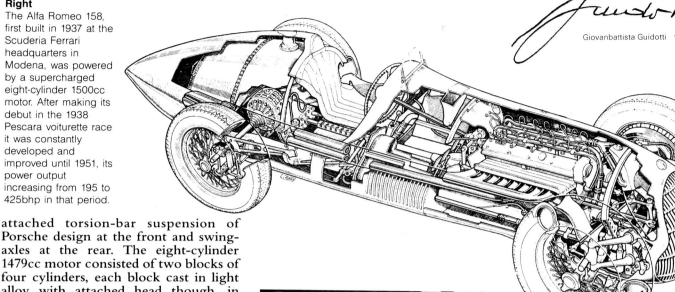

Right
The Alfa Romeo 158, first built in 1937 at the Scuderia Ferrari headquarters in Modena, was powered by a supercharged eight-cylinder 1500cc motor. After making its debut in the 1938 Pescara voiturette race it was constantly developed and improved until 1951, its power output increasing from 195 to 425bhp in that period.

attached torsion-bar suspension of Porsche design at the front and swing-axles at the rear. The eight-cylinder 1479cc motor consisted of two blocks of four cylinders, each block cast in light alloy with attached head though, in contrast to earlier Alfa Romeo practice, the cylinders had steel liners attached at top and bottom. Each block was separately cast in light alloy in one piece with the cylinder-head. A single-stage Roots supercharger operating at 0.8kg/cc boost was fitted to the first models, in which form the engine developed 195bhp at 7200rpm, though considerably more power was made available when two-stage supercharging was adopted during the 1947 racing season. The cylinder dimensions of 58 x 70mm remained unchanged throughout the car's life, from its debut on July 31st 1938 in the Coppa Ciano at Leghorn, when Emilio Villoresi and Clemente Biondetti took the cars to the first two places, until its last season of racing, 1951. A year after its inception the 158 was given a facelift when the nose was redesigned, and this made the car one of the most attractive of any racing at that time.

Factory records show that total production of the Alfetta was 16 units. Six cars were built in 1937 and 1938, and raced through to the end of 1939, and another six laid down in 1940. These cars were constantly rebuilt, modified and updated throughout their racing lives, which continued right up until 1950. The last four cars, to Type 159 specification, were built in 1951. The Alfetta's first major defeat was early in its career when on May 7th 1939 the V8 Mercedes W165s driven by Lang and Caracciola took first and second places at Tripoli ahead of the Italians. But the Alfetta was Alfa Romeo's most successful car, certainly since the 1932–35 P3 model.

Left
Jean-Pierre Wimille in an Alfa Romeo 158. On the extreme left is Alfa racing manager and occasional driver Giovanbattista Guidotti.

Below
The first postwar Grand Prix was the GP des Nations, held at Geneva in 1946. Giuseppe Farina, shown leading his team-mate Jean-Pierre Wimille, won in an Alfa Romeo 158.

The First Formula One

The Alfettas are unbeatable, and Jean-Pierre Wimille their most successful driver. Ferrari builds a V12. Cisitalia builds a car to Porsche designs.

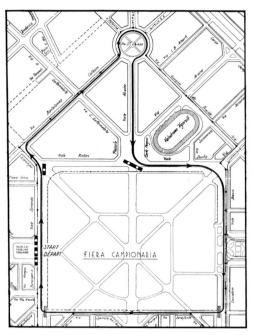

Above

As the Monza Autodrome had been used for years as a dumping ground for war materials, the Italian Grand Prix was held on a 3.447km street circuit around the Milan fairgrounds.

Conte Carlo Felice Trossi

Below

The eight-cylinder Alfetta's long run of successes began in 1946 (it was beaten only once before 1951). In 1947 the motor was fitted with two-stage super-charging, which dramatically increased the engine output.

At the end of 1946 the newly formed *Fédération Internationale de l'Automobile* decided to establish new rules for Grand Prix racing, and for the first time the term "Formula One" was applied. The rules laid down maximum capacities of 1500cc for supercharged engines and 4500cc for unsupercharged engines, which represented a change in the ratio between supercharged and unsupercharged engines from 1:1.5 (or 3 litres to 4.5 litres) which had existed since 1938, to 1:3. But in spite of this the supercharged motors still developed more power than their unsupercharged counterparts. The Alfa Romeo Type 158, now with two-stage supercharging which increased boost from 0.8kg/cc to 2.5kg/cc, was putting out 275bhp at 7500rpm in 1947. And although dry weight went up at the same time, from 630kg to 700kg, the power-to-weight ratio increased from 314bhp/tonne to 393bhp/tonne; by 1951 this had grown still further, to almost 600bhp/tonne.

The 1489cc (78 x 78mm) four-cylinder supercharged engine of the Maserati 4CL, the best car after the Alfetta, developed 220bhp at 6000rpm which, for a dry weight of 630kg, gave a power/weight ratio of 349bhp/tonne. Both in terms of pure power and of power to weight, these engines were far superior to the 4.5-litre Talbots which were not only less powerful, but at the same time weighed a lot more too.

An interesting new 12-cylinder contender, far ahead of its time, was under construction in Italy at this time, being built to Porsche designs by the Cisitalia company in Turin. The Cisitalia company had been founded by Piero Dusio in 1946 and produced a batch of popular little 350kg racing cars. Powered by 65bhp Fiat 1100 engines (other tuners were getting 80bhp from these units by now), no fewer than 16 examples of the D46 Cisitalia, driven by some of the best-known drivers of the day, took part in a special one-make race at Cairo early in 1947.

But Piero Dusio had his sights set on Formula One. At the end of 1946 he had contacted Professor Porsche and bought the rights to the Porsche 360 Grand Prix project, which had been designed by Porsche GmbH at Gmünd in Austria. Among those actively involved in the project were Carlo Abarth, at the time employed by Scuderia Scagliarini looking after Fiat-powered Cisitalia racing and sportscars, and later a manufacturer in his own right, and the engineer Rudolf Hruschka, who was engaged in an advisory capacity.

The Cisitalia-Porsche was a complicated and futuristic design with engine mounted behind the cockpit and driving via a five-speed gearbox to all four wheels, though the front-wheel drive could be switched off when not required. Suspension followed Auto-Union practice in its use of double torsion bars at the front and trailing arms at the

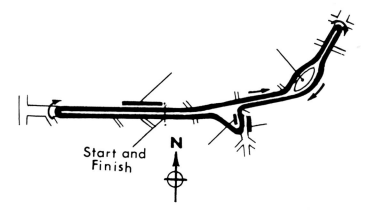

Start and
Finish

N

Left
The first postwar ACF
Grand Prix race took
place on the 7.296km
Lyon-Parilly street
circuit in 1947. Louis
Chiron in a Talbot won.

rear. The fuel tanks were located on
either side of the cockpit.

Slung low into this set-up was a
complex 12-cylinder Porsche-designed
Boxer motor with four overhead
camshafts and, mounted with the
carburettors above the engine, two
single-stage superchargers which
produced 1.96kg/cc boost. The 1492cc (56
x 51mm) engine developed 296bhp at
8500rpm but it was anticipated that the
motor could ultimately be developed to
produce more than 400bhp. With a dry
weight of 630kg, the initial power/weight
ratio was 470bhp/tonne, with a potential
for an increase to something in excess of
600.

But Cisitalia, in the midst of liquidity
problems, was unable to raise finance to
complete the project, which because of
the complexity of its design was an
expensive one, and at the end of 1949 the
factory was closed down. Dusio moved
to Argentina and took his Grand Prix cars
with him, and in 1953 Clemar Bucci in
one of them established an Argentinian
speed record. But the 1.5-litre formula
had ceased to exist by then, and no
purpose was to be served by persevering
with development. In 1960 the Cisitalia

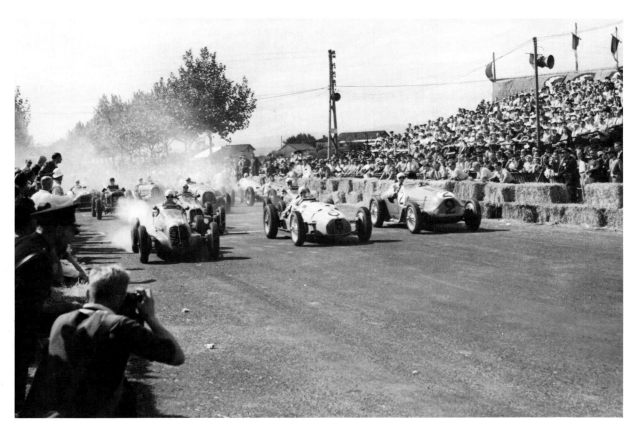

360 was rediscovered in Argentina by Huschke von Hanstein, then manager of Porsche's racing team, and transported to the Porsche factory museum.

A new name appeared on the racing circuits in 1947 — Ferrari. The first models had the classic overhead-camshaft

Gioachino Colombo

Gioachino Colombo

V12 motor designed by Gioachino Colombo, the former Alfa Romeo engineer, which would become a Ferrari trademark. At the same time Maserati experimented with two-stage super-charging. Britain was represented by the old-fashioned "square-rigged" ERA with its large diameter wheels and super-charged six-cylinder 1488cc (62.8 x 80mm) engine developing around 190bhp and also by the newer four-cylinder (68.75 x 100mm, 1488cc) Alta, but this country's Formula One supremacy was still a long way off. Britain had not won a major Grand Prix since Sir Henry Segrave's victories in the ACF race at Tours in 1923 and the San Sebastian Grand Prix in 1924, and would in fact have to wait another decade for a repeat, when Moss and Brooks were first over the finishing line in the British Grand Prix at Aintree in a four-cylinder Vanwall on July 20th 1957.

Meanwhile in 1947 the Alfa Romeo team of Jean-Pierre Wimille, Achille Varzi, Count Carlo-Felice Trossi and Consalvo Sanesi went from victory to victory, the Type 158 winning the Swiss and Belgian Grands Prix and also races at Bari and Milan. Those were the only races they contested.

The French continued to campaign their unsupercharged 4.5-litre Talbot, Delage and Delahaye designs, which were markedly inferior to the supercharged opposition. A serious French contender did not appear until the following year's Grand Prix des Nations when Talbot unveiled their T26C, of which some 20 examples were built at the Suresnes factory.

The 1947 French challenger, the car that was supposed to bring Grand Prix glory to France, was the CTA Arsenal, built by the *Centre d'Etudes Techniques de l'Automobile*. Design of this car was under the direction of Albert Lory, the famous engineer who had built the successful 1.5-litre Delage in 1926–27, and was based around a two-stage supercharged V8

engine of 1482cc capacity (60 x 65.5mm) which developed 266bhp at 7500rpm. Sadly however the car did not live up to expectations. Raymond Sommer had to abandon the car at the start of the ACF Grand Prix at Lyons when it developed clutch trouble, and a second attempt a year later, when two CTA Arsenals were entered in the Grand Prix at Rheims, ended when they were withdrawn after practice. They were never heard of again.

The Alfa Romeos did not take part in the 1947 ACF Grand Prix at Lyons, which allowed Louis Chiron in a six-cylinder Talbot to come home winner.

The brilliant Ettore Bugatti died in 1947 after a long illness, at the age of 66, bringing an era to an end, for his death closed a wonderful chapter in automobile history. Louis Delage died shortly after Ettore Bugatti.

During the year the Maserati brothers finally severed their links with the company that bore their names, selling their remaining interests to the Orsi family. The Maserati brothers meanwhile set up *Officine Specializzate Costruzioni Automobili* near Bologna, and began building OSCA cars.

In Britain at the same time plans were announced for a national racing car, promoted by ERA driver Raymond Mays and the engineer Peter Berthon under the name of British Racing Motors. More than one hundred British companies pledged their support through the BRM Trust.

Above
Poster of the 1938 Italian Grand Prix at Monza.
Overleaf left
Contemporary drawing by the Swiss artist Giorgio Guglielmetti. Subject: Mercedes Benz W 154.

Overleaf right
Cover picture of the magazine "Alfa Corse", 1940 edition.

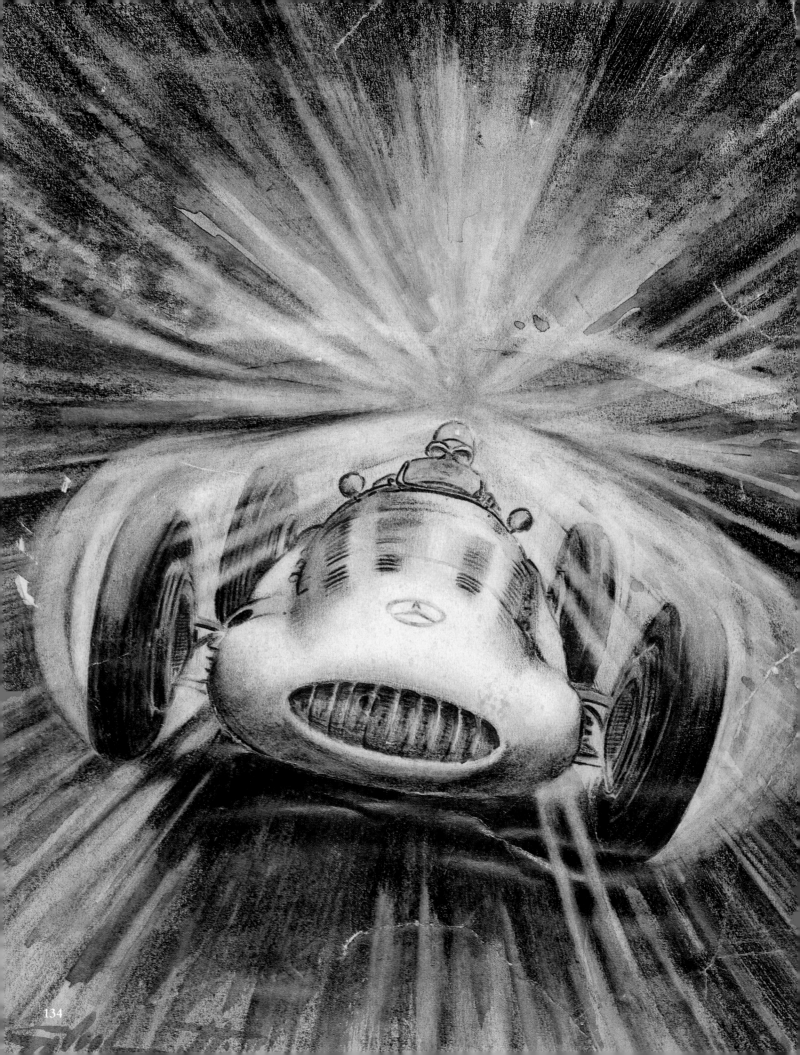

A contemporary drawing of the 1939 Talbot "Monoplace".

Another Alfetta Year

The Type 158 wins race after race. The first Ferrari Formula One car appears on the starting line. Talbot modifies its 4.5-litre engine. A certain Juan Manuel Fangio races at Rheims.

Nothing appeared capable of competing with the Alfa Romeos, which this year were producing 310bhp at 8000rpm, and their No. 1 driver Jean-Pierre Wimille was the best-known driver of the period.

The previous year several Italian drivers had accepted invitations to take part in the first Temporada series of races in Argentina and Brazil, and in 1948 they took note of a somewhat quiet and sad-looking Argentinian driver who performed well in an underpowered Simca-Gordini. His name was Juan Manuel Fangio and he would become World Champion five times between 1951 to 1957.

In sportscar racing this year a Ferrari driven by Clemente Biondetti won both the Mille Miglia and the Targa Florio.

But the real star of the Mille Miglia, as in 1947, was the veteran Tazio Nuvolari. In the earlier year, in spite of driving an 1100cc Cisitalia against much more powerful opposition, the 55-year-old ace showed his unique skills — as he had so

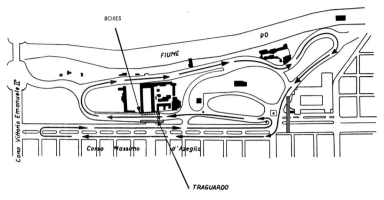

many times in the past — by leading almost all the way. But on the long straight roads near the finish he was unable to match the sheer speed of Biondetti's Alfa Romeo 2900, and was overtaken just before the finish. But

Nuvolari was now suffering the results of years of inhaling petrol fumes and almost collapsed when he climbed out of his car at the end. It was the beginning of a five-year struggle which ended with his death in 1953.

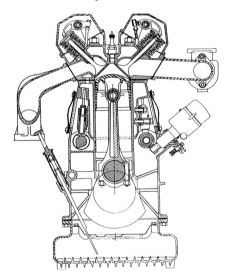

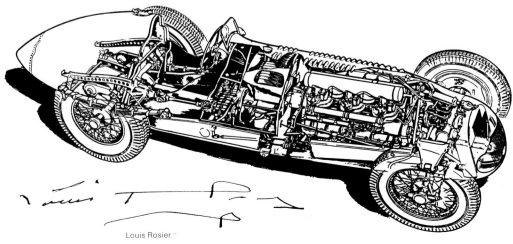

Louis Rosier

Above
The unsupercharged six-cylinder motor of the Talbot-Lago T26C (93 x 110mm, 4483cc) had twin camshafts positioned in the centre, driving the overhead valves through push rods and rocker gear. The performance was progressively increased from 240bhp at 4700rpm in 1948 to 280bhp at 5000rpm in 1951.

Right
The Talbot-Lago T26C made its debut in Louis Rosier's hands in the Grand Prix des Nations at Geneva in 1948. The Talbot, with its five-speed Wilson preselector gearbox, was not as fast as the supercharged Alfa Romeo, Maserati and Ferrari opposition, but could complete an entire race without having to stop to refuel.

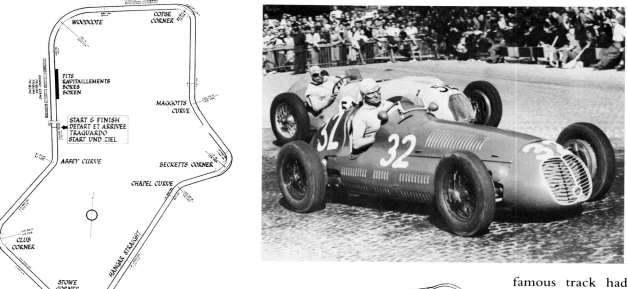

In spite of this, Nuvolari's drive in the 1948 Mille Miglia was every bit as sensational. This year driving a 2-litre Ferrari, he led for 1300km of the 1600km race. After half the race, the car's bonnet had come off in Rome and he later lost a mudguard in a brush with a stone wall, but still he continued, until finally, the rear axle broke. It was the end of the race for Nuvolari, a truly heroic driver and a man who was honoured and lauded by everyone. He fought his last race with an iron will and tremendous determination. However, as a father he had suffered greatly, when his two sons died in early years from serious illnesses.

Towards the end of his life Nuvolari gave some of his close friends to understand that he wanted to die at the wheel, and it was later claimed that this was a factor in his last desperate drives. But his last wish was not to be granted for Nuvolari, the dare-devil hero, died in a hospital bed.

When the Alfettas were absent, most races of 1948 fell to the four-cylinder Maseratis driven by Giuseppe Farina, Luigi Villoresi and Alberto Ascari. A new Maserati model, the Type 4CLT/48, was built for this year, and first appeared in the San Remo Grand Prix on the Ospedaletti circuit in June, with a tubular chassis, independent front suspension and a rigid rear axle. It retained the old 4CL engine (78 x 78mm, 1489cc) with two-stage supercharging which gave it 270bhp at 7000rpm. This new Maserati, with its familiar emblem of Neptune's trident, won the San Remo event (and was known ever after as the San Remo Maserati) in the hands of 30-year-old Alberto Ascari, and would win numerous other races until 1950.

Alfa Romeo now competed only in selected races, this year contesting the European Grand Prix at Berne, the ACF race at Rheims, the Italian Grand Prix at Turin and the Monza Autodrome Grand Prix. The Italian Grand Prix was held on an improvised circuit in the Valentino Park, as Monza was not available. The

famous track had incurred a lot of damage during the war, when it had been used as a dump for military vehicles. The circuit was rebuilt with modified corners for the Autodrome race on October 17th 1948. Alfa Romeo took the first four places at Monza with Wimille, Trossi, Sanesi and Taruffi driving.

Before the Italian Grand Prix, Ferrari cars had appeared in a number of races, but these were two-seater sportscars stripped of mudguards and headlamps, and powered by unsupercharged V12 motors of either 1.5-litre or 2-litre capacity. Now however the first genuine

Jean-Pierre Wimille

Ferrari Formula One car, the Colombo-designed Type 125, appeared, with a V12 1498cc (55 x 52.5mm) engine which employed single-stage supercharging and developed 225bhp at 7500rpm. Three of the 552kg 125s appeared in the nineteenth Italian Grand Prix, held on the Valentino circuit in Turin on September 5th, driven by the Frenchman Raymond Sommer, the Italian Nino Farina and the Siamese Prince Bira. The Turin race was held in pouring rain, and Farina collided with a fence and had to abandon the race, while Bira's car developed a clutch defect and he also had to withdraw. But Raymond Sommer kept going to finish the Italian

Raymond Sommer

Below
The Monza circuit, damaged during the war, was rebuilt in October 1948. It was based on the old road course but with realignment making a new distance of 6.3km. The original high speed oval was not rebuilt until much later.

Left
The first Formula One Ferrari appeared at the Italian Grand Prix in 1948, driven by Farina (pictured), Sommer and Bira. The car was the Type 125, a supercharged 1.5-litre V12.

Below
The elegant tail of the Alfa Romeo 158. This car was originally built in 1938 but underwent constant modification and improvement.

Bottom
This old-fashioned monoposto, with its large diameter wheels, is not a product of the 'twenties but a contemporary Iddings Special with Meyer chassis and four-cylinder Offenhauser engine. Lee Wallard took seventh place with this car in the 1948 Indianapolis 500; he won in a different car three years later.

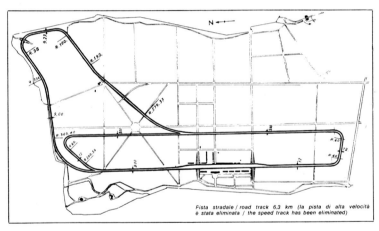

Pista stradale / road track 6,3 km (la pista di alta velocità è stata eliminata / the speed track has been eliminated)

LEE WALLARD
INDIANAPOLIS MOTOR SPEEDWAY, 1948

Grand Prix in third place, behind Wimille in an Alfa Romeo and Villoresi in a Maserati. It was the start of a Formula One tradition which has continued to this day, for there has not been a year since then when Ferrari cars have not taken part in Grand Prix races.

Among the competitors in this year's ACF Grand Prix at Rheims was the 37-year-old Argentinian Juan Manuel Fangio. Driving one of the beautifully built but grossly underpowered and notoriously fragile Simca-Gordinis, the South American had mechanical troubles in his European debut and was unable to finish the race. He had more luck the following season.

But there was tragedy this year too. Achille Varzi was killed on July 1st on a slippery Bremgarten track during practice for the Swiss and European Grand Prix. His Alfetta spun several times and then, after almost coming to a stop, flipped over and crushed its driver. Varzi

was an excellent driver who rarely made mistakes and had had few accidents in a racing career of more than 20 years. It was a sad ending for one of the great driving stylists of all time. Then on the second lap of the race, on July 4th, another accident took the life of the Swiss driver Christian Kautz, in a Maserati. He had been a racing mechanic for the Mercedes team before the war and was a cadet driver for that factory and also for Auto Union in the late thirties. Kautz had taken a Mercedes 125 to third place in the 1937 Monaco Grand Prix and was fourth in the Belgian Grand Prix at Spa. Ten years later he won the Rheims Grand Prix in a 1.5-litre Maserati, passing Louis Chiron in a Talbot and leaving him behind.

The first Formula Two was introduced this year, for cars with unsupercharged engines of less than 2000cc. There was also provision for supercharged 500cc engines, though in fact there was never

any serious consideration of this option.

The first British Grand Prix since 1927, when Benoist in a Delage had won at Brooklands, was held in 1948 on a disused military airfield at Silverstone. The first two places, again in the absence of the "invincible" Alfa Romeos, went to the 4CLT/48 Maseratis of Villoresi and Ascari. Earlier in the year Ascari had had a one-off drive in an Alfetta, and taken third place in the ACF Grand Prix at Rheims, behind team-leader Wimille.

The Ferrari name assumed greater significance at the end of the racing season when the Formula One Type 125 won its first race, a minor event at Lake Garda on October 24th. Nino Farina, the driver responsible for this historic success, went on to win at Rosario in Argentina on February 13th the following year, during the 1949 Temporada, though he was to switch to a 4CLT Maserati for the 1949 European season.

Ferrari Shows its Teeth

Alfa Romeo takes a break. The supercharged Ferraris and Maseratis take most of the Formula One laurels. Swiss driver de Graffenried wins the British Grand Prix. Many races are held on street circuits.

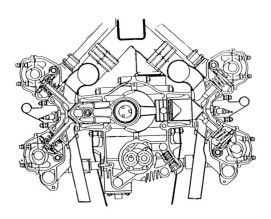

Before the 1949 season Alfa Romeo announced it would not be racing this year. On January 28th their leading driver, Jean-Pierre Wimille, had lost his life racing a little Simca-Gordini on an improvised circuit in Palermo Park in Buenos Aires, possibly after taking sudden evasive action to avoid spectators crossing the track during the race. Then on May 9th 1949 Count Carlo-Felice Trossi died after a long and serious illness. Within ten months the élite Alfa Romeo team had lost all their top drivers, Achille Varzi, Jean-Pierre Wimille and Count Carlo-Felice Trossi. The Milan factory's withdrawal left Maserati, Ferrari and Talbot to share the 1949 spoils.

Ferrari hired the leading Maserati drivers, Luigi Villoresi and Alberto Ascari, and at the end of the season produced a two-stage version of the 125. This modification boosted power to 300bhp at 7500rpm and enabled Ascari to take victory on the car's first appearance in the European Grand Prix at Monza, backing his Swiss Grand Prix victory earlier in the year.

The ACF Grand Prix was run for sportscars this year and won by Charles Pozzi in a 12-cylinder Delahaye. A race called the Grand Prix de France was however held at Rheims, and this went to

Above
The Porsche-designed 12-cylinder Cisitalia boxer engine with four overhead camshafts and two superchargers theoretically developed over 400bhp.

Right
The mid-engined four-wheel-drive Cisitalia 360 was conceived in Porsche's design office and built in Turin.

Far right
A group of drivers and supporters aboard the *Conte Grande* on their way to the South American Temporada in Argentina. Standing (from left): Alberto Ascari, journalist Corrado Filippini, Emanuel de Graffenried, Gigi Villoresi, Clemente Biondetti, Dorino Serafini and Omar Orsi (Maserati's owner). Kneeling: chief Ferrari mechanic Meazza, and Pietro Carini.

Below right
The start of the 1949 San Remo Grand Prix on the Ospedaletti street circuit.

Louis Chiron in a Talbot T26C, which Anthony Lago promptly presented to him as a token of appreciation for his win. The Belgian Grand Prix also fell to Talbot, the driver this time being Louis Rosier. Rosier was the most successful Talbot driver of the immediate postwar period, winning a total of six Formula One races as well as the 1950 24-hour race at Le Mans. These unsupercharged cars had shown since their debut in the previous year's Grand Prix des Nations at Geneva that they could cover entire race-distances without stopping for fuel, while the faster supercharged cars required at least one refuelling stop. This made the less powerful unsupercharged cars a worthwhile compromise. The British Grand Prix, held on May 14th at Silverstone, was won by a Maserati 4CLT/48 driven by the Swiss enthusiast Emanuel de Graffenried. With financial help from the Argentinian Government, Juan Manuel Fangio toured Europe, racing Maserati and Ferrari cars. The trip was a tremendously successful one, and Fangio chalked up no fewer than six major victories.

The 24-hour Le Mans sportscar race was held in 1949, for the first time in ten years. A Ferrari Type 166 with 2-litre V12 engine won, with Luigi Chinetti and Lord Selsdon driving. This car was going from success to success in races all over Europe.

Right
Alberto Ascari wins the 1949 Swiss Grand Prix at Berne in a supercharged Ferrari 125.

Below
The Ferrari 125 had two-stage supercharging for the 1949 European Grand Prix at Monza. The 12-cylinder engine now developed 300bhp.

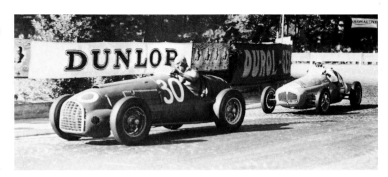

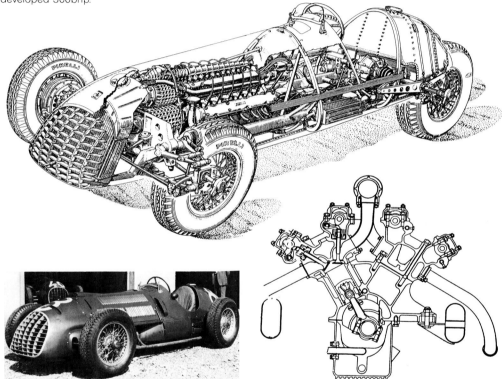

Above
The Maserati 4CLT/48 (here at Monza) which Nino Farina drove during the 1949 racing season. This car still had a rigid rear axle.

Centre
The new two-stage Ferrari 125 which competed in the Italian and European Grand Prix. Driven by Alberto Ascari, it won.

Far right
Cross-section of the Ferrari 4-OHC V12 Type 125 engine with two-stage supercharging. The cylinder dimensions were 55 x 52.5mm, giving a swept volume of 1496cc.

Formula One cars 1947 to 1949

Year	Make & model	Cylinders	Capacity	Bore	Stroke	bhp	rpm	Gears	Max. speed km/h	Dry weight
1947	Alfa Romeo 158	8	1479	58	70	275	7 500	4	270	700
1947	Maserati 4CL	4	1489	78	78	220	6 600	4	250	630
1947	Talbot (monopl.)	6	4485	93	110	210	4 500	4	260	850
1947	CTA Arsenal	8	1482	60	65.5	266	7 500	4	250	620
1947	Cisitalia 360	12	1492	56	50.5	296	8 500	5	285	630
1947	Alta Special	4	1490	78	78	230	7 000	4	245	650
1947	Donmartin	8	3619	80	90	200	5 800	4	220	700
1948	Maserati 4CLT/48	4	1489	78	78	260	7 000	4	260	625
1948	Talbot Lago T26C	6	4485	93	110	280	5 000	4	270	850
1948	Ferrari 125	12	1496	55	52.5	230	7 000	5	240	700
1949	Ferrari 125	12	1496	55	52.5	260	7 500	5	260	700
1949	Ferrari 125 (DS)	12	1496	55	52.5	300	7 500	5	270	730
1949	BRM Type 15 Mark 1	16	1488	49,5	48,26	420	10 000	5	290	730

First World Title to Farina

The Alfetta wins all Formula One races in the first modern World Championship. Ferrari drops its supercharged 1500cc engine in favour of unsupercharged 4500cc designs.

Alfa Romeo returned to racing after their year off with a new team, Giuseppe Farina, Juan Manuel Fangio and Luigi Fagioli. In the interim the Alfetta Type 158 had been further developed and now produced 350bhp at 9300rpm. In this form it remained unbeatable, and in 1950 took 11 wins from 11 starts, including all six qualifying events for the newly instituted World Drivers' Championship. It was a busy time for Alfa Romeo, as at the same time they were launching their first mass-produced model, the Berlina 1900, built on a conveyor-belt production line.

The *Fédération Internationale Motocycliste* had organised the first motorcycle World Championship in 1949, and the FIA followed their lead in 1950 by staging the first World Drivers' Championship for Formula One Grands Prix. Although a similar series had been promoted in the 1920s, those earlier championships are usually ignored by motor racing historians.

First event counting towards the 1950 World Championship was the British and European Grand Prix, held on May 13th on the former airfield at Silverstone. Nino Farina won in an Alfa Romeo with his Alfa team-mates Luigi Fagioli and Reg Parnell second and third; Parnell, a leading British driver, had been taken onto the team for this one race.

The other events counting towards the Championship were the Monaco Grand Prix, the Swiss Grand Prix at Berne, the Belgian Grand Prix at Spa, the ACF Grand Prix at Rheims and the Italian Grand Prix at Monza, as well as the Indianapolis 500. The American race would remain in the World Championship programme till 1960, though only American drivers competed in it, and it was run to a different formula (the 3-litre formula introduced in 1938 was still in use, though in 1957 the engine limits were reduced to 2.8 litres for supercharged engines and 4.2 litres unsupercharged).

The points systems under which the World Championship was initially run awarded eight points to the winner of each qualifying round, six for second place, four for third, three for fourth and two for fifth, with an additional point awarded to the driver returning the fastest lap in the race. The system was changed in 1953 when one point was allocated for sixth place, again in 1960 when the point for fastest lap was dropped, and in 1961 when the winner's points were increased to nine. Until 1957, drivers who took turns in a car shared the points awarded; after 1958 no points were awarded where a car was driven by more than one driver. Giuseppe Farina and Juan Manuel Fangio won all the qualifying events for the 1950 Championship (except Indianapolis) between them, and Farina took the inaugural World Championship with 30 points, followed by Fangio on 27 points and Fagioli with 24.

Ferrari made a major policy change this year. In spite of its experience with supercharged Grand Prix cars, the Modena firm switched to unsupercharged engines during 1950. Ferrari was convinced that the bigger units should be capable of beating the highly stressed supercharged motors and hired Aurelio Lampredi to design such an engine. A 12-cylinder development of the Ferrari sportscar motor was produced, retaining unaltered the single overhead-camshaft cylinder-head layout. The engine had a capacity of 3322cc (72 x 68mm) and developed 300bhp at 7300rpm, and Alberto Ascari drove a car

Left

A multiple pile-up in the 1950 Monaco Grand Prix. Farina is standing in the middle with de Graffenried on his right. Although fuel was spilt onto the track, luckily no fire broke out. Fangio threaded his way through the mess and carried on to win.

Giuseppe Farina

Right

Start of the 1950 British and European Grand Prix at Silverstone, very first race in the new World Championship. The Alfa 158s are leading.

with one of these engines in the Belgian Grand Prix at Spa. By the time the Grand Prix des Nations was run at Geneva the engine had been bored out to 80mm, to bring it up to 4101cc, and it now developed 335bhp at 7000rpm. The final version of this engine was a 4493cc (80 x 74.5mm) unit developing 350bhp at 7000rpm, and made its appearance at Monza, where it provided serious competition for the Alfettas. The race was won by Farina in a 370bhp Alfetta, but Ascari, in spite of his oil pressure having dropped to a dangerously low level in the closing laps of the race, took a promising second place.

Behind the Alfas and Ferraris, cars such as Maserati, Talbot and Simca-Gordini had to be content with filling the placings. The little Gordini's four-cylinder 1490cc (76 x 79mm) engine was supercharged this year, but still developed only 195bhp at 6500rpm.

The Maserati 4CLT/48 now developed around 300bhp but the engines had become notoriously unreliable. Talbot did however manage an important win, when Louis Rosier won the non-championship Dutch Grand Prix at Zandvoort.

The German Grand Prix was also held again this year, for the first time since 1939. It was held at its traditional venue, the Nürburgring, though not on this occasion for Grand Prix cars. Instead only cars complying with Formula Two (2-litre unsupercharged engines) regulations were admitted. In addition to entries from Ferrari, Gordini, HWM and others, the field also included several examples of the home-grown AFM and Veritas designs. Ascari in a V12 Ferrari Type 166 was a convincing winner of the German race.

The Le Mans 24-hour sportscar race was notable for an incredible display of tenacity and endurance by Louis Rosier. He was at the wheel for almost the entire 24 hours, except for a 44-minute stop for repairs just after half-distance, and two laps later in the race when his son took over. Rosier and his son won the race at an average speed of 144.38km/h, ahead of their team-mates Meyrat/Mairesse. In a

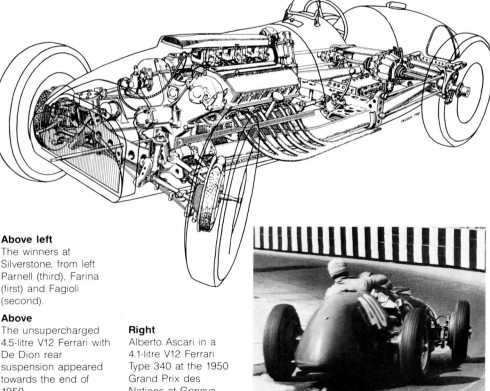

Above left

The winners at Silverstone, from left Parnell (third), Farina (first) and Fagioli (second).

Above

The unsupercharged 4.5-litre V12 Ferrari with De Dion rear suspension appeared towards the end of 1950.

Right

Alberto Ascari in a 4.1-litre V12 Ferrari Type 340 at the 1950 Grand Prix des Nations at Geneva.

near-repeat of this performance two years later the Frenchman Pierre Levegh, also in a Talbot, led for 23 hours before he had to give up when his camshaft broke, allowing Lang and Riess in a 300SL Mercedes through to victory. The almost superhuman feats of endurance performed by Rosier and Levegh had their detractors however, many people believing that safety would be jeopardised by any loss of concentration, and the organisers subsequently brought in regulations requiring drivers to change at regular intervals during the 24 hours.

In 1950 Mexico was the scene of the first of what was later to become a famous road race, the Carrera Pan-Americana. Initiated to mark the opening of the Pan-American Highway, the race was held every year for five years and quickly became one of the most important events on the international sportscar racing calendar. Later, it was run over a distance of 3000km through the length of Mexico and was divided into several days of racing. The 1950 Carrera Pan-Americana was restricted to production saloons and was won by the American McGriff in an Oldsmobile; the 2500 model Alfa Romeos, driven by Taruffi and Bonetto, took fourth and eighth places. In ensuing years the Mexican race was dominated by European sportscars: a Ferrari driven by Taruffi/Chinetti won in 1951, Kling/Klenk in a Mercedes in 1952, Fangio in a Lancia in 1953 and Maglioli in a Ferrari in 1954. But there had been many accidents over the years and the 1954 race was the last.

The Tourist Trophy race was held again in 1950 for the first time since 1938, and won by 21-year-old Stirling Moss in a Jaguar. This was the first big success for the young Englishman who later became one of the élite of the racing world. British drivers became more and more

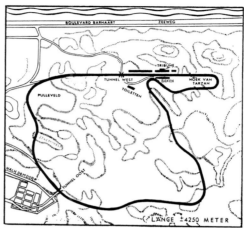

successful in the early 1950s, and a so-called "British School" formed. During that time there was a great deal of racing in Great Britain and a number of circuits were built on disused wartime airfields. This provided British drivers with the opportunity of practising somewhere nearly every weekend, and they were thus able to develop their driving skills to a degree without parallel in racing history.

At the same time a great deal of pioneering occurred with the introduction of Formula Three, for which many super-light, mid-engined designs with 500cc motorcycle engines were built. Many English racing enthusiasts found their way into the international racing arena as a result of the introduction of this small-engined racing car category.

This was also the year the BRM national Grand Prix car made its debut. In theory the BRM's V16 engine was the best and most efficient Grand Prix motor ever developed, but although the design was technically very advanced the project was heavily under-capitalised and the car was never able to fulfil its potential on the

circuits. The motor took a long time to develop its expected potential and proved to be very unreliable.

But there was never any question about the advanced design of the original car, which was first shown to the press at the end of 1949. Designed by Peter Berthon, Stuart Tresilian and Raymond Mays, the BRM was based on a chassis of tubular construction with independent front suspension and a De Dion rear axle.

But it was the V16 engine, theoretically capable of producing 615bhp at 12,000rpm, which was the real point of interest. Considered the ultimate in design at the time, the 1488cc (49.5 x 48.3mm) motor had two banks of eight cylinders inclined at an angle of 135°. The blocks were cast in one piece from light metal alloy and had wet cylinder liners. Each row of cylinders had two overhead camshafts with valves positioned at 90° to each other. The camshafts were driven from the crankshaft by a complex gear-chain, as was the Rolls-Royce twin-stage supercharger. It was intended to fit the motor with fuel injection but two SU carburettors were used instead. In 1950 form it developed 495bhp at 10,500rpm, and that was increased to 528bhp at nearly 12,000rpm by 1952, but it never achieved its full potential. Its power output remains however the greatest of any engine built for the 1948–51 Formula One.

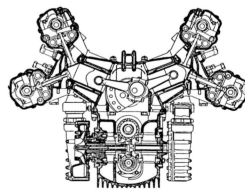

Reginald Parnell

Top
A permanent 4.25km racing circuit was built among the sand-dunes at Zandvoort in Holland in the late 1940s.

Left
Reg Parnell on a test run in the Mark I BRM V16 Type 15. The car proved thoroughly unreliable in its early races.

Above
BRM V16 (135° motor (49.53 x 48.26mm, 1488cc) with Rolls-Royce centrifugal supercharger.

An artist's impression of an Alfa Romeo battle during the late-1940s.

An extremely rare very early colour photo. Corrado Milanta took the photograph of Juan Manuel Fangio in an Alfa Romeo at the 1951 Spanish Grand Prix at Barcelona, where Fangio won the World Championship.

146

The Alfa Romeo driver becomes World Champion after a duel with Ascari of Ferrari. The last year of the 1.5-litre formula. The disc brake appears at Indianapolis.

The V16 BRM had been disappointing in its few 1950 appearances, but during 1951 Reg Parnell managed to take fifth place in the British Grand Prix, at Silverstone on July 14th.

The race was a historic occasion, for it was here that the Alfettas were beaten for the first time in five years, when the Argentinian Froilan Gonzalez won the race in an unsupercharged 380bhp 4.5-litre Ferrari. The Alfettas that took part in the race were the latest Type 159 models. Since the previous season the Milan factory had been bristling with activity, for the arrival on the scene of the unsupercharged Ferrari Type 375 had meant that, for the first time, the Alfettas had a serious competitor. The maximum power of the familiar 158 engine was boosted to 430bhp at 9300rpm, and roller bearings used for the main and big-end bearings. Consumption of the special fuel mixture was tremendous — no less than 120 litres were consumed every 100 racing kilometres — so additional fuel tanks were fitted to the sides of the car. Even so, at least two refuelling stops were needed in each race. The final modification was the use of a De Dion rear end in place of the swing-axle suspension. Four of the new wider Type 159 cars were built for the 1951 season and they won three World Championship races. But just as many victories went to the 4.5-litre Ferrari. Fangio took the World Drivers' Championship title for Alfa with 31 points, Ascari followed with 25 for Ferrari with Gonzalez, also driving Ferraris, third with 24.

At the end of the season Alfa Romeo, having won no fewer than 33 major races

with the 158 and 159 between 1938 and 1951, decided to withdraw from Grand Prix racing.

The significant development which had occurred during the life of the 1.5-litre supercharged/4.5 unsupercharged formula was an increase in the performance per litre. The Alfa Romeo 159 developed 287bhp/litre and the BRM 352bhp/litre. These figures could be achieved in the highly-developed supercharged engines only with the use of special fuels which contained a high percentage of alcohol in order to help keep engine temperatures low.

There had however been no significant development in chassis design since the 750kg racing formula of 1934-37. The Cisitalia-Porsche Type 360 was the most modern design concept of the immediate postwar era, and could well have revolutionised chassis design had it been able to race.

The 1.5-litre formula tempted Daimler-Benz to return to Grand Prix racing but when the CSI announced at the end of 1951 that the World Championship for the next two years would be run to Formula Two regulations, the Mercedes project was abandoned. In a document dated June

15th 1951, the Daimler-Benz company had expressed its intention of building five 1.5-litre cars based on the 1939 Type W165, the famous car with which Lang and Caracciola had demoralised the Italian voiturette teams at Tripoli just before the war.

The final years of the old formula were notable for a number of exciting wheel-to-wheel battles between Alfa Romeo, Ferrari, Maserati and Talbot. These were the last classic races until recent times in

Juan Manuel Fangio

Alberto Ascari

Right
Juan Manuel Fangio wins the 1951 Swiss Grand Prix in his Alfa Romeo. It rained heavily during the race.

Above
Juan Manuel Fangio was 40 when he gained the first of his five World Championship titles in 1951.

Top
Alberto Ascari won the 1951 Italian Grand Prix at Monza in a Ferrari 375, beating the Alfa Romeo 159.

which spectators were able to enjoy the spectacle of regular fuel stops. Refuelling procedures had developed into a fine art, crews practising every day with each move timed to the split second, so that in a race the operation could frequently be carried out in less than 20 seconds. Fuel stops were reinstated in 1982 and 1983 when the Formula One teams started races with half-full tanks and soft-compound tyres.

The handling characteristics of the racing cars of the early 1950s called for special skills, as the heavy and imprecise steering required a great deal of strength on the part of the driver. Although the ease of steering had improved considerably, compared with the cars of the first and second decades of the

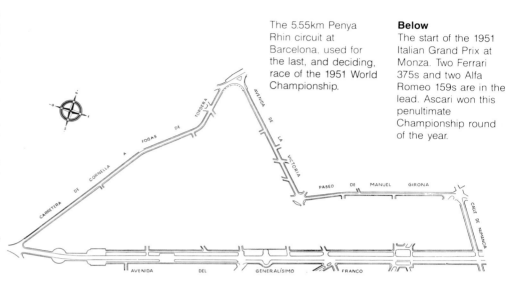

The 5.55km Penya Rhin circuit at Barcelona, used for the last, and deciding, race of the 1951 World Championship.

Below
The start of the 1951 Italian Grand Prix at Monza. Two Ferrari 375s and two Alfa Romeo 159s are in the lead. Ascari won this penultimate Championship round of the year.

century, it was still hard work. Today's direct steering and super-wide tyres which stick to the road enable drivers to handle their small-diameter steering wheels with millimetre precision. But in the Alfetta's time drivers had to work hard at the steering, constantly correcting the direction of travel through large wooden steering wheels.

The straight-armed driving style which gives much more relaxed control was an idea pioneered by Giuseppe Farina and Stirling Moss. Early drivers, in cars with their large steering wheels, had to manoeuvre their way carefully into curves and if the superchargers or engines were irregular, or missed a beat, the vehicle spun on the spot.

Drivers in the older vehicles did however have the advantage of being able to pick up early signs of the car reaching its limit of adhesion, as the "feel" of the steering gave advance warning of that

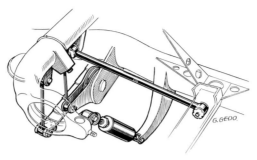

limit. Modern racing cars race through curves as though they are on rails and there is only a very fine margin between adhesion and "breaking away". Even the finest steering adjustment can have catastrophic effects and only the best drivers are able to avoid disaster. The roadholding and steering qualities of the older monopostos were more "user-friendly"; slight mistakes by the driver during cornering could still be controlled and corrected.

Different racing cars all required different methods of driving, so that comparing the skills and abilities of drivers from different eras becomes difficult; for this reason it is not really possible to determine who was the best driver of all time.

The first cars to be raced with disc brakes were seen at Indianapolis in 1951. The new system was enthusiastically taken up by British racing manufacturers, who were subsequently responsible for its introduction first to sportscar racing and then to Grand Prix vehicles. But although the Americans were the first to use disc brakes in racing, they were years behind the British and Continental manufacturers in adopting them for production passenger cars, the speed limits in force on American roads having a decidedly limiting effect on technical progress.

Left
The last version of the Alfetta, the Type 159, had De Dion rear suspension and leaf springs. It used both friction and hydraulic shock absorbers on each side.

Below
The rear tank of the Alfa 159 held 150 litres and the two side-tanks a total of 75 litres, giving the car a total capacity of 225 litres.

Far below
The sketch illustrates the two-stage supercharging set-up which produced a pressure of 3kg/cm² at 1.32 times the engine speed. A triple-choke carburettor was mounted over the first supercharger.

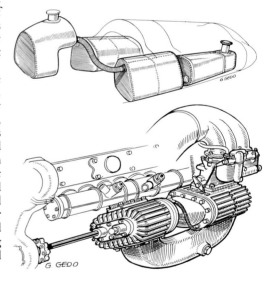

José Froilan Gonzalez

Above
The historic first defeat of the supercharged Alfa Romeo by the unsupercharged Ferrari 375. Froilan Gonzalez

winning the 1951 British Grand Prix at Silverstone.

Formula One cars 1950 to 1951

Year	Make & model	Cylinders	Capacity	Bore	Stroke	bhp	rpm	Gears	Max. speed km/h	Dry weight
1950	Alta	4	1490	78	78	250	7 000	4	250	
1950	BRM Type 15 Mark 1	16	1496	49,53	48,26	525	10 500	5	310	736
1950	Gordini Type 15 s/c	4	1490	78	78	164	5 250	4	240	680
1950	Ferrari 275	12	3322	72	68	280	7 300	5	280	820
1950	Ferrari 340	12	4101	80	68	335	7 000	5	280	850
1950	Ferrari 375	12	4493	80	74,5	350	7 000	4	300	850
1950	Alfa Romeo 158	8	1479	58	70	370	8 500	4	290	700
1951	Osca V12	12	4472	78	78	295	7 500	4	270	725
1951	Alfa Romeo 159	8	1479	58	70	425	9 300	4	305	710

Ferrari Wins the Series

The World Championship is run under Formula Two and most victories are chalked up by Ascari in Ferraris. Intensive work is carried out on the unsupercharged motor.

In 1951 the FIA decided the Grand Prix formula for the 1952 and 1953 World Championships would be the 1948 Formula Two, for cars with unsupercharged 2-litre engines, as the existing 1.5-litre supercharged formula, due to finish at the end of 1953 anyway, seemed in danger of having no support. Alfa Romeo had announced its withdrawal from Grand Prix racing, the Type 159 having reached the end of its long stage of development. The BRM V16 was unsatisfactory, both in performance and reliability, and no new models had been built by Maserati or Talbot. To continue with the 1.5-litre supercharged/4.5-litre unsupercharged

formula appeared senseless as the 4.5-litre Ferrari would have won hands down. (Nobody then knew of Daimler-Benz's intention to re-enter racing with a new 1.5-litre car in 1952.)

The replacement Grand Prix formula to take effect in 1954 had been announced in February 1951, stipulating a maximum size of 2.5 litres for unsupercharged engines (or 750cc supercharged) and the current 2-litre class was seen as a suitable compromise for the interim period. A great many Formula Two races had been held all over Europe since 1948, and considerable numbers of cars built, in England and Germany as well as Italy and France, which, due to their relatively

simple construction, were cheap to produce. The formula also admitted under its regulations cars with 500cc supercharged engines but this was a complicated and costly alternative and no manufacturer pursued that course. The change to Formula Two meant the end of supercharged engines in Grand Prix racing but the writing had been on the wall anyway since the defeat of the supercharged Alfetta at Silverstone in 1951.

The change of emphasis brought with it a change of internal engine design priorities. Until now the supercharger had been almost the only device for increasing performance, but now new methods had to be found of increasing the flow of fuel/air mixture into the engines, of running unsupercharged engines at higher compression ratios, and

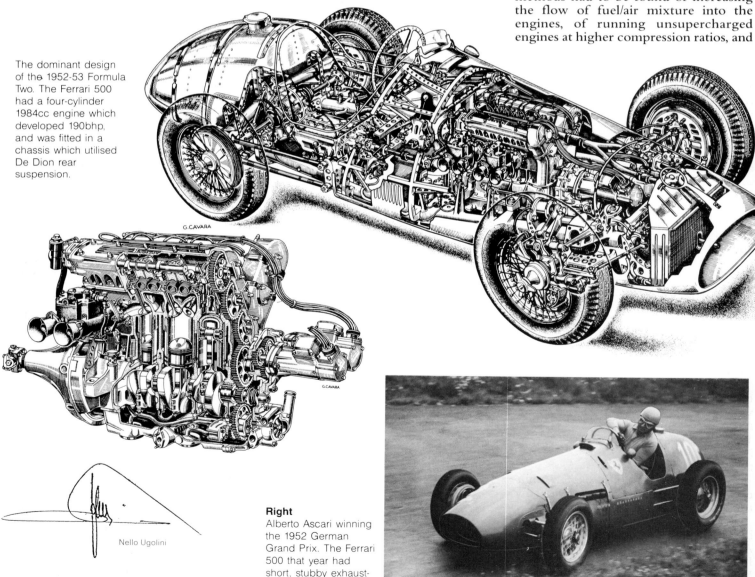

The dominant design of the 1952-53 Formula Two. The Ferrari 500 had a four-cylinder 1984cc engine which developed 190bhp, and was fitted in a chassis which utilised De Dion rear suspension.

G.CAVARA

G.CAVARA

Nello Ugolini

Right
Alberto Ascari winning the 1952 German Grand Prix. The Ferrari 500 that year had short, stubby exhaust-pipes, with no tail-pipe.

of increasing crankshaft revolutions. As a result of the changed requirements, research into combustion-chamber shape was accelerated and valve-timing principles reassessed. New theories in intake-manifold and carburettor design were developed, leading to the use of one carburettor per cylinder. At the same time, close study was made of the shape of the exhaust manifold and the configuration and length of pipes.

Much of the technology from the old supercharged formulae had little application to ordinary production-car use, but the new formula on the other hand encouraged developments that would have spin-offs for ordinary passenger models. One outcome of the research carried out in this period was the return to the short-stroke motor which gave more revolutions for a given swept volume. This had a direct application for road use.

The era of the 2-litre formula falls into two periods, the years from 1948 to 1951 when it was a "voiturette" formula for minor racing events, and the period from 1952 to 1953 when it was the premier international category, used for races in the World Drivers' Championship.

During these last two seasons a single driver/car combination was virtually unbeatable.

The driver was Alberto Ascari, born in Milan in 1918, the son of Antonio Ascari who was killed racing an Alfa Romeo in the 1925 ACF Grand Prix at Montlhéry.

The car was Ferrari. The first Ferrari

seen in Formula Two had been the V12 Type 166. When it first ran in 1948 its rivals were the four-cylinder 1460cc Simca-Gordini and the six-cylinder 1978cc Maserati A6G which, like the Ferrari, was to all intents and purposes a stripped sportscar. The following year Cooper built a light mid-engined car with a 1000cc V-twin JAP motor while in Munich Alex von Falkenhausen built the AFM with an improved version of the prewar six-cylinder 1971cc BMW 328 motor and at Bologna OSCA produced a four-cylinder 1355cc car. In 1950, the English Connaught, with four-cylinder 1767cc Lea-Francis engine, appeared, while another British firm, HWM, built

Charles Cooper

Charles Cooper

Amédée Gordini

Amédée Gordini

a two-seater with four-cylinder 1960cc Alta engine. In Germany the AFM was joined by the Veritas, also using the BMW 328 engine. In 1951 Gordini produced a new 1490cc engine with twin camshafts.

Following the news that the World Championship would be run to Formula Two regulations came support from many more manufacturers: in Britain alone, no fewer than seven firms signified their intention of taking part. Ferrari had meanwhile been actively supporting the class, starting in 1949 with Formula One cars adapted to take the unsupercharged 2-litre V12 Type 166 engine, and the following year with a new and lighter Formula Two chassis. With this model Ferrari had become a household world, winning nearly every race in that class; the only time that other makes won was when the Maranello V12s were not competing.

In the World Championship years, the most successful cars apart from the Ferraris were Maserati, HWM, Gordini, Cooper-Bristol, Connaught and AFM, the last driven by former Auto Union star Hans Stuck and now with a four-camshaft V8 engine.

Ferrari's contender for the 1952 races was the four-cylinder Type 500, developed in 1951 under the capable direction of the engineer Aurelio Lampredi. This proved to be the best design around, and Ascari took it to victory after victory. Its principal advantages over the V12 which it succeeded were in improved torque and better fuel consumption. The engine's flexibility was such that changing gear-ratios to suit specific circuits was not the crucial factor it had been in the past. Lampredi's four-cylinder motor had a short stroke of 78mm (which combined with a bore of 90mm to give a capacity of 1980cc) with twin overhead camshafts, dual ignition and four Weber carburettors, and developed 180bhp at 7000rpm. It had De Dion rear suspension and the gearbox mounted in unit with the differential.

At the start of the 1952 season Maserati was represented only by privately owned four-cylinder cars from Enrico Platé's team. Using the old 4CLT, Platé had removed the supercharger and increased the bore from 78 to 90mm, bringing the capacity to 1980cc.

The Maserati factory meanwhile built a new six-cylinder car under the direction of Gioachino Colombo, who had worked for Alfa Romeo and Ferrari but was now

The only serious accident Fangio had in his Grand Prix career was at Monza in 1952 driving a Maserati A6GCMF2. As a result of this accident he had to wear a plaster cast for many weeks, and was out of racing for the rest of the season.

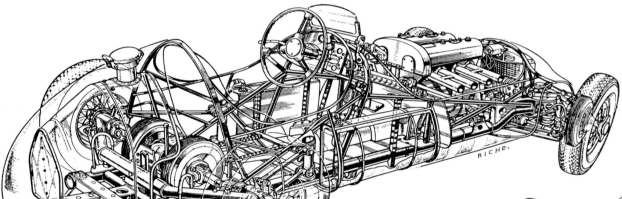

The British HWM started in Formula Two with cars fitted with four-cylinder Alta engines. The cars had tubular chassis with De Dion rear suspension and drum brakes.

Piero Taruffi

employed by Maserati. This car made its debut during the course of the season and carried the Type identification A6GCM. The 1958cc (76 x 72mm) A6GCM motor had two overhead camshafts and dual ignition and was initially rated at 160bhp.

The car's first appearance at the Gran Premio dell'Autodromo at Monza in June ended in disaster when its driver, Juan Manuel Fangio, suffered what was the only serious accident of his Grand Prix career. On the previous day the Argentinian had raced a BRM V16 in Northern Ireland, then flown to Paris the same night to catch a train to Italy, arriving at Monza one hour before the start of the race, without having had any sleep. As he had not practised, he had to start from the back of the grid, but in spite of this, and in spite of being in an advanced state of exhaustion, he had managed to move up to sixth position by the end of the first lap. On the second lap however the Maserati ran off the track and somersaulted several times. The World Champion sustained injuries to his face and back, which put him out of action for the rest of the season.

The 1952 Ferrari team, under the management of Nello Ugolini, consisted of Alberto Ascari, his friend and mentor Luigi Villoresi, Dr Giuseppe Farina, Piero Taruffi and the Frenchman André Simon. Fangio, Froilan Gonzalez and Felice Bonetto were all driving official Maseratis. The Swiss, Rudolf Fischer, drove a private Ferrari, and Emanuel de Graffenried drove a four-cylinder Platé-Maserati. Amédée Gordini had now split with Simca which led to years of tremendous financial hardship for the Paris-based racing organisation: donations to help keep the team going were collected at French petrol stations. Members of the Gordini team included the former motorcycle champion Jean Behra, Maurice Trintignant, Robert Manzon and the Siamese Prince Bira, known from his prewar races in ERAs and as a Maserati driver in the forties. Gordini built a "square" (75 x 75mm) six-cylinder 1989cc engine for 1952, with twin overhead camshafts, but the 155bhp it developed at 6000rpm failed to match the performance of Ferrari or Maserati. In spite of its underpowered engine

Below
Freddie Agabashian
drove this Cummins
Diesel Special (with
supercharged 6.7-litre
six-cylinder engine) at
Indianapolis at an
average speed of
222.058km/h.

Below
Freddie Agabashian
drove this Cummins
Diesel Special (with
supercharged 6.7-litre
six-cylinder engine) at
Indianapolis at an
average speed of
222.058km/h.

Centre
1952 World Champion
Ascari tried his luck at
Indianapolis with a
4.5-litre V12 Ferrari 375
but had to withdraw
after losing a rear
wheel with only a
quarter of the distance
completed.

Right
Ken Wharton with the
1952 Formula 2 Frazer
Nash fitted with a front-
mounted six-cylinder
Bristol engine. This
light car had a rigid
rear axle.

however Behra in a Gordini managed to beat the Ferraris in the non-championship Grand Prix de la Marne at Rheims.

An interesting Gordini story is told of that time concerning Behra's adventures in the days leading up to the Swiss Grand Prix. The car had not been completed in time to be taken to the circuit by transporter, so Behra drove it on the road from Paris to Berne. It is alleged that the police and customs officers who saw the Gordini approaching obligingly turned their backs to it!

Among the large British contingent this year the HWM team comprised George Abecassis, Stirling Moss, Lance Macklin and Peter Collins, while Alan Brown, Eric Brandon and Mike Hawthorn drove the Mk20 Cooper-Bristols. There was only one Frazer Nash, with six-cylinder Bristol motor, driven by Ken Wharton.

Based on weight, the updated and modified AFM driven by Hans Stuck should have been one of the fastest cars racing in 1952. Its 1978cc (67 x 70mm) V8 motor with four overhead camshafts and two twin-choke carburettors, built by Küchen in Stuttgart, developed 180bhp at 7500rpm, which gave the German car a power-to-weight ratio of 265bhp/tonne, compared with the figure of just over 300 for the Ferrari Type 500. But although he made a very fast start at Berne, Hans Stuck lost valuable time in the pits later in the race as the AFM's new motor required constant attention.

A new star who appeared on the

racing scene in Britain this year was Mike Hawthorn. Still a student at the Automobile Engineering College at Chelsea he became a serious rival to the established aces with his driving of the new Cooper. This car had a lightweight chassis with all-independent suspension (by transverse leaf springs) and was fitted with a six-cylinder twin-over-head-camshaft Bristol engine based on the BMW 328 design.

Alberto Ascari won six of the seven World Championship qualifying races, the Belgian, ACF, British, German, Dutch and Italian Grands Prix. The exception was the Swiss Grand Prix at Berne won by Piero Taruffi, also in a Ferrari. Ascari did not take part in this race as he was racing a Type 375 Ferrari at Indianapolis. After showing initial promise in the American race, and getting up to eighth place, the 4.5-litre car developed a hub fault and Ascari was

forced to withdraw from the race.

A new six-cylinder Maserati model was introduced at the end of the season with an engine that developed close to 180bhp at 8000rpm, and with one of these Gonzalez caused an upset when he led Ascari for the first 36 laps of the Italian Grand Prix. The Maserati engineers knew their high-compression engine was harder on fuel than the Ferrari, and the car would not be able to complete the Monza race without refuelling. They had therefore sent Gonzalez out with a light fuel load in the hope that he could build up a lead. Ascari's Ferrari, with 160 litres of fuel in the tank, could not keep pace, but after Gonzalez stopped the Ferrari went into the lead and notched up yet another win.

By the end of the season Ascari had accumulated 36 points and became World Champion, ahead of Giuseppe Farina with 24 points and Piero Taruffi with 22 points. Mike Hawthorn, in the Cooper-Bristol, and Rudolf Fischer, competing privately in a Ferrari, scored 10 points, whilst the Gordini factory driver Robert Manzon received nine. Fischer had won the Eifelrennen on the Nürburgring in his Ferrari.

Daimler-Benz made an appearance in sportscar races this year with the prototype Mercedes 300SL. It raced for the first time in the Mille Miglia but was defeated by Giovanni Bracco in a Ferrari. The Stuttgart coupé received world-wide attention later with victory at Le Mans and in the Carrera Pan-Americana.

Ascari's Second World Championship

Six-cylinder Maseratis are Ferrari's most feared rivals. An unsupercharged engine achieves 100bhp/litre for the first time. A fuel-injected engine wins the "Indy 500". Farina has a Grand Prix victory at the age of 47.

The leading Grand Prix teams in 1953 were announced as follows: Ferrari with Ascari, Farina, Villoresi and, as a new member, Mike Hawthorn; Maserati with the Argentinians Juan Manuel Fangio, Froilan Gonzalez and Onofre Marimón, and the Italian Felice Bonetto; and Gordini with Behra, Trintignant, Manzon, the American Harry Schell and the Argentinian Roberto Mieres.

The World Championship season started with Ascari chalking up another victory in a new event on the programme, the Argentine Grand Prix on the new Buenos Aires Autodrome.

With the 2-litre formula going out of force at the end of 1953, there were no new designs at the start of the year, the various manufacturers contenting themselves with simply improving the cars they had run in 1952. At the end of the season however Ferrari, with an eye to 1954, revealed the Type 553, an all-new design with side-mounted fuel-tanks and a 1997cc (93 x 73.5mm) motor which developed 190bhp at 7500rpm. This engine had a relatively low compression ratio and thus moderate fuel consumption: running on a blend of 90% petrol and 10% methanol it used 22 litres/100km on medium-speed circuits, though this increased to 24 litres/100km on faster courses.

Fuel consumption of the six-cylinder Maserati was 33 litres/100km, considerably more than its Maranello rival, and it was only in the second half of the season that design modifications enabled the car to complete an entire Grand Prix without the necessity of a refuelling stop. Running on a fuel mixture of benzol, water, methanol and acetone, the Type A6SSG Maserati was reputed to develop 200bhp at 7500rpm. This made it the first unsupercharged car engine in motor racing history to produce more than 100bhp per litre, a figure achieved in the past only by supercharged engines or single-cylinder motorcycle engines. The Ferrari was however said to have delivered the same figure on the test bench, before Lampredi reduced output to ensure a margin of safety in actual racing conditions, where different stresses are evident. On fast tracks with long straights, such as Monza and Rheims, where the Maserati was able to make full use of its power, it proved capable of matching the Ferraris' lap times, but on circuits with a greater number of corners, the changing of gear ratios was insufficient to overcome the handling disadvantage of its rigid rear axle.

The first European Grand Prix of the season was held at Syracuse in Sicily at the end of March and brought a real surprise, for not one of the four factory Ferraris made it to the finishing line, three having to withdraw for the same reason, broken valve springs. A modified Maserati driven by Emanuel de

Bottom
Young Mike Hawthorn after his astonishing victory in a Ferrari 500 at Rheims in 1953, when he beat the cream of the racing establishment.

Below
Ascari about to test-drive the new Ferrari Type 553 "Squalo" at Monza at the end of 1953. Standing on the right is Lampredi, designer of the unusual side-tank car.

Right
A moment in the exciting 1953 Italian Grand Prix as Ascari, Farina, Fangio and Marimon lap some tail-enders.

Graffenried kept going and came to the finish line as winner while second place went to 54-year-old veteran Louis Chiron at the wheel of a new OSCA built by the Maserati brothers. This car's six-cylinder 1987cc (76 x 73mm) engine developed 170bhp at 6500rpm.

The increasing number of sportscar races being held in the early 1950s led the FIA to launch the first World Championship for sportscars in 1953. Qualifying rounds were the 12-hour race at Sebring in Florida, which had been held for the first time in 1950, the Mille Miglia, the 24 hours at Le Mans, the 24 hours at Spa, the first 1000km race on the Nürburgring, the Tourist Trophy and the Carrera Pan-Americana. Ferrari won three races (the Mille Miglia, the Spa 24 hours and the Nürburgring 1000km) and became the first winner of the new sportscar World Championship title.

The World Drivers' Championship was more or less a repeat of the previous year's, Ascari winning in Argentina, Holland, Belgium, England and Switzerland. He lost a wheel when leading the German Grand Prix and had to limp to the pits on the brake drum, leaving Giuseppe Farina to win. This was the last Grand Prix success that the 1950 World Champion (and, incidentally, a Doctor of Economic Science) achieved in a career which had begun in the thirties and in 1953 he was, at the age of 47, the oldest Grand Prix winner in the history of the Nürburgring. There had however been older winners of other Grands Prix: in 1951 Luigi Fagioli was 53 when he shared the wheel of Fangio's winning Alfetta in the ACF Grand Prix at Rheims.

The two other races, the ACF Grand Prix at Rheims and the Italian Grand Prix at Monza, were the highlights of 1953. In practice at Rheims the stars — Ascari, Gonzalez, Villoresi, Fangio and Farina — all lapped within 1.3 seconds of each other. As at Monza the previous year, Gonzalez started the race with his Maserati's tank only half full in an attempt to force the Ferraris into going faster than they might otherwise have, and at the end of the twentieth lap the timekeepers recorded a 20-second advantage for the Maserati. He had to refuel ten laps later, and came out on the tail of his erstwhile pursuers Ascari, Fangio, Hawthorn, Farina, Marimón and Villoresi, who were still in incredibly close company.

Fangio and Hawthorn eventually got a break and fought a desperate battle for

1953 Formula Two contenders seen from exactly the same place during practice for the 1953 Italian Grand Prix at Monza. The spot was in the Porfido bend, later rebuilt as the Parabolica.

From top to bottom
Mike Hawthorn in a four-cylinder Ferrari Type 500, Elie Bayol in a six-cylinder OSCA, Maurice Trintignant in a six-cylinder Gordini Type 16, Stirling Moss in a four-cylinder Cooper-Alta T24, Emanuel de Graffenried in a six-cylinder Maserati A6GCM53.

the lead. On the last lap, with only the Thillois Hairpin and the sprint to the finish-line remaining, Fangio was ahead, but on that last bend the Maserati got itself a little sideways, due apparently to a gearbox problem, and Hawthorn got alongside. The young Englishman crossed the finishing line 2 metres ahead of the Maserati. Gonzalez was third only a few lengths behind his compatriot, and Ascari came in fourth, 3 seconds later.

The last World Championship Grand Prix under the 2-litre formula was the 24th Italian Grand Prix at Monza. Nearly 30 cars took part and it was alleged that the lead Maserati developed over 200bhp. Stirling Moss appeared on the line with a Cooper T24 fitted with a fuel-injected Alta engine and disc brakes. The Cooper had been modified to his order by his mechanic Alf Francis and was the first Grand Prix car fitted with disc brakes, but neither this feature nor the Hilborn fuel-injection system lived up to expectations and the car made little impression.

Hilborn fuel-injection was also used by Connaught this year but, even with such advances, the British motors were not by and large able to match the performance of the Italian engines, and would not for two or three more years yet. Fuel-injection engines were also used at the Indianapolis 500 in 1953 when Bill Vukovich won this most famous American race in a Kurtis-Kraft with four-cylinder Meyer-Drake engine, to which a Howard Keck injection system had been fitted. The most successful fuel-injected Grand Prix car would be the Mercedes-Benz W196 of 1954–55.

In the 1953 Italian Grand Prix there was very little difference in lap-times between the four top competitors, Fangio and Marimón in Maseratis and their opponents from Ferrari, Ascari and Farina. In the first 46 laps these four were all within 20 metres of each other, and the lead changed 26 times. Then Marimón had to go to the pits with radiator damage, rejoining one lap behind the

three champions, Farina, Fangio and Ascari. As the race drew to a close the result seemed decided, and with two corners to go the timekeepers prepared to name the finishing order Ascari, Fangio and Farina.

But then fate took a hand. In the Porfido curve (today called the Parabolica, having been rebuilt and renamed in 1955), with only a few hundred metres to the finish, Ascari had to go out of his way to overtake a Connaught driven by Jack Fairman. Ascari tried to pass on the inside but his tyres lost adhesion and the car started to slide. It was clipped by Marimón and both cars slid onto the grass. In a repeat of the 1950 Monaco Grand Prix situation, Fangio's superb reactions enabled him to find his way through the general upheaval and race across the line into first place.

This victory meant that Maserati had at last won a World Championship race.

Many contemporary reports described

Emanuel de Graffenried

Below
In the last phase of its development the six-cylinder Maserati A6GCM (76 x 72mm, 1987cc) developed 200bhp at 8000rpm. It was the first multi-cylinder unsuper-charged engine in Grand Prix history to develop 100bhp per litre.

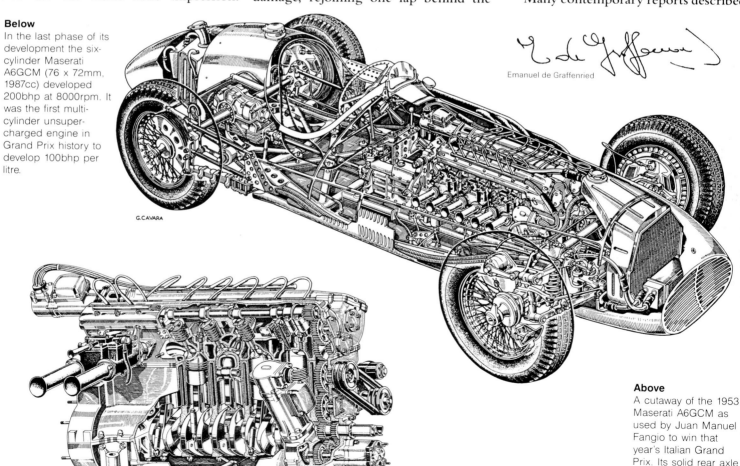

G.CAVARA

Above
A cutaway of the 1953 Maserati A6GCM as used by Juan Manuel Fangio to win that year's Italian Grand Prix. Its solid rear axle meant its handling was inferior to that of the Ferrari 500.

97.5km/h. Lang's time had been set in a 3-litre supercharged Mercedes W163 which developed nearly 500bhp, while Ascari's Formula Two Ferrari developed only 190bhp. It was only on the faster circuits that the 2-litre cars were unable to approach the speeds of their predecessors. At Monza Fangio recorded the fastest 1953 lap at 182.17km/h; the record was 200.4km/h, set in 1951 by a 430bhp Alfetta.

The best Formula Two engines in 1953 developed between 95 and 100bhp per litre, the same values as had been achieved by the supercharged engines of the first 1.5-litre Grand Prix formula approximately a quarter of a century earlier. The 560kg Ferrari of 1953 had a power-to-weight ratio of 303bhp/tonne; the Maserati, although 20kg heavier, was also more powerful, and so produced about the same. The Gordini, at 165bhp, was clearly underpowered by comparison with the two Italian cars and also weighed more (630kg): its ratio was 262bhp/tonne. Most of the other competitors were even heavier. The Ferrari, Maserati and

Gordini designs were all subsequently adapted to the 1954 2.5-litre Formula One which followed, simply by increasing cylinder measurements to comply with the new limit.

In sportscar racing in 1953, Jaguar won at Le Mans, with Rolt and Hamilton driving, a historically significant victory in that it was the first for a car fitted with disc brakes. The C-Type Jaguar's Dunlop brakes were considered to have played an important part in the success, and over the second half of the decade this type of braking system came to be generally accepted and nearly all racing vehicles so equipped, though Ferrari did not make the change until 1958. These brakes are now fitted to all passenger cars — at least to the front wheels.

The racing season ended on a sad note in Mexico, for although Lancia took the first three places in the Carrera Pan-Americana, Fangio winning from Taruffi and Castellotti, the fourth member of the team, Felice Bonetto, never reached the finishing line: he died as a result of an accident.

A modern autodrome was built in Buenos Aires in 1952 to replace the old road circuits in city parks, which had been used since the late '40s. The new facility, with imposing grandstands, could be used in a number of different configurations. A 3.912km circuit was used for the World Championship Argentine Grand Prix at the opening meeting in 1953.

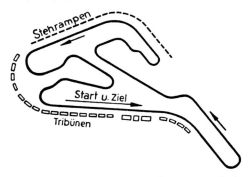

this race, the last in the era of the interesting and successful Formula Two, as the most exciting race of all time; others said the same about the Rheims race. Alberto Ascari became World Champion with 34.5 points followed by Juan Manuel Fangio with 28 and Farina with 26.

These 2-litre monopostos, powered by relatively simple four- or six-cylinder engines, were not as spectacular nor as attractive as their predecessors of the 1.5-litre supercharged formula, but they performed well. In winning the German Grand Prix Farina's four-cylinder Ferrari averaged 135km/h, the highest average recorded at the Nürburgring to that time. Alberto Ascari's 4.5-litre Ferrari had averaged 132.2km/h in 1951 and Rudolf Caracciola's 1937 figure in the legendary 646bhp Mercedes-Benz W125 was 133.2, though it should not be forgotten that the supercharged cars needed frequent stops for refuelling and tyre changes.

Taking Berne as another example, Ascari made the fastest postwar lap time of 162.48km/h in 1953 against the 168.108km/h Fangio had clocked in practice with an Alfetta two years before; Bernd Rosemeyer's official, legendary and never-repeated time of 2 minutes 34.5 seconds in an Auto Union in 1936 translates to 169.632km/h. At Pau Ascari not only bettered his own 1951 lap record, set with a 4.5-litre Ferrari, but also raised the race average, which had been held by Hermann Lang since 1939, from 88.6 to

Formula Two cars 1948 to 1953

Year	Make & model	Cylinders	Capacity	Bore	Stroke	bhp	rpm	Gears	Max. speed km/h	Dry weight
1948	Ferrari 166	12	1995	60	58,8	155	7000	5	200	700
1948	Gordini Type 15	4	1491	78	78	114	5250	4	210	450
1948	Maserati A6-GCS	6	1978	72	81	130	6000	4	195	630
1949	AFM V8 Küchen	8	1976	67,3	70	150	5900	4	230	680
1949	AFM	6	1971	66	96	140	5800	4	225	650
1949	Cooper T12 JAP Twin	2	1097	84	99	95	6000	4	185	410
1949	Osca MT4	4	1342	75	76	90	6000	4	190	480
1949	HRG	4	1998	83	92	130	5900	3	185	530
1950	HWM-Alta	4	1970	83,5	90	125	5700	4	210	600
1950	Veritas Meteor	6	1988	75	75	125	5800	5	225	660
1951	Alta	4	1970	83,5	90	150	5800	4	220	630
1951	Connaught Type A	4	1964	79	100	130	6000	4	235	585
1951	Ferrari 166	12	1995	63,5	52,5	160	7200	5	230	600
1951	Ferrari 500	4	1984	90	78	170	7000	4	240	560
1951	Maserati A6-GCM/F 2	6	1969	72,6	80	160	6500	4	240	560
1952	Maserati A6-GCM/F 2	6	1989	75	75	180	7000	4	250	600
1952	Alta	4	1970	83,5	90	160	6000	4	230	630
1952	Aston Butterworth	4	1986	87,5	82,5	138	6500	4	215	520
1952	Cooper T20 Bristol	6	1971	66	96	140	5800	4	225	510
1952	Ferrari 500-F2	4	1984	90	78	175	7200	4	240	560
1952	Frazer-Nash	6	1971	66	96	140	5800	4	215	610
1952	Gordini Type 16/20	6	1989	75	75	155	6000	5	257	644
1952	HWM	4	1970	83,5	90	150	6400	4	230	560
1952	Nardi-Lancia	6	1991	72	81,5	130	5500	4		600
1952	Maserati Platé	4	1980	90	78	150	7000	4	225	570
1952	Osca F2	6	1985	76	73	135	5800	4	210	510
1952	Sacha-Gordine	8	1970	70	64	195	8000	5	260	530
1953	Cooper T24-Alta	4	1970	83,5	90	186	6100	4	257	510
1953	Ferrari 553-F2	4	1997	93	73,5	190	7500	4	260	560
1953	Maserati A6-GCM	6	1987	76,2	72	197	8000	4	250	580
1953	Osca F2	6	1985	76	73	155	6000	4	230	540

The 2.5-Litre Formula

Mercedes-Benz and Lancia join the existing competitors in Grand Prix events. The advanced new Mercedes W196. Fangio becomes World Champion again in Maserati and Mercedes.

The 1954–60 Formula One — the era of unsupercharged 2500cc Grand Prix cars — was a progressive and changeable period, certainly more so than the stopgap Formula Two of the previous two years. Supercharged engines up to 750cc were also admitted under the new formula but the option was considered too complex and none was seriously campaigned. The choice of fuel remained optional — at least until the end of 1957. Originally devised to run for a period of four years (to the end of 1957), the formula's life was extended by the CSI first to 1959 and ultimately to the end of the 1960 season.

It was an interesting time which saw the perfection of fuel injection and other advances in engine design, but a genuine revolution in layout. Chassis design and the general shape of racing cars had advanced little since the days of the 750kg formula in the mid 1930s but this era brought significant progress, particularly during the years from 1958 to 1960, when British designers initiated a trend back to mid-engined configuration: this concept of course had its origins in the 1923 Benz *Tropfenwagen* and had subsequently been revived in the 1934–39 Auto Union and the unraced 1947 Cisitalia-Porsche. By definition a mid-engined car is one whose engine is located between the driver and the rear axle; the term rear-engined should, strictly speaking, be applied only when the motor is behind the rear axle.

No fewer than 14 different makes took part in Grand Prix races over the seven years of the 2.5-litre formula's life. Apart from the well known specialist names such as Ferrari, Maserati, Gordini and Connaught, large manufacturing firms such as Daimler-Benz and Lancia were also represented. Even a Bugatti took part, in a single 1956 race, and Aston Martin appeared later. The principal British brands were Connaught, BRM, Vanwall and, later, Cooper and Lotus. After nearly 40 years' absence the United States was represented once again, albeit briefly in the last year of the formula, by the Scarabs campaigned by Lance Reventlow.

It was during this era that the modern idea of "kit" racing-car manufacture was born, as companies bought motors and gearboxes from outside suppliers to build into their own chassis. It was in this context that the British Coventry Climax engine, used by both Cooper and Lotus, first made a name for itself during the

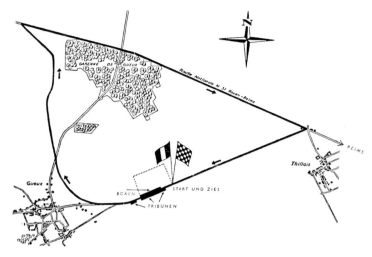

The new 8.347km Rheims circuit which bypassed the village of Gueux; it was half a kilometre longer than the old course.

1957 and 1958 Grand Prix racing seasons.

Ferrari, Maserati and Gordini all entered the new formula with developments of their existing Formula Two cars, enlarging the engines but leaving chassis design and body shape virtually unchanged. Ferrari modified the dimensions of its successful four-cylinder car to 94 x 90mm (2498cc) in which state the Type 625, as it now became, developed 250bhp at 7200rpm. At the same time Aurelio Lampredi produced a new design, based on the side-tank car that had made its debut in Formula Two guise in the 1953 Italian Grand Prix when it was driven by Umberto Maglioli. The engine of this Ferrari model, the Type 555, had cylinder measurements of 100 x 79.5mm (capacity 2497cc) and developed 260bhp at 7200rpm. The side-mounted tanks gave the 555 a rather bulbous shape, and it was familiarly known as the "Squalo", or shark. Its handling was always considered a problem by comparison with the more conventional 625, though Mike Hawthorn did take a Squalo to victory in the Spanish Grand Prix at Barcelona.

Maserati's contender was the six-cylinder Type 250F, a model whose design would remain virtually unchanged till the end of the formula. Based on the Formula Two A6SSG, the new car had a tubular frame designed by Valerio Colotti (later famous for his gearbox designs) while the engine was developed by Bellentani and, until he left the project after a difference of opinion, Gioachino Colombo; the 250F was further developed and improved upon in later years by Giulio Alfieri. Throughout its racing lifetime the 250F Maserati was a very successful car, and a total of 34 examples (in three basic versions) were built between 1953 and 1958.

As first tested by Guerino Bertocchi at Modena in December 1953, the six-cylinder 250F had cylinder dimensions of 81 x 80mm (2473cc) and developed 260bhp at 7000rpm; experiments with

Karl Kling

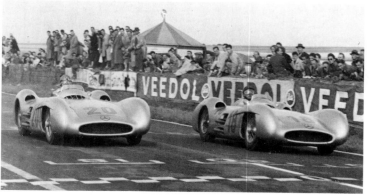

A great moment for German motor sport as Fangio and Kling in their streamlined W196 Mercedes-Benz Grand Prix cars cross the finish line side by side at the end of the French Grand Prix on July 4th 1954.

fuel-injection were carried out later in the year, but then put aside for a later date. The rigid rear axle, for years considered the Achilles heel of Maserati Grand Prix cars, was finally replaced by a De Dion axle on the 250F, while the gearbox and differential were mounted in unit at the rear. The fuel mixture used was a blend of 50% methyl alcohol, 35% petrol, 10% acetone and 5% benzol, though under hot weather conditions the proportion of methyl alcohol was increased to 60% and the petrol reduced to 25%.

Gordini did not make any significant alterations to his familiar six-cylinder Type 16. The cylinder dimensions were increased to 80 x 82mm (2473cc) which gave it 220bhp at 6000rpm, but the rigid rear axle was retained and the chassis unaltered. Nobody expected the Gordinis to be able to realise their full potential, as the amount of work the Paris stable could undertake was severely limited by its strained financial resources.

Neither of the two new contenders, Mercedes-Benz and Lancia, was ready to race at the start of the season. The new formula brought several changes to the manning of the various teams: Daimler-Benz hired Fangio and the Germans Karl Kling and young Hans Herrmann, but as the much feared "Silver Arrows" would not appear until the ACF Grand Prix at Rheims on July 4th, Fangio was released to drive for Maserati in the first World Championship races. Ferrari hired Froilan Gonzalez, Mike Hawthorn, Giuseppe Farina and the Frenchman Maurice Trintignant, with the young

Right
The Mercedes W196 (1954 version) had the front brakes mounted inboard, behind the water and oil radiators.

Centre right
The desmodromic valve mechanism of the Mercedes-Benz W196.

Below
The cockpit of the W196. The brake and clutch pedals are 60cm apart.

Right
Ascari in a Ferrari 625 chases Fangio's Mercedes W196 in the Italian Grand Prix at Monza. The 1952 and 1953 World Champion had signed for Lancia in 1954, but the new D50 was not ready until the last race of the season, in Spain, and he drove for Maserati and Ferrari until then. With the Ferrari, he hounded Fangio for many laps at Monza.

Below
The W196 was raced with enclosed bodywork on the fast tracks (Rheims, Silverstone, Monza and Avus).

Bottom
The open-wheeled version of the Mercedes-Benz W196. The chassis was constructed of light alloy tubing, with the fuel and oil tanks positioned behind the rear wheels.

Italian Umberto Maglioli standing by as relief driver. Gianni Lancia, the son of Vincenzo Lancia (who had been unbeatable as a Fiat driver before the First World War), engaged Ferrari's top driver Alberto Ascari and the 45-year-old Luigi Villoresi, together with their young compatriot Eugenio Castellotti, considered at that time to be Italy's great hope for the future, but again Lancia's late entry into the season meant Ascari and Villoresi drove for Maserati or Ferrari on occasions.

Maserati had the largest line-up, due to the fact that the 250F was manufactured for sale to private entrants. The six-cylinder cars were driven this year by

Hans Herrmann

Onofre Marimón, the young Italian Sergio Mantovani, the American Harry Schell, the Argentinian Roberto Mieres, the Siamese Prince Bira and British drivers Roy Salvadori, Ken Wharton and Stirling Moss. Moss had until this time insisted on driving British cars, but had finally decided that, in the absence of a competitive British car, he had no option but to change to an Italian make. Gordini's team for 1954 consisted of Jean Behra, the Argentinian Clemar Bucci, the Belgian André Pilette (father of the later Formula 5000 driver Teddy Pilette) and another Belgian, the journalist Paul Frère.

Although it wasn't known until much later, Alfa Romeo had intended to return to Formula One in 1954, and an engine, designated the Type 160, had actually been completed for this purpose and tested in 1952. The Type 160 was a

12-cylinder Boxer unit of 68 x 57mm (2498cc), with no fewer than 12 side-draught carburettors (one for each cylinder). The chassis was a tubular construction with front-mounted motor but designed for four-wheel drive. An even more unorthodox feature of the Type 160 though was the positioning of the cockpit, for the intention was to locate the driver's seat, dragster style, behind the rear axle. The Alfa Romeo engineers hoped this bizarre innovation would improve weight distribution and thereby provide better roadholding. Interestingly, a Type 159 Alfetta was rebuilt in 1952 with its seat relocated behind the rear axle and Consalvo Sanesi

Paul Frère

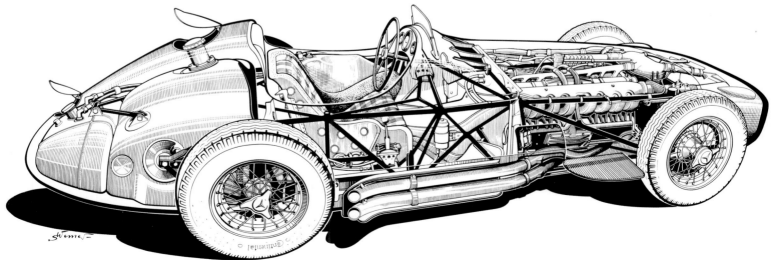

secretly tested it at Monza in October that year, returning with very satisfactory reports about the car's performance. But the increasing demands placed on Alfa Romeo engineering staff by the development of the popular 1.3-litre Giulietta, whose sales were a great financial success for the company, led to a decision to abandon the Formula One project before it got any further. The plan to race the new Type 160 in 1954 was never made public at the time and in fact remained secret until 1967 when the Italian journalist Count Johnny Lurani stumbled across the plans.

The World Drivers' Championship of 1954 began with the Argentine Grand Prix and then moved to Belgium, both races falling to Fangio in a Maserati 250F. The European racing season had started with a circuit race in the southern French township of Pau, where Ferrari, Maserati and Gordini all had teams on the starting line, though Fangio was absent and that gave the other drivers a chance of winning. Farina had a slight collision at the start from which he never quite recovered, and Gonzales was forced out when leading the race when his Ferrari broke its crankshaft. Marimón's Maserati also abandoned the race due to a mechanical fault and this left the Ferrari driver Trintignant leading from Jean Behra. The Gordini driver was given tremendous encouragement from the partisan crowd in the wake of these various mishaps and, shortly before the end of the race, his blue car overtook his rival and raced to victory, 30 metres in front of the red Ferrari.

A considerable amount of excitement greeted the arrival of the new Mercedes-Benz cars at Rheims on July 4th. The first July weekend of 1954 was of great significance for Daimler-Benz, for 40 years earlier, on July 5th 1914, Mercedes had taken the first three places at Lyons with Lautenschlager, Wagner and Salzer driving, beating their arch-rival Goux in the Peugeot. Then 20 years later, on July 1st 1934, the 750kg formula Mercedes-Benz Type W25s raced in the ACF Grand Prix at Montlhéry on their first appearance outside Germany, though neither Mercedes nor Auto Union finished that race and the Alfa Romeo P3 took the first three places with Chiron, Varzi and Moll/Trossi driving.

The sight of the three fully streamlined eight-cylinder Mercedes on the starting line, with Fangio, Kling and Herrmann in the drivers' seats, was one that had not been seen since the Avus races in the 1930s. In practice Fangio had, for the first time at Rheims, taken the lap average over 200km/h. Ascari and Villoresi were present in Maseratis but they did not appear to be a serious threat. Fangio and Kling slid effortlessly to the front, and took the first two places ahead of Robert Manzon in a Ferrari and Prince Bira in a Maserati. Ascari's Maserati and the Ferraris of Gonzalez and Hawthorn all had to abandon the race. Hans Herrmann broke the lap record but had to withdraw

Gianni Lancia

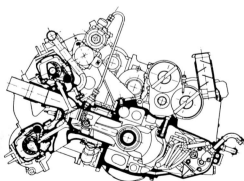

Above
The eight-cylinder motor of the Mercedes-Benz was inclined at 20 degrees to the horizontal.

Above right
Ascari tested the Lancia D50 exhaustively throughout the summer of 1954, but it did not make its debut until October 24th.

Right
View of the V8 Lancia D50, showing the side location of the fuel tanks in panniers between the wheels.

on the 17th lap after over-revving his engine and blowing it up.

The Mercedes-Benz was the best-known and most successful Grand Prix car of the year. After the company had made its decision to proceed with the project in 1952, the Daimler-Benz engineers had used the most up-to-date technical knowledge available and incorporated a number of new developments in this model. Its contemporaries all had some innovations, but the W196 was the best thought-out "package". The most revolutionary of its features were desmodromic valve operation and direct fuel injection, similar to the principle used in diesel engines. The eight-cylinder motor was inclined at 20° from the horizontal, which allowed for a low, flat body shape with low wind resistance and a low centre of gravity. Torsion-bar suspension was employed front and rear, with swing-axles at the rear and large-diameter turbo-cooled brake drums mounted inboard at the rear to reduce unsprung weight and improve roadholding still further. In common with every other Grand Prix car of the time except Gordini, the W196 had its gearbox and differential in unit. The

completely enclosed streamlined body was said to result in a one-second gain in a two-minute lap time on fast circuits (such as Rheims), but a more conventional body with exposed wheels was introduced for the tighter courses later in the year. In line with Mercedes practice since 1914, the eight-cylinder W196 motor consisted of two iron blocks of four cylinders separated by an alloy housing, with central drive to the overhead camshafts. The cylinders were connected to a base plate and surrounded by welded steel water jackets. The combustion chambers had two spark plugs per cylinder and the intake and exhaust manifolds were in unit, which reduced engine weight and provided greater reliability. Each cylinder had mechanically-closed valves, an innovation which had first appeared in Grand Prix racing on the French Peugeot before the First World War, and had been used on and off by other manufacturers since then with varying success. Although the W196's valves were operated by cams and rocker arms, the desmodromic actuation dispensed with the necessity for valve springs, and valve-bounce at high engine revs was thus eliminated. This in turn

meant the valves were able to remain open for a split-second longer, leading to more efficient gas flow. The problems caused by frictional heat in valve-gear operation were avoided and failure due to breakages was minimised.

The W196 was built under the direction of Professor Fritz Nallinger. Dr Lorenscheid and the engineer Rudolf Uhlenhaut were also involved in its development. Dr Scherenberg and a number of leading technicians were responsible for the construction of the car. The fuel injection system on the W196 had been developed in cooperation with the Bosch organisation and was unlike the American Hilborn system which had been in use for some years in the four-cylinder Offenhauser engines which were raced at Indianapolis; the Hilborn system had also been used by Connaught in Grand Prix racing in 1953. The American system injected the fuel into the intake manifolds, but the Bosch direct-injection system, later adopted by Ferrari from 1963 to 1965, fed fuel direct to the combustion chambers. The Mercedes had an eight-chamber pump which injected fuel at a pressure of 100 kg/cc. Since 1966 this system has been

INTERNATIONALE RENNEN

XIV. GROSSER PREIS VON DEUTSCHLAND

UM DIE AUTOMOBIL-WELTMEISTERSCHAFT

Freiexemplar

CONTINENTAL

MUNDORFF

NÜRBURGRING IN DER EIFEL

29. JULI 1951 · 10 UHR · VERANSTALTET VOM
AUTOMOBILCLUB VON DEUTSCHLAND A. v. D.
OFFIZIELLES PROGRAMM · PREIS DM 1,00

Left Start of the British Grand Prix at Silverstone. Froilan Gonzalez makes the best start in the Ferrari 625 (No. 9) which will eventually win. Moss in a Maserati 250F (7) and Fangio in a Mercedes W196 (1) lead the pursuit.

Above Cover of the programme for the 1951 German Grand Prix.

Cover of the programme for the 1952 German Grand Prix.

Below
Froilan Gonzalez in a Ferrari 625 during the European Grand Prix on the Nürburgring. His compatriot Onofre Marimon was killed during practice for this race.

Below
The open-wheeled version of the Mercedes W196 made its first appearance in the European Grand Prix. Making up for his defeat at Silverstone, Fangio had an easy win here.

Left
The men responsible for the Mercedes W196. From left: Ludwig Kraus, Hans Scherenberg, Fritz Nallinger and Rudolf Uhlenhaut.

superseded in racing applications by improved indirect-injection systems, where pumps are used to deliver the fuel to the intake manifold.

The cylinder dimensions of the Mercedes-Benz were 76 x 68.8mm, giving a capacity of 2496cc, and the engine developed 280bhp at 8500rpm. A special, secret fuel mixture was used but this had a corrosive effect on all metal parts and was never allowed to remain in the tank or fuel lines overnight. After every race the fuel was drained and the system flushed out with ordinary petrol. Within the Mercedes organisation the mixture, supplied by Esso, was referred to as RD1 and appeared to be made up principally of 25% methyl alcohol, 45% benzol, 3% acetone and 2% nitrobenzol. The pistons achieved a mean speed of 19.5 m/sec with a specified performance of 112bhp/litre, which was the best of the time.

In spite of the light tubular steel chassis the car was quite heavy: the streamliner's dry weight was 680kg and the open-wheeled car's 640kg, giving a power-to-weight ratio of 410 to 440bhp/tonne. The Ferrari, which weighed 590kg, had a ratio of 440bhp/tonne, Maserati, at 630kg, 415 and Gordini (590kg) 370. Although these figures were competitive, the W196 was as yet in its infancy and better figures could be expected in the future. Ferrari, Maserati and Gordini on the other hand had little room for improvement, as their 1954 designs were the outcome of several years of development.

The performance of the Mercedes team at Rheims in 1954 caused much concern in the opposition ranks, but the result of the next race, the British Grand Prix at Silverstone, was a great disappointment for the Germans. Ferrari took the first two places with cars driven by Gonzalez and Hawthorn, ahead of Marimón in a Maserati: Fangio could manage only fourth. The Argentinian found the car's wide body a hindrance, especially entering corners, when it blocked his view of the track, something which had not mattered at Rheims. Thus hindered, he had trouble keeping up with Gonzalez in the Ferrari and on more than one occasion rammed the marker-drums, running off the circuit on one occasion and finally developing a transmission fault.

An intriguing coincidence occurred at the British Grand Prix when the fastest lap was shared by no fewer than seven competitors: Gonzalez and Hawthorn in Ferraris, Moss, Ascari and Marimón in Maseratis, Fangio in the Mercedes and Behra in a Gordini. All of them clocked 1 minute 50.0 seconds, 154.2km/h, due to the fact that timing was only to the second, and not in tenths as it was elsewhere.

The next event was held at the Nürburgring, where the Mercedes appeared for the first time with conventional bodywork and exposed wheels. During practice the Argentinian Marimón, whose father had once been

among the best known South American long distance specialists, had an accident in his Maserati and was killed. In spite of the shock caused by this accident Fangio won with ease. Gonzalez, deeply affected by the death of his fellow countryman and friend, had to stop at the halfway mark and hand his car over to Hawthorn.

The Swiss Grand Prix held at Berne was a sad one too, but for a different reason: it was the last time the difficult Bremgarten circuit was used. In 1955 all racing activities in Switzerland were cancelled in the aftermath of the Le Mans disaster and the following year the Government of Switzerland withdrew permission for the running of all circuit races. The Bremgarten circuit had not been kept up to date anyway, and only the injection of a considerable amount of money would have brought it up to an acceptable level of safety. But the Berne races had been very successful events and attracted large crowds of spectators, with the record gate of 110,700 (practice and race days included) being reached in 1948. Statistics kept from the end of the war to 1952 showed the following: 1947, 109,500; 1948, 110,700; 1949, 89,200; 1950, 83,900; 1951, 83,800; 1952, 96,600. The 1952 takings from racing were 563,267 Swiss francs which left a relatively small deficit of 30,040 francs, which was made up by contributions from the organizer of the race, the Canton and the town. The 1952 events showed a deficit of 22,500 Swiss francs offset by ticket sales of 75,500 francs which resulted in a profit for the Canton and the town of 53,000 Swiss francs.

Gonzalez in a Ferrari was fastest in practice for the 1954 Swiss Grand Prix, ahead of Fangio and Moss, but Fangio won the race.

The Italian Grand Prix was the penultimate event in the 1954 World Drivers' Championship series and was in many ways the most interesting. Alberto Ascari drove a Ferrari in this event and

held the lead until the 49th lap, fending off a very strong challenge from his rival Juan Manuel Fangio in a streamlined Mercedes until the Italian was finally forced to give up due to a transmission fault. Stirling Moss took over the lead for Maserati and increased it lap by lap so that by the 60th lap he led Fangio by 22 seconds. Then he was forced to drop back due to falling oil pressure and lost his lead to Fangio, who swept past him and drove his Mercedes first over the finishing line.

A new British four-cylinder car built for Grand Prix racing in 1954 was the Vanwall, whose design owed a lot to Ferrari ideas and which was driven by Alan Brown in its debut race, the International Trophy race at Silverstone in May. Peter Collins drove it in the British Grand Prix, also at Silverstone, and subsequently in its first foreign race, the Italian Grand Prix at Monza. The car had been built by the industrialist Tony Vandervell in collaboration with the Norton motorcycle company. The first version had a 2-litre engine and the second a 2.3-litre, but by Monza the car was powered by a full 2.5-litre motor. This motor, fed by four Amal carburettors, developed 225bhp. The Vanwall was fitted with Dunlop disc brakes and some years later — in 1957 and 1958 — these streamlined, long-bodied green vehicles turned in some impressive performances.

The last race of the 1954 season was the Spanish Grand Prix at Barcelona and this provided another interesting twist. The new D50 Lancias finally made their appearance here, driven by Ascari and Villoresi. Ascari clocked the best time during practice, better than Fangio and Hawthorn. The Italian took the lead in the race and increased it in the first ten laps by two seconds per lap over his rivals, but was then forced to withdraw due to trouble in the clutch hydraulic system. Harry Schell in a factory Maserati then took over the lead, but on the 20th lap Trintignant in a Ferrari went past and a cat and mouse game developed between Schell and Trintignant. Mike Hawthorn in a Ferrari 555 Squalo then passed both to take his turn in the lead. During the race strong winds whirled up clouds of dust and paper which blocked the radiators of some of the cars, notably Fangio's, whose motor overheated and lost oil as a result. Hawthorn held the lead for the remainder of the race and won from the young Italian Maserati driver Luigi Musso, whilst Fangio came in third. The fastest lap was recorded by Ascari in the new Lancia with full tanks.

The Lancia D50, powered by a powerful V8 motor, was the brainchild of the former Alfa Romeo designer Vittorio Jano, the father of the successful P2 and P3. In spite of the fact that the firm's founder, Vincenzo Lancia, had been a successful Fiat Grand Prix driver, the Lancia company had for years refused to take part in official competitions. When Vincenzo's son Gianni Lancia took over the business however there was an immediate change of policy, and the company supported the Gran Turismo class from 1951 before producing the successful V6 racing sportscar Types D20, D23 and D24 in 1953 and 1954.

Two versions of the Formula One D50 engine were built, each with slightly different cylinder dimensions: the first had cylinders of 73.6 x 73.1mm (capacity 2488cc) and this developed 260bhp at 8000rpm; the dimensions of the second motor were 76 x 68.5mm (2486cc), which gave 255bhp at 8000rpm. The cylinders were in two cast alloy blocks, each with its own camshaft and two plugs per cylinder, the blocks being set in a 90° vee. The fuel — a mixture of 50% 130-octane aviation fuel, 25% benzol and 25% alcohol — was supplied to the motor through twin-choke Solex Fallstrom carburettors. The motor was diagonally positioned in the chassis at an angle of 12° to the car's longitudinal axis, to enable the driveshaft to bypass the driver's seat and thus provide a lower seating position. An interesting feature was that the motor was used as a load-bearing structural member, a feature now common in racing car design. Front suspension was by double wishbones and the rear by a De Dion axle, with gearbox and differential in unit.

Giving the D50 a unique squat appearance was the location of the fuel tanks, which were suspended in pontoons between the wheels on either side of the car. This arrangement guaranteed a constant weight distribution and at the same time improved airflow along the sides. Significantly the car weighed only 600kg, which gave it a power/weight ratio of around 430bhp/tonne.

After two wins with Maserati and four for Mercedes, Fangio won the World Championship title with 42 points, Gonzalez taking second place with 25 and one-seventh and Hawthorn third with 24 and nine-fourteenths. The first racing season of the Mercedes W196 had not been an overwhelming success, as the Italians had notched up most of the victories: the four which Daimler-Benz achieved had been due to the enormous driving skills and ability of Fangio. He had the uncanny ability of understanding how to drive even a "sick" car and still be able to win a place without major faults developing. Mercedes engineers later maintained that vehicles driven by Fangio showed less wear and tear than those of his team-mates. He not only drove fast but treated his equipment gently at the same time.

Ferrari took the World Sportscar Championship title for the second time in 1954, the 12-cylinder Maranello cars winning the Buenos Aires, Le Mans, Tourist Trophy and Carrera Pan-Americana (the last) races. Alberto Ascari, in a Lancia, was first in the Mille Miglia and an OSCA driven by Moss/Lloyd won at Sebring.

Fangio wins race after race in the W196 and is World Champion for the third time. Ascari dies in an accident at Monza. Lancia makes a gift to Scuderia Ferrari.

The 1955 season was a black one in the history of motor racing. In May, Alberto Ascari and double Indianapolis winner Bill Vukovich both lost their lives and the following month the Le Mans disaster occurred. There was an immediate reaction. The Swiss, ACF and German Grands Prix were cancelled. The American Automobile Association withdrew from the international organising body, although two other bodies, the United States Auto Club (USAC) and the Sports Car Club of America (SCCA), immediately stepped in to sanction the major American races together, since 1980, with Championship Auto Racing Teams, CART).

At the beginning of the year Daimler-Benz team manager Neubauer hired Stirling Moss so that with Juan Manuel Fangio as well the firm had an invincible Grand Prix duo. The wheelbase of the W196 was reduced, and the front brake drums were mounted outboard, while the engine now developed 290bhp at 8500rpm, against the 260/270bhp of the Italian opposition. Daimler-Benz also introduced a new sportscar, the 300SLR, which played a dominant role in sportscar racing and took the World Championship title for that category. Stirling Moss, partnered by the English journalist Denis Jenkinson, took one of these 3-litre cars to victory in the Mille Miglia at an average speed of 157.65km/h, a record which was never beaten. The 2992cc engine was of different construction from the Grand Prix unit, the cylinder blocks being cast from a light alloy with no components welded onto them, as the welded and reheated steel was found to have a tendency to deform.

Fangio and Moss were joined in the Mercedes-Benz team by Kling and Herrmann, with Taruffi joining later in the year. Ferrari meanwhile had Hawthorn, Gonzalez, Farina, Trintignant and Maglioli, and Lancia's drivers were

Stirling Moss

Maurice Trintignant

Ascari, Villoresi and Castellotti. The Maserati team was made up of Behra (who had left Gordini), the Argentinians Carlos Menditeguy and Roberto Mieres and the Italians Cesare Perdisa and Sergio Mantovani, while the private Maserati entrants included 50-year-old Louis Rosier. Gordini competed with Élie Bayol, da Silva Ramos and Harry Schell.

Fangio in the revised Mercedes won the Argentine Grand Prix at Buenos Aires, an extraordinary race in unbearably hot conditions. Shade temperatures soared to 37°C, and the grandstands were full to capacity 6 hours before the start. The ground temperature meanwhile reached 52°C and virtually every driver in the race, which lasted just over three hours, had to stop and let someone else take over their car while they rested in the pits. There were some 50 pit stops in the 96-lap race. Only two drivers covered the distance without relief, Juan Manuel Fangio in the Mercedes and Roberto Mieres in a Maserati — both Argentinians. After 28 laps Moss was simply too exhausted to continue and left his Mercedes on the side of the track. Of the 21 cars that started the race, 11 were driven by two drivers, and Behra and Trintignant each drove three cars. One of the Ferraris had five different drivers, at one stage remaining in the pits for an entire lap as none of the

drivers was fit enough to continue.

Finally Gonzalez, after an injection against back pain, climbed into the driver's seat; the Argentinians called him "Cabezon", the stubborn one, after that. Gonzalez caught up with race-leader Fangio at the rate of five seconds per lap but the Mercedes driver, himself close to collapse (he thought of giving up on several occasions), summoned his last reserves of energy and got the W196 to the line at the end of the 381.2km in first place, after 3 hours and 38.6 seconds of torture, three of the most tense hours in racing history. Drained of all energy, Fangio could hardly stand up at the prize-giving ceremony and slumped into a chair in front of that great racing enthusiast, President Peron of Argentina. The tough "Chueco" (the bow legged) from the town of Balcarce had lasted thanks only to his iron will, having to draw on the last reserves of his strength. Nearly every night he was in bed not later

than 10pm and was not even available for interviews organised by his publicity manager.

The unpredictable continued at the next Championship race, the European Grand Prix at Monte Carlo. First, Hans Herrmann suffered a serious accident in practice, and the Frenchman André Simon was given the third Mercedes for the race. Lancia, for whom Alberto Ascari had won the non-championship Valentino Grand Prix at Turin on March 27th and the Naples Grand Prix on May 8th, also made a change to their line-up, offering their fourth car to the 56-year-old Grand Prix veteran and Monte Carlo citizen Louis Chiron. The four-cylinder Vanwall appeared with Bosch direct petrol-injection and driven by Mike Hawthorn; later in the season however he returned to Ferrari and the Vanwalls were driven by Ken Wharton and Harry Schell.

For the first 50 laps of the Monaco race Fangio and Moss in the W196s were unchallenged, running as they pleased ahead of Ascari and Castellotti in the fastest Lancias and Behra in the best of the Maseratis. But in the second half of the race all three Mercedes cars developed faults in their valve mechanisms and had to withdraw from the Grand Prix. Fangio was first to go, allowing Moss to lead, but on the 80th lap the Englishman's engine also developed the fault and he was forced to follow Fangio in throwing in the towel.

Ascari took over the lead for Lancia but before the lap was over he shot off

the track and dived straight into Monaco harbour. He was unhurt in this accident, though his fellow countryman, Lorenzo Bandini, would die in an accident at the same spot 12 years later.

But four days after the Monaco race, on May 26th, Ascari died in a testing accident with a Ferrari 750 sportscar on the Monza track. The car shot off the track at the Vialone Curve, a corner which has since been renamed in his

honour, in circumstances which have never been satisfactorily explained.

The Monaco Grand Prix was finally won by the Frenchman Maurice Trintignant in an old Ferrari Type 625 with 24-year-old Castellotti second in a Lancia and Behra/Perdisa in third place in a Maserati. The Monaco race was the only 1955 Grand Prix in which Mercedes was unplaced.

Following Ascari's death, Lancia team manager Gianni Lancia, whose enterprise was in financial difficulties, decided to quit racing and shut down the competition department. On July 26th he presented Scuderia Ferrari with all the equipment of his racing division: cars, spare motors, spare parts etc. Eugenio Castellotti and the engineer Jano also joined the Maranello firm. In spite of tremendous efforts made by Ferrari to update the unsuccessful four-cylinder Squalo into the 555 Super Squalo, it had not been able to provide the Mercedes with serious competition.

Fangio won all remaining World Championship events with the exception of the British Grand Prix, held at Aintree near Liverpool and won by Stirling Moss — the first time a British driver had won the British Grand Prix. Fangio became World Champion for the third time, with 40 points to his credit, against the 23 of his team-mate Moss and the 12 of Lancia and Ferrari driver Castellotti.

A future racing ace had a modest start in that Aintree race: the Australian Jack Brabham drove a modified Cooper sportscar with a six-cylinder Bristol engine mounted in the rear. The car's 2-litre single overhead-camshaft motor developed a modest 140bhp and Brabham was one of the slowest in the race. But in spite of its lack of pretension the Cooper T40 was in fact the forerunner in the technical revolution which would develop at the end of the fifties; an era of lighter metals and motors located behind the driver. This was still the age of the

heavy front-engined cars however and it would be some time before the Brabham/Cooper combination made a name for themselves. The only British car which put up any sort of performance in the Aintree race was the Vanwall driven by Harry Schell.

The last Grand Prix for the year was held at Monza, on a track modified to incorporate a high-speed section with 38°

Umberto Magglioli

Umberto Magglioli

Robert Manzon

Robert Manzon

Below left
Jack Brabham, the Australian racing ace, started his Grand Prix career in the 1955 British Grand Prix at Aintree, where he drove a Cooper T40 with 2-litre six-cylinder 140bhp Bristol engine in the rear.

Below
In the middle of the 1955 season Gianni Lancia decided to withdraw from racing, following the death of Alberto Ascari. On July 26th he donated the six Type D50 cars and all spare parts to Scuderia Ferrari.

banked curves surfaced with reinforced concrete. At the same time the road circuit was reduced from 6.3km (the length it had been since its 1948 rebuild) to 5.75km, which, with the banked section, gave a total circuit length of exactly 10km. Right from the first practice laps the reinforced concrete section of the new Monza circuit, opened by the President, Giovanni Gronchi, was seen to be very bumpy, requiring the chassis of competing cars to absorb tremendous amounts of vibration. During its years of use the surface settled and this increased the unevenness, also making the cost of repair prohibitive.

At Monza Amédée Gordini unveiled what was to be his last Formula One model, the Type 32. This had an eight-cylinder 75 x 70mm (2498cc) twin-camshaft motor which developed 256bhp at 7200rpm and was equipped with four-wheel independent suspension and disc brakes. Driven by Jean Lucas, the Type 32 Gordini lasted only seven laps of the race. The Lancia D50 was entered under the Ferrari banner, but didn't start because Ferrari had no suitable tyres.

Ferrari had come up with a completely new project in 1955. The company designer, Lampredi, had built a two-cylinder 118 x 114mm (2493cc) motor

which, on the test bench, apparently developed 175bhp at 4800rpm. This unusual engine, designated the Type 116, was intended for tight tracks such as Monte Carlo for, in spite of its moderate power, the large cylinder dimensions gave it excellent torque characteristics. The twin-cylinder project never came to fruition however, Maranello abandoning the concept after it had been given the Lancia cars and equipment. During 1955 Lampredi, Ferrari's long-serving chief design engineer, left the firm to work for Fiat in Turin, where he was to play a leading role over the years in the development of that company's range of production-line models.

At the end of the season Daimler-Benz made the surprise announcement that it was withdrawing from all racing activities. During a ceremony in October to honour the drivers and the racing department, and in the presence of the management and a number of invited guests, technical director Fritz Nallinger announced that Mercedes-Benz would retire from Formula One and sportscar racing for an unspecified time. Dr Nallinger revealed later that the reason for this decision was the enormous work-load placed on the Research and Development section, which had responsibility for work on production cars as well as on the racing and sportscars. The time and effort spent developing the racing machinery had meant less could be devoted to passenger-car research. He did however pay tribute to the contribution that racing had made to the big passenger-car manufacturers such as Daimler-Benz. "The knowledge gained from racing has been used to its fullest extent in the development of production cars for private motoring," Dr Nallinger said.

At the end of 1955 the W196 and 300SLR cars were rolled into the Daimler-Benz Museum to take up places of honour. In their two Formula One seasons the single-seaters had started in 15 races and taken 12 firsts. Seven of those were 1-2 results, in one they took the first three places and in another the first four — a remarkable achievement.

Mercedes had built no fewer than 15 Grand Prix cars during the Formula One period. The cars were far in advance of their competitors, and were clearly the product of a well-trained and highly disciplined complement of engineers and technicians, which only a large, well-organised and financially sound motor

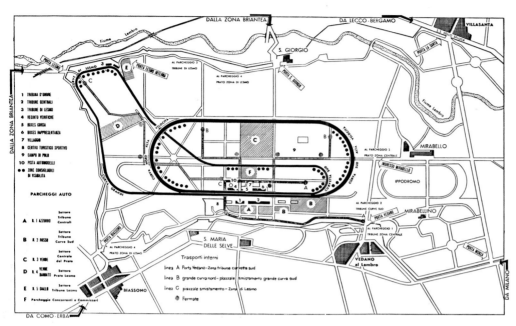

Above and right
The rebuilding of the Monza Autodrome was completed in 1955. The road circuit remained unchanged apart from the old Porfido curve connecting the back straight with the start/finish straight, which was realigned and renamed Parabolica. New length of the road circuit was 5.75km (against the earlier 6.3km). In addition a new 4.25km high-speed oval (pictured at right under construction) was added, with two curves banked at 38 degrees. The banked track proved to be very bumpy however. The combined circuit was exactly 10km long.

Below
The last Formula One Gordini was the eight-cylinder Type 32, but it was far too heavy to be competitive. Robert Manzon takes it out for a test run on the fast Montlhéry circuit late in 1955.

Right
The high speed track at Monza was opened for the 1955 Italian Grand Prix. Fangio is in the lead.

company could provide. Firms such as Ferrari, Maserati, Gordini, Cooper, Connaught and HWM understood their trade just as well, and had as much skill and knowledge, but never had the resources that a large enterprise such as Daimler-Benz had at its disposal.

In Ferrari's case, a large proportion of the funding of the racing operation came from the Fiat company, which in those days paid Ferrari an annual fee of 50 million lire. The Turin manufacturer believed that Ferrari racing successes helped the Italian drive to secure foreign markets for the sale of their passenger cars.

On the other hand — in contrast to Italy, France and later Great Britain — Germany never had small "backyard" specialist firms building internationally successful Grand Prix cars or sports racing machinery. That country's racing history was written by only a few marques, first Mercedes-Benz and Auto Union, and later Porsche and BMW.

The Mercedes-Benz engineer Uhlenhaut, one of the originators of the W196, was an enthusiastic and excellent driver and, given the opportunity by his firm (and his wife), would have taken an active part in racing. During test drives Uhlenhaut showed a degree of skill which amazed not only his colleagues but the professional drivers as well. Years later, at a banquet, he told the author that, during private practice in the W196 at the Nürburgring in 1955, he had set the fastest lap of the session, in 9 minutes 48 seconds — three seconds better than Fangio managed the same day. But, Uhlenhaut was quick to point out, "That

did not mean I could drive as fast as Fangio; he never went faster than he absolutely had to." There was no German Grand Prix that year, so the fastest official Nürburgring lap clocked by a W196 remained Karl Kling's 1954 time of 9 minutes 55.1 seconds, though in private testing with the short-wheelbase W196 the following year Fangio lapped at 9 minutes 33.9 seconds. In 1956 the Argentinian set a new official Nürburgring lap record in a Lancia-Ferrari in 9 minutes 41.6 seconds, and a year later in a 250F Maserati reduced that to 9 minutes 17.4 seconds, an incredible effort considering the technical standards of the time.

Between the two seasons there was an upset in the non-championship Syracuse Grand Prix in October when Tony Brooks, a 22-year-old British dental student, won the race in a Connaught. This was the first time since 1924, when Henry Segrave was first at San Sebastian in a Sunbeam, that a British Grand Prix car had beaten the Continental opposition and, what's more, Brooks was competing in his first Formula One Grand Prix. The performance of the Connaught, which had a fuel-injected Alta engine, coupled with Brooks's driving, took the Maserati and Gordini opposition by complete surprise. After the race the Sicilian race organisers demanded the engine's capacity be checked — and found that it complied with its declared specification.

The Connaught was built and raced between 1949 and 1957 by a small company backed by Kenneth McAlpine, who occasionally raced the cars himself, as did their designer, Rodney Clarke. Lea-Francis motors had been used for sportscars and Formula Two machinery until 1953 but, with the introduction of the 2.5-litre formula, the switch was made to Altas.

The British Vanwall appeared regularly in Grand Prix events after 1954 carrying the colours of the industrialist Tony Vandervell, already well-known as entrant of the "Thinwall Special" cars in British Formula One and later Formule Libre races between 1949 and 1954. These cars, developed from 12-cylinder Grand Prix Ferraris, enjoyed many a battle with the supercharged V16 BRMs. The first Formula One Vanwall had a chassis designed by John Cooper and a 2-litre four-cylinder motor built in conjunction with Norton motorcycle engineers Joe Craig and Gilbert Smith. Some time later

Aurelio Lampredi

its capacity was increased to 2.3 litres and, later still, to 2.5 litres. Over the course of years, especially in 1957 and 1958, these green Vanwalls were the Italians' strongest rivals.

It was during the mid-fifties that the cornering technique known as the "four-wheel drift" was developed to perfection. The four-wheel drift represented the fastest speed at which a car could be driven through a fast curve. In a four-wheel drift a car adopts a position where its longitudinal axis is at a slight angle to that of the road, but aligned with the approaching corner. It is the position where the wheels are beginning to lose their grip on the road, where the limit of adhesion has been reached, and the car is starting to slide, but is controlled by careful use of throttle and steering. This cornering technique has only limited application these days when cars have such low centres of gravity and are so aerodynamically efficient that they can corner as if on rails.

Formula One cars in the 2.5-litre formula era 1954 to 1955

Year	Make & model	Cylinders	Capacity	Bore	Stroke	bhp	rpm	Gears	Max. speed km/h	Dry weight
1954	Mercedes W196	8	2496	76	68,8	260	8500	5	280	758
1954	Lancia D50	8	2487	73,6	73,1	260	8000	5	280	600
1954	Lancia D50	8	2485	76	68,5	255	8000	5	280	600
1954	Maserati 250F	6	2493	84	75	260	7000	5	290	630
1954	Gordini Type 16	6	2473	80	82	220	6000	4	240	590
1954	Vanwall	4	2340	93	86	210	6500	5	245	570
1954	HWM-Alta	4	2448	93	90	195	6000	4	220	560
1954	Connaught Type B	4	2464	93,5	90	220	6000	4	235	590
1954	Arzani Volpini	4	2496	94	90	210	7100	4	265	650
1954	Ferrari 625	4	2498	94	90	240	7000	4	250	600
1954	Ferrari 553	4	2497	100	79,5	250	7500	4	250	590
1955	Mercedes W196	8	2496	76	68,8	290	8500	5	300	730
1955	Lancia D50	8	2480	74	72	260	8200	5	280	600
1955	Vanwall	4	2490	96	86	250	7000	5	270	570
1955	Bugatti 251	8	2432	75	68,8	250	8500	5	250	750
1955	Gordini Type 32	8	2480	75	70	250	8200	5	250	650
1955	Connaught	4	2464	93,5	90	240	6500	4	245	590
1955	BRM P25	4	2497	102,8	74,9	255	8000	4	265	580
1955	Ferrari 555	4	2497	100	79,5	270	7500	4	270	590
1955	Ferrari 252	2	2493	118	114	174	4800			
1955	Cooper T40-Bristol	6	1971	66	96	140	5800	4	240	

GRAND PRIX BERN

21./22. August 1954

Offizielles Programm mit Startliste

Los Nr. 14803

(Preis Fr. 2.– inkl. Loszuschlag)

Cover of the programme for the 1954 Swiss Grand Prix.

Cover of the programme for the 1955 British Grand Prix.

Poster of the 1956 Monaco Grand Prix.

AINTREE

GRAND PRIX D'EUROPE

Incorporating the 10th R.A.C. British Grand Prix

Saturday **20th July, 1957**

Racing organised by the

British Automobile Racing Club

OFFICIAL **2/-** PROGRAMME

The Grand Prix d'Europe 1956 was won by Stirling Moss, driving a Maserati, using

BP Energol

MOTOR OIL

Cover of the programme for the 1957 European Grand Prix at Aintree.

Lancia-Ferraris Victorious

Ferrari further develops the Lancia D50 and Fangio becomes World Champion again. The fast British Vanwall with fuel injection. A short and final Bugatti appearance at Rheims.

Following the Daimler-Benz withdrawal from racing, Ferrari and Maserati were able to share the Grands Prix between themselves in 1956 but, for the first time, the British also made their presence felt. The Modena and Maranello stables, both used to winning, now had to consider the new competitors as serious rivals.

On paper the season promised to be a one of wheel-to-wheel duels between former Mercedes-Benz drivers Juan Manuel Fangio and Stirling Moss, the Argentinian going to Ferrari in 1956 and the Englishman to Maserati. Their respective teams were the only competitors at the Argentinian Grand Prix where Carlos Menditeguy, a local polo, golf and tennis ace, caused a stir in a Maserati 250F when he pulled away from the other competitors until the 43rd lap when, with a lap in hand over Fangio, his car's axle broke. Fangio won the race in his Ferrari, a modified eight-cylinder 1954–55 Lancia D50, which was now known as the Ferrari-Lancia or, more usually, the Lancia-Ferrari. Alterations over the winter months had included incorporating the side fuel tanks into the main part of the car, although the panniers remained for aerodynamic purposes. The suspension system was also

revised, with coil springs replacing the leaves at the front and the De Dion rear also undergoing modification. Ferrari also tried a V8 Lancia in a Super Squalo chassis but it was not a success and was immediately abandoned.

After a long absence from Formula One races, BRM once again appeared before the Monaco Grand Prix, the second World Championship round of 1956. Mike Hawthorn drove the new Type 25 which was tremendously fast but still suffered teething troubles. BRM was now part of the organisation owned by the British industrialist Sir Alfred Owen, and the new front-engined car was designed by Peter Berthon. It had a short-stroke 2486cc (102.8 x 74.9mm) four-cylinder motor with unusually large valves and, fed by Weber carburettors, developed 270bhp at 8000rpm. It had unique oleo-pneumatic front suspension and a De Dion rear, and was fitted with disc brakes. Its real advantage was its weight, for at 550kg it was considerably lighter than the Italian cars, and had a power-to-weight ratio of 490bhp/tonne.

At Monte Carlo Moss was winner for Maserati, with Fangio, who had exchanged Lancia-Ferraris with a team-mate, the young Englishman Peter Collins, second. This exchange of cars was a quite common event in the fifties. As soon as a fault developed in the car driven by the No 1 driver, one of his team-mates was flagged down and the senior man took over.

The Ferrari team had been disappointed in the non-championship Silverstone race one week earlier, for both Fangio and Collins had to retire, without either having led the race. Hawthorn in the lightweight BRM had led for the first ten laps, until the motor developed a fault, and then Moss, driving

a Vanwall in this race, won ahead of two Connaughts. The Vanwall was a new model for 1956, Colin Chapman having been co-opted from Lotus to design a new chassis and the aerodynamic specialist Frank Costin to attend to the body. (Costin's half-brother, Mike Costin, was a well-known engine-tuner who would, in 1960, join with Keith Duckworth to found the famous engine firm Cosworth.) The distinctive Vanwall body shape would be repeated in the front-engined Lotus designs of a year or two later. Vanwall had also done a lot of work on their Bosch fuel-injected four-cylinder motor, which now produced 285bhp and, coupled with the aerodynamic body-shape and powerful disc brakes, made it a strong challenger.

After a long absence a European driver once again took part in the Indianapolis 500 meeting at the end of May when 1950

Above
The eight-cylinder Bugatti Type 251 made its debut at the 1956 ACF Grand Prix.

Right
The Bugatti 251's eight-cylinder motor was mounted transversely in front of the rear axle. The car had a solid front axle and De Dion rear end, and was fitted with four side tanks.

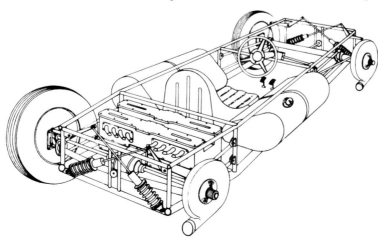

Top
The 1956 version of the Vanwall. The body shape was designed by Frank Costin and the chassis by Colin Chapman, and in this form the car proved competitive with the Ferrari and Maserati opposition.

Above
From left: Ferrari drivers Luigi Musso, Peter Collins and Juan Manuel Fangio at Monaco in 1956.

World Champion Giuseppe Farina drove a Bardahl-Ferrari (an American chassis with a Ferrari engine), but unfortunately failed to qualify. The race was won by a car with a 4.5-litre four-cylinder Offenhauser engine developing approximately 400bhp.

Another wheel-to-wheel duel developed between Moss in Maserati and Fangio in Lancia-Ferrari at the Belgian Grand Prix but both retired and the race was won by young Peter Collins in another Ferrari. Second was the Belgian sports journalist Paul Frère, who had come to Spa as a spectator but, much to his surprise, was engaged to drive a Ferrari.

The eyes of the racing world turned next on the ACF Grand Prix at Rheims, where a new car with a well known name made its first appearance. This was the Type 251 Bugatti, two examples of which had been built at Molsheim to a design by Gioachino Colombo, the former Alfa Romeo, Ferrari and Maserati engineer. The new Bugatti was a very unconventional design with its eight-cylinder motor mounted in a tubular chassis transversely behind the driver, complicated front suspension based on coil springs and a De Dion rear axle. The 75 x 68.8mm (2430cc) engine was built in two blocks of four cylinders with a centrally positioned power take-off and, using twin camshafts and Weber carburettors, produced 245bhp at 8000rpm. This however was insufficient for the car to compete successfully against the best of the time, and the chassis design, revolutionary though it may have been, was no match for the other 1956 cars. Maurice Trintignant drove the car in the race at Rheims but abandoned after 18 laps when an accelerator linkage broke. This was Bugatti's last public appearance; after this they dropped out of sight forever. The Bugatti factory in Molsheim was taken over by Hispano-Suiza in 1963, to be passed on a little later to SNECMA. In due course Concorde air-frames would be built where famous racing and sportscars were once produced.

At Rheims, Lancia-Ferrari drivers Fangio, Collins and Castellotti fought for the lead, joined in the later stages by Harry Schell in the Vanwall, a contender for the first time. Fangio had to stop to change spark plugs on the 40th lap however and Schell, his Vanwall having expired, took over Hawthorn's, leaving Collins to win the race from Castellotti.

The BRM made its Grand Prix debut at Silverstone, where Hawthorn led the British Grand Prix for the first few laps before the car broke down. Moss took over the lead but he, too, had to withdraw from the race when his Maserati broke its rear axle. Fangio pushed ahead and won, and then celebrated another victory at the Nürburgring, where he led from start to finish.

At Monza the four-man Lancia-Ferrari team — Castellotti, Fangio, Collins and Musso — fought a neck-and-neck battle with the Maserati 250F driven by Moss. Fangio's car then developed a fault and he took over Collins's, which left Luigi

Right
Stirling Moss took the lead shortly before the end of the Italian Grand Prix at Monza in a new Maserati 250F.

Above
On the Sound Curve of the Nürburgring just after the start of the German Grand Prix. Peter Collins in a Lancia-Ferrari leads Fangio (Lancia-Ferrari), Moss (Maserati 250F) and Castellotti (Lancia-Ferrari). Fangio won the race.

Left
Scuderia Ferrari brought no fewer than six Lancia-Ferraris from the team base at Maranello to Monza for the 1956 European Grand Prix.

Right
A new version of the Maserati 250F appeared at Monza in late August 1956. The engine was angled diagonally across the car, making it possible for the driver to be seated lower down in the vehicle.

Musso in front until just three laps from the end, when he retired with broken steering, which left Moss to take first place for Maserati. This victory had not however been achieved without controversy, for Moss had run out of fuel earlier in the race and his team-mate Piotti, quickly summing up the situation, gave the faster car a nudge towards the pits, where it was refuelled. The bumps of the banked part of the circuit caused a lot of damage to some of the cars, and was very hard on tyres, particularly the Ferraris'.

The Maserati which won at Monza was a new version of the 250F with its six-cylinder motor set diagonally across the longitudinal axis, allowing for a very low seating position. This enabled a lower body style which, with high cockpit sides,

Peter Collins

Eugenio Castellotti

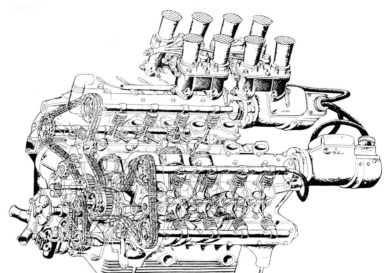

Ferrari used the V8 Lancia motor until 1957. The four-overhead-camshaft engine with four dual-throated carburettors was the same as the unit which took Fangio to the 1956 World Championship.

was very pleasing to the eye. The engine developed 275bhp at 7200rpm on the day.

The 1956 season had been a very interesting one, during which all records established by the Mercedes W196 were beaten, the power output of the Italian and British motors having climbed to between 270 and 285bhp. Juan Manuel Fangio became 1956 World Champion with 30 points, ahead of Moss with 27 and Collins with 25 points. The multiple World Champion from Argentina, now 45 years old, was the greatest on the tracks but he had strong opposition in such drivers as Moss, Collins, Hawthorn, Castellotti and Musso.

At the end of the 1956 season Gordini withdrew from racing. Its drivers had never been very happy with the heavy eight-cylinder Type 32, and financial problems had also hampered research and development. Amédeé Gordini joined Renault and many Gordini variations of Renault production cars became available in ensuing years, receiving an enthusiastic public reception.

Maserati, Ferrari, Aston Martin and Jaguar were fierce competitors for the World Sportscar Championship. Jaguar won at Le Mans with Flockhart and Sanderson at the wheel, but the title went to Ferrari.

Fangio's Fifth World Championship

The Argentinian shows the younger generation who is best. Fangio receives his title after a successful campaign in the 250F Maserati. The Vanwalls are hard to beat in the last races of the year.

1957 was the great Juan Manuel Fangio's last successful season in Grand Prix racing. No new models appeared, the leading manufacturers being content to update their existing cars. But while the Italians kept to their traditional form, the British resorted to more up-to-date solutions, and the majority of their contenders were lighter in weight than the opposition; all had disc brakes. Vanwall, no longer content to limit its participation to one or two cars in selected races, planned a full season with a three-man team comprising Stirling Moss, Tony Brooks and Stuart Lewis-Evans. Ferrari this year fielded a new development of the Lancia D50, which used Ferrari's own tubular chassis and was fitted with conventional bodywork without the familiar sidepods. This new model, called the Type 801, made its debut at the Monaco Grand Prix in May. World Champion Fangio changed teams again, switching from Ferrari back to Maserati.

The Vanwalls did not take part in the Argentine races, so Moss was released for a final Maserati drive, but it was Fangio who won. The Buenos Aires race was Eugenio Castellotti's last Grand Prix, the 26-year-old Italian being killed at Modena

during a Ferrari test session on March 14th. Shortly after this Maranello lost another works driver when the Spanish Marquis Alfonso de Portago lost control of his Ferrari during the Mille Miglia on May 12th, apparently when the rear axle broke. The car careered off the road, killing de Portago and several spectators. As a result of this accident, by no means the first in this classic race, the historic Mille Miglia was banned in its familiar form.

Monte Carlo marked the first appearance of Type 43 Cooper, the car which started the mid-engined design revolution. As driven at Monaco by Jack Brabham the 370kg car was fitted with a 1960cc version of the four-cylinder Coventry Climax engine. At the same

meeting Maserati appeared in practice with a new V12 2491cc (68.7 x 56mm) motor for the 250F. Test bench results indicated that the 60° V12 motor developed 306bhp at 9500rpm on carburettors but it did not live up to expectations and only raced once before being abandoned. The power was however the highest output of any motor built for the 2.5-litre formula. Maserati retired from racing at the end of 1957 but the V12 motor was revived in 1966 and used by Cooper.

The 1957 Monaco race was an eventful one. On the fourth lap Moss, who was leading in a Vanwall, took the famous chicane too fast and slammed into the barriers, to be joined immediately by the Ferraris of Collins and Hawthorn, and

6 km 542

Left
The 6.542km Rouen-Les Essarts circuit, venue of the 1957 ACF Grand Prix.

Below left
Early stages of the 1957 European Grand Prix at Aintree. Peter Collins and Luigi Musso in Ferrari 801s sandwich the Vanwall of Tony Brooks, the car which Moss took over and took to victory. The Ferraris were the final version of the Lancia D50 design, with the side-mounted fuel tanks replaced by tail tanks.

the three English aces were out in one blow. Fangio, in a six-cylinder 250F Maserati, immediately responded and, just as he had done with the Alfetta in 1950, slid through the gap and raced to victory. Jack Brabham in the little Cooper-Climax T43 was in third position at 100 laps, until then the complete distance of the Monaco races: this year though there were 105 laps and on the 102nd a blockage developed in the Australian's petrol tank and he had to push the car over the finishing line, in sixth place.

The Belgian and Dutch Grands Prix were not held in 1957, which meant the next big race was the ACF Grand Prix, held this year at Rouen, and Fangio led from start to finish and moved further into the World Championship points lead, even though World Championship events had to be run for a minimum of three hours and the Maserati was not always able to get through races without refuelling.

The European Grand Prix at Aintree resulted in the first British victory in a World Championship event. Moss in his green Vanwall led till the 18th lap, at which point a mechanical defect forced the car onto the sidelines. His team-mate Tony Brooks was flagged in and Moss took over the No 2 Vanwall, rejoining the

race in ninth place. The son of a dentist, pig farmer and former racing driver (Alfred Moss had taken part in the 1924 Indianapolis 500 in an American Barber-Warnock Ford Special) then overtook one competitor after another till he crossed the finishing line in first place at the end of the race, to a loud roar of appreciation from the spectators. This day, July 20th 1957, was a most memorable one for British motor racing, for no British car had a won a *Grande Épreuve* for over three decades.

A week later came another British victory, though this time in a non-championship race, at Caen in the west of France. Jean Behra, who normally drove Maseratis, took the opportunity to try out the latest development of the four-cylinder BRM, as the Italian team was not taking part. He won the race. The BRM Type 25 in 1957 form had coil-spring front suspension in place of the earlier

Jean Behra

pneumatic set-up, and had a single disc brake operating on the transmission.

The experts all agree that the 1957 German Grand Prix on the Nürburgring was the greatest race in Fangio's eventful career. Before the race the official lap record, which the Argentinian himself had set with the Lancia-Ferrari the year before, was 9 minutes 41.6 seconds. In practice for the 1957 race he took the 250F around in 9 minutes 25.6 seconds, and the experts shook their heads in disbelief. Although not an official record

(lap records must be established during an actual race), the improvement in one year was a phenomenal 16 seconds. The younger drivers began to wonder about their ability. The Vanwalls were not in their element on this difficult track and BRM did not start.

Fangio in the 250F Maserati and Hawthorn and Collins in Ferrari 801s wrote the story of this memorable race, a race which covered 501.82km in 22 laps. The Maserati used about 50 litres of fuel per 100km and had a tank which held 258 litres, which meant it was going to have to stop to refuel during the race, and would also have to have its rear tyres changed. The Ferraris on the other hand were going to be able to get through without a stop.

In the first two laps Fangio allowed the "young lions" to let off steam. But then as his fuel-load lightened he passed them, on the third lap, with a new official lap record of 9 minutes 34 seconds, and set about improving his advantage to allow for his planned pit stop. On the eighth lap he lowered the record further, to 9 minutes 30.8 seconds, followed a lap later by yet another new time, 9 minutes 29.5 seconds. Then, with 28 seconds lead over Hawthorn and Collins, who were still neck and neck, he made his stop. After 56 seconds the Maserati was back on the circuit, refuelled and its rear tyres changed, but now 30 seconds behind the Ferraris. But they weren't wasting time either: while the Maserati was in the pits Collins had lowered Fangio's new lap record to 9 minutes 28.9 seconds. Had Fangio underestimated the young lions?

Now the real fight began, as Fangio fought to get back to the front, clipping

Above
Mike Hawthorn (left) and Stirling Moss during a break in practice at Monte Carlo.

Above right
After several decades a British car once again wins a Grand Prix, as Moss takes the Vanwall over the finishing line at Aintree.

six to eight seconds off the Ferraris' lead each lap. On his 18th lap came another new record, 9 minutes 25.3 seconds, but there was still more to come. The Argentinian's 20th lap took 9 minutes 17.4 seconds, i.e. 147.8 km/h, set — as were the earlier record times — on a track made greasy not only by 20 laps of a Grand Prix but also by the 39 Gran Turismo cars which had taken part in a curtain-raiser. The spectators roared their approval, for nobody had thought such times possible.

Fangio was in a class of his own. At the end of that 20th lap Fangio was still two seconds behind the Ferraris, having clipped 11 seconds off the times of the much younger Englishmen in just one lap. (Fangio was then 46 years old; Hawthorn and Moss were 28 and Collins 25.) The young lions had no answer. At the Hatzenbach Corner on the 21st lap the Maserati slipped between the two

Ferraris, and within a few kilometres more was in the lead. The whole of the last lap was a triumph for Fangio. In just one year he had bettered his record time by 24.2 seconds, a result which no one else had been able to do with Grand Prix cars in this formula.

After the race the respected German sports journalist Günter Molter wrote in the Swiss magazine *Automobil Revue*: "Fangio's younger colleagues will now look up to him as someone unsurpassed, the grand old master of Grand Prix racing who can drive like no-one else. Let them look up to Fangio who, as a poor mechanic from a little Pampas township in Argentina, started racing in dilapidated cars in very minor events, but has now become king of the world's famous racing circuits. He is a man who will be esteemed wherever he goes, who will remain the same in spite of fame, what

the British refer to as 'a nice chap' and his own people mean with 'Muchacho'. He is a great ambassador for his country, a man of modest disposition, never losing his temper and, most importantly, always behaving fairly. To his 73-year-old father and his mother he always remained the little boy Juan (Author's Note: Loreto Fangio emigrated from Italy to Argentina and died in October 1972, aged almost 89 years). In the half-light of the room where he grew up his mother would pray with her rosary when he competed against the world's best, while his nephews drew racing cars in the sand in front of the simple house in Balcarce. This Fangio is a phenomenon."

No event in Grand Prix history has ever been more discussed or written about than that record-breaking Nürburgring drive by Juan Manual Fangio, culminating in his fantastic lap

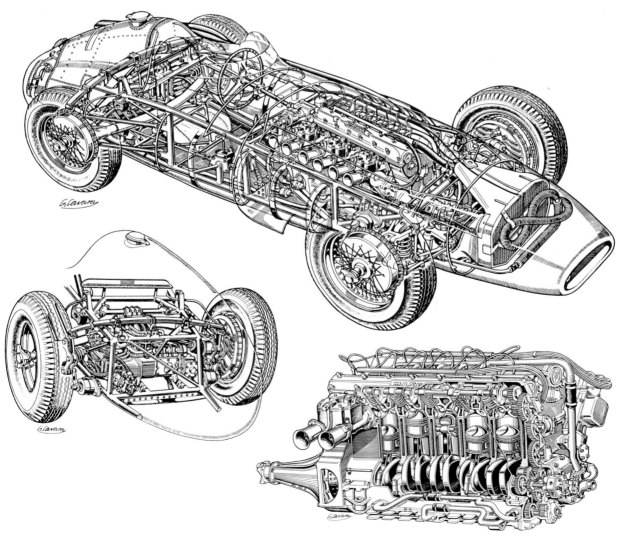

Above
Juan Manuel Fangio, at the age of 46, becomes World Champion for the fifth time.

Left
The 250F Maserati Fangio used to win the 1957 title was a development of the car that had appeared at Monza at the end of the 1956 season. The top drawing shows how the six-cylinder motor was offset in the chassis; the other illustrations depict the De Dion rear suspension with combined gearbox/differential unit, and the classic 250F engine.

Below
Ferrari introduced the Dino 246 model fitted with a V6 engine at the end of the 1957 season. The engine was named after Ferrari's son, Dino, who died in 1956. Collins is shown going out to practice at Modena.

Right
Second place at Monza was enough to ensure that Fangio was World Champion for 1957.

Below
Togetherness at Monza. Peter Collins in the Ferrari 801 shares the track with World Motorcycle World Champion Carlo Ubbiali on an MV Agusta.

time of 9 minutes 17.4 seconds. The quiet "Muchacho" from Balcarce was a driver who never drove faster than was absolutely necessary to win. On August 4th 1957 the necessity showed how brilliant he was.

The new competitiveness of the British cars became more and more obvious in the next few weeks, starting when Moss in the Vanwall won the Pescara Grand Prix, which this year counted towards the World Championship. Then in the Italian Grand Prix at Monza the Vanwalls of Stuart Lewis-Evans, Stirling Moss and Tony Brooks set the three fastest practice times, ahead of Fangio's Maserati, and Moss carried on for another win. Jean Behra gave the V12 Maserati its first actual race, but was delayed by an overheating engine.

But in spite of the Vanwalls' late-season charge, Fangio had enough points in the bag to take his fifth World Championship. The Argentinian's score was 46 points to the 25 of Moss, the 16 of Musso and Hawthorn's 14. At the end of the season Maserati retired from racing, for financial reasons, though the company returned in 1966 and 1967 with an updated V12 engine.

A new Formula Two, for cars with engines under 1500cc, had been introduced this year and the little cars occasionally competed in Grands Prix; Cooper, Ferrari, Lotus and Porsche were the most successful makes in this class which, in slightly modified form, would become the Grand Prix formula in 1961. Among the other Formula Two contenders in 1957, the OSCA concern unveiled a new four-cylinder engine with desmodromic valve design along the lines of the all-conquering 1954–1955 Mercedes-Benz W196, but the cylinder-head design proved less than satisfactory.

Ferrari, for the first time since the series began, did not win a single World Championship race in 1957. At the same time as the team was running the V8 Type 801s, work was also proceeding on the next generation of Formula One Ferraris, powered by a new six-cylinder motor.

This engine, a V6 OHC unit, was named after Enzo Ferrari's son, Dino, who had died in 1956. First appearing as a Formula Two unit, the Dino V6 engine was stretched to Formula One size before the end of the year and was the first step in a long and successful tradition of V6 Ferrari engines. The engine, for which Jano and Bellentani had been responsible, had first appeared in Formula Two guise at the Naples Grand Prix in April 1957, in a chassis designed by Massimino and his staff, the car being driven by Luigi Musso. By the time the Formula One car appeared, in the non-championship Moroccan Grand Prix at Casablanca in October, Ferrari had promoted former Alfa Romeo engineer Carlo Chiti to the position of chief engineer. Two cars appeared in the North African race, similar in concept to the Formula Two car and carrying the same long, sleek

Right
Last in the Connaught line. Stuart Lewis-Evans with the very special-bodied B-Type nicknamed "Dart" or the "Toothpaste Tube". The British make made its reputation when Tony Brooks beat the Italians to win the 1955 Syracuse Grand Prix.

Right
Last in the Connaught line. Stuart Lewis-Evans with the very special-bodied B-Type nicknamed "Dart" or the "Toothpaste Tube". The British make made its reputation when Tony Brooks beat the Italians to win the 1955 Syracuse Grand Prix.

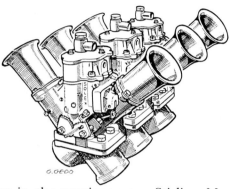

Below left
The 7.602km Ain-Diab circuit at Casablanca, venue of the 1957 and 1958 Moroccan Grands Prix.

Below
Solex developed a special carburettor for mounting on the X-shaped manifolds of an experimental Ferrari Dino V6 motor.

bodywork. Although they had identical chassis and weighed 540kg however, one car was designated the Dino 226, and had a 2.2-litre motor, while the other, the Dino 246, was of 2.4 litres. Drivers were Collins and Hawthorn. Significantly, they ran on a mixture of petrol and benzol in compliance with the new regulation to be introduced in 1958, banning special fuel blends and requiring Grand Prix cars to run on aviation fuel with a maximum rating of 130 octane; the other competitors at Casablanca still used their nitro-methane blends. Vanwall driver Stirling Moss became ill with Asian 'flu after practice, as did Fangio, but although the English driver chose not to start the race the World Champion did take part; he finished fourth. His team-mate Jean Behra won.

On June 29th 1957 a match-race had taken place between American Indianapolis drivers and Europeans on the high speed track at Monza. The race was divided into three heats totalling 500 miles but attracted little European support. Jimmy Bryan in an Offenhauser-powered Dean Van Lines Special won the race for the United States at an average speed of 257.504km/h.

The Monza 500 was run again in 1958, and this time Luigi Musso in a 4023cc Ferrari V12 Type 412MI was the fastest over three qualifying laps, at an average of 281.077km/h. Juan Manuel Fangio, in a Dean Van Lines Special powered by an Offenhauser engine, reached 275.481km/h. Winner of the race though was Jim Rathman in a Zink-Offenhauser with an overall average of 267.75km/h, Jimmy Bryan returning the same average

as in the previous year. Stirling Moss drove a 4.2-litre V8 Maserati Italia sponsored by the Eldorado ice-cream company but had to withdraw with a problem in his steering.

A new movement which started in Italy in 1957 was Formula Junior, based on single-seater cars with production engines under 1100cc. In 1959 this formula was given international recognition as a first step on the international ladder, an inexpensive alternative to Formula Two or the small sportscar classes. It soon became the accepted "nursery" formula and remained so until it was replaced in 1964 by Formula Three which, retained the production-engine base.

Formula One cars in the 2.5-litre formula era 1956 to 1957

Year	Make & model	Cylinders	Capacity	Bore	Stroke	bhp	rpm	Gears	Max. speed km/h	Dry weight
1956	Ferrari-Lancia D50	8	2487	76	68,5	265	8 000	5	290	645
1956	Vanwall	4	2490	96	86	280	7 500	5	285	570
1956	Maserati 250F	6	2493	84	75	270	7 400	5	290	630
1956	BRM P25	4	2491	102,8	74,9	260	8 000	4	275	550
1956	Gordini 32	8	2480	75	70	256	7 300	5	260	650
1956	Connaught B	4	2470	93,5	90	250	6 800	4	260	580
1956	Bugatti 251	8	2432	75	68,8	265	7 500	5	250	750
1956	Ferrari 625	4	2498	94	90	250	7 500	5	265	620
1956	Ferrari 555 Squalo	8	2496	76	68,8	270	8 600	5	250	630
1957	Ferrari 801	8	2494	80	62	285	8 800	5	270	650
1957	Ferrari 226	6	2195	81	71	240	8 500	5	270	560
1957	Cooper T43-Climax	4	1960	86,4	86,8	176	7 250	4	255	368
1957	Maserati 250F	6	2493	84	75	280	7 600	5	290	630
1957	Maserati 250F/T2	12	2490	68,7	56	306	10 000	5	300	680
1957	BRM P25	4	2497	102,8	74,9	280	8 250	4	285	550
1957	Vanwall	4	2490	96	86	285	7 600	5	300	550

Britain's First World Champion

Stirling Moss wins four Grand Prix events in Coopers and Vanwalls but Mike Hawthorn becomes World Champion for Ferrari with just one victory. The amazing Cooper-Climax.

The 1958 season was unusual in many ways. The Vanwalls driven by Moss and Brooks dominated the racing scene, winning no fewer than six World Championship races, while Hawthorn and Collins won one each in Ferraris. But it was Mike Hawthorn, with only a one-point advantage over Moss, who became World Champion. At the same time Cooper registered its first successes.

The season started with a series of hastily-arranged races in Argentina. The organisers announced the events only a few weeks before the start and BRM and Vanwall, requiring more time to prepare their cars, were unable to take part. In fact only ten cars appeared on the starting line: six Maseratis (all private), three Ferraris and one small dark blue Cooper-Climax T43 entered by the Rob Walker Racing Team and driven by Stirling Moss. Moss did not want to miss out on the opportunity of collecting points for the World Championship and, released by Vanwall, offered his services to Walker's stable. Nobody gave the Englishman the slightest chance. Fangio was taking part in his last race in his home country and although his Maserati lost time due to a tyre change, he still managed to take fourth place. Moss meanwhile, against all predictions, slipped into first place. Musso in a V6 Type 256 Ferrari, misinformed by his pit, made his final bid too late and the unexpected happened. The tiny mid-engined Cooper-Climax crossed the finishing line 2.7 seconds ahead of the Ferrari. It was an historic milestone.

The Cooper, with a 2-litre engine developing 175bhp, had beaten the Ferrari, which had 280bhp available (but weighed 100kg more). For the first time since the Auto Union era a mid-engined car had defeated the conventional models.

There was a second surprise for the conventional vehicles at Monte Carlo, when a Rob Walker Cooper-Climax won again, this time driven by Maurice Trintignant. A new British team, Lotus, took part in its first World Championship race with its ultra-light Mark 12, with a 2.2-litre Coventry Climax engine similar to the Coopers' but mounted in the front. The cars were driven by Graham Hill and Cliff Allison.

The question that was now being asked was: how was it possible for these Coopers to win against cars with vastly more power? The mid-engined layout was in fact superior to the conventional front-engined design for a number of reasons. First, by locating the engine in the middle of the car with fuel tanks on each side and the driver between, all the heavy components were concentrated towards the centre. Steering was thus more responsive. Furthermore, under acceleration, the tendency of the car was to lift the front and to "dig in" at the back, thus applying more force on the rear wheels which allowed the available torque to be better utilised and, in turn, provided better acceleration. But the greatest advantage of the mid-engined design lay in the area of weight saving. By dispensing with a driveshaft, the overall design could be more compact, and further weight saved through careful

selection of construction materials. In spite of its smaller engine capacity and relatively low power, the Cooper actually achieved the same power-to-weight ratio as the larger-capacity front-engined cars, while at the same time providing superior braking and acceleration because of its smaller size.

Yet another advantage of the mid-engined concept came from its lower air resistance. With the driver seated lower in the car through the elimination of the driveshaft, the frontal area could be smaller, and airflow over the body less impeded. Later, at the end of the sixties, a lot more research would be carried out into the aerodynamics of car bodies, with downforce increased by the use of front and rear air spoilers. At the same time, as the mid-engined concept was increasingly refined over the years, more and more attention was paid to the distribution of weight between front and rear axles.

After the upset of the Cooper successes in Argentina and Monaco, the front-engined Vanwalls and Ferraris dominated the remainder of the 1958 season.

The banning of special fuels mixtures for Grand Prix engines in favour of 130-octane aviation fuel halted — at least temporarily — the march towards more powerful engines. The 2417cc (85 x 71mm) Dino 246 engine in the 1958 Ferrari developed 280bhp at 8500rpm, the fuel-injected four-cylinder Vanwall 290bhp and the four-cylinder BRM engine, as fitted to the Type 25s driven this year by Behra and Schell, 280bhp at

Tony Vandervell (above), proud owner of the Vanwall team. Three Vanwalls on the front row of the grid for the 1958 Dutch Grand Prix, driven by (from left) Lewis-Evans, Moss and Brooks.

8800rpm. The "square" (88.9 x 88.9mm) 2207cc Coventry Climax engine as fitted to the Cooper and Lotus cars had a considerably lower output, 194bhp at 6750rpm. The Ferrari (which weighed 560kg) had a power-to-weight ratio of 500bhp/tonne, the Vanwall (550kg) 527bhp/tonne and the BRM (550kg) 509hp/tonne. The 380kg Cooper's power-to-weight ratio however was better than 510bhp/tonne, while the 370kg front-engined Lotus 12's was even better, 524bhp/tonne. Cooper and Lotus were constantly competing with each other to produce the lightest car, but though Cooper was now on a par with its front-engined rivals in straight power-to-weight terms, its roadholding and cornering abilities were clearly superior.

Stirling Moss and Vanwall were back on top in the Dutch Grand Prix at Zandvoort, and Tony Brooks won the Belgian Grand Prix, also in a Vanwall. Mike Hawthorn went on to take first place for Ferrari in the ACF Grand Prix at Rheims on July 6th. But it was an event marred by tragedy when the Italian ace Luigi Musso was killed when he crashed his Ferrari in the midst of a wheel-to-wheel duel with his team-mate Hawthorn. He was the last top-line Italian driver of his generation.

After the Argentine Grand Prix, Fangio had finally decided to try the Indianapolis 500, accepting an offer to drive an Offenhauser-powered American car. But after trying the car in practice he declared it unraceworthy, and did not race. He in fact drove in only two more events, the Monza 500 on June 29th, where he drove an Offenhauser-powered Dean Van Lines Special, and the ACF Grand Prix one week later, in a Maserati. This race was held on the same circuit that, ten years earlier, had witnessed his European debut in a little Simca-Gordini. After the 1958 Rheims race he retired from racing altogether. One of racing's all-time stars had left the racing scene.

The World Championship continued with the British Grand Prix at Silverstone and another Ferrari win, this time with Peter Collins at the wheel. But in the next Grand Prix, the German race at the Nürburgring, came tragedy when the handsome young Englishman ran off the track and was killed instantly. Collins's accident coming so soon after Musso's meant that Ferrari had now lost two top drivers within a period of four weeks. Brooks won the German race for Vanwall.

The Neapolitan Maria-Teresa de Filippis, who drove a Maserati 250F, was the first woman to take part in a World Championship Grand Prix.

Below
Waiting for the start of the ACF Grand Prix at Rheims are Mike Hawthorn in a Ferrari 246 (nearest camera), Luigi Musso in another Ferrari 246 and Harry Schell in a BRM P25. This was Musso's last race. He was killed when his car swerved and ran off the track on the Muizon Curve during the sixth lap while he was chasing team-mate Hawthorn. The race was won by Brooks in a Vanwall.

The Portuguese Grand Prix at Oporto, included in the World Championship for the first time, was won by Stirling Moss in a Vanwall. Brooks then took first place in the Italian Grand Prix and Moss won the last World Championship event of the year, the Moroccan Grand Prix at Casablanca. Another life was taken in this event when Stuart Lewis-Evans lost control on some oil which had been dropped on the track, the Vanwall spinning off the track. He was badly burned and died a week later.

The Ferrari Dino 256 was finally fitted with Girling disc brakes for the Monza and Casablanca races, its traditional large-diameter drums by now being outmoded and quite unable to match the performance of the British cars. Disc brakes had been one of the major

Right
The Mk 16 was the first true Formula One model produced by Lotus. Also known as the "Mini-Vanwall", the car was designed by Colin Chapman with body by Frank Costin, and used the four-cylinder Coventry Climax motor.

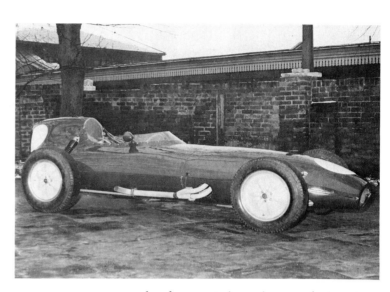

Below
The successful V6 Ferrari 246 which carried Mike Hawthorn to the 1958 World Championship. The drive-shaft was positioned on the left-hand side of the driver.

Overleaf
A historic victory for mid-engined design was achieved by Stirling Moss (No 14) in the 1958 Argentine Grand Prix. Here he is about to take the lightweight T43 Cooper Climax past Jean Behra's Maserati 250F. The 1960cc Coventry-Climax engine in the Cooper developed only 175hp.

developments in racing car design since they had first won a major race in 1953, when Jaguar won the Le Mans 24-hour sportscar race with a car fitted with disc brakes.

Stirling Moss had won the World Championship rounds in Argentina, Holland, Portugal and Morocco, but he did not win the coveted title. That went instead to his countryman Mike Hawthorn, who had won only once, at Rheims, but picked up numerous second and third placings. Hawthorn earned 42 points, one more than Moss, with Brooks third on 24.

The first FIA Cup for Formula One manufacturers was awarded this year and went to Vanwall, whose four-cylinder cars had won no fewer than six of the ten qualifying races. Vanwall scored 48 points for its win, Ferrari 40 and Cooper 31.

The Vanwall motor was now a famous engine and deserves special mention. In its original 2-litre form, it was basically built from four 500cc Norton motorcycle engines mounted on a common crankshaft and converted from an air-cooled to a water-cooled design. In its final 2.5-litre (96 x 86mm) configuration, as developed by the Vanwall engineers at their premises just outside London, the engine remained in many ways an unusual design. The crankshaft, in a separate alloy housing, was supported by five bearings and the cylinders were fitted with wet sleeves and a special light metal water-jacket, with a cast cylinder head. The twin overhead camshafts, each contained in a separate magnesium alloy housing, were gear-driven from the front of the motor. The valves were operated by cam followers, with the motorcycle

heritage obvious in that the valve springs could be seen protruding into the open air.

The original 2-litre motor had been fitted with four Amal racing carburettors, as on the Norton racing engine, but the 2.5-litre version was equipped with a Bosch fuel-injection system which,

Below
Feverish activity during a testing session with the Ferrari Type 246 at Monza in June 1958. Engineer Carlo Chiti (with tie) had resumed work with Ferrari at the end of 1957. Also in the picture are Luigi Bazzi (nearest camera) and an interested priest!

Right
The Portuguese Grand Prix, until then a sportscar race, was a World Championship round for the first time in 1958. The race was held on a 7.407km road circuit in Oporto, at Lisbon in 1959, then back at Oporto again in 1960.

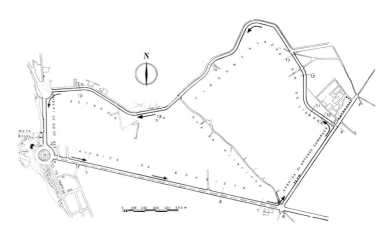

controlled by a complex mechanism, pumped precise amounts of fuel into each inlet port separately.

It was entirely due to the efforts of one man, Tony Vandervell, that Vanwall ranked so high amongst the world's great cars. He had led the small enterprise he backed to a degree of technical perfection that resulted in their bringing the World Manufacturers' Championship home to Britain.

Ferrari may not have won the Formula One prize but they did succeed in winning the World Sportscar Manufacturers' Championship in 1958, for the fifth time since the award was introduced in 1953, the only interruption

to their successes having been brought about by Daimler-Benz with the 300SLRs in 1955.

At the end of the 1958 season Tony Vandervell withdrew his cars from Grand Prix racing. They appeared occasionally over the next two years — at Aintree in 1959 and in two Formula One races in 1960 — but the heyday of these distinctive-shaped green vehicles was over. Tony Vandervell and his Vanwall racing cars represented a very successful era in automobile history, for they were the first British cars to win a Grand Prix after a lapse of several decades. A mid-engined design was produced in 1961, and raced in an Intercontinental Formula (3

litres) event in the hands of John Surtees. It was not much of a threat however, though its fifth-place finish was respectable enough. But that was the Vanwall's last race: Tony Vandervell and his Vanwall cars then disappeared forever from the racing scene.

Mike Hawthorn

A tragic event occurred on January 22nd 1959 when Mike Hawthorn, the first British World Champion, was killed in a road accident near London, only days after he had announced his retirement from racing at the age of 29. It was especially tragic that, after the blond young Englishman had made his decision to retire from the perils of racing, he could not resist a moment of dare-devilment, a daring which had so often led to his winning races. It is even sadder when one considers that this champion had exhibited a great deal of self-discipline, both on and off the track, in his last racing season, which put him in true championship class. Whilst driving on a country road near Guildford he recognised in front of him a Mercedes-Benz driven by Rob Walker, owner of the dark blue Coopers which had won two Grand Prix races the previous year. Hawthorn indicated that he would overtake on the downhill road, waved to his friend, and accelerated past to almost track speed. A few seconds later his Jaguar went out of control on a wet patch of road, slid across the other carriageway and slammed into a tree. Hawthorn was killed instantly.

Australian Jack Brabham becomes World Champion in a lightweight Cooper-Climax. Bruce McLaren wins the United States Grand Prix at Sebring at the age of 22. BRM's first Grand Prix victory at Zandvoort.

No significant technical innovations were made in 1959, and for the moment it seemed that developments originating out of Formula One had come to a standstill. Aston Martin, well known for its racing sportscars, entered Formula One with a new car, the six-cylinder Type DBR4/1, but the front-engined design was out of date almost as soon as it appeared, its power-to-weight ratio far below those of its competitors. At the end of the season BRM followed the Cooper lead and introduced a mid-engined design.

Stirling Moss, undisputedly the leading driver of the time, was sought by every team and tried a variety of cars without finding one he was satisfied would be a consistent winner. The Rob Walker team built him a Cooper with a four-cylinder BRM engine but this did not prove satisfactory and Moss reverted to a Cooper-Climax. He appeared at Rheims and Aintree with a light-green front-engined BRM Type 25, and during the year also tried the new Aston Martin and the latest development of the successful 1958 Vanwall. His constant search for the right car ruined his chances for the 1959 World Championship, on which he had had his sights firmly set.

For 1959 the Ferrari team, under the management of Romolo Tavoni, comprised the American Phil Hill, the Frenchman Jean Behra, Englishmen Tony Brooks and Cliff Allison, and the Belgian long-distance specialist Olivier Gendebien, though during the season the young American star Dan Gurney also joined the team. Cooper engaged Jack Brabham, 22-year-old New Zealander Bruce McLaren and the American

Masten Gregory to drive their lightweight mid-engined cars, while the Frenchman Maurice Trintignant drove a similar car for the private Rob Walker team. The BRM colours were represented by Swedish driver Joakim Bonnier (like Gregory a Maserati privateer until now), Scotsman Ron Flockhart and Paris-resident American Harry Schell. The Lotus team, with the front-engined Climax-engined Mk 16s, consisted of Graham Hill and the Scotsman Innes Ireland, and finally the Aston Martin DBR4/1s were driven by Englishman Roy Salvadori and American Carroll Shelby (of later Shelby Cobra fame).

The principal contenders appeared before the season to be the well-proven front-engined Dino V6 Ferrari and the T51 Cooper-Climax. Carlo Chiti, Ferrari's design engineer, had modified the chassis and the new Type 256 had independent suspension with coil springs, as well as a facelifted body. The Coopers this year had for the first time a full 2.5-litre (95 x 89.9mm, 2495cc) engine which developed 243bhp at 6800rpm. The Rob Walker team had adapted one of these cars to take a BRM engine and five-speed Colotti gearbox but after testing in the spring Moss decided he preferred the Climax motor.

Although the Aston Martin DBR4/1 made its debut in the International Trophy race at Silverstone in May it had been under test since 1957, and the design was already obsolete at the time of its release. The Aston had a six-cylinder in-line 2493cc (83 x 76.8mm) engine developing 260bhp at 7500rpm on carburettors and mounted in the front of the chassis. (The Vanwall withdrawal

Above
The Rob Walker team in a discussion around the one-off T51 Cooper-BRM at Modena. To the left of the car is famous mechanic Alf Francis;

Stirling Moss is in the centre and team owner Rob Walker on the right. After testing the Cooper-BRM, the team switched back to Coventry Climax power.

Above
Jack Brabham celebrates his first World Championship race win, the 1959 Monaco Grand Prix.

Left
The Australian Jack Brabham (then 33) sticks like glue to the steeply banked North Curve of the Avus circuit with his T51 Cooper-Climax during the 1959 German Grand Prix.

meant there were no longer any fuel-injected cars in Formula One.) Weighing 575kg, the Aston Martin was a heavy vehicle and produced a power-to-weight figure of 452bhp/tonne compared with the Ferrari 256's 536 and the 528 of the T51 Cooper-Climax. A Vanwall made a one-off appearance in the British Grand Prix at Aintree, driven by Tony Brooks, released for the occasion by Ferrari because a strike at the Italian factory meant the red cars could not be prepared in time for the British race.

The Aston Martin not only had the disadvantage of a lower power-to-weight ratio but, in addition, the tubular chassis with double-wishbone front suspension and De Dion rear axle with Watts linkages proved uncompetitive in modern conditions.

The 1959 season opened with the Monaco Grand Prix, won by Jack Brabham in a T51 Cooper-Climax. He also won the British Grand Prix, while Stirling Moss in the similar Rob Walker car was first in Portugal and Italy. After the best part of ten years of trying, BRM finally won a Grand Prix this year when the Swede Joakim Bonnier brought a four-cylinder front-engined Type 25 over the line in first place in the Dutch Grand Prix at Zandvoort, defeating the Coopers of Brabham and Gregory. The high power output of the Ferrari 256 was unequalled on the faster circuits and Tony Brooks won both the ACF Grand Prix at

The 246 Ferraris of Tony Brooks (who won) and Dan Gurney (second) lead Masten Gregory's Cooper-Climax T51 out of the South Curve at the Avus during the 1959 German Grand Prix. This was the first time the race was held on the Berlin circuit, rather than the Nürburgring, since 1926, though this time on the shorter circuit used for non-championship events since the war.

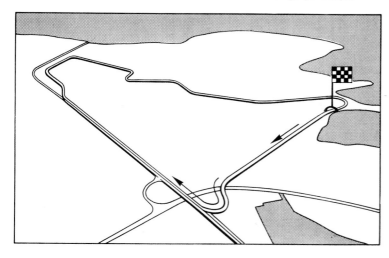

Above
The 1959 Portuguese Grand Prix was held on the Monsanto circuit on the outskirts of the capital, Lisbon. The 5.44km circuit incorporated a stretch of motorway.

Right
Stirling Moss won in Portugal and Italy (picture) in 1959 with the Rob Walker T51 Cooper-Climax.

Above
BRM scored their first World Championship win in the 1959 Dutch Grand Prix. Joakim Bonnier in the winning four-cylinder P25.

Bonnier's BRM and Moss's Lotus duel at Monaco in 1960. Moss won; Bonnier was side-lined with rear suspension failure.

The BRMs of Graham Hill and Richie Ginther in the 1962 French Grand Prix at Rouen. Ginther finished third, but Hill dropped back to ninth with fuel injection problems. Dan Gurney won to give Porsche their first (and only) Grand Prix victory.

Below
The last of the dinosaurs; Phil Hill's front-engined Ferrari was a distant fourth in the non-Championship Silver City Trophy race at Brands Hatch in 1960.

Below
Rodger Ward joined the Formula One field for the 1959 United States Grand Prix at Sebring with a Kurtis Midget powered by a four-cylinder 1.7-litre Offenhauser engine. Ward had won the Indianapolis 500 earlier in the year but, in spite of spectacular cornering, the dirt-track car was completely outclassed.

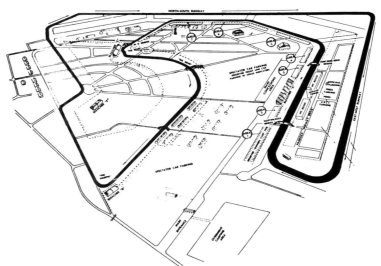

Left
The 8.36km Sebring airfield circuit in Florida was already well known as venue of the international 12-hour sportscar race when the first World Championship United States Grand Prix was run there in December 1959. Winner was 22-year-old Bruce McLaren, still the youngest-ever Grand Prix winner.

Rheims and the German Grand Prix on the Avus at Berlin. The Avus meeting was another sad one in Grand Prix history. Shortly before, following a dispute with his Ferrari team-mates, Jean Behra had left Ferrari. He drove a Porsche in the sportscar race at the Avus but crashed on the steeply banked North Curve and was killed.

The season ended with the first United States Grand Prix of the modern era (the American Grand Prize had been held on several occasions before the First World War). The venue for this event was the disused military airfield at Sebring in Florida. The New Zealander Bruce McLaren, aged 22, unexpectedly won the race in a T51 Cooper-Climax. McLaren, who later became a constructor in his own right, entered the record books as the youngest-ever winner in Grand Prix history.

During practice for the Italian Grand Prix at Monza, BRM's first mid-engined car, the Type 48, appeared. It had the familiar four-cylinder P25 engine mounted in a chassis based on Cooper principles, but with suspension on all four wheels by coil springs and wishbones, and the rear disc brake operating on the transmission. In spite of their win in Holland in 1959, the BRM had remained very much an outsider in a Grand Prix year during which events were dominated by the cars from Cooper-Climax and Ferrari.

Part of the reason for the Cooper team's success was that it was a small close-knit operation whose members worked well together. Jack Brabham was a man of great technical ability — indeed, he later competed in Grand Prix races in cars of his own design. He worked closely with team owner John Cooper in fine-tuning the new designs, particularly in regard to suspension behaviour, to an extent that they were easily adaptable to any sort of circuit or conditions. Cooper cars always had a reputation for ease of driving. With no large-scale factory to divert their attention, the small operation at Surbiton in South London was able to concentrate their effort on Formula One and the continual development of the cars.

At the end of the year it was clear that the 33-year-old Australian Jack Brabham would become World Champion. He had scored 31 points, followed by Ferrari driver Tony Brooks with 27 and Stirling Moss, in Cooper-Climax and BRM, with 25. In addition, Cooper won the Formula One Manufacturers' Championship.

Contrary to expectations, Ferrari were beaten to the World Sportscar Championship by Aston Martin, whose crowning moment was victory in the 24-hour race at Le Mans. The British manufacturer accumulated a score of 24 points to the 18 each of Ferrari and Porsche.

In September 1959 the great Rudolf Caracciola died of a liver complaint, at the age of 58. The popular "Caratsch" had lived in Lugano since the end of the thirties, and had become a Swiss citizen during the war. In 1946 he was severely injured in an accident during practice at Indianapolis, but returned to racing again to drive a Mercedes-Benz 300SL in 1952. In his long and successful career he had three severe accidents, Monte Carlo in 1933, Indianapolis in 1946 and Berne in 1952. Caracciola was rated as Germany's most famous driver and his name is deeply engraved in the history of motor racing.

Rodger Ward

Brabham the Champion Again

A complete changeover to mid-engined designs. Colin Chapman's brilliant Lotus 18 sets new standards. The superior British racing industry leads the way in the last year of the 2.5-litre formula.

Below
Jack Brabham after his 1960 British Grand Prix victory at Silverstone. Pictured with him is team owner John Cooper, whose father Charles founded the race engineering business in Surbiton, a suburb of London.

Far below
A wheel-to-wheel race between two generations of motor cars. At the ACF Grand Prix at Rheims a mid-engined T53 Cooper-Climax driven by Jack Brabham overtakes the Ferrari Type 246 of Wolfgang von Trips. The long reign of the front-engined concept was now at an end.

At the end of 1959 the critics were still not quite convinced about Jack Brabham's ability. They questioned whether he was a deserving World Champion, suggesting he had profited from Stirling Moss's constant bad luck. But by the time the 1960 season had come to an end the sceptics all had to change their opinion, for Brabham, driving the low-line T53 Cooper-Climax, had won the Dutch, Belgian, ACF and Portuguese Grands Prix on the way to winning his second consecutive World Championship title, this time by a clear margin.

Many people were coming to the conclusion that Stirling Moss may have been the world's best driver, but he was unlikely ever to be World Champion. He did not possess Jack Brabham's fine feeling for the machinery, and was accused of being too hard on his cars. Certainly there were many occasions in his career when his cars broke under him; perhaps that was the fault of the cars.

This was the last year of the 2.5-litre Formula One, and many of the new designs which appeared were prototypes for the 1.5-litre Formula One which was to come into force in 1961. The 1960 Ferrari team was made up of the American Phil Hill, the German Count Wolfgang Berghe von Trips, little Richie Ginther (a new arrival from America), the Englishman Cliff Allison and the Belgian daredevil Willy Mairesse. Cooper's colours were carried by Jack Brabham and Bruce McLaren, with a number of others at the wheel of cars run by private stables: these included Tony Brooks, Olivier Gendebien and Henry Taylor. The BRM team consisted of Joakim Bonnier, Dan Gurney and Graham Hill while Lotus had Innes Ireland and Alan Stacey, though during the season they took on two newcomers. These young men were the talented Scot Jim Clark and multiple World Motorcycle Champion John Surtees, both World Champions in future years. Stirling Moss elected to drive exclusively for the Rob Walker team this year, first (in the Argentine Grand Prix) in a Cooper T51 but thereafter with a Lotus 18.

There were two surprises in the opening round of the 1960 World Championship, in Argentina. The first was that victory went to an outsider, 22-year-old New Zealander Bruce McLaren in a Cooper, the same combination which had, equally unexpectedly, won the previous year's United States Grand Prix at Sebring. The

second surprise was the appearance on the starting grid of a new mid-engined Lotus. Fitted with the familiar Coventry Climax engine and driven by Innes Ireland, the Lotus 18 was the sensation of the Buenos Aires race. The car was identical in concept to the Lotus Formula Junior car which had appeared at the Boxing Day meeting at Brands Hatch, near London, and in Formula One guise had a "dry" weight of only 390kg. Fitted with the four-cylinder Coventry Climax engine (which developed 243bhp at 6800rpm on Weber carburettors) it therefore had the very impressive power-to-weight ratio of 623bhp/tonne, which compared more than favourably with the Cooper T53's 538 and the 500 of the latest front-engined Ferrari.

The Lotus 18 was the last word in modern design thought, designer Colin Chapman having studied the Cooper design and set out to improve on it. Built with a tubular frame and glass fibre body, the Lotus 18 had the further advantage of an extremely low centre of gravity. The suspension was novel too, for although the familiar system of coil springs and double wishbones was employed at the front, the rear set-up was a new design, and one which later became almost universally copied by other designers. Each wheel was mounted on a light-alloy hub-carrier to which was mounted a bottom wishbone parallel to the half-shaft and with its base to the wheel. It was located by radius arms at the top, the half-shaft acting as the upper wishbone. Although brilliant in concept this system had the disadvantage that the wheel was unsupported in the event of an axle or structural break. The consequence of this shortcoming became very apparent during the racing season.

The new Lotus was finished only a few days before the Argentine Grand Prix, allowing time for only a short test-run around the factory yard before the car was airfreighted to South America. The inevitable teething problems meant only a few practice laps could be completed at the circuit. And yet on the first lap Innes Ireland was in the lead, the tiny low-slung car making the towering front-engined machinery suddenly appear very old-fashioned. It was a brief moment of glory, for Joakim Bonnier in a front-engined BRM Type 25 took the lead on the second lap, and Bruce McLaren was the eventual winner; the Lotus 18 came sixth.

At Monte Carlo Stirling Moss made his first appearance with the dark blue Rob

Romolo Tavoni

Left
The Scarab, brainchild of Lance Reventlow (Barbara Hutton's son), was fitted with a fuel-injected four-cylinder engine, but after appearing briefly in 1959 and 1960 it was seen no more. The American front-engined car had no chance against the mid-engined British lightweights.

Centre
The most successful Formula One car of 1960 was the Cooper T53 fitted with the four-cylinder 2495cc Coventry Climax motor. Cooper was the most experienced builder of mid-engined cars at the time, and the car was fast and light with exceptional roadholding.

Below
Ferrari's heavy front-engined Type 246 won only one Grand Prix race during 1960, at Monza in Italy, and then only because there was no British competition. The motor was inclined at an angle so that the tailshaft ran alongside the driver. Ferrari had now discontinued the use of the De Dion axle for its Grand Prix cars, using instead a system of double wishbones and coil springs.

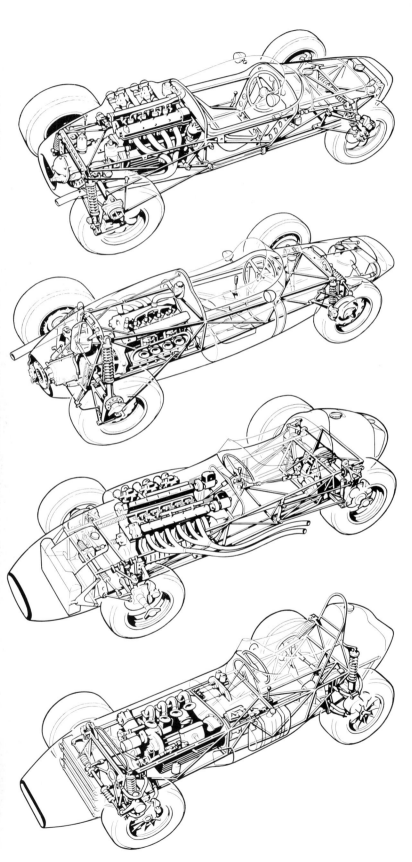

From top to bottom
The Lotus 18 was the most interesting new design of 1960. Colin Chapman had put a great deal of emphasis on weight reduction in this model.

In 1960 BRM changed its Type 48 to a mid-engined design. The car was fitted with the four-cylinder Type 25 engine. An interesting feature of the Type 48 was the disc brake on the transmission.

The six-cylinder Aston Martin DBR4/250 with De Dion rear end took part in a few races in 1959 and 1960, but its heavy construction and front-engined layout made it uncompetitive.

The American Scarab appeared in Europe in 1960 and raced at Monaco and Spa. Its four-cylinder engine featured desmodromic valve operation and Hilborn fuel injection, with power transmitted from the front through a Corvette gearbox.

Right
The Riverside circuit in California during the running of the 1960 United States Grand Prix.

Walker Lotus 18 and won the event. There had been a tragic accident earlier in the month when Harry Schell lost control of his private Cooper during practice on a wet track at Silverstone, and crashed to his death. Two more new designs made their first appearance in the Monaco Grand Prix. One was the first mid-engined Ferrari, and the other the American Scarab, a front-engined car backed by Lance Reventlow, son of the Woolworths heiress Barbara Hutton. The Ferrari was driven at Monaco by Richie Ginther, and took sixth place. At the same time Ferrari had also built a 1.5-litre version for Formula Two, and this was driven by Count von Trips to a very popular victory in the Solitude race near Stuttgart later in the year. The Tuscan engineer Carlo Chiti was put in charge of changing the Maranello factory over to the construction of mid-engined cars, for the 1960 Formula Two car formed the basis of the 1961 Ferrari Formula One contender. The Scarab was a beautifully-built car but suffered from the same drawback as the Aston Martin: it was born old, appearing at a time when designers were changing over to mid-engined designs.

The Scarab story had started in California, where Reventlow opened a factory in 1957, and built a batch of Scarab sportscars which were unbeatable against the imported Ferraris and Lister-Jaguars in American sportscar races in 1958. Work on the Formula One car started immediately, based around its own four-cylinder 2443cc (95.2 x 85.7mm) engine designed by Leo Goosen of Offenhauser. It had twin overhead camshafts and a desmodromic valve system with American Hilborn indirect fuel-injection, and in 1960 delivered 220bhp at 7500rpm. The engine was mounted in a light tubular frame with independent suspension and Girling disc brakes. The car's performance was not good enough to enable it to qualify for the Monte Carlo race, where the field was restricted to 16 starters. Drivers Lance Reventlow and Chuck Daigh finally qualified for the Belgian Grand Prix at Spa but had to withdraw due to engine trouble. The Scarab Formula One cars then vanished from the racing circuits and were seen no more. Reventlow himself lost interest in racing after that: he lost his life in an air accident in July 1972.

Jack Brabham's winning streak continued at the Dutch Grand Prix, the

race in which Jim Clark made his World Championship debut in a Lotus. Brabham also won the Belgian, ACF and British Grands Prix. In this last race though Graham Hill in the new mid-engined BRM Project 48 fought the Cooper for the lead until the Englishman spun off the track, leaving the way clear for Brabham to win yet again. Two six-cylinder Aston Martins appeared in this race, driven by Trintignant and Salvadori, but their performance was so disappointing that team owner David Brown decided not to race them again.

There had been a spate of serious accidents in the Belgian Grand Prix. Two young English drivers, Chris Bristow in a Cooper and Alan Stacey in a Lotus 18, lost their lives and two other Lotus drivers, Stirling Moss and Mike Taylor, were badly injured in separate accidents. The three accidents involving Lotus cars raised questions about the strength of these cars, questions which would arise on many future occasions, for Moss's crash was the result of a half-shaft failure and Taylor's of broken steering. The Stacey accident however cannot be blamed on any structural failure, for the unfortunate driver lost control at high speed after having been hit in the face by a bird.

Multiple motorcycle champion John Surtees made his Formula One debut in a thrilling British Grand Prix and came second.

The Germans restricted their 1960 Grand Prix, back on the Nürburgring, to 1.5-litre Formula Two cars and the spectators hoping for a Porsche victory were not disappointed: Joakim Bonnier was winner in one of the silver German

Roy Salvadori

cars. Ferrari scratched their entries, though the mid-engined car had won the Solitude race, also in Germany, a week earlier.

Back on the Formula One trail Brabham won the Portuguese Grand Prix with his Cooper team-mate McLaren second and Jim Clark in a Lotus third.

There was a lot of argument before the Italian Grand Prix, as the organisers, the Milan Automobile Club, had decided to incorporate the high-speed banked oval into their circuit. The British teams, recalling the damage done to competing cars the last time this bumpy track had been used, for the 1956 race, and anticipating the effect it would have on the latest generation of cars, wanted the race run on the road circuit only, and

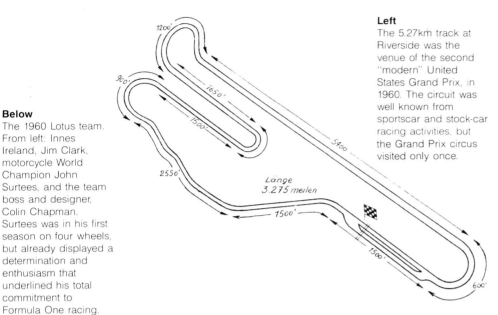

Left
The 5.27km track at Riverside was the venue of the second "modern" United States Grand Prix, in 1960. The circuit was well known from sportscar and stock-car racing activities, but the Grand Prix circus visited only once.

Länge
3.275 meilen

Below
The 1960 Lotus team. From left: Innes Ireland, Jim Clark, motorcycle World Champion John Surtees, and the team boss and designer, Colin Chapman. Surtees was in his first season on four wheels, but already displayed a determination and enthusiasm that underlined his total commitment to Formula One racing.

lightweight mid-engined car, carrying this concept from Formula Three to sportscars and Formula Two, and ultimately to Formula One. With the exception of the Formula Two models built in 1952 and 1953, all single-seater racing Coopers were built to this format.

The front-engined Ferrari proved to be hopelessly outclassed in 1960, for although it had the most powerful motor, it was hampered by its old-fashioned chassis and high tyre wear, particularly on the faster tracks. The mid-engined Formula One Ferrari raced at Monte Carlo had not been further developed, attention being concentrated instead on the Formula Two car with an eye to the 1961 Grand Prix formula.

1960 was a season of transition. Not only was it the last year of the 2.5-litre Grand Prix formula, it was also the last year in which front-engined Formula One cars took part in Grand Prix races. In spite of Ferrari's year of disappointment and frustration in Formula One however they were able to clinch the World Sportscar Championship title once again. The Italian manufacturer scored 22 points, the same as Porsche, but was awarded the title because they had won more races than Porsche. Maserati returned to the racing scene with the famous "Birdcage" model, run by private teams, and took third place.

the Formula One Manufacturers' Championship for the second successive year.

The Cooper company had been set up just after the war and made their first racing cars in 1946. These were tiny 500cc cars built for a new category which became the very popular Formula Three. Cooper cars were enormously successful in this class, and many famous British drivers served their apprenticeships in them. Cooper was the pioneer of the

when the organisers refused, they boycotted the race. This meant that Ferrari was in fact the only factory team in the race, and the field was made up of private entrants and Formula Two cars. Ferrari accordingly took first, second and third places, with Phil Hill, Richie Ginther and Willy Mairesse as the respective drivers. Another Ferrari, the mid-engined 1.5-litre Formula Two car, was fifth, driven by Count von Trips, who made full use of the slipstream of his team-mates' cars to shake off the Formula Two Porsche competition.

The Italian team did not however go to the last World Championship race of the year, the United States Grand Prix at Riverside in California, which was won by Stirling Moss in Rob Walker's Lotus 18. Even before that race Jack Brabham had sufficient points to give him an unbeatable lead in this year's World Drivers' Championship, which he duly took with 43 points. Bruce McLaren with 34 points was second and Stirling Moss with 19 third. In addition, Cooper won

Formula One cars of the 2.5-litre formula era 1958 to 1960

Year	Make & model	Cylinders	Capacity	Bore	Stroke	bhp	rpm	Gears	Max. speed km/h	Dry weight
1958	Cooper T45-Climax	4	2207	88,9	88,9	195	6750	4	265	380
1958	Lotus 16-Climax	4	2207	88,9	88,9	195	6750	4	265	360
1958	Ferrari 246	6	2417	85	71	270	8300	4	270	560
1958	BRM P25	4	2491	102,8	74,9	280	8250	4	285	550
1958	Vanwall	4	2490	96	86	285	7600	5	300	550
1959	Cooper T51-Climax	4	2495	94	89,9	240	6750	4	280	460
1959	Lotus 16-Climax	4	2495	94	89,9	240	6750	4	280	410
1959	Ferrari 256	6	2474	86	71	300	9000	4	270	560
1959	Aston Martin DBR4/250	6	2492	83	76,8	280	8250	5	275	575
1959	Scarab	4	2441	95,2	85,7	230	7500	4	265	560
1959	Tec-Mec	6	2494	84	75	280	7600	5		
1960	Cooper T53-Climax	4	2495	94	89,9	240	6750	5	285	435
1960	BRM P48	4	2499	102,8	74,9	285	8000	5	285	550
1960	Lotus 18-Climax	4	2495	94	89,9	240	6750	5	290	390
1960	Ferrari 246	6	2417	85	71	280	8500	5	290	560
1960	Ferrari 256	6	2474	86	71	290	8500	5	260	540
1960	Ferrari 246 rear eng.	6	2497	86,4	71	290	8500	5	260	550
1960	Cooper-Castellotti	4	2498	94	90	250	6500	5	265	525
1960	Cooper-Maserati	4	2489	96	86	238	7000	5	270	450
1960	Vanwall	4	2490	96	86	285	7600	5	300	485
1960	Aston Martin DBR4/250	6	2492	83	76,8	280	8250	5	285	575

Another Ferrari Season

The V6 cars from Maranello dominate in the first year of the 1.5-litre formula. The British V8s make a late appearance. German cars return to Formula One.

When the Formula One rules for 1961 had been announced in October 1958, they had been greeted by an immediate outcry, for they represented little more than a renaming of the 1500cc Formula Two, which had been introduced in 1957 and was to run until 1960. The British motor racing industry was, at the time of the announcement, equally competitive in Formula One and Formula Two, but considered the switch to smaller cars would lack spectacle. They launched an immediate campaign to have the life of the existing 2.5-litre Formula One extended.

The CSI would not budge from its decision, even in the face of a boycott threat by the British, though in time a second series, called Formula Inter-Continental, was sanctioned, for cars with engines between two and three litres. This series did in fact run in 1961 but there were only a few events, all in Britain, and the category soon disappeared from the international calendar. The old Formula One cars, and updated versions of them, continued to race in international events in New Zealand and Australia, subsequently evolving into the 2.5-litre Tasman Series.

By the time 1961 dawned and the 1.5-litre Formula One became fact, the British teams found themselves very much on the back foot. Their lobbying for the continuation of the old class had left them unprepared for the inevitability of the new class. At the same time, their concentration on Formula One had been at the expense of Formula Two, where they had, by the last year of the 1957–60 Formula Two, been overtaken by the V6 Ferrari 156 and the air-cooled four-cylinder Porsche 718/2. The advent of the 1500cc Formula One was accordingly welcomed in both Italy and Germany with far more enthusiasm.

The rules for the new Formula One, which would govern World Championship Grand Prix events between 1961 and 1965, called for engines between 1300cc and 1500cc, but for the first time in an international Grand Prix formula there was no provision for a supercharged alternative. Special fuel mixtures were no longer allowed, which meant that normal, commercially available petrol with a maximum octane rating of 100 had to be used (since 1958 130 octane had been allowed). There was also a minimum weight requirement. This was first suggested as 500kg, though the CSI finally admitted this was too heavy and agreed to a 450kg limit for car plus tyres, oil and water, but without fuel; ballast was not permitted. This weight stipulation was incorporated into the regulations in the interests of vehicle safety, as there was a widely-held view that the latest ultra-lightweight British designs lacked sufficient structural strength.

Wolfgang Berghe von Trips

Carlo Chiti

Phil Hill

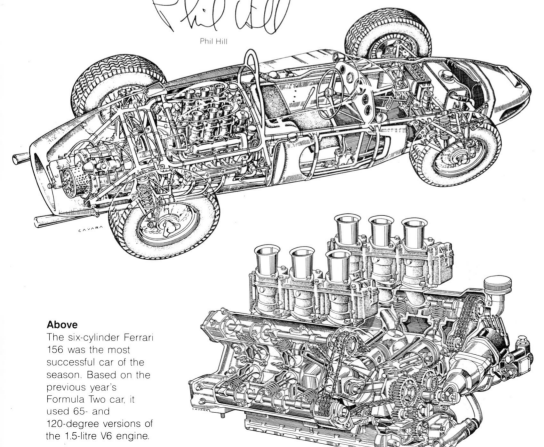

Above
The six-cylinder Ferrari 156 was the most successful car of the season. Based on the previous year's Formula Two car, it used 65- and 120-degree versions of the 1.5-litre V6 engine.

Left
The 120-degree V6 motor, designed by the engineer Carlo Chiti, with cylinder dimensions of 73 x 58.8mm (1476cc), was superior to any of the other manufacturers' engines in 1961. The motor was fitted with two triple-choke Weber carburettors; it developed 190bhp at 9500rpm. Later versions had four valves per cylinder (1962) and Bosch direct fuel-injection (1963).

Above
Engineer Carlo Chiti (right) talking to Wolfgang Berghe von Trips, who was one of the favourites for the 1961 World Championship, during a break in practice for the European Grand Prix at the Nürburgring. Von Trips was killed on the Monza track some weeks later. Chiti left Ferrari at the end of the season to build the V8 Formula One ATS.

Safety was in fact the by-word of the new formula. Cars now had to be fitted with electric self-starters (push-starts were not permitted), ignition cut-out switches, dual braking systems and roll-over bars. The strength of the roll-bars was not specified however, so that the first examples tended to be rather token efforts: it was considered sufficient to weld a tube of reasonable strength behind the cockpit, onto the chassis. Enclosed wheels were banned, meaning that streamlined bodies such as had been seen on the Mercedes W196 would no longer be permissible.

The British racing teams' protests about the 1500cc Grand Prix formula had cost them dearly as far as the new Formula One was concerned, for they started 1961 with no suitable engines to face the Continental contenders. Coventry Climax and BRM were both working on new V8 designs but until they were ready the only available motor was a new (81.8 x 71.1mm) 1496cc version of the four-cylinder Coventry Climax

Formula Two engine, developed by Harry Mundy, and this was used by all British racing manufacturers, Cooper, Lotus and even BRM. It developed 145 to 155bhp at 7500rpm.

Porsche's air-cooled four-cylinder Boxer, the 1498cc (85 x 66mm) four-camshaft Type 547/3, was developed from the firm's sportscar designs and produced 155 to 165bhp at 8500rpm. The Porsche racing cars still used the classic torsion-bar front suspension developed by Professor Ferdinand Porsche which was also used by Auto Union and, later, by Volkswagen.

Ferrari, however, started the season from the position of greatest strength, for in addition to the successful 65° Dino 156 Formula Two motor they also had a new and more powerful 120° version on the stocks. The older 67 x 70mm (1481cc) engine developed 185bhp at 9300rpm in 1961, whereas the newer short-stroke (73 x 58.8mm) 1476cc unit was good for 190bhp at 9600rpm. In either case the output was far in excess of anything available to the opposition.

Three other Italian engines appeared in Formula One during the year: Maserati with an ageing four-cylinder sportscar design, Alfa Romeo with a Giulietta engine developed by Conrero, and OSCA. But none made any lasting impression. All Grand Prix engines at the start of the year were fitted with car-burettors, though fuel injection would be reintroduced on a large scale in 1962 and 1963. Indeed the only fuel-injected car to race in 1961 was the BRM V8, which did

not make its appearance until the end of the season.

Ferrari had an excellent season of 1.5-litre Grand Prix racing, the mid-engined Type 156 being virtually unbeatable. The Maranello cars, with distinctive "twin-nostril" air-intakes, were on a par with their British counterparts in terms of chassis design, being constructed on tubular frames with four-wheel independent suspension by double trapezoid wishbones. But their superiority in the engine department coupled with excellent reliability made the results of each race almost a foregone conclusion.

There was a brief appearance by a single front-engined design during the year, the four-wheel-drive Climax-engined Ferguson P99 which had been built primarily for experimental purposes, but raced in the British Grand Prix.

The De Dion rear axle had also passed into history, but on the other hand disc brakes found almost universal acceptance, all manufacturers except Porsche using the British braking systems. The German company did experiment with a new type of disc brake, which was used on their eight-cylinder car in 1962, but otherwise remained faithful to drum brakes.

The only important technical advances during the year were in the area of power increases, for the 120° Ferrari V6 had a relative power output of 127bhp/litre. Some progress had also been made in respect of tyre technology and aerodynamics which led to reduced wind resistance, as the new cars had an edge on

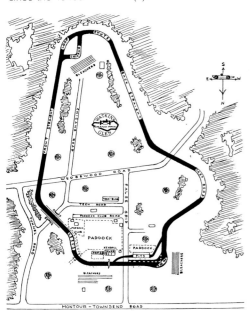

their more powerful predecessors on winding and difficult tracks. But on the whole, progress remained at the level of the last years of the 2.5-litre Grand Prix formula.

Giancarlo Baghetti

Ferrari won the Dutch and British Grands Prix with von Trips driving, and the Belgian and Italian races with Phil Hill at the wheel. A new Italian driver, Giancarlo Baghetti, achieved something nobody else had managed before or since when he won a World Championship Grand Prix at his very first attempt. This was the ACF race at Rheims in which Baghetti brought a Ferrari to the line in first place after a breathtaking slipstreaming battle with Gurney's Porsche. Baghetti had given a foretaste of this when he won the non-championship Syracuse Grand Prix, also in a Ferrari, earlier in the year: that had been his first race in a Grand Prix car.

Ferraris took the first four places in Belgium — just as Mercedes had at Aintree in 1955 — the drivers on this occasion being Phil Hill, Count von Trips, Richie Ginther and Olivier Gendebien. The Dutch race was unique in Grand Prix history as every car which started the race was still running at the finish.

Perhaps the high points of the season were Stirling Moss's victories with the Walker Racing Team's Lotus 18 in the Monaco and German Grands Prix, on the two most difficult circuits on the schedule, where his extraordinary skills were able to offset the car's inferior power. The Monte Carlo victory was a direct result of his tremendous tenacity and sheer determination for, although hounded mercilessly by the Ferraris, he drove like one possessed.

The front-engined Ferguson P99 which appeared in the British Grand Prix at Aintree was the most technically interesting newcomer of the year. Apart from its four-wheel drive, the disc brakes were fitted with an anti-locking device, a forerunner of the ABS system which would gain increasing use on passenger cars in later years. The brakes themselves were mounted inboard on the tubular chassis, in aid of reducing unsprung weight. Although built only as a test-bed, the car was raced at Aintree, with Jack Fairman at the wheel, and its roadholding in the conditions — the race was held in teeming rain — was exceptional. Stirling Moss drove the P99 at Oulton Park at the end of the season and won the race. The car was later used for mountain racing in Switzerland by Joakim Bonnier and Peter Westbury.

The new 90° Coventry Climax V8 motor, eagerly awaited by all the British constructors, finally made its first appearance at the Nürburgring in August, fitted to a Cooper T58 driven by Jack Brabham. Although the chassis had not been designed specifically for the new engine, Brabham showed the car's potential in practice, though in the race he left the track on the second lap. Weighing only 115kg, the new 1496cc engine, with "oversquare" dimensions of 62.0 x 57.4mm, was designed by a team led by Wally Hassan, with help from Leonard Lee and Harry Spears. The design incorporated a rather complicated exhaust system with the four pipes from each cylinder block feeding into a single

tail-pipe. Fitted with Weber carburettors and transistorized ignition, the new motor developed 185bhp at 8500rpm; a Lucas fuel-injection system was developed a year or two later. The aim of the special exhaust design was to provide torque over a wide engine-speed band, and the motor indeed developed useful power over the entire range between 5500 and 8500 rpm. This motor, as fitted to Cooper, Lotus and later Brabham cars, was the most successful over the five-year period of the 1.5-litre Grand Prix formula. Coventry Climax did not however build racing engines after that, having been bought out by Jaguar.

The European part of the World Championship came to a catastrophic end at the Italian Grand Prix at Monza when Jim Clark's Lotus 21 and von Trips's Ferrari collided under braking for the Curva Parabolica. The Ferrari somersaulted along the fence line and came to a halt amongst the spectators. Count von Trips, who had been leading

Innes Ireland

Left
First appearance of the V8 Coventry Climax motor was in Jack Brabham's T58 Cooper at the German Grand Prix in 1961.

Above
Innes Ireland won at Watkins Glen in a Lotus 21 Climax.

Left
Baghetti, driving a Ferrari 156 in his first World Championship Grand Prix, managed to beat the Porsches of Bonnier and Gurney to win the ACF Grand Prix at Rheims.

the Championship at this point, was killed, and so were several bystanders.

The debut of the eight-cylinder Coventry Climax engine was quickly followed by BRM's own V8, which was first seen in practice at Monza. Designed by Peter Berthon and Tony Rudd, the 90° V8 P56 engine was fitted with a Lucas vacuum petrol-injection system which enabled the engine to operate with greater flexibility and provided better acceleration. Like the Coventry Climax, the 1498cc (68.5 x 50.8mm) BRM used transistorized ignition. In its initial form it had a compression ratio of 13:1 and developed 185bhp at 10,000rpm, but the high compression was found to cause detonation and consequently burnt out pistons, and was reduced to 10.5:1. In this form output was 188bhp at 10,250rpm. The T56 BRM was fitted with a six-speed gearbox so that full use could be made of the extraordinarily high engine speeds.

After the tragic accident at Monza Ferrari withdrew from all racing events for the remainder of the season. The United States Grand Prix at Watkins Glen was won by the Scotsman Innes Ireland in a Lotus 21, the updated and modernised version of the well-proven Mk 18. Bodywork of the 1961 car was lower and narrower, and the ingenious Colin Chapman had moved the coil springs inboard, out of the airstream. The wishbones were fabricated from welded sheetmetal and shaped to provide better aerodynamics.

Phil Hill became World Champion with 34 points, with von Trips a posthumous second on 33 points; third was shared by Moss (Lotus) and Gurney (Porsche) with 21 points each. Double World Champion Jack Brabham was not so lucky with his Coopers as in 1961.

At the end of the season the racing world was surprised by news from Maranello that many of the leading Ferrari personnel had left the firm. They included team manager Romolo Tavoni and the engineers Carlo Chiti (technical manager of the racing division) and Giotto Bizzarini (responsible for the development of Gran Turismo Ferraris), as well as a number of other senior staff men. It was a severe blow to Ferrari to lose the best members of a team who had worked so well together and who had made the last models so successful. Chiti and Tavoni joined a new project whose aims were made public in the spring of 1962. This was *Automobili Turismo e Sport*, or ATS, founded by a partnership

Left
Moss's superior driving skill enabled him to win the 1961 Monaco Grand Prix in a Lotus 18 ahead of the Ferraris.

Below
A group of drivers before the 1961 Monaco Grand Prix. In the front (from left) are Ginther, Phil Hill, von Trips and Surtees.

comprising the Italian textile magnate Giorgio Billi, South American Jaime Ortiz Patino (nephew of the zinc king Antenore Patino) and the young Venetian Count Giovanni Volpi di Misurata. The new enterprise, working from a factory in Pontecchio Marconi in Bologna, was not however a success, its downfall accelerated when Count Volpi withdrew at the end of 1962, followed by Patino a little later.

Another end-of-year shock was Colin Chapman's firing of Innes Ireland from Team Lotus. In his own words Innes Ireland said at the time, "I visited the motor show in London where I met Colin. Although we had had a good working relationship up till then, he came up to me at Earls Court and told me abruptly that I would not be needed for the 1962 season. I had brought a lot of fame to Lotus between 1959 and 1961 and had won the United States Grand Prix. I have experienced the bad times with Lotus, when wheels came off during races or when vehicles ran off the track due to fractures in the chassis. Once I jumped into the cockpit shortly before the start, and noticed that a weld in a chassis member had broken. Without any hesitation Colin Chapman welded it into position. Imagine my feelings when I started the race a few minutes later. And now I am thanked in such a brutal fashion for all the risks I took. He just wants to promote Jim Clark who has moved into the foreground in 1961."

The Formula One Manufacturers' Championship went for the first time to Ferrari, following Vanwall's success in 1958 and Cooper's in 1959 and 1960. Lotus and Porsche took the next positions.

Ferrari also won the World Sportscar Championship, using the 3-litre V12 Testarossa and also the first mid-engined sports Ferrari, the Type 246, which was powered by the 2.4-litre V6 engine from

the old Formula One cars.

In these years Dunlop was the leading tyre company in Grand Prix racing; the firms of the fifties, such as Michelin, Pirelli, Continental and Engelbert, were no longer in evidence. The British company provided the rubber for all the teams and, in one sense, there were no longer any tyre problems, because everyone had the same material. Wear had improved to the stage where tyre changes were no longer necessary during a Grand Prix, and brake problems had virtually disappeared too: a set of linings or disc-pads generally lasted for the duration of a race without any difficulty.

It is worth referring to Jack Brabham's participation in the Indianapolis 500. His car was the Cooper T54, with a 2.7-litre four-cylinder Coventry Climax engine, a bored-out unit from the old Formula One. This was the first sowing of the seeds of change from front to mid-engined racing cars in the United States, though it took a little longer for the revolution to be completed there, for the Americans were rather conservative and hung onto their outmoded front-engined roadsters with rigid suspension, a feature which had remained unchanged for years. Brabham came ninth, for although the Cooper had a vastly inferior power output, it was a more modern design, and weighed 300kg less than the opposition.

The First Monocoques

The World Drivers' Championship title is decided on the last race in favour of Graham Hill in a BRM V8. Jim Clark in the brilliant Lotus 25 Climax V8 misses the title by inches. Moss retires after a bad accident.

Ferrari was unable to maintain the superiority in 1962 World Championship events it had shown in the 1961 season, and suffered defeat after defeat. The eight-cylinder engines from Coventry Climax, BRM and Porsche were now fully proven, and right from the first trials it was patently obvious that the British cars would lead the way in respect of motor as well as chassis development. Ferrari had done very little compared with the British teams, and although a new V6 motor with four valves per cylinder and a power output of 240bhp was forecast, it never appeared. Ferrari sorely felt the loss of their top engineering brains to ATS. The young engineer Mauro Forghieri was promoted to Carlo Chiti's vacant position of technical chief of the racing team and nail-polish manufacturer Eugenio Dragoni was appointed manager of the team which, since 1960, had been officially known as SEFAC Ferrari.

On Easter Monday, before the start of the World Championship season, Stirling Moss suffered a serious crash in a

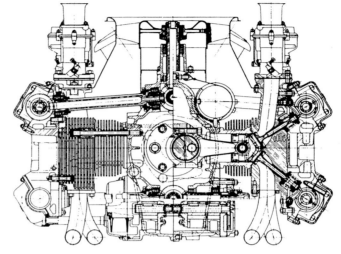

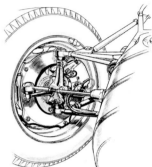

Below
Porsche developed a disc brake with an interior positioned brake "saddle".

Graham Hill [signature]

Formula One Lotus in a race at Goodwood. He was badly injured, and in spite of surgery, his sight remained impaired. About a year after the accident, and after much speculation about his driving future, Moss returned to the track in a private run to test his ability, and afterwards announced that he was convinced he could not reach his former skill again. His reactions were as good as ever, but he found he was having to think about what should have come naturally. And so the man who should have been

World Champion several times retired from racing.

The 1962 World Championship opened with the European Grand Prix at Zandvoort in Holland, won by Graham Hill in a BRM Type 56 V8. Four new cars had been seen on the starting line: Colin

Colin Chapman [signature]

Chapman's monocoque Lotus 25 (private Lotus customers had the spaceframe 24), the Lola Mark 4 designed by Eric Broadley, the Cooper T66, which was the work of Owen Maddock, and the Porsche 804, whose new bodywork had a frontal area 75% that of its predecessor. The Porsche was fitted with a new eight-cylinder Boxer engine while the other three all used the Coventry Climax V8. In these times of increasing "kit-car" manufacture, the Climax motor was available to private teams as, for the first time, was the new BRM V8.

The smaller frontal area was a feature of the new breed of Grand Prix car. The aim of this exercise was to improve straight-line speed without increasing power, and reducing wind resistance over the car was the method employed, so that the bodies now looked like torpedoes. In 1956–57, the cross-sectional area of a typical front-engined Formula One car had been 0.85 square metres, but by 1962 that had come down to 0.54 square metres for the Ferrari 156, 0.45 for the BRM and a remarkable 0.37 for the Lotus 25. It didn't stop there either, for the ATS which appeared in 1963 had a cross-section of

Top
Porsche developed the air-cooled eight-cylinder Type 753 motor for their Formula One 804 model, with four overhead camshafts. The cylinder dimensions were 66 x 54.6mm (1494cc), but the engine was later enlarged to 2 litres and 2.2 litres for sportscar applications.

Above right
Graham Hill in a V8 BRM Type 56 at the 1962 Belgian Grand Prix. In its earliest form this car was distinguished by its vertical exhaust-stacks.

Left
Joseph Siffert in a space-frame Lotus 24 (the Lotus 25 had a monocoque chassis) with four-cylinder Coventry Climax engine, at the 1962 Belgian Grand Prix.

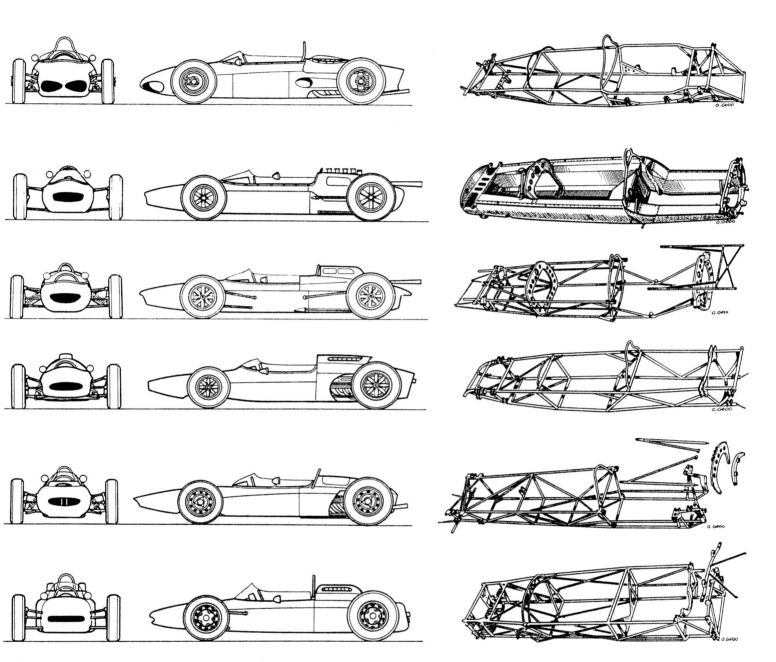

0.34 square metres. The narrow cockpits of the new cars almost totally encased the driver, and to reduce height even further, the cars were designed so that the driving position was virtually prone.

Gone too were the traditional steering wheels for, with the exception of the Ferraris, the large wooden wheels had been replaced by much smaller leather-bound wheels. Controlling the lightweight racing car of 1962 no longer required brute strength, for everything could be done with the flick of a finger. What was required with these fast, responsive cars, with their direct steering,

was a high degree of concentration. There was not room for even the slightest of errors.

The most remarkable of the new 1962 designs was the Lotus 25, designed and built by Colin Chapman in his small factory in the London suburb of Cheshunt and driven so brilliantly by Jim Clark. The Lotus 25 became the Type 33 in 1964 and raced until the end of the 1.5-litre formula in 1965, and also in the 3-litre formula in 1966.

Its key feature was the monocoque chassis, likened to a bathtub in which the driver sat, with the engine bolted on

From top to bottom

Ferrari 156 with V6 motor (either 65 or 120 degrees).

The Lotus 25 with V8 Coventry Climax engine was the most successful design of the 1962 season.

The Lola Mark 4 with Coventry Climax motor.

The Cooper T60 with Coventry Climax V8 motor.

The BRM P56 was the first car in the 1.5-litre formula to have indirect fuel injection for its eight-cylinder motor.

The Porsche 804 with eight-cylinder air-cooled motor.

Jim Clark in a Lotus 25 had a clear lead in the South African Grand Prix and seemed assured of the World Championship when a bolt came loose and the rear of the car disappeared in a cloud of oil vapour; that was the end of his race.

Below
The 1962 South African Grand Prix, last round in the World Championship, was held on a 3.918km track at East London.

Bottom
A new De Tomaso with eight-cylinder Boxer engine appeared during practice for the 1962 Italian Grand Prix, but was withdrawn before the race and never seen again.

behind. The chassis consisted of riveted sheetmetal boxes, with the hollows of the D-shaped side-members filled with rubber fuel tanks. The beauty of the monocoque chassis was its torsional rigidity which allowed for more compact design, and incidentally provided the driver with more protection in the event of an accident, as there were no chassis tubes to twist and bend. The Lotus monocoque was reinforced with cross-members made from sheet steel level with the dashboard and surrounding the driver. The monocoque construction method was quickly adopted by other racing designers and soon became the accepted form. The Climax motor in the Lotus 25 was connected to a German five-speed gearbox from *Zahnradfabrik Friedrichshafen* (ZF).

Both Coventry Climax and BRM used transistorized ignition on their engines, a system developed by Lucas which had an advantage over the traditional type of circuit-breaker in that the transistors could handle a significantly stronger electrical impulse. Electricity generated in these special coils remained constant, even at high revolutions. Climax also adopted Lucas fuel injection, at the end of the season, and within another twelve months virtually all Grand Prix engines had completed the change from carburettors. Porsche had carried out extensive tests on their four-cylinder engines with the Kugelfischer injection system but decided to retain the conventional carburettor system for 1962, and Ferrari did not introduce its first

injection system until 1963 either.

The advantages of this type of fuel-air mixture delivery into high performance engines should be pointed out. The injection system enabled accurate amounts of fuel to be delivered at any engine speed, which yielded better acceleration throughout the rpm range, improved cooling in the combustion chamber, reduced fuel "swirl", gave better fuel consumption for the same performance and made cornering safer (by eliminating flat spots). A further advantage of the fuel injection system was

its immunity to changes in temperature or humidity.

Porsche retained their traditional air-cooling in the new eight-cylinder 1494cc (66 x 54.6mm) Boxer engines with their four camshafts and dual ignition. The former torsion-bar suspension system was dropped in favour of a new system with wishbones located by longitudinal radius arms. The German manufacturer also developed an interesting new braking system which first appeared on this model. In place of a disc, the brake was a flat ring mounted on the outside of the

Right
Bonnier in an air-cooled eight-cylinder Porsche 804 chased by three Ferraris (Giancarlo Baghetti, Ricardo Rodriguez and Willy Mairesse) in the 1962 Italian Grand Prix. The Porche's pressed steel wheels have been covered with sheet metal discs to reduce air resistance. Mairesse's Ferrari is the new model with lighter chassis, new body, six-speed gearbox and four-valve-per-cylinder engine. Mauro Forghieri was appointed chief engineer after Carlo Chiti left the Ferrari enterprise.

hub, worked by an internally-operated caliper.

The performance of the various motors in 1962 were as follows: Coventry Climax V8 with four Weber carburettors, 185bhp at 8500rpm; BRM V8 with Lucas fuel injection, 185 to 192bhp at 10,250rpm; Porsche air-cooled 804 Boxer eight-cylinder, 185bhp at 9200rpm; and Ferrari 120° V6 Type 156 with two triple-throated Weber carburettors, 195bhp at 9600rpm. All competing engines this year gave performance in the range of between 123bhp and 130bhp per litre, but there was more variation in power-to-weight ratios. Among the principal contenders, the 450kg Lotus-Climax 25 had a ratio of 411bhp/tonne, the 460kg BRM P56 417bhp/tonne, the 455kg Porsche 804 and the 455kg Lola-Climax both 406, the 470kg Cooper-Climax T66 394 and the 490kg Ferrari 156 398. A slimmer and lighter version of the Ferrari 156 was introduced from the German Grand Prix, weighing only 455kg, and

this had a power-to-weight ratio of 428bhp/tonne. Mean piston speeds of the various 1962 Formula One engines were: Ferrari 21.9, BRM 16.9, Porsche 16.7 and Coventry Climax 16.2m/sec.

On the gearbox front, the six-speed units built by Colotti in Modena were much in demand this year, and were used by BRM and Lola (also fitted with a five-speed gearbox) as well as the new Brabham, which appeared during the season. BRM also built their own five-speed gearbox, while Porsche, Cooper and Ferrari all used six-speed units of their own design and the Lotus 25, as mentioned, used a ZF gearbox. As a rule, cars fitted with the Coventry Climax engine could get by with five-speed gearboxes but six-speed boxes were needed to take full advantage of the higher-revving Ferrari, BRM and Porsche engines. The Colotti enterprise had been established by Valerio Colotti, a former Maserati engineer who had specialised in gearboxes and trans-

missions, in association with Alf Francis, the one-time Polish refugee who had long served as Stirling Moss's racing mechanic. Francis suffered badly as a result of this association as before long the British Hewland firm, which started soon afterwards, was able to meet all the potential Italian requirements. Francis once said: "In the years I had been Stirling Moss's racing mechanic I was paid a percentage of his winnings and my savings grew steadily, as Moss won many races in the fifties. My association with him occurred at the time of the World Championships. Now I have invested my money in Colotti's firm and am his business partner. I can see now that we cannot compete with the British firm, as they are larger and better equipped. I have lost all my money."

The 1962 British Grand Prix cars had alloy wheels, which considerably reduced unsprung weight. Ferrari still used wire-spoked wheels in 1962, but would change to alloy rims in 1963. Porsche's Formula One models retained the traditional pressed-steel rims, as on their sportscars. At the same time some designers were changing to 13-inch wheels not only to reduce unsprung weight, but also in the interests of decreasing air resistance.

The drivers of the leading racing teams in 1962 were: Jim Clark and Trevor Taylor for Lotus, Graham Hill and Richie Ginther for BRM, Dan Gurney and Joakim Bonnier for Porsche, John Surtees and Roy Salvadori for Lola (backed by the Yeoman Credit finance company), Bruce McLaren and Tony Maggs for Cooper, and Phil Hill, Willy Mairesse, Lorenzo Bandini, Giancarlo Baghetti and the 20-year-old Mexican Ricardo Rodriguez for Ferrari. Jack Brabham founded his own firm and, after racing a Lotus-Climax 24, brought out his new Brabham-Climax BT3 at the German Grand Prix.

The heroes of the season were Graham Hill in the BRM P56 and Jim Clark in the Lotus-Climax 25. Hill won the European (at Zandvoort), German, Italian and South African Grands Prix and Clark the Belgian, British and United States races. Bruce McLaren in a Cooper-Climax T60 won the Monaco Grand Prix, following the withdrawal of the faster competitors, and Dan Gurney in a Porsche was first in the ACF Grand Prix at Rouen. This was Porsche's only victory in a World Drivers' Championship event.

The World Championship title was not settled until the final round, the South

African Grand Prix at East London. Would it be Graham Hill and BRM or Jim Clark and Lotus? At the start the Lotus shot to the front and, as he built his advantage to 30 seconds, the scales were tipped towards the Scotsman becoming the new World Champion. But on the 63rd of the 82 laps luck stepped in and upset the balance: a small bolt had worked loose and caused all the engine-oil to drain out. Clark was forced to retire, and Graham Hill won the title.

Ferrari had not taken part in any races for some time, partly due to strikes in the metal industries in Italy, but also because the once-invincible six-cylinder cars had been pushed into the background by the superior British machinery. Then to add insult to injury Ferrari's top driver, Phil Hill, left at the end of the season and joined the new ATS outfit, for which Carlo Chiti had built a new car. The first Type 100 with ATS V8 motor and Colotti transmission was built in a house somewhere in the country, as the factory had not been completed. As a replacement for Hill, the 1961 World Champion, Ferrari hired John Surtees to lead the team in 1963.

Huschke von Hanstein

Dan Gurney

Another new car appeared at the Italian Grand Prix. It carried the name of Alessandro de Tomaso, an Argentinian living in Modena (and later owner of Maserati), and had an eight-cylinder Boxer motor designed by the former Ferrari and Maserati engineer, Massimino. Driven by the Argentinian Estefano Nasif, the car was seen in practice but did not take the start of the race, and was in fact never seen again.

A car with a bigger future appeared in the German Grand Prix at Nürburgring. This was the first Brabham, fitted with a Coventry Climax motor. As with all Brabham cars until 1971, it was built by the Australian engineer/driver in collaboration with his fellow countryman, Ronald Sydney Tauranac, an expert in chassis design and construction.

At the end of the year Graham Hill was awarded the Drivers' World Championship for 1962, the BRM driver having accumulated 42 points to Jim Clark's 30 with the Lotus 25, and Cooper driver Bruce McLaren's 27. BRM won the World Manufacturers' title ahead of Lotus and Cooper, a welcome reward for the Bourne (Lincolnshire) team after so many years of disappointment and defeat.

The World Championship for endurance racing was held not for sportscars this year, but for Gran Turismo vehicles, which bore closer relationship to production models, and Prototypes which, as their name suggests, were supposed to be the production cars of the future. The organisers of the 24-hour Le Mans race, and subsequently the International Sports Commission, decided that the two-seater racing cars should be replaced by cars which corresponded more closely to the rules

The first Mexican Grand Prix was held in 1962 on the 5.0km Magdalena Mixhuca circuit near Mexico City. The Central American race became a round in the World Championship the following year.

laid down for ordinary production vehicles. The aim of having vehicles which corresponded with everyday cars was, of course, pure delusion. A higher windscreen, or an enclosed cockpit, or a boot with specified dimensions, could not change a wild tiger into a domestic cat. Be that as it may, the 1962 Championship was split into three divisions, up to 1000cc, 1001–2000cc and over 2000cc, and the respective titles went to Abarth, Porsche and Ferrari, though it was Ferrari who won all the classic races.

At the end of the season Porsche racing manager Huschke von Hanstein, the former Mille Miglia winner, announced that the Stuttgart firm was withdrawing from Formula One racing at the end of 1962 to concentrate on long-distance racing and the European Mountain Championship.

The Grand Prix season finished on a sad note. The youngest of the top drivers, Ricardo Rodriguez, was killed in an accident during practice for the non-championship Mexican Grand Prix: he was not quite 21 years old. Gary Hocking, a motorcycle champion from Rhodesia (now Zimbabwe), had been trying his luck in racing cars after a successful career on two wheels, but lost his life practising for the Natal Grand Prix at Durban in South Africa. Coincidentally, both these promising young men had been driving Lotus-Climax 24 cars for the Rob Walker Racing Team.

The eight-cylinder Porsche Type 804 won only one World Championship race, the 1962 ACF Grand Prix at Rouen, when American Dan Gurney, who later built his own Eagle Grand Prix cars, took first place.

The Invincible Jim Clark

The Scot becomes World Champion in a Lotus 25. Lotus makes a sensational debut at Indianapolis. A general trend to fuel-injection engines. Jack Brabham's success in a Brabham.

The dominant role in 1963 was played by Jim Clark in the Lotus 25 with Lucas fuel-injected Coventry Climax motor. The Scot won seven of the ten races on the Championship calendar, the Belgian, Dutch, ACF, British, Italian, Mexican and South African Grands Prix. The Monaco and United States Grands Prix were won by Graham Hill in a BRM P56, and the German Grand Prix by John Surtees in a V6 Ferrari Type 156B. The Nürburgring result was Ferrari's first victory after the devastating defeats of the previous season. Jack Brabham's young team achieved excellent results considering that it was their first full season and that there were only two drivers, Dan Gurney and Brabham himself.

The installation of the Lucas low-pressure fuel-injection system increased the output of the Coventry Climax V8 engine to 200bhp at 9800rpm, and of the eight-cylinder BRM unit to 205bhp at 11,000rpm. Ferrari's 120° V6 motor was also equipped with fuel injection this year, a Bosch system adapted by the Swiss engineer Michael May. Bosch, May and Ferrari had been brought together on this project by German motoring journalist Günther Molter, who later became public relations manager for Daimler-Benz. The Bosch system injected the fuel directly into the combustion chamber, a method similar to that used by Mercedes-Benz in the W196 in 1954–55, and boosted Ferrari power to 205bhp at 10,200rpm.

Ferrari engineers were working on a number of new design ideas, and it was widely known that the car with which the team started the season was an interim model. This had a tubular spaceframe chassis and was clothed in a

Jim Clark

Left
The Lotus 29 built for the 1963 Indianapolis 500 was powered by a 4.2-litre Ford V8 pushrod engine.

Below
The V8 Coventry Climax was the most successful 1.5-litre Grand Prix motor. Cylinder dimensions were 62.9 x 57.4mm (1496cc) and power rose from 190bhp originally to 213bhp in the 32-valve version.

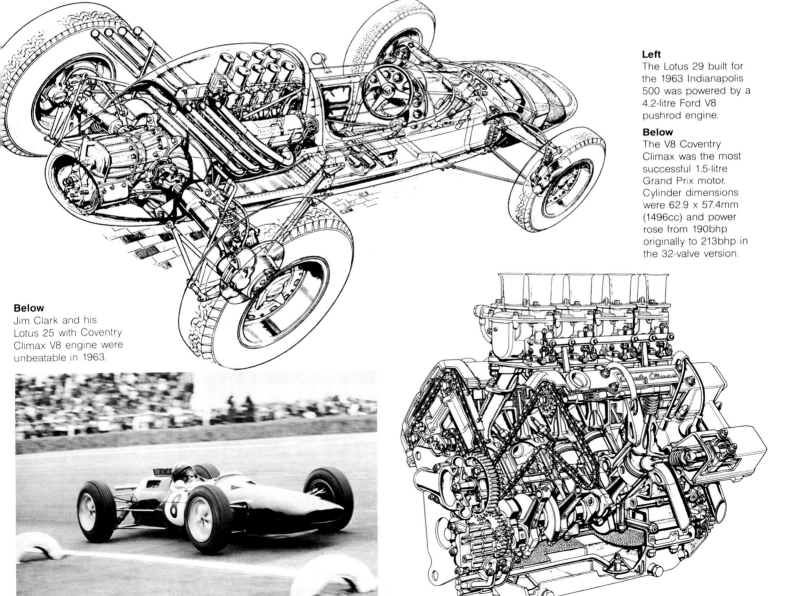

Below
Jim Clark and his Lotus 25 with Coventry Climax V8 engine were unbeatable in 1963.

VIC BERRIS

Autocar
copyright

body with smaller frontal area, to minimize wind resistance. Most importantly, the Maranello firm once again had a top driver in John Surtees, and this made them competitive once more.

Later in the year the semi-monocoque "Aero" 156 model with inboard suspension appeared and with this Surtees led the opening lap of the Italian Grand Prix at Monza before the car broke. Inspired by aeronautical practice, the new car was built on a chassis comprising a framework of small-diameter tubes, to which were riveted metal sheets, a method of construction which was to be a Ferrari practice for many years. Rubber fuel tanks were enclosed within these boxed sections. Following what was now common practice with other constructors, the front coil springs and shock absorbers were mounted inboard, which reduced unsprung weight and at the same time improved airflow. The rear brakes were also located inboard, next to the differential rather than on the wheels. The car retained the familiar Dino 156 motor.

A new make on the scene in 1962 was the BRP, designed for the British Racing Partnership by Tony Robinson. The monocoque car was in fact a virtual copy of the Lotus 25, even the suspension being similar. The BRP, powered by a BRM V8 motor and fitted with a six-speed Colotti-Francis gearbox, first appeared in Belgium and was driven by the former Lotus driver Innes Ireland.

The new BRM P61, outwardly distinguishable by its much smaller frontal area, was seen for the first time during practice at Zandvoort. Its construction combined spaceframe and monocoque principles, the centre section being made from riveted sheetmetal to which were attached tubular subframes front and rear. The P61 also had inboard coil-spring and wishbone suspension front and rear but the rear-end design never worked very well and was subsequently replaced by a more conventional design. The BRM P61 was driven by Graham Hill in the fast Rheims and Monza races but on other circuits, where roadholding was more important, the tubular-spaceframe P56, which had better handling characteristics, was used. The P61 incidentally used BRM's own six-speed gearbox. At the same time Lotus experimented with Colotti and Hewland gearboxes but in the end remained faithful to the five-speed ZF transmission.

The 1963 version of the Ferrari 156 was inspired by British designs. Wheels with cast alloy rims were used instead of the previous wire spokes. Under the direction of engineer Michael May, the V6 was fitted with Bosch direct fuel injection and the engine developed 200bhp. From the left: Mairesse, chief mechanic Vecchi, engineer Forghieri, engineer May and the driver, Surtees.

Above
Jim Clark takes Colin Chapman on a lap of honour after their victory at the 1963 Italian Grand Prix. Clark won the World Drivers' Championship and Lotus the Manufacturers' Championship.

Above right
Jack Brabham winning the 1963 Solitude Grand Prix at Stuttgart, the first time anyone had won a Formula One race in a car of their own manufacture. The Brabham BT3 Coventry Climax designed by Ron Tauranac used spaceframe construction, which the team persevered with until 1972.

The new V8 ATS Type 100 launched by Carlo Chiti at the end of 1962 did not appear until the Belgian Grand Prix at Spa, where first results were disappointing. The 1494cc (66 x 54.6mm) motor was fed by four twin-choke Weber carburettors but developed only 188bhp at 10,100rpm. After a few races the ATS was withdrawn, having never proved a competitive mount for Phil Hill and Giancarlo Baghetti.

A similar fate befell the tubular-framed Scirocco, which used a BRM motor and Colotti transmission. Commissioned by the American driver Tony Settember and built in England by Hugh Powell, the Scirocco appeared in several races during the year but was not a great success and ultimately vanished from the tracks also.

At the end of the season Ferrari started testing a new V8 model in preparation for the 1964 racing season, which Surtees would open with victory in the non-championship Syracuse Grand Prix, and end with victory in the World Championship. Based on the car which had appeared at Monza, the Type 158 Aero was fitted with a 1487cc (64 x 57.8mm) V8 engine which, running with Bosch direct fuel-injection, developed 190bhp at 10,700rpm, with superior torque characteristics to those of the Type 156.

Ferrari's No 2 driver for the first races of the 1963 season was the Belgian Willy Mairesse but he suffered severe injuries as the result of an accident on the Nürburgring and was replaced by Lorenzo Bandini. Having been dropped

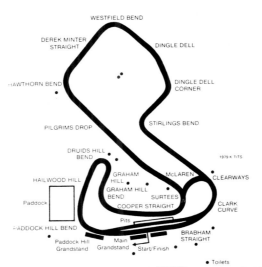

Willy Mairesse

from the Ferrari Grand Prix team at the end of the 1962 season, the Italian had been racing a BRM P56 for the Italian Scuderia Centro Sud in the earlier 1963 World Championship rounds. Mairesse was never brought back onto the Formula One team, competing only in long-distance races after his convalescence.

The Brabham-Climax BT3 had its first Formula One victory at the Solitude race at the edge of the city of Stuttgart, which was the first time any such event had been won by a driver/constructor. The team also recorded excellent results in World Championship events, Dan Gurney taking second place in both Holland and South Africa and Brabham himself repeating the effort in Mexico.

Brands Hatch near London has one of the most picturesque settings of any Grand Prix circuit, affording spectators a view of much of the 4.265km from hilly parkland. The British Grand Prix was first held there in 1964, and thereafter alternated with Silverstone for more than 20 years.

WESTFIELD BEND
DEREK MINTER STRAIGHT
DINGLE DELL
HAWTHORN BEND
DINGLE DELL CORNER
PILGRIMS DROP
STIRLINGS BEND
DRUIDS HILL BEND
1979 K TITS
HAILWOOD HILL
GRAHAM HILL
GRAHAM HILL BEND
McLAREN
CLEARWAYS
Paddock
SURTEES
COOPER STRAIGHT
CLARK CURVE
PADDOCK HILL BEND
Pits
BRABHAM STRAIGHT
Paddock Hill Grandstand
Main Grandstand
Start/Finish
• Toilets

There have been very few occasions in which a World Drivers' Championship favoured one particular driver as clearly as in the 1963 series. Jim Clark and the Lotus-Climax 25 were always one step ahead of their rivals.

And on top of the Clark/Lotus domination of Formula One racing they very nearly won the Indianapolis 500 as well. For the American race a Formula One chassis was modified to take an engine supplied by Ford. The American motor giant had decided to take a prominent part in racing, though whether this was done to collect technical know-how and experience or purely for monetary gain and publicity is open to interpretation. A pushrod V8 Ford Fairlane production engine was modified to produce some 370bhp at 7000rpm, but in spite of its power deficiency the Lotus, fitted with a four-speed Colotti gearbox, was far and away the lightest car on the circuit. The suspension arms on the right-hand side of the car were longer than those on the left in order to provide better weight distribution in the four left-hand bends of the Indianapolis circuit. Alongside the ultra-narrow low-slung

Right
ATS (Automobili Turisimo e Sport) was founded in Bologna by a group of disenchanted Ferrari personnel in the spring of 1962. The chief engineer was Carlo Chiti (in the middle of picture) who designed the new Formula One car with its own V8 engine. The ATS made its debut at the Belgian Grand Prix (picture) but was withdrawn at the end of the season. Phil Hill and Giancarlo Baghetti, both of whom had previously driven for Ferrari, were the drivers.

Below
Graham Hill in a BRM P56 leads Jim Clark's Lotus 25 and Richie Ginther's BRM in the Monaco Grand Prix, which Hill won. Note the slimmer body of the Lotus.

Right
Graham Hill and BRM with the victory laurels at Monaco in 1963. The Englishman won this race again in 1964, 1965, 1968 and 1969.

Parnelli Jones

Lotus 29, the traditional American cars, with their front-mounted Offenhauser engines, looked like dinosaurs.

In the race Clark and the Lotus took second place, 34 seconds behind Parnelli Jones. Jones's "Offy" Roadster lost oil on the last lap and should have been disqualified, but the officials closed their eyes to the breach. The Lotus 29's appearance at Indianapolis revolutionised American ideas of chassis design and more modern designs immediately started appearing in the New World.

Another vehicle that raised eyebrows at the 1963 Indianapolis 500 was the car built by American dragster and speed-record man Mickey Thompson. Powered by a fuel-injected Chevrolet engine mounted in the rear, the car had a most unusual appearance because of the very flat shape of its body and its 12-inch wide racing tyres, which Thompson had had specially manufactured by Firestone. This vehicle ushered in a new era in racing technology, which very soon spread to Europe.

At the end of the season, Jim Clark, the farmer's son from the Scottish borders, had accumulated 54 points towards his World Championship, BRM drivers Graham Hill and Richie Ginther each having 29 and John Surtees of Ferrari 22. The World Manufacturers' Championship went to Lotus followed by BRM, Brabham and Ferrari.

Joseph Siffert and his private team had survived their first Formula One season. He had driven a spaceframe Lotus 24 fitted with a BRM V8 motor and during the year took sixth place at the ACF Grand Prix at Rheims, for the first World Drivers' Championship point of his career. And in the Syracuse Grand Prix in Sicily the promising Swiss driver celebrated his first Formula One victory. At the end of the season Siffert was awarded the Von Trips Memorial Trophy for the most successful private competitor of 1963; this award was made by the Grand Prix Drivers' Association, whose president was Rob Walker's T60 Cooper-Climax driver Joakim Bonnier.

Close Decision in Mexico 1964

Three drivers are in line for the World Championship going into the last event. John Surtees wins the title. Jackie Stewart, a new ace, makes a name for himself in Formula Three racing.

The 1964 World Championship was an exciting one, with no fewer than four makes — Lotus, Ferrari, Brabham and BRM — winning races. The tension reached its height at the Mexican Grand Prix, final round in the Championship, when three drivers from three different teams all had a chance of winning the title. The outcome was in the balance till three laps from the end, but John Surtees in a Ferrari Type 158 Aero V8 took second place in the race — and first in the Championship.

This year, for the first time, there was competition from Asia when Honda, the world's largest motorcycle producers, made their Formula One debut on the Nürburgring.

Modifications had been made to existing motors over the winter to improve performance: BRM's V8 produced 208bhp at 11,000rpm in 1964, the Mark 2A Coventry Climax 204bhp at 9600rpm, the Ferrari 156 200bhp at 10,200rpm and the new Ferrari 158 210bhp at 11,000rpm. (Another new Ferrari, with 12-cylinder Boxer engine, appeared at the end of the season.) The Brabham Racing Organisation used German Mahle pistons in their Coventry Climax motors this year and these proved to be better than the original ones: before long most of the other users of Climax engines had also changed over to Mahle pistons. The performance per litre was now between 133 and 140bhp and the dry weight of the 1964 Formula One cars between 450kg and 470kg, which put the average power-to-weight ratio between 445 and 455bhp/tonne. As far as chassis of the main contenders were concerned, Lotus, BRM and Ferrari all now used monocoque or semi-monocoque construction, only Brabham remaining faithful to the tried and proved tubular spaceframe design.

Ferrari engines seemed to be the most reliable on the tracks, the British engines tending to be more prey to mechanical defects. A trend to 13-inch wheels with wider rims was noticeable, and for the first time in some years there was competition among tyre manufacturers, Dunlop being joined by the American firm, Goodyear. The Cooper's shine had faded a little by now. In addition to Bruce McLaren, Phil Hill also drove one of the Surbiton products this year, but the former champion seemed to be losing his touch. The best drivers of this period were Jim Clark, Dan Gurney, John Surtees and Graham Hill, and there was very little to chose between any of the four whenever they met.

Graham Hill celebrated his second Monaco Grand Prix win, the Monte Carlo circuit seeming to be especially well-suited to him. He was at the wheel of the new BRM Type P261 which had a full monocoque chassis without any tubular steel subframes, and with the rear coil springs once more located outboard. Jim Clark in the latest derivative of the Lotus 25, called the 33, won the Dutch, Belgian and British Grands Prix, the last-named race being held for the first time at Brands Hatch this year. Dan Gurney took first place in the ACF Grand Prix at Rouen in a Brabham-Climax BT7 (the first Brabham victory in a World Championship event) and also won the last race of the series, the Mexican Grand Prix. Graham Hill meanwhile had his second major win of the year in the United States Grand Prix at Watkins Glen.

Ferrari had embarked on an intensive

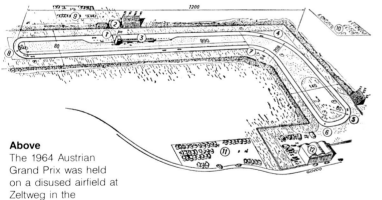

Above
The 1964 Austrian Grand Prix was held on a disused airfield at Zeltweg in the Steiermark. The L-shaped 3.2km circuit was badly prepared and its very bumpy surface caused most of the field to retire.

Above right
Ferrari driver John Surtees, World Champion in 1964, fetches a jack from the Zeltweg pits in the forlorn hope of repairing his car, which has broken suspension.

John Surtees

Left
The Ferrari team, led by engineer Forghieri, cheer John Surtees over the line as he wins the 1963 World Championship in Mexico.

programme of long-distance sportscar racing in the first half of the season, and had been unable to devote itself fully to sorting out the new Aero V8 Grand Prix car, but once priorities were reordered John Surtees won both the German and Italian Grands Prix.

Between these races Lorenzo Bandini had taken a surprise victory with an older V6 Ferrari in the Austrian Grand Prix, a World Championship round for the first time this year, but held on the airfield at Zeltweg rather than at the Autodrome which was built later. The original L-shaped Zeltweg circuit was concrete-surfaced and known as a chassis-killer, and most of the leading competitors were forced out of the race with either chassis or suspension breakages.

Making his World Championship debut in this race with a Brabham-Climax was a talented youngster from Graz, Jochen Rindt, who had been achieving remarkable results in Formula Two races (for cars under 1000cc). Although born in Germany, Rindt had grown up in Graz, and drove under an Austrian licence.

Another dramatic race this year was the Belgian Grand Prix at Spa, in which several of the top drivers ran out of fuel in the closing stages. Dan Gurney was leading in a Brabham-Climax on the 30th lap when he started to run low on petrol.

He stopped at the pits to refuel but when no petrol was found to be immediately available he kept going in the hope of finishing. He ran out on the last lap.

Graham Hill in a BRM had taken the lead when Gurney pitted, but the unfortunate Englishman also came to a halt on the last lap, due in this case to a fault in the pump for the reserve tank. Jim Clark in a Lotus had had to stop earlier in the race to top up his radiator with water, and he, too, ran out of fuel on the last lap. He coasted over the line, not knowing he had in fact won the race. John Surtees had abandoned the race a few laps earlier due to mechanical failures in his Ferrari.

An interesting new design appeared during practice for the British Grand Prix at Brands Hatch. This was the BRM Type P67, built by the Owen Organisation as a research project for the 1966 Formula One and incorporating Ferguson four-wheel drive. The V8 motor was mounted in a tubular frame behind the cockpit, with the fuel tanks located along the sides. Power was transmitted through a six-speed gearbox located on the driver's left and level with his seat. The four-wheel-drive P67 was never in fact raced in a Grand Prix but was later used for mountain races in Switzerland.

Honda had been successful in motorcycle racing for some years and had made a tentative foray into four-wheeled sport with their own little production sportscars, also supplying engines for Formula Two. Their RA271 Formula One car, unveiled at the German Grand Prix at the Nürburgring, showed that the Japanese designers had come up with an unusual theory for mounting the V12 engine, placing it transversely across the back of the chassis, as had already been tried on the last Grand Prix Bugatti in 1956. The central part of the chassis was of monocoque construction, with a tubular steel subframe carrying the motor and providing a solid base for the suspension.

The 1498cc (58.1 x 47mm) V12 four-camshaft Honda motor was fitted with six twin-choke Japanese Keihin carburettors. It was claimed that the engine developed 200bhp at 10,500rpm on its six carburettors, but that increased to 206bhp at 10,800rpm by Monza, when the V12 used an indirect fuel-injection system designed by Keihin in collaboration with the Honda company. It was said that this engine had produced 230bhp at 13,000rpm for a short period of time on the test-bench. Unfortunately the Honda engineers, under the management of Yoshio Nakamura, had not been able to devise a chassis to match the engine's performance. The Japanese car was raced in

Just before the start of the 1964 United States Grand Prix at Watkins Glen. On the right, Clark has his Lotus in pole position, with Surtees (Ferrari No. 7) alongside and, on the second row, Gurney (Brabham No. 6) and Graham Hill (BRM No. 3). The Ferrari is entered by the North American Racing Team rather than the works, and sprayed in the US racing colours of blue and white, as the Italian team was in the midst of a row with the Italian racing authorities.

Right
John Surtees in the Ferrari 158 "Aero" in which he took the 1964 World Championship. The chassis consisted of an alloy skin riveted to a thin tubular framework, and the V6 engine had been replaced by a V8 (though the second Ferrari, driven by Bandini, was a V6). Both cars were fitted with direct Bosch injection.

Right
Californian Ronnie Bucknum tests the Honda RA271 at Zandvoort prior to its debut in the German Grand Prix. The Honda's V12 motor, which developed 215bhp at 11,000rpm, was mounted transversely across the chassis.

Europe by an unknown Californian, Ronnie Bucknum.

A similar car to the Honda RA271 in concept, with a transverse V12 engine, had been devised in Modena between 1961 and 1963 by Maserati's chief designer, Giulio Alfieri. The existence of the 55.2 x 52mm (1493cc) engine was first made public in 1964, but unfortunately Maserati's policy of no racing meant neither the car nor the engine ever saw the light of day.

Ferrari's 12-cylinder Boxer, the Type 512, was first seen in practice for the Italian Grand Prix. The car was of semi-monocoque construction and incorporated a number of features carried over from the 158 Aero. The 1489cc (56 x 50.4mm) motor, unlike the V6 and V8, was not fitted with Bosch direct fuel-injection, as the German company had not designed a system for 12-cylinder motors, but instead used a Lucas low-pressure system. Bosch did develop a direct-injection system for engines larger than eight-cylinder in 1965, but by then Ferrari was no longer interested. During testing the Type 512 engine produced an output figure of 220bhp at 12,000rpm.

Ronnie Bucknum

The car was raced by Lorenzo Bandini in the United States and Mexican Grands Prix at the end of the season.

Joseph Siffert, who had taken fourth place in the German Grand Prix at the Nürburgring, came to an arrangement to run his Brabham-BRM BT11 as part of the British Rob Walker team from the American Grand Prix at Watkins Glen. Swedish driver Joakim Bonnier, who at the time lived in Switzerland, had arranged for Siffert to drive for Rob Walker, an arrangement which proved to be of benefit to all parties concerned. Siffert was third at Watkins Glen.

Lorenzo Bandini

Going into the last round of the World Drivers' Championship in Mexico Graham Hill led the table with 39 points, John Surtees had 34 and Jim Clark 30, and any of the three could still win the title. Hill was the first contender to drop out when, in the second half of the race, his front wheels received a nudge from Bandini's 12-cylinder Ferrari in a sharp bend, and sent the Englishman's BRM spinning into a trackside fence, which bent his exhaust pipes. He was able to make his way to the pits where the exhaust pipes were cut, but the delay meant that Hill had lost any chance of getting back into the points. Bandini on the other hand was able to continue unabated.

With 60 of the 65 laps run Jim Clark was in the lead and it seemed he would retain the World Championship title. But the last few laps were the most dramatic of the whole Grand Prix, and the result of the race, and of the Championship, were decided — literally — in the last four minutes. Clark's Lotus 33 began to slow, imperceptibly at first but then more dramatically, and on the penultimate lap Dan Gurney in his Brabham-Climax BT7 shot past the Scot and won at the fall of the chequered flag on the 65th lap. The Lotus, with no oil left in its engine, finally crept over the line in fifth place. Clark had lost the Championship under very similar conditions in South Africa in 1962 when a loose bolt and subsequent oil leak cost him both the race and the World Championship title to Graham Hill. Surtees in the Ferrari Aero V8 finished second in Mexico and became World

Champion with a score of 40 points, one more than Hill, and Clark had to be content with third place. The Manufacturers' Championship went to Ferrari.

Joseph Siffert had started to earn a name for himself and in August took his private Brabham-BRM BT7 to victory in the nail-biting Mediterranean Grand Prix on the fast Enna-Pergusa track circuit in Sicily. From the start Siffert fought a bitter wheel-to-wheel battle with Jim Clark in a Lotus-Climax 33 and Innes Ireland in a BRP-BRM, and at the end of the race crossed the finishing line 0.1 second ahead of World Champion Clark with Innes Ireland coming through 0.7

Right
Graham Hill won the Monaco Grand Prix for the second time in succession in 1964, with a monocoque V8 BRM P261, the most successful of all BRM designs. Hill only narrowly missed the World Championship title.

Below
The BT7 Brabham-Climaxes of Jack Brabham and Dan Gurney lead Graham Hill's BRM P261 in the 1964 Monaco Grand Prix.

second later. The Swiss driver's defeat of Jim Clark was a sensation, for Siffert, a private competitor, had beaten the world's best driver. Siffert would have a repeat victory in a Brabham-BRM in this race the following year, when he once again beat Clark in a Lotus, this time by 0.3 second.

Lotus and Ford made a second attempt on the Indianapolis 500 in 1964. For this year's race Ford in Detroit had developed a new high-performance version of the 4186cc (95.2 x 72.9mm) motor, with four overhead camshafts and Hilborn fuel-injection, and this developed 424bhp at 8500rpm. Jim Clark in the Lotus-Ford,

again with asymmetric suspension, was fastest in qualifying and took the lead during the actual race, only to be forced to quit after 46 laps due to a suspension breakage. Three cars with supercharged Novi motors developing 700bhp started the race, but none finished. Winner was A J Foyt in his old-fashioned roadster with front-mounted Offenhauser motor. But, as a sign of the times, 12 of the 33 cars which started the race this year were mid-engined, and seven of those were Ford-powered.

The Ford company had now given a full commitment to motor racing, and in addition to the Indianapolis programme this year had begun to campaign the promising GT40 prototype in long-distance sportscar races. Most of the first year's outings were marred by teething troubles but they laid the groundwork for the Ford successes in the classic endurance races between 1966 and 1969.

Making a name for himself in the Formula Three category, which had replaced Formula Junior this year, was a talented 25-year-old Scotsman by the name of Jackie Stewart. A champion clay-pigeon shot, Stewart was a member of Ken Tyrrell's racing team and drove a Cooper-BMC in Formula Three, which was for modified production engines under 1000cc. After winning race after race in 1964 he was invited to join the BRM Grand Prix team for 1965.

The last year of the 1500cc formula singles out one driver in particular in a way that rarely happens. Jim Clark wins six Grands Prix and also the Indianapolis 500.

Left

Jim Clark dominated the racing scene in 1965, just as he had in 1963. This year's Lotus, the 33, was fitted with a 32-valve Climax V8 engine, and is shown here giving team-mate Mike Spence a lift back to the pits during practice at Clermont-Ferrand. Clark also won the 1963 Indianapolis 500 in a Lotus-Ford V8.

The 8.055km circuit around the Puy de Charade (an extinct volcano) near Clermont-Ferrand was opened in 1958, and used for the 1965 ACF Grand Prix. The undulating Charade track with its 51 bends also hosted the ACF Grand Prix in 1969, 1970 and 1972.

The last World Championship run under the 1.5-litre formula in 1965 was a repetition of 1963, with Jim Clark in the Lotus-Climax 33 absolutely dominating the racing scene. The Scot won six out of the ten 1965 races, the South African, Belgian, ACF, British, Dutch and German Grands Prix. Whenever he started he usually finished in first place, except when he was foiled by mechanical troubles, and won his second World Championship. Also for the second time, Lotus won the Formula One Manufacturers' Championship.

Clark did not start the Monaco Grand Prix, preferring to contest the Indianapolis 500 which took place at about the same time. This time Clark, Lotus and Ford worked together perfectly and won the big American race, Clark becoming the first European in almost five decades to win this most important of American races. The triumph of Lotus and Ford was completed by the American driver Parnelli Jones, who finished second in a similar car. This year's Lotus was the monocoque Type 38 with asymmetric suspension and the Ford V8 motor fitted with a Hilborn fuel-injection system. The four-camshaft Ford engine now developed 495bhp at 8800rpm and was superior to the four-cylinder Offenhauser which had a maximum output of 450bhp at 7200rpm. 1965 was not only the first victory for Lotus and Ford at Indianapolis, but also the track's first victory by a mid-engined car. With this race the age of the front-engined American Roadster finally came to an end.

Graham Hill in a BRM won the Monaco Grand Prix for the third time in succession; at the end of the season he also won the United States Grand Prix.

The American Richie Ginther, Hill's BRM team-mate for the past three years, went to Honda to drive the new RA272 alongside fellow countryman Ronnie Bucknum. Grand Prix newcomer Jackie Stewart won the Italian Grand Prix for BRM in September, in his first Formula One season. He shadowed his team-mate Graham Hill until the more experienced man was delayed at the exit of the Parabolica Curve on the second-to-last lap. Jackie Stewart was the rising star on the racing tracks and everybody predicted that he would have a great career. By the end of the year most observers considered the very talented Scot to be already in the same class as Jim Clark, Dan Gurney, Graham Hill and John Surtees.

The last World Championship race of the 1.5-litre formula was held on October 3rd 1965 on the Autodrome Magdalena Mixhuca in Mexico City. Run at an altitude of 2300 metres above sea level, the Mexican race is always a nightmare for engineers as it is very difficult to tune the engines to run properly in the thin atmosphere. Jim Clark had to quit after a few laps due to an engine defect, which left the 12-cylinder Honda 272 driven by Richie Ginther in the lead. Honda had a good day. While most of the opposition fell by the wayside, the white Japanese car with its east-west motor ran like a charm. The result meant a number of firsts. It was Honda's first win in a Formula One race. It was also Ginther's first (and only) Grand Prix victory. And the Mexican race was the first Grand Prix success for the American Goodyear tyres.

With a new Grand Prix formula, which would allow engines up to 3000cc, due to come into force in 1966, there was little in the way of major technical development in 1965, apart from wider racing tyres and a new version of the V8 Coventry Climax motor with two inlet valves and two exhaust valves per cylinder. Cars of the year were again the Lotus-Climax and the well-engineered BRM, but Ferrari, whose V8 had been in the same class the previous year, lost ground with the newer 12-cylinder car. On top of that, team leader John Surtees suffered serious injuries in an accident in Canada in September, when the Lola-Chevrolet T70 he was driving in a Can-Am sportscar race crashed. His injuries were such that he had to miss the last two Formula One races of the season, at Watkins Glen and Mexico City, where his place on the Ferrari team was taken by the Mexican Pedro Rodriguez. The Brabham-Climax BT11 was very fast but prone to engine failures which earned it the reputation of being unreliable, but Dan Gurney was nevertheless able to come fourth in the World Championship.

Lotus and Brabham each obtained a newly-developed, more powerful Coventry Climax motor this year, the 32-valve Type FWHK, on which the camshafts were driven by gears rather than the timing-chain used on the 16-valve engine. The new engine gave better performance than the 16-valve unit but appeared over-developed, and was highly susceptible to breakdown. On more than one occasion Jim Clark had to race with a 16-valve engine after faults had developed with the more powerful version during practice. A case in point was the ACF Grand Prix, held this year on the mountainous Charade circuit at Clermont-Ferrand, when Clark won with a 16-valve engine. Dan Gurney and Jack Brabham took turns at running the new engine in their cars.

The following power-output figures were recorded in the last year of the 1.5-litre formula: 32-valve Coventry Climax FWHK, 213 bhp at 10,800rpm; 16-valve Coventry Climax Mark 3, 205bhp at 10,000rpm; BRM Type 56 V8, 222bhp at 11,700rpm; Ferrari Type 158 V8 210bhp at 12,000rpm; V12 Honda RA272 220bhp at 12,000rpm. Ferrari did not fare well in 1965 in spite of the power of their V8 Type 158 and 12-cylinder 512 motors, and neither John Surtees nor Lorenzo Bandini was able to win a World Championship race. While Coventry Climax had increased power outlet between 1961 and 1965 from 155bhp (for the four-cylinder engine) to 220bhp, the increase at Ferrari had been much less, the V6 having produced 190bhp in 1961.

In the same period per-litre output had increased from 103/117 to 136/147bhp, while the power-to-weight ratios of Grand Prix cars at the end of the 1.5-litre formula was between 455 and 485bhp/tonne.

At the end of 1965 Coventry Climax withdrew from Grand Prix racing, having won 34 World Championship Grands Prix between 1958 and 1965, first with the 2.5-litre four-cylinder engine between 1958 and 1960, then with the four-cylinder 1.5-litre model in 1961, and finally with the 1.5-litre V8. During their last year Coventry Climax had been developing a compact new 16-cylinder Boxer engine, the Type FWMV. This complex 54.1 x 40.64mm (1495cc) unit required no fewer than eight camshafts (four to each bank of cylinders), which were driven by a central gear-train, and

Right
Between 1962 and 1965 Jim Clark won no fewer than 19 World Championship Grands Prix in Lotus cars. He is seen here in a Lotus 33 after winning the 1965 British Grand Prix at Silverstone.

Below
The start of the 1965 Belgian Grand Prix on a wet Spa-Francorchamps track. The BRMs of Jackie Stewart (left) and Graham Hill sandwich Jim Clark's Lotus on the front row.

Above
The spectacular 16-cylinder Coventry Climax engine, built for the 1.5-litre formula as a successor to the 32-valve V8. Bore and stroke of the H16 were 54.1mm and 40.6mm, capacity 1494cc.

had a similar Bosch fuel-injection system to that used on the successful V8. This 16-cylinder engine produced 220bhp at between 11,000 and 12,000rpm in bench tests, but although both Brabham and Lotus designed and built new models in

Richie Ginther

Below
Honda competed in Formula One for the first time in 1964, in the 1.5-litre formula. Richie Ginther won the last race of this formula, the 1965 Mexican Grand Prix, in a Honda RA272 with east-west V12 engine.

Bottom
Graham Hill, in a BRM P261, in the last race of the 1.5-litre formula (1965).

readiness for the exciting new engine, it was never actually seen in a race. Jim Clark's continued domination with the eight-cylinder engines, and the fact that 1966 was the year of a new formula, made Coventry Climax decide not to proceed with the complicated 16.

Cooper still won some good places but the Surbiton firm was no longer able to match the successes of earlier years, in spite of the skills of John Cooper's two drivers, the long-experienced Bruce McLaren and Grand Prix newcomer Jochen Rindt. Bruce McLaren was making his own way and had already opened a small factory, Bruce McLaren Motor Racing Ltd, at Colnbrook near London's Heathrow airport, to build racing cars.

The principal technological advance of the 1.5-litre formula had come from refining the mid-engined concept: new theories of weight distribution, aerodynamics and suspension geometry were all progressively applied between 1961 and 1965. The monocoque chassis, revived by Colin Chapman for his Lotus 25 in 1962, totally revolutionised chassis construction. The principle, which originated in the aircraft industry, was copied over the years by all racing car manufacturers. British chassis and suspension design consequently influenced Continental designs and led to a degree of technical uniformity, where all racing cars looked more or less the same. The principal area of differentiation was in the number of cylinders and the engine configuration.

Concurrent with this was a new era of specialisation, for whereas Grand Prix constructors had until now built complete cars, including chassis, engine and transmission, they now bought finished components for incorporating into their own designs. At the end of the fifties Cooper and Lotus had led the British trend in this direction. The initiating company bought in proprietary motors and transmissions and fitted them to their own chassis.

The small-engined 1.5-litre formula had been introduced to reduce speeds in the interests of safety, but the history of Grand Prix racing shows that, whenever engine sizes are reduced for safety reasons, the reduced speeds are quickly offset by technical innovations in other areas, so that the previous limits set are equalled and often surpassed. In a sense, the modern racing car had become dangerous because its excellent roadholding demanded tremendous driving skill. The manoeuvrability which

characterised the old front-engined cars had vanished.

Jim Clark won his second World Drivers' Championship with a score of 54 points, ahead of Graham Hill with 40 and Jackie Stewart with 33. During the period of the 1.5-litre formula, 1961 to 1965, Clark had taken part in 47 World Championship events in Lotus 25 and 33 cars, and won 19 Grand Prix races. In the same period Graham Hill had won ten races in BRMs, while John Surtees in Ferraris and Dan Gurney in Porsche and Brabham had won three races each. Two-time winners were Stirling Moss in Lotus cars and Ferrari drivers Wolfgang von Trips and Phil Hill, and single victories had fallen to Bruce McLaren in a Cooper, Innes Ireland in a Lotus, Giancarlo Baghetti and Lorenzo Bandini in Ferraris, Jackie Stewart in a BRM and Richie Ginther in a Honda. As far as the constructors were concerned, 22 of the 47 races had fallen to Lotus, 11 to BRM, nine to Ferrari, two to Brabham and one

Double World
Champion Jim Clark
with Lotus designer
Colin Chapman in the
Steering Wheel Club in
London. At that time
Lotus were successful
in many different
racing classes.

Formula One cars of the 1.5-litre formula era 1961 to 1965

Year	Make & model	Cylinders	Capacity	Bore	Stroke	bhp	rpm	Camshafts	Induction	Gears	Chassis	Dry weight
1961	BRM P56	8	1498	68,5	50,8	185	10 000	4	I	6	T	460
1961	BRM-Climax	4	1496	81,8	71,1	155	7 500	2	C	5	T	470
1961	Cooper T55-Climax	4	1496	81,8	71,1	155	7 500	2	C	5	T	465
1961	Cooper T58-Climax	8	1496	62,9	57,4	183	8 500	4	C	6	T	465
1961	Cooper-Maserati	4	1484	81	72	165	8 500	2	C	5	T	460
1961	De Tomaso-Osca	4	1492	78	78	158	7 500	2	C	5	T	445
1961	Ferguson P99-Climax	4	1496	81,8	71,1	155	7 500	2	C	5	T	480
1961	Ferrari 156 65°	6	1481	73	59	180	9 000	4	C	5	T	460
1961	Ferrari 156 65°	6	1480	67	70	185	9 500	4	C	5	T	460
1961	Ferrari 156 65°	6	1496	81	48,2	190	10 500	4	C	5	T	460
1961	Ferrari 156 120°	6	1476	73	58,8	190	9 500	4	C	5	T	460
1961	Lotus 21-Climax	4	1496	81,8	71,1	155	7 500	2	C	5	T	455
1961	Porsche 718	4	1498	85	66	165	8 500	4	C	5	T	440
1961	Porsche 787	4	1498	85	66	175	9 000	4	I	5	T	440
1962	ATS 100	8	1494	66	54,6	185	9 200	4	C	6	T	460
1962	Brabham BT3-Climax	8	1496	62,9	57,4	190	9 000	4	I	6	T	485
1962	BRM P56	8	1498	68,5	50,8	192	10 000	4	I	6	T	450
1962	De Tomaso-Boxer	8	1488	68	51	180	9 800	4	C	5	T	459
1962	Ferrari 156 65°	6	1480	67	70	190	9 400	4	C	6	T	470
1962	Ferrari 156 120°	6	1476	73	58,8	200	10 000	4	C	6	T	490
1962	Gilby-BRM	8	1498	68,5	50,8	185	10 000	4	C	5	T	470
1962	Lola Mk4-Climax	8	1496	62,9	57,4	190	9 000	4	I	5	T	455
1962	Lotus 25-Climax	8	1496	62,9	57,4	190	9 000	4	I	5	M	450
1962	Porsche 804	8	1494	66	54,6	185	9 200	4	C	6	T	465
1963	ATS 100	8	1494	66	54,6	188	10 100	4	I	6	T	462
1963	Brabham BT7-Climax	8	1495	67,9	51,5	198	9 500	4	I	6	T	475
1963	BRM P61	8	1498	68,5	50,8	205	11 000	4	I	6	M	470
1963	BRP-BRM	8	1498	68,5	50,8	205	11 000	4	I	6	M	465
1963	Cooper T66-Climax	8	1495	67,9	51,5	198	9 500	4	I	6	T	470
1963	Ferrari 156 120° Aero	6	1476	73	58,8	200	10 200	4	I	6	M	460
1963	Ferrari 156 120°	6	1476	73	58,8	200	10 200	4	I	6	T	470
1963	Ferrari 158	8	1489	67	52,8	200	10 500	4	I	6	M	460
1963	Lotus 24-BRM	8	1498	68,5	50,8	205	11 000	4	I	6	T	480
1963	Lotus 33-Climax	8	1492	68,4	50,8	200	9 800	4	I	5	M	455
1963	Scirocco-BRM	8	1498	68,5	50,8	205	11 000	4	I	5	T	475
1964	ATS 100	8	1494	66	54,6	216	10 200	4	I	5	T	460
1964	Brabham BT11-Climax	8	1496	68	51	203	9 800	4	I	6	T	470
1964	BRM P26	8	1498	68,5	50,8	210	11 000	4	I	6	M	465
1964	BRM (4 × 4) P67	8	1498	68,5	50,8	210	11 000	4	I	6	T	525
1964	BRP-BRM	8	1498	68,5	50,8	210	11 000	4	I	6	M	465
1964	Cooper T73-Climax	8	1496	68	51	203	9 800	4	I	6	T	460
1964	Ferrari 158	8	1489	67	52,8	210	10 500	4	I	5	M	460
1964	Ferrari 512	12	1489	56	50,4	220	12 000	4	I	5	M	465
1964	Honda RA271	12	1495	58,1	47	215	11 000	4	I	5	T	520
1964	Lotus 33-Climax	8	1496	68	51	203	9 800	4	I	5	M	455
1964	Maserati 8/F1	12	1493	55,2	52	—	—	4		6	—	—
1965	BRM P261	8	1498	68,5	50,8	222	11 750	4	I	6	M	460
1965	Coventry-Climax FWMW	16	1494	54,1	40,6	225	12 000	4	I	—	—	—
1965	Ferrari 158	8	1489	67	52,8	210	12 000	4	I	5	M	460
1965	Ferrari 512	12	1489	56	50,4	220	12 000	4	I	5	M	465
1965	Honda RA272	12	1495	58,1	47	220	12 000	4	I	6	T	485
1965	Lotus 33-Climax (32-valve)	8	1496	73,3	45,4	213	10 800	4	I	5	M	450

Key: C = carburettors; I = injection; T = tubular; M = monocoque

each to Cooper, Porsche and Honda. It was in this period that Lotus moved into modern new premises at Wymondham in Norfolk. The old Cheshunt facility had become too small, and there was also a need to provide for commercial production, which was growing steadily all the time.

Significant progress had been made in tyre design in these years. In the era of the supercharged car, drivers had to compromise between speed and tyre wear on corners, as bad surfaces or unsympathetic driving methods could cause the tread to part from the casing. Substantial gains had been made in the early 1950s when the lining material was changed from a cotton fibre to nylon yarn, which better withstood the higher temperatures brought about by increased speeds. At the same time both wear and adhesion were constantly improved through the use of synthetic compounds. During the sixties tyres became wider, but the diameter was reduced at the same time, so that the area of contact with the road remained the same as with the narrower, larger diameter tyres. By 1964 13-inch wheel rims were common on Formula One cars, but the contact area of Grand Prix tyres in 1965 was a little more than 200mm, a figure which was considered to provide optimum adhesion on a dry track. Wider tyres would not have been a viable proposition in earlier years, as wear would have increased due to higher roll resistance and the resultant heat build-up. The new nylon casings and special rubber compounds eliminated these drawbacks, and at the same time reduced the weight of the tyres. The days of the ultra-soft "rubber rollers" were however still in the future.

The disadvantages of wider tyres is the reduced pressure on the contact area, especially on wet tracks. In unfavourable conditions the film of water between the contact area of road and tyre cannot be dispersed quickly enough and this leads to aquaplaning. The effect was later minimized through improved tyre tech- nology, by using profile ridges leading towards the outside of the tyres, which facilitated the drainage of the trapped water film. In the years of the 3-litre formula after 1966 tyre technology progressed at a rapid rate as wider tyres, softer compounds and treadless contact areas were introduced. The "tyre war" had begun.

Above
Jackie Stewart leads Graham Hill to a BRM 1, 2 in the 1965 Italian Grand Prix. This was the first of Stewart's 27 World Championship victories.

Following pages
Even on the fast Rheims circuit, the Ferrari of Michael Parkes could only finish second to Jack Brabham's less powerful Repco Brabham in the 1966 French Grand Prix.

225

Jackie Stewart's 2-litre BRM comfortably beat all the new 3-litre cars to win the 1966 Monaco Grand Prix.

228

Return to Power 1966

Most teams are unprepared. Jack Brabham takes out his third World Drivers' Championship with his simple Brabham-Repco. Surtees leaves Ferrari in the middle of the season.

The end of the 1.5-litre formula was greeted by enthusiasm in all quarters. The theory that cars with smaller engines were safer had not been proven: in emergency situations, a car with a reserve of power has a higher safety margin. Cars with much more powerful engines had been used in the USAC formula (Indianapolis etc) in the United States and in international endurance racing, with no corresponding increase in the number or severity of accidents. By increasing the Formula One limit to three litres the European administrators also hoped to attract American interest, though all indications in the recent history of US racing showed they preferred their own racing formulae, and did not seek any unification with European racing regulations. American adoption of the international formula would have meant greatly increased competition in US racing from technically skilled foreign manufacturers, and the home side would have lost a lot of prize money to European teams. This in fact occurred with the Cam-Am series of sportscar races in the United States and Canada, where for years great sums were taken to Europe.

The first steps towards a free exchange of ideas were taken by the president of the International Sports Commission, Maurice Baumgartner, in 1963, when he began collecting ideas and opinions about the introduction of the new Grand Prix formula for 1966.

Comments were invited from participating nations and also from other interested parties such as oil and tyre companies, drivers and the specialist press. These were discussed at a meeting in Monte Carlo two days before the Monaco Grand Prix. This meeting showed however that there was little common ground among the various groups, and a great divergence in viewpoints. The principal suggestions were as follows:

The Italian delegation: no limitation of engine capacity or type of motor, but only commercially available 100-octane fuels to be used, with weight between 550 and 600kg, minimum rulings for cockpit measurements, and a minimum race distance for World Championship qualifying events of 600km.

The British delegation: retention of the present Formula One, as high development costs would make the change to another formula too expensive, and the performance of the existing Formula One motors would not peak until 1966 anyway: inclusion of rotary engines.

The German delegation expressed very similar thoughts to the British but preferred an increase in engine capacity to two litres.

The US delegation (represented by Colin Chapman on the advice of American engineers): engine capacity three litres or more.

Grand Prix drivers: increase of engine capacity to two litres, to provide a distinct differentiation between Formula One and Formula Two and to attract further participation in racing.

Oils and tyre companies: agreement with British suggestions, but sought a general cost reduction.

The press: unrestricted formula (though opinions differed as to whether there should not be limitations on weight or fuel use) but with regulations defining cockpit measurements and increased safety measures (eg, reinforced cockpits).

The Formula One drivers made a further presentation to the International Commission after a meeting held prior to the United States Grand Prix at Watkins Glen, chaired by Joakim Bonnier, president of the Grand Prix Drivers Association (GPDA). The new suggestion was for a maximum engine limit of three litres, and a minimum weight of 525kg. While the drivers had expressed support

Joakim Bonnier

for a 2-litre formula at Monaco, they now preferred the higher limit, as discussions with designers had revealed that research and development costs for a 3-litre engine were no greater than those for a 2-litre motor.

The Grand Prix formula for the future was finally specified by the CSI at the end of November, 1963. The rules were: (a) conventional piston engines, maximum of 3000cc for unsupercharged engines or 1500cc supercharged, running on normally available commercial fuel, with a minimum weight (with oil and water but without fuel) of 500kg; (b) rotary engines of the Wankel type, no size limit specified (though an equivalence formula was to follow), running on normally available commercial fuel; (c) turbine engines: no capacity limit (though again an equivalence formula was later produced), fuel optional. The formula was to remain valid until December 31st 1970.

The position of the British contenders became critical when Coventry Climax announced, in 1964, that they would withdraw from Grand Prix racing at the end of the 1.5-litre formula in 1965. Lotus,

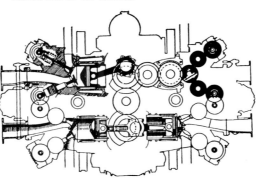

Above
The BRM H16 motor consisted of two flat-eight engines, developed from the V8, bolted together. The complicated 16-cylinder engine had two crankshafts and eight camshafts.

Right
Rear view of the BRM P83 with its H16 engine which, in its first year, developed 400bhp. The four exhaust tailpipes can be seen. The P83 was not a successful design.

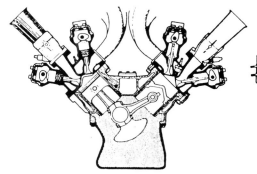

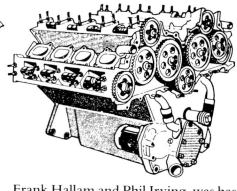

Brabham and Cooper were suddenly left without a source of engines, and they applied to the CSI to extend the 1.5-litre formula by a further year. This was followed by a request for a variation to be incorporated in the formula to allow production-based engines with larger capacities than 3000cc. As so often happens however, these requests were seen not as representing any technical value, but merely as personally-motivated ways of effecting change, and the CSI did not allow any changes to the formula it had already laid down.

Although the 3-litre formula had been announced nearly two and a half years before, the acute engine shortage meant that the only manufacturers ready for its inception on January 1st 1966 were Ferrari, Brabham and Cooper. Lotus and BRM, with no 3-litre engines yet available, bored out their 1.5-litre engines, Coventry Climax and BRM respectively, to two litres. Later in the year McLaren modified the Indianapolis Ford V8 motor, reducing it to three litres, and at the end

of the season Honda appeared with a new 12-cylinder engine. The new American firm Eagle, founded in California by Dan Gurney and Carroll Shelby, chose the old 2.7-litre four-cylinder Coventry Climax as an interim unit until their new Weslake V12 engine was ready.

For the first race Ferrari used a two-valve 3-litre Type 312 and a 2.4-litre V6 in a 1.5-litre 12-cylinder Type 512 chassis. Four Continents were represented in the new formula: Europe with Lotus, Cooper, BRM and Ferrari; America with the Eagle (built in Britain); Asia with Honda and Australia with the Repco-Brabham (built in Britain with Australian motors). In addition the Anglo-American McLaren-Ford was built by the New Zealander Bruce McLaren. There had never before been greater international participation in Grand Prix racing.

Ferrari was better prepared for the new formula than any other contender and was the logical bet for success in its first year. The Italian company had 20 years' experience with 12-cylinder engines and had gained an excellent reputation for robustness and reliability. The new Maranello contender was a 60° 2989cc (77 x 53.5mm) V12 with four camshafts and Lucas fuel-injection, which developed 360bhp at 9800rpm. It had the classic Ferrari chassis, a small-diameter tubular frame reinforced inside and out with riveted sheetmetal.

Brabham's spaceframe Type BT19 closely resembled the previous year's Formula One model, and used a five-speed Hewland gearbox. Like all Brabham cars at this time it was designed by Brabham and his friend Ron Tauranac — hence the BT prefix which is still used on Brabham cars today. The Australian Repco V8 motor however was completely new. In February 1964 Jack Brabham had approached Repco, a car-parts manufacturer based in Melbourne, and they had agreed to build a Formula One engine. The whole programme was a fairly simple and cost-effective exercise with no expensive research and development. The Type 620 V8 motor, built under the direction of chief engineer

Frank Hallam and Phil Irving, was based on the aluminium engine block of an Oldsmobile F85, but carefully rebuilt with new cylinder heads which had an overhead camshaft positioned over each row of cylinders. The 2996cc (86 x 66mm) engine was fitted with Lucas fuel-injection and produced 308bhp at 8500rpm. This made it the least powerful of the 1966 Formula One engines, but its reliability and consistency enabled Jack Brabham to win his third World Championship with it. New Zealander Denis Hulme, a newcomer to Grand Prix racing and Brabham's No 2 for 1966, had to use the old 2.5-litre Climax four for the first events.

John Cooper

Tim Parnell

John Cooper produced the new Formula One Type T81 with a sturdy monocoque chassis and a 2989cc (70.4 x 64mm) Maserati motor which, fitted with Lucus fuel-injection, developed 340bhp at 9000rpm. ZF transmission was used. A shorter-stroke (75.2 x 56mm, 2984cc) engine was used later and this produced an extra 20bhp at 9200rpm. The V12 Maserati with its two valves per cylinder was not a new design, having been used in 1957, albeit without success, in the old 2.5-litre Formula One category. Engineer Giulio Alfieri had modified the unit by increasing its capacity to three litres. Maserati motors were used because the small Cooper company had been taken over the previous year by the Chipstead Motors group, which imported Maserati road cars into England. The operation moved from its traditional base at Surbiton to a new factory at Byfleet, and John Cooper was joined on the board by Jonathan Sieff, the principal shareholder of Chipstead Motors. Another Chipstead

Above
Tyres, tyres and more tyres. These items became more important in the mid 'sixties with three companies, Dunlop, Goodyear and Firestone, becoming fierce competitors during the era of the 3-litre formula.

Top right
McLaren initially used a reduced-capacity 4.2-litre Ford 4OHC "Indy" engine in the 3-litre formula, the modification having been carried out under the direction of the German engineer von Rücker.

Giulio Alfieri

director, the former Maserati and Aston Martin driver Roy Salvadori, was appointed manager of the racing team. With this new association Maserati once again, though indirectly, competed in the Formula One class. This was achieved mainly through the personal initiative of Alfieri and some enthusiastic colleagues, for Maserati management kept a low profile in the project.

McLaren was a Formula One newcomer, though the company had worked with Trojan on the production of large-capacity cars for other formulae, notably sportscars. The Formula One prototype, designated the Mk 2A, had been built in 1965, and fitted with a 4.5-litre Oldsmobile V8 motor for testing purposes, primarily on behalf of the Firestone tyre company. The monocoque Mk 2B was designed to take the Indianapolis Ford V8 motor, converted to Formula One specification. In original form, the 4186cc Ford engine had cylinder dimensions of 95.2 x 72.9mm, but under the direction of the German engineer von Rücker, a former BMW and Porsche designer, the stroke was shortened to 52.3mm. This brought the capacity down to 2999cc. The engine had four valves per cylinder and was fitted with Tecalemit fuel injection. In spite of its incredibly noisy exhaust, the engine developed only about 320bhp at 9000rpm, and as this was well below expectation, the project was soon abandoned.

Instead Bruce McLaren turned to a Serenissima V8 motor, originally designed by Massimino for use in a mid-engined sportscar planned by a company founded by Count Giovanni Volpi di Misurata. That enterprise had not been very successful however and had quickly disappeared. The Serenissima motor did not perform for McLaren any more successfully than the Ford had, and for the Mexican race at the end of the season he switched back to the American unit.

Designer of the Formula One McLaren was the Englishman Robin Herd, who in 1969 would become one of the founders of the March enterprise. Herd had been trained in the aircraft industry and had been actively involved in the Anglo-French Concorde project at the Aeronautical Establishment at Farnborough (another experienced member of the McLaren team was Owen Maddock, formerly with Cooper). Herd brought to Colnbrook some very

advanced ideas, and the most interesting design feature of the new Formula One McLaren was its chassis, which consisted of a triple-layered sandwich, two outer alloy skins with a 3mm balsa-wood filling. This laminate, known as Mallite, is used for aircraft cabin floors and interior panelling, and provides a sturdy, safe and stable material.

Bruce McLaren

The most complicated new Grand Prix motor was the BRM H16. Built with the latest technical know-how and with no expense spared, the 16-cylinder engine should have wiped the competition from the tracks. But the motor, which consisted of two combined Boxer units geared together in a common crankcase, was a great disappointment. Responsible for the ingenious concept was Tony Rudd, a Rolls-Royce trained engineer who had joined the Owen Organisation as assistant to Peter Berthon. By coupling two of the 1.5-litre V8 engines from the old Formula One into a new unit, he devised an arrangement which made it possible for many parts from the existing eight-cylinder motors to be used, a saving not only in cost but also in design development. The two banks of each V8 engine were separated and reformed into two horizontally-opposed eights, each of which retained its own crankshaft: one of these new units was placed on top of the other, and the crankshafts geared together, and there was the H16 engine. The crankshaft housing and cylinder blocks were cast in one piece. Bolting the two eight-cylinder Boxer engines

Left
Bandini in a V12 Ferrari 312 in the 1966 ACF Grand Prix.

Below
World Champion once again. Brabham in 1966.

Tony Rudd

together gave a 2998cc (69 .8 x 48.8mm) unit with 32 valves (two per cylinder) driven by eight camshafts. The H16 motor was fitted with Lucas fuel-injection and in 1966 was reported to develop 400bhp at 10,750rpm. Later, in 1968, the engines were fitted with four-valve cylinder-heads (a total of 64 valves and no fewer than 128 springs) and this increased output to 480bhp. But, right from the outset, the BRM H16 engine rarely ran satisfactorily, and continued to cause problems until work on the project finally came to a halt in 1968 in favour of another new BRM engine. The replacement was a V12 which had appeared during the 1967 season and was intended originally for sportscar applications. Like the supercharged V16 which had come into being at the end of the 1940s, the H16 was too complicated and had too many moving parts, which multiplied the potential for faults to occur. The H16 followed its V16 predecessor into oblivion. In 1966, the BRM H16 motor was used to power the new Lotus Type 43 as well as BRM's own Type P83. In both models the motor formed a structural part of the chassis, the monocoque in each design ending behind the cockpit. The motor, coupled to BRM's own six-speed gearbox, carried the suspension direct.

BRM intended to increase the capacity of the H16 and to race it in the Indianapolis 500, but the constant problems with the Formula One unit meant this plan never came to fruition.

With the introduction of the new Grand Prix formula, a third tyre company became involved in Formula One, the American Firestone company joining the two established suppliers, Dunlop and Goodyear. Firestone had opened a European research centre for racing tyres in Britain at Brentford in Middlesex, and this year signed contracts to ensure that Ferrari, Lotus and McLaren used only their tyres. At the same time Goodyear supplied Brabham, Eagle and Honda, leaving Dunlop with only Cooper this year. BRM did not enter into a contract but mainly used either Dunlop or Firestone as the situation arose.

The Grand Prix season opened on May 22nd with the Monaco Grand Prix. The BRM H16 had been completed and tested but BRM works drivers Graham Hill and Jackie Stewart came to the starting line with the old V8 cars bored out to two litres; likewise, in the absence of the H16 Lotus-BRM 43, Jim Clark appeared with a 2-litre Lotus-Climax 33. The new 3-litre Ferrari Type 312 was driven by John Surtees, and Lorenzo Bandini drove the interim model, the 2.4-litre V6 Type 246. Jack Brabham introduced his new 3-litre Repco-Brabham BT19, while his teammate Denis Hulme had the same model but fitted with a 2.5-litre four-cylinder Climax motor. The new T81 Cooper-Maserati V12 was driven for the factory team by Jochen Rindt and Richie Ginther; the American was under contract to Honda but the new Japanese

V12 was not yet ready to race. There were also three private Cooper-Maseratis, entered by the Rob Walker Racing Team (for Joseph Siffert), Joakim Bonnier and French amateur Guy Ligier. Other privately-entered cars included four-cylinder Brabham-Climax, 2-litre BRM V8 and 2-litre Lotus-BRM V8. Only seven of the 16 starters in fact had 3-litre engines.

John Surtees in the V12 Ferrari took the lead but had to quit due to a differential problem. Jackie Stewart in a 2-litre BRM took over and held the position to the end. Only four competitors in this opening race were officially classified: Jackie Stewart in a 2-litre BRM, Lorenzo Bandini in the 2.4-litre Ferrari, Graham Hill in a 2-litre BRM and Bondurant in a similar car; not one 3-litre car crossed the finishing line. There was still a lot of work to be done.

The Belgian Grand Prix on the fast Spa-Francorchamps circuit was won by John Surtees in the V12 Ferrari ahead of the Cooper-Maserati of Jochen Rindt and the Ferrari V6 of Lorenzo Bandini. This was the last Formula One race John Surtees drove for Ferrari as he left the Italian team in the wake of a steadily worsening rift with the management in general and Enzo Ferrari in particular. Both parties, Enzo Ferrari and John Surtees, talked over their grievances in the Ristorante Cavallino opposite the entrance of the Ferrari factory, but after dining together they finally parted. Each

realised the separation would probably cost him the chance of winning the 1966 World Championship, but they parted friends. Enzo Ferrari said goodbye with the words: "Let's think of the proud times of our mutual successes and not of the sad moment of this separation."

Making its debut in the Belgian Grand Prix was the American Eagle, built by the All American Racers organisation founded by Dan Gurney and Carroll Shelby. The monocoque chassis, which gave the body a very elegant shape, was designed by the Englishman Len Terry, a former Lotus team member who would later do design work for BRM, Surtees and Leda. Dan Gurney used a 240bhp 2.5-litre four-cylinder Climax motor at Spa as the new Weslake V12, which was being built for the Eagle at Rye in Sussex, had not been completed. The 12-cylinder engine, designed by Harry Weslake, did not in fact appear until the Monza race at the end of the season.

The Belgian Grand Prix could have ended in catastrophe. A sudden deluge of rain flooded the track on the first lap,

sending cars spinning off the circuit in all directions: only seven cars were still in the race at the end of the second lap. Jackie Stewart crashed and broke his collarbone, but it was amazing under the circumstances that no-one else was hurt. Jim Clark had to abandon the race 1.5km from the start due to mechanical failure.

The Ferraris showed well in the ACF Grand Prix on the fast Rheims track. Lorenzo Bandini, who with the departure of Surtees had been given a V12, took the lead and held it until his accelerator pedal broke. He was able to effect repairs with a piece of wire and rejoined the race, but by then of course he was well out of

Carroll Shelby

contention. Jack Brabham had taken the lead and carried on to win, with his team-mate Denis Hulme taking third place behind the British engineer Mike Parkes, who had replaced John Surtees in the Ferrari team. The new Lotus 43, with the BRM H16 engine, made its first appearance at Rheims, driven by the Englishman Peter Arundell, but unfortunately had to retire with transmission problems. The young New Zealander Chris Amon had a one-off drive in a Cooper-Maserati in this race.

Brabham and Hulme went on to take the first two places in the British Grand Prix at Brands Hatch, where the Ferrari team was not able to participate as there was a metalworkers' strike in Italy at the time, but John Surtees made his debut in a works T81 Cooper-Maserati.

Jim Clark in the 2-litre Lotus-Climax 33 led most of the way in the Dutch Grand Prix at Zandvoort but eventually dropped back to place third at the end. Brabham in his Repco-Brabham was winner once again, with Graham Hill in a 2-litre BRM second.

The German Grand Prix on the Nürburgring provided evidence of the enormous driving skills of Jack Brabham, John Surtees and Jochen Rindt in coping with terrible weather conditions and teeming rain. They crossed the line in that order.

There was plenty of interest at Monza, for Honda started with their V12 RA273,

Michael Parkes

Chris Amon

Dan Gurney introduced his new Weslake V12 engine, designed by the cylinder-head specialist Harry Weslake, the BRM works drivers displayed their H16 cars for the first time and so did Jim Clark, with the Lotus-BRM H16.

A striking feature of the monocoque Honda driven by Richie Ginther was that its V12 engine had the unusual cylinder angle of 90°. The 2991cc (78 x 52.2mm) engine had four camshafts, four valves per cylinder and an indirect fuel-injection system developed by Honda's own engineers. The V12 engine, said to produce 360bhp, was designed by the 25-year-old engineer Irimagiri and coupled to a five-speed Honda gearbox, but the car itself was somewhat heavier than its rivals. Richie Ginther had a slight accident during the race which forced him to abandon the event.

The dark-blue Eagle, with a radiator opening symbolizing the characteristics of the beak of an eagle, suffered from teething troubles, and Gurney was forced to retire after the oil temperature rose. The 2998cc (72.8 x 90.3mm) Harry Weslake engine had four camshafts, four valves per cylinder and Lucas fuel-injection, and initially developed 390bhp at 9500rpm. The V12 Eagle-Weslake performed better in the following season, after a number of changes were made, but the engine was never really trouble-free.

Ferrari had prepared new cylinder heads for the Monza race with three valves per cylinder (two inlet and one exhaust), which increased the performance from 360 to 380bhp at 10,000rpm, and during the race the three 312 Ferraris, driven by Bandini, Scarfiotti and Parkes, fought an exciting slipstreaming battle with Jack Brabham's Repco-Brabham BT19. Brabham had to quit due to oil loss (a screw had not been tightened before the race) and so did Lorenzo Bandini, when a defect developed in his car's ignition system. Enzo Ferrari had expressed the wish before the race that an Italian driver should win if possible and Mike Parkes provided his team-mate Lodovico Scarfiotti, who was leading, all the help he was able to give, by covering his rear. The British driver placed himself right in front of his pursuers in the curves, slowing them down, and trailed in their slipstream on the straights, making it possible for Scarfiotti to increase his lead. The former hillclimb champion won the Italian Grand Prix, ahead of Mike Parkes and Denis Hulme. Neither the BRM H16 nor the Lotus H16 put up a convincing performance.

Jim Clark was a surprise winner of the United States Grand Prix at Watkins Glen, scoring the Maurice Phillippe designed Lotus 43's only victory and also the only win for the complicated BRM H16 engine. The BRM H16s of Hill and Stewart both withdrew from the Watkins

Lodovico Scarfiotti

Glen race, and the following season did nothing to improve the engine's tarnished image. Bandini, who was leading at Watkins Glen in a Ferrari, and Brabham in the Repco-Brabham, both dropped out of the race leaving the T81 Cooper-Maseratis of Jochen Rindt, John Surtees and Joseph Siffert to take the next places.

Ferrari did not compete in Mexico, and John Surtees in his T81 Cooper-Maserati scored a win after a long spell trailing Jack Brabham, who had taken the early lead. Richie Ginther in the Honda RA273 set the fastest lap and finished fourth. Bruce McLaren, after a long absence, rejoined the circus in Mexico with the Indianapolis Ford engine which was however still not a convincing performer and the New Zealander did not use it again.

Jack Brabham was declared World Champion for the third time at the end of the season with 42 points, adding the 1966 title to those he had won in 1959 and 1960. At the time he was 40 years old and many critics considered that too old for competitive driving. They were obviously forgetting that Fangio had become World Champion in 1957 at the age of 46 and Tazio Nuvolari had won Grands Prix in 1938 and 1939 at 46 and 47. Championship runner-up in 1966, having scored 28 points with Ferrari and Cooper-Maserati, was John Surtees, and Cooper-Maserati driver Rindt was third with 22 points.

The Brabham organisation's greatest success of the year however was its winning of the Formula One Manufacturers' Championship, a significant honour for such a fine-tuned team. Out of all the new designs the Repco-Brabham displayed by far the simplest and cheapest solution. The eight-cylinder BT19 was very light (540kg) and reliable, with a simple but effective chassis which provided superb roadholding. The uncomplicated twin-camshaft Repco engine had a very broad power-band which was a considerable advantage in winding, hilly terrain. The car won four of the nine Grands Prix of the year.

Jack Brabham was the first driver in the history of the World Drivers' Championship to win the title in a car of his own manufacture. He did not have an

Jack Brabham

easy life, as in addition to driving in Formula One races, he also managed several other technical enterprises from his little workshop near the Surrey town of Byfleet, a small London suburb close to the abandoned Brooklands circuit which was famous before the war but now had grass and weeds growing on its steeply banked bends. One of the Brabham enterprises produced highly successful Formula Three and sports racing cars for sale to private teams and another sold modified engines for production Vauxhall saloons. He and Ron Tauranac were also involved at first hand in other forms of single-seater racing, notably Formula Two, which was for cars with 1000cc four-cylinder motors. The Brabham cars in this class were fitted with 944cc Honda engines which developed 147bhp at 11,000rpm and which brought him victory after victory. Partly because of the pressure of his various interests, he flew his own twin-engined Beechcraft Queen Air 65 between races.

In spite of Jack Brabham's extraordinary efforts and achievements he never became a popular international racing hero hailed by the international press with the same enthusiasm that, for example, Fangio had been, or Jackie Stewart would be later. He appeared to be the personification of the "English understatement". Of all the Grand Prix drivers of the day he was the man of fewest words: he would say very little after a victory and merely smile when complimented or congratulated. Although Fangio, like Brabham, was a man of few words, he had a charisma and personality which the Australian seemed to lack. Brabham was always sober in habits and never "made a show" like so many of his racing contemporaries.

In theory, the 1966 World Championship should have been won by Ferrari, but the departure of John Surtees from the Maranello stable at a critical time in the development programme spelt an end not only to the Englishman's title hopes, but also to the Italian company's. Other difficulties, such as a strike in the Italian metal industries, also contributed to a lean year.

Amongst the younger drivers, Jochen Rindt displayed convincing evidence of considerable talent. His driving was sometimes rather wild, but at least some of the reason for that was the inferior roadholding of the T81 Cooper-Maserati.

After four successful years between

1962 and 1965, Graham Hill had no Grand Prix wins in 1966: even the Monaco race, in which he had scored a hat-trick over the previous three years, eluded him. Victory in the Indianapolis 500 was the only high point in a meagre Formula One season.

The British driver's victory in the American classic came at the wheel of a Lola-Ford entered by the American Mecom team. At the start there was a mass collision of no fewer than 16 cars, 11 of which had to abandon proceedings. The race was restarted after an hour and a half and the lead taken by young Italian-born American Mario Andretti, until he had to stop with a valve defect. Jim Clark in a Lotus-Ford V8 took over but unfortunately lost a minute in the pits. Jackie Stewart in a Lola-Ford now had his turn in this race of changing fortunes and held the lead right up to the 191st lap (of 200) when he had to withdraw due to engine failure. Graham Hill slipped his similar car through into first position and won the race, with Jim Clark second.

During the summer of 1966 Dr Giuseppe (Nino) Farina, the 1950 World Champion and 1938 and 1939 Italian Champion, was killed in a road accident at the wheel of his Ford Lotus-Cortina near Chambéry in the French Alps. He

they developed methods of forming wide cross-section tyres with flat sidewalls.

And it was in the spring of 1966 that the beautifully engineered and very successful V8 Ford-Cosworth DFV engine, the envy of its competitors, had its origins. This ingenious engine, which won no fewer than 155 Grand Prix races between 1967 and 1983, was the brainchild of Keith Duckworth, part owner of the British racing engine company Cosworth Engineering. When the new 3-litre formula had come into force, Lotus boss Colin Chapman had appealed to the British motor industry, and even the government, to support the construction of a suitable engine which would aim for Grand Prix success. This would not only secure the future of the racing industry, but also promote Britain's image abroad. Chapman did not appear to be particularly impressed with the BRM H16 motor, as the manufacturer could be expected to use the best engines in their own works cars. The idea of the Cosworth Formula One and Formula Two engine project originated at a dinner party at Colin Chapman's house, when he entertained the Vice-President of Ford of Europe, Walter Hayes. A month later Hayes received the nod from Henry Ford II in Detroit and, on March 1st 1966, a four-point contract came into force. Ironically Keith Duckworth only signed the contract months later.

The first point of the contract was: "In return for a £100,000 grant from Ford to Cosworth, Cosworth and Duckworth are to design and build Formula One and Formula Two engines for Ford, which will compete in motor racing activities under the Ford logo." Point No 2 contained more precise definitions: "(A): to build a 1600cc four-cylinder in-line engine carrying the Type designation FVA which will comply with the regulations governing the international Formula Two valid for 1967, using an alloy cylinder-head with four valves per cylinder in conjunction with Ford's 120E (Cortina) cylinder-block. (B): to build a 90° V-eight-cylinder engine of 3000cc capacity using cylinder heads designed and developed from the FVA motor."

Point No 4 said: "Cosworth and Duckworth will be required to have the first motor operational by May 1967. Five motors are to be available and handed over by Cosworth to Ford by January 1st 1968. Ford is to appoint a Formula One team whose manning is Ford's prerogative and remains secret."

was a nephew of Battista Pininfarina, the famous Turin coachbuilder. A few months before his death, Giuseppe Farina had told the author that, in the course of a quarter of a century racing experience, he had spent five years in hospital as a result of accidents on the tracks. It was tragic that this man had to die in an ordinary saloon.

In general, the lap times of the new 3-litre Grand Prix cars of 1966 had differed very little, if at all, from those of their predecessors of half the engine capacity, though the power-to-weight ratio of the 3-litre cars was now around 600–700bhp/tonne. The figure for the BRM H16 was 580, the Lotus-BRM H16 690, the V12 Ferrari 657, the Cooper-Maserati 595 and the Repco-Brabham 593bhp/tonne. The Brabham BT19 was the lightest car, with a dry weight of 540kg, and the 680kg Honda RA 273 the heaviest; all the other contenders in the 1966 series weighed between 550 and 620kg.

Fastest lap time in the 1966 Monaco Grand Prix was recorded by Lorenzo Bandini in the 2.4-litre V6 Ferrari at 1 minute 29.8 seconds — 1.9 seconds faster than Hill had recorded with the 1.5-litre

BRM the previous year. But the fastest time by a full 3-litre car in practice had been the 1 minute 30.1 seconds recorded by Surtees in the V12 Ferrari, appreciably slower than his team-mate achieved in the race. In 1964 Jim Clark had lapped the Brands Hatch course in 1 minute 35.4 seconds in a 1.5-litre Lotus-Climax, and that time was not bettered by the 3-litre machines in 1966. The larger-capacity machines were also slower at Zandvoort than their predecessors had been in earlier years. The reason for this apparent anomaly was that the 1500cc cars had been able to take at full speed some corners which the newer cars could not: although they were more powerful, they were also heavier, and required greater distances to slow before corners.

The new Formula One engines were also very thirsty. The following consumption figures were established at the Nürburgring in 1966: Brabham-Repco 41 litres per 100km, Cooper-Maserati 45, V12 Ferrari 42 and Eagle-Climax 35; the bored-out interim 2-litre V8 engines of both BRM and Coventry Climax used 35 litres per 100km. The 1500cc cars of the last year of the old formula had used, on average, between 32 and 36 litres per 100km.

The 1966 season also marked the beginning of widespread changes in the design of tyres. Firestone and Goodyear introduced new low-profile tyres with very wide cross-sections and squared sidewalls, leaving Dunlop the only company manufacturing tyres with the traditional rounded sidewalls. It was said that Dunlop was more or less forced to produce tyres with the classic cross-section as it was some time yet before

This Time it's Hulme

The simple Repco-Brabham concept predominates. Sensational Zandvoort debut of the Lotus 49 with V8 Ford-Cosworth motor. A turbine car narrowly misses victory at Indianapolis.

There were quite a few personnel changes amongst the drivers at the beginning of the 1967 season. John Surtees went to Honda, Richie Ginther to Eagle, Graham Hill to his former firm, Lotus, Pedro Rodriguez to Cooper, Mike Spence to BRM and Chris Amon to Ferrari.

The World Championship opened with the South African Grand Prix on January 2nd, held for the first time on the Kyalami circuit near Johannesburg rather than at East London. Ferrari did not take part in this race, and other competitors came to the line with their previous season's cars. Gurney's Eagle was still fitted with the old four-cylinder Coventry Climax motor and Lotus again ran Type 43s with BRM H16 engines for Clark and Hill while continuing work on the new Type 49, which was to be powered by the new DFV Cosworth-Ford V8. The race held more than one surprise.

Denis Hulme in a Brabham BT19 with Repco motor had a substantial lead until he had to stop for more brake fluid, and the lead passed to Rhodesian John Love in an old four-cylinder Cooper-Climax. Fortune did not remain with the local man for very long however, as six laps before the end he had to stop for more

Keith Duckworth

Above
Keith Duckworth, father of the Cosworth DFV motor.

Right
The V8 four-camshaft Ford-Cosworth DFV motor with four valves per cylinder and Lucas fuel injection. Cylinder dimensions were 85.6 x 64.8mm, giving a capacity of 2993cc.

The South African Grand Prix was held on the 4.094km Kyalami circuit near Johannesburg for the first time in 1967.

Left
Thirty-year-old New Zealander Denis Hulme, the 1967 World Champion. He won only the Monaco and German Grands Prix, but was well placed in the ACF, British and Canadian rounds.

Denis Hulme

fuel and the Mexican Pedro Rodriguez slipped past into the lead. He was first over the finishing line with Love second and Surtees in a V12 Honda RA273 third.

In March Dan Gurney gave the V12 Eagle-Weslake a win in the Race of Champions at Brands Hatch, but only by a margin of 0.4-second over Lorenzo Bandini in a new Ferrari 312 with the exhaust pipes on top of the motor. Joseph Siffert in a Cooper-Maserati was third, another two seconds behind. After this victory great things were predicted for the Gurney/Eagle combination for the rest of 1967. The new Ferrari had a much slimmer chassis, but although a four-

valve version of the well-known V12 motor was being prepared, Bandini's Brands Hatch car retained a three-valve configuration. The cylinder head had however been modified since the previous year's Italian Grand Prix, the inlet and exhaust valves being reversed so that the exhaust pipes could be located in the vee of the motor. This repositioning allowed a better aerodynamic shape at the rear of the vehicle.

A new Maserati motor with three valves and two spark-plugs per cylinder appeared in one of the Coopers during practice at Monte Carlo, where Jack Brabham unveiled his latest car, the Brabham BT24. The compact design of this car, with which Brabham hoped to retain his World Championship title, was based on the spaceframe Formula Two car and it was fitted with a new light-alloy Repco V8 motor. The 2996cc (88.9 x 60.3mm) Type 740 motor still had one camshaft per cylinder-bank but had flat cylinder-heads and the combustion chamber in the piston. Initially this engine developed 330bhp at 8500rpm with Lucas fuel-injection and ignition systems.

The Monaco Grand Prix ended sadly with the tragic accident involving the Milan-based Lorenzo Bandini. The Ferrari driver rammed the walls at the exit of the chicane and suffered terrible burns to his body, as a result of which he died four days later. Denis Hulme made up for his bad luck at Kyalami by winning the Monaco race with the older Repco-Brabham BT19, followed by Graham Hill in a Lotus 33 whose BRM V8 engine had been bored out to 2070cc, a similar unit being fitted to the old BRM V8 driven in

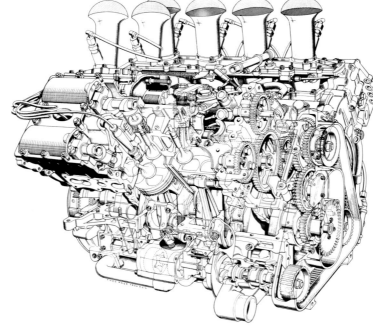

the Monaco race by Jackie Stewart. In this form the engine developed 283bhp at 10,000rpm. New Ferrari driver Chris Amon was third, but Richie Ginther was a non-starter after failing to qualify his Eagle-Weslake, and decided to give up active motor racing.

Lorenzo Bandini's terrible accident resulted in a close examination of the safety provisions in the event of an outbreak of fire. War was declared on fire at international racing circuits, and fire marshals in asbestos suits were placed along the tracks and in front of the pits during most races. All possible contingencies to minimise fire were considered. The chemicals industry introduced more flame-resistant overalls for drivers, notably a very impressive new material called Nomex, introduced by the American Dupont company. Within the year spectacular results were achieved in respect of safety and protection.

The Dutch Grand Prix at Zandvoort on June 4th 1967 was of great historical significance, as it marked the debut of the Lotus 49 and, with it, the V8 Cosworth-Ford DFV engine. Their combined attributes resulted in a truly sensational debut, when Jim Clark conducted the car to victory.

The Lotus 49 had an incredibly small monocoque chassis designed not by Colin Chapman personally but by the very talented engineer Maurice Phillippe. Another of Phillippe's designs was the four-wheel-drive Lotus 63 of 1969, and he was also responsible for the ingenious wedge-shaped Lotus 72 with side-

radiators, which the factory raced with considerable success from 1970. Phillippe then went to the United States and designed an Offenhauser-powered USAC car for the Parnelli Jones team, and with one of these cars Joe Leonard became USAC Champion in 1972.

Forming the rear of the Lotus 49 chassis was the new eight-cylinder Ford-Cosworth DFV motor which, under the terms of the Ford contract, was initially for the exclusive use of Lotus. Constructed in light alloy, the V8 engine actually consisted of a combination of two Formula Two Ford-Cosworth Type FVA motors which used the Ford Cortina cast-iron block. This four-cylinder engine project had also been financed by the Ford Motor Company and developed by Keith Duckworth under very similar contract conditions.

The FVA and the DFV were both successful engines which gained many victories in their respective categories of international racing. The 2993cc (85.7 x 64.8mm) Formula One motor was a 90° V8 with four valves per cylinder, inclined at 32° to each other and operated by two gear-driven overhead camshafts. The exhaust ports were located on the outside of the heads and the inlets on the inside of the vee. The motor was fitted with a Lucas 12-volt ignition system and Ford claimed 400bhp for the unit in its initial form.

The Lotus 49, with five-speed ZF gearbox, was an overnight success, but although it was universally considered to be the best design of 1967, it nevertheless

had its share of teething troubles. There were weaknesses in the chassis and some suspension difficulties too. In spite of all this however Jim Clark won four World Championship Grands Prix with the car in 1967.

The Repco-Brabham remained the most reliable Formula One car of the year, although it did not have the ultra-modern shape of the Lotus 49 nor the sheer power of the Ferrari, Eagle, Honda or BRM H16. In spite of its lack of spectacular technical innovation, the Brabham was a harmonious and functional design, its very simplicity aiding its reliability, and in Holland Brabham and Hulme were beaten to the line only by the victorious Jim Clark. The three Ferraris, driven by Amon, Parkes and Scarfiotti, followed the Brabhams over the line, the death of Lorenzo Bandini having apparently cast a damper on the fighting spirit of the whole of Scuderia Ferrari.

The heavy burden of leading the team now fell on the shoulders of the 24-year-

Left
Jim Clark after his victory with the Lotus 49, with new Ford-Cosworth engine, in the 1967 Dutch Grand Prix.

Overleaf
Denis Hulme in a Brabham BT19 racing towards his first Grand Prix win at Monaco in 1967.

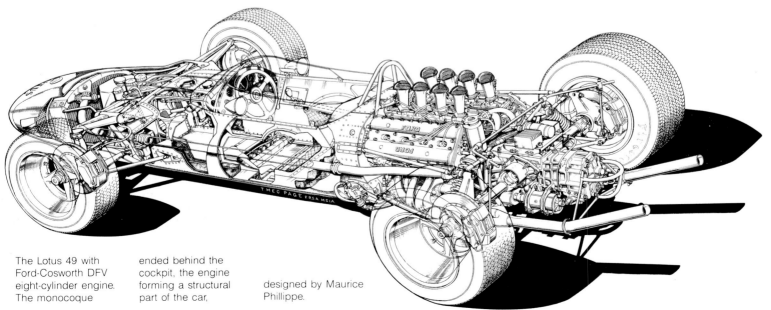

The Lotus 49 with Ford-Cosworth DFV eight-cylinder engine. The monocoque ended behind the cockpit, the engine forming a structural part of the car, designed by Maurice Phillippe.

old New Zealander Chris Amon, as there was no longer any other top driver at Ferrari. Amon had been racing Formula One cars since he was 20, having been helped into Grand Prix racing in 1963 by former Grand Prix driver Reg Parnell (father of Tim Parnell, who later became BRM team manager).

The 1967 Indianapolis 500 was historically significant as it was nearly won by a gas-turbine car. The STP-Paxton entry, driven by Parnelli Jones, was financed by the STP fuel-additive company, headed by its ambitious president, Andy Granatelli. No limitations had at that stage been imposed on gas turbines at Indianapolis and engines of all sizes were allowed. The motor was a 540bhp Pratt & Whitney gas-turbine, which had been built by United Aircraft in Canada. The chassis of the STP-Paxton consisted of a centrally located backbone constructed on monocoque principles with the cockpit on the right-hand side and the gas-turbine motor on the left, coupled to a Ferguson four-wheel-drive system. This layout gave the car an unusually wide, bulbous shape but it revealed superior characteristics during the race. In qualifying Parnelli Jones and the STP-Paxton were a promising sixth fastest. Among the European-based drivers, Jim Clark in the latest Lotus-Ford qualified for a midfield start, Denis Hulme in an Eagle-Ford was further back, Jackie Stewart in a Lola-Ford on the second to last row and both Graham Hill in another Lotus-Ford and Jochen Rindt in an Eagle-

Ford on the last of the starting-grid's 11 rows.

In the course of the race the STP-Paxton turbine car showed that it was the equal of most of the cars using normal internal-combustion engines, and as the end approached Jones had it in the lead, with 30 seconds in hand over A J Foyt in a Coyote-Ford. But on lap 197, with only three to go, a small component in the transmission broke, and the gas-turbine failed to take its deserved victory, leaving A J Foyt to win his third Indianapolis 500.

The European contingent generally had a miserable time, Jim Clark and Graham Hill withdrawing fairly early in the proceedings and Jochen Rindt and Jackie Stewart during the second half. Denis Hulme gained an excellent fourth place however while Parnelli Jones, the big loser, came sixth.

After the very promising demonstration of his revolutionary

vehicle, STP company president Andy Granatelli decided to collaborate with Lotus in the development of a new gas-turbine-powered car, the wedge-shaped Lotus Type 56.

The 1967 Grand Prix season resumed at Spa in Belgium where Jim Clark's Lotus 49 appeared for the first time with small wings on its nose to deflect the air and front-end lifting in the interests of improving roadholding.

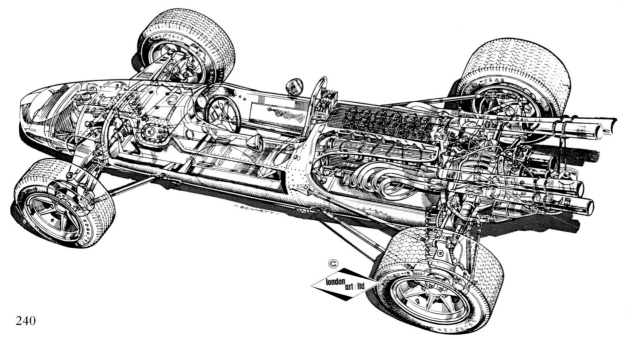

The Eagle-Weslake had an excellent monocoque chassis with V12 motor built under the direction of Aubrey Woods at the Harry Weslake company at Rye. Cylinder dimensions of the 60° engine were 72.8 x 60.3mm and the capacity 2997cc. The four-camshaft engine developed 390bhp at 9500rpm.

Before long, all Grand Prix cars would be fitted with these spoilers which became larger and larger and increased enormously the downforce on the cars at high speeds. Jim Clark had to retire while leading at Spa and Jackie Stewart, who took over the lead in his BRM H16 (running perfectly for once), was slowed by a transmission fault, which allowed Dan Gurney to take his second Formula One race victory of the year. This was the first — and only — Grand Prix victory achieved by the excellent Eagle chassis, designed by the young English engineer Tony Southgate.

The very fast Ardennes circuit was the scene of a very nasty accident involving English engineer Mike Parkes who, like his countryman Mike Hawthorn before him, had to have special long-wheelbase Ferrari Grand Prix cars built to accommodate his tall frame. Parkes suffered leg injuries in this accident which immobilised him for a long period of time and cost him all chance of pursuing his driving career, in which he had shown considerable promise of a big future. This was a bad period for Ferrari team manager Franco Lini, a well known journalist and PR man, and chief engineer Mauro Forghieri, for the following month the German driver Günther Klass, who had been engaged by Ferrari for sportscar racing, was killed during

Maserati modified the V12 engine in 1967 by fitting a new cylinder-head with three valves per cylinder, as well as Lucas fuel injection and Lucas transistorized ignition. This engine, the Type 10F1, had cylinder dimensions of 75.2 x 56mm, giving a capacity of 2987cc (against the 70.4 x 64mm of the earlier 9F1 unit) and developed 390bhp at 10,000rpm.

practice for the Mugello race in Tuscany, at the wheel of the ultra-lightweight Dino Mountain Spider.

The 1967 ACF Grand Prix was held at Le Mans, as it had been in 1906 and 1921, but this time on the new Bugatti Circuit which the *Automobile Club de l'Ouest* had built inside the famous 24-hour course. Although incorporating part of the finishing straight of the old track and another, shorter, stretch, most of the Bugatti circuit was constructed in the huge parking area behind the pits. The new layout was not at all popular with the drivers as the engineers responsible for its design and construction had shown very

little imagination, incorporating a number of slow hairpin bends. The race was a non-event for the organisers with very few spectators bothering to attend, and the ACF Grand Prix was never again held at Le Mans.

The Lotus 49 suffered teething troubles in the Le Mans race and the Brabham team of Jack Brabham and Denis Hulme took the first two places. Bruce McLaren was still waiting for the new BRM V12 motor for his Type M5A, designed by Robin Herd, so drove one of Dan Gurney's Eagle-Weslakes at the Sarthe; in the previous Formula One race the New Zealander had driven an interim Formula One McLaren, the M4B. This comprised a monocoque McLaren M4A Formula Two chassis modified to take a 2.2-litre BRM V8 motor.

The British Grand Prix at Silverstone was won by Jim Clark in the Lotus 49, his fifth victory in this race. During practice Graham Hill had been lucky to escape injury when his Lotus 49 rammed a wall

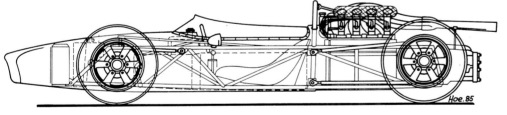

Above
The Brabham BT24 with Repco V8 motor. Ron Tauranac had built a simple spaceframe chassis that could easily be adapted to other formulae.

Right
Pedro Rodriguez in a T81 Cooper-Maserati leads Chris Amon's four-valve Ferrari 312 and Jochen Rindt in another Cooper in the 1967 Belgian Grand Prix.

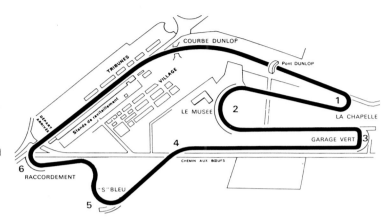

The 4.442km Bugatti circuit at Le Mans, used for the 1967 ACF Grand Prix.

Below
Start of the ACF Grand Prix at Le Mans. From left: Hill and Clark in Lotuses, Brabham in a Brabham and Gurney in an Eagle.

due to an imbalance caused by a suspension defect. During the race a similar problem developed and Hill was just able to roll to the pits with a rear wheel at a peculiar angle; a screw had not been tightened! Behind Clark at the end of the race came Hulme in a Brabham BT24, Amon in a Ferrari 312 and Brabham in a Brabham, the last two flying to the finishing line neck and neck. Jochen Rindt appeared at the Silverstone meeting with the T86 Cooper, which, although still fitted with the three-valve V12 Maserati engine, had an all-new chassis. Designed by Tony Robinson, the new car had a very slim lightweight chassis slung low on the wheels. The new Cooper, like the Lotus 49, had outboard disc brakes, mounted away from the wheels for improved cooling. So efficient was the cooling on the Lotus in fact that the cars appeared in the German Grand Prix with the wide perforated discs replaced by smaller more conventional units.

Jim Clark in the Lotus 49 took the lead on the Nürburgring, but was again forced to give up, this time with tyre trouble on the fifth lap. Dan Gurney took his Eagle-Weslake into the lead and it was obvious to everybody watching that the American was having a great day. But although he was able to shake off all his competitors, the Eagle's driveshaft snapped on the unlucky 13th lap, leaving the way open for Denis Hulme in a Repco-Brabham BT24 to win his second Grand Prix of the year.

Special mention should be made of the driving in this race of Jacky Ickx, 22-year-old son of a well-known Belgian motor racing journalist. Although at the wheel of a Formula Two (1600cc) Matra-Ford he was in fourth position among the Grand Prix cars when the front suspension broke and he had to retire.

The Canadian Grand Prix at Mosport was included in the World Championship schedule for the first time in 1967. Held in teeming rain, the race went to Jack

Brabham with his team-mate Denis Hulme second. Jim Clark quit once more, due to an ignition fault.

It was at Mosport that Bruce McLaren unveiled his new Formula One M5A car, with monocoque chassis designed by Robin Herd and fitted with the first example of the new V12 BRM motor which Tony Rudd had adapted from the old V8 design. The never-ending reliability problems with the H16 engine led, the following year, to the works BRM team using this 2988cc (74.6 x 57.2mm) V12 engine.

The Italian Grand Prix was a sensational race, from its breathtaking start to a cliffhanger finish. The Ferrari 312 made its first appearance with the new four-valve cylinder-head, and Honda unveiled their new Type RA300. Still using the well-known V12 motor, the RA300 dispensed with the earlier cars' heavy chassis in favour of an all-new monocoque designed by Eric Broadley of Lola, a firm in which Honda driver John Surtees at that time had interests. The RA300 is listed in the Lola register as the Lola Type 130, and the wags instantly dubbed it the "Hondola". Jacky Ickx, having given ample proof of his skill at the wheel of the Formula Two Matras of the British Tyrrell team, made his Formula One debut in this race in a T81 Cooper-Maserati.

By the second half of the 1967 season the various engines had achieved the following performances: the 48-valve V12 Ferrari developed 408bhp at 10,500 rpm, the 36-valve V12 Ferrari 390bhp at 10,000rpm, the 36-valve V12 Maserati 400bhp at 10,000rpm, the 24-valve V12

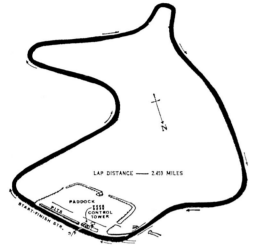

LAP DISTANCE — 2.459 MILES

Maserati 365bhp at 9200rpm, the 32-valve H16 BRM 400bhp at 11,000 rpm, the 24-valve V12 BRM 375bhp at 10,000rpm, the 32-valve V8 Ford-Cosworth 405bhp at 8600rpm, the 48-valve V12 Weslake 400bhp at 10,000rpm, and the 48-valve V12 Honda 405bhp at 10,000rpm.

The Monza race was another demonstration of why Jim Clark was considered the best driver of his time. He took the lead right from the start, but then had to stop at the pits to replace a tyre, and by the time he rejoined the race he was in 15th place, and a lap behind the leaders. Driving like one possessed however the Scot was back up to second place, with only team-mate Hill ahead, by the 59th lap. Then Hill had to withdraw and the maestro was in first place again. Behind him Brabham and Surtees were fighting a wheel-to-wheel battle and an intriguing game of slipstreaming developed as they caught up with Clark. On the last lap, as the three cars shot into the Curva Grande in one 260km/h bunch, Clark suddenly found himself without power — his fuel had run out. Brabham and Surtees shot past the slowing Lotus and at the apex of the Curva Parabolica were side by side. Brabham tried to outmanoeuvre the "Hondola" on the inside but Surtees did not give an inch. At the exit of the corner Brabham trailed in the slipstream of Surtees's car but the ploy did not come off and, with only half

a car's length advantage, Surtees won the Italian Grand Prix for Honda.

Clark's Lotus spluttered over the finishing line in third place, but the Scot was the hero of the day. Never before in the modern history of Grand Prix racing, in which every little bit of reserve from A to Z is used, had a competitor lost a lap in the pits and fought back to regain the lead. This had been possible only due to Clark's tremendous skill and determination and the performance of the Lotus, which had been brought to a high degree of technical perfection.

The finish of the United States Grand Prix at Watkins Glen was also an exciting one, though in a different way. Clark in his Lotus was again in front two laps from the end of the race, with a clear lead over Graham Hill's Lotus 49, but on the last lap a bolt in the leader car's suspension broke. In spite of the wheel leaning at an odd angle however, the Scot was able to continue at only slightly reduced speed to win from Hill, Hulme and Siffert, the Walker team's ageing T81 Cooper-Maserati simply unable to match the speed and handling of the newer cars. Clark also won the Mexican Grand Prix, with Brabham and Hulme second and third in their reliable BT24 Repco-Brabhams, ahead of Surtees in the Honda. Clark's success in Mexico was his 24th Grand Prix win, putting him level

with the record set by the great Juan Manuel Fangio.

Denis Hulme and Jack Brabham had each won two World Championship events in 1967 to the four achieved by Jim Clark in the Lotus-Ford 49, but Hulme became World Driver's Champion as a result of the additional placings he had taken. His final point score was 51, ahead of Jack Brabham with 46 and Jim Clark with 41. Ferrari driver Amon and Honda team-leader Surtees each received 20 points, to share fourth place.

The World Championship had been a very exciting contest in the second year of the 3-litre formula. The athletic Denis Hulme, a driver of outstanding ability, had won, effortlessly overcoming the greatest physical strain. As cool and collected in the cockpit of the car as he was outside it, the quiet and unassuming Hulme was, like his employer, a man who never sought publicity or press attention in the way that many of his predecessors had. He was tough and strong but anything but a showman. The reliability of the Repco-Brabham in this class was again quite evident, and confirmed by Brabham's victory in the World Formula One Manufacturers' Championship.

At the end of the 1967 season Maserati gave up building Formula One engines for Cooper. Their heavy V12 motor, designed in 1956, was now outdated and there was insufficient money for new ventures. A close technical association between Maserati and Citroën had been developed for the manufacture of luxury sportscars, the Italian company researching and building the V6 motor for the Citroën SM. In the spring of 1969 the French company bought a 60% shareholding in Maserati, and some time later completely took over the historic Bologna company, with its insignia of Neptune's trident.

Racing Cars Sprout Wings

The Ford-Cosworth engine wins the World Championship for Graham Hill. Jim Clark dies at Hockenheim. Siffert wins the British Grand Prix in a Rob Walker Lotus.

The V8 Ford-Cosworth DFV motor's run of successes really began with the 1968 Grand Prix season. Between 1968 and 1982 12 World Championships were won by drivers whose cars used this engine, its supply no longer confined exclusively to the Lotus team. More and more designers made use of the engine's availability, McLaren switching to the DFVs in 1968, and the new Matra team using them too. In its second season the British V8 won no fewer than 11 of the 12 World Championship Grands Prix. Ferrari's V12 was an equally outstanding unit, but it won only one race.

The 1968 season also became known as the season of the aerofoils or wings, the aerodynamic aids which were attached to the Grand Prix cars to improve their grip on the road. By the end of the season all competing cars were fitted with these stabilising wings front and rear, and Brabham had gone so far as to use two wings mounted direct to the front and rear suspension, this system immediately being dubbed the "double decker".

Not all wings however were built in accordance with the laws of the science of aerodynamics: some gave the appearance of having been knocked up at random and their effectiveness left much to be desired. There were also instances where the uprights supporting the wings broke under the additional stresses, as occurred with the Lotus 49. The positioning of the spoilers had a marked effect on wind pressure on the car and thus affected the downforce on its suspension. This effect varied according to the size of wing and also its angle which, in those days of rudimentary aerodynamic knowledge, was set by spirit-level in the pits rather than by systematic wind-tunnel tests: these did not come for some years.

Some wing designs, like the Matra's, were adjustable, the idea being to have a fairly steep angle on corners, so as to increase downforce (and thus increase adhesion), but then to be able to change the wing to a flatter position to reduce air resistance (and increase speed) on the straights. In the Matra system, the wing angle was controlled automatically by an electric motor actuated by impulses from the brake pedal, but at Monza Ferrari experimented with a hydraulic-operated wing, linked to the engine's lubrication system. This meant the wing angle changed with every gear change or depression of the brake pedal. The various developments became a matter of

concern to the administrators and as the wings started to become dangerous it became necessary to implement rules to limit their development.

Three 1968 Grands Prix were held in terrible weather and pelting rain, the Dutch, French and German races. The choice of which tyres to use in these conditions was critical and Dunlop's special rain tyres, made from a super-soft compound and with wide grooves down the centre, proved excellent for the job. Driving in the rain with these super-wide tyres did however cause quite a few problems, as aquaplaning caused them to throw up enormous amounts of water, reducing visibility for the following drivers to a minimum. The normal dry-weather tyre had a road contact width of 38cm.

Most of the research and development in Grand Prix racing up to 1966 had been directed towards progress in the manufacture of chassis and engines and also with safety, but by 1967 a start had been made towards improving aerodynamics and reducing vehicle weight, with greater use of titanium and magnesium alloys. Although very expensive, titanium was capable of withstanding the same forces as steel, but was only a fraction of its weight. Magnesium was mainly used for bodies, as well as for wheels.

A new chapter in international motor racing was begun this year with the introduction of advertising on racing cars, a policy which, until then, had been permitted only in the United States. In Europe the money supply was tightened up in 1967 when two major oil suppliers, BP and Esso, withdrew. Firestone quickly followed their example: there were no more free supplies, and anyone wanting to use their tyres had to buy them. This situation placed some Grand Prix teams in very difficult positions financially, and it was in response to this that the CSI changed their long-standing policy and

allowed advertising on cars competing in their championships.

Overnight the whole appearance of Grand Prix racing changed as cigarette, drink, ski and cosmetic advertisements appeared on cars. Products with no direct relationship with the motor industry now helped to finance the spiralling costs of Grand Prix racing, though not without considerable opposition from the traditionalists. Many enthusiasts considered this sort of "foreign" advertising immoral, and its monetary emphasis a blow to the image of Grand Prix drivers, who were now seen as money-hungry businessmen rather than sportsmen. Furthermore the familiar colours of the cars, until now chosen according to each car's country of origin, became meaningless. The Lotus 49s, traditionally green with a yellow stripe, appeared at the Monaco Grand Prix in the predominantly red colours of Gold Leaf tobacco, and the team was officially renamed Gold Leaf Team Lotus. Before long only Ferrari continued to appear in its national colours.

The 1968 season produced a further series of fatal accidents amongst the top drivers. Mike Spence was killed during practice at Indianapolis on May 7th, Lodovico Scarfiotti in practice for the Rossfeld hillclimb on June 8th and the French driver Jo Schlesser in the French Grand Prix at Rouen-Les-Essarts on July 7th. But the greatest loss of all was Jim Clark, who died in a Formula Two accident at Hockenheim on April 7th.

The dynamic young French space rocket firm of Matra made its Formula One debut in 1968. In October 1964 Matra had founded a motor company, Société Matra Sport, with offices at Vélizy near Paris, and launched straight into the construction of Ford-engined Formula Three and Formula Two cars. The Formula Three model won its first race at Rheims in 1965 and the Formula Two version won on the Nürburgring the

Matra appeared in Formula One for the first time in the 1968 season. The MS9 model seen here in Jackie Stewart's hands in the 1968 Race of Champions was powered by a Cosworth motor and carried the colours of Matra International, Ken Tyrrell's team.

Left
Joseph Siffert

Right
Joseph Siffert scoring his first World Championship Grand Prix win, with the Walker-Durlacher Lotus 49 in the 1968 British Grand Prix at Brands Hatch.

Jo Siffert

Rob Walker

Mike Spence

Jacky Ickx

following year, and many other successes came their way as well.

With an excellent international reputation already established, the company was given a French government subsidy of six million francs in April 1967 for research into and development of a Formula One car, for France was eager to recover some of the prestige it had held amongst Grand Prix nations in earlier times, but which had been absent in more recent years. The government subsidy covered half the development project's costs, and Matra received additional support from the Elf petrol company, which was a heavy backer of smaller racing classes in France and became the major sponsor of the Matra Formula One project.

Matra formed two Formula One teams to run the new cars. Elf-Matra was the works team, led by Jean-Pierre Beltoise, while Matra International was operated from England by the well-known team of former timber merchant Ken Tyrrell.

Matra International's No 1 driver was Jackie Stewart, whose international career Tyrrell had launched in Formula Three, and who had continued to drive for the team in Formula Two.

Rindt meanwhile left Cooper and went to Brabham for 1968, replacing Hulme, who had joined his countryman McLaren. Clark and Hill stayed with Lotus, with Jackie Oliver replacing the lamented Clark during the year. The BRM team consisted of Pedro Rodriguez, Mike Spence and Richard Attwood, while Cooper engaged Englishman Brian Redman, Belgian Lucien Bianchi and Italian Lodovico Scarfiotti. Ferrari had two very talented young drivers in Chris Amon and Jacky Ickx and Surtees stayed with Honda, but Gurney raced his Eagles only sporadically, appearing on other occasions in Brabham or McLaren cars. Gurney was, this year, the first Grand Prix driver to wear a face-protecting crash helmet, a Bell Integral of the type which would soon by adopted by all the drivers. Lotus changed from ZF gearboxes on their 49s to Hewland units, which allowed ratios to be changed more rapidly.

Lotus started the season by taking the first two places in the opening event, the South African Grand Prix at Kyalami, Clark leading Hill over the line. Matra made their Formula One debut in this race with a Type MS9 entered by Ken Tyrrell. Using a modified Formula Two monocoque chassis, the car had a Ford-Cosworth motor and Hewland gearbox and the car, driven by Jackie Stewart, created an outstanding impression. BRM appeared in the same race with their new Type 126, a monocoque with Hewland transmission and the V12 motor, all work on the H16 engine now having ceased. The V12 BRM motor, designed by Aubrey Woods, was also used in the Cooper T86B.

Clark's Kyalami victory was his 25th, but it was also his last, for before the first European round of the World Championship, his career ended with his still-unexplained death in a Formula Two race at Hockenheim in West Germany. There were very few spectators on the stretch of road where the accident happened, in very wet conditions, and no-one witnessed the tragedy: it has never been discovered whether the accident was caused by a chassis defect or a momentary loss of attention. It is a fact however that safety measures at the high-speed Hockenheim track were not up to standard, with trees lining the edge of the circuit with no safety barriers to minimise the effect of any car striking trouble. At the time of his death Jim Clark was not only the outstanding driver of his time, he was also universally liked as a pleasant personality.

Just one month after Clark's death, Mike Spence was killed during practice at Indianapolis: his was the 34th fatality at Indianapolis. The unfortunate Englishman was killed when his Lotus 56 turbine car lost a front wheel (which spun into the cockpit) and hit the wall.

The 1968 Indy 500 was the second — and last — in which gas-turbine engines were admitted. New rules had been brought in limiting the air intake for these motors to 15.99sq inches, or 103.21cm² and STP placed an order with Lotus for six new cars fitted with the newly approved Pratt & Whitney gas-turbine engines. This Lotus model, the 56, was fitted with Ferguson four-wheel drive and was another futuristic design. A wedge-shaped monocoque was built which acted as a natural aerofoil, forcing the car down onto the road. The first tests with the Type 56 had been carried out by Jim Clark before his death but the three STP

Lotus drivers who qualified to start the Indianapolis race were Graham Hill, Joe Leonard and Art Pollard, Leonard qualifying to start from pole position.

The race was tremendously exciting with the lead constantly changing between Joe Leonard's Lotus gas turbine and the Eagle-Offenhauser driven by Bobby Unser. Graham Hill took no part in this, having crashed his "wedge" into a safety-fence and out of the race on the 11th lap.

Jochen Rindt also took part in this race, driving a Brabham BT25 with four-camshaft Repco motor, but gave up on the fifth lap with a broken piston.

Twenty laps before the finish, Leonard's Lotus led Unser's Eagle by eight seconds, but by the 193rd of the 200 laps this had been reduced to five seconds. Would this be the first win for a turbine car? No — seven laps before the finish a shaft broke in the fuel pump of the gas turbine and Leonard had to let his car roll to a stop and watch Bobby Unser win the race. The age of the turbine car at Indianapolis was however to all intents and purposes over, as the area of the air-intake was reduced to 11.99 sq inches or 77.3cm² in 1969, which made the gas turbine no longer a viable prospect. A year later four-wheel-drive cars were also banned from the 500-mile race.

But these measures didn't stop all technical development at the Brickyard, for both Ford and Offenhauser were

Bobby Unser

making increasing use of exhaust-driven turbochargers in this period. This was the beginning of the turbo era in top-flight racing, though the turbocharger did not make its appearance in Formula One until 1977. Although turbocharged Indy-car motors were limited to 2.8 litres (the same as for supercharged units), the Ford developed 700bhp and the Offy 630.

Back in Europe the World Drivers' Championship resumed with the first Formula One Spanish Grand Prix since Mike Hawthorn in the Super Squalo Ferrari had beaten Juan Manuel Fangio's Mercedes-Benz at Barcelona in 1954. A modern circuit had been built at Jarama, about 24km outside Madrid, as a new home for the race. Several new cars made their first appearance in Spain, among them the new Cosworth-Ford-powered McLaren, the M7A. Designed by Robin Herd, the M7A had been tried with side-mounted fuel tanks, similar to the 1954–55 Lancia D50, but this idea was scrapped. Jack Brabham appeared in practice with his new BT26 which no longer had the classic tubular spaceframe but instead was a semi-monocoque on Ferrari principles, constructed from sheetmetal riveted to a tubular frame. The car was powered by a new four-camshaft Repco V8 engine, a smaller version of the unit that Jochen Rindt had used at Indianapolis. The 2996cc (88.9 x 60.3mm) Type 760 Formula One Repco engine had four valves per cylinder and developed 390bhp at 9000rpm. The new Australian eight appeared to have reached its limit of development however and suffered from a seemingly never-ending number

of problems. It rarely ran satisfactorily and at the end of the year Repco decided to cease design and production of Formula One engines. Also appearing for the first time at Jarama was a new Lotus design, the 49B. Compared to the Mark 49, the 49B had a 50mm longer wheelbase and stronger suspension, the modifications having been made under the direction of Maurice Phillippe with the assistance of young Swiss technician Josef Marquart from Winterthur, who would later succeed Robin Herd as chief designer for McLaren. John Surtees drove the new V12 Honda RA301 with a wide monocoque chassis engineered by Yoshio Nakamura.

The Spanish Grand Prix was won by Graham Hill in a Lotus-Ford 49B from Denis Hulme in a McLaren-Ford M7A and Brian Redman in a T86B Cooper-BRM V12, but it had been a very gripping event, with a number of surprises. Pedro Rodriguez took the early lead in the new V12 BRM P126 but came off the track and was forced to retire. That gave the lead to Jean-Pierre Beltoise, driving the Matra-Ford MS10 in place of Jackie Stewart, who had broken his wrist. The Anglo-French car developed an oil leak however, causing the former French

Josef Marquart

Joshio Nakamura

Graham Hill in a Lotus-Cosworth 49 laps the LDS-Repco of South African driver Sam Tingle during the 1968 South African Grand Prix while Jochen Rindt in a BT24 Brabham-Repco passes the local man on the inside. The Lotuses carried their traditional green racing colours for the last time at Kyalami; when next seen they were in Gold Leaf colours. This race was the 25th, and last, Grand Prix won by Jim Clark, killed shortly afterwards in an accident at Hockenheim.

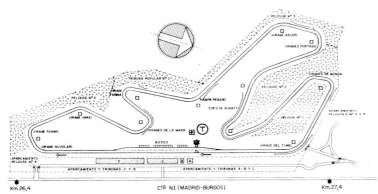

Spain finally has a permanent racing circuit. The 3.404km Jarama track, 20km from Madrid, hosted the Spanish Grand Prix ten times between 1968 and 1981.

motorcycle champion to drop out of the race, and this enabled Chris Amon at the wheel of a Ferrari 312/015-68 to take the lead. But Amon had no more luck than the Matra driver, a faulty fuel pump depriving the New Zealander of victory and allowing Graham Hill to lead the field over the line. Siffert had raced the ageing Cooper-Maserati in South Africa but in Spain had his first Grand Prix drive in the Rob Walker team's Lotus 49.

Matra Elf arrived at the Monaco Grand Prix with their new MS11, powered not by the Cosworth-Ford V8 engine but by their own V12. The new 2999cc (79.7 x 50mm) Matra V12 engine, which was coupled to a British Hewland gearbox, had been built by Matra in consultation with the Moteur Moderne enterprise under the direction of engineer Georges Martin. It had four camshafts, four valves per cylinder and Lucas fuel-injection, and developed 390bhp at 10,500rpm. The Matra MS11 was the first car to carry the French blue racing colours on the Formula One circuits since Gordini's withdrawal from Grand Prix racing in 1957. Another French company, Alpine, had however shown an interest in joining the field before then: in 1967 Alpine director Jean Rédélé had expressed his intention of making the move, using a modified version of the Gordini-built V8 Renault engines which at that time powered the successful Alpine sports prototype cars. The Formula One car was completed during the summer of 1968 and tested by Alpine works driver Mauro Bianchi on the Belgian Zolder circuit in August of that year, but the project never came to fruition as, although Alpine was substantially controlled by Renault, it required government support to continue and this was not approved.

The French Formula Two ace Johnny Servoz-Gavin drove the Tyrrell team's second Matra-Ford at Monaco, and

actually held the lead for a while before he was forced to retire from the race with a broken axle. This allowed Graham Hill to win his fourth Monaco race. Hill's Lotus had two short wings in the front and a wedge-shaped cover over the rear to increase downforce, and also used a new design of magnesium alloy wheel.

After Lorenzo Bandini's fatal accident the previous year, safety measures on and off the track had been increased, though not always without controversy. Ferrari withdrew its Monaco entries without giving any reason, but it was widely believed to have been in connection with new safety requirements. The Monte Carlo race distance was shortened from 100 laps to 80, and the chicanes relocated, but of the 16 cars that started the race, only seven were still running by the 15th lap and only five crossed the line at the end of the 80 laps. Dickie Attwood, driving a new V12 BRM P126 designed by Len Terry, recorded fastest lap of the race and finished in second place.

The Belgian Grand Prix was held on June 9th, a date of some historic significance, as the Ardennes race marked the first occasion on which Grand Prix cars ran with rear-mounted stabilising wings. Lotus had an additional metal foil fitted to the wedge-shaped engine cover of their cars to increase downforce on the rear axle, while Ferrari mounted an aerofoil wing over the 312's engine, and with this Chris Amon was fastest in the first practice session. Soon after that the Brabham was also seen with a rear wing mounted over the engine, which distributed downforce more evenly over the whole car and not just on the rear suspension.

Stewart led the Belgian race in the Matra-Ford MS10 but ran out of petrol and McLaren in his McLaren-Ford M7A came home a surprise winner. Cooper driver Lodovico Scarfiotti did not take part in this race, but instead honoured a

commitment to drive a Porsche in the Rossfeld round of the European Mountain Championship, at Berchtesganten the same weekend. During practice however Scarfiotti's ultra-light Porsche Spyder left the road just after the start and the car crashed, killing its unfortunate driver instantly.

The Dutch Grand Prix at Zandvoort was the first of three World Championship events this year run in rain. The first two places at the end went to Jackie Stewart in the Matra-Ford MS10 and Jean-Pierre Beltoise in the heavier MS11 with Matra V12 engine, both drivers providing ample evidence of their skills in driving under very difficult weather conditions. This was Matra's first Formula One victory, and the excellent Dunlop rain tyres used by the Matras were a major contributing factor in their success.

Since the first Grand Prix in 1906, the French race had always officially been called the *Grand Prix de l'Automobile Club de France* (ACF), although it would be true to say that most historians refer to the series as the French Grand Prix. In 1968, for the first time, French Grand Prix became the official as well as unofficial title, coinciding with the ACF's change of name to the *Fédération Francaise du Sport Automobile* (FFSA).

The Lotus 49B appeared at Rouen, where the race was held this year, with a new rear wing, not mounted on the chassis or above the motor but instead mounted high in the airstream and bolted by thin metal supports direct onto the suspension. These exerted considerable downforce on the rear wheels, and were much more effective than anything tried until now by opposition teams. By the same token they added stress to the suspension, as irregularities in the road were transmitted to the wing and thence to the chassis. Indeed during practice Jackie Oliver had a high-speed accident with his works 49B when the suspension broke and it was a miracle that the little Englishman walked away with hardly a scratch, for the car was a total wreck with all its wheels torn off. Oliver was the victim of a fault in the design which had come about through insufficient study of aerodynamics.

The advantage of the high-mounted rear wings of the Lotus was that they provided a stabilising effect from air pressure, by leaving the turbulence created by the car in its slipstream. On later models Colin Chapman increased the height of the wings even more.

Joe Leonard

Andy Granatelli

Joe Leonard narrowly missed winning in the 1968 Indianapolis 500 in the Lotus 56 fitted with a Pratt & Whitney gas turbine engine. Seven laps before the finish the fuel-pump drive broke and the car, owned by the corpulent Andy Granatelli (in the background), was forced to withdraw.

Right
Competitors had to choose whether or not to use ''wings'' in the 1968 Italian Grand Prix at Monza. Those with wings were slower on the straights but faster on the corners. Bruce McLaren in a McLaren-Cosworth M7A leads at the start ahead of Graham Hill in a Lotus-Cosworth 49 and John Surtees in a Honda RA301.

Although these aerodynamic aids added to the air resistance in the straights, and thereby decreased maximum speed, they were of great assistance in corners, and faster lap times were achieved in most instances. The improved roadholding meant that corners could be taken faster and the cars could accelerate faster out of corners due to the greater downforce on the driving wheels.

Also new at Rouen was a brand new Honda, the Type RA302 with air-cooled V8 motor, the first air-cooled motor seen in Formula One racing since the eight-cylinder Porsches in 1962. After a considerable amount of testing with the new car John Surtees refused to drive it, considering it to be unsafe, and it was offered instead to Frenchman Jo Schlesser. Although a Formula One first-timer, Schlessser was a highly-rated driver, with considerable experience in Formula Two and long-distance endurance events. Sadly however he was killed on the third lap, when the air-cooled Honda crashed at the exit of the right-hand curve before the Nouveau Monde corner and was completely burnt out.

The cylinders of the new 2987cc (88 x 61.4mm) Honda motor were set at an angle of 120°, and, fed by Honda indirect fuel-injection, it produced 390bhp at 10,500rpm. The car was fitted with Honda's own five-speed gearbox. The engine was cooled by way of air intakes on either side of the cockpit and many parts of the RA302 were built of magnesium alloy which is, of course, highly inflammable. The ultra-light alloy not only catches fire easily, but the high temperatures it then generates makes it very difficult to put the fire out. The Honda RA302 appeared again in practice at Monza, but was put away after John Surtees had completed only a few laps, and was not seen again.

Like the Dutch Grand Prix, the French race was also held in teeming rain, and convincingly won by Jacky Ickx in a Ferrari 312 fitted with Firestone's improved rain tyres. The young Belgian controlled his car in a masterly fashion in the rain and led practically from start to finish. John Surtees in a Honda RA301 (water-cooled V12) was second ahead of Jackie Stewart in the Matra-Ford MS10 and British Formula One beginner Vic Elford, driving a T86B Cooper-BRM designed by Tony Robinson. Elford was a former international rallying ace who had gone on to build himself a first-class reputation in long-distance sportscar races as well.

The next major event was the British Grand Prix, held at Brands Hatch on July 20th 1968 and won by Joseph Siffert. This was his first victory in a World Championship race, though he had won three non-championship Formula One Grands Prix, the 1963 Syracuse event and the Enna race in 1964 and 1965. Rob Walker had now taken stockbroker Jack Durlacher into partnership and they provided the Swiss driver with a brand new Lotus 49B for this race, equipped with the high-mounted rear wings first seen at Rouen. So new was the car in fact that finishing touches were still being put to it in the transporter on the way to the circuit.

All cars in the Brands Hatch race except BRM and Cooper were now fitted with wings, Honda following the Lotus example and mounting the wings on the rear suspension.

The Lotuses dominated the race, though Chris Amon in a Ferrari fought a lengthy battle with them later in the race. Lotus driver Jackie Oliver took the early lead but was passed by his Gold Leaf Team Lotus team-mate Graham Hill on the fourth lap. The younger man regained the lead on lap 27 when Hill's car broke its driveshaft but Oliver's smile soon vanished as his car also developed a transmission fault and ground to a halt on the 44th lap. Siffert and his dark blue Lotus had been glued to the tail of Oliver's red example and now took the lead, but Chris Amon's red Ferrari 312 went with him, and there followed an enthralling demonstration of driving skill from both men as Siffert brought his new Lotus to the line to beat Amon by 4.4 seconds.

The German Grand Prix was run in atrocious weather conditions, the Eifel mountains hidden by dense fog and the circuit continuously lashed by wind and rain. The pits appeared only as a shadowy silhouette from the grandstand on the other side of the track. Nobody could remember worse conditions, here or anywhere else, and there was some debate about whether the race should in fact take place. But it did, and, just as he had at Zandvoort, Jackie Stewart in the Tyrrell team's Matra-Ford once again displayed his enormous skill in the heavy Nürburgring rain to come home to victory, the blue Matra seemingly guided through the fog by radar. Hill crossed the finishing line in second place, but he was four minutes behind the Scot.

The advantages of the winged cars were put to their toughest test in the Italian Grand Prix, for the Monza circuit was the fastest of the year. It was debatable whether the improved

cornering provided by the wings would offset the loss of speed on the long Monza straights, and during practice extraordinary combinations of adjustable wings were tried by the various teams. Several competitors chose to run no wings at all, and one of them, the McLaren-Ford of Denis Hulme, was the ultimate winner.

In the best Monza tradition, the race developed into an intense battle, with a large group of cars bunching on the straights, driving in each other's slipstream. The lead in fact changed no fewer than 16 times during the race. Bruce McLaren led in a McLaren-Ford, so did Jackie Stewart in the Matra-Ford, Joseph Siffert in his Lotus-Ford, Denis Hulme in another McLaren-Ford and John Surtees in a V12 Honda. Jacky Ickx was sure of a high placing for Ferrari but ran out of fuel near the end and second place behind Hulme went to Johnny Servoz-Gavin in a Matra-Ford. The Monza race marked the last Grand Prix appearance of the Eagle-Weslake as Dan Gurney's enterprise now concentrated its efforts increasingly on the construction of USAC cars.

After the Italian Grand Prix, with three World Championship races still to go, Graham Hill was leading the scores with 30 points, Jacky Ickx had 27, Jackie Stewart 26 and Denis Hulme 24, which meant the title was still wide open.

At Monza an Italian journalist, the engineer Enrico Benzing, published the results of a study he had made on the effects of wings on Grand Prix cars.

Basing his calculations on wing areas of 25 to 30cm deep by 100 to 130cm wide, he worked out the theoretical downforce produced by different wing angles at speeds between 200km/h and 300km/h, and at the same time calculated the power loss resulting from the increased air resistance they created. The results of his study were as follows:

Angle of Wing	Downforce in kg
0°	25–55
5°	40–110
10°	60–170
15°	70–250

	Performance loss in hp
0°	1–2.5
5°	2–8
10°	5–15
15°	7–25
20°	12–40

The World Championship continued on the Mont Tremblant circuit in Canada where Chris Amon in the Ferrari led from the first lap to the 72nd, when a clutch fault developed and he was forced to change gears without it. However this was more than the car's transmission could stand, and the Italian car finally had to drop out. The race went to Denis Hulme in his M7A McLaren-Ford. During practice Jacky Ickx had an accident in his Ferrari, breaking a leg which of course prevented him from taking part in the race and effectively destroyed his World Championship hopes.

The title was still undecided after the United States Grand Prix at Watkins Glen, which Jackie Stewart won from Graham Hill, John Surtees, Dan Gurney (in a McLaren-Ford) and Joseph Siffert.

This left the Championship to be decided at the last race of the year in Mexico, from among Stewart, Hill and Hulme. Here, as always, tuning of engines was crucial at the Magdalena Mixhuca circuit, where adjustments have to be made to take the thinner air into account.

Joseph Siffert was the star of this race. After an indifferent start the Swiss driver took his Walker-Durlacher Lotus 49B to the front and built up a good lead until his throttle-linkage broke on the 26th lap. For two laps he sat immobile in the pits while the fault was repaired and his hopes of a second Grand Prix victory evaporated. But, back on the track, he was again the fastest man of the day. He broke the lap record time and again, won back one of the laps he had lost, and crossed the finishing line in sixth position. Siffert's heroic drive in Mexico did not go unnoticed, as, for the second time, he was presented with the BP Racing Trophy, which had been awarded every year since 1965 to the driver, personality or institution considered to have made the most outstanding effort in motorsport during the year.

Graham Hill was winner of the race, his third of the year, and this success ensured that the 39-year-old Londoner secured his second World Championship. He had scored 48 points against the 36 of Stewart (also with three wins), the 33 of Hulme (two wins) and the 27 of Jacky Ickx, who had missed the last two races. The Manufacturers' Championship went to Lotus, who thus repeated their

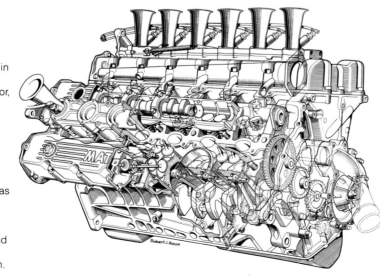

The Canadian Grand Prix was held for the first time on a 3.324km circuit at Mont Tremblant near St Jovite in 1968, but this venue was only used till 1970.

victories of 1963 and 1965.

Graham Hill's World Championship title was well deserved, although he did not quite seem to have the easy skill of Jim Clark. In his last years Clark had unquestionably been the outstanding driver, and his death left a large group of top drivers more or less in the same class as each other: in 1968 there was little to choose in terms of sheer skill between Graham Hill, Jackie Stewart, Denis Hulme, Jacky Ickx, Jack Brabham, Dan Gurney, Jochen Rindt, Chris Amon, John Surtees and Joseph Siffert. Gurney, Brabham and Rindt had not however been quite so much in the limelight in 1968, due mainly to the unreliability of their cars.

Several companies withdrew from Formula One racing at the end of the season. Dan Gurney decided to build Eagles only for USAC racing, Honda withdrew completely after a disappointing season with their machines and Cooper followed suit. In addition Matra started 1969 with the Ford-Cosworth engine but reverted to their own motor again in 1970.

Cooper's departure ended a successful era which had begun with the construction of the first 500cc Cooper-JAPs for Formula Three racing in 1946. The company had written a large portion of the history book of Grand Prix racing since that time, but in 1969 they vanished from the tracks forever. A prototype, the T90, had been developed for Formula 5000 racing, but was never marketed. All the Formula One materials were put up for auction and John Cooper himself sold his shares in the business and moved to Sussex, where he bought an ordinary garage. A great name disappeared.

Matra took part in Formula One events in 1968 with their own V12 engine. The motor, with four camshafts and 48 valves, was built in cooperation with the Moteur Moderne enterprise. The engineer responsible for the 12-cylinder engine was Georges Martin. Cylinder dimensions were 79.2 x 50mm (capacity 2999cc) and it developed just on 400bhp at 10,500rpm.

The Scot becomes World Champion for the first time, driving a Matra-Ford. The Ford-Cosworth motor wins every Grand Prix event. Disappointing start for four-wheel-drive Formula One cars.

The Ford-Cosworth DFV motor monopolised the 1969 season. Used this year by Matra, McLaren and Brabham as well as Lotus cars, it won every round in the World Championship. Best results achieved by the 12-cylinder cars were third place, by the Ferrari 312 at Zandvoort and the BRM P139 at Watkins Glen.

Ford's run of successes with the Cosworth V8 was a unique one: they took the first six places in South Africa and Monaco, the first nine at Clermont-Ferrand, the first ten at Silverstone, the first six on the Nürburgring and the first seven in Canada. When the DFV engine had first been used in the Lotus 49 at the 1967 Dutch Grand Prix it developed between 400 and 410bhp at 9000rpm, but after two years of development it now delivered 430bhp at 9500rpm, mainly due to alterations made to the exhaust system and the cylinder head. The engine's popularity was due in large part to its high degree of reliability: Matra for example had no motor faults on their records in 22 races in 1969. But the almost universal use of the Cosworth engine meant that all Formula One vehicles tended to be similar, with an individual monocoque chassis fitted with the Ford motor and Hewland transmission.

Ferrari and BRM now found themselves left behind. The Ferrari engine now developed 430bhp, the same as the Cosworth, but the Italian V12 lacked the eight's flexibility. Furthermore, Ferrari had only one top driver, Chris Amon, in 1969, as Jacky Ickx had left Ferrari and joined Brabham. BRM tried out new cylinder heads with four valves per cylinder on their transitional P139 model but the car was not a success. Their No 1 driver this year was John Surtees, who after Honda's withdrawal had also set up a company to build Formula 5000 cars under his own name. Brabham's previous year's BT26 chassis was adapted to take the Ford engine instead of the four-camshaft Repco, the team also losing Jochen Rindt to Lotus.

The only new model, apart from the four-wheel-drive cars, was the monocoque Matra MS80. A policy of technical co-operation had been developed over the years between Matra and Simca, a firm controlled by Chrysler, and Matra road cars were later sold through the enormous Chrysler/Simca dealer network. The Ford-powered Matra MS80 appeared in practice for the South African Grand Prix at Kyalami but did not actually race until the Spanish Grand Prix at Barcelona, which it won. With this car, built by Matra and maintained in peak condition by the Ken Tyrrell team, Jackie Stewart went on to win six of the 11 World Championship races of the year and by the time of the Italian Grand Prix at Monza had clinched his first world title, with three races still to go.

Jackie Stewart

As in the Lotus 49, the motor formed a structural part of the car, but the Matra was shorter and wider than its contemporaries, and had a bulbous appearance due to its fuel tanks being mounted on the sides. This idea of locating the tanks on the sides to concentrate the weight near the centre of the car was picked up over the following year or two by the McLaren, BRM and Tyrrell teams.

Matra was the leader in experimentation with aerodynamic wings and fins. The front nose-fins were adjustable and mounted onto the front suspension. The angle of the fin increased with acceleration, forcing the car's nose down, and decreased under braking in a similar system to that used by the Porsche factory in the development of their highly successful sports-racing cars. The Matra's large rear wing was also adjustable, and mounted on the suspension. Its angle was adjusted with the aid of a small electric motor, which increased the angle when applying the brakes or changing to lower gears, when the greatest roadholding is required. However all this came to nought when the urgently needed wing legislation was finally introduced, in time for the Monaco Grand Prix. This banned the use of adjustable wings, and rendered all Matra's development work obsolete.

From 1969 all racing cars had to be equipped with an automatic fire-extinguishing system. The most popular

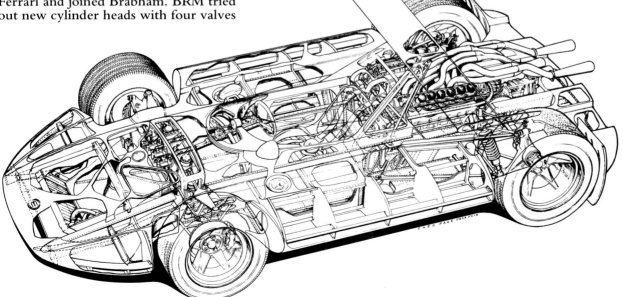

In 1968 the management of *Automobil Revue* in Berne came up with the idea of a safety racing car. An international consortium of specialists and experts was called together to formulate ideas, and the resultant Sigma Safety Car was built by Pinin Farina in Turin, using the mechanical parts of the 1966 Ferrari 312. The numerous integrated safety features included the provision of "soft impact zones" around the vehicle.

system used was the British Graviner, designed to react automatically to excess heat by releasing extinguishing gas into the cockpit and engine bay by means of a system of perforated pipes.

Jackie Stewart opened his season by winning the South African Grand Prix, driving the previous year's Matra-Ford MS10. The two BT26 Brabham-Fords developed fractures in their wings and suspension at this race.

The race in Spain marked the end of the road for the original types of wing. During the event, on the Montjuich Park street circuit in Barcelona, Graham Hill and Jochen Rindt both crashed their Lotus 49s into the safety barrier on the side of the road following wing breakages, causing considerable damage to their cars. Jacky Ickx also retired with a broken wing. Stewart won the Spanish Grand Prix in the new Matra MS80 but the spate of wing accidents had become alarming, and the CSI took action.

Winged cars appeared in the Thursday practice sessions at Monte Carlo but the CSI held an emergency sitting and announced that unrestricted use of wings would be banned from all future races, with immediate effect. The ruling met with a lot of opposition from the constructors, who argued that cars designed to use wings could become unstable in some situations without them; fortunately events did not prove their fears to have been justified. Graham Hill won the Monaco Grand Prix — for the fifth time — in a Lotus-Ford 49B after initial leader Jackie Stewart lost his chances of success when the new Matra MS80 retired with a broken driveshaft.

In the wake of the new wing ruling, the cars appeared for the Dutch Grand Prix at Zandvoort with washboard-like angled deflectors mounted on the rear.

Two new and much talked about four-wheel-drive cars made their appearance in this race, the Matra MS84, with Ferguson transmission, and the Lotus 63, which used a system developed by Lotus's own engineers. The wedge-shaped monocoque Lotus, designed by Maurice Phillippe, had its cockpit positioned well to the front, with the pedals mounted in front of the front axle, so that the driver's legs had to stretch under the axle. Matra's MS84 had the same outward appearance as the MS80 but used, as an interim measure, a tubular frame. This gave it the advantage that individual tubes could be easily cut off and relocated as development progressed and different layouts were tried. No four-wheel-drive cars in fact started the Zandvoort race as there was already considerable uncertainty about the advantages of the concept. McLaren were however proceeding with the preparation of their own four-by-four M9A, designed by the Swiss engineer Jo Marquart, and Ferrari and Cosworth were both working on four-wheel-drive Formula One Grand Prix cars too.

Jochen Rindt in a Lotus-Ford was the early leader in the Dutch race, but he was overtaken by Jackie Stewart in the Matra MS80. The Scot held his position to the end and won his third World Championship Formula One Grand Prix of the year. Rindt retired, leaving Joseph Siffert to take second place in his Rob Walker Lotus-Ford 49B, with Chris Amon third for Ferrari.

The CSI was convened in Amsterdam the day following the Dutch Grand Prix to discuss once more the key issue of wings in Formula One, this time with representatives of the constructors also attending the meeting. As a result of this meeting the CSI introduced another set of rules governing the use of wings. Suspension-mounted wings could no longer be moveable or adjustable, and the highest point of any wing had to be within 80cm of the lowest point of the fully sprung vehicle. The width of the body parts in front of the front wheels (air deflectors or fins) wider than 100cm could be no higher than the front wheel rims. The maximum width of any protrusion in front of the front wheels nevertheless had to be less than 150cm.

These rules provided a satisfactory solution to the wing problems. Aerodynamic devices now had to be mounted either in a fixed position, or forming an integral part of the body, and the designs could, at last, be controlled.

The four-wheel-drive Lotus 63 started in the French Grand Prix at Clermont-Ferrand, driven by the Englishman John Miles, but had to drop out on the second lap when mechanical problems intervened. Matra International, the Tyrrell team, won with Stewart first and Beltoise second, ahead of the Brabham-Ford of Jacky Ickx.

Stewart's Matra MS80 was damaged in practice for the British Grand Prix at Silverstone and he had to take over Beltoise's car for the race. Lotus driver Rindt was again early leader but once again struck trouble, this time losing half a minute in the pits after a small wing component had worked loose, causing heavy vibrations. Stewart, in spite of driving a strange car, won yet again, and moved yet further into the World Championship points lead. Three four-wheel-drive cars started in this race, the Lotus and Matra entries being joined by McLaren's M9A, which was driven by the Englishman Derek Bell. During the race Bell fought an enthralling neck-and-neck battle with Jean-Pierre Beltoise in the four-wheel-drive Matra MS84, but Bell had to retire when the new McLaren developed a suspension fault. Beltoise went on to finish ninth, with Miles tenth in the Lotus.

Cosworth had already built their four-wheel-drive car, but it never raced. The engineers behind the project were Keith Duckworth and Mike Costin together with former McLaren designer Robin Herd. The design was originally intended to be a Ford project, but the multinational company withdrew its support and the car never appeared at a racing event.

Below left
Jochen Rindt
(foreground) and
Graham Hill, each in a
Lotus 49, crashed into
the safety barriers in
separate incidents
during the 1969
Spanish Grand Prix at
Barcelona. The
accidents were caused
by breakages in the
wing mountings.
Shortly afterwards
wings of these
dimensions were
prohibited.

Right
Graham Hill in the
Lotus 49 during the
South African Grand
Prix at Kyalami, prior
to the wing restrictions.
The wing supports
were fitted directly on
to the suspension and
were very effective.

Below right
Mario Andretti in the
new Lotus 63 at the
German Grand Prix on
the Nürburgring. The
four-wheel-drive car
had its rear wings fitted
to the chassis to the
correct height in
accordance with the
new regulations.

After a few secret test sessions it was put away forever and has been in a British museum ever since. The four-wheel-drive Cosworth's shape was not its most attractive feature. Built within severe specification constraints, the car's body was slightly shorter than the outside of front and rear tyres, with fuel tanks accommodated within the rather angular bodywork. The four-wheel-drive mechanism, developed and built by Cosworth, was positioned immediately behind the cockpit, which was offset slightly to the left, and in front of the Cosworth-Ford V8 engine.

The merits or otherwise of four-wheel-drive racing cars came under serious discussion at the time. After prolonged tests by some of the top drivers the consensus of opinion was that four-wheel drive did not provide any distinct advantage.

It might be appropriate here to examine an article written by Belgian journalist Paul Frère, which appeared in *Automobile Year* at the end of 1969 under the heading, "The present failure of four-wheel-drive cars".

"It is possible to calculate that a modern Grand Prix car carries its greatest weight, 70% in fact, on the rear wheels. With modern racing tyres acceleration is at an approximate rate of 10 m/sec² (mean torque value between road and tyre under dry weather conditions 1.2). With today's engines developing in excess of 400bhp, it should be feasible, subject to proper gearing, for cars to achieve much faster acceleration, but this would require roadholding, torque and wheel pressure on the road to be sufficient. In practice, under full acceleration, with the optimum gearing, the wheels spin up to a speed of between 150 and 160km/h and are unable to transmit full engine power onto the road. A rate of acceleration greater than 10m/sec² can be achieved only by using the front wheels to increase roadholding. The limitation to acceleration is theoretically governed by roadholding x gravity (G = 9.81m/sec²). The maximum acceleration for a four-wheel-drive vehicle with a roadholding value of 1.2 and a corresponding power output of 430bhp is therefore approximately 12m/sec², as ineffective rotation of the wheels (wheelspin) occurs only up to 120-130km/h.

"Armed with this knowledge four firms produced four-wheel-drive cars: Matra, Lotus, McLaren, and Cosworth, though the Cosworth never passed beyond the private testing stage. A further advantage of four-wheel-drive is that the rear tyres can be narrower than generally used at present, reducing air resistance. In wet conditions the advantages of four-by-four increase substantially. The driving wheels of a conventional car spin at full acceleration up to 250-270km/h and full power can never be utilized. In a four-wheel-drive car wheelspin ceases between 200-220km/h and the acceleration of cars up to that speed is 20% more effective. As very few of this year's races took place in rain however, the theory could not be tested in practice.

"Four-wheel-drive cars do of course have disadvantages as well as advantages. By its very nature the vehicle is heavier (though some of the additional weight could be reduced by between 30 and 40kg) and the additional transmission requirements absorb some of the engine's power. It is largely because of these two factors that four-wheel-drive racing cars have not caught on to any great extent, even though the four-by-four has a clear advantage in corners under 130km/h. Corners under 130km/h are however relatively rare in modern circuits.

"But it must be said that four-wheel-drive cars have not yet been fully exploited. It should also be stated that the cars require a different technique of driving.

"The location of the motor is about the same in all four-wheel-drive cars. In all cases Ford motors have been used, installed back to front with the clutch to the front and the gearbox mounted directly behind the driver's seat. From there power is transmitted, slightly offset, to a differential. The constructors of four-wheel-drive cars are not very forthcoming with information regarding the power distribution ratio but it appears

First lap of the 1969
Dutch Grand Prix. The
midfield cars race
through the corner
before the Hunze Rug.
Pictured are: Piers
Courage (16) in the
Brabham BT26 of the
Frank Williams team,
Joseph Siffert (10) in a
Lotus 49B from the
Walker team, Jean-
Pierre Beltoise (5) in a
Matra MS80 from
Matra International,
John Surtees (10) in a
BRM P138, Jackie
Oliver in a BRM P133
and Vic Elford
(obscured) in a
McLaren M7A. Right at
the back of the picture
is Silvio Moser in his
private Brabham BT24.

Vic Elford

that in all cases the power is distributed
from the differential at a ratio of about
25% to the front and 75% to the rear. The
reason for applying more power to the
rear is because the greatest weight rests
on the rear wheels: static strain is greater
and dynamic force increases as
acceleration takes place. It is important
that the rear wheels are the first to spin,
otherwise the car could not be steered. A
small change in this ratio has a marked
influence on the car's roadholding
though at the same time it appears that
slight deviations from the accepted ratio
of 25:75 do not have a substantial effect
on the mode of driving. A limited-slip
differential is now used on the rear axles
of all racing cars and it appears that they
also have the same in front but here, too,
the experts are very guarded with their
information. It is a fact, however, that
only the Matra MS84 used the Ferguson
system which transmits power through
the differential from one axle to another
as soon as a pre-calculated percentage of
force is exceeded.

"None of the other cars use this sort
of power transfer system. The greatest
success achieved by a four-wheel-drive
car was Jochen Rindt's second place with
the Lotus-Ford 63 in the non-
championship Oulton Park Gold Cup
race, one lap behind the Brabham-Ford
driven by Jacky Ickx, and in the absence
of several of the leading Grand Prix
drivers.

"It is a fact, however, that the ever-
increasing power outputs of Grand Prix
motors will be heavily in favour of a
return to four-wheel drive in time to
come. Today's experiments, although not
of immediate use, will be of advantage in
the future. In wet conditions the speed
and safety of four-wheel-drive cars
already outweigh those of conventional
cars, and it would be no surprise if, in
years to come, four-wheel-drive Grand
Prix cars have the edge even in the dry
on circuits such as Monte Carlo."

255

Bottom
Several firms
introduced four-wheel
drive Formula One
cars in 1969. The
Matra MS84, in
contrast to the MS80,
had a tubular
spaceframe chassis
rather than a
monocoque. The four-
wheel-drive system,
incorporating inboard
brakes at front and
rear, was manufactured
by Ferguson.

Below
Graham Hill, defending
World Champion,
stands beside his
Lotus 49. The car is
still fitted with the
incredibly high rear
wings, but they were
banned soon
afterwards.

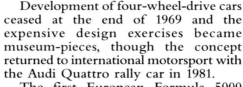

Development of four-wheel-drive cars ceased at the end of 1969 and the expensive design exercises became museum-pieces, though the concept returned to international motorsport with the Audi Quattro rally car in 1981.

The first European Formula 5000 races, derived for the American Formula A, were held in 1969 for cars with modified production engines with a maximum capacity of 5000cc. One of the most successful cars in the new class in both Europe and America was the TS5, designed with a Chevrolet motor by the former Eagle engineer Len Terry and built by the new company set up by John Surtees. Although himself racing BRMs in Formula One, Surtees was working on his own Grand Prix car for 1970.

As a result of continuing disappointment at BRM, chief engineer Tony Rudd gave notice at the end of 1969 and joined Lotus. In the internal shake-up that followed his departure Aubrey Woods and Jeff Johnson were given responsibility for engine design and Tony Southgate brought in to look after chassis development. Woods had been with BRM since the late forties, first working under Peter Berthon on the V16 and then the four-cylinder P25, and had become one of the leading lights in the 1.5-litre V8 Formula One engine project in 1960. Southgate joined BRM from All American Racers, the company responsible for Eagle cars, and at Bourne was assisted by Alec Osborne and Peter Wright, while Alec Stokes was put in charge of transmission development. This team was responsible for developing the rather hefty BRM P139, which had made its first appearance at Zandvoort in 1969, into the P153 in 1970 and the P160 the following year. Tim Parnell, son of the former Formula One driver Reg Parnell, was appointed BRM team manager.

The 1969 Grand Prix season meanwhile continued with the German Grand Prix where, on the sixth lap, Jacky Ickx took his Brabham-Ford BT26 past Stewart's Matra-Ford MS80 to lead the race. The Belgian, always something of a wizard on the Nürburgring, carried on for a clear win over the Scot. Siffert had bad luck in this race, having to retire when in third place on the last lap after his car's suspension broke. During practice Indianapolis winner Mario Andretti, who had never been to the Nürburgring before, put up some excellent times in the four-wheel-drive Lotus 63, but in the race left the track and retired.

The Italian Grand Prix was as exciting as ever, with the usual high-speed slipstreaming battle for the lead throughout. It was believed that the use of lower body-mounted wings would reduce speeds on the long Monza straights by between 15 and 20km/h, and many drivers accordingly decided against them. In the photo finish, Jackie Stewart's Matra crossed the line half a car's length ahead of Jochen Rindt's Lotus, with Jean-Pierre Beltoise in another Matra and Bruce McLaren in a McLaren a further car's length behind.

In Modena, Ferrari had been carrying out the first tests of their new Formula One car, the flat-12 Type 312B1, in the days leading up to the Italian Grand Prix. In typical Ferrari fashion, the outer sheetmetal skin was riveted to the tubular frame and the 12-cylinder motor was hooked onto rear of the chassis. This was the model which would bring Ferrari those much hoped-for victories once again.

Ickx again interrupted Stewart's string of successes in the Canadian Grand Prix at Mosport, the Scot losing control and careering off the track. Team boss Brabham followed his No 2 over the line for a double Brabham victory.

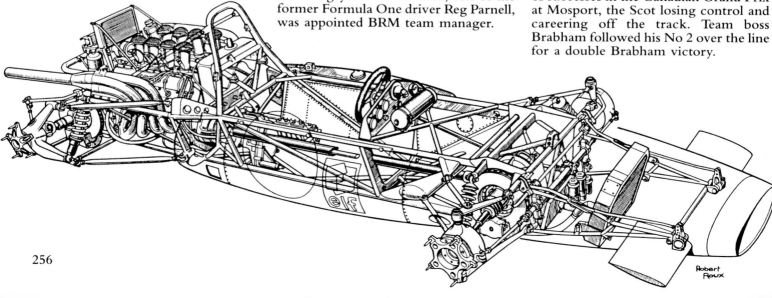

Franco Gozzi

Jackie Stewart won his first World Championship in 1969. Pictured here, Stewart takes his Matra-Cosworth MS80 through a bend during the French Grand Prix.

At Watkins Glen Jochen Rindt in the Lotus 49B won his first Grand Prix, and took home $52,000 in prize money. The German, although racing on an Austrian licence, had now emigrated to Switzerland where he spent his prize money building a luxurious house near Jackie Stewart's in a romantic village overlooking Lake Geneva. Graham Hill had a serious accident at Watkins Glen, breaking several bones, and the 1962 and 1968 World Champion was forced to spend several months recuperating.

The McLaren team celebrated another victory in the Mexican Grand Prix when Denis Hulme in an M7A beat the Brabhams of Jacky Ickx and Jack Brabham.

The fight for the 1969 World Championship had been decided long before this: not since Jim Clark's day had it been so obvious who the next

Silvio Moser

Champion would be. Jackie Stewart, with 63 points, took the title, ahead of Jacky Ickx with 37, Bruce McLaren with 26 and Jochen Rindt with 22. The World Manufacturers' Championship went to Matra.

As most of the leading Grand Prix contenders now used the same motor, greater attention was now paid to those other elements in the car's makeup which had previously played only a minor role. With chassis design no longer making much difference, driver ability counted for more than ever. Also increasingly important in this era was the quality and durability of tyres. Dunlop had become very popular because of Stewart's Championship win, but Goodyear and

Firestone now matched the British company's products in every respect. Lower-profile tyres (with the height in cross-section between 0.4 and 0.45 of the width) were now almost universally adopted, and were superior on dry roads. Wheels of 15-inch diameter (13-inch rims were usually used in the front to reduce wind resistance) were now in common use, and this also allowed the use of bigger brakes, as well as providing better handling at limits of centrifugal force. The norm for rim widths became 14-inch to 16-inch at the rear and 10-inch to 12-inch in front. In 1969 the official Matra and BRM teams both used Dunlop tyres, while Lotus and Ferrari stuck with Firestones, and McLaren and Brabham used Goodyears.

In June of 1969, months of negotiations ended when Fiat, the Turin automotive giant, became a 50% shareholder in the Ferrari enterprise. Enzo Ferrari remained as president of the company and was also in charge of racing while Fiat engineer Giuseppe Dondo became managing director and another Fiat man, Francesco Bellicardi, was also appointed to the Ferrari board. Commendatore Bellicardi was previously a director of the Weber carburettor company in Bologna, a subsidiary of Fiat, and was a long-standing friend of Ferrari. The engineer Mauro Forghieri remained technical manager of the racing division and Dr Franco Gozzi public relations manager, a position he had held for the previous two years. Fiat had no intention of changing the traditional character of the Maranello stable, whose organisation and structure had been, and would continue to be until his death in 1988, greatly influenced by the personality of its founder. A few years earlier Henry Ford II had made an unsuccessful bid to take over the prestigious Ferrari enterprise, and it was only due to the personal

influence of Fiat's president, Gianni Agnelli, that the 1969 arrangement succeeded.

The 1969 Indianapolis 500 had been won by Mario Andretti in an American-built Hawk car with turbocharged Ford V8 motor. Andretti's entrant, Andy Granatelli of STP, had commissioned a new Ford-engined four-wheel-drive car from Lotus for the race but the British car, the Lotus 64, had failed to come up to expectations during testing and the team changed over to the older car shortly before the race. The Indianapolis 500 had by now lost its appeal for European Grand Prix drivers, the exception this year being Denis Hulme, but British designers such as McLaren and Lola continued to supply cars for American teams and United States drivers.

In 1969 a new British make, March, was born. Behind the enterprise were four men, Alan Rees, Robin Herd, Max Mosley and Graham Coaker (the company name actually came from their initials, *M*osley, *A*lan *R*ees, *C*oaker and *H*erd). Rees was a former Formula Two driver who had later become manager of the Roy Winkelmann Formula Two racing team (for which Jochen Rindt competed), Herd, a former school friend, had designed the first Formula One McLaren in 1965 and had subsequently worked for a short period for Cosworth, where he designed the four-wheel-drive car, and Mosley, a solicitor and one-time Formula Two driver, was a friend of Herd's from their Oxford University days; the three had met Coaker, who had once worked for Hawker-Siddeley, at a motor race meeting. The March firm was established at Bicester in Oxfordshire in April 1969 and ambitious plans were released in the summer. By September a prototype had already taken part in a Formula Three race, and new Formula Two and Formula One cars were promised for the 1970 season. Mosley, who was responsible for financial control of the newly founded firm and who also handled public relations, succeeded in obtaining financial support from the Italo-American president of STP, Andy Granatelli, and Herd immediately started work on the Type 701 for Formula One. The car was ready at the beginning of the 1970 season.

Jochen Rindt wins the World Championship for Lotus but dies on the track at Monza. The ingenious wedge-shaped Lotus 72. In the second half of the season the flat-twelve Ferrari dominates the circuits. Stewart in a Tyrrell.

Jochen Rindt won the World Championship in 1970 with the Lotus 49B and 72 models, but his fatal accident during practice for the Italian Grand Prix at Monza meant the title was awarded posthumously.

Jochen Rindt

After the absolute dominance of the Ford-Cosworth engine in 1968 and 1969, the 12-cylinder Ferrari, BRM and Matra engines started to make up for lost time in 1970 and the Ferrari in fact won several races. In this they were aided by the mid-year onset of something of a Ford-Cosworth crisis, a result of practical rather than technical factors. A new approach was also evident in the question of materials, their utility and application being reappraised more closely than had been done for many years before.

Most established teams had new models for this season's World Championship and in addition several new makes appeared in Formula One, notably March, De Tomaso and, later, Surtees and Tyrrell. At the same time the ranks of Formula One masters were boosted by an influx of talented new drivers from Formula Two and long-distance racing, men such as the Swiss driver Gianclaudio Regazzoni, the Swedes Ronnie Peterson and Reine Wisell, Frenchmen François Cevert and Henri Pescarolo, Brazilian Emerson Fittipaldi, the Italian Ignazio Giunti, German Rolf Stommelen, Englishman Peter Gethin and Australian Tim Schenken. Among the young newcomers, "Clay" Regazzoni and Emerson Fittipaldi each won a Formula One race in their first World Championship year, and there were indications that they both had brilliant racing futures.

But 1970 was also a tragic year, with accidents taking the lives of Bruce McLaren, Piers Courage and Jochen Rindt. Rindt was leading the World Championship after the German Grand Prix but was killed during practice for the

Italian Grand Prix. At the end of the season, for the first time, motorsport had to honour a World Champion posthumously.

Car of the year, without question, was the striking new wedge-shaped Lotus 72 with unique side-mounted radiators. Right from this car's first appearance in the Spanish Grand Prix, it was clear that the Norfolk firm had once again produced a trend-setting design for other Formula One constructors to follow. By the Dutch Grand Prix the car had already reached a state of development which enabled Jochen Rindt to score an easy win.

Like the Lotus 18 of 1960, the Mark 25 (the first successful monocoque Grand Prix car) two years later and the 1967 Mark 49, the Lotus 72 was an entirely new design which was years ahead of its time. Designed by Maurice Phillippe, the 72's wedge shape with flat sloping nose provided built-in downforce to improve cornering efficiency. Furthermore, as it had no air intake at the front (the radiators were fed by low-mounted intakes on the sides of the cockpit), wind resistance was dramatically reduced and straight-line speed improved. Indeed back-to-back tests with a Lotus 49C, fitted with the same Ford-Cosworth motor showed that the new car was 14km/h faster in terms of straight-line speed, due entirely to its aerodynamically superior body shape.

Phillippe's suspension design for the Lotus 72 was on the torsion-bar principle, reviving the concept applied by Professor Porsche on his Auto Union designs in the 1930s but not used very much since that time. On the Lotus a torsion bar constructed from nickel-chrome molybdenum was positioned inside a tube and connected at one end to the spring-steel suspension arm. To reduce unsprung weight further, and also to increase aerodynamic efficiency, both front and rear brakes were mounted inboard, though a problem arose with the front brakes in the car's first few races. Repeated applications of the brakes gave rise to difficulties of heat dissipation, and the grease in the wheel-bearings began to liquify. This was ultimately corrected by the use of forced ventilation (by an electric motor) to cool the brakes as the car was slowed.

Brabham produced their first true monocoque this year, the BT33. The chassis ended just behind the cockpit and the Ford-Cosworth motor served as a

structural member at the rear.

At BRM the new Type P153 was produced under the direction of Tony Southgate, with a very fat body enclosing the fuel tanks and the familiar V12 engine further developed by Aubrey Woods.

The ranks of the Cosworth users were reduced by one when Matra director Jean-Luc Lagardére announced at the end of 1969 that, due to the company's impending amalgamation with Chrysler-Simca, Matra cars would in the future be fitted exclusively with Matra's own V12 engines. Ken Tyrrell and Jackie Stewart wanted to continue with Cosworth engines however, and ended their technical collaboration with the Vélizy firm.

The only company offering to provide Ford-powered Grand Prix cars to private teams in 1970 was the new March company, founded the year before, and thus it was that Tyrrell placed an order for three new March 701 cars. The French Elf petrol company remained the Tyrrell team's principal financial backer.

Even before their car turned a wheel, it looked as if the new March firm would take their fair share of laurels, as they also planned to run a two-car works team,

Above
In 1970, the Tyrrell team changed from Matras to the March-Ford 701, in which Jackie Stewart (pictured here at Monaco) won the Spanish Grand Prix at Jarama. The March's small side-mounted fuel tanks were designed to provide extra aerodynamic downforce.

Top right
Jean-Pierre Beltoise in a V12 Matra MS120 leads Jack Brabham's Cosworth-Ford-powered Brabham BT33 during the Spanish Grand Prix at Jarama.

Andrea de Adamich

with Chris Amon and Joseph Siffert as drivers. In addition, the factory supported Indianapolis winner Mario Andretti who competed with a team consisting of STP personnel from the United States under the direction of Vince Granatelli, Andy's son. The tall, blond Swede, Ronnie Peterson, competed in privately owned March 701. He had proved himself racing Tecno cars in Formula Three and Formula Two over the past four years and had a reputation of being hard to beat.

Robin Herd had decided his first Formula One March would be a conservative design with no great technological breakthroughs, and the March 701 monocoque was indeed orthodox in every sense, even to outboard-mounted coil springs and shock absorbers. The new car did however have aerodynamically-shaped fuel tanks mounted on the sides of the chassis, their wing form providing built-in downforce, but this was not a principle that was followed up by other constructors until the end of the decade when Colin Chapman rediscovered the "wing-car" concept and revolutionized Formula One design. The hasty construction of the new March Grand Prix cars was immediately apparent, and both Amon and Siffert were driven to despair by a constant succession of teething troubles, though the Tyrrell team's Marches seemed better prepared than the factory team's own examples.

The Matra V12 motor reappeared in Formula One this year after an absence of 12 months, during which time it had been seen only in endurance racing, and was fitted into a new box-shaped Matra Type MS120. The combustion chambers and valve angles of the compact V12 had been modified and the camshafts placed in a common housing.

At McLaren, Jo Marquart had designed the new M14A model, which was little more than an improved version of the M7A. The works cars continued to use Ford-Cosworth motors but McLaren had come to an arrangement with Alfa Romeo to supply additional chassis to the Italian company. For their first tentative steps towards a return to Grand Prix racing, Alfa Romeo fitted to the McLaren chassis their own V8 engines, 2933cc (86 x 64.4mm) units which had been used very successfully in sportscar racing. There were however considerable difficulties in adapting them to the British cars for Grand Prix use, as the engine was approximately 30kg heavier than the

Cosworth-Ford, and problems with oil circulation were encountered in its Formula One application. The cars were built and maintained by Alfa Romeo's racing division, Autodelta, with Andrea de Adamich from Milan as the principal driver, first with an M7 (designated M7D in its Alfa Romeo application) and later with new M14D cars.

The new monocoque De Tomaso Type 505-38 was designed for Italian-resident Argentinian Alejandro de Tomaso by the former Maserati and Lamborghini engineer Giampaolo Dallara, and run during the season by a small British team run by Frank Williams, with Piers Courage, of the brewing family, as driver. The previous year Courage had raced a Brabham for the Williams team, which in those days was far from the successful operation it later became.

Ferrari's weapon for 1970 was the new Type 312B which had been completed, but not raced, the previous year. Its engine was a 12-cylinder four-camshaft 2991cc (78.5 x 51.1mm) Boxer unit which, running on a compression ratio of 11.8:1, developed 464bhp at 11,600rpm. The flat-12 engine was fitted with Lucas fuel-injection and Marelli Dinoplex ignition. The chassis was the familiar Ferrari combination of tubular framing and monocoque construction with cross-bracing behind the cockpit. Into this the motor was fitted underneath, onto longitudinal supports.

To minimise frictional losses, the Ferrari engineers had decided to reduce the number of main bearings from seven to four, and this — predictably perhaps — led to many early problems, even to broken crankshafts. There were also early difficulties with oil circulation but the

problems were all overcome and by the second half of the season the 312B proved to be a very competitive vehicle. Jacky Ickx and Clay Regazzoni in fact finished first and second with their 312Bs in the Austrian, Canadian and Mexican Grands Prix.

Two new makes appeared later in the season, Tyrrell and Surtees. Jackie Stewart had won the Spanish Grand Prix in Ken Tyrrell's March 701 but the team was not satisfied with the car's outmoded design and its lack of development potential, and Tyrrell had already decided to build a car which would carry his own name. To design the first Tyrrell car, the one-time timber merchant obtained the services of Derek Gardner, a former Ferguson engineer who had been actively involved in the four-wheel-drive Matra MS84 project. Gardner started his first drawings for the car, which would be powered by the Cosworth-Ford V8 engine, in February 1970, and produced an excellent monocoque design which made its race debut in August.

Team Surtees had been set up in premises at Edenbridge in Kent in 1969 and immediately began building cars for the Formula 5000 class. John Surtees himself started the 1970 Grand Prix season at the wheel of an M7A McLaren but at the British Grand Prix at Brands Hatch appeared with a small Cosworth-powered monocoque, the Surtees TS7. He thus became the fourth Grand Prix driver in modern history to race his own make in Formula One events, following Jack Brabham, Dan Gurney and Bruce McLaren.

This year's large influx of new young drivers to the top level of the sport had meanwhile led to many changes in the

Formula One teams. Jacky Ickx, who had taken over Chris Amon's position as No 1 driver at Ferrari, was joined by two newcomers, Clay Regazzoni and Ignazio Giunti, though both young drivers had apparently been given only vague promises of opportunities to take part in Grand Prix races. Regazzoni, who came from the Swiss canton of Tessin, had been a works driver for the Bologna-based Tecno factory since 1967, driving in their

Rolf Stommelen

Formula Three team for two years with considerable success in races all over Europe and graduating to Formula Two during the 1968 season. Ferrari was in fact only the second team he had driven for. Regazzoni had gained a reputation for being a tough driver, and his temperament marked him as something of a black sheep, but he was a fearless dare devil renowned for his late braking. Ignazio Giunti came to Ferrari from Alfa Romeo, where he had gained considerable experience in long-distance endurance racing.

On Ickx's return to Ferrari, Jack Brabham took on the German driver Rolf Stommelen, whose drive was reportedly paid for by *Auto Motor und Sport* magazine.

The McLaren team consisted initially of team boss Bruce McLaren and his countryman Denis Hulme, but in quick succession Hulme had an accident at Indianapolis and burnt his hands, and McLaren was killed in a testing accident. The paprika-coloured cars were then driven by Dan Gurney and British Formula 5000 specialist Peter Gethin.

The Matra-Simca MS120s were handled by Jean-Pierre Beltoise and Formula Two graduate Henri Pescarolo while the Tyrrell team consisted of Jackie Stewart and Johnny Servoz-Gavin. Then at the end of May, after the Monaco Grand Prix, Servoz-Gavin suddenly announced his retirement from racing, saying he felt he was getting too old to make a name for himself, and adding that he was losing his nerve. Many admired him for this courageous decision. The Elf petrol company had made it a condition of their sponsorship of the Tyrrell team that one of the drivers should be a Frenchman, and this opened up the

opportunity for François Cevert, a brother-in-law of Jean-Pierre Beltoise, to join the team.

Graham Hill, following several months' convalescing after his Watkins Glen accident, left the Lotus factory team after three years to drive the private cars of Rob Walker, first a Lotus 49C and later a new Lotus 72. Jochen Rindt was thus top man at Gold Leaf Team Lotus in 1970, with John Miles as No 2. Later in the season however the promising young Brazilian Emerson Fittipaldi joined the team and so, at the end of the year, did the Swedish Formula Three star Reine Wisell.

The BRM team of P153 cars, sponsored this year by Yardley cosmetics, were driven by Pedro Rodriguez, the Englishman Jackie Oliver and wealthy Canadian George Eaton. Eaton had only average ability as a Grand Prix driver, and joining the team had reputedly cost him a lot of money.

Joseph Siffert's signing with the March Formula One team had caused quite a stir in the Swiss press, as he had been approached by Ferrari at the end of the previous year with the offer of a contract for both Grand Prix racing and endurance events. However, he already had a contract with Porsche for long-distance events, and another with BMW for Formula Two, so had to turn the Maranello offer down in order to continue his association with these two important German firms and remain in Formula One racing at the same time. His position as No 2 to Chris Amon at March was actually paid for by the Porsche company.

The attention paid to the quality and reliability of tyres, evident over the previous few years, continued, for the most powerful motor and the best driver were of little use if the car was fitted with tyres of the wrong compound. Quite often the tyre engineers at Firestone, Goodyear or Dunlop experimented with compounds between one race and the next and the results of their tests could be the deciding factor between winning or losing. Tyres became softer and softer, so that a set lasted just long enough for one Grand Prix. Tyres were also made lighter and thinner and, in the second half of the sixties, tubeless tyres had appeared, though their soft compounds made them very susceptible to puncturing. Driving over sharp, pointed stones was often enough to cause damage.

World Champion Jackie Stewart was

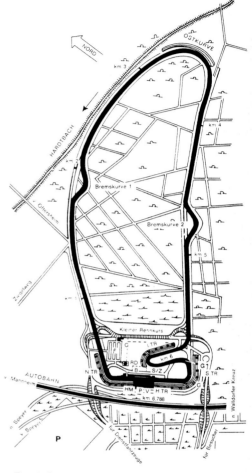

The AvD was forced to change the venue of the 1970 German Grand Prix to Hockenheim after the drivers threatened to boycott the Nürburgring. Two chicanes were built into the Hockenheim circuit's long and slightly curving straights, which were considered to have become too fast. A lap measured 6.788 kilometres.

Right
Clay Regazzoni in a Ferrari 312B leads a snake of cars through the Lesmo Curve during the 1970 Italian Grand Prix at Monza, which he won. It was only his fifth Grand Prix start. Here he is followed by Jackie Stewart's March-Ford 701 and the BRM P153 driven by Rodriguez.

probably the best prepared of any driver for the start of the new Grand Prix season, having undertaken an intensive tyre-testing programme for Dunlop. This often required days of test driving with various types of tyres to determine their optimum performance and safety. This year was however to be the last Grand Prix year for the British tyre manufacturer, who announced at the end of 1970 that they would be turning their attention to less expensive categories.

Stewart had covered thousands of kilometres in tyre-testing before the 1970 World Championship opened with the South African Grand Prix at Kyalami, and he led from the start. The Tyrrell-entered March 701 was however overtaken by the BT33 Brabham-Ford of 44-year-old Jack Brabham, who crossed the finishing line winner. Hulme in a McLaren M14A was second, with Stewart third and Beltoise in the Matra-Simca MS120 fourth.

During 1970 representatives of the CSI, the racing teams and the Grand Prix organisers convened in Geneva to discuss the vexed question of starting money. A number of drivers and their teams had been demanding an increase in payments, but the organisers had responded that they were in no position to meet such demands. It was a delicate matter, and on more than one occasion it appeared that stalemate had been reached. However, the meeting ended in agreement, even though it caused a great deal of confusion and complaint until it was finally accepted.

Under the system in operation before this an organiser merely invited specific competitors, with whatever starting money the organiser thought necessary to pay. The Geneva Accord however specified a fixed scale, taking transportation costs into account, and also introduced a new system of incentive payments. Under this new scheme drivers were paid according to their positions at the one-quarter, half and three-quarter distance stages of the race, in addition to the prize money for which each final place was entitled. With all the various expenses such as starting money, transport costs and prize money now fixed, Grand Prix organisers were able to secure the participation of major competitors, while at the same time the teams were able to work to a fixed budget for the season.

There was some confusion at the Spanish and Monaco Grands Prix over whether the Geneva Accord was yet in force, or was only to apply in the future, and some of the more prominent drivers were guaranteed starts, while others had to qualify for the right.

Jackie Stewart in the Team Tyrrell March-Ford 701 led the Spanish Grand Prix at Jarama from start to finish with Bruce McLaren second at the end in his McLaren-Ford M14A and Mario Andretti, also in March-Ford 701, third. The March maiden victory came from the combination of Jackie Stewart's driving skill, the Tyrrell team's first-class preparation and the choice of Dunlop tyres.

During the first lap of the race there was an accident which could have had tragic consequences. Jackie Oliver lost his brakes entering a slow corner and his BRM P153 rammed Jacky Ickx's Ferrari in the side, ripping a hole in the Italian car's fuel tank. Both vehicles immediately burst into flame, but although Oliver was able to free himself from the cockpit of his car straight away Ickx was not quite so fast. When the Belgian finally appeared from behind the burning car, with overalls ablaze, he ran towards the trackside fire marshals and rolled on the ground. A fire extinguisher was immediately turned on him but the unfortunate Belgian suffered burns to his legs and hands. After a few weeks of rest however he was able to take part in the Monaco Grand Prix.

The Monaco race ended dramatically. Jackie Stewart in his dark blue March-Ford had been well ahead when an engine fault forced him to throw in the towel on the 21st lap. Jack Brabham in his Brabham-Ford BT33 took the lead with Chris Amon in the works March second. When the New Zealander also had to give up second place was taken over by Jochen Rindt, having one last drive in an old Lotus-Ford 49C as the new 72 had failed to come up to expectations during practice. Brabham seemed certain of victory, even though Rindt was steadily closing the gap, but at the Gasometre Hairpin on the last lap the Australian braked too late and slid straight into the safety barrier. Rindt took the lead in the last 150 metres and won the Grand Prix unopposed. Even though the circuit had become very slippery towards the end, Rindt's last lap was a new record.

The Austro-German driver had once again displayed his outstanding driving skills in this race. Once considered a rather wild and undisciplined driver, he had now matured into a remarkable driver with exceptional skills who had not however lost his killer instinct. Brabham was able to extricate his car and crossed the finishing line in second place with Henri Pescarolo third in a Matra-Simca MS120.

On June 2nd Bruce McLaren lost his life at Goodwood while testing the McLaren-Chevrolet M8D CanAm sportscar which he and Denis Hulme were planning to use later in the year. The rear engine-cover flew up at high speed and the M8D slammed into a marshal's post.

BRM returned to the winner's circle after many disappointing years when Pedro Rodriguez won the Belgian Grand Prix at Spa. The marque's last Grand Prix success had been at Monaco in 1966, when Jackie Stewart won the first World Championship event of the new 3-litre

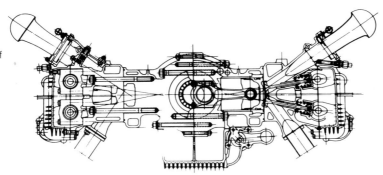

The flat-12 Type 312 Ferrari motor which appeared at the end of 1969, and had only four main bearings.

formula in the old BRM V8. One of the new Ferraris took fourth place in the 1970 Belgian race, driven by Ignazio Giunti.

The distinctive side-radiator Lotus 72 was ready for the Dutch Grand Prix, and Jochen Rindt was the envy of every driver at Zandvoort. He took the new wedge-shaped car to its first victory, with Stewart in the March 701 second and Ickx in a Ferrari 312B third. Clay Regazzoni made his Formula One debut in this race and was fourth in his Ferrari 312B1.

After the promising Grand Prix debuts of both Giunti and Regazzoni, Ferrari decided to let them take part in the following World Championship events, alternating as No 2 driver to Jacky Ickx for the rest of the season. Dan Gurney, brought in as a substitute driver at McLaren, did not show his earlier confidence at Zandvoort, and never really regained it. There was another accident, when Piers Courage's De Tomaso careered off the track and burst into flames and the driver was killed.

In the French Grand Prix at Clermont-Ferrand the initial lead was disputed by the 12-cylinder Matra of Beltoise and the 12-cylinder Ferrari driven by Ickx, but both cars developed faults which forced them to quit. Beltoise had tyre problems and Ickx valve damage, leaving Rindt in the Lotus 72 to win his third Championship event in a row. It appeared after Clermont-Ferrand that the 12-cylinder cars were having something of a revival, for although there were fewer multi-cylinder engines racing it looked as if the Ford-Cosworth domination might soon be broken.

In the days leading up to the French Grand Prix the Formula One drivers had let it be known that they were not willing to drive in the German Grand Prix on the Nürburgring, considering the track to be in poor condition and no longer in keeping with modern safety requirements. There were no safety fences to protect cars from the many trees

growing close to the track. The drivers had made their demands too late however, as there was not enough time available before the race to rebuild the 22.8km northern Eifel circuit; that would take many weeks of work. The organisers therefore decided to hold the race on the fast Hockenheim circuit which had been equipped with the necessary safety features.

All the major names were represented at the British Grand Prix at Brands Hatch. Jack Brabham in his BT33 seemed assured of victory until he ran out of petrol on the last lap, literally 200 metres from the finish-line. In a repeat of the Monaco result, Jochen Rindt in the Lotus 72 swept past to take an unexpected last-minute victory. This race was Clay Regazzoni's second Grand Prix and, after a hard fight with Hulme, he took fourth place.

Eighth across the line, in his first Grand Prix, was the 24-year-old Brazilian Emerson Fittipaldi, whom Colin Chapman had given a Lotus 49C for the race. Fittipaldi had arrived in England in 1968 and competed in the Formula Ford class, for single-seater racing cars with Ford Cortina 1600 motors. His talent was immediately obvious, and before the

season was out he was driving for Lotus in Formula Three, where he was instantly as successful as he had been in Formula Ford. For his second season in Europe, with the financial support of sponsors in Brazil, young Fittapaldi was able to progress to Formula Two, again with Lotus.

The grandstands were filled to capacity when the starting flag fell at the German Grand Prix at Hockenheim. The spectators were held spellbound by a gripping neck-and-neck race between Rindt in the Lotus 72 and Ickx in a Ferrari 312 while behind them Regazzoni in the second Ferrari ran for the first half of the race in close company with March drivers Amon and Siffert. Rindt and Ickx continued their battle right until the end of the race, which the Lotus finally won, just ahead of the Ferrari. With five Grand Prix victories already under his belt at the beginning of August, Jochen Rindt was almost certain to be the new World Champion. Fittipaldi made everyone take

Pedro Rodriguez

Pedro Rodriguez

Above
The 1970 Belgian Grand Prix at Spa was won by Pedro Rodriguez in the V12 BRM P153.

Left
Jochen Rindt gave the Lotus 72 its first victory in the 1970 Dutch Grand Prix. He had earlier won at Monaco with the earlier 49B model.

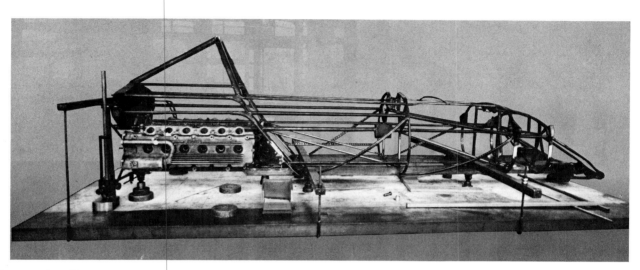

The chassis of a Type 312B laid out on its jig at Maranello showing the small-diameter tubular frame before the alloy sheeting is welded on to provide rigidity. This method of chassis construction was used by Ferrari till 1982. The flat-12 engine was mounted from underneath onto an extension of the chassis.

notice with fourth place in the old Lotus 49C.

By the middle of the year Cosworth had reached a crisis point. The increasing Ferrari threat made it necessary for the Northampton company to devote its energies to research and development into improving their design, yet company personnel were fully occupied with the regular overhaul and maintenance of the existing engines of their large number of customers. By this time approximately 70 Ford-Cosworth DFV engines were in circulation, and the factory had to overhaul a dozen engines after each Grand Prix, which was beyond their capacity. Drivers had to be asked to treat their engines with the utmost care during practice and to keep the number of practice laps to a minimum. The top drivers — Rindt, Stewart and Brabham — had the privilege of using the so-called "Super Cosworth" which had a few additional horsepower. But in spite of the engine's successes, all the Cosworth V8s still seemed to have the same weaknesses, the camshaft being susceptible to breakages on the last cylinder on the right-hand side. Drivers also became familiar with a small exploding noise inside the motor, which was the sound of broken pushrods shattering against the block. It seemed there had never been a motor in Grand Prix history with more problems, though in time Cosworth was able to overcome them all.

By 1970 cylinder heads with four valves per cylinder and Lucas fuel-injection systems were common to all Formula One engines. They delivered the following specific performances:

Ferrari 312B: flat-12-cylinder motor, 78.5 x 51.1mm capacity 2991cc, developing 464bhp at 11,600rpm; performance per litre 155bhp, mean piston speed 19.7m/sec.

Matra Simca MS120: 60° V12, 79.7 x 50mm, 2999cc, 430bhp at 11,500rpm; 143bhp/litre, 19.1m/sec.

BRM P153: 60° V12, 74.5 x 57.2mm, 2998cc, 425bhp at 10,500rpm, 142bhp/litre, 20m/sec.

Ford Cosworth DFV: 90° V8, 85.6 x 64.8mm, 2993cc, 436bhp at 10,000rpm, 145bhp/litre, 21.6m/sec.

Alfa Romeo 33.3: 90° V8, 86 x 64.4mm, 2993cc, 424bhp at 9600rpm, 141bhp/litre, 20.6m/sec.

The 1970 Austrian Grand Prix was held for the first time on the newly built Österreichring circuit at Zeltweg in the Steiermark, rather than on the bumpy tarmac of Zeltweg airport, where the last World Championship Austrian Grand Prix had been held in 1964. This time there was a major change in fortunes and Ferraris took the first two places, Ickx winning from the improving Regazzoni.

A few days after the Austrian Grand Prix, Derek Gardner's Tyrrell 001 design was unveiled to the public. A monocoque chassis fitted with Cosworth-Ford motor and Hewland transmission, the car was raced for the first time by Jackie Stewart in the Oulton Park Gold Cup race, where it failed to finish, and Stewart reverted to the March 701 for the Italian Grand Prix.

It was during practice for this meeting that World Champion elect Jochen Rindt was tragically killed. As he approached the Parabolica Curve on one lap, a front brake-shaft on his Lotus 72 broke and the car turned sharp left into the safety fence at high speed. Rindt died in the ambulance on the way to the hospital, and the mood of the drivers was understandably subdued in the days leading up to the Grand Prix.

The Italian Grand Prix was a gripping race and after Ickx was forced out with a clutch problem his team-mate Regazzoni took over. The Swiss driver outran Stewart, Beltoise and Hulme and won the race; it was only his fifth start in a World Championship Formula One Grand Prix.

The new Tyrrell's first Grand Prix was the Canadian race at Mont Tremblant, and Stewart took it straight to the front. He led the Ferraris until the 31st lap when a suspension fault forced him out, leaving Ickx and Regazzoni to score another 1-2 result for Ferrari. The Tyrrell's performance caused a stir at Ferrari, though some tried to explain away the British car's superiority by saying that Stewart used Dunlop tyres; these reached optimum operating temperature after only a few laps, whereas the Firestones on the Ferraris required a longer time to warm up. But overall, Ferrari personnel considered the Tyrrell-Ford 001 a serious rival to their hitherto superior flat-12.

A very similar story unfolded in the United States Grand Prix. Stewart in the Tyrrell led from the first lap, driving the car to its limits in an effort to put as much distance as possible between himself and his competitors. Unfortunately however an oil leak forced him to drop out of the race after 83 laps. The Mexican Pedro Rodriguez in a BRM 153 took over the lead and it looked as if BRM would take their second victory of the season. Eight laps from the end however Rodriguez had to refuel and the time that took cost him victory. Winner in a Lotus 72, in only his fourth Grand Prix start, was the Brazilian Emerson Fittipaldi, whose grandfather had emigrated from Calabria to Brazil to find his fortune. Rodriguez took second place and the Swede Reine Wisell celebrated his Formula One debut by bringing his Lotus 72 in third, ahead of Ickx's Ferrari.

Last World Championship race of the year was the Mexican Grand Prix, run under very dangerous circumstances which could easily have resulted in catastrophe. Many spectators scaled the safety fences and rows of them were standing, closely packed, right on the edge of the track.

The race was delayed for several hours while efforts were made to move the spectators to safer positions, but even a direct plea by the drivers had little effect and the race started amid mixed feelings. The Ferraris of Ickx and Regazzoni dominated the race and once again took the first two places. Jackie Stewart retired from the fray after colliding with a dog, which damaged the chassis of his car.

Jochen Rindt had already notched up 45 World Championship points before his accident, and was awarded the title ahead of Ickx with 40 points, Regazzoni with 33, Hulme with 27 and Brabham and Stewart with 25 each. Clay Regazzoni's ranking was remarkable; the other Grand Prix newcomer, Fittipaldi, was in tenth place with 10 points. The Formula One Manufacturers' Championship went to Lotus, and the curtain fell on a season tinged with sadness.

Clay Regazzoni

Clay Regazzoni at Hockenheim in 1970, where he led a Formula One race for the first time in his career. He had the reputation of being a daredevil, earned in Formula Three and Formula Two events. He became European Formula Two Champion with Tecno in 1970.

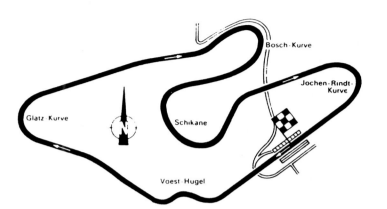

The 1970 Austrian Grand Prix was held for the first time on the Osterreichring at Zeltweg, though the 5.911km circuit did not initially have the chicane illustrated here.

Formula One cars of the 3-litre formula era 1966 to 1970

Year	Make & model	Cylinders	Capacity	Bore	Stroke	bhp	rpm	Valves	Camshafts	Gears	Dry weight
1966	Brabham BT12-Repco	8	2996	88,9	60,25	320	7 500	16	2	5	515
1966	BRM P83-H16	16	2997,86	69,85	48,89	400	11 000	32	6	6	690
1966	Cooper T81-Maserati	12	2989,48	70,4	64	360	9 500	24	4	5	605
1966	Ferrari 312 (24V)	12	2989,5	77	53,5	360	10 000	24	4	5	548
1966	Ferrari 312 (36V)	12	2989,5	77	53,5	390	10 000	36	4	5	540
1966	Ferrari Dino 246	6	2417	85	71	280	8 500	12	4	5	505
1966	Lotus L43-BRM	16	2997,86	69,85	48,89	425,8	10 500	32	6	6	580
1966	McLaren M2B-Ford	8	2999,174	95,5	52,32	321	9 000	32	4	5	530
1966	Honda RA273	12	2992	78	52,2	400	11 000	48	4	5	720
1967	Brabham BT20-Repco	8	2996	88,9	60,25	360	8 500	16	2	5	515
1967	Cooper T81-Maserati	12	2990	75,2	56	390	10 000	36	4	5	580
1967	Eagle TG2-Weslake	12	2997	72,8	60,3	390	9 500	48	4	5	530
1967	Honda RA300	12	2992	78	52,2	420	11 000	48	4	5	600
1967	Lotus 49-Ford	8	2993	85,7	64,8	400	9 000	32	4	5	510
1967	Ferrari 312 (48V)	12	2989,5	77	53,5	410	10 000	48	4	5	530
1967	McLaren M5A-BRM	12	2998	74,6	57,2	380	10 000	24	4	5	535
1968	Brabham BT24-Repco	8	2986	89	60	400	8 500	32	4	5	530
1968	BRM P133	12	2998	74,6	57,2	380	10 000	24	4	5	565
1968	Cooper 86B-BRM	12	2998	74,6	57,2	380	10 000	24	4	5	545
1968	Ferrari 312 (48V)	12	2989,5	77	53,5	415	10 000	48	4	5	530
1968	Honda RA301	12	2993	78	52,2	410	11 000	48	4	5	580
1968	Honda RA302	8	2987	88	61,4	380	10 500	32	4	5	500
1968	Lotus 49-Ford	8	2993	85,6	64,8	415	9 200	32	4	5	510
1968	Matra MS 11	12	2999	79,7	50	390	10 500	48	4	5	540
1968	McLaren M7A-Ford	8	2993	85,6	64,8	415	9 200	32	4	5	545
1969	Brabham BT26-Ford	8	2993	85,6	64,8	425	9 000	32	4	5	535
1969	BRM P138	12	2998	74,6	57,2	420	9 500	48	4	5	540
1969	Cosworth 4WD-Ford	8	2993	85,6	64,8	425	9 000	32	4	5	560
1969	Ferrari 312(48V)	12	2989	77	53,3	436	11 000	48	4	5	530
1969	Lotus 49-Ford	8	2993	85,6	64,8	425	9 000	32	4	5	530
1969	Lotus 63-Ford (4 × 4)	8	2993	85,6	64,8	425	9 000	32	4	5	600
1969	Matra MS10-Ford	8	2993	85,6	64,8	425	9 000	32	4	5	540
1969	Matra MS11	12	2985	79,7	50	420	9 000	48	4	5	560
1969	Matra MS80-Ford	8	2993	85,6	64,8	425	9 000	32	4	5	540
1969	Matra MS84-Ford (4 × 4)	8	2993	85,6	64,8	425	9 000	32	4	5	600
1969	McLaren M7A-Ford	8	2993	85,6	64,8	425	9 000	32	4	5	540
1969	McLaren M9A (4 × 4)	8	2993	85,6	64,8	425	9 000	32	4	5	565
1970	Brabham BT33-Ford	8	2993	85,6	64,8	450	10 000	32	4	5	540
1970	De Tomaso 505-38-Ford	8	2993	85,6	64,8	450	10 000	32	4	5	552
1970	Ferrari 312B	12	2998	79	52,8	458	11 500	48	4	5	540
1970	Matra MS120	12	2999	79,7	50	450	11 000	48	4	4	555
1970	McLaren M7D-Alfa	8	2993	86	64,4	425	10 000	32	4	5	530
1970	McLaren M14A-Ford	8	2993	85,6	64,8	450	10 000	32	4	5	545
1970	BRM P153	12	2998	74,6	57,2	450	11 000	48	4	5	530
1970	Lotus 72-Ford	8	2993	85,6	64,8	450	10 000	32	4	5	530
1970	March 701-Ford	8	2993	85,6	64,8	450	10 000	32	4	5	540
1970	Bellasi-Ford	8	2973	85,6	64,8	450	10 000	32	4	5	560
1970	Surtees TS7-Ford	8	2973	85,6	64,8	450	10 000	32	4	5	553
1970	Tyrrell 01-Ford	8	2973	85,6	64,8	450	10 000	32	4	5	540

Victory for Tyrrell

Stewart wins his second World Champion title. Treadless tyres prove to be useless in the rain. Lotus tries a turbine car. Siffert loses his life at Brands Hatch.

After the convincing performance of the 12-cylinder Ferrari in the second half of the 1970 season, the experts believed that the 1971 World Championship would be dominated by the red Italian cars with their high-revving flat-12 engines. The Cosworth DFV motor was now four years old, and the general consensus of opinion was that it had only a minimal chance of success. But Keith Duckworth's engine was in fact nowhere near the end of its racing life, and a new Series 2 model was produced this year, developing between 440 and 450bhp at 10,500rpm. Ferrari's latest 12-cylinder creation was said to develop 480bhp at 12,500rpm, but there is reason to believe these claims were exaggerated. The 12-cylinder Matra and BRM engines both developed 440bhp. But, output aside, the Cosworth factory had now succeeded in building reliability into their V8s, and the problems of 1970 were a thing of the past.

At the end of 1970 Ferrari had tried to hire Jackie Stewart, but the Scot remained with Tyrrell and Ford. As always, the Tyrrell organisation's standards were unequalled in every respect and set an example for every other team. Each member of the team had his set tasks, and there was never any haste or disorder. Accordingly the cars designed by Derek Gardner were maintained and operated at the peak of efficiency, and Stewart in

The Scot Jackie Stewart, pictured during the French Grand Prix at Le Castellet, became World Drivers' Champion for the second time in 1971, driving the well-balanced Tyrrell 001. Note the high "air box", a fashionable feature at the time.

Tyrrell-Fords 001 and 002 finished nine of the 11 World Championship races of 1971. Stewart's driving skills matched the reliability of his cars and he won six Championship Grand Prix races, which gave him his second World Drivers' Championship. The Scottish driver's domination of the season drew parallels with his late countryman Jim Clark.

There were the usual changes before the season started. Chris Amon, Joseph Siffert and Mario Andretti all left the

Francois Cevert

young March firm after their disappointments of 1970. Amon signed a two-year contract with Matra, Siffert joined the Mexican Pedro Rodriguez at BRM and Andretti went to Ferrari, thus fulfilling an ambition the Italian-born American had held since boyhood. The Swede Ronnie Peterson, who in 1970 had driven a March 701 owned privately by vintage car enthusiast Colin Crabbe, was hired by the March factory for a period of two years. Rob Walker gave up his independent team this year and amalgamated with John Surtees, where Rolf Stommelen, the former Brabham driver, was now on the driving strength. Walker's driver Graham Hill joined Brabham as a works driver, his team-mate being the Australian Tim Schenken. Jack Brabham had retired from driving at the end of 1970 and his Formula One team was managed this year solely by his friend Ron Tauranac.

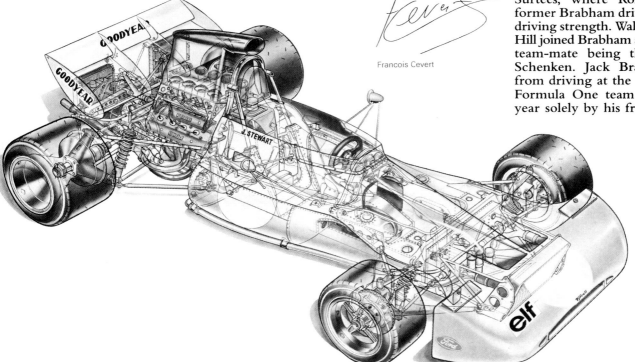

The Tyrrell-Ford 001, designed by Derek Gardner, appeared in the middle of 1970. The first Tyrrell had been built secretly and was greeted with great surprise at Oulton Park. It was an instant success.

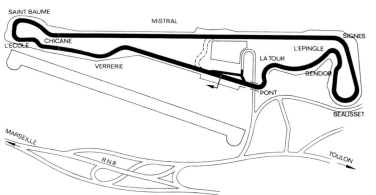

The promising Emerson Fittipaldi remained with Lotus and so did Reine Wisell, while Colin Chapman continued his policy of promoting from the ranks by offering the Australian Formula Three specialist Dave Walker the chance of driving in Formula One later in the year.

The 1971 racing season began tragically in January when the Italian driver Ignazio Giunti died at the wheel of his Ferrari 312 sports prototype in the Buenos Aires 1000km race, first round of the World Championship of Makes. The Matra driven by Jean-Pierre Beltoise had run out of fuel and its driver was pushing it across the finishing-straight to the pits. Giunti, who was leading the race at the time, saw the almost-stationary blue Matra moving across the road too late to avoid colliding with it. There was a tremendous explosion and the Ferrari burst into flames, in which the unfortunate Italian died. Beltoise was held by the Argentinian authorities to have acted negligently, and was stripped of his licence for six months.

By the start of the Grand Prix season a number of new models were ready. Ralph Bellamy, formerly on the Brabham design staff, unveiled the McLaren M19A, a low, flat car with its fuel tanks mounted on the sides in BRM and Tyrrell fashion. Feature of the M19A was its new type of "rising rate" suspension with inboard coil springs and shock absorbers, but the innovative system did not work effectively in practice, and towards the

end of the season was replaced by more conventional suspension. The new Ferrari 312B2 also employed a new suspension design, with the coil springs mounted almost horizontally over the rear axle. The B2 had many initial chassis problems however and its performance did not match that of its predecessor, the B1. In spite of this however Clay Regazzoni took a 312B2 to victory in the non-championship Race of Champions at Brands Hatch in March, though it is fair to add that his victory was assisted by a lucky choice of tyres.

The new March 711 was built under the direction of Robin Herd with streamlined bodywork by aerodynamics expert Frank Costin, who had earlier been responsible for the first Lotus sportscar bodies and subsequently the Formula One Vanwall. The new March had no frontal air intake but instead a rounded nose, on top of which an oval wing was mounted in the centre. This concept did not work out well in practice, as the design had not made sufficient provision for engine cooling. The March

711 also had its front disc brakes mounted inboard with shafts running to the wheels, in Lotus practice, but after Ronnie Peterson had an accident due to a broken shaft — and with Jochen Rindt's Monza accident still fresh in everyone's mind — Herd repositioned the brakes of the 711 on the outside of the chassis.

Ron Tauranac came up with the Brabham BT34 with two separate front-mounted radiators mounted on either side of the front spoiler, and looking something like a lobster-claw. The Surtees TS9 was an only slightly modified development of the TS7, and likewise Tony Southgate's BRM P160 was almost identical to the P153, though its roadholding was much improved.

After collaborating with McLaren in 1970, Alfa Romeo this year came to a similar arrangement with March, whereby the British team ran cars with the Italian engines for Alfa's drivers Andrea de Adamich and Nanni Galli. The hoped-for Formula One victories remained elusive however.

Following the Dunlop tyre company's withdrawal from Grand Prix racing, their test driver, Jackie Stewart, signed a three-year contract with Goodyear. Tyre technology had progressed markedly and lower and lower profiles were being adopted. Research had shown that the contemporary racing tyre was responsible for 65% of a car's total wind

For the first time in 1971 the French Grand Prix was held on the modern new circuit built by the drinks manufacturer Paul Picard at Le Castellet, between Toulon and Marseilles. The 5.81km circuit was considered one of the safest in use at that time.

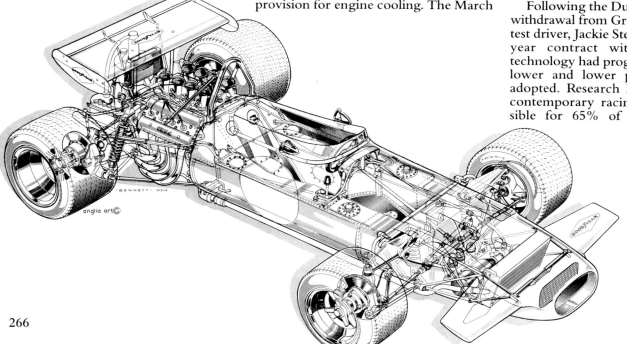

The Brabham BT33, raced with Ford-Cosworth DFV motor from 1970 to the beginning of 1972, was Ron Tauranac's first true monocoque design. It was in one of these cars that Jack Brabham drove his last Formula One races in 1970.

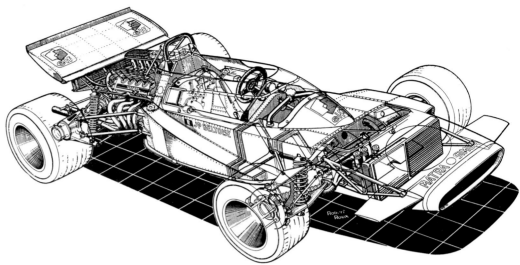

resistance, but on the latest low-profile tyres, whose width was approximately three times their height, that percentage fell to 30. To reduce wind resistance still further, and also to reduce unsprung weight, many designers revised their idea of having 15-inch rear tyres and fitted 13-inch units instead. This in turn brought dramatic improvements in road-holding, to the extent that Grand Prix cars were typically generating centrifugal force of around 1.6g through corners.

It was not long after this that tyres completely devoid of treads started appearing in European Grand Prix events. These "slicks", as they were called, had been used by dragsters in the United States and also for kart racing, and their smooth contact area provided maximum roadholding. They were however quite useless, and indeed dangerous, in wet weather conditions.

The 1971 World Championship series opened with the South African Grand Prix at Kyalami. Denis Hulme took the lead in the new McLaren M19A and held his position for much of the race, only to fall back due to a suspension problem. This enabled Mario Andretti in a previous year's 312B1 Ferrari to take over the lead and he stayed there for his first Formula One victory.

The Matra appeared in this race fitted for the first time with a high air-scoop above the engine. This was designed to increase the pressure of air to the engine, and in the months which followed most Formula One designers modified their cars by fitting these tall air-scoops.

At the end of January Chris Amon in a Matra won the Argentine Grand Prix, a non-championship event this year and run in the absence of many of the top teams, notably Ferrari, Tyrrell and BRM. This Buenos Aires victory was the first Formula One success for the V12 Matra engine. The local Formula Two driver Carlos Alberto Reutemann made his Formula One debut in this race at the wheel of Joakim Bonnier's privately-owned McLaren-Ford M7A and took third place; at the end of the season he would take part in his first World Championship race as a Brabham works driver.

As already mentioned, Clay Regazzoni won the Race of Champions in March with the new Ferrari 312B2, designed by Mauro Forghieri. A few weeks later the Maranello team celebrated another Formula One victory when Andretti in the older 312B1 won the non-championship Questor Grand Prix on the new Ontario circuit in California. The next Championship successes however went

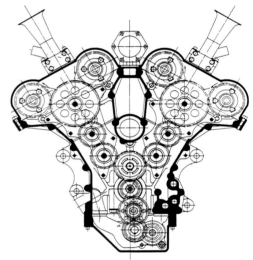

Below
The Lotus 72, with wedge-shaped body, torsion-bar suspension and inboard brakes, was continuously developed between 1970 and 1975.

Above
The Lotus 56B with a Pratt & Whitney gas turbine.

Above right
The V12 Matra MS120 engine with centrally positioned fuel-injected trumpets. These had previously been located (centre right) between the camshafts.

to Jackie Stewart, who won both the Spanish and Monaco Grands Prix in Tyrrell-Fords. At Barcelona Jacky Ickx in a Ferrari 312B1 followed him like a shadow without being able to pass, but nobody could match the Stewart/Tyrrell combination at Monaco.

During practice at Monaco the Tyrrell appeared for the first time with new Girling front brakes, which employed a dual-disc system designed to overcome the overheating problems which had arisen at the time that 13-inch wheel-rims were adopted and discs were moved inboard; before that they had been exposed directly to the cooling effects of the airstream.

Tyres were the deciding factor in the Dutch Grand Prix at Zandvoort. The track was made wet by a very fine rain which fell from the start, and it was soon clear that those competitors using Firestone tyres had the advantage over those on Goodyears. Ickx in a Ferrari 312B2 and Rodriguez in a BRM P160 soon left the pack behind them and fought for the lead until Ickx, an outstanding wet-weather driver, was able to shake off his Mexican rival. Many drivers, amongst them Jackie Stewart,

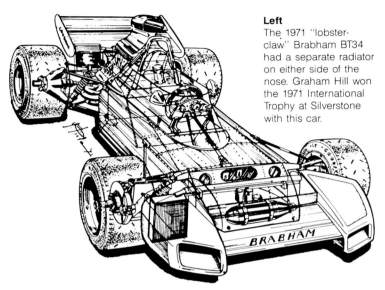

Left
The 1971 "lobster-claw" Brabham BT34 had a separate radiator on either side of the nose. Graham Hill won the 1971 International Trophy at Silverstone with this car.

Below
Joseph Siffert started the 1971 Austrian Grand Prix from pole position and recorded an impressive start-to-finish victory. Siffert's BRM P160 started losing air from the left rear tyre towards the end but this was not enough to let Fittipaldi's Lotus 72 get past.

were caught in nose-to-tail collisions or careered off the track. Among those whose races ended in the barriers was Dave Walker, driving the Lotus 56. This car, fitted with a Pratt & Whitney gas-turbine engine, was derived from the Indianapolis Lotus models of earlier years, but this sort of propulsion was difficult to adapt to European-style road courses. Jochen Rindt had forecast a great future for the concept but Emerson Fittipaldi and Reine Wisell encountered the same problems with the car as Walker had. Gas-turbine engines required a different driving technique, as smooth acceleration out of corners depended on the engines

being at peak revs going in. To achieve this the driver had to apply the throttle before the bend, at the same time as he was braking!

Jackie Stewart in the Tyrrell had another clear victory in the French Grand Prix, held for the first time on a new circuit at Le Castellet near Marseilles. Prior to the race it was thought the power of the Ferrari motors on the long Mistral Straight would decide the outcome of the race, but Stewart in the Tyrrell-Ford anticipated the opposition's every move and proved to have the advantage over them in every situation. The Tyrrell was seen at Le Castellet with a new full-width nose-section extending right to the wheels. This considerably improved downforce, and the concept was soon being tried by other designers. Rumours had flown around Le Castellet that the Tyrrell engines were not using standard petrol, but that was discounted after the fuel was tested. Rumours persisted however, and at the British Grand Prix the car's engine capacity was checked — and found to be within the legal limits.

In the middle of the season both BRM and Ferrari started experiencing problems with chassis vibration. On the British car these led to problems in the ignition coil, which was mounted on the roll-bar. This was a location particularly susceptible to vibration, and repositioning the component on the cylinder-head cured

the problem. This was done just before the Austrian Grand Prix. At the same time the Ferrari technicians had similar problems with vibration and all sorts of tests were conducted in an effort to trace the cause. These were not successful however and the vibration problem in the cars continued throughout the year. It was only later that it was discovered that the problems at both BRM and Ferrari were caused by the Firestone tyres, and magnified by changes in diameter. In 1971 Dr Peter Schetty of Basle, winner of the 1969 European Mountain Championship with a 2-litre 212E Ferrari, was appointed manager of the Ferrari racing department. Although no longer racing, Schetty continued as Ferrari test driver.

In July came tragedy when the 31-year-old Mexican Pedro Rodriguez was killed in an unimportant sportscar race on the Nürnberg circuit in West Germany. He was having a one-off drive in a privately owned Ferrari 512 but during the race was baulked by a slower competitor and the two cars collided. The 5-litre Ferrri immediately burst into flames and there was no hope for

Rodriguez. It was tragic that a daredevil driver of such skill had to die in an accident that was in no way any of his making.

Jackie Stewart's string of successes continued in the British Grand Prix at Silverstone and then in the German race. This latter event was held once again on the Nürburgring, which had been completely rebuilt and brought up to modern safety standards. François Cevert in the second Tyrrell followed his second place in France with a repeat here, setting a new lap record of 7 minutes 20.1 seconds (186.8km/h) for the difficult circuit. The Tyrrell successes were not only due to the ability and talents of Jackie Stewart, but also to the excellence of their technically advanced cars.

Joseph Siffert had his day in the Austrian Grand Prix at Zeltweg. The Swiss showed his determination to win by setting fastest time in practice with his BRM P160, and led the race from start to finish. Even Jackie Stewart in the Tyrrell-Ford was unable to pass the Swiss driver, finally losing a wheel on the 34th lap and careering off the track.

On the last lap the leading BRM started to lose air from its left rear tyre, and Emerson Fittipaldi in his Lotus 72 closed the gap hand over fist. But Siffert still managed to cross the line in first place, 5.1 seconds ahead of the Brazilian, for what was to be his last victory.

Taking part in his first World Championship Grand Prix here, at the wheel of a March, was a local Formula Two driver called Niki Lauda.

Matra scratched their entries from the Austrian Grand Prix while the MS120s

Above
The circuit at Watkins Glen was completely rebuilt in 1971 and extended to 3.906km.

Right
The very original body shape of the March 711 was designed by Frank Costin. The car was usually driven by Ronnie Peterson, though in a few events, Andrea de Adamich and Nanni Galli drove an Alfa Romeo V8-powered version.

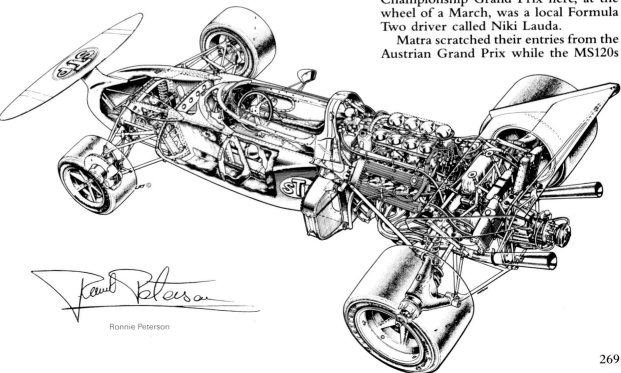

Ronnie Peterson

underwent revision in Vélizy but they were back in the field for the Italian Grand Prix at Monza, where Amon set fastest time in practice. In the race the usual slipstreaming battle took place. Regazzoni, Amon, Siffert, Peterson and Stewart all held the lead at one time or another, and so did a couple of newcomers to the big time, Mike Hailwood and Peter Gethin. Hailwood, a former World Motorcycle Champion, was making a return to Formula One with a factory Surtees TS9, having tried with private Lotus cars several years before, while Gethin, who was the son of a famous English jockey, was in a BRM P160. Amon fell back from the leading bunch when the blue Matra developed a fault in its fuel-feed system, and Siffert fell victim to faulty transmission. It was a photo-finish, with Gethin emerging as the surprise winner, by one metre from the Swede Ronnie Peterson in his March 711, and François Cevert in the second Tyrrell taking third place by mere lengths from Hailwood.

Emerson Fittipaldi drove the Lotus 56 turbine car at Monza in the colours of an imaginary entrant as Colin Chapman and the official Lotus team were concerned about legal difficulties in the wake of Jochen Rindt's fatal accident the previous year. Fittipaldi finished eighth, the turbine engine failing to perform satisfactorily even on this fast track.

Gethin's victory was actually achieved as much by luck as good management, as a slipstreaming race is always something of a lottery. The diminutive Englishman had managed to outfox his rivals with a risky late-braking manoeuvre at the Parabolica Curve on the last lap, though no amount of controversy could dampen his joy.

The V12 BRM P153 raced in 1970 (when Rodriquez won the Belgian Grand Prix) and 1971. The P160 model which followed it had a very similar bulbous appearance.

The next Grand Prix, the Canadian, was held at Mosport in teeming rain. The Goodyear wet-weather tyres, which had not fared very well at all in Zandvoort, were every bit as good as the Firestone product at Mosport and Jackie Stewart scored a clear win over Ronnie Peterson. American Mark Donohue, in his first Grand Prix, took third place at Mosport in a McLaren-Ford M19A prepared by Roger Penske's team, one of the leading Indianapolis entrants.

The World Championship ended with the United States Grand Prix on the Watkins Glen circuit, which had been extended, overhauled and made safer. Stewart led initially but his motor started to slow down. His team-mate Cevert took over the lead and carried on to win his first Grand Prix, ahead of Siffert and Peterson. It was the first Grand Prix victory for a Frenchman since Maurice Trintignant's success at Monaco in 1958.

The International Sporting Commission cancelled the last World Championship race, the Mexican Grand Prix, as they had been unable to obtain a guarantee from the organisers that safety could be improved from the previous year's debacle, when spectators had swarmed onto the edges of the

The fashionable "fat-belly" shape was also adopted by Ralph Bellamy for his successful McLaren M19 design of 1971-/2. The M19 made its debut in 1971 at Kyalami, where Denis Hulme held the lead for most of the event.

Mark Donohue

Mike Hailwood

circuit. It was also probable that the Mexican race would not have attracted much spectator interest as the death of the Mexican idol, Pedro Rodriguez, was fresh in local minds.

After 11 World Championship events, Jackie Stewart was acclaimed the best driver in the world, and won the title with a points score of 62. Ronnie Peterson, who had picked up a lot of ground in the second half of the season, was runner-up for March with 33 points, followed by Stewart's team-mate François Cevert with 26 points and, with 19 each, Jacky Ickx (winner in Holland) and Joseph Siffert (first in Austria). Emerson Fittipaldi was ranked sixth on the World Championship ladder after his first full Grand Prix season. Tyrrell won the World Manufacturers' Championship at their first attempt, a truly remarkable achievement.

The Grand Prix series had begun with a number of Ferrari victories and these were followed by the astonishing run of successes by the Stewart/Tyrrell combination as the Ferraris' performance fell further and further behind over the second half of the season. BRM had made a lot of progress at their Bourne base and moved back into the limelight in the last few races but Matra, McLaren and Brabham were able to chalk up only a few minor successes. During the season the experimental suspension systems of both the McLaren M19A and the Ferrari 312B2 were replaced by more conventional inboard systems. The Ford-Cosworth DFV motor had won its fourth World Championship in 1971. This ingenious, and relatively simple engine was still very much alive, despite predictions to the contrary.

The 1971 racing season was yet another that finished on a tragic note. As a substitute for the Mexican Grand Prix which had been cancelled, a non-championship Formula One race was held at Brands Hatch on October 24th. It was here that Joseph Siffert died at the wheel of his BRM P160. The precise cause of the accident has never been made public, but it is believed that Switzerland's best driver was the victim of a technical fault. The BRM burst into flames immediately after hitting an earth bank and Siffert suffocated in the cockpit. The fire marshals and emergency services arrived too late to be of any help.

Formula One cars of 1971

Make/model	Chief designer(s)	Engine	Gearbox (speeds)	Chassis	Wheelbase	Track	Tyre make	Dry weight
Brabham BT 33	Ron Tauranac	Cosworth DFV (V8)	Hewland DG 300 (5)	SM	2413	F 1486 R 1556	Goodyear	560
Brabham BT 34	Ron Tauranac	Cosworth DFV (V8)	Hewland FG 400 (5)	FM	2413	F 1575 R 1600	Goodyear	570
BRM P 153	Tony Southgate	BRM P 142-60 (V12)	BRM (5)	SM	2438	F 1524 R 1499	Firestone	550
BRM P 160	Tony Southgate	BRM P 142-60 (V12)	BRM (5)	SM	2464	F 1473 R 1448	Firestone	540
Ferrari 312 B	Mauro Forghieri	Ferrari 312 B (12 cyl 180°)	Ferrari (5)	TS	2380	F 1480–1545 R 1485–1555	Firestone	550
Ferrari 312 B2	Mauro Forghieri	Ferrari 312 B (12 cyl 180°)	Ferrari (5)	TS	2300–2350	F 1380–1420 R 1380–1420	Firestone	560
Lotus 72	Colin Chapman Maurice Phillippe	Cosworth DFV (V8)	Hewland DG 300 (5)	SM	2540	F 1448 R 1448	Firestone	550
Lotus 56 B	Colin Chapman Maurice Phillippe	Pratt & Whitney gas turbine	Ferguson/ZF	SM	2616	F 1587 R 1587	Firestone	600
March 711	Robin Herd Geoffrey Ferris	Cosworth DFV (V8)	Hewland FG 400 (5)	FM	2438	F 1524 R 1524	Firestone	560
March 711	Robin Herd Geoffrey Ferris	Alfa Romeo 33/3 (V8)	Hewland FG 400 (5)	FM	2438	F 1524 R 1524	Firestone	580
Matra MS 120 B	Georges Martin Robert Morin	Matra MS 71 (V12)	Hewland FG 400 (5)	FM	2500	F 1640 R 1600–1700	Goodyear	560
McLaren M 19	Ralph Bellamy	Cosworth DFV (V8)	Hewland DG 400 (5)	FM	2540	F 1600 R 1575	Goodyear	560
Surtees TS 7	John Surtees	Cosworth DFV (V8)	Hewland DG 300 (5)	FM	2438	F 1473 R 1524	Firestone	550
Surtees TS 9	John Surtees	Cosworth DFV (V8)	Hewland FG 400 (5)	FM	2534	F 1524 R 1549	Firestone	540
Tyrrell 01-03	Derek Gardner	Cosworth DFV (V8)	Hewland FG 400 (5)	SM	2388–2535	F 1590 R 1590–1648	Goodyear	560

Chassis construction: SM = semi-monocoque; FM = full monocoque; TS = tubular frame with stressed skins.

Another South American

Fittipaldi becomes World Champion in a Lotus 72. Beltoise wins BRM's last Grand Prix at Monaco. Ecclestone takes over the Brabham team. The 500bhp figure approaches.

Bernie Ecclestone

Emerson Fittipaldi was born in 1946 in Sao Paulo, son of a radio reporter. He came to Europe in 1968 and, after taking part in Formula Ford and Formula Three races, made his Formula One debut at Brands Hatch in 1970. Two years later, at the age of only 25, he became the youngest World Champion. Never had a driver achieved so much in such short time as this quiet, fast, but safe driver.

The 23rd World Championship series was made up of 12 events and five of them were won by Fittipaldi in the redeveloped Lotus-Ford 72 (correctly the Lotus 72D). Jackie Stewart won four others for Tyrrell-Ford, and single victories went the way of Jean-Pierre Beltoise in a BRM, Jacky Ickx in a Ferrari and Denis Hulme in a McLaren-Ford.

In the re-forming of the various Formula One teams at the beginning of the season, Fittipaldi remained No 1 driver at Lotus, with the Australian Dave Walker as his No 2, Colin Chapman not wishing to renew Reine Wisell's contract. The wedge-shaped side-radiator Lotus 72s were officially renamed John Player Specials this year after the John Player tobacco company bought the exclusive rights to the prestigious model; in fact most people continued to refer to the cars by their more familiar name. The cars were sprayed black with gold lines, similar to John Player Special cigarette packets.

The successful Tyrrell cars designed by Derek Gardner were again driven by Jackie Stewart and François Cevert, though the French Formula Two driver Patrick Depailler also drove in two races during the season. Ronnie Peterson was joined on the March team by 23-year-old Niki Lauda. Lauda, the son of a Vienna industrialist, had bought his way into

Arturo Merzario

Formula One racing by means of a loan from an Austrian bank. The Ferrari team remained unchanged, with Jacky Ickx, Clay Regazzoni and Mario Andretti as permanent members; in addition, Arturo Merzario was given two Grand Prix drives during the season and Nanni Galli one.

A major change occurred at BRM when the Philip Morris tobacco company invested two million francs in the Bourne team for the right to have the cars called Marlboro-BRMs for one year. The plan was for five cars to take part in every race, three in the official team plus two drivers from the so-called Marlboro National teams. The "A-team" drivers were Jean-Pierre Beltoise, the New Zealander Howden Ganley and Peter Gethin, with the other cars being entrusted to the Austrian Dr Helmut Marko and Alex Soler-Roig, son of a Spanish surgeon;

Helmut Marko

Reine Wisell also raced for BRM on a few occasions. It seemed however that Marlboro-BRM had set their sights a bit high, as the preparation involved in getting five cars ready for each Grand Prix required a lot of manpower. Jean-Pierre Beltoise did nevertheless win the Monaco Grand Prix, in teeming rain. The victory was a big morale booster for BRM, but it was also the last in BRM's history.

Matra decided for financial reasons to run only one car, for Chris Amon, in 1972, while Denis Hulme remained as No 1 driver at McLaren with the American Peter Revson as his No 2. The team was sponsored this year by the Yardley cosmetics company, which was a rather ironic situation as Revson was heir to the American Revlon cosmetics concern, a competitor of Yardley. A third McLaren was provided on occasion for the Englishman Brian Redman, while the talented young South African Jody Scheckter was also given a try-out at the end of the year. John Surtees retired from active driving to devote more time to developing his cars and to managing the team, leaving the TS9s to be driven by Mike Hailwood, Tim Schenken and Andrea de Adamich. Trieste-born de Adamich was married to the daughter of a director of Alfa Romeo, but after two years struggling to make his mark in Formula One with Alfa-powered cars, McLarens in 1970 and Marches in 1971, he joined the Cosworth-Ford side this year with sponsorship from the Italian ceramics concern, Pagnossin.

Frank Williams renewed contracts with the Frenchman Henri Pescarolo and the young Brazilian Carlos Pace, who had made quite an impression with his performances in Formula Two races in 1971. The Italian toymaker Politoys became the sponsor of this small team and a car called the Politoys-Ford, designed for Williams by the Ford engineer Len Bailey, appeared during the year. This was not an outstanding success however and the Williams team relied heavily on March-Ford cars for much of the year.

The aerodynamics and cooling system of the BRM P160 were continuously modified between 1971 and 1973. This is the 1972 P160B version, with an air-scoop above the V12 motor and the oil radiator at the extreme rear.

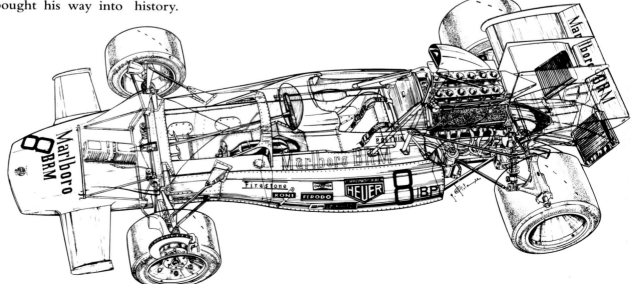

John Wyer

Emerson Fittipaldi

Wilson Fittipaldi

The Brabham team was bought by wealthy London businessman Bernie Ecclestone who, in the course of the next few years, would become an increasingly important figure in the Formula One world. Ecclestone and Tauranac soon parted company, apparently as a result of a clash of personalities, and Ralph Bellamy, the originator of the famous McLaren M19A, was brought in as designer. Ecclestone's drivers were Graham Hill, the Argentinian Carlos Reutemann, and the Brazilian Wilson Fittipaldi, older brother of Emerson.

Rolf Stommelen and John Surtees went their separate ways in 1971 due to differences of opinion, the German driver securing the backing of Gunter Hennerici of the Eifelland caravan company. The new team bought a March-Ford 721, replaced its British body with a rather bizarre body designed in Germany by Luigi Colani, and renamed it Eifelland. The car was not a success however and, before the season ended, the team had disbanded due to lack of finance.

An all-new make in Formula One in 1972 was Tecno. The small Bologna company had first made a name for itself in kart racing, subsequently producing its first Formula Three cars in 1966 and moving on to Formula Two in 1968 and proving very successful in both these categories. Tecno boss Luciano Pederzani was a businessman who had started building racing cars as a hobby, and decided to go the whole hog with the new Formula One car, and build his own engine rather than follow the obvious route of fitting a Cosworth-Ford engine to his own chassis, though he did employ a Hewland gearbox in his design. The new Tecno engine was a 12-cylinder 2996cc (81 x 48mm) unit modelled after the Ferrari, and said (by Pederzani) to develop 440bhp at 11,000rpm. Pederzani was lucky enough to attract the drinks manufacturer Martini & Rossi into Formula One as his team sponsor; they already supported the Porsche factory sportscar team in long-distance racing. The Tecno PA123, first shown to the press at the end of 1971, was unusual for the time in employing a tubular spaceframe, but initial tests showed that this was not up to standard. Pederzani went back to work and built a new monocoque, also called the PA123. Tecno hired the Italian Nanni Galli and the Englishman Derek Bell as drivers, with David Yorke, from

John Wyer's famous sportscar team (and before that with Vanwall), as team manager. The new car made its first World Championship race appearance in the Belgian Grand Prix at Nivelles, but its performance did not match the team's expectations of it.

The regular Formula One field was completed by the British driver Mike Beuttler, whose private March was backed by a group of London stockbrokers.

The tendency in 1972 Grand Prix cars was to have a greater proportion of the weight over the rear axle than before. This was achieved by repositioning various components such as oil tanks, oil coolers, fuel tanks and even — as in the new BRM P180 — radiators more towards the rear. The wings were then mounted further back, behind the rear axle, so that a leverage action occurred, further increasing downforce on the rear wheels. Without some sort of balancing force at the front however cars would have suffered severe understeer on corners, tending to run straight off the track instead of taking the corner. Designers therefore introduced a corresponding increase in downforce at the front by aerodynamic means, using either wedge-shaped nose-cones or angled nose-fins to compensate. Tyres became still wider and fitted to 13-inch rims which were up to 18 inches (45.7cm) wide on, for example, the Surtees TS9. The successful Lotus 72D was fitted with nine-inch wide tyres at the front and 14-inch wide at the rear.

A tug-of-war developed between Goodyear and Firestone to produce special tyres of even softer compound than before, to provide maximum roadholding for short periods purely for qualifying. These special tyres wore out

after just three or four laps, but their superior adhesion allowed favoured competitors to obtain the best starting positions possible. The "qualifying tyre" phenomenon of course added considerably to costs.

There were new developments in the field of braking too. The introduction of the twin-disc system by Tyrrell in 1971 was followed this year by laterally drilled discs, which were used by Matra, Brabham and Tecno. Until then cooling of individual discs had been provided by radial channels, but the new technique was more efficient in dissipating the heat. The system had actually been pioneered by the Porsche sportscar prototypes. Laterally drilled discs were particularly effective in wet conditions. The next development in braking was the adoption of four-piston calipers which increased the total brake pad area.

After a break of 12 years, the Argentine Grand Prix returned to the World Championship calendar again this year. There was a sensation during practice when local ace Carlos Alberto Reutemann — a farmer's son from Santa Fe who had been hired by Brabham to drive a Brabham-Ford BT34 — set the fastest time, and qualified to start the race from pole position on the starting grid.

Reutemann was supported by the state-owned YPF oil company which in earlier years had been sponsor of the Argentine Temporada. Jackie Stewart in Tyrrell-Ford 003 led the race from the first lap to the last and won from Denis Hulme in a McLaren M19A and Jacky Ickx in a Ferrari 312B2. Reutemann started well but lost time with a tyre change; Emerson Fittipaldi had to retire with suspension problems.

The next major event was the South African Grand Prix at Kyalami where Stewart led until the 45th lap, when he fell victim to a transmission problem. Hulme in his McLaren-Ford M19A took over and won from Fittipaldi in a Lotus 72, Peter Revson in another McLaren and Mario Andretti in a Ferrari. The Brazilian Carlos Pace made his Grand Prix debut in this race in a March 721 entered by Frank Williams.

The first European Grand Prix of the year was the Spanish race at Jarama, at which several new cars made their appearance. Graham Hill drove the new Brabham BT37, Ralph Bellamy's development of the BT34, which had a conventional frontal treatment in place of the previous model's distinctive "lobster-claw" nose. The Argentinian Reutemann had won the non-championship Brazilian Grand Prix on the Interlagos circuit at Sao Paulo with a BT34 some weeks earlier after the leading Lotus, driven by Fittipaldi, dropped out. But after showing such tremendous early-season promise Reutemann had an accident during practice for a British Formula Two race

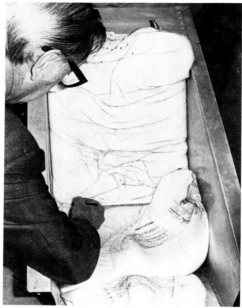

when a wheel came off his Brabham. He suffered a broken bone in his foot, which meant he had to miss both the Spanish and Monaco Grands Prix.

Another new car in Spain was the BRM P180, driven by Peter Gethin. Its designer, Tony Southgate, had placed great emphasis on the distribution of weight over the driving wheels by locating water and oil radiators in air-intake funnels over the rear wheels. The body of the P180 was wedge-shaped in the front, not unlike the Lotus 72, but the car did not live up to expectations and was raced only spasmodically.

Two new March-Ford models

Max Mosley

Peter Revson

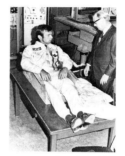

Peter Revson is fitted for his seat at Shadow. Seats are moulded to the shape of individual drivers, who sit on a sack filled with soft resin fibre, in a dummy cockpit. The seat is subsequently shaped to this form.

appeared, the 72IX for works drivers Peterson and Lauda, and the 721G of the independent driver Mike Beuttler. With the 721X, designer Robin Herd had taken a different approach to that of Lotus and BRM by avoiding any attempt to place maximum weight over the rear wheels. His aim was to concentrate the weight in the middle of the car, and he accordingly located the transmission — of the type used by Alfa Romeo on their Type 33/T3 sportscars — in front of the rear axle-line, and placed the cockpit, enclosed in a safety cage, far forward. But the 721X, like the BRM P180, was not a successful design and was replaced after the French

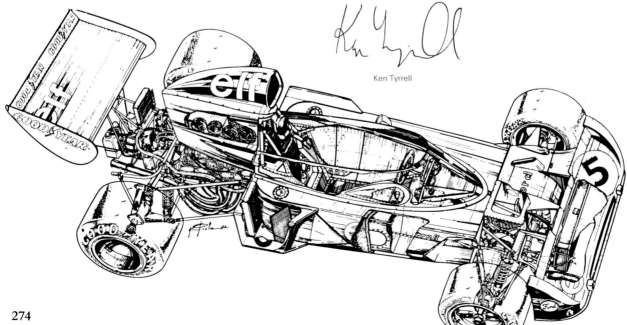

Ken Tyrrell

Left
The Tyrrell 005 appeared mid-1972 and, like the previous model, was very successful. Initially the front brakes were positioned inboard. The large air-intake above the motor served to increase the pressure of the air supply.

Right
Standing with the oddly shaped March-Ford 721X are (from left) new driver Niki Lauda, team manager Max Mosley, designer Robin Herd and chief mechanic Pete Kerr.

Carlos Pace

Grand Prix by the 721G, which was based on the company's Formula Two model with conventional weight distribution and radiators mounted on the sides of the monocoque.

Emerson Fittipaldi's run of 1972 successes began with the Spanish Grand Prix. The Brazilian moved from fifth position to the lead in only a few laps, and stayed there to the end of the race. The Ferrari 312B2s of Jacky Ickx and Clay Regazzoni took the next places, ahead of a four-car bunch comprising Andrea de Adamich in a Surtees-Ford TS9, Peter Revson in a McLaren-Ford M19A, Carlos Pace in a March-Ford 721 and Grand Prix newcomer Wilson Fittipaldi in a Brabham-Ford BT33. Jackie Stewart retired after spinning his Tyrrell.

The Monaco Grand Prix was held in a tremendous downpour, from which the Frenchman Jean-Pierre Beltoise emerged victorious in a BRM P160. He held the lead under the adverse conditions from start to finish, making no mistakes while most of the field had collisions of some sort or lost time manoeuvring their way around obstacles.

For safety reasons the organisers had shifted the pits to a place near the old chicane, and constructed a new chicane nearer to the *Bureau de Tabac*. This was narrower than the old one, and could be negotiated by only one car at a time. It was a most unsatisfactory solution.

It was obvious at Monaco that Jackie Stewart and the Tyrrell-Ford were no longer the top combination. The competition's equipment had improved and Firestone tyres were now faster than the Goodyears which Stewart still used. In passing, it should be mentioned that the first Tyrrells, built between 1970 and 1972, had no special model designations but were identified by their chassis numbers, 001 to 004.

Monaco was one of the most eventful races ever with cars spinning off virtually every lap. The modern super-wide racing tyres were useless in the rain, as they could not cope with dispersing water at a sufficient rate. But Beltoise was master of his car and the conditions, and nobody could outsmart him on the day. His Monte Carlo victory, the only World Championship win of his career, was well-earned.

The Belgian Grand Prix was not held

Jacky Ickx in a Ferrari 312B2 leads Jackie Stewart's Tyrrell 001 and Fittipaldi's Lotus 72 in the 1972 British Grand Prix at Brands Hatch. The Ferrari suffered from handling difficulties at this time, and won only on the Nürburgring. Stewart won the last two World Championship events of the season.

this year on the fast Spa circuit, as this was considered too dangerous for modern racing. The modifications necessary to update the track would have meant the investment of immense amounts of capital, so it was decided to hold the 1972 race on a newly-built track at Nivelles near Brussels. This decision was not universally welcomed however, as the Nivelles circuit was only 3.72km long, and could not approach the character of the historic Ardennes circuit. Jackie Stewart was unable to take part due to a stomach ulcer having been diagnosed. He was forced to pull out of the CanAm sportscar series in North America, in which he was to have campaigned a works McLaren. Fittipaldi was fastest in practice at Nivelles with Regazzoni second, and the Lotus 72 driver won the Belgian Grand Prix from Cevert in a Tyrrell and Hulme in a McLaren. The 12-cylinder Tecno PA123 made its Grand Prix debut in this race,

driven by Nanni Galli, but the Tuscan was involved in a collision with Regazzoni which put both cars out of the race.

A few days after the Belgian Grand Prix, Tyrrell's new 005 model was introduced to the press, at Le Mans. Designer Derek Gardner had developed a rather wide, box-shaped chassis, with inboard brakes and a well-thought-out aerodynamic shape incorporating a high air-box at the rear. The new car was due to make its debut in the French Grand Prix at Clermont-Ferrand but during practice Cevert ran off the road and put it into a safety fence, so the big moment had to be postponed until the European Grand Prix at Brands Hatch two weeks later. The Dutch Grand Prix had been cancelled as the Zandvoort circuit was in the process of being up-graded to meet increased safety requirements.

Also new for the French Grand Prix was Matra's new Type MS120D, designed by Georges Martin and Robert Morin.

The car was not dissimilar to the MS80 dating back to 1969, and had a rather bulbous middle section. The new model proved to be a good choice by the Vélizy firm and with it Chris Amon was fastest in the practice sessions. Absent from the French race though was Regazzoni, who had broken his wrist playing soccer with Ferrari mechanics at the 1000km sportscar race at Zeltweg. Ferrari offered Tecno driver Nanni Galli the opportunity of driving the 312B2 at the Charade circuit, which left the Englishman Derek Bell to drive the Tecno.

The Matra looked unbeatable at Clermont-Ferrand. Amon took the lead and nobody was able to get close to the New Zealander and his blue car. Then the most unfortunate piece of bad luck occurred when a tyre punctured. After the tyre change, Amon drove as if possessed and fought his way back up to third place at the end behind Stewart and Fittipaldi.

Important characteristics of 1972 Formula One cars

Make	BRM	Cosworth	Ferrari	Matra	Tecno
Model	P 142 60	DFV	312 B	MS-72	PA 123
Cylinder configuration	V12 60°	V8 90°	V12 180°	V12 60°	V12 180°
Bore & stroke	74,61 × 57,15	85,7 × 64,8	78,5 × 51,5	79,7 × 50	80,98 × 48,46
Capacity	2998	2990	2991	2993	2995
Main bearings	7	5	4	7	7
Fuel injection	Lucas	Lucas	Lucas	Lucas	Lucas
Ignition	Marelli	Lucas	Marelli	Ducellier	Marelli
Power (bhp) at (rpm)	440 10 800	450 10 000	470 11 600	470 11 500	430 11 000

Right
Emerson Fittipaldi,
here at the
Nürburgring, won the
1972 Spanish, Belgian,
British, Austrian and
Italian Grands Prix and
became World
Champion with a clear
margin over Stewart.

Below
Rolf Stommelen driving
the Eifelland team's
rebodied March 721.
The special body was
designed by Luigi
Colani and had a high
central rear-vision
mirror but was not a
success.

In the weeks leading up to the French Grand Prix the Charade circuit, which wound through mountainous volcanic terrain, had been completely resealed but although the road surface was quite acceptable, nothing had been done about tidying up the broken edges, which should have been sealed with concrete strips. A tight line by any car on one of the corners quite often resulted in the front tyres whipping up loose stones from the outer edges of the road and hurling them into the middle of the track. These sharp volcanic rocks caused a number of punctures over the weekend as the casing of a modern racing tyre is no more than a very thin and sensitive rubber skin. In addition to Amon's misfortune, another stone was thrown up and smashed a hole in Stewart's windscreen, and he was lucky to escape unhurt. Not so fortunate was the Austrian driver Helmut Marko. A small rock penetrated the visor of his helmet and injured his left eye with serious consequences, for his vision was sufficiently reduced to force him to abandon what had been a very promising career.

During practice for the European and British Grand Prix at Brands Hatch, Jackie Stewart had an accident when the inboard front brakes on the new Tyrrell 005 malfunctioned, severely damaging the car. After this the 005's designer Derek Gardner decided to reposition the brakes in the conventional manner outside the chassis. Ferrari appeared set to celebrate a long overdue victory in England when Jacky Ickx in a 321B2 took the lead and held it in spite of all attempts by Stewart in the Tyrrell-Ford 003 and Fittipaldi in a Lotus-Ford 72C to wrest the lead for themselves. However, the Belgian had to give up when oil leaks developed on the 48th lap and Fittipaldi won the race ahead of Stewart and Peter Revson. The Brazilian was leading the World Championship points table by this time, well ahead of reigning Champion Stewart. Sportscar driver Arturo Merzario made his Formula One debut in the Brands Hatch race at the wheel of a Ferrari 312B2, the wiry little Italian finishing in sixth place after an excellent race and earning one World Championship point. He also received the *Prix Rouge et Blanc,* a Marlboro distinction in honour of Joseph Siffert, which was awarded for the first time at Brands Hatch. This prize, which consisted of a small gold ingot, was awarded from this time after every World Championship event to the driver showing the greatest "fighting spirit". The panel awarding the prize consisted of journalists of the International Racing Press Association (IRPA).

Ferrari and Ickx had their great day at Germany's World Championship round

on the Nürburgring. In practice the Belgian achieved an unbelievable best time of 7 minutes 0.07 seconds and led from the first lap of the race to the end. Ickx steadily improved his lap record during the race with his final best time being 7 minutes 13.6 seconds, 189.6km/h. Behind him Stewart in the older-model Tyrrell 003 and Regazzoni in a Ferrari 312B2 disputed second place in a tremendous battle which saw them passing and repassing many times until Stewart's car suddenly spun; Regazzoni carried on and crossed the finishing line in second place. Following a disappointing start to the season with their 721 and later the 721X, March achieved their first really good results for the year on the Nürburgring when Ronnie Peterson brought the Formula Two based 721G into third place. Fittipaldi was forced to give up in the Eifel race when his car developed a transmission fault.

But after winning the Austrian Grand Prix on the Österreichring Fittipaldi had the World Drivers' Championship title well within reach. Stewart finally got to race the new Tyrrell 005 here and led initially, but chassis damage forced him to slow down and gave Fittipaldi the opportunity of securing his fourth victory. The Austrian Grand Prix was held under extremely hot conditions which led to the petrol vaporising in the Ferrari pipes and a drop in engine performance. A new car in the field here was the Connew-Ford, a monocoque car designed and built on a shoestring as a virtually one-man effort by the young British engineer Peter Connew, who had formerly worked for Surtees. The driver of the Connew-Ford PC1 was French newcomer François Migault, but it was sad to see that there were obvious weaknesses in the vehicle, due entirely to the lack of financial backing.

Following the Austrian Grand Prix it was still theoretically possible for Stewart, Hulme or Ickx to overhaul Fittipaldi and win the World Championship, but to do this one of those drivers would have had to win all three remaining World Championship events without Fittipaldi scoring a point, which was highly improbable.

The Monza circuit, venue of the Italian Grand Prix, was another which 1970s thinking had deemed too dangerous for modern racing; the fast racing cars had outgrown the 50-year-old track. Early in the spring the Grand Prix Drivers'

Left
Denis Hulme won the South African Grand Prix at Kyalami in the squat, low-slung McLaren-Ford M19A, but this was the team's only success of the season.

Below
After a number of successful years in Formula Three and Formula Two, Tecno tried their luck in Formula One racing in 1972, with their own flat-12 motor, but the project was a failure. This is the PA123 with Derek Bell at the Nürburgring.

Association demanded an upgrading of the track as slipstreaming, especially on the long straight, had become a dangerous practice. The cheap and simple solution was to enforce a reduction in speed by introducing two new chicanes. There had been no shortage of ideas nor lack of finance for more imaginative alternatives, but local bylaws prohibited the cutting down of trees and a thorough overhaul of the track was prevented by political considerations. The decision was therefore taken to build one chicane on the start/finish straight just before the entrance to the banked circuit, and another in the Ascari Curve. This meant that competitors had to reduce their speed sharply twice per lap, which made for a severe test of the durability of brakes. There was no longer any slip-streaming as drivers had to negotiate the chicanes in single file. The introduction of the chicanes did not meet the drivers' approval but they certainly served the purpose of reducing speed and increasing safety.

Jacky Ickx was fastest in practice, ahead of Chris Amon, and the Ferrari driver led the race from the start until the 13th lap, at which point he was overtaken by his team-mate Regazzoni. The Swiss driver led for three laps but then collided in one of the chicanes with the March of Carlos Pace, which had struck difficulties and was rolling slowly through the chicane. Regazzoni, although having noticed the yellow warning flag, failed to reduce speed sufficiently and a collision was unavoidable. It was fortunate that it wasn't more serious, though the leading Ferrari was forced to retire. Ickx took

over the lead again and held it till the 45th lap when an ignition fault put an end to his ambitions. Fittipaldi now took the lead and was able to celebrate his fifth Grand Prix success of the year, and clinch the World Championship title. Jackie Stewart in the Tyrrell-Ford 005 was put out of action by a burnt-out clutch right at the start.

The first car complying with the 1973 safety regulations, the Surtees-Ford TS14, appeared in this race. The following year Grand Prix cars were required to be constructed with deformable structures or "crumple zones" which were designed to collapse on impact in the event of an accident and absorb much of the force of the crash. The Surtees had these structures on the sides, with the radiators built into them. A rather similar construction had been developed by Ferrari and this car, designated the 312B3, had undergone its first trials in August on the Ferrari test track at Fiorano. These trials were disappointing however and the results were not considered satisfactory.

Jackie Stewart picked up momentum in the last World Championship events of the year, winning both the Canadian Grand Prix at Mosport and the United States Grand Prix at Watkins Glen in the Tyrrell-Ford 005. Fittipaldi had no luck in North America but had of course already secured the World Championship title. François Cevert drove a new Tyrrell in the Canadian Grand Prix, and at Watkins Glen the Tyrrells took first and second places. A third, older-model, Tyrrell finished seventh, driven by the Frenchman Patrick Depailler, and the three Tyrrell drivers took out a record total

amount of prizemoney.

The Formula One debut of the 23-year-old South African Jody Scheckter at Watkins Glen was sensational. Scheckter had had good results in the Formula Two class during the season, and the McLaren team now offered him an opportunity of racing an M19A in Formula One. The South African set the fourth best time in practice and was in third place, behind Stewart and Hulme, by the second lap of the race. He was then overtaken by Cevert in fourth place from lap 17 to 39 but then, as light rain began to fall during the latter part of the race, he spun his car and lost time. He finished the race in ninth place.

With the 1972 World Championship now finished, Emerson Fittipaldi had won the title with a score of 61 points, ahead of Jackie Stewart with 45, Denis Hulme with 39 and Jacky Ickx with 27. The Manufacturers' Championship was won by Lotus from Tyrrell, McLaren and Ferrari.

Jackie Stewart's Watkins Glen win was the 51st Grand Prix win for Keith Duckworth's Cosworth-Ford DFV engine design, out of the 68 World Championship Grands Prix it had contested between 1967 and 1972. This was a unique record, made the more remarkable by the fact that the eight-cylinder unit had undergone no major change during those six seasons, minor improvements having been sufficient to increase power output from 400bhp in 1967 to 470bhp in 1972. Furthermore the success story of this British engine, originally financed by Ford, was to continue for another 12 seasons.

Lotus and Tyrrell had been the most prominent constructors in 1972, but McLaren had some good results too, Denis Hulme winning the South African Grand Prix with an M19A. Ferrari had suffered a lot of teething problems with their new 12-cylinder model and, although the Maranello engineers claimed that the engine developed about 500bhp, its overall performance was disappointing. Jacky Ickx did win the German Grand Prix for Ferrari in no uncertain fashion, but the Belgian driver was eliminated by engine failures when leading at both Brands Hatch and at Monza. The achievements of the large BRM team were also disappointing, Jean-Pierre Beltoise's Monaco Grand Prix victory aside. The magnitude of the five-car operation meant manpower and other resources were stretched to their limits and this had a detrimental effect on the development of the new Type P180. The 12-cylinder Matra was also disappointing on balance, and by the end of the season the French team had become so discouraged that they decided to withdraw from Formula One and to concentrate their efforts solely on endurance racing instead. They had come close to victory at Clermont-Ferrand, where only the necessity to change a tyre had prevented Chris Amon from winning his first World Championship event, something he had been trying to do since 1967. Several times victory had been within his reach, but it always eluded him, and although he belonged to the Formula One driving élite of his time, Amon never did win a Grand Prix.

March contested the series with three different models, but their performances were disappointing. The best results came from the Formula Two-based 721G but they came too late to make an impact. Bernie Ecclestone's Brabham team meanwhile suffered many handicaps due to mechanical failures.

The 1972 season was the year of the South Americans. Emerson Fittipaldi became World Champion and his brother Wilson started to earn a name for himself in Grands Prix as did the Brazilian Carlos Pace and the Argentinian Carlos Reutemann. It was almost like a return to the days of Fangio, Gonzalez, Marimón, Mieres and Menditeguy.

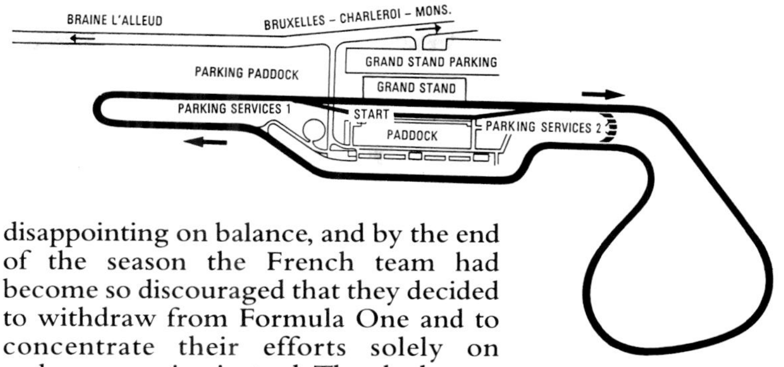

The 1972 and 1974 Belgian Grands Prix were held on the 3.724km Nivelles track near Brussels. The circuit was closed soon after due to financial difficulties.

Formula One cars of 1972

Make/model	Chief designer(s)	Engine	Gearbox (speeds)	Chassis	Wheelbase	Track	Tyre make	Dry weight
Brabham BT 37	Ron Tauranac Ralph Bellamy	Cosworth DFV (V8)	Hewland FG 400 (5)	FM	2413	F 1575 R 1600	Goodyear	570
BRM P 160	Tony Southgate	BRM P 142-60 (V12)	BRM (5)	SM	2464	F 1473 R 1448	Firestone	560
BRM P 180	Tony Southgate	BRM P 142-60 (V12)	BRM (5)	SM	2540	F 1473 R 1499	Firestone	550
Connew PC 1	Peter Connew	Cosworth DFV (V8)	Hewland DG 300 (5)	SM	2489	F 1574 R 1577	Firestone	580
Ferrari 312 B2	Mauro Forghieri	Ferrari 312 B (12 cyl 180°)	Ferrari (5)	TS	2350	F 1420 R 1420	Firestone	560
Lotus 72 D	Colin Chapman Maurice Phillippe	Cosworth DFV (V8)	Hewland FG 400 (5)	SM	2540	F 1448 R 1448	Firestone	560
March 721	Robin Herd	Cosworth DFV (V8)	Hewland FG 400 (5)	FM	2438	F 1524 R 1524	Goodyear	570
Matra MS 120 C	Georges Martin Robert Morin	Matra MS 72 (V12)	Hewland FG 400 (5)	FM	2500	F 1640 R 1700	Goodyear	560
McLaren M 19 C	Ralph Bellamy	Cosworth DFV (V8)	Hewland FG 400 (5)	FM	2540	F 1600 R 1575	Goodyear	560
Politoys FX 3	Len Bailey	Cosworth DFV (V8)	Hewland FG 400 (5)	SM	2413	F 1600 R 1549	Goodyear	580
Surtees TS 9 B	John Surtees	Cosworth DFV (V8)	Hewland FG 400 (5)	FM	2534	F 1524 R 1549	Firestone	560
Tecno PA 123	Luciano Pederzani Gianfranco Pederzani	Tecno B 12 (12 cyl 180°)	Hewland FG 400 (5)	TS	2470	F 1440 R 1434	Firestone	580
Tyrrell 005	Derek Gardner	Cosworth DFV (V8)	Hewland FG 400 (5)	FM	2386	F 1590 R 1590	Goodyear	560

Chassis construction: SM = semi-monocoque; FM = full monocoque; TS = tubular frame with stressed skins.

Stewart's Third Championship

Stewart retires at the end of the season with a total of 27 Grand Prix victories (from 99 starts). Tyre choice becomes more crucial than ever.

Three drivers, Jackie Stewart, Emerson Fittipaldi and Ronnie Peterson, dominated the 1973 Grand Prix season as far as winning was concerned, but it was Stewart who won the World Championship title — his third. He then retired to his home in Waadtland, Switzerland with 27 Grand Prix victories to his credit, beating the earlier scores of Jim Clark (25) and Juan Manuel Fangio (24).

There were 15 races in the 1973 World Championship, and Stewart in a Tyrrell 006 won five. Peterson in a Lotus 72D won four of the others and Fittipaldi, also in a Lotus, won three. Fittipaldi and Peterson finished second and third respectively on the World Championship table. But although less successful in terms of victories, the new McLaren M23 ranked with Tyrrell and Lotus as one of the dominating makes of the season. On the other hand, 1973 was a crisis year for both Ferrari and BRM, and while Ferrari was able to work their way up again in later years, BRM came to a virtual standstill. This situation continued until 1977, when the British team finally disappeared from the scene.

The tyre war became even more aggressive this year, Goodyear producing the best qualifying rubber but Firestone appearing to have developed a better tyre for the wet. Lotus, Tyrrell, McLaren, Brabham, Ferrari and March all used Goodyear tyres while BRM, Surtees, Iso (Williams) and various private teams ran on Firestones. Lotus and Ferrari had made the switch to Goodyear as Firestone had indicated their intention of retiring from this field at the end of 1972.

As the choice of tyres became more and more critical in Formula One, a computer was used to assist decision-making. Computer analysis of data from an entire racing season showed that in a lap of 1 minute 30 seconds the driver and chassis could affect the time by half a second each and the motor could make a 0.7-second difference, but the right choice of tyres could result in up to 2 seconds being gained — or lost. The tyre companies constantly tested their products in order to determine the best mix of chemicals to obtain the optimum balance between maximum roadholding and wear. Ed Alexander, director of the Goodyear racing service, was quoted as saying that in the course of a season tests were made with approximately 300 rubber compounds, of which probably only 30 would leave the laboratory to be

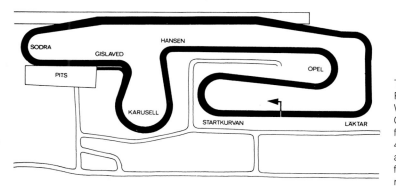

The Swedish Grand Prix was a round in the World Drivers' Championship for the first time in 1973. The 4.018km Anderstorp airfield circuit suffered from being located in a rather isolated area.

tested in the field. The companies even went so far as trying to ascertain the optimum compound for each different make of car at each circuit, as no one tyre suited every type of car or every chassis. It was quite common for the outcome of a race to be dependent on the selection of the right compound tyre for the day.

The increasing trend towards softer rubber compounds led to a corresponding increase in their sensitivity, and small, sharp stones were quite often sufficient to puncture a tyre. This was compensated for to a certain degree by the fact that, because the modern soft-compound tyres ran at relatively low pressures, the rate of air escape from a punctured tyre was reduced, and it was often possible for a driver to keep going for a few more laps, possibly to finish a race. This actually happened in the Spanish Grand Prix when Fittipaldi had a slow puncture in the last third of the race: he not only carried on to the finish, but won the race into the bargain.

At the end of 1972 Tyrrell raced on a tyre whose external diameter was 26.5 inches (until then 24 inches had been the widest used) on a 13-inch rim and this tyre incorporated a "tangential spring" effect which assisted in acceleration out of corners. There is a split-second delay between the moment when the hub increases speed and the moment when the outside surface of the tyre transmits

that increased speed and the spring effect of the new tyre, inspired by those used in drag racing, provided a catapulting action which pushed the car forward during that tiny delay.

There was little to report from the engine development field in 1973, as the Ford-Cosworth DFV continued its triumphant success. Ferrari experienced difficulties with their chassis, BRM had diverse problems and endless troubles were reported from Tecno with regard to their flat 12-cylinder engines. Matra had of course withdrawn from Formula One at the end of 1972 and their V12 was now used only for long-distance racing — with some success. It later returned to Formula One with the Ligier team. The Cosworth DFV now developed 460bhp, about 20 or 30bhp less than the Ferrari, while the BRM V12 produced about 450bhp.

The Tyrrell team started with their 005 and 006 cars (006 was initially the chassis

Above
Jackie Stewart in conversation with team boss Ken Tyrrell.

Left
The short-wheelbase Tyrrell 006, designed by Derek Gardner, was a successful model in which Jackie Stewart became the 1973 World Champion. Note the characteristic squat appearance and high cockpit sides.

number but it was later used to identify the model), now with their front brakes mounted outboard after the vibration problems encountered with the inboard positioning in 1972. Although Jackie Stewart was to win the 1973 World Championship with the shortened and widened Tyrrell, the vehicle did not have the best roadholding. Initially, the rear wings were in a forward position to provide for high speed on the straights but after the Argentine and Brazilian Grands Prix designer Derek Gardner positioned them further to the rear to put more pressure on the driving wheels, and this improved the handling qualities quite significantly. At first only Stewart and Cevert drove the dark blue cars but, towards the end of the season, Chris Amon, after a troubled time with Tecno, joined the little team.

The Lotus 72, raced for the first time in 1970, competed this year in B, C and D versions in which Fittipaldi and Peterson between them won seven World Championship events. The many detailed

changes and improvements increased to 650kg the dry weight of the car, which was officially known as the John Player Special. During the season Lotus tested no fewer than five different air-intake housings. The rear wings were set well back and low in order to ensure the least amount of turbulence yet still provide maximum downforce at the rear axle line. Maurice Phillippe, who had been actively involved in the design of the Lotus 72, had left to join the Parnelli team in California and the Australian designer Ralph Bellamy, formerly with Brabham and McLaren, took over the vacant position. Colin Chapman still retained his executive position however, and had the final word on the design of new models.

Maurice Phillippe

Bellamy's successful McLaren M19A model was replaced this year by the M23, from the drawing-board of Gordon Coppuck. The new car made a most impressive debut in Denis Hulme's hands in the South African Grand Prix, and would continue to be raced by the factory for some time. The wedge-shaped M23 with side-mounted radiators was an especially well-balanced design, constructed in such a way that a variety of design options could be used. The chassis was built to comply with the new regulations, with the space between the monocoque skins filled with hardened foam to create a cushion. This afforded greater driver protection in the event of an accident, and also provided better insulation for the petrol tanks. The M23 had a long and successful career, from the time of its inception in 1973 until the end of 1977; private teams continued to run the M23 into 1978. The model took Emerson Fittipaldi to his 1974 World Championship and James Hunt to victory in the 1976 competition.

The much modified V12 BRM V12 in its 1973, 160E, form. In order to increase downforce, the car was fitted with a wider nose and wings mounted well to the rear.

Overleaf
Many helping hands for the World Champion, Jackie Stewart.

Right
The 1973 Brabham-Ford BT42 was the first Formula One car designed by the South African Gordon Murray. The trapezium-shaped monocoque and separate front radiators were unique. The BT44 which superseded it was almost identical.

Left
The American racing stable UOP Shadow, which had previously contested the CanAm series, appeared in Formula One with the DN1 in 1973. Founder was the former career army officer Don Nichols, with sponsorship from the chemicals concern UOP. From left: driver George Follmer, Nichols, team manager Alan Rees, designer Tony Southgate, and driver Jackie Oliver.

Below
The 1973 Surtees TS14A at Monte Carlo, with the Brazilian Carlos Pace at the wheel. Founded in 1969 by John Surtees, the former multiple World Motorcycle Champion and 1964 Formula One Champion, the Surtees factory had moved on to making Grand Prix cars after a number of successes in Formula 5000.

Below
The Formula One Ensign MN01, financed and driven by Rikky von Opel, made its debut in 1973. It was built by former Lotus mechanic and Formula Three driver Maurice (Mo) Nunn, whose Formula Three designs had been a great success.

Taking charge of the Brabham design office in 1972 was young Gordon Murray, a tall, slim South African who had worked at Brabham for several years under Ron Tauranac and then Ralph Bellamy. Later recognised as one of the most brilliant of all Grand Prix designers, Murray was responsible in 1973 for the compact Brabham BT42. In cross-section, the narrow chassis of this car was trapezium-shaped, which gave it strength with lightness. Driven by Carlos Reutemann and Wilson Fittipaldi, the BT42 did not win any races, but the BT44 which followed it in 1974 was the most successful Formula One Brabham model for some time.

Ferrari reached an all-time low in 1973, but it was only a lull while efforts were concentrated on the next generation of cars, for in 1974 the red Italian cars were once again on top. The Ferrari B312B3 built at the end of 1972 was an odd-looking low-slung car with a plough-like front, but this proved to be quite unsuccessful in testing and the car never raced. Instead work started on a completely different design and this car, also designated 312B3, appeared for the first time at the 1973 Spanish Grand Prix. To save time, Ferrari had commissioned the chassis from the English engineer John Thompson of Northampton, whose company specialized in chassis building. Working to Ferrari's plans, Thompson manufactured a chassis which was a full monocoque rather than the familiar Ferrari set-up of a tubular frame with riveted sheetmetal skins, though Maranello reverted to their usual method

of construction for the 312T model which followed. On Thompson's 312B3 the radiators were located longitudinally in the sides but several problems arose with the car and these had to be ironed out during the season. The team in fact gave both the Dutch and German Grands Prix a miss while they thoroughly overhauled the design.

The American firm Shadow, previously a contender in the CanAm sportscar series, joined the Formula One circus in 1973, starting at the South African Grand Prix. The team was financed by the UOP chemical concern whose founder was former professional soldier Don Nichols, who had commissioned Tony Southgate, the British BRM engineer, to design the new Shadow DN1. Nichols engaged Jackie Oliver and George Follmer (who had won the 1972 CanAm Championship in a Porsche) as drivers with Alan Rees, one of the founding partners of March, as team manager. Follmer took the new Shadow to sixth place in the South African Grand Prix and was then third across the finish line in Spain. Double World Champion Graham Hill also competed with a Shadow DN1 this year, running a private team in the colours of the Embassy cigarette firm.

Another new Formula One car this year was the Ensign, developed by former Lotus mechanic and Formula Three driver, Maurice "Mo" Nunn. Ensign had already made a reputation with a competitive Formula Three car, and the Formula One project was financed by its driver, the young Liechtenstein businessman Ricky von Opel. Von Opel took the big step into the world of Formula One racing following tremendous success in Formula Three, but soon realised that the Grand Prix class was beyond him, and withdrew from racing in 1974.

Clay Regazzoni celebrated his departure from Ferrari for BRM by qualifying his P160B on pole for the Argentine Grand Prix, first round in the 1973 World Championship, but this would be the last time one of the Bourne V12s achieved this honour. In the race Regazzoni led till the 28th lap and then Cevert in a Tyrrell took the lead until the 85th lap, when he yielded to Fittipaldi in a Lotus 72D. The Brazilian won, followed by the Tyrrell 006s of Cevert and Stewart.

The next Grand Prix was at Sao Paulo, the first time a World Championship race had been held in Brazil, and Fittipaldi won this too, from Stewart and Hulme.

The new McLaren M23 made its debut in South Africa and Hulme promptly qualified it on pole, and then led the race for four laps. Local hero Jody Scheckter, in a McLaren M19A, soon took over the lead but he held it for only two laps before

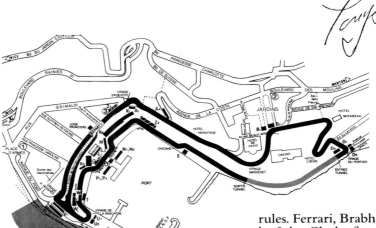

George Follmer
George Follmer

Jackie Oliver
Jackie Oliver

Tony Southgate
Tony Southgate

The modified 3.278km Monte Carlo harbourside circuit was used for the first time in 1973. The new track went around the swimming pool as well as the Rascasse Restaurant.

Stewart went past and carried on to win. Stewart had had a bad accident during practice and started from only tenth position on the grid but, to the sorrow of his rivals, this did not deter him from slicing through the field and scoring one of his most remarkable victories. Stewart's triumph was however soured by a protest from the McLaren team claiming the Tyrrell driver had overtaken another car during the race while the yellow flags were displayed. The protest was rejected. Peter Revson finished second in a McLaren, ahead of Fittipaldi. The unfortunate Regazzoni had a very bad accident in his BRM and Mike Hailwood, who braved the flames to free the Swiss driver from his burning car, received severe burns to his hands.

The new safety regulations came into force at the Spanish Grand Prix. All new Formula One cars had to be built to these standards, while the existing models were adapted as far as possible to meet the rules. Ferrari, Brabham and Iso (designed by John Clarke for the struggling Frank Williams team) had new models for this race. Emerson Fittipaldi won the Spanish race, but it was to be his last victory of the season. Peterson in the second Lotus led for several laps but was forced to abandon the race due to a transmission fault.

The Belgian Grand Prix was run for the first time at Zolder this year, but there was strong criticism of the track surface. This was new, and tended to lift in places. Endless discussions took place during and after practice, with the drivers at one point threatening to strike, but the matter was finally settled and the race started. Stewart and Cevert took the first two places in their Tyrrell 006s, the former World Champion having started from eighth position. Fittipaldi finished third behind the "Tyrrell Twins".

Stewart then enjoyed an end-to-end victory at Monaco, followed all the way by the Lotus 72Ds of Fittipaldi and Peterson. Eyebrows were raised in this race at the performance of Niki Lauda. Driving a BRM P160E, Lauda held third position from the fourth to the ninth laps.

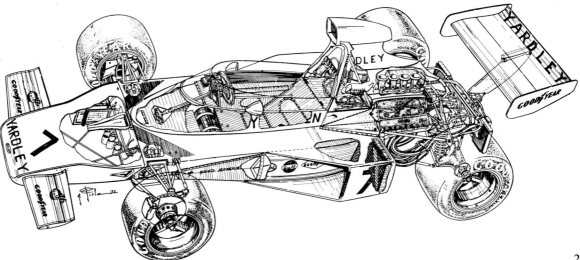

The McLaren-Ford M23, designed by Gordon Coppuck, was raced with considerable success from 1973 to 1978. Emerson Fittipaldi won the World Championship with this model in 1974 and James Hunt in 1976. The wedge-shaped chassis and side-mounted radiators were inspired by the Lotus 72 design. This drawing shows the 1973 version.

Until now the young Austrian had been competing on a race-by-race basis, but BRM team owner Louis Stanley recognised the youngster's ability and replaced the trial contract with a fixed one.

Taking part in his first World Championship race at Monaco was blond English driver James Hunt, who drove a March for the private team of young Lord Alexander Hesketh.

The next event was the first World Championship Swedish Grand Prix, held on the Anderstorp airfield circuit, and here Denis Hulme gave the new McLaren M23 its first success. The French Grand Prix at Le Castellet was however another success for Lotus, Ronnie Peterson coming in first ahead of Francois Cevert in his Tyrrell and Carlos Reutemann in a Brabham. The British Grand Prix at Silverstone started badly when Jody

Louis Stanley

Scheckter spun his McLaren and triggered a multi-car pile-up. The race was immediately brought to a halt and it took an hour to clear the track. Several competitors were unable to restart, among them Andrea de Adamich, who was trapped in the cockpit of his private Brabham BT42 and had to be cut free. This accident led to de Adamich's early retirement from Formula One. The American Peter Revson in a McLaren M23 had his first World Championship success in the restarted race.

There was a worse tragedy in the Dutch Grand Prix at Zandvoort when the young Englishman Roger Williamson

crashed the March he was driving for Tom Wheatcroft (owner of the famous Donington Collection of Grand Prix cars housed at his race circuit). The circuit safety marshals were ill-prepared for such an emergency, and while fellow driver David Purley struggled heroically to save his colleague his efforts were in vain, and Williamson burnt to death before the eyes of millions of TV viewers. The Tyrrell Twins, Stewart and Cevert, were again first and second in the Zandvoort race, with James Hunt third in the private Hesketh March. Ferrari did not take part in this race, or the German Grand Prix which followed, the time being spent by Ferrari engineer Mauro Forghieri to redesign and rebuild the 312B3.

The Belgian Ferrari driver Jacky Ickx was released from his contract to drive a McLaren M23 on his favourite circuit, and came third in the Nürburgring race behind Stewart and Cevert. Fastest lap — a new record — was set by the Brazilian Carlos Pace in a Surtees TS14A and he repeated that effort in the next race, the

Above
The Brazilian Grand Prix, held on the 7.96km Interlagos circuit near Sao Paulo, was included in the World Championship for the first time in 1973.

Left
The Ferrari 312B3 was modified by the engineer Mauro Forghieri in the middle of the 1973 season, with large radiators accommodated in the car's sidepods.

Right
The Lotus 72 was one of the most significant designs of the seventies, and took Rindt to the World title in 1970 and Fittipaldi in 1972. Shown here is the 72D version built in 1973, with rear wing mounted far to the rear. Interesting features were the torsion bar suspension and the inboard-mounted brakes.

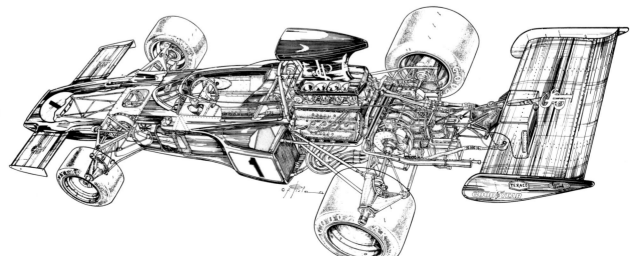

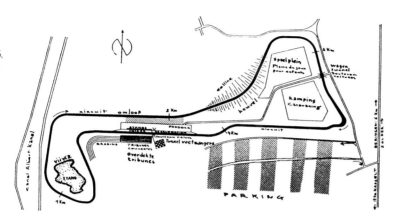

The Belgian Grand Prix, first held in 1925, found a new home in 1973 in the 4.221km Zolder circuit, built in the sixties. The fast Spa circuit was still considered too long and dangerous.

was killed during practice. Jackie Stewart, who had already earned sufficient points to win the 1973 World Championship, did not start in the race. He had reached a decision to retire from racing earlier in the year, on April 5th to be exact, when he revealed his thoughts to his team boss Ken Tyrrell, and also to Walter Hayes, vice-president of Ford of Europe. The death of his team-mate merely underlined his decision. Ronnie Peterson led the Watkins Glen race from start to finish, but he was hounded all the way by James Hunt in his March, who eventually had to settle for second place.

Austrian Grand Prix, in which he finished third. Peterson won this one for Lotus, relegating Stewart to second.

At Monza Peterson and Fittipaldi took the first two places for Lotus but the Canadian Grand Prix was a chaotic event, partly due to lack of organisation and partly through very poor weather conditions, and there were a number of accidents during practice. In the race Niki Lauda led from the second lap to the 19th,

when he fell back with transmission failure, leaving McLaren driver Revson to score his second, and last, Grand Prix success, with Fittipaldi second. Due to the chaotic conditions many spectators could not believe the final victory announcement and expressed their opinion that the victory should have gone to Fittipaldi.

The World Championship ended tragically with the United States Grand Prix when Tyrrell driver François Cevert

After the 15 events of the 1973 World Championship Jackie Stewart was declared Champion with 71 points; Fittipaldi followed with 55, Peterson with 52 and their dead colleague Cevert with 47. Stewart's last season made him the most successful driver in Grand Prix history, with 27 victories out of 99 starts since 1965. Lotus won the World Manufacturers' Championship for the season, ahead of Tyrrell and McLaren.

Formula One cars of 1973

Make/model	Chief designer(s)	Engine	Gearbox (speeds)	Chassis	Wheelbase	Track	Tyre make	Dry weight
Brabham BT 42	Gordon Murray	Cosworth DFV (V8)	Hewland FG 400 (5)	FM	2388	F 1422 R 1448	Goodyear	575
BRM P 160 E	Tony Southgate	BRM P 142-60 (V12)	BRM (5)	SM	2464	F 1473 R 1448	Firestone	580
Ensign MN 01	Morris Nunn	Cosworth DFV (V8)	Hewland FG 400 (5)	SM	2565	F 1549 R 1498	Firestone	585
Ferrari 312 B3	Mauro Forghieri Franco Rocchi Bussi	Ferrari 312 B (12 cyl 180°)	Ferrari (5)	FM	2500	F 1625 R 1605	Goodyear	578
ISO IR	John Clarke	Cosworth DFV (V8)	Hewland FG 400 (5)	FM	2489	F 1575 R 1524	Firestone	576
Lotus 72 D	Colin Chapman Maurice Phillippe	Cosworth DFV (V8)	Hewland FG 400 (5)	SM	2540	F 1448 R 1448	Goodyear	578
March 731	Robin Herd	Cosworth DFV (V8)	Hewland FG 400 (5)	FM	2438	F 1448 R 1448	Goodyear	576
McLaren M 23	Gordon Coppuck	Cosworth DFV (V8)	Hewland FG 400 (5)	FM	2565	F 1464 R 1588	Goodyear	575
Shadow DN 1	Tony Southgate	Cosworth DFV (V8)	Hewland TL 200 (5)	SM	2540	F 1473 R 1524	Goodyear	575
Surtees TS 14 A	John Surtees	Cosworth DFV (V8)	Hewland FG 400 (5)	FM	2565	F 1524 R 1549	Firestone	590
Tecno PA 123	Alan McCall Edy Wyss	Tecno B12 (12 cyl 180°)	Hewland FG 400 (5)	FM	2450	F 1600 R 1473	Firestone	590
Tyrrell 006	Derek Gardner	Cosworth DFV (V8)	Hewland FG 400 (5)	FM	2386	F 1590 R 1590	Goodyear	578

Chassis construction: SM = semi-monocoque; FM = full monocoque

McLaren Just Beats Ferrari

Ferrari driver Regazzoni and Fittipaldi in a McLaren start the last Grand Prix of the year on equal World Championship points — the Ferrari performs disappointingly and Fittipaldi becomes World Champion.

Right
Emerson Fittipaldi, World Champion for the second time in 1974.

Far right
Lauda in a Ferrari 312B3 winning the Spanish Grand Prix, his first Formula One victory.

Ferrari was the technically superior car of 1974, but in spite of this, the World Championship was won by Emerson Fittipaldi, who had switched camps and was now driving a McLaren M23 rather than a Lotus.

The last of the 15 rounds in the Championship was an exciting affair, as there were still three drivers in with a chance of winning the title when the Watkins Glen race started: Fittipaldi in the McLaren, Clay Regazzoni in a Ferrari 312B3 and Jody Scheckter in a Tyrrell 007. Fittipaldi took the lead when both Ferraris retired and carried on to win his second World Championship title.

The Ferrari 312B3, which had been redesigned in 1973 under the direction of engineer Mauro Forghieri, was once again subjected to close examination after its disappointing performance that year. The company did not contest long-distance sportscar races in 1974, and was thus able to concentrate all its efforts on Formula One, with the result that the 12-cylinder Italian car started from the front row in the first World Championship race of the year, in Argentina. Regazzoni had returned to Maranello after his unlucky BRM year, and brought with him his team-mate Niki Lauda. Testing for 1974 had started at Fiorano and Vallelunga in October and by the time the starting flag fell for the Argentine Grand Prix, the Ferraris had covered many thousands of kilometres and the drivers and cars were better prepared for the season than at any time in recent memory. Fiat, as a major shareholder in Ferrari, had injected a significant amount of capital into the racing team, which had made it possible for much more thorough pre-season work to be carried out; the generous Fiat budget gave the Ferrari racing operation a new lease of life. In Niki Lauda, the Ferrari works had obtained a driver with excellent technical know-how and an intuitive feel for setting up a car, a man who tested untiringly until the best

method was found. The Roman Luca di Montezemolo, who was related to the Agnelli family and was being groomed for a high-ranking career in the Fiat concern, was made team manager, with the little Sicilian engineer Giacomo Caliri technical manager at the circuits. Separate mechanics and equipment were used for the two team entries, Giulio Borsari looking after Regazzoni's car and Ermanno Cuoghi Lauda's.

With their M23, introduced in 1973, McLaren had a well-proven model at their disposal for 1974 and an equally proven team with Emerson Fittipaldi and Denis Hulme as drivers. The McLaren team was sponsored this year by two wealthy companies, Texaco and Marlboro, which enabled the Colnbrook team to have the best that money could buy. A third works-run McLaren in the colours of the Yardley cosmetics company was driven by the former motorcycle champion Mike Hailwood, though unfortunately Hailwood had a serious accident on the Nürburgring and suffered a complicated leg injury which resulted in his having to abandon his Formula One racing career. A well-

organised and well-disciplined team was set up under American Teddy Mayer, a former barrister, as team manager and Gordon Coppuck as technical chief, this pair having worked together since the early seventies.

Lotus had a poor start to the 1974 season. The new Lotus 76, which was to have been used from the beginning of the year, was not ready in time, so that Jacky Ickx, who had moved from Ferrari to Lotus, and Ronnie Peterson had to compete in the old 72Ds. The 72D was still one of the best Grand Prix cars of the time, with its concentration of mass towards the rear, its wedge-shaped body and inboard-mounted disc brakes, but it was only ever intended to be an interim design under the new safety regulations. Ralph Bellamy's all-new 1974 contender, the 76 — officially named "John Player Special Mark 1" — had some revolutionary design features. The clutch could be actuated either electronically with a button on the dashboard or in the conventional way with a pedal, and the gold-trimmed black body had dual wings at the rear. However, early testing with the new car proved that it was inferior to

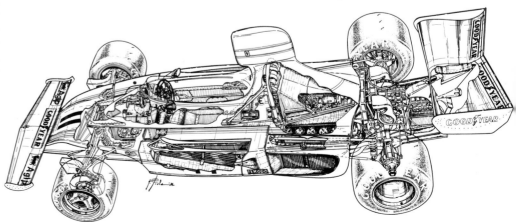

the older model, and the 72Ds were used for most of the season. It was with this model that Peterson scored Lotus's three Grand Prix victories of 1974, in Monaco, France and Italy, and also won the non-championship Race of Champions at Brands Hatch.

After Jackie Stewart's retirement and François Cevert's fatal accident, Ken Tyrrell engaged two relatively inexperienced young drivers for his 1974 team, the Frenchman Patrick Depailler and the impatient curly-haired Jody Scheckter.

The short, squat 006-model Tyrrell which had been campaigned in 1972 and 1973 and with which Stewart had won the third World Championship title of his racing career in 1973, was an unpredictable car in some circumstances, and for 1974 Derek Gardner developed the 007 model. In contrast to its predecessor, the new car had a sleek wedge-shaped body with side-mounted radiators and a significantly longer wheelbase. It was easy to set up and maintain and both Depailler and Scheckter were soon at home with it. The Tyrrell 007 had a few unusual technical characteristics, such as "progressive" front suspension, torsion-bar rear suspension similar to the Lotus 72's and inboard-mounted front brakes, though during the 1975 season the rear suspension reverted to a conventional set-up and the front brakes were relocated outboard.

South African Gordon Murray was responsible for all Brabham designs from 1973 on.

Gordon Coppuck, designer of the McLaren M23. John Barnard later took over a lot of Coppuck's influence at McLaren.

Gordon Murray

Gordon Coppuck

The tall air-intake mounted on the engine-cover was slim enough to allow airflow to be directed relatively unhindered onto the rear wing. After 1974 the rear wing was modified to make it shorter, as new regulations meant that aerodynamic aids (wings) were not allowed to protrude more than 100cm in the horizontal plane beyond the centre of the rear wheels. This of course meant a

reduction in downforce on the rear wheels.

Brabham had a new car for 1974 too. Outwardly very similar to the BT42, the new BT44 model, built under the direction of Gordon Murray, had progressive front suspension with the radiators positioned at either side of the wide front. The cross-section of the monocoque chassis was, as was now a tradition with Brabhams, a trapezium, which facilitated downforce at high speeds. The new Brabham lost victory in its first race, the Argentine Grand Prix, only when Carlos Reutemann's example ran out of petrol on the second to last lap. The local hero had shaken off all his rivals by then and his first Grand Prix victory was in reach. A few weeks later, Reutemann won the South African Grand Prix.

The BRM team, sponsored this year by the Motul fuel concern, consisted of the French drivers Jean-Pierre Beltoise, Henri Pescarolo and François Migault. Tony Southgate had left BRM at the end of 1972 and joined Shadow, where the DN1 had been built under his direction. His vacated position was taken by Mike Pilbeam, who became chief designer at BRM, where he was responsible for the new P201 model for 1974. This car had two radiators, one on either side of the engine, accommodated in separate air ducts, and inboard front brakes. The

Left
The 1974 Ferrari 312B3 was the dominant model of the year, bringing many successes to Lauda and Regazzoni.

Right
Regazzoni in a Ferrari 312B3 leads in the 1974 Monaco Grand Prix ahead of his team-mate Lauda, Jarier in a Shadow DN03, Peterson in a Lotus 72D and Reutemann in a Brabham BT44.

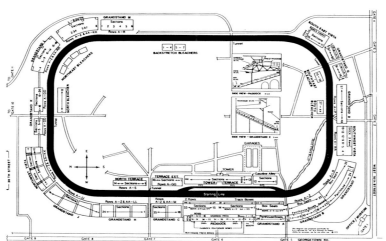

The 2.5-mile (4.064km) Indianapolis track has been in existence since 1909, and the 500-mile race held there each year (apart from during World Wars) since 1911. The track has remained unaltered except for the surface but, over the course of the years, many grandstands and other facilities have been built around the track.

Bottom
Emerson Fittipaldi in his sharp-nosed McLaren M23 leads John Watson's private Brabham BT42 during the 1974 Monaco Grand Prix. Ferrari drivers led the World Championship events throughout the season but it was Fittipaldi who won the title.

Below
After the 1974 Argentine Grand Prix, from left: Niki Lauda (second), Denis Hulme (first) and Clay Regazzoni (third) on the dais. The Argentinian Carlos Reutemann led in a Brabham from the first lap until he ran out of petrol on the last lap.

BRM P201 showed considerable promise in its first appearance in Jean-Pierre Beltoise's hands in South Africa, but the car which everyone hailed at Kyalami proved a dismal failure in subsequent races.

At Shadow, Tony Southgate's new DN3, looking very much like the previous model, was introduced in Argentina. Drivers under contract to Shadow were the former McLaren driver Peter Revson and the 1973 European Formula Two Champion, the young Frenchman Jean-Pierre Jarier. Unfortunately however Revson was killed during testing for the South African Grand Prix when a fatigued suspension part of the Shadow broke. The Englishman Brian Redman took Revson's place on the team on a temporary basis, and the Welshman Tom Pryce, who had shown up well in Formula Three, was later appointed permanently.

The Hesketh team, which had competed the previous year with a March driven by James Hunt, built their own car for 1974. The car's designer, Dr Harvey Postlethwaite, decided on a very simple construction for the Cosworth-powered Hesketh 308, eschewing such innovations as progressive suspension and inboard brakes. In its first year the Hesketh 308, with Hunt at the wheel, had mixed results. There were a number of teething problems, defects and even accidents, but in spite of everything Hunt succeeded in winning the *Daily Express* International Trophy race at Silverstone with the 308, although this was not a World Championship event.

The Surtees team had a rather dismal season in 1974, despite the arrival of the

new TS16 model. Drivers were initially the Brazilian Carlos Pace and the German Jochen Mass but during the season both young men, disappointed, left the team, Pace to continue his career

Harvey Postlethwaite

with Brabham. Even the important sponsor left the sinking ship. Surtees engaged drivers (Bell, Jabouille, Dolhem and Koinigg) on a race by race basis from then on, but at the end of the season Helmut Koinigg, the young Austrian, was killed during practice for the United States Grand Prix.

The March team also existed on a limited budget this year. Hans-Joachim Stuck, son of the prewar Auto Union driver, made his Formula One debut with a 741 in Argentina, while a second car was driven by Vittorio Brambilla, brother

of the former Ferrari driver Ernesto Brambilla. This was sponsored by the Italian tool company Beta.

Lola returned to the Formula One category after a long absence in 1974, when Eric Broadley supplied his T370 to Graham Hill's team, which was again backed by the Embassy tobacco people. The Embassy-Hill Lolas were driven by Guy Edwards as well as Graham Hill. The Frank Williams team stuck with their Iso-Fords, again supported by the Italian luxury-car manufacturer and further developed by the well-known engineer Giampaolo Dallara. When the Iso company fell victim to the general economic crisis, Dallara went to Lancia to work on their production-based competition cars and was replaced as designer by John Clarke, the cars being

Tom Pryce
Tom Pryce

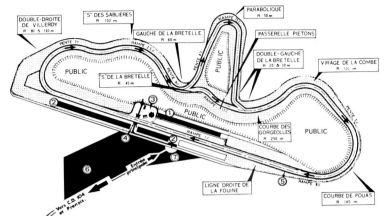

The 1974 French Grand Prix was held for the first time on the 3.289km Dijon circuit. The second time this circuit was used, in 1977, the Bretelle section (in the middle of sketch) was used, increasing the track length to 3.8km.

Hans-Joachim Stuck

renamed Williams at the same time. Best known of the Iso drivers was Arturo Merzario, but the Frenchman Jacques Laffite made his Formula One debut in an Iso later in the year.

Several other small firms produced Formula One cars in 1974, some never managing to qualify and others being consistent tail-enders. Included in this category were the products of Trojan (designed by Ron Tauranac), Token (Ray Jessop), Amon and Lyncar, all of which very quickly disappeared from the scene. New Zealander Chris Amon's Formula One project ran completely out of money before he had a chance to drive, placing him in an especially precarious financial position. The only small manufacturer to survive the crisis for any time was Ensign, which continued to be financed by Rikky von Opel, though he withdrew his support during the course of the season. Another of these teams came from Japan — the Maki — though its results were very disappointing, and towards the end of the season, two American racing stables announced that they would be taking part in the Canadian Grand Prix. The teams of both Roger Penske and Parnelli Jones were sound enterprises with solid experience in the Indianapolis 500 races. The new Penske was driven by Mark Donohue and the Parnelli by Mario Andretti. Without exception, these teams used the Ford-Cosworth engine and Hewland transmission.

The World Championship race was a gripping one. The combination of Niki Lauda and the Ferrari 312B3 was theoretically the fastest as Lauda led for a total of 338 laps over the 15 World Championship rounds. On a number of occasions however he was forced to retire

when in a clear lead, and managed only fourth place on the Championship table. Emerson Fittipaldi in the McLaren M23 was World Champion, even though he led only 77 laps over the season. Second and third in the contest were Ferrari driver Regazzoni, who led for 80 laps and was narrowly beaten to the title, and Tyrrell man Scheckter, in front for 86 laps during the year.

Parnelli Jones

Ferrari team-mates Lauda and Regazzoni took the first two places in the Spanish Grand Prix, and again in Holland. At the Nürburgring Lauda came off the track on the first lap after a daring braking manoeuvre failed to come off, leaving Regazzoni to lead the race till its end. At Monaco Regazzoni was initial leader but fell back after constant pressure from his team-mate; Lauda later had to drop out with mechanical problems. The Ferraris gained more and more ground on the opposition during the season, and Regazzoni performed remarkably consistently, collecting points in virtually every race. Lauda's luck on the other hand completely ran out over the second

Jody Scheckter

Niki Lauda

half of the year. He couldn't do anything right after the German Grand Prix, and didn't add a single point to his score during the latter part of the season.

By contrast, Emerson Fittipaldi was very successful with the McLaren M23, winning the Brazilian, Belgian and Canadian Grands Prix. Three victories also went to Carlos Reutemann in the Brabham BT44, the South African, Austrian and United States races. Scheckter and Depailler took the first two places for the Tyrrell 007 in Sweden and Scheckter also won the British Grand Prix after Lauda's Ferrari had to abandon the race due to a flat tyre. Even the good old Lotus 72D was not without a victory, Ronnie Peterson winning at Monaco in the black JPS after the Ferrari misfortunes. Lauda and Regazzoni also had to retire with mechanical troubles when well ahead in both France and Italy.

There was a considerable amount of tension in the air on the eve of the United States Grand Prix at Watkins Glen, for

Patrick Depailler

going into the 15th and final World Championship round Fittipaldi and Regazzoni each had 52 points, followed by Scheckter with 45. Tyrrell driver Scheckter still had a theoretical chance of becoming champion if he won this last event.

The Ferraris had incredibly bad luck at Watkins Glen. Lauda started from the third row of the grid and Regazzoni from the fifth, but in the race both had problems with their cars' shock absorbers and weren't able to play any part in the battle for the lead. Lauda eventually dropped out of the race and Regazzoni was unable to get beyond the midfield positions. As the Swiss driver fell further and further behind in the race Fittipaldi's Championship became only a matter of finishing. Easing up and avoiding taking risks the Brazilian finished in fourth place in the race, and that was enough to assure him of his second title.

Brabham driver Carlos Reutemann enjoyed a start-to-finish victory in this race, leading his team-mate Carlos Pace over the line, while James Hunt was third in the Hesketh. It was here that Denis Hulme took part in his last race, in a McLaren, before retiring to New Zealand.

The World Manufacturers' Championship was won by McLaren from Ferrari and Tyrrell. Although Ferrari possessed the better cars, the rivalry between Lauda and Regazzoni, and the lack of team strategy, cost the Maranello team the World Championship.

The two American Grand Prix newcomers had made their debuts in the second to last World Championship event of the year, the Canadian Grand Prix at Mosport. Mario Andretti drove the Parnelli-Ford VPJ4, designed by former Lotus engineer Maurice Phillippe, and Mark Donohue the Penske-Ford PC1, the work of Englishman Geoffrey Ferris. The Penske Grand Prix team, based at Poole in England, suffered a major setback soon afterwards when they lost their team manager, the Swiss enthusiast Heinz Hofer, in a road accident.

1974 had been a good Grand Prix season for Goodyear — all 15 Grands Prix had gone to cars using their tyres. Firestone had almost completely withdrawn from racing, carrying out no new development work, and this led to a noticeable general trend towards their rivals. Vehicles fitted with Firestone tyres were BRM, Hesketh, Surtees, Iso, Ensign, Lola and Parnelli (which was driven by Firestone's star driver Mario Andretti), but Goodyears were run by McLaren, Ferrari, Brabham, Lotus, Tyrrell, March, Shadow and Penske.

Formula One cars of 1974

Make/model	Chief designer(s)	Engine	Gearbox (speeds)	Chassis	Wheelbase	Track	Tyre make	Dry weight
Brabham BT 44	Gordon Murray	Cosworth DFV (V8)	Hewland FG 400 (5)	FM	2413	F 1519 R 1424	Goodyear	576
BRM P 201	Mike Pilbeam	BRM P 142-60 (V12)	BRM P 161/193 (5)	SM	2591	F 1524 R 1524	Firestone	585
Ensign MN 01/02	Morris Nunn	Cosworth DFV (V8)	Hewland FG 400 (5)	SM	2565	F 1549 R 1498	Firestone	585
Ferrari 312 B3	Mauro Forghieri	Ferrari 312 B (12 cyl 180°)	Ferrari (5)	FM	2500	F 1600 R 1640	Goodyear	578
Hesketh 308	Harvey Postlethwaite	Cosworth DFV (V8)	Hewland FG 400 (5)	SM	2540	F 1473 R 1549	Firestone	589
ISO IR	John Clarke	Cosworth DFV (V8)	Hewland FG 400 (5)	FM	2489	F 1575 R 1524	Firestone	576
Lola T 370	Eric Broadley	Cosworth DFV (V8)	Hewland FG 400 (5)	SM	2591	F 1626 R 1626	Firestone	592
Lotus 72 D	Colin Chapman Maurice Phillippe	Cosworth DFV (V8)	Hewland FG 400 (5)	SM	2540	F 1448 R 1448	Goodyear	578
Lotus 76	Ralph Bellamy	Cosworth DF (V8)	Hewland FG 400 (5)	FM	2565	F 1473 R 1575	Goodyear	578
March 741	Robin Herd	Cosworth DFV (V8)	Hewland FG 400 (5)	FM	2489	F 1473 R 1473	Goodyear	580
McLaren M 23	Gordon Coppuck	Cosworth DFV (V8)	Hewland FG 400 (5)	FM	2565 – 2579	F 1575 R 1578	Goodyear	575
Parnelli VPJ 4	Maurice Phillippe	Cosworth DFV (V8)	Hewland FG 400 (5)	FM	2540	F 1499 R 1549	Firestone	578
Penske PC 1	Geoff Ferris	Cosworth DFV (V8)	Hewland FG 400 (5)	SM	2540	F 1473 R 1524	Goodyear	582
Surtees TS 16	John Surtees	Cosworth DFV (V8)	Hewland FG 400 (5)	FM	2438	F 1524 R 1524	Firestone	595
Shadow DN 3	Tony Southgate	Cosworth DFV (V8)	Hewland FL 200 (5)	SM	2667	F 1473 R 1524	Goodyear	580
Token RJ 02	Ray Jessop	Cosworth DFV (V8)	Hewland DG 300 (5)	FM	2464	F 1575 R 1575	Firestone	585
Trojan T 103	Ron Tauranac	Cosworth DFV (V8)	Hewland DG 500 (5)	SM	2591	F 1556 R 1626	Firestone	580
Tyrrell 007	Derek Gardner	Cosworth DFV (V8)	Hewland FG 400 (5)	SM	2591	F 1602 R 1501 – 1603	Goodyear	588

Chassis construction: SM = semi-monocoque; FM = full monocoque

A clear World Championship title for Niki Lauda and the flat-twelve
Ferrari. The new Lotus models are disappointing. A Hesketh victory for
James Hunt in Holland. An absolute tyre-supply monopoly for Goodyear.

The 3-litre Grand Prix formula had its tenth season in 1975. Although originally intended to end in 1970, the formula had attracted a well-balanced range of designs with no domination by any one make, and provided interesting racing. The continuing research and development possible in a long-lasting formula had however brought a new trend to motorsport, as Grand Prix racing now tended to become little more than a branch of show business. The concept of different racing formulae being introduced to further technical development in the motor industry as a whole, disappeared. In the ten seasons of the 3-litre formula until that time, all World Championship titles had been won by cars with V8 engines, the Repco in 1966 and 1967 and then, from 1968 to 1974, the ubiquitous Ford-Cosworth DFV.

Mauro Forghieri

But 1975 was the year of the 12-cylinder 3-litre engine. At the end of 1973 Scuderia Ferrari had launched a very sophisticated and scientific programme under their energetic technical manager Mauro Forghieri who, apart from a short break in 1972, had fulfilled that role with the company since 1962. The continual testing the team was able to carry out on its private track at Fiorano finally bore fruit in 1975 when, by the Italian Grand Prix, Niki Lauda's World Championship for Ferrari was almost a mathematical certainty. At the end of the season Lauda had scored 64.5 points, 19.5 more than the defending Champion, McLaren driver Emerson Fittipaldi, with Carlos

Reutemann third for Brabham with 37 points. Lauda won the Monaco, Belgian, Swedish, French and United States Grands Prix, and in addition his team-mate Clay Regazzoni won in Italy. Of the 14 World Championship events, six were won by Ferrari.

The 312B3, which had brought the Ferrari name back to the fore in 1974, was superseded after the first World Championship races of 1975 by a new model, the 312T. This car, which had first appeared in the autumn of 1974, replaced the 312B3 from the 1975 South African Grand Prix. The car once again utilised a tubular-frame chassis with riveted sheetmetal skin, but in order to concentrate more weight towards the centre of the car, the gearbox was mounted transversely (hence the "T" suffix). Its success seemed to confirm that Ferrari had got the balance right. In the 312T, the 12-cylinder engine developed more than 500bhp at 12,500rpm, in spite of running on only four main crankshaft bearings.

McLaren further modified the M23 for 1975, changing the suspension at least five times during the season. Under Gordon Coppuck's direction, alterations were made to wheelbase and track as well as suspension geometry, but the car, driven by Emerson Fittipaldi and Jochen Mass, was not particularly competitive on winding hilly circuits. Fittipaldi did however win the Argentine Grand Prix and also the totally washed-out British Grand Prix, where a flooded circuit led to the race ending in chaos. In addition Mass won the Spanish Grand Prix, which was stopped early due to a bad accident.

The crisis which had overcome Lotus in 1974 was still present in 1975, but was now a specifically technical problem. Following the failure of the 76 model in 1974 the old 72D (with significantly

altered wheelbase) had to be resurrected once again, and Ronnie Peterson and Jacky Ickx had to make the best of what had become a hopeless situation with old and outdated cars. Indeed after the French Grand Prix a disappointed Ickx left the team, and was replaced by John Watson. During the latter part of the season Watson's car was adapted to a conventional coil-spring suspension system in place of the torsion-bar set-up, but finally in September Colin Chapman unveiled his new Lotus 77. This car was unusually narrow with a sharply pointed front, but its most unusual feature was its ingenious suspension system, specifically designed with quick adjustments of track width and geometry in mind. Again the way-out suspension design was not persevered with, and the 1976 design by Ralph Bellamy and Chapman once again reverted to coil springs.

Brabham was one of the most successful teams in 1975 with Gordon Murray's BT44B model which, apart from minor details, was identical to the BT44. Brabham owner Bernie Ecclestone was successful in enticing the drinks manufacturer Martini & Rossi to sponsor the team, whose drivers were

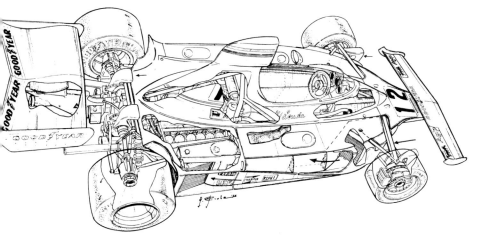

Reutemann and Pace. Carlos Pace won his first, and only, Grand Prix in Brazil, after the retirement of Jarier in a Shadow DN5, and Reutemann took first place at the Nürburgring when Niki Lauda's Ferrari fell back with a punctured tyre.

The Tyrrell 007, driven once more by Jody Scheckter and Patrick Depailler, had a simplified chassis this year, Derek Gardner abandoning the torsion-bar rear suspension and relocating the inboard front brakes into the wheels. The Tyrrell 007 first appeared in this modified form in practice for the South African Grand Prix at Kyalami, where Scheckter came off the track, which led to the suspension being further revised. Then during the race-morning warm-up session the car developed an engine fault, and the unit had to be replaced in record time. In spite of all the pre-race headaches however Scheckter came through to score a brilliant win in his home Grand Prix.

Creating a big stir in both South American races was Tony Southgate's latest Shadow, the DN5. With this basically conventional car Frenchman Jean-Pierre Jarier started from pole position at Buenos Aires, at the car's first appearance, only for the differential to break on the warm-up lap so that he could not take part in the race. Then at Interlagos Jarier was once again fastest

qualifier, and started the Brazilian Grand Prix from pole position. This time the car was able to start, and Jarier took the lead on the fifth lap, shaking off his rivals with ease. But on the 32nd of the 40 laps a fault developed in the fuel-injection system and this enabled Brabham driver Carlos Pace to pass and win the race.

Jarier was unable to match his South American showing in subsequent events but a Shadow was again on pole position for the British Grand Prix, this time with Tom Pryce as driver. Jarier's secret had been the Cosworth "Super" motor, which had been installed in the Frenchman's car on a trial basis. The special version of the eight-cylinder engine had now been built in sufficient numbers for it to be sold to the top competitors.

The Hesketh team again consisted of just one driver, James Hunt, this year and he celebrated his first Grand Prix success in Holland. Lauda in his Ferrari had been fastest in practice and took the lead at the start. When rain started everyone changed to "wet" tyres but Hunt scored tactically when he was one of the first to change back to dry-weather slicks when the rain started to ease. In the last few laps Lauda launched a strong attack against the leading Hesketh, but Hunt held on to lead the Ferrari over the line.

Since the previous year's United States Grand Prix, the Hesketh 308B had been fitted with rubber front suspension. In this arrangement the shock absorber was mounted on the outside of the chassis, with a piston, fitted at an angle, exerting pressure onto a rubber cylinder. The rubber elements, developed from Aeon

Bottom
The Ferraris of Lauda and Regazzoni were both eliminated from the 1975 Spanish Grand Prix as the result of a multiple collision triggered just after the start by Mario Andretti in a Parnelli. The race was later called off following a serious accident.

Below
Graham Hill retired from active racing in 1975 in order to concentrate on the management of his own team, whose principal driver was 23-year-old Englishman Tony Brise (right). Both died in an air accident on November 29th 1975.

Carlos Reutemann

Below
The Automobile Club of Switzerland held the well-patronised non-championship Grand Prix on the Dijon circuit in 1975. Ferrari entered a single 312T for Regazzoni, who won.

Above left
Brazil had its own Formula One car in 1975. The Copersucar, built mainly with British parts, was financed by the sugar-cane industry and driven by Wilson Fittipaldi, but never managed to obtain anything better than midfield placings.

Left
Carlos Reutemann and Carlos Pace (an Argentinian and a Brazilian) in their BT44B Brabham-Fords.

products, were meant to save weight, but designer Harvey Postlethwaite abandoned the concept for his next model, the Hesketh 308C.

Robin Herd's new March 751 amazed the sporting world in Belgium when the exuberant driving style of Vittorio Brambilla took the car into the lead on the fourth lap, but he was unfortunately forced to quit with braking problems later in the race. In Sweden Brambilla qualified the orange March 751 on pole position and led the race till the 16th lap when bad luck struck again, first with a tyre problem and then with a broken half-shaft. Then at Zeltweg Brambilla celebrated his first — and only — Grand Prix victory when he easily shook off his competitors, led by James Hunt in the Hesketh, during a heavy thunderstorm, and raced across the finishing line with a 24-second lead when the race was cut short. The Zeltweg event was held under a different sort of cloud as well however, as during practice the American Mark Donohue ran his Penske-entered March off the track following a tyre failure. Donohue, a former CanAm and Indianapolis winner, did not appear badly hurt, but in fact died a few hours after the accident. Donohue's widow sued Goodyear and, after several years of claims and counter-claims, the tyre

company was ordered to pay her compensation of several million dollars.

There was tragedy too in the Spanish Grand Prix, held on the Montjuich Park circuit in Barcelona. During practice matters of safety were the subject of considerable discussion, and the drivers finally refused to race because the organisers would do nothing to improve the inadequate precautions, such as missing bolts in safety barriers. The drivers agreed to resume practice and, ultimately, to take part in the race itself only when the organisers threatened to seize the cars and equipment to cover their contractual losses, and the team owners in turn brought pressure to bear on their drivers. World Champion Emerson Fittipaldi completed only sufficient laps, at low speed, to guarantee his team their starting money, and sat the race out in protest.

The race was full of incident, much of it involving the top drivers. Soon after the start Lauda's Ferrari was rammed by Mario Andretti as the Parnelli tried to force a way to the front. The American

car spun into Regazzoni's, and both Ferraris were eliminated from the race in the one incident. Worse was to come however, as on the 26th lap the wing on Rolf Stommelen's Hill-Ford GH2 came loose shortly after a pit-stop. The car immediately went out of control and smashed into the safety barrier, killing four people who were standing behind it, a track marshal, two fire marshals and a reporter. Three laps later the organisers waved the cars down and stopped the Grand Prix prematurely. At that time the McLaren of Jochen Mass was leading and the organisers declared him winner, though because such little distance had been completed he was allocated only half the World Championship points available for first place.

Graham Hill was now turning his efforts more and more to managing his

Jochen Mass

Embassy team and at Monaco he climbed into the cockpit for what was expected to be his last race. Sadly, the five-times Monaco winner did not qualify for the race. Prior to the British Grand Prix the 46-year-old Hill said goodbye to his public by driving slowly around the circuit — his last laps. On November 29th 1975 Graham Hill and several members of his Embassy team died in an aeroplane accident. The plane, piloted by Hill, was on a flight home from a test session at Le Castellet when it crashed into trees during its descent in fog. Amongst the dead was the promising young driver Tony Brise, who had just made his Formula One debut in Belgium, at the age of 23. The others were Hill's designer Andy Smallman and several mechanics.

In his 17 years of racing in Formula One, Hill had taken part in 176 Grand Prix races. He had broken many Grand Prix records and in addition had won the Indianapolis 500 in 1966 and the 24-hour race at Le Mans in 1972.

A Brazilian constructor had joined the Formula One family in Argentina at the start of the 1975 season. This was the Copersucar-Fittipaldi, financed by the Brazilian sugar-cane industry and built up by Wilson Fittipaldi, the older brother (by three years) of the double World Champion. The new Copersucar-Ford FD01 was built under the direction of

Richard Divila, initially with its radiator behind the transmission though, to increase cooling efficiency, this was later positioned in the front. 1975 was a bad year for BRM, with Bob Evans in the P201 as well as Surtees, but Frank Williams, who was teetering on the edge of bankruptcy, had his first real scoop when Jacques Laffite took second placing

Silverstone, the British racing track, was converted from a former airfield built during the war and served as the venue for many races from the end of the forties. Over the years the circuit was completely overhauled. Average speeds of over 200km/h made it necessary to install a chicane at Woodcote corner, immediately before the start. The lap length measured 4.719km.

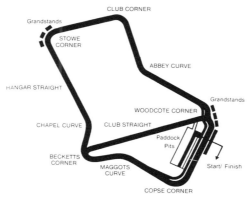

at the Nürburgring with the Williams FW04, designed by Ray Stokoe. Laffite took advantage of many of the top competitors falling back with tyre failures to give the struggling team its best result until then.

The Nürburgring had a sad record of tyre failures: this year there were 26 tyre changes during practice and 12 in the race. The lack of competition in the tyre industry had now become critical, and there were few developments in the tyre sector in 1975. Goodyear ruled the market with an absolute monopoly, Firestone having withdrawn after the Argentinian Grand Prix. In that race Mario Andretti in the Parnelli raced on Firestones, but by the next race, in Brazil, that team, too, had changed over to Goodyears. A second tyre company did not reappear on the circuits until 1977, when Michelin joined the field for the British Grand Prix.

The Goodyear monopoly meant an end to the tyre war, for with only one tyre now available to all teams, the special compounds for individual makes of cars disappeared. This meant that, as not all soft mixtures were suitable for all brands of cars, chassis had to be built to suit the only tyre now available. The compounds became harder which meant they were less susceptible to punctures, but it also meant slower lap times and generally slower races.

The 1975 Belgian Grand Prix at Zolder. Jody Scheckter, winner of the South African Grand Prix in his Tyrrell 007, leads Bob Evans in the V12 BRM P201 and one of the Hill-Fords. The BRM concern, now under Louis Stanley's management, was nearing the end of its life, and never regained its former glory.

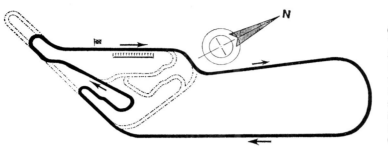

Another factor contributing to the
lack of progress in race averages in 1975
was the wet weather that prevailed
throughout the season. Many Grands
Prix were held in teeming rain and this
necessitated not only different driving
techniques, but also tyre changes in the
middle of races. The Monaco, Dutch and
British races all saw frequent tyre changes
being made, while in the Austrian Grand
Prix, where it rained from before the
start, rain tyres were used throughout.
The British Grand Prix was quite
extraordinary, the weather so changeable
that as many as three tyre changes were
made by some teams. At one stage the

cars were on treadless slicks when the heavens opened, and half a dozen skated into the catch-fencing on one corner alone, though at least a mass collision was avoided. Events at Silverstone demonstrated how dangerous modern tyres could be as soon as conditions were not perfect. Emerson Fittipaldi won the race in his McLaren in circumstances that reflected his clever tactics. The car was fitted with slicks when the first shower of rain came but he stayed out on those and only changed to "wets" after the second downpour. As the rain persisted, and cars slithered uncontrollably across the track, the race had to be terminated prematurely with Fittipaldi still in first position.

Formula One cars of 1975

Make/model	Chief designer(s)	Engine	Gearbox (speeds)	Chassis	Wheelbase	Track	Tyre make	Dry weight
Brabham BT 44 B	Gordon Murray	Cosworth DFV (V8)	Hewland FG 400 (5)	FM	2413	F 1422 R 1549	Goodyear	578
BRM P 201	Mike Pilbeam	BRM P 142-60 (V12)	BRM (5)	SM	2591	F 1524 R 1524	Goodyear	585
Ensign MN 04	Morris Nunn	Cosworth DFV (V8)	Hewland FG 400 (5)	FM	2565	F 1499 R 1524	Goodyear	605
Ferrari 312 T	Mauro Forghieri Franco Rocchi	Ferrari 312 B (12 cyl 180°)	Ferrari (5)	TS	2500	F 1500 R 1480—1540	Goodyear	580
Fittipaldi	Richard Divila	Cosworth DFV (V8)	Hewland FG 400 (5)	FM	2410	F 1500 R 1550	Goodyear	602
Hesketh 308	Harvey Postlethwaite	Cosworth DFV (V8)	Hewland FG 400 (5)	SM	2540	F 1473 R 1549	Goodyear	589
Hesketh 308 C	Harvey Postlethwaite	Cosworth DFV (V8)	Hewland FG 400 (5)	SM	2565	F 1397 R 1422	Goodyear	580
Hill GH 1	Andy Swallman	Cosworth DFV (V8)	Hewland FG 400 (5)	SM	2573	F 1626 R 1600	Goodyear	603
Lotus 72 D	Colin Chapman Maurice Phillippe	Cosworth DFV (V8)	Hewland FG 400 (5)	SM	2540	F 1448 R 1448	Goodyear	590
Lotus 72 D (long wheelbase)	Colin Chapman Maurice Phillippe	Cosworth DFV (V8)	Hewland FG 400 (5)	SM	2667	F 1549 R 1626	Goodyear	625
Maki F 101 C	Kenij Mimura Masao Ono	Cosworth DFV (V8)	Hewland FG 400 (5)	SM	2540	F 1460 R 1610	Goodyear	620
March 751	Robin Herd	Cosworth DFV (V8)	Hewland FG 400 (5)	FM	2540	F 1473 R 1473	Goodyear	576
McLaren M 23	Gordon Coppuck	Cosworth DFV (V8)	Hewland FG 400 (5)	FM	2692	F 1651 R 1651	Goodyear	589
Parnelli VPJ 4	Maurice Phillippe	Cosworth DFV (V8)	Hewland FG 400 (5)	FM	2540	F 1499 R 1562	Goodyear	580
Penske PC 1	Geoff Ferris	Cosworth DFV (V8)	Hewland FG 400 (5)	SM	2489	F 1372 R 1473	Goodyear	584
Surtees TS 16	John Surtees	Cosworth DFV (V8)	Hewland FG 400 (5)	FM	2489	F 1549 R 1600	Goodyear	610
Shadow DN 5	Tony Southgate	Cosworth DFV (V8)	Hewland FL 200 (5)	SM	2667	F 1499 R 1575	Goodyear	589
Shadow DN 7	Tony Southgate	Cosworth DFV (V8)	Hewland FL 200 (5)	SM	2667	F 1473 R 1549	Goodyear	612
Tyrrell 007	Derek Gardner	Cosworth DFV (V8)	Hewland FG 400 (5)	FM	2593	F 1590 R 1575	Goodyear	625
Williams FW 04	Ray Stokoe	Cosworth DFV (V8)	Hewland FG 400 (5)	FM	2540	F 1570 R 1570	Goodyear	591

Chassis construction: SM = semi-monocoque; FM = full monocoque; TS = tubular frame with stressed skins.

World Champion Lauda has a bad accident at the Nürburgring but is back again at Monza, then throws in the towel during the final race in Japan. Hunt in a McLaren is Champion.

The 1976 World Championship was one of the most unusual and gripping in motor racing history and was not decided until the last laps of the last race, in Japan. The championship was contested for the first time over 16 races, and Ferrari driver Niki Lauda dominated the first half of the season. His second consecutive World Championship title was in reach when events took a different turn, and the English driver James Hunt in a McLaren became the 1976 World Champion.

There were two significant team changes. In November 1975 it became known that Emerson Fittipaldi would drive the Copersucar, financed by the Brazilian sugar-cane industry. Until then the car had been driven by Wilson Fittipaldi but had not performed convincingly, and this situation did not in fact change even with a driver of Emerson's ability. At about the same time, Lord Alexander Hesketh withdrew his team from Formula One as he had found the cost of racing to be too much of a strain on his resources. McLaren boss Teddy Mayer immediately hired James Hunt, the Hesketh team driver from 1973 to 1975, to fill the vacancy created by Fittipaldi's departure. The Hesketh cars and parts were meanwhile taken over by the Frank Williams team and carried the name of the new team. Harvey Postlethwaite, the Hesketh designer, also joined the Williams team, while during the course of the season the Austrian-

Guy Ligier's Vichy-based team entered Formula One for the first time in 1976. Driver was Jacques Laffite, who by finishing fourth at Long Beach gave Ligier their first World Championship points. A feature of the car was the large airbox above the V12 engine, a feature much appreciated by the sponsor, Gitanes!

Canadian oil millionaire Walter Wolf became the principal team sponsor.

A new Lotus team had been formed with Ronnie Peterson and Mario Andretti, but after the Brazilian Grand Prix the blond Swede parted company with Colin Chapman. He was replaced on the Lotus team before the South African event by another Swede, Formula Three driver Gunnar Nilsson. The Lotus 77 had been converted to a conventional suspension system for this season but still did not perform as well as had been expected, though many of the car's problems seemed to have been overcome by the time the Spanish Grand Prix was run. The Lotus showed a noticeable improvement in this race, thanks in part at least to the experience and testing abilities of Mario Andretti.

Ferrari dominated the racing scene for the first half of the season, with Lauda winning the Brazilian and South African Grands Prix (Argentina had been cancelled in 1976 due to political unrest) with the 312T.

A second United States Grand Prix, run on the Long Beach street circuit in California, was added to the World Championship schedule this year, and here Clay Regazzoni demonstrated his abilities with the 312T Ferrari to the full. He set fastest lap in qualifying and then led the race unchallenged from the first

James Hunt

James Hunt became World Champion in 1976 in Gordon Coppuck's McLaren M23, with which Emerson Fittipaldi had won the 1974 title. A young John Barnard used this car as a basis for his first Indianapolis project. The M23 first appeared with its divided airbox in the 1976 Spanish Grand Prix.

lap till the end, again setting fastest lap. The Ferrari 312T2, which strongly resembled the earlier model and retained the transverse transmission, made its debut in the Spanish Grand Prix. With this new car Lauda won the Monaco and Belgian Grands Prix and, after finishing second to Hunt in the British Grand Prix at Brands Hatch, was subsequently awarded first place in this race too when Hunt was disqualified following a protest from Ferrari.

Between 1974 and 1976 Ferrari had carried out tests with Michelin tyres and De Dion rear axles on their private track at Fiorano, but although the new T2 had a De Dion rear when first shown to the press, it was never actually raced in this form.

New Formula One regulations, devised to restrain designers from producing cars which were too fast, came into force on May 2nd, and applied from the Spanish Grand Prix. All Grand Prix cars now had to have a cushion zone in front of the pedals to protect the drivers' feet from impact in the event of an accident, and a second roll-hoop had to be fitted level with the instruments in the cockpit. At the same time rear-wing overhang was reduced from 100cm between the wheel hub and the furthest point of the wing to 80cm, and the front wing was limited to 120cm. The highest

point of the air-intake funnel, or air-box, was not allowed to be more than 85cm from the lowest sprung point of the chassis. Total vehicle width now had to be under 215cm, the width of the rear wheels was not to exceed 21 inches, or 53.4cm, and wheel-diameter was restricted to 13 inches.

While the Lauda/Ferrari combination had dominated the first half of the World Championship season, the man to beat in the second half was James Hunt with the McLaren M23. The tall, long-haired, blond Englishman won the French Grand Prix at Le Castellet after the Ferraris of Regazzoni and Lauda both withdrew from the race with broken crankshafts, and also crossed the line first in the British Grand Prix at Brands Hatch, though he was subsequently disqualified and the victory awarded to Niki Lauda. The Hunt/McLaren successes continued in the German, Dutch, Canadian and United States Grands Prix, giving their World Championship point score an enormous boost.

The technical breakthrough of the 1976 season was the six-wheeled Tyrrell P34. When the prototype appeared in September 1975 it caused a sensation, though there were many who considered it some sort of practical joke. But Ken Tyrrell and his designer Derek Gardner

were deadly serious and when the car was first raced, by the Frenchman Patrick Depailler in the Spanish Grand Prix at Jarama, it made quite an impression. The rear section of the P34 was quite conventional, with two normal-sized driving wheels. At the front however were four small-diameter wheels, all steerable. Each pair of wheels had its own steering geometry, which interconnected by a steering plate and geared shaft to the steering column.

The size of the front wheels, which had ten-inch rims, and the car's narrow track provided a considerable reduction in wind resistance. Apart from the extra number of wheels, the front section of the car was of conventional design, though its odd appearance was accentuated by the wheels being mounted close in to the chassis. The P34's first trials were quite impressive but in the long run the car failed to show any advantage over more orthodox designs. Notwithstanding this it had a good record with numerous placings, the highlight being first and second (Scheckter from Depailler) places in the Swedish Grand Prix at Anderstorp. The six-wheeler's wheelbase was increased and the track widened for 1977 under the onslaught of increased competition but roadholding was not improved, and some of the advantages of reduced air resistance were lost. In 1978

Niki Lauda in a Ferrari 312T leading the 1976 French Grand Prix at Le Castellet, ahead of Hunt in a McLaren M23 and Regazzoni in a Ferrari. Lauda and Hunt were the stars of the season, fighting a gripping duel for the Championship. The title was not decided, in Hunt's favour, until the last race.

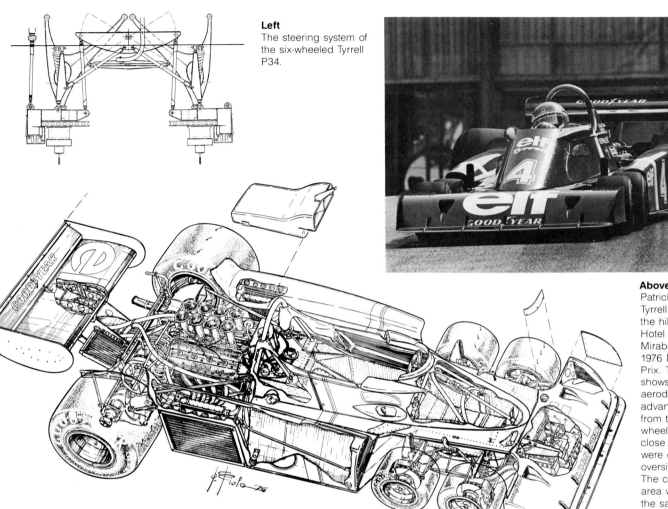

Left
The steering system of the six-wheeled Tyrrell P34.

Above
Patrick Depailler in the Tyrrell P34 races down the hill between the Hotel de Paris and Mirabeau during the 1976 Monaco Grand Prix. This picture shows how the aerodynamic advantages gained from the small front wheels, positioned close in to the chassis, were offset by the oversized rear tyres. The car's overall frontal area was in fact about the same as those of more conventional models. The cockpit sides were fitted with tiny windows through which the driver could see the front wheels. On the whole, the six-wheeled design was not a success.

Above
The six-wheeled Tyrrell P34, designed by Derek Gardner, first appeared in the 1976 Spanish Grand Prix at Jarama, though a prototype had been tested as early as September 1975. The P34 took the first two places in the 1976 Swedish Grand Prix at Anderstorp, with drivers Scheckter and Depailler.

the P34 was replaced by the more conventional 008 model.

All Formula One cars in 1976 used Goodyear tyres, but this seems to have resulted in the supplying company becoming complacent, for all research and development work into racing tyres was shelved. The tyre was made from a hard compound, which made it impossible for cars to match the lap times achieved in previous years.

Following the change to harder rubber, Ferrari complained of inferior roadholding, the 312T2s being worse affected than most because of the high percentage of weight they had distributed on the front axles. This meant the rear tyres took longer to reach operating temperatures. The Ferrari in fact had more of its weight (36.5%) on its front axle than any of the other 1976 Formula

One cars: the McLaren figure was 35.4%, the Lotus 34.5% and the Shadow 32.5.

In 1976, John Watson from Northern Ireland was promoted to drive the Penske PC04 in the Austrian Grand Prix, which he won. He also displayed his skills in the Dutch Grand Prix at Zandvoort, where he fought a wheel-to-wheel duel for the lead with James Hunt. After a year's break since Brambilla won the 1975 Austrian Grand Prix in heavy rain, March returned to the winner's circle at Monza when Ronnie Peterson won the Italian Grand Prix in a March 761. The fast Swede had missed out on a number of earlier victories through mechanical problems.

Alfa Romeo's indirect support of Formula One racing provided one of the most interesting developments of 1976 when the Milan company made their successful Type 33 endurance-racing engines available to Brabham. These were 2995cc (77 x 53.6mm) flat-12s with only four main crankshaft bearings, for which Brabham designer Gordon Murray built the BT45 model. Initially, the car was very heavy and the engine proved to be very thirsty, repeatedly leaving Carlos Reutemann and Carlos Pace frustrated. But in 1977 the improved BT45B model Brabham-Alfa would be counted amongst the Formula One élite.

Carlos Reutemann had however left the Brabham team, disappointed and disillusioned, before the end of 1976, and raced for Ferrari at Monza. For his sins, Reutemann lost a large percentage of his Brabham income, as Bernie Ecclestone did not take kindly to a top driver changing to an opposition camp. Following Reutemann's engagement, Ferrari indicated that Regazzoni's 1977 contract would not be extended, for the Swiss driver had fallen out of favour at Maranello.

The 1976 season was exciting and colourful, with more than the usual amount of controversy surrounding several events. There were disqualifications and reinstatements to a degree never before seen in the Grand Prix arena. This unpleasant chapter of events began at the Spanish Grand Prix where the winner, James Hunt, was disqualified two hours after victory. During a post-race inspection of his McLaren, it was found that the rear of the car exceeded the maximum allowable width (2150mm) by 18mm. At the same time the scrutineers found that the wings of

The Monza circuit, originally built in 1922, became too fast for modern cars, and was slowed down with a chicane in the Vialone, or Ascari, Curve. Further chicanes were built in 1976 at the end of the start/finish straight and before the first Lesmo Curve. The road circuit now measured 5.8km.

Above
The drawing, left, shows the effect of the new rules which came into force at the 1976 Spanish Grand Prix and stipulated a total chassis height of 85cm. The rear wings had to be moved 20cm forwards (measured from their rearmost point). The drawing on the right shows the Ligier-Matra JS5 with its imposing airbox, another casualty of the new regulations.

Right
Jacky Ickx, past his prime as a Formula One driver by 1976, but still a successful endurance-race driver, parks his Ensign MN176 on the side of the road during the Dutch Grand Prix.

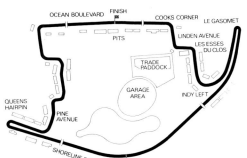

Jacques Laffite's Ligier-Matra JS5 were out by 15mm. James Hunt's win was withdrawn and Lauda, who was still suffering the effects of a chest injury resulting from a tractor accident, was declared winner. The authorities in Jarama had made a very courageous decision, indicating that the CSI meant business in its enforcement of the new regulations. But two months later, an appeal by McLaren to the FIA was sustained and the CSI's decision overturned. The victory was awarded to James Hunt for the second time and, in recognition of this victory, he was presented with the winner's laurels for the Spanish Grand Prix, and Lauda was relegated to second place.

The Court of Appeal's decision on behalf of the FIA did little for the reputation of Grand Prix racing and the controversy continued at the British Grand Prix at Brands Hatch, following a first-lap multiple collision. Ferrari team-mates Regazzoni (who had started from the second row) and Lauda entered the first corner after the start side by side and then touched. Regazzoni's 312T spun around and rammed Hunt's McLaren. Several other cars were damaged in the ensuing confusion. The officials of the meeting immediately stopped the race and, after a long delay, allowed the vehicles to line up for a second attempt. James Hunt's damaged McLaren was repaired for the restart and, after following Niki Lauda's Ferrari for much of the race, the English driver took the lead when the Ferrari developed gearbox problems and slowed. Hunt won, but Ferrari lodged a protest against the McLaren on the grounds that the car had been rendered unraceable in the accident after the first start, and had been able to race only because of repairs carried out during the period between the stopping of the race and its restarting. This work, Ferrari claimed, should have been carried out during actual racing time, and the car should not therefore have been allowed to start. And so, two months later, James Hunt lost his British Grand Prix win, and the victory was awarded instead to Lauda.

Left
James Hunt, 1976
World Champion,
during the victory
ceremony following the
French Grand Prix at
Le Castellet.

Many observers expressed the view that this decision was most unfair, particularly in view of the fact that the collision had been caused by Ferrari in the first place. It was believed at the time that the decision was intended as a form of compensation to appease the Ferrari team for Hunt's Spanish reinstatement.

The controversy did not end there. During practice for the Italian Grand Prix technical inspectors took test samples of fuel and ruled that the McLaren and Penske teams were both using fuel with a higher octane rating than permissible. The Friday qualifying times of McLaren drivers Hunt and Mass, and Watson (Penske) were disallowed, which meant they had to do it all again on the Saturday. Unfortunately it rained that day, but in the end Hunt and Watson were offered starting positions on the third row. This deprived them of any chance to take part in the battle for the lead.

But the lowest point of all in the 1976 World Championship season was not a political matter, but Niki Lauda's accident. On the second lap of the German Grand Prix at the Nürburgring Lauda, his second World Championship title in reach, lost control of his Ferrari. The car spun across the track and crashed into the barriers, where it immediately burst into flames and was then rammed by a following car. Drivers Arturo Merzario, Guy Edwards, Harald Ertl and Brett Lunger ran to the burning vehicle, pulling their colleague free and saving his life, although he was very seriously injured. The World Champion had lost his helmet when the car overturned and suffered severe burns to his head, face, arms and hands. His lungs were also

Brett Lunger

In November 1976 Walter Wolf unveiled his new contender for the following year. The Wolf WR1, designed by Harvey Postlethwaite, caused a sensation in 1977 when Scheckter drove it to victory first time out.

severely damaged from the effect of poisonous gases inhaled while he was trapped in the car. He was taken to a special hospital where he was under intensive care for several days and was in fact given the last rites.

But, with superhuman effort, he made a miraculous recovery and, only a few weeks after the Nürburgring accident, competed in the Italian Grand Prix at Monza, finishing in fourth place. He came eighth in the Grand Prix that followed in Canada and third at Watkins Glen.

Going into the 16th and final World Championship Grand Prix of the year, in Japan, the World Championship position was very close. Lauda had led on points ever since the first round in Brazil and now had 68 points, just three more than James Hunt. The Austrian, driven by ambition, was determined to make up for the two Grands Prix he had missed through his hospitalisation after the Nürburgring accident. It was raining heavily and the circuit at the foot of Mount Fujiyama was shrouded in fog when the Japanese Grand Prix was due

to get under way. The start was delayed while everyone waited for conditions to improve, but the flag finally dropped and James Hunt set off in the lead, pushing his McLaren further and further ahead.

But on the second lap the unthinkable happened: Niki Lauda pulled up at the pits and clambered out of his completely intact Ferrari. His short comment was, "My life is more important than the World Championship." Lauda's decision was kept quiet and Ferrari, to protect him, gave out that a technical fault was the reason for his withdrawal from the race. But Lauda ignored the Ferrari excuses and stood by his words. He had just managed to escape death's clutches at the Nürburgring and was no longer prepared to take risks endangering his life.

This withdrawal meant that he had said goodbye to his World Championship hopes, for James Hunt kept going in fog and rain, driving as though the devil were after him, and shaking off all opposition. But then on the 62nd lap of the 73, with victory in sight, the Englishman had to slow down with tyre trouble and steadily lost his advantage. Patrick Depailler in the six-wheeled P34 Tyrrell took over the lead and then Andretti in a Lotus 77 passed Depailler. On the 68th lap Hunt finally stopped at the pits and had all four tyres changed, so the order now was Andretti (Lotus), Regazzoni (McLaren), Jones (Surtees), Depailler (Tyrrell) and Hunt (McLaren).

But it was still not all over, for Jones and Regazzoni both struck last-minute tyre trouble and fell back, and Hunt was able to take third place at the end. The four points he earned for that place meant he had beaten Niki Lauda by one point, and became World Champion for 1976. The World Manufacturers' Championship went to Ferrari.

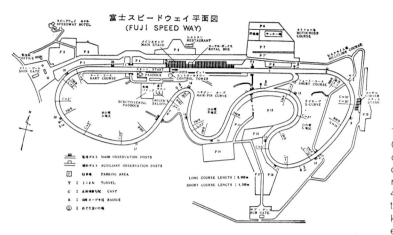

The 1976 World Championship was decided on the Fuji circuit in Japan. The race was held on the 4.359km combination track (without the kidney-shaped extension).

Formula One cars of 1976

Make/model	Chief designer(s)	Engine	Gearbox (speeds)	Chassis	Wheelbase	Track	Tyre make	Dry weight
Brabham BT 45	Gordon Murray	Alfa Romeo 115-12 (12 cyl 180°)	Hewland TL 2-200 (6)	SM	2502	F 1422 R 1524	Goodyear	605
Ensign MN 05	Morris Nunn Dave Baldwin	Cosworth DFV (V8)	Hewland DG 400 (5)	FM	2616	F 1473 R 1575	Goodyear	604
Ferrari 312 T2	Mauro Forghieri Franco Rocchi	Ferrari 312 B (12 cyl 180°)	Ferrari (5)	TS	2560	F 1403 R 1430	Goodyear	595
Fittipaldi FD 04	Richard Divila	Cosworth DFV (V8)	Hewland DG 400 (5)	FM	2506	F 1510 R 1563	Goodyear	610
Hesketh 308	Harvey Postlethwaite	Cosworth DFV (V8)	Hewland TL 200 (5)	SM	2540	F 1473 R 1543	Goodyear	590
Ligier JS 5	Paul Carillo	Matra MS 73 (V12)	Hewland TL 2-200 (5)	SM	2608	F 1536 R 1600	Goodyear	605
Lotus 77	Colin Chapman Ralph Bellamy	Cosworth DFV (V8)	Hewland DG 400 (5)	FM	2616 — 2794	F 1473 R 1575	Goodyear	593
March 761	Robin Herd	Cosworth DFV (V8)	Hewland DG 400 (5)	FM	2591 — 2794	F 1397 R 1422	Goodyear	580
McLaren M 23	Gordon Coppuck	Cosworth DFV (V8)	Hewland DG 400 (5)	FM	2743	F 1651 R 1626	Goodyear	595
McLaren M 26	Gordon Coppuck	Cosworth DFV (V8)	Hewland DG 400 (5)	FM	2743	F 1651 R 1626	Goodyear	585
Penske PC 4	Geoff Ferris	Cosworth DFV (V8)	Hewland DG 400 (5)	FM	2692	F 1422 R 1473	Goodyear	590
Shadow DN 5 B	Tony Southgate	Cosworth DFV (V8)	Hewland TL 200 (5)	SM	2667	F 1499 R 1575	Goodyear	590
Shadow DN 8	Tony Southgate Dave Wass	Cosworth DFV (V8)	Hewland TL 200 (5)	SM	2667	F 1473 R 1549	Goodyear	580
Surtees TS 19	John Surtees Ken Sears	Cosworth DFV (V8)	Hewland FGA 400 (5)	FM	2489	F 1448 R 1473	Goodyear	594
Tyrrell P 34	Derek Gardner	Cosworth DFV (V8)	Hewland FG 400 (5)	SM	2453/1993	F 1234 R 1473	Goodyear	587
Williams FW 05	Harvey Postlethwaite	Cosworth DFV (V8)	Hewland DG 400 (5)	SM	2565	F 1397 R 1422	Goodyear	595

Chassis construction: SM = semi-monocoque; FM = full monocoque; TS = tubular frame with stressed skins.

Dawn of the Turbo Era

Lotus starts a technological revolution with its "wing car" — Renault starts another with its turbocharged V6, which runs for the first time in the British Grand Prix. Lauda in a Ferrari is World Champion again.

The 1977 season saw the beginning of a new chapter in Formula One racing, one of great technical importance, for this was the dawn of the era of the "wing" car. With this new idea Colin Chapman, the Lotus boss, once again proved himself to be an inventor of genius, for although the concept had appeared as early as 1970, on the March-Ford 701, it was Chapman's Lotus 78 which made it work. Robin Herd's design had had additional fuel tanks built on its sides in the shape of upside-down aircraft wings, but the first Formula One March was not a successful design and not much notice was taken of Herd's experiment. The breakthrough came in 1977 when the Lotus-Ford 78 made its first appearance in the Argentine Grand Prix. During the remainder of the season the combination of Mario Andretti and Lotus 78 proved to be practically unmatched in terms of lap speeds, though it was robbed of certain victory on a number of occasions by mechanical breakdowns.

The wing car concept can be described as the most important technical Formula One achievement of the seventies, but in order to chart its development it is necessary to go back to the 1975 season. At that time Lotus were going through a low period, for they had still not succeeded in producing a car which was able to duplicate the successes of the brilliant 72 model. In July of that year, 1975, Colin Chapman came to the conclusion that a completely new Formula One car would have to be constructed, and by August had come up with the idea for the first Lotus wing car. But the concept could not be produced right away, for before proceeding with the wing car it was necessary to take a number of intermediate steps.

The first was to build a conventional car so that the chassis problems which the new concept was likely to produce could be ironed out. That was the plan for 1976, with a view to the revolutionary new 78 being ready to start at the beginning of the 1977 season. Ralph Bellamy and Tony Rudd were the engineers and they had already begun construction of the wing car by the end of 1975. The actual aerodynamic experiments were the responsibility of Peter Wright, who had worked out a wing-car concept when working with Rudd at BRM as long ago as 1969. The idea was never put to the test, however, and the 1970 March has therefore gone down in history as the first wing car.

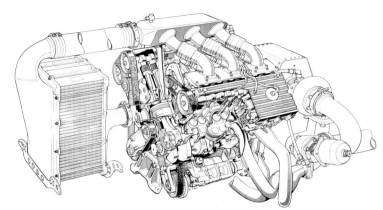

Left
The 1492cc V6 Renault-Gordini engine initially had only one turbocharger.

Below
The Renault turbo made its debut at the 1977 British Grand Prix at Silverstone. Jean-Pierre Jabouille here leads Fittipaldi in a Fittipaldi and Lunger in a McLaren.

In the development of the Lotus 78, 400 hours were spent in the wind tunnel testing the various wing/radiator combinations alone. Using the knowledge gained in the wind-tunnel experiments, Bellamy and Martin Ogilvie started work on the final form of the wing car in September 1976. The chassis had already been completed and was standing by, so that tests could begin as soon as the body was built, and the completed car was in fact unveiled to the press on December 21st 1976. The Lotus 78 had a smaller than usual central monocoque, with the two side-wing sections, which contained the radiator and fuel tanks, fixed between the front and rear wheels. The front and rear wings of the previous year's conventional Formula One Lotus model were retained but the new sidepods produced additional downforce to the extent that total downforce achievable by the Lotus 78 was something like 15% more than on the cars of its competitors. During the 1977 season it became more and more obvious that when braking, or when accelerating from a low speed, the Lotus 78 was always the fastest car, giving it a

considerable advantage over its rivals.

The principle behind this increase in downforce is pure aerodynamics. On an aircraft, lift is created when the wings, with curved upper surfaces and almost flat undersides, pass through the airstream, because the air passes faster over the flat surface and therefore creates more pressure. By rotating the wing through 180°, exactly the opposite effect is produced, the thrust becoming downward rather than upward. On a racing car, this downforce pushes the car onto the road and allows for improved roadholding. But the wing-car concept did have one disadvantage: wind-resistance was greater, and that meant the car was slower than its rivals in terms of maximum possible speed.

The outcome of the Argentine Grand Prix, which opened the 1977 World Championship season, was a turnup for the books for the winner was not a Lotus, nor a Ferrari, nor a McLaren, but a brand new car, making its race debut in the hands of Jody Scheckter. This was the Wolf-Ford WR1, the product of a new team set up by wealthy Canadian enthusiast Walter Wolf. The team had

Walter Wolf

Below
John Watson in a Brabham-Alfa Romeo BT45B. The Ulsterman led the French Grand Prix at Dijon right up until the last lap, when he ran out of fuel and Lotus driver Andretti snatched victory.

The Brabham BT45B with flat-12 Alfa Romeo engine and side-mounted tanks was very fast but plagued by minor faults.

been officially founded on June 5th 1976, and on January 9th 1977 they took their first victory. Wolf had chosen people of proven reliability for his team: his racing manager Peter Warr came from Lotus, designer Harvey Postlethwaite from Hesketh, and Scheckter from Tyrrell. Niki Lauda and Carlos Reutemann were the Ferrari drivers, in the 312T2. Clay Regazzoni's contract with the Italian team had expired at the end of 1976 and the Swiss driver transferred to the Ensign team; in doing so, he left his winning streak behind.

The second round of the World Championship was the Brazilian Grand Prix at Interlagos, where before the final practice session Ferrari produced their own "winged wonder", with which Reutemann boosted himself onto the front row of the grid. Lauda, on the other hand, was not given the same treatment, for the Austrian's withdrawal from Japanese Grand Prix the year before had weakened Ferrari's trust in him. Tensions between the 1975 World Champion and his team were high, and would mount as the season wore on, fuelled no doubt by Reutemann's winning in Brazil.

The next Grand Prix, in South Africa, had a tragic conclusion when a freak accident took the life of a driver and a track marshal. This had been innocently triggered by Renzo Zorzi's Shadow

stopping on the side of the track with a mechanical problem. An over-enthusiastic marshal leapt from the pits to go to Zorzi's aid with a fire extinguisher but ran across the track, right in the path of the other Shadow, driven by Welshman Tom Pryce. The marshal was killed by the impact but the fire extinguisher caught Pryce's head and he, too, was killed instantly. The Shadow continued along the home straight with its dead driver in the cockpit, colliding with Jacques Laffite's Ligier-Matra at the next corner and sending the French car off the track as well. Pryce's Shadow, its momentum undiminished, then crashed heavily into the barriers. Niki Lauda was one of those who drove over a piece of wreckage from the accident, and the Ferrari's oil pressure fell to an alarmingly low level over the last few laps. But Lauda kept going by the skin of his teeth to gain

Important characteristics of Formula One cars of 1977

Make	Alfa Romeo	BRM	Cosworth	Ferrari	Matra	Renault
Model	115-12	P 142 60	DFV	312 B	MS-77	EF 1
Cylinder configuration	V12 180°	V12 60°	V8 90°	V12 180°	V12 60°	V6 90° Turbo
Bore & stroke	77 × 53,6	74,61 × 57,15	85,7 × 64,8	80 × 49,6	79,7 × 50	86 × 42,8
Capacity	2995	2998	2990	2992	2993	1492
Main bearings	7	7	5	4	7	4
Fuel injection	Lucas	Lucas	Lucas	Lucas	Lucas	Kugelfischer
Turbocharger	—	—	—	—	—	1 × Garrett
Ignition	Marelli	Lucas	Lucas	Marelli	Ducellier	Marelli
Power (bhp) at (rpm)	525 12 000	480 11 500	480 10 600	520 12 000	510 12 000	500 11 000

Antony Joseph Foyt

his first victory since his dreadful accident on the Nürburgring.

Lauda in the Ferrari, Jody Scheckter in the Wolf and Mario Andretti in the Lotus 78 dominated the United States Grand Prix West in a great three-way battle which lasted throughout the whole Long Beach race. At the end Andretti took a historic victory, the first for the Lotus 78 wing car. Tom Pryce's was not the only familiar face missing at Long Beach, for the Brazilian Carlos Pace had been killed in a private plane crash on March 19th; his place on the Brabham team was taken by the German Hans-Joachim Stuck.

The outstanding superiority of the Lotus 78 was clearly demonstrated for the first time at the Spanish Grand Prix at Jarama, when Mario Andretti qualified in pole position and had a trouble-free drive to a runaway win. Niki Lauda withdrew shortly before the race. The reason he gave was that, rounding a corner during practice, he had suddenly felt an extremely sharp pain in his ribs. His unexpected refusal to start did nothing to quench the flames of controversy which his critics were ever ready to fuel. After the Lotus victory in Spain it was generally believed that the car's superiority was due to a new kind of differential which had been developed by the Getrag firm in Germany, for public opinion could still not accept the full significance of the wing concept. The new McLaren M26 made its first appearance in the Spanish Grand Prix, driven by James Hunt. This had a honeycomb-sandwich chassis, but 1977 marked the beginning of a lengthy fall from form for both Hunt and the McLaren team.

There was heavy rain at the start of the Belgian Grand Prix at Zolder and things went from bad to worse. Andretti in the Lotus had been fastest in practice but on the first lap collided with Watson's Brabham-Alfa Romeo which had started alongside him. Both cars skidded off the track into retirement. The rain caused untold confusion and the lead changed several times. The ultimate winner was the Swede Gunnar Nilsson in the second Lotus 78, this being the only Formula One victory of his short Grand Prix career; a year and a half later he succumbed to cancer.

Jody Scheckter scored a runaway victory in the Monaco Grand Prix on May 22nd 1977, this being the 100th World Championship race win for the Ford-Cosworth DFV engine. It had been almost exactly ten years since the eight-cylinder engine had made its debut in Jim Clark's Lotus 49 and won the Dutch Grand Prix on June 4th 1967 by a clear margin. Keith Duckworth, father of the DFV, could be justifiably proud of this anniversary. At this time Cosworth was running tests with magnesium alloy blocks and heads with the aim of reducing weight, but these units were to prove unreliable, because the very light metal had such a high coefficient of expansion. The bearings were susceptible to damage, particularly when the engines were cold. In its long career the Ford-Cosworth V8 had not only won 100

Grand Prix victories but had also won the 24-hours Le Mans race in 1975 (with the Gulf-Mirage driven by Derek Bell and Jacky Ickx) and had a tally of eight World Drivers' Championships.

The talented young Italian driver Riccardo Patrese made his Formula One debut at Monaco in a Shadow and took a meritorious ninth place, ahead of such drivers as Ickx, in an Ensign, and Jarier, in an ATS. Ickx was driving Clay Regazzoni's Ensign MN177 here because the Swiss driver was competing in the Indianapolis 500 the same day: he drove a McLaren-Offenhauser M16 but had to drop out after 25 of the 200 laps because of a leaking tank.

As far as tyres are concerned, conditions were similar for all teams during the 1977 season. Goodyear provided several suppliers with tyres but all teams still ended up with identical tyres. There was no longer any need for tyres to be submitted to qualifying tests, as they now used harder compounds. This also made them wear better, and there were fewer instances of defective tyres.

Mario Andretti once again made full use of the Lotus 78 superiority in the Swedish Grand Prix at Anderstorp, but when he was well ahead of the field his engine's regulating mechanism developed a fault which slightly increased his fuel consumption, and he ran out of fuel two and a half laps before the finish. For the

Above
Anthony Joseph Foyt is congratulated by 1925 Indianapolis winner Pete De Paolo after becoming the first man to win four 500-mile races at The Brickyard.

Right
Mario Andretti in a Lotus 78 winning the 1977 Spanish Grand Prix. The Lotus 78 was the first genuine "wing car" but in the years to come Colin Chapman's concept was copied by all the other designers.

Above
Francois Castaing, father of the Renault-Gordini V6 turbo.

Overleaf
Jody Scheckter in the Wolf-Ford WR1 and Jochen Mass in a McLaren-Ford M23 fight an exciting duel for third place in the 1977 Spanish Grand Prix. Scheckter got the verdict.

first time in years the French had a genuine victory to celebrate, as Jacques Laffite took the V12 Matra-powered Ligier JS7 to victory. This was in fact the only World Championship Grand Prix success achieved by the 12-cylinder Matra engine (the 1971 Argentine Grand Prix, which Amon won in a Matra, was not at that time a World Championship qualifier).

Brabham-Alfa Romeo seemed finally about to realise a long-awaited victory when John Watson led the French Grand Prix at Dijon right up to the very last lap, with Andretti following him, but the 12 then ran out of fuel and Andretti in the Lotus 78 won again. Watson only just managed to get across the finish line in second place.

There were two important Grand Prix debutantes in the British Grand Prix at Silverstone, Renault and Michelin both entering the battle at the top level. Renault had not competed in a Grand Prix since 1908 and neither had Michelin, though the tyre company had been producing racing rubber for several years. The French tyres were unusual in that they were of radial-ply rather than the otherwise universal crossply construction.

Renault had undertaken a broad-based sporting programme in the seventies, ranging from rallies and the Le Mans 24-hour race to Formula Two and now

Formula One. The Formula One engine was of the same type as had been used in sportscar events, being a 90° V6 with the cylinder block constructed with a particularly thin-walled iron casting. Developed by Renault Gordini at Viry-Chatillon near Paris, under the direction òf François Castaing, this unit was characterised by its narrow angle between the inlet valve and exhaust valve which could be made to work only by the use of very long valve stems. The engine had first appeared in the two-seater Alpine A440 running in the 2-litre sportscar class in 1973, and then Jean-Pierre Jabouille had won the 1975 European Formula Two Championship in an Elf-Renault using the same engine. René Arnoux repeated this success in a Martini-Renault in 1977. For the Le Mans event Renault Gordini built a turbo-charged version of the 2-litre engine which, in 1978, brought Renault a much coveted victory in the 24-hour classic.

A 1.5-litre version of this V6 unit was adapted for use in Formula One, with cylinder dimensions of 86 x 42.8mm, giving 1492cc capacity, for the rules allowed supercharged (or turbocharged) engines to be only half the size of atmospherically aspirated, i.e., fuel-injected or carburettor-fed, units. The Renault RS01, which made its debut at Silverstone with Jean-Pierre Jabouille at the wheel, was the first Grand Prix car

in history to be equipped with an exhaust-driven turbocharged engine. Renault claimed 500bhp at 11,000rpm for their four-valve V6 engine, and readings on straight sections of circuits showed it to be one of the fastest of all Formula One cars. But the Renault V6 suffered from hesitation (or "turbo lag") under acceleration, which made the car difficult to drive on twisty sections of circuit, or in close company with other cars. Furthermore, it suffered more than its fair share of teething troubles, and more than a year would elapse before Jabouille was able to complete an entire Grand Prix without breaking down. There were early problems with the turbocharger itself, then the pistons and the piston rings. At first the turbocharged engine was not taken seriously, but in time, of course, all other teams, one by one, switched to using the same sort of engine.

In the 1977 British Grand Prix at Silverstone, meanwhile, Watson in the Brabham-Alfa Romeo once again had victory almost within his grasp when his fuel supply packed up. James Hunt was finally able to win another Grand Prix to end what had been for him a very lean period. Making his Formula One debut in the Silverstone race at the wheel of a McLaren M23 was the 25-year-old French-Canadian Gilles Villeneuve. He made an excellent impression and, a few weeks later, was offered a Ferrari contract.

The German Grand Prix was held again at Hockenheim as the Nürburgring had now been declared unsuitable for Formula One racing. The race was won by Niki Lauda in a Ferrari, the victory marking Goodyear's 100th Grand Prix success. To celebrate this centenary in style Goodyear invited Nakamura, Honda's engineer, and the former American Formula One driver, Richie Ginther, to Hockenheim, as it had been Ginther in the transverse-engined V12 Honda RA271 who gained the very first Goodyear Formula One victory when he won the 1965 Mexican Grand Prix, the

Above
Niki Lauda was World Champion for the second time in 1977. His face still shows the scars from his serious accident the previous year. Towards the end of the season the atmosphere between Lauda and Scuderia Ferrari worsened and he finally transferred to Brabham.

Left
Niki Lauda in the Ferrari 312T2 at the 1977 Monaco Grand Prix, where he finished second to Scheckter. Lauda, in his fourth season with Ferrari, won the South African, German and Dutch Grands Prix.

Above left
Ferrari's temperamental but talented chief engineer Mauro Forghieri, responsible for designing all Ferrari Grand Prix cars from 1973. His father also worked for Ferrari.

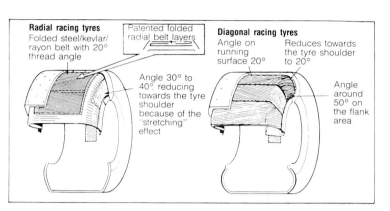

Michelin displayed its radial tyres for Formula One cars for the first time on the 1977 Renault. Later, Goodyear changed to radial tyres and when Pirelli reappeared in Formula One they, too, adopted this design.

Radial racing tyres
Folded steel/kevlar/rayon belt with 20° thread angle

Patented folded radial belt layers

Angle 30° to 40° reducing towards the tyre shoulder because of the "stretching" effect

Diagonal racing tyres
Angle on running surface 20°

Reduces towards the tyre shoulder to 20°

Angle around 50° on the flank area

last race of the 1.5-litre racing formula.

Rain once again caused confusion, this time in the Austrian Grand Prix, and produced a surprise winner in the form of Australian Alan Jones in a Shadow-Ford DN8. This was the first time that Shadow had won a World Championship race and it was especially gratifying for the principal sponsor, Swiss cigar manufacturer Heinrich Villiger. It would probably have been welcomed just as much by another Shadow sponsor, Neapolitan businessman Franco Ambrosio, but he was unable to be there to see the victory as his business practices had brought him into conflict with the law...Mario Andretti again had to retire in Austria because of an engine fault.

At this stage in the World Championship Lauda was clear leader, and he consolidated that position in the next race, the Dutch Grand Prix, with yet another victory. But the following day Ferrari fans received a shock when it was announced that the partnership between Ferrari and the prospective World Champion would cease at the end of the season. The circumstances surrounding this "divorce" were rather unpleasant at

times, and were well aired in the press. Never before in the long history of Grand Prix racing had the fact that a leading driver was changing teams created such an uproar.

As a precaution Lauda surrounded himself with bodyguards for the subsequent Italian Grand Prix. There were no disturbances, but no victory either. Mario Andretti in the Lotus 78 won the race with Lauda second. The Austrian needed just a single point to clinch the 1977 World Championship and he achieved this at Watkins Glen when he came in fourth behind Hunt, Andretti, and Scheckter in the United States Grand Prix. By this time though the tension between Ferrari and Lauda had become almost unbearable, and this came to a head when, out of the blue, Ferrari fired Ermanno Cuoghi, the mechanic in charge of Lauda's car. At the Canadian Grand Prix Niki Lauda, the newly crowned World Drivers' Champion,

refused to start as a protest against Ferrari, and also forewent the last race of the year, the Japanese Grand Prix. Ferrari promptly signed on Gilles Villeneuve to drive the 12-cylinder Italian car in Canada, but the hard-charging little man from Quebec came off the track in both practice and the race. Jody Scheckter won the Mosport race in the Wolf WR1, the third victory for the new make in its first year of racing.

After a long run of bad luck Patrick Depailler in the six-wheeled Tyrrell finally recorded a second place in Canada, but the season had shown that the six-wheel design was not altogether the inspiration it had appeared. Designer Derek Gardner had attempted to improve the P34's road-holding by widening the track but the Tyrrells lost more and more ground as the season progressed and finally Gardner had to pack his bags and go. Ken Tyrrell replaced him with Maurice Phillippe, formerly on the design staffs of Lotus, Parnelli and Copersucar, and he immediately took charge of the design of a conventional four-wheeled car, the Tyrrell 008. James Hunt's season had started unhappily but closed with victory on the Fuji circuit in Japan, with Reutemann's Ferrari second and Depailler's Tyrrell third. The event was marred by a tragic accident when Villeneuve tried to outbrake Peterson's Tyrrell going into a corner. The cars touched and the Ferrari was thrown into the air. It killed two spectators who were watching from a prohibited area.

When the 16 races which made up the 28th World Drivers' Championship had been run, Niki Lauda was the Champion for the second time, ahead of Scheckter and Andretti. Once again Ferrari won the Constructors' World Championship.

The year 1977 marked the last

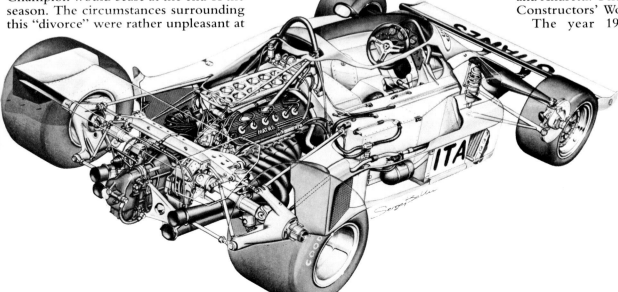

A V12 Matra-powered Ligier JS7 of the type with which Jacques Laffite won the 1977 Swedish Grand Prix, his and Ligier's first Formula One victory. The JS7 was designed by Gérard Ducarouge, who later moved to Alfa Romeo and Lotus, and Paul Carillo.

appearance of BRM. This once famous make, one of the proud British names, had introduced its complicated V16 cars in 1949 but they had not become competitive until the supercharged-1.5-litre formula was out of date. Joakim Bonnier had given BRM their first Grand Prix success in the 1959 Dutch Grand Prix, and then in 1962 Graham Hill became World Champion in the V8. British Racing Motors achieved their final Grand Prix success in 1972, with Beltoise

in Monte Carlo, but from then on began to lose more and more ground. At the end of 1974 Sir Alfred Owen resigned from the concern and his brother-in-law Louis Stanley took over as sole proprietor. Mike Wilds and Bob Evans tried their luck with the V12 Stanley-BRM in 1975 but the car was clearly inferior. In the following season Ian Ashley occasionally appeared in a Stanley-BRM and, at the end of 1976, Stanley unveiled his new model P107, which had been designed by Len Terry.

The Australian driver Larry Perkins was signed on in 1977, but he was not able to achieve much with the inferior 12-cylinder car, and the team was finally disbanded. In 1981 the factory's own collection of racing cars came under the hammer at Christie's in London. Part of the collection was bought by the building contractor Tom Wheatcroft, owner of the famous racing car museum at Donington. Thus was closed the final chapter of the BRM story.

Formula One cars of 1977

Make/model	Chief designer(s)	Engine	Gearbox (speeds)	Chassis	Wheelbase	Track	Tyre make	Dry weight
ATS-Penske PC 4	Geoff Ferris	Cosworth DFV (V8)	Hewland FGA 400 (5)	FM	2692	F 1422 R 1473	Goodyear	585
Brabham BT 45 B	Gordon Murray	Alfa Romeo 115-12 (12 cyl 180°)	Hewland-Alfa Romeo (6)	FM	2489	F 1422 R 1524	Goodyear	615
Ensign MN 06	Morris Nunn Dave Baldwin	Cosworth DFV (V8)	Hewland FGA 400 (6)	FM	2616	F 1473 R 1575	Goodyear	590
Ferrari 312 T2	Mauro Forghieri Franco Rocchi	Ferrari 312 B (12 cyl 180°)	Ferrari (5)	TS	2560	F 1500—1550 R 1480—1520	Goodyear	590
Fittipaldi FD 05	Dave Baldwin	Cosworth DFV (V8)	Hewland FGA 400 (6)	FM	2718	F 1524 R 1575	Goodyear	601
Hesketh 308 E	Frank Dernie Nigel Stroud	Cosworth DFV (V8)	Hewland FGA 400 (6)	SM	2667	F 1651 R 1524	Goodyear	602
Ligier JS 7	Gérard Ducarouge Paul Carillo	Matra MS 76 (V12)	Hewland TL 2-200 (5/6)	FM	2608	F 1536 R 1600	Goodyear	603
Lotus 78	Colin Chapman Ralph Bellamy	Cosworth DFV (V8)	Hewland FGA 400 (6)	FM	2741	F 1702 R 1600	Goodyear	588
March 761 B	Robin Herd	Cosworth DFV (V8)	Hewland FGA 400 (6)	FM	2500	F 1422 R 1473	Goodyear	593
March 771	Robin Herd Martin Walter	Cosworth DFV (V8)	Hewland FGA 400 (6)	FM	2600	F 1422 R 1473	Goodyear	600
McLaren M 23	Gordon Coppuck	Cosworth DFV (V8)	Hewland-McLaren (6)	FM	2718	F 1651 R 1664	Goodyear	600
McLaren M 26	Gordon Coppuck	Cosworth DFV (V8)	Hewland-McLaren (6)	FM	2743	F 1600 R 1626	Goodyear	589
Renault RS 01	Andre de Cortanze Jean-Pierre Jabouille	Renault-Gordini EF 1 (V6 Turbo)	Hewland FGA 400 (6)	SM	2500	F 1425 R 1525	Michelin	607
Shadow DN 8	Dave Wass Tony Southgate	Cosworth DFV (V8)	Hewland FGA 400 (6)	SM	2642	F 1473 R 1524	Goodyear	605
Stanley-BRM P 207	Len Terry	BRM P 142-60 (V12)	BRM T 193 (5)	FM	2642	F 1422—1549 R 1486—1549	Goodyear	615
Surtees TS 19	John Surtees Ken Sears	Cosworth DFV (V8)	Hewland FGA 400 (6)	FM	2489	F 1475 R 1499	Goodyear	585
Tyrrell P 34	Derek Gardner	Cosworth DFV (V8)	Hewland FGA 400 (6)	SM	2563/2103	F 1589 R 1473	Goodyear	620
Wolf WR 1	Harvey Postlethwaite	Cosworth DFV (V8)	Hewland FGA 400 (6)	SM	2489	F 1524 R 1524	Goodyear	589

Chassis construction: SM = semi-monocoque; FM = full monocoque; TS = tubular frame with stressed skins.

Lotus "Wing Car" Dominates 1978

Mario Andretti and the Lotus 79 are undisputed World Champions. Most designers copy the Lotus "wing car" concept. Skirts greatly increase downforce. Ferrari wins with Michelin radial tyres.

Mario Andretti

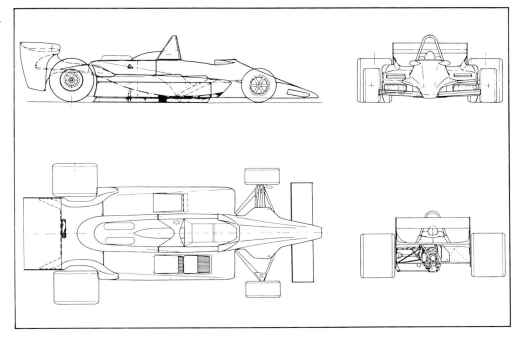

The value of the wing car was finally accepted in 1978, and a number of other designers adopted Colin Chapman's concept for their new cars. But Lotus had got a head start, and remained on top, winning no fewer than eight of the 16 World Championship races, six falling to Mario Andretti and two more to Ronnie Peterson, who had transferred from Tyrrell to Lotus. The established 78 model won the Argentine and South African rounds and then its successor, the 79, won a debut victory in Andretti's hands in the Belgian Grand Prix at Zolder. The Lotus superiority in 1978 is underlined by the fact that on four occasions during the year, in the Belgian, Spanish, French and Dutch Grands Prix, Andretti and Peterson finished first and second.

Mario Andretti profited greatly from his 1977 experiences. He had learnt that sudden demands should not be made on the car and that, while the Lotus was fast, it had to be driven carefully and only as fast as was necessary for victory. Andretti used to try to shake off the rest of the field at the start and to establish a good lead. As the leader he was in the best position to control his rivals. The American won in Argentina, Belgium, Spain, France, Germany and Holland.

The Lotus 79 was an improved version of the 78, with the odd defects of the first wing car design rectified. Martin Ogilvie and Geoff Aldridge had drawn up the new Lotus 79 in August 1977 with the intention of improving streamlining and saving weight rather than increasing the downforce on the car. It was again Peter Wright who devised the aerodynamic modifications, concentrating on improving the upper body shape of the Lotus 79 compared with that of the 78.

The rear dampers were relocated out of the airstream, next to the gearbox, and the exhaust pipes were raised and integrated into the sidepods. At the same time the fuel tanks were removed from the sides and relocated within the chassis, being mounted right behind the cockpit. This not only improved weight distribution, but, as a result of the repositioning, airflow under the side-wings was improved and the car became more aerodynamically effective, for the sidepods of the Lotus 79 generated more downforce than had those on the 78. By making the rear wing slightly less effective at the same time as the other improvements were effected, the Lotus engineers achieved their aim of keeping the total downforce generated by the old

and new models the same, but improving wind resistance. The Lotus 79 was in fact something like 15% more efficient aerodynamically than the 78.

During the development of the Lotus 78 and 79 models, experiments had been carried out into the use of vertical side-pieces or "skirts", fixed to the outside of the car between the chassis and the road. The purpose of these was to prevent air from outside being sucked into the pressure area under the car. In the first experiments, the bottom of the skirt was fitted with bristles but these wore down after only a few laps of scraping the ground. Next, plastic edgings were tried but the friction arising from continual contact with the track surface heated them to such an extent that the plastic

Above
The Lotus 79, a logical development of the 78 with improved aerodynamics, was a winner from its debut race in Belgium in 1978. The dotted line in the side view shows the "wing" profile.

Above
Andretti (the winner) with Peterson (left, second) and Hunt (right, third) after the French Grand Prix.

Right
In 1978 Mario Andretti's Lotus 79 was virtually "glued" to the track surface and there was nothing anyone could do about it.

Right
Jacques Laffite in the V12 Ligier-Matra JS7 at the 1978 Argentine Grand Prix.

Below
A view of the underside of the Lotus 79 showing the wing profiles and also the skirts which maximised downforce.

Centre
Chassis of the Ferrari 312T3. This was again a construction of thin square tubing with aluminium plates riveted onto it.

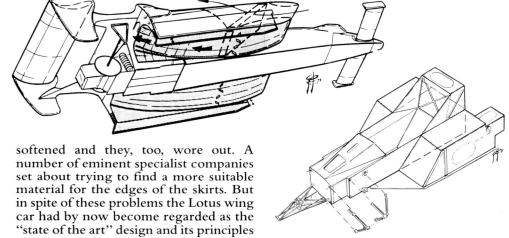

softened and they, too, wore out. A number of eminent specialist companies set about trying to find a more suitable material for the edges of the skirts. But in spite of these problems the Lotus wing car had by now become regarded as the "state of the art" design and its principles were soon adopted by others.

One early imitator, which appeared at Rio de Janeiro in practice for the 1978 Brazilian Grand Prix on the Jacarepagua circuit, was from a brand new company, Arrows. This company had been set up by Alan Rees, Jackie Oliver, Tony Southgate and a number of their colleagues from the Shadow team. Southgate, the former Lotus and BRM engineer, had drafted a wing-car design before leaving Shadow and the Arrows FA1 was in fact all but identical to the Shadow DN9, differing only in minor details. These similarities were to have legal repercussions before the season was over.

Southgate's sidepod design was not a slavish copy of the Lotus, for he had sought the advice of scientists at the Imperial College and in fact the final shape of the Shadow/Arrows was determined by Dr Harvey, a lecturer at the College. In Dr Harvey's wing-car design downforce was obtained largely by constructing an area of excess pressure on the upper side of the body, which made

its concept quite distinct from the Lotus idea.

By the end of the 1978 season other wing cars had appeared. During practice for the Dutch Grand Prix the ATS HS2/1, designed jointly by the German Gustav Brunner and Englishman John Gentry, made its debut, though it was not raced at that stage. McLaren unveiled their new M28 in October; both the ATS and the McLaren were to all intents and purposes Lotus copies. At the end of the following month the new Ligier JS11 (reverting once again to the Ford-Cosworth engine) became the latest addition to the ranks of wing cars. The concept was also adopted on cars competing in smaller single-seater formulae such as F2, F3 and Formula Super Vee.

Gilles Villeneuve

Those Formula One designers who used flat-12 engines, such as Ferrari and Alfa Romeo, found themselves handicapped because they could not take full advantage of the wing-car concept. The width of their engines meant there was less space for aerodynamic aids and it was for this reason Alfa Romeo replaced their flat-12 with a 60° V12 version for 1979.

As has been already mentioned the Lotus was superior in 1978 and notched up a record eight Grand Prix victories. Next most successful model was Ferrari's transverse-gearbox 312T3, which was first raced in South Africa. With this Carlos Reutemann won four Grands Prix, the Brazilian, the United States West (at Long Beach), the British and the United States East (Watkins Glen). Ferrari's new acquisition, Gilles Villeneuve, was developing into a very fast driver although he wrote off several cars initially. He was however winner on the new Notre Dame circuit in Montreal, in his home Grand Prix.

The Ferrari victory in Brazil at the beginning of the season created a sensation, for it was achieved on Michelin radial tyres, until then seen only on the Renaults. It was thanks largely to these tyres that Carlos Reutemann was able to completely outclass the field on his way to victory. This was a euphoric year for Michelin. The Brazilian victory was their first in a Grand Prix in modern times, but a few days earlier Michelin tyres had been used on the winning car in the Monte Carlo Rally, the Porsche driven by Nicolas, and in June they won the Le Mans 24-hours endurance race on the Renault-Alpine A442 turbo driven by Pironi and Jaussaud.

The Brazil result spurred Goodyear on to new efforts, and the Michelin/Ferrari combination suffered a resultant setback in the next Grand Prix, in South Africa. Riccardo Patrese, driving the Arrows-Ford FA1 in only its second race, held a clear lead for many laps, and when an engine fault forced him out, Ronnie Peterson in a Lotus 78 took over. Peterson was however strongly challenged by Patrick Depailler in the four-wheeled Tyrrell 008, the duel between these two drivers lasting right up to the very last bend, when the Tyrrell ran out of fuel, its engine stuttering over the final kilometres. Ferrari might have been beaten in South Africa but they had excellent engines and were able to take revenge at

Long Beach, where Reutemann and Villeneuve started from the front row. The young French-Canadian led the race for several laps but then collided with Regazzoni's Shadow when lapping the slower car and had to withdraw, leaving Reutemann to be first past the chequered flag. The Australian Alan Jones made quite an impression at Long Beach in his Williams-Ford FW06, designed by Patrick Head, and sponsored by Saudia, the Saudi Arabian airline. This race in fact signalled the end of the years of struggling for

Frank Williams

Frank Williams and his team as for a while at Long Beach it seemed as if Jones could dislodge Reutemann's Ferrari from the lead. The Williams was however forced back with a misfire near the end of the race.

After a turbulent race the Frenchman Patrick Depailler in the Maurice Phillippe-designed Tyrrell 008 was declared winner of the Monaco Grand Prix. This was Depailler's first Formula One success but was to remain the Tyrrell team's sole victory of the 1978 season.

Brabham had a surprise in store for the opposition in the Swedish Grand Prix at Anderstorp, for the flat-12 Alfa Romeo-engined BT46, designed by Gordon Murray, arrived with a strange attachment at the rear. The device in question was a fan, which was intended

The Renault RS01 competed in its first full Grand Prix season in 1978. The 90° V6 1492cc (86 x 42.8mm) engine employed a single Garrett turbocharger and developed slightly over 500bhp at 11,000rpm. Ignition was by Marelli and fuel injection by Kugelfischer, but engine problems were still frequent.

to increase downforce by sucking air, like a vacuum cleaner, from under the car. The large tail-mounted fan was driven by a shaft running from the gearbox. The monocoque chassis was completely surrounded by skirts and these assisted the fan in sucking the car down onto the track. More efficient engine cooling was a bonus. The Swedish race illustrated the enormous advantages of the fan system for, once Niki Lauda had dislodged Andretti's Lotus from the lead, he very quickly left him well behind. The fan did have one disadvantage, though this affected other competitors more than the Brabham drivers: stones and dust sucked under the car by the fan were thrown out behind, which was particularly unpleasant for those competitors driving behind — the more so when the Brabham drove off the edge of the track! Thanks to this device Brabham recorded their first Formula One victory since 1975, and Alfa Romeo engines their first since 1951, when Fangio was World Champion in an Alfetta.

There was however considerable debate about the legality of the Brabham "fan car". Its secret had in fact leaked out a few weeks before the car's appearance and after Anderstorp other teams immediately started to design their own similar systems. But within days of the Brabham success the CSI ruled them illegal, pointing out that "moveable aerodynamic aids" had been banned since the Lotuses of Hill and Rindt had had their accidents at Barcelona in 1969. But the authorities allowed Lauda's win to remain on the books.

The "vacuum cleaner" concept itself

Below

In 1978 Alfa Romeo produced a new 60° V12 2991cc (78.5 x 51.5mm) engine to replace the previous flat-12.

Below right

The infamous "vacuum cleaner" of the Brabham-Alfa Romeo BT46B "fan car" which won in Sweden. The fan sucked air from under the car, causing a vacuum which increased downforce.

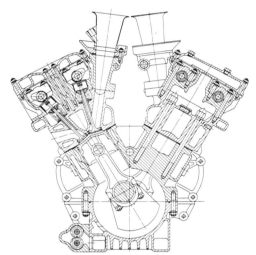

Left

Hans-Joachim Stuck in the Shadow-Ford DN9 which was never very successful, either in his hands or Clay Regazzoni's. Designer Tony Southgate, together with a number of former Shadow colleagues, had now left Shadow to found the new Arrows make.

was not new, for as early as 1970 Jim Hall had used the same principle on his Chaparral-Chevrolet J2 in the CanAm series of sportscar races in North America. In this design two large fans were mounted in the tail and driven by a 750cc motorcycle engine.

After the fan interlude in Sweden, the World Drivers' Championship settled back into its normal pattern for the French Grand Prix which followed. Once again it was an Andretti-Peterson one-two for Lotus. The Lotus cars were again out in front at Brands Hatch but this time they had to withdraw quite early on and the race was finally a Ferrari victory with Reutemann driving the 312T3. But even so, Mario Andretti and Ronnie Peterson were well in the lead at this point in the World Championship.

The rivalry in the Formula One tyre sector had increased dramatically since Michelin's successful arrival on the scene. The degree of manufacturer commitment was illustrated by their provision of ultrasoft tyres for qualifying as well as better racing rubber. Goodyear stocked their best tyres only for the use of their top drivers and considered themselves no longer in a position to provide the best tyres for the two dozen competitors at each Grand Prix. Their

new policy was made public at the Belgian Grand Prix.

In future only seven named drivers would be guaranteed the special racing tyres at every race: Andretti and Peterson at Lotus, Lauda and Watson at Brabham, Hunt at McLaren, Scheckter at Wolf, Depailler at Tyrrell and Fittipaldi at Copersucar. In addition the fastest competitor of those forced to use "slow" tyres in practice for each Grand Prix would also be provided with the better rubber for that race. The lucky drivers who gained access to Goodyear's select circle in the races that followed were Riccardo Patrese at Arrows, Jacques Laffite at Ligier and Alan Jones at Williams. The rest had to be satisfied with the "hard" normal tyres which were scornfully described as "wooden tyres". With such tyres it was almost a foregone conclusion that drivers would not make it into the 12 or 14 front positions on the starting grid.

This rationalisation policy on the part of Goodyear was particularly hard on such drivers as Regazzoni and Stuck at Shadow, Mass at ATS, Stommelen at Arrows and Pironi at Tyrrell. The combination of the "wooden" tyres and insufficient preparation of the Shadow cars led to a situation where Stuck and

Regazzoni were hardly ever successful. Regazzoni, who had won four Grands Prix between 1970 and 1976, failed to qualify five times during 1979.

The dispute between Shadow and the newly-founded Arrows team, which had been going on since late 1977, came before the courts in 1978. Shadow claimed that, while Tony Southgate was still in their employ, he had designed the Shadow DN9 according to wing-car principles. Then in November 1977 Southgate, together with fellow Shadow personnel Alan Rees and Jackie Oliver, had left to set up their new Arrows team. When the new company's Grand Prix car was subsequently unveiled it was, Shadow contended, simply a copy of the new Shadow which had not yet made its first appearance. In August 1978 the British judge who had heard the case found in Shadow's favour. He ruled that the Arrows FA1 was in fact a copy of the Shadow DN9, and that the Arrows team and its principals had thus violated the laws of copyright. He decreed that, with immediate effect, the Arrows FA1 was not to be raced again.

Arrows must have expected such a decision for, at the time the judgement was made public, they were already putting their new Mark 2 car through its paces at Zandvoort. Although in principle a direct development of the FA1 wing car, the new contender boasted a great number of alterations. The rear suspension was quite new, with the coil springs and shock absorbers moved further forward to create more effective airflow behind the sidepods which, in turn, produced greater downforce than on the FA1.

There was uproar in Formula One circles at the Dutch Grand Prix when, after a meeting at Zandvoort on the

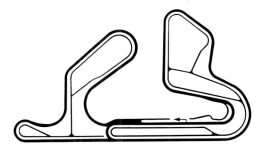

Saturday, the CSI announced that sealing devices (i.e., skirts) would be prohibited from January 1st 1979. As these were necessary for obtaining maximum possible downforce, the whole concept of wing cars was thrown into question. Furthermore, as a number of designers had wing cars on the drawing boards, they were reluctant to accept the ban at such short notice. As a result the Formula One Constructors' Association (FOCA) convened a hasty meeting and the next day issued a communique saying they would ignore the ban at the 1979 Argentine Grand Prix. FOCA was becoming a very powerful force in Grand Prix racing at this time: in 1978, for example, they demanded more than $385,000 in expense, starting and prize money for a Formula One field of 25 cars, and this succeeded in bringing concessions from the CSI.

Last European Formula One race of the year was the Italian Grand Prix at Monza, but this was marred by a multiple collision just after the start which caused the race to be stopped. In this accident Ronnie Peterson suffered severe injuries from which he was to die the following day. The race was restarted after a halt of several hours, with Andretti and Villeneuve as favourites. They dominated the race but had both jumped the start and were consequently penalised one minute each. This relegated them to sixth and seventh places and allowed Niki Lauda and John Watson to take the first two places in the Brabham-Alfa Romeos. Andretti was now confirmed as World Champion but no-one felt like celebrating after the race as Peterson's fatal injuries had cast a pall over proceedings.

The Monza accident provided plenty of material for the critics. The Clerk of the Course was reproached for having released the field too soon after the warm-up lap, before the back rows of the grid had come to a stop. Some drivers accused Riccardo Patrese of making a dangerous start, and blamed him for triggering the collision. This was never proven, but some of the leading drivers turned their anger on the Italian driver and at the next race, the United States Grand Prix (East), set up a Drivers' Safety Committee which succeeded in having him banned from the race.

Ferrari won both the final races in the 1978 Grand Prix series, Reutemann leading the field home at Watkins Glen and Villeneuve at Montreal. Villeneuve's victory was achieved in his first full Grand Prix season, on the new circuit which had been hurriedly laid out on Notre Dame Island in the St Lawrence River. After Ronnie Peterson's death Colin Chapman had hired Jean-Pierre Jarier for the two North American

Below
From 1978 the Canadian Grand Prix, originally held either at Mosport or Mont Tremblant, was always run on the 4.670km circuit on Notre Dame Island in Montreal.

Grands Prix, and the Frenchman responded by setting fastest lap at Watkins Glen as he fought his way through the field after having stopped to have a tyre replaced. He eventually got his Lotus 79 up to third but then, four laps from the end, ran out of fuel. Jarier was similarly competitive at Montreal, qualifying on pole position and shooting off like a rocket in the race. He in fact led until the 47th of the 70 laps, when an oil-leak put an end to the Lotus's chances. Villeneuve took victory in spite of very cold temperatures, but egged on by a home crowd which was going wild with excitement. After clinching the 1978 World Championship at the Italian Grand Prix, Mario Andretti did not perform well in North America. He had an engine failure at Watkins Glen and rammed Watson's Brabham-Alfa at Montreal.

The final placings in the World Drivers' Championship were: winner, Mario Andretti with 64 points, second his team-mate Ronnie Peterson, who had been killed in Monza, with 51 points, then Reutemann on 48 and Lauda with 44. Andretti, who had made his Grand Prix debut in the United States Grand Prix ten years before, thoroughly deserved his championship victory: at 38, he was one of the oldest active Formula One drivers, only Brambilla (41) and Regazzoni (39) being older. Lotus were convincing

winners of the 1978 World Manufacturers' Championship, with second and third places falling to Ferrari and Brabham respectively.

The McLaren team did not manage a single victory in 1978. Their lead driver, James Hunt, seemed unable to regain the form which had won him the 1976 World Championship, and was in fact involved in collisions in several races. His team-mate this year was Patrick Tambay, who had joined the team as successor to Jochen Mass. Mass in turn had transferred to the German ATS team, owned by alloy-wheel manufacturer Gunter Schmid. ATS had taken over the Formula One division of March, but results in 1978 were unsatisfactory. The Copersucar team, on the other hand, made real progress this year after several seasons of disappointment. They engaged former Ferrari engineer Giacomo Caliri as consultant and in the 1978 Brazilian Grand Prix Emerson Fittipaldi was able to bring his yellow Copersucar home in second place behind Reutemann. Jody Scheckter in the new Harvey Postlethwaite-designed Wolf WR5 was one of the fastest competitors in the field, but the car did not manage to win anything this year. At the end of 1978 Scheckter transferred to Ferrari and Walter Wolf replaced him with James Hunt for the following year. Tyrrell used the 008 with

conventional chassis in 1979 and Patrick Depailler succeeded in winning the Monaco Grand Prix; a possible second victory eluded him when he ran out of fuel at Kyalami. For the Surtees team of Vittorio Brambilla, Rupert Keegan and René Arnoux the season was a disappointing one, and at the end of the year John Surtees decided to withdraw the team from further Formula One Grand Prix competition.

Alfa Romeo had expressed their intention of entering Formula One with a car of their own, rather than supplying their engines to other manufacturers, and in the spring of 1978 a car was completed under the direction of Carlo Chiti at the Autodelta workshops in the Milan suburb of Settimo. It was first tested by Brambilla at the Balocco test track at the end of May and Niki Lauda completed a few laps with it at Le Castellet later in the year. As the year ended however Alfa Romeo's policy was still unclear, though they renewed their contract to supply the Brabham team with 12-cylinder engines for 1979, while their own car continued its test programme at Balocco. The Formula One Alfa Romeo was unique in that its tyres were neither Goodyears nor Michelins, but Pirellis. Pirelli's P7 radial tyres had been used successfully in other racing formulae and in rallies and the company was now anxious to introduce them to Formula One.

The Canadian Grand Prix at Montreal marked the last appearance of the name Matra in Formula One. Since the end of 1975 the French V12 engine had been used to power the Ligier Grand Prix contenders but the end of 1978 saw the last of these, Ligier reverting to the Cosworth-Ford DFV for its JS11 which was introduced in 1979.

The 1978 World Drivers' Championship was the 29th. Since 1950 a total of 302 races had been held and 52 drivers had engraved their names on the long list of race winners. Jackie Stewart headed that list with 27 wins, followed by Jim Clark with 25, then Juan Manuel Fangio with 24, Niki Lauda with 17, Stirling Moss with 16, Graham Hill, Jack Brabham and Emerson Fittipaldi with 14 each, Alberto Ascari with 13, Mario Andretti with 12, and Ronnie Peterson and James Hunt with 10 wins apiece. Of the makes, Ferrari had been the most successful with a total of 73 Grand Prix victories, though Lotus was a close second with 71.

Formula One cars of 1978

Make/model	Chief designer(s)	Engine	Gearbox (speeds)	Chassis	Wheelbase	Track	Tyre make	Dry weight
Arrows FA 1	Tony Southgate Dave Wass	Cosworth DFV (V8)	Hewland FGA 400 (5/6)	SM	2565	F 1600 R 1549	Goodyear	589
ATS HS 1	Robin Herd John Gentry	Cosworth DFV (V8)	Hewland FGA 400 (5/6)	FM	2720	F 1500 R 1525	Goodyear	585
Brabham BT 46	Gordon Murray	Alfa Romeo 115-12 (12 cyl 180°)	Hewland-Alfa Romeo (6)	FM	2591	F 1422 R 1524	Goodyear	595
Ensign MN 06	Morris Nunn Dave Baldwin	Cosworth DFV (V8)	Hewland FGA 400 (6)	FM	2616	F 1473 R 1575	Goodyear	590
Ferrari 312 T3	Mauro Forghieri	Ferrari 312 B (12 cyl 180°)	Ferrari (5)	TS	2580	F 1600—1650 R 1450—1550	Michelin	598
Fittipaldi F 5 A	Ralph Bellamy	Cosworth DFV (V8)	Hewland FGA 400 (6)	FM	2718	F 1689 R 1588	Goodyear	615
Hesketh 308 E	Frank Dernie Nigel Stroud	Cosworth DFV (V8)	Hewland FGA 400 (6)	SM	2667	F 1651 R 1524	Goodyear	602
Ligier JS 7	Gérard Ducarouge Paul Carillo	Matra MS 76 (V12)	Hewland FGA 400 (5/6)	FM	2760	F 1625 R 1600	Goodyear	595
Ligier JS 9	Gérard Ducarouge Paul Carillo	Matra MS 78 (V12)	Hewland FGA 400 (6)	FM	2700	F 1625 R 1611	Goodyear	590
Lotus 78	Colin Chapman Ralph Bellamy	Cosworth DFV (V8)	Hewland FGA 400 (6)	FM	2718	F 1702 R 1600	Goodyear	588
Lotus 79	Colin Chapman Martin Ogilvie	Cosworth DFV (V8)	Hewland FGA 400 (5)	FM	2743	F 1730 R 1630	Goodyear	578
Martini Mk 23	Tico Martini	Cosworth DFV (V8)	Hewland FGA 400 (5/6)	SM	2670	F 1540 R 1525	Goodyear	610
McLaren M 23	Gordon Coppuck	Cosworth DFV (V8)	Hewland-McLaren (6)	FM	2743	F 1600 R 1626	Goodyear	589
Merzario A 1	Arturo Merzario	Cosworth DFV (V8)	Hewland FGA 400 (5)	FM	2420	F 1530 R 1570	Goodyear	595
Renault RS 01	André de Cortanze Jean-Pierre Jabouille	Renault-Gordini EF 1 (V6 Turbo)	Hewland FGA 400 (6)	SM	2500	F 1540 R 1520	Michelin	605
Shadow DN 9	Tony Southgate	Cosworth DFV (V8)	Hewland FGA 400 (5/6)	SM	2686	F 1600 R 1549	Goodyear	587
Surtees TS 19	John Surtees Ken Sears	Cosworth DFV (V8)	Hewland FGA 400 (6)	FM	2489	F 1475 R 1499	Goodyear	585
Surtees TS 20	John Surtees Ken Sears	Cosworth DFV (V8)	Hewland FGA 400 (5/6)	FM	2667	F 1651 R 1600	Goodyear	583
Theodore TR 1	Ron Tauranac Len Bailey	Cosworth DFV (V8)	Hewland FGA 400 (6)	FM	2544	F 1448 R 1493	Goodyear	610
Tyrrell 008	Maurice Phillippe	Cosworth DFV (V8)	Hewland FGA 400 (5/6)	SM	2700	F 1626 R 1524	Goodyear	578
Williams FW 06	Patrick Head	Cosworth DFV (V8)	Hewland FGA 400 (6)	SM	2540	F 1575 R 1550	Goodyear	588
Wolf WR 1	Harvey Postlethwaite	Cosworth DFV (V8)	Hewland FGA 400 (6)	SM	2489	F 1524 R 1524	Goodyear	589
Wolf WR 5	Harvey Postlethwaite	Cosworth DFV (V8)	Hewland FGA 400 (6)	FM	2642	F 1600 R 1575	Goodyear	577

Chassis construction: SM = semi-monocoque; FM = full monocoque; TS = tubular frame with stressed skins.

Historic Turbo Victory

Jody Scheckter becomes World Champion in the reliable Ferrari 312T4 but Williams dominates the second half of the season. A turbocharged Renault wins the French Grand Prix at Dijon.

Most successful makes in 1979 were Ferrari (who won six of the World Championship qualifying rounds), Williams (five), Ligier (three) and Renault (one) and it was the South African Jody Scheckter, who had switched from Wolf to Ferrari, who won the World Championship. Ferrari also claimed the runner-up spot in the table through Gilles Villeneuve, but it was the Australian Alan Jones who dominated the second half of the season in the Williams FW07. For Ferrari, the flat-12 engine had more than paid its way. Its horizontal layout made it impossible to take full advantage of the wing-car concept, but although the engine's width did not allow the use of wings to provide maximum downforce, it was a strong and extremely reliable unit, and allowed a low centre of gravity. By the 1979 season all the leading teams had adopted at least some elements of the wing-car concept.

An event of historic significance this year was Jean-Pierre Jabouille's victory in the French Grand Prix at Dijon on July

Jean-Pierre Jabouille

Jean-Pierre Jabouille in the Renault RS10 took the first turbo victory in the history of Formula One on July 1st 1979 in the French Grand Prix at Dijon. In the same year Arnoux was twice placed second in an RS10 but Jabouille was unable to win any more World Championship points.

1st, for his Renault RS10 was the first turbocharged car in the history of Grand Prix racing to win a race. The 1.5-litre V6 Renault turbo engine had been constantly developed and improved since its first appearance in the middle of 1977, and both Ferrari and Alfa Romeo had now taken decisions to build turbocharged engines of their own for Formula One. Both engines were however still in the planning stage.

For 1979 all designers used the

brilliantly conceived Lotus 79 as their reference point, and the car became the prototype of the new generation of Formula One cars. A typical wing car had a very small monocoque with the fuel tank incorporated into it, behind the driver. This placement of the tank between the engine and the cockpit meant that the driving position had to be moved forward, which in turn left the driver rather exposed, his legs being particularly vulnerable to serious injury

Below
A separate KKK turbocharger supplied each bank of cylinders on the Renault V6 engine in 1979.

Right
The Dijon-winning Renault RS10, showing its wing-car characteristics, twin turbochargers and intercoolers.

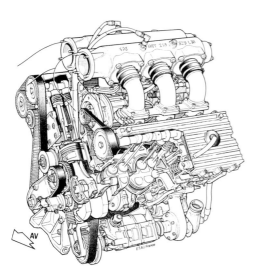

Below
Jean-Pierre Jarier in the Tyrrell 009, an almost exact copy of the Lotus 79, in the 1979 Argentine Grand Prix. But whereas the Lotus had been extremely successful in 1978, the Tyrrell did not win a single race.

Below right
Toasting the Brazilian Grand Prix success in Paris. From left: Patrick Depailler, Guy Ligier, Jean-Marie Balestre and Jacques Laffite. For Ligier, a former rugby international, 1979 was one of his most successful seasons.

Left
The Ligier-Ford JS11s proved to be extremely fast at the beginning of the 1979 season. Jacques Laffite won the Argentine Grand Prix and Patrick Depailler (pictured) the Spanish.

Jacques Laffite

in the event of an accident — a far cry from "the good old days" when the driver sat upright in the cockpit with arms bent. Although the fuel tank was situated between the cockpit and engine for purely aerodynamic reasons, the arrangement had a positive side-effect, because the internal bag-tanks were now better protected, which minimised the risk from fire. The water and oil radiators were built onto the sides of the monocoque and enclosed in the longitudinal sidepods. Vertically adjustable skirts, which scraped along the track surface, were used to shield the resultant downforce zone from the surrounding airstream, counteracting the balance of pressure from within and without. To improve the airflow under the sidepods further, suspension systems were now invariably mounted inside the bodywork, out of the airstream, at both front and rear. Alterations to chassis design meant that suspension systems were now restricted in their operation, and levers were used to tilt the shock absorber and suspension units. To some extent the front spoilers could also be dispensed with, as there was less wind resistance, and for the same reason smaller wings could be used at the rear.

At the end of 1978 the administration of international motor sport was completely restructured. The CSI was replaced by a new body, the *Fédération Internationale du Sport Automobile,* or FISA. This was given more autonomy from the *Fédération Internationale de l'Automobile* (FIA) than its predecessor, but was still subordinate to the parent body. President of the new association was French journalist and publisher Jean-Marie Balestre, a wilful, authoritarian and often controversial figure. While FISA took over the role of administering the sport

Jean-Marie Balestre

on behalf of the organising clubs, the teams' interests continued to be looked after by FOCA, the Formula One Constructors' Association. This was headed by Bernie Ecclestone, himself a clever man, though in Balestre he found an opposite number who was both eloquent and familiar with all the regulations. Their relationship was not

always an easy one.

One of FISA's first moves was to tighten up the regulations governing participating in the World Championship. Only those teams and drivers who had registered in writing with FISA in Paris before November 15th 1978 would be entitled to World Championship points; any team which wanted to participate in the Championship at a later date would have to register at least three months in advance, and pay a penalty of $30,000. Only 28 cars would be allowed to participate in qualifying at each Grand Prix, and only the fastest 24 (20 for the Monaco Grand Prix) permitted to take part in the actual race.

But FOCA won an early victory over FISA when it stuck to its guns over its resistance to the ban on skirts for 1979. The teams claimed they had invested too much in the development of skirt technology, and FISA ultimately gave way.

Missing from the circuits this year was Team Surtees, the stable founded by former motorcycling and motor racing World Champion John Surtees, after years of struggling without much success.

Again, several prominent drivers changed teams for the new season. Carlos Reutemann left Ferrari after two seasons and joined World Champion Mario Andretti at Lotus, hoping no doubt that the team would continue to call the tune in 1979 as it had in 1978. Jody Scheckter left Wolf to take Reutemann's place at Ferrari, where he joined the French-Canadian Gilles Villeneuve, who was rapidly gaining in popularity with the crowds and was something of a hero in Italy. Tyrrell entrusted his cars to Jean-Pierre Jarier, who had previously been

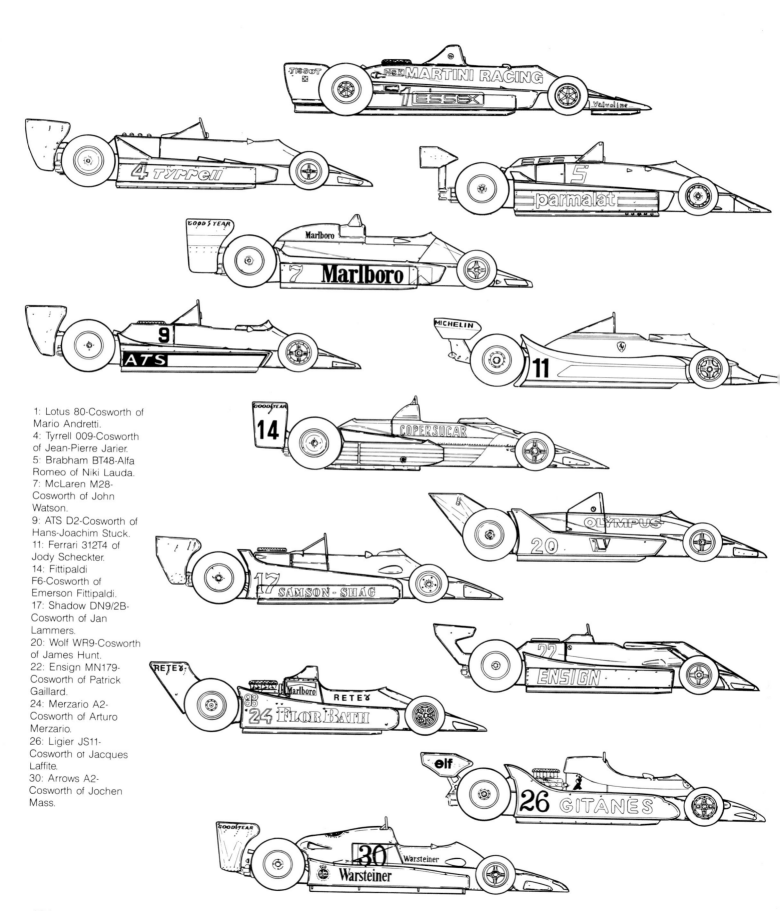

1: Lotus 80-Cosworth of
Mario Andretti.
4: Tyrrell 009-Cosworth
of Jean-Pierre Jarier.
5: Brabham BT48-Alfa
Romeo of Niki Lauda.
7: McLaren M28-
Cosworth of John
Watson.
9: ATS D2-Cosworth of
Hans-Joachim Stuck.
11: Ferrari 312T4 of
Jody Scheckter.
14: Fittipaldi
F6-Cosworth of
Emerson Fittipaldi.
17: Shadow DN9/2B-
Cosworth of Jan
Lammers.
20: Wolf WR9-Cosworth
of James Hunt.
22: Ensign MN179-
Cosworth of Patrick
Gaillard.
24: Merzario A2-
Cosworth of Arturo
Merzario.
26: Ligier JS11-
Cosworth ot Jacques
Laffite.
30: Arrows A2-
Cosworth of Jochen
Mass.

Right
Clay Regazzoni gives Williams their first Grand Prix victory in the 1979 British Grand Prix at Silverstone. Here his FW07-Ford leads Pironi's Tyrrell 009.

Below
The British Grand Prix has always been lucky for Swiss drivers. Here Emanuel de Graffenried, winner of the 1949 Silverstone race, congratulates Regazzoni on his 1979 success; in addition to these two, Joseph Siffert won at Brands Hatch in 1968.

the Irishman Derek Daly, and Alfa Romeo, which had such a long tradition of motor racing, was preparing for its Formula One comeback, former European Formula Two Champion Bruno Giacomelli continuing the testing programme on the Balocco circuit.

On the tyre front the competition was again between Goodyear, still using crossply tyres, and Michelin, with their radials. The French company continued to supply just two teams, Renault and Ferrari, which enabled them to provide a good service. The American manufacturer on the other hand was faced with the task of supplying the remainder of the field. They therefore decided to provide a normal service to most, but to single out leading drivers for privileged treatment. These selected few were supplied with the best compounds for qualifying while the other competitors had to be content with harder tyres. Arrows, Brabham, Fittipaldi, Ligier, Lotus, McLaren, Tyrrell, Williams and Wolf were supplied with both qualifying and racing Goodyears at no cost, but the qualifying tyres were strictly rationed. In fact only the four World Champions — Lauda, Hunt, Andretti and Fittipaldi — received the "qualifiers" as of right, then the fastest of the rest of the Goodyear drivers.

The Lotus wing-car design had been phenomenally successful: during 1977 and 1978 the Lotus 78 and 79 — driven by Andretti, Peterson, Nilsson and Jarier — had achieved an unbelievable 19 pole positions, 13 victories and a World Championship (Andretti). It is hard to imagine a more impressive testimony of the quality of Colin Chapman's revolutionary concept. But while he was the inspiration behind the wing car, much credit for its execution must go to his aerodynamics adviser, Peter Wright.

The factor now determining success in Formula One was the relationship between aerodynamics and tyres. The enormous pressure on the tyres, achieved by the increased aerodynamic forces, did have some negative effects, for the cars now gripped the road so well that cornering forces increased to more than 3g, and this presented the drivers with new problems. In the fifties, before the general changeover to mid-engined designs, centrifugal force in corners tended to be between 0.6 and 0.7g. By the beginning of the sixties, when all Grand Prix cars were fitted with wider tyres and had their engines behind the driver, the once mythical figure of 1g became a

with ATS and Lotus, and Didier Pironi, while Niki Lauda remained Brabham's No 1, Northern Irishman John Watson transferred to McLaren however and was replaced at Brabham by the talented young Brazilian Nelson Piquet. After a brilliant Formula Three season in Britain in 1978, Piquet had already competed in a handful of Grands Prix for Ensign and Brabham. Joining Watson at McLaren was the Frenchman Patrick Tambay, while Ligier retained the faithful Jacques Laffite and added Patrick Depailler, formerly with Tyrrell, to the team. Renault expanded its team to two cars, Jean-Pierre Jabouille being joined by René Arnoux, an up-and-coming young driver who had represented Martini and Surtees in several Formula One races; Martini now left the Grand Prix scene

after a very short involvement.

Williams included Alan Jones in his team after some promising results with the FW06 during the previous year, and also took on Clay Regazzoni from Shadow. James Hunt left McLaren and joined Walter Wolf's team while Riccardo Patrese and Jochen Mass (formerly with ATS) now drove for Arrows. Fittipaldi continued to carry the colours of his Brazilian Copersucar team and Shadow took on two talented young newcomers,

Derek Daly

Hector Rebaque

the Dutchman Jan Lammers and Italian Elio de Angelis, a specialist in Formula Two and Three. Arturo Merzario drove a car of his own construction as did the wealthy Mexican Hector Rebaque, who virtually had a Lotus 79 specially built for him. The Ensign team was represented by

reality, and in the early seventies the best designs had created a further sensation by passing the 1.5g mark. During the winter of 1978–79 Ferrari carried out back-to-back tests at Fiorano using a 1978-model 312T and a redesigned version with sidepods and sliding skirts. The test track has a bend with a 100m radius and the normal 312T3 was timed through this at a speed of 142km/h. The car which had been redesigned with sidepods and skirts was however able to take the same corner (with the same engine and the same driver) at a speed of 157km/h. In terms of the centrifugal force generated in each case, the figure registered by the older car was 1.8g, but the modified version produced 2.2g. This new knowledge resulted in a 10.5% increase in cornering speeds.

Lotus might have invented the wing car but when they tried to improve on it further for the 1979 season they failed. Chapman's aim with the new Lotus 80 was to increase downforce even more without a corresponding reduction in wind resistance. There was no front spoiler, and in place of conventional rear wings the sidepods were extended back to the tail of the car. But the first test sessions mercilessly revealed the weaknesses of the new Lotus, downforce being less than expected, so that rear wings had to be fitted as well, and this in turn produced more wind resistance. The factory reverted to the earlier 79 model while continuing work on the new car, so that in effect they were developing two cars at once. This was not a Lotus year: they did not win a single race.

The successful new Williams FW07, designed by Patrick Head, made its debut in the hands of Jones and Regazzoni in the Spanish Grand Prix. Modelled on the

Patrick Head

Lotus 79, the new Williams had an extremely small monocoque chassis, so small in fact that the driver had to twist his feet forwards to reach the pedals, and Regazzoni was not enthusiastic about the restricted legroom, particularly when contemplating the result of any frontal collision. Head still preferred not to use exotic materials, so the tub was made of alloy sheetmetal. During the design stages weeks were spent in the wind-tunnel at London's Imperial College, and one of the first tasks of the new research and development section set up by Williams in the middle of the season was the construction of a wind-tunnel of their own. The new department, which would function separately from the racing department, was placed under the direction of Frank Dernie, formerly a designer at Hesketh. The new wind-tunnel was Dernie's first task, and he built it with a conveyor-belt so that more realistic aerodynamic conditions could be achieved by having the models' wheels turning.

Gérard Ducarouge

Guy Ligier

The car that proved virtually unbeatable at the beginning of the season was the Ligier JS11, fitted with a Ford-Cosworth DFV engine after several years of using Matra V12 units. Ligier commissioned the Paris firm of SERA to carry out all the aerodynamic work on this car; Paul Carillo designed a small monocoque wing car and Gérard Ducarouge was in overall charge of the design. It was immediately evident that the pale blue Ligier was extremely fast on twisty sections of circuit, but slower than the opposition on the straights.

Brabham had had their new BT48 model ready by December 1978. This was another wing car with narrow monocoque and longitudinal sidepods. Like the Lotus 80, it did not initially have a rear wing, designer Gordon Murray trying it with the sidepods extended to behind the rear axle. But — again as with

the Lotus — the car then did not have enough downforce, and a normal wing set-up had to be substituted. Murray was the first of the modern designers to return to mounting the rear brakes outside the chassis, which allowed for improved airflow through the sidepods, though it did of course increase unsprung weight. The narrow monocoque of the Brabham was made of exotic materials such as honeycomb or graphite fibres combined with the traditional aluminium foil.

The Alfa Romeo engine was also a novelty. The 12-cylinder previously had an angle of 180° but a narrow-angle version had been developed at Autodelta in Milan, under the direction of their engineer Carlo Chiti. This 60° V12 had cylinder dimensions of 78.5 x 51.5mm, giving a capacity of 2991cc. Ferrari's own 12-cylinder retained its Boxer configuration, which meant the sidepods could not be widened at the rear, but Alfa's switch to a V12 enabled better use to be made of the wing-car principle.

With the V12 Alfa Romeo engine, the Brabham BT48s of Lauda and Piquet were usually in the front one-third of the field in qualifying but were plagued by mechanical problems in the races themselves. The BT48 was last used in the non-championship Dino Ferrari Grand Prix at Imola, which Lauda won. This was Brabham's sole success of the year and at the Canadian Grand Prix at the end of the season a new Brabham, the BT49, appeared. This was to all intents and purposes a shortened version of the BT48, fitted with the old faithful eight-cylinder Ford-Cosworth DFV engine in place of the 12-cylinder Alfa unit. With this car Piquet qualified to start from the front row of the grid for the last race of the year, at Watkins Glen.

Another Lotus 79 copy was the Tyrrell 009; in fact it was rumoured that Tyrrell had obtained the plans of the Lotus 79 from a Japanese model-car firm, and used these to build his 009! Tyrrell designer Maurice Phillippe employed an alloy monocoque using a sandwich construction with intermediate honeycomb layer, which provided superior torsional rigidity. The body was a copy of the Lotus almost to the last detail. Phillippe strove to increase the total downforce all season, redesigning the underside of the sidepod and then adding a trim to its originally flat upper side. This was all done very scientifically, as Tyrrell used computers to work out suspension geometry. Unfortunately however the car suffered several

Prix, even though this car still retained the flat underside, its turbo power was sufficient to put Jabouille on pole position for the race. By the fifth World Championship race of the season however, the Spanish Grand Prix, Renault had their new RS10 wing car. Since 1977 they had been using a single American Garrett turbocharger on their Grand Prix engines but at the Monaco Grand Prix they appeared for the first time with twin German KKK devices. Having one turbo unit for each bank of three cylinders made the engine smoother at lower revs. The main disadvantage of the turbo engines was that they reacted relatively slowly to the accelerator pedal but the KKK twin-turbo set-up reduced this "turbo lag", and made the car much easier to drive.

The turbocharged Renault engine was by far the most powerful in Formula One but development was an extremely expensive business. Initially endless problems were experienced with the intercoolers, resulting in numerous engine failures. But in 1979, in the French Grand Prix at Dijon, Renault finally reached its goal when it won a Formula One race: this was also the first Grand Prix victory for a turbocharged engine, of any make. Francois Castaing had responsibility for Renault engine

Michel Têtu

suspension breakages and consequently played no part in the battle for victory in 1979.

Teddy Mayer's McLaren team were in a very sad state in 1979. The M28, intended as the car for the 1979 season, had been completed by the previous October but unfortunately grave errors had been made in the chassis design. This car, a wing car, was somehow an unbelievable 70kg overweight, so work

immediately began on a modified version. The new M28B was ready for the Spanish Grand Prix, but this did not bring the hoped-for results either, and designer Gordon Coppuck immediately turned his attention to the M29. Although this made its debut in the British Grand Prix, 1979 was to remain an unsuccessful year for McLaren.

Renault started the season with the old RS01 and in the South African Grand

Left
South African Jody Scheckter in his Ferrari 312T4 well deserved his 1979 World Championship title. The Ferrari was very reliable even though its flat-12 engine was not the most easily adapted to the wing-car concept.

Above
Prince Rainier and Princess Grace of Monaco present the winner's cup to Jody Scheckter.

Right
Nelson Piquet in the Brabham-Alfa Romeo BT48 in the 1979 Monaco Grand Prix.

development while Michel Têtu was in overall charge of the chassis.

In both races at the start of the season, in Argentina and Brazil, the Ligier JS11 was unbeatable, and Jacques Laffite was the victor both times. A Ligier was also second in Brazil, driven by Depailler. Ferrari was still using the previous year's 312T3, with virtually flat underside and achieving very little downforce, in South America, but the replacement car, the 312T4, made its debut in South Africa. This had smaller sidepods than most of the opposition, and the inevitable adjustable skirts. Gilles Villeneuve and Jody Scheckter drove them straight into the first two places at Kyalami, then just as promptly repeated the result in the United States Grand Prix West at Long Beach. This Ferrari superiority was perhaps surprising in view of the T4's wide engine and transverse gearbox, which took up space which could otherwise have been used to aerodynamic advantage.

Ligier struck back in the Spanish Grand Prix at Jarama, when Patrick Depailler took the chequered flag in front of the Lotuses of Reutemann and Andretti; the Argentinian was driving the previous year's model, the faithful 79, while the American was in the new Mark 80. The Williams FW07 made its debut in this race, and was very impressive right from the start; before long it would be almost invincible.

The lead in the Belgian Grand Prix changed a total of six times but it was Jody Scheckter who finally won the race in his Ferrari, which seemed almost indestructible. The Alfa Romeo factory made their first reappearance in the Zolder race with their Type 177, which they had been testing for almost a year. Instead of using the new 60° unit as seen in the Brabham BT48 however, Alfa Romeo's car still had the old flat-12 engine which Brabham had used the previous year. The Type 177 was not a wing car but retained an old-fashioned "flat bottom" design, for racing was as yet being approached merely as an extension of the test programme. Bruno Giacomelli qualified the new car 14th fastest but the car was eliminated in a collision during the race.

The Monaco Grand Prix was a very exciting race. Over the last laps Clay Regazzoni got his Williams so close to Scheckter's leading Ferrari that only 0.44 second separated the two cars as they shot over the finish line. This race was the last

Grand Prix contested by 1976 World Champion James Hunt, for after the finish he suddenly left the Wolf team and retired from racing.

As already mentioned, Renault celebrated their first Formula One success with Jabouille at the wheel in the French Grand Prix at Dijon. This historic victory for the turbos followed Renault's success in the previous year's 24-hour Le Mans with the 2-litre version of their

turbocharged V6. Another high spot at Dijon was the fierce duel fought in the closing stages for second place behind Jabouille. Villeneuve in his Ferrari and Arnoux in the second Renault passed and repassed all the way around the circuit. Several times these two hotheads threatened to drive each other off the track as they "polished" the sides of each other's car with their wheels in the middle of corners. Millions of television viewers witnessed this unprecedented battle, which ended with Villeneuve retaining the upper hand.

The Williams FW07s were able to make full use of their advantage on the fast track at Silverstone, as the well-balanced wing car was unbeatable on fast corners. Alan Jones held the lead for a long time but his engine then overheated and he was forced to withdraw. This enabled his team-mate Clay Regazzoni to win, for the first time since his 1976 Long Beach victory in a Ferrari. The Silverstone race was Regazzoni's fifth, and last, Grand Prix victory, but was the first success for the Williams team.

Alan Jones and Williams completely dominated the rest of the season. They were the winning combination in the German Grand Prix at Hockenheim, with Regazzoni second. They were also the winning combination at Zeltweg in Austria, at Zandvoort in Holland and at Montreal in Canada. At Monza Ferrari returned to the top, with Scheckter and Villeneuve taking the first two places, and Scheckter also won the washed-out United States Grand Prix at Watkins Glen.

Alfa Romeo produced their new wing car, the Type 179, in time for the Italian Grand Prix at Monza. This car used the 60° V12 engine of the type used by Brabham, and an aerodynamic chassis developed by Robert Choulet of SERA in Paris. In the Italian race Bruno

Giacomelli drove the new car and Vittorio Brambilla the old flat-12, and the new model showed its potential by getting as high as seventh position before Giacomelli put it off the road.

South African Ferrari driver Jody Scheckter won the 1979 World Championship title from his team-mate Gilles Villeneuve, with third in the final placings going to Australian Alan Jones in the Williams, who had so definitively called the tune throughout the second half of the season. The Ferrari might not have been the most advanced design but reliability enabled it to more than pay its way, for Scheckter earned points in no fewer than 12 of the 15 Championship races. He won three times, and started from pole position once. Villeneuve also achieved three first placings, but although Alan Jones's score of four victories was better than either Ferrari driver, he did not have the lesser placings to back him up. By qualifying on pole position six times, Renault had demonstrated the potential of the turbo engine, but although this unit did indeed point the way to the future it was still unreliable, and Renault managed to finish in the first three placings only three times during the season.

Ligier lost the dominance it had achieved at the beginning of the season, for after winning in Argentina, Brazil and Spain the French cars were unable to retain their excellent form. The season

had been disappointing for both Brabham and McLaren, and even more so for Lotus.

Together, Ferrari and Renault took a total of seven wins, showing the development of the radial tyre to be a good investment, though by winning the other eight races, with Ligier and Williams, Goodyear emerged with a slight advantage over the other tyre manufacturer.

The biggest shock of the season came during practice in Canada when Niki Lauda suddenly climbed out of his car, and declared that he was finished with

racing. Retiring immediately, he turned his energies instead to running the airline he had founded in Austria. After two seasons away from the circuits however he would reappear in 1982 to drive for McLaren.

On May 25th 1979 the former Grand Prix constructor, Amédée Gordini, died in Paris at the age of 79. Known as "The Sorcerer", Gordini was a modest, likeable figure who, in the fifties, had been an integral part of the Grand Prix scene. He had first driven his own designs under France's colours in the late thirties, but his fragile lightweight cars first became an international force in 1948, after which they were a Grand Prix fixture for many years. Gordini initially worked in conjunction with Simca but severed all links in 1952, and was thereafter continu-ally plagued with financial problems. Gordini entered the 2.5-litre Grand Prix formula with a six-cylinder design, followed by the eight-cylinder car in 1955, but at the beginning of 1957 the team finally had to be disbanded. During the sixties Gordini, who was actually Italian-born, worked closely with Renault on the development of tuned Gordini versions of their production saloons.

Formula One cars of 1979

Make/model	Chief designer(s)	Engine	Gearbox (speeds)	Chassis	Wheelbase	Track	Tyre make	Dry weight
Alfa Romeo T 177	Carlo Chiti	Alfa Romeo 115-12 (12 cyl 180°)	Hewland-Alfa Romeo (6)	FM	2740	F 1660 R 1610	Goodyear	610
Arrows A 2	Tony Southgate Dave Wass	Cosworth DFV (V8)	Hewland FGA 400 (5)	FM	2692	F 1765 R 1524	Goodyear	589
ATS D 2	—	Cosworth DFV (V8)	Hewland FGA 400 (5)	FM	2731	F 1600 R 1600	Goodyear	590
Brabham BT 48	Gordon Murray	Alfa Romeo (V12 60°)	Hewland-Alfa Romeo (6)	FM	2743	F 1702 R 1626	Goodyear	595
Ensign MN 09	Morris Nunn	Cosworth DFV (V8)	Hewland FGA 400 (5)	FM	2667	F 1778 R 1626	Goodyear	612
Ferrari 312 T4	Mauro Forghieri	312 B (12 cyl 180°)	Ferrari (5)	TS	2700	F 1700 R 1600	Michelin	584
Fittipaldi F 5 A	Ralph Bellamy	Cosworth DFV (V8)	Hewland FGA 400 (5)	FM	2780	F 1706 R 1596	Goodyear	605
Fittipaldi F 6	Ralph Bellamy	Cosworth DFV (V8)	Hewland FGA 400 (5)	FM	2780	F 1956 R 1621	Goodyear	582
Ligier JS 11	Gérard Ducarouge Paul Carillo	Cosworth DFV (V8)	Hewland FG 400 (5/6)	FM	2794	F 1738 R 1600	Goodyear	582
Lotus 79	Colin Chapman Martin Ogilvie	Cosworth DFV (V8)	Hewland FG 400 (5)	FM	2819	F 1778 R 1626	Goodyear	590
Lotus 80	Colin Chapman Martin Ogilvie	Cosworth DFV (V8)	Hewland FGA 400 (5)	FM	2789	F 1700 R 1638	Goodyear	580
McLaren M 28	Gordon Coppuck	Cosworth DFV (V8)	Hewland FG 400/6 (6)	FM	2870	F 1778 R 1626	Goodyear	588
McLaren M 29	Gordon Coppuck	Cosworth DFV (V8)	Hewland FG 400/6 (6)	FM	2870	F 1740 R 1590	Goodyear	586
Merzario A 2	—	Cosworth DFV (V8)	Hewland FGA 400 (5)	SM	2720	F 1680 R 1640	Goodyear	591
Renault RS 10	Michel Têtu	Renault-Gordini EF 1 (V6 Turbo)	Hewland FGA 400 (5)	FM	2860	F 1720 R 1570	Michelin	600
Shadow DN 9/B	Tony Southgate John Baldwin	Cosworth DFV (V8)	Hewland FGA 400 (5)	SM	2692	F 1715 R 1588	Goodyear	603
Tyrrell 009	Maurice Phillippe	Cosworth DFV (V8)	Hewland FGA 400 (5)	FM	2794	F 1702 R 1613	Goodyear	592
Williams FW 07	Patrick Head	Cosworth DFV (V8)	Hewland FGA 400 (5)	FM	2692	F 1738 R 1600	Goodyear	579
Wolf WR 9	Harvey Postlethwaite	Cosworth DFV (V8)	Hewland FGA 400 (5)	FM	2667	F 1626 R 1626	Goodyear	585

Chassis construction: SM = semi-monocoque; FM = full monocoque; TS = tubular frame with stressed skins.

Williams and Brabham in Front

The Australian Alan Jones becomes World Champion for Williams just ahead of Brazilian Brabham driver Nelson Piquet. Ferrari and Alfa Romeo both work hard on turbo engines. Lotus remains unsuccessful.

The 1980 season was dominated by the ongoing power struggle between FISA and FOCA. There was also friction within the Formula One teams themselves. And it was a season when the downforce of the skirted wing cars sent cornering speeds rocketing to an alarmingly high level, cutting lap times by an average three seconds from the previous year.

When centrifugal force of an unbelievable 2.7g was registered on one corner at Hockenheim the drivers were forced to reconsider this dangerous trend, for cornering at such speeds brought new problems. Because of the additional adhesion caused by the increased downforce, the cars no longer slid around corners but instead remained glued to the track and cornered as if on rails. This was not particularly spectacular to watch, and, more seriously, caused the drivers severe neck strain, because their muscles were continually having to flex to counteract the centrifugal forces trying to move their heads outwards on corners. At the same time they had to force their feet onto the pedals as the lateral forces kept pushing their feet to one side.

Renault had been alone in developing turbo engines since 1977, but in the spring of 1980 Ferrari introduced its own turbo car, the 126 model with 120° V6 engine. At the same time there were rumours that Alfa Romeo were working on a turbocharged V8, and a certain degree of anxiety became evident in the British camp. Indeed, the British teams made full use of the regulations to counter the sudden bustle of turbo development, to try to keep turbo engines out of the running.

But although Renault drivers Jabouille and Arnoux won a total of three Grands Prix in 1980, this was not a turbo year. The French supercar may have produced between 50 and 70 more horsepower than the normally aspirated 3-litre cars, but in other respects it was very much prone to defects, and Renault had to deal with a large number of valve-spring breakages and piston damage.

The Australian Alan Jones and the talented Brazilian Nelson Piquet quickly became favourites for the 1980 Championship. Jones drove the Williams FW07 until Patrick Head's FW07B design was ready, while Piquet was in the Brabham BT49. Both contenders relied on the Ford-Cosworth DFV engine, a winner since its debut in Jim Clark's Lotus 49 at the 1967 Dutch Grand Prix but now,

because of its small and compact size, the perfect unit for taking most advantage of the wing-car concept.

The Ford's chief rival was Ferrari's reliable 12-cylinder unit, whose success story dated back to 1970. With these engines behind them Jody Scheckter and Gilles Villeneuve had taken the first two places in the 1979 World Championship but, although now running at 12,000rpm and with an undeniable horsepower advantage, this was no longer enough for the Ferrari engine to combat the wing cars, and the horizontal layout of its cylinders continued to preclude its own adaption to full wing-car principles. Downforce had become the principal factor in determining victory or defeat, and cornering speeds had increased to the extent that even a car with an engine as powerful as the Ferrari's could not compete on equal terms.

The 312T4 which had been so successful in 1979 was succeeded in 1980 by the 312T5 but this was an inferior design. Jody Scheckter only just managed to qualify, on the second to last row, for the British Grand Prix and at Montreal did not even make the field. That race was Scheckter's 112th Grand Prix, but he only competed in one more. And for this sort of performance the Ferrari drivers were risking their lives.

Michelin once again provided Renault and Ferrari with radial tyres, leaving Goodyear to supply their crossplies to all the other teams. The American company was now manufacturing its racing tyres in the United States rather than in Britain, and was forced to limit both the number of tyres it produced and the variety of compounds. Nevertheless Goodyear tyres were used by the winners of 11 of the 14 Grands Prix of 1980, while Michelin had to be content with the three Renault victories.

By now the costs of organizing a Grand Prix had increased dramatically. An organiser had to pay out a massive $540,000 for a 25-car field, the sum then being divided into fractions, known as the famous "key", and distributed among the teams according to individual performances.

A record number of entrants took part in Formula One events in 1980. Some continually faltered at the qualifying hurdles and were thus excluded from entry into the field on a regular basis. The 1980 teams were Alfa Romeo, Arrows, ATS, Brabham, Brands Hatch Racing (with the South African lady driver Desiré Wilson), Ensign, Ferrari, Fittipaldi, Ligier, Lotus, McLaren, Osella, RAM, Renault, Shadow, Theodore-Shadow, Theodore-Rainbow, Tyrrell, Williams-Leyland (as the official Williams team became known for a while) and Williams Grand Prix Engineering, its more usual name.

Among the leading teams, Ferrari retained their 1979 line-up, reigning World Champion Jody Scheckter and the impetuous Gilles Villeneuve. Bruno Giacomelli remained with Alfa Romeo and was joined by Patrick Depailler, formerly with Ligier. After Niki Lauda's departure from Brabham, the talented Nelson Piquet was promoted to No 1, the second car being shared by the rather

Alan Jones

Above
The 1980 World Champion, Australian Alan Jones, pictured here with his wife.

Left
Alan Jones in the Williams FW07.

Just after the start of the 1980 Belgian Grand Prix at Zolder. Didier Pironi in the Ligier-Ford JS11 leads the field, ahead of the Williams FW07s of Jones and Reutemann. Pironi's victory here was his first Grand Prix win, and was also Ligier's first success for more than a year.

Overleaf
The Australian Alan Jones dominated the second half of the 1979 season. The Williams-Ford FW07 he drove had been designed to achieve the optimum downforce, the side-skirts "sealing" the car's body to the track surface.

lacklustre Zunino (from Argentina) and Rebaque (Mexico). Despite the disappointing 1979 season Mario Andretti remained with Lotus but Carlos Reutemann left the team and went to partner Alan Jones at Williams. Reutemann was replaced at Lotus by Elio de Angelis, who was in fact still under contract to Shadow and had to buy his way out of his former team. Tyrrell took on Jean-Pierre Jarier and Derek Daly, releasing Didier Pironi to join Jacques Laffite on the Ligier team. Clay Regazzoni, who had given Williams their first victory at Silverstone in 1979, was not able to renew his contract and was taken on by Mo Nunn's small Ensign team. McLaren was still in a state of crisis but took on the talented young French Formula Three ace Alain Prost to run alongside Northern Irishman John Watson. Patrick Tambay was thus left without a drive and took himself off to the United States, where he won the

Marc Surer

Giorgio Stirano

CanAm Championship in a Lola. Osella, formerly a Formula Two make, entered the Grand Prix arena with the young Rome-resident American Eddie Cheever as their driver and a car designed by young engineer Giorgio Stirano, who subsequently went on to found his own Alba make. Swiss driver Marc Surer, the 1979 European Formula Two Champion, meanwhile signed for his first Formula One season with the ATS team owned by German alloy-wheel magnate Gunter Schmid. Most of the other teams competed only sporadically and had little, if any, chance of winning.

Some of the prominent teams — such as Lotus, McLaren and Arrows — had had little success with their wing-car experiments in 1979 and their designers accordingly drew up comparatively conventional cars for the new season. These were very similar both in construction and in the way the aerodynamics were applied.

It had become apparent to many other teams that their cars were very difficult to steer around slow bends, so for 1980 designers altered weight distribution to place more load on the front once again. This was achieved by moving the driver's seat even further forward, so that his feet were now protected only by a polyester casing and a metal plate. At the same time shortcomings in torsional rigidity which had come to light in 1979 chassis design were tackled this year by increasing use

of the expensive new honeycomb sandwich method of construction, rather than aluminium.

The oil and water radiators were fixed onto the monocoque walls at about the same level as the driver, though most teams were now experimenting with using heat exchangers integrated into the water circulation system instead of the traditional type of oil cooler. In this system air-cooled water, instead of air, was used as the cooling medium for the oil radiators. The new process required larger water radiators, but this had positive aspects, for the relatively heavy oil coolers could now be dispensed with and at the same time, because more oil-cooling surface area was lost than water-cooling surface gained, wind resistance was reduced, which made a positive contribution to effective aerodynamics.

As early as 1979 the shaping of aerodynamic sidepods had proved to be an extremely exacting process for although all the cars may have looked like wing cars, very few of them were able to achieve optimum downforce. But in 1980 nearly all the teams were conducting research programmes in wind-tunnels, and the new season looked more promising. Intensive study of the characteristics of sidepods at a constant resistance resulted in much more downforce being generated than in the previous year. This meant that the front wings could be partly, or even wholly,

done away with and the size of the rear wing also reduced, resulting in even less wind resistance. The size of the rear wing was, to some extent, an indicator of the effectiveness of the sidepods.

The Williams designer, Patrick Head, went to great lengths to optimize sidepod design, even redistributing various engine accessories. The fuel pump, on a Ford-Cosworth engine normally found underneath, was placed on top of the motor to remove it from the all-important underside airstream, where it had tended to produce turbulence. The crankcase could thus be made narrower and more aerodynamically effective.

The chassis of the Brabham BT49, which appeared at the end of 1979, was constructed mainly of carbon fibre and, although this material was extremely expensive, it greatly reduced any tendency of the chassis to twist. Within a very few years carbon fibre monocoques would be the norm for Formula One cars. Unlike most of his contemporaries, Brabham designer Gordon Murray did not use a wind-tunnel, preferring to test all his modifications on the track — something only a team with a very generous budget could afford to do. Murray also experimented with the American Weismann

gearbox, familiar from Indianapolis applications. This was narrower than the English Hewland FGB400 gearbox then in general use in Formula One and thus, once again, could lead to an improvement in downforce.

The Ligier JS11/15, like the Brabham and the Williams, was an improved version of the previous year's model. The aerodynamic improvements on this car were planned in the Paris engineering offices of SERA, who also contributed to Renault and Alfa Romeo design work. The Ligier cars themselves were designed by Paul Carillo and Hervé Guilpin at the team's workshops in Vichy, under the direction of former aircraft engineer Gérard Ducarouge. In line with the general trend Ligier relocated the rear brakes outboard this year in order to improve the effectiveness of the sidepods, even though doing so resulted in a weight increase. Indeed by now only Ferrari continued to use inboard brakes, because the width of the 312T5's 12-cylinder engine meant the brakes were not directly in the path of the airflow which was directed backwards by the small sidepods.

The Renault RS10, which had been so successful at Dijon, was further improved and renamed the RS20. This well-

balanced wing car still had the most powerful engine of all, and by using titanium and magnesium alloys the Renault engineers had succeeded in reducing the weight further. They then worked on improving the aerodynamics as well.

At Lotus Martin Ogilvie designed the 81 under the eye of Colin Chapman, employing a short wheelbase to decrease understeer. This was not much faster than its predecessor however so Nigel Stroud designed a new monocoque, in which the cockpit was moved forward by about 12cm. This chassis was torsionally more rigid and, by using 15-inch wheels as well, they were able to control the car's understeer tendencies. But, again, 1980 was not to be a Lotus year.

Autodelta made great progress with the Type 179 Alfa Romeo which had appeared at the end of 1979. With a very blunt nose, this car was not the most aesthetically pleasing design but, aerodynamically, it was very effective. The body and wings were designed by Robert Choulet and closely resembled the Ligier design; this was understandable as both came from the SERA drawing-boards. The Alfa Romeo was very unreliable at the beginning of the season and was continually forced out of races

Right

Right
Mario Andretti was never able to regain his earlier form at the wheel of the 1980 Lotus-Ford 81.

Below
Ligier team-members (left to right) Jacques Laffite, Gérard Ducarouge and Didier Pironi.

Above
A rousing welcome for the Renault team at Roissy Airport after René Arnoux's victory in the 1980 Brazilian Grand Prix. Left (with tie) racing manager Jean Sage; right (foreground) chief engineer Gérard Champion.

René Arnoux

Left
The two Renault RE20s at Kyalami in 1980. Jabouille (who started from pole position) is in front, Arnoux (the winner) behind.

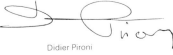

Didier Pironi

because of minor problems which, in most cases, should have been avoidable. In this respect the test work carried out by Patrick Depailler was invaluable, and the 12-cylinder car gradually moved nearer to becoming a leading contender.

Maurice Phillippe, the former Lotus and Parnelli employee, designed the new Tyrrell 010 but although this proved to be faster than the old 009 it was still not a winner. Patrick Depailler's 1978 Monaco win apart, this team had not been able to recapture the success it had enjoyed before Derek Gardner's departure in 1977. It is interesting to note that the development of the 010 was assisted by the American Karl Kempf, a specialist in applied mathematics with a doctorate in physics. Using electronic probes, he measured the most important dimensions in racing car construction such as downforce, movement of the car on its three axes (lateral, longitudinal and vertical), engine speed and the transverse flexing of steering under load. The results were fed into an on-board computer, and Phillippe was able to use the data to make an assessment of the car's behaviour independent of the driver's opinion, which had until then been the only alternative.

Tyrrell also used computer technology for a new suspension system, which was tested in the spring of 1980. On this system the upper wishbones at the front and rear followed conventional design but the lower wishbones could be continually adjusted by means of computer-controlled hydraulics to keep the camber of the wheels constant under all driving conditions. The computer continually monitored the camber of all four wheels and guided the hydraulic system as required. The system functioned in practice but did not bring any noticeable improvements in performance and, in spite of its revolutionary concept, was eventually abandoned.

The McLaren company underwent a major restructuring in 1980. With generous support from its sponsor, Marlboro, the old company was replaced by a new organisation, McLaren International, headed by Ron Dennis and John Barnard. As a young man in the sixties Dennis had worked as a mechanic for Brabham, and had then founded his own successful Formula Two team. Barnard, who became the new company's chief designer, had assisted Gordon Coppuck on the design of the successful McLaren M23 some years before, and had later been responsible for the design of the Chaparral car which had caused such a sensation in CART racing in the United States. Coppuck stayed on to work on the M29 which, in the second half of the 1979 season, had still failed to produce any worthwhile results. The M29 was developed during 1980 into the M29B and then the M29C, which made its debut at the Spanish Grand Prix, but neither was a success. Then at the Dutch Grand Prix the M30, in which the driver's seat was placed far forward, appeared, again without any noticeable improvement in results.

Ron Dennis

John Barnard

Barnard helped Coppuck with the design of the M30 while concentrating his energies on the first of the new-generation cars from McLaren International. When this first appeared, in 1981, it was not designated M31 but rather, in keeping with other changes, was called the MP4. By then Gordon Coppuck had left, after 15 years with McLaren. There was a new face on the McLaren driving strength in 1980 too. During the winter Teddy Mayer had invited the talented young Frenchman Alain Prost, who had just won the European Formula Three Championship, for a test at Le Castellet, and Prost returned better lap times than the old hand, John Watson. The young French-man would confirm his potential during the season.

The remaining teams — Arrows, ATS, Ensign and Fittipaldi — all campaigned unexceptional wing cars in 1980 and played only minor roles, but Shadow disappeared from the scene during the season. Unable to find another sponsor, the team's American owner Don Nichols was forced to sell his equipment to Hong Kong millionaire enthusiast Teddy Yip.

But the biggest tragedy of the season, one which continued into 1981, was the continuing power struggle between FISA and FOCA. FISA continued to press for the institution of its ban on skirts while the teams represented by FOCA (in other words, all the Formula One teams except Ferrari, Alfa Romeo, and Renault) united in their determination to stand fast on their own viewpoint. There were flare-ups at Zolder and Monaco when the FOCA drivers, in support of the stand their teams were making, refused to take part in the compulsory drivers' briefings, which brought a response from FISA president Jean-Marie Balestre in the form of $2000 fines for each offending driver and withdrawal of their licences.

The matter reached crisis point just prior to the Spanish Grand Prix, with Ferrari, Alfa Romeo and Renault remaining loyal to FISA, but the remaining teams ranged against them. Hours of discussion preceded the race and Formula One seemed about to collapse when FISA declared the race invalid. FOCA went ahead and sanctioned the race themselves, with the "banned" drivers taking part, but without those teams loyal to FISA. Alan Jones was the victor at Jarama but did not receive any World Championship points, for FISA had withdrawn the event from the World Championship schedule.

The crisis continued, and as the date for the French Grand Prix grew closer that race seemed under threat. On June 24th, just five days before the race was due to be held, representatives of all Formula One teams met at a London hotel and, after nine hours of discussions, finally reached agreement and the race at Le Castellet was allowed to run. Skirts remained. But the question remained a thorn in FISA's side, for although these aids vastly increased downforce they could also be very dangerous. If a skirt suddenly stopped functioning, as could easily happen if it were damaged (for example when a car ran over a kerb when cornering), then the downforce was immediately negated, which could cause sudden loss of control in the middle of a corner.

The intrigues and politicking of

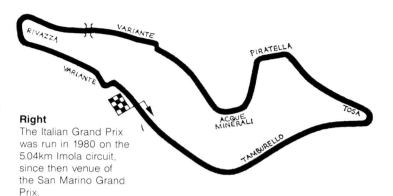

Formula One had resulted in a loss of the sport's credibility among the public. Spectator numbers dropped and television stations began to question whether they should continue to transmit the races live. The sponsors then took up arms, for if the races were not televised they would not get the coverage they had paid for. The power of hard cash told, and the teams reached agreement to ensure the continuation of the World Championship.

But back to the racing. The season produced an exciting duel between Alan Jones, whose father had been one of the leading Australian drivers in the fifties, and the young Brazilian Nelson Piquet, son of a doctor and former member of the Brazilian cabinet. At the opening race in Argentina Jones in the Williams-Ford FW07B was winner from Piquet in his Brabham-Ford BT49. But thanks to the superior performance of the turbo, Renault was able to strike back in Brazil, and René Arnoux won his first Grand Prix. The young Roman Elio de Angelis was second in what would be the best Lotus-Ford placing of the entire season, and Jones in the Williams was third. Arnoux won again in South Africa, where the race was run at an altitude of about 1800 metres and the Renault's turbocharged engine, less affected by changes in atmospheric pressure than its competition, had an even greater advantage. In the next race, the United States Grand Prix West at Long Beach, Nelson Piquet celebrated the first Grand

Prix victory of his career, while Jones was eliminated from the race in a collision. The Arrows, usually very much the underdogs, performed very well here, and Riccardo Patrese brought an A3 home in second place.

But the race on the Long Beach street circuit had a tragic twist when Clay Regazzoni suffered a very serious accident. On the 51st lap the brake pedal on his Ensign MN11 broke on the long straight and the car careered straight into Zunino's Brabham, which was parked up the escape road, and then crashed head-on into a concrete wall. Miraculously Regazzoni survived but the crash ended his career, for he was paralysed from the waist down and has been confined to a wheelchair ever since.

Another newcomer was winner of the Belgian Grand Prix at Zolder, when Didier Pironi in the Ligier-Ford JS11/15 left the Williams cars of Reutemann and Jones well behind.

But Williams turned the tables on Ligier at Monte Carlo, Reutemann winning from Laffite. Piquet finished third but Jones retired with gearbox trouble. This race was the scene of a spectacular — though relatively harmless — accident when Irishman Derek Daly in a Tyrrell 010 was involved in a mass collision as the field raced towards Sainte-Devote in a tight bunch just after the start. In the excitement Daly's Tyrrell flew across the top of several other cars. Collisions at Monaco are common, particularly at the Sainte-Devote "eye of the needle", and as a consequence the camera lenses are always at the ready. Fortunately there were no casualties but the spectacular sequence of events went right round the world via the television cameras and the press.

There was a positive side to the accident as well, for Tyrrell's sponsor, the Milan-based Candy washing-machine company, were delighted. Never before

had their name received such intensive coverage as it was given by the repeated slow-motion replays!

Monaco was followed by the "illegal" Spanish Grand Prix at Jarama, run in the absence of the non-FOCA teams (Ferrari, Alfa Romeo and Renault) and consequently removed from the official calendar. Fortunately the clouds gathering on the Formula One horizon were dispelled by the June 24th London meeting, after which the season returned to normal.

Alan Jones in the Williams won the French Grand Prix at Le Castellet from the Ligiers of Pironi and Laffite, but Renault's proceeds from its home Grands Prix were meagre, Jabouille retiring and Arnoux having to be content with fifth place. Jones also won the next race, the British Grand Prix at Brands Hatch, but the next victor, in the German Grand Prix at Hockenheim, was Jacques Laffite. Then in the Austrian round on the fast Osterreichring, Renault, with Jabouille driving, came to the line in first place ahead of the two Williams.

On August 1st, just ten days before the Italian Grand Prix, the Formula One world was shattered by the death of Patrick Depailler, in an accident during testing at Hockenheim. He crashed at the Ostkurve, for reasons which remain unclear to this day. Depailler had all the makings of a World Champion and the racing world lost a great sportsman. Alfa Romeo also lost an outstanding test driver whose efforts had made no small contribution towards putting them back on the path to success.

For the first time since 1949 this year's Italian Grand Prix was not held on the famous Monza autodrome which had opened in 1922. In 1979 the owners of the Imola circuit had begun campaigning for the right to hold a World Championship Grand Prix. The Autodromo Dino Ferrari had been continually expanded and improved over the years, and the original circuit, which led through the streets of Imola, had now been replaced by a permanent circuit. The region around Imola is home to an enthusiastic racing public, and they were finally

allowed their day when it was announced that the 1980 Italian Grand Prix would be held on their circuit. To the Milanese this decision was incomprehensible.

The Ferrari team had had a chronically bad run so far in 1980 but there was new hope on the horizon when the turbo era opened for them at Imola, and Gilles Villeneuve appeared in practice with the new Ferrari Turbo Type 126. Villeneuve qualified the new car 0.6-second faster than his times with the normally-aspirated 312T5, but used the older car in the race. He left the track when a tyre burst on the sixth lap.

The Ferrari 126, built to replace the normally-aspirated 312T5, was designed from the ground up as a wing car. The 1496cc (81 x 48.4mm) engine was a 120° V6, with twin KKK turbochargers, though Ferrari were also working on another version of the engine. This was to have a Comprex turbocharger produced by the firm of Brown Boveri, but after comprehensive testing preference was finally given to the KKK version.

Alfa Romeo also had a surprise in store in the Imola pits when they unveiled their new turbo engine, a 90° V8 with dimensions of 74 x 43.5mm, giving a capacity of 1496cc. This was not actually an immediate successor of the V12, for Alfa Romeo did not make the final switch to turbo engines until 1983.

After the British Grand Prix Jody Scheckter had hinted that he would be retiring at the end of the season, and Enzo Ferrari lost no time in making his plans for 1981. The day after the Italian Grand Prix, the Commendatore announced that Didier Pironi would be joining Villeneuve on the team for the following year.

With two rounds now left in the World Championship, Brabham driver Nelson Piquet headed the points table with 54 points, just one point more than Williams driver Alan Jones. The Montreal air was understandably alive with tension at the start of the next race, the Canadian Grand Prix on Notre Dame Island. Jones and Piquet duly started from the front row but at the very first corner Jones boxed his rival in against the crash barriers. There was a massive collision and the race had to be stopped. Piquet climbed into his spare car but after 24 laps of the new race, when in the lead, he had to withdraw because of engine failure. Jones took a comfortable victory, so that the Australian was now in the lead with 62 points while Piquet remained on 54.

But the fastest qualifier in the last race, the United States Grand Prix at Watkins Glen, was neither of the title contenders,

but Bruno Giacomelli in the improved version of the V12 Alfa Romeo 179.

Bruno Giacomelli

Giacomelli put up a good show in the race too, and for 32 laps the Alfa Romeo was a clear leader. Its jinx then returned and its electrical system failed, forcing the

car out of the race.

Jones had gradually been working his way towards the front and came home winner, of the race and the Championship. Piquet, who had been forced out after 25 laps, had to console himself with the thankless title of runner-up, followed by Reutemann, Laffite, Pironi and Arnoux. Williams won the Manufacturers' Championship for the first time, ahead of Ligier and Brabham; the previous year's champion, Ferrari, had to be content with tenth place in the table.

Formula One cars of 1980

Make/model	Chief designer(s)	Engine	Gearbox (speeds)	Chassis	Wheelbase	Track	Tyre make	Dry weight
Alfa Romeo 179	Carlo Chiti	Alfa Romeo 33 TT 12 (V12 60°)	Alfa Romeo (6)	FM	2740	F 1720 R 1570	Goodyear	595
Arrows A 3	Tony Southgate	Cosworth DFV (V8)	Hewland FG 400 (5)	FM	2591	F 1727 R 1600	Goodyear	581
ATS D 4	Nigel Stroud Gustav Brunner	Cosworth DFV (V8)	Hewland FGA 400 (5)	FM	2692	F 1702 R 1600	Goodyear	579
Brabham BT 49	Gordon Murray	Cosworth DFV (V8)	Hewland FGA 400 (5)	FM	2642	F 1702 R 1626	Goodyear	580
Ensign MN 10— MN 14	Ralph Bellamy Nigel Bennett	Cosworth DFV (V8)	Hewland FGA 400 (5)	FM	2743	F 1676 R 1588	Goodyear	598
Ferrari 312 T5	Mauro Forghieri	Ferrari 312 B (12 cyl 180°)	Ferrari (5)	TS	2700	F 1650 R 1610	Michelin	610
Ferrari 126 CK	Mauro Forghieri	Ferrari 126 C (V6 Turbo)	Ferrari (5)	TS	2700—2850	F 1760—1780 R 1680—1650	Michelin	620
Fittipaldi F 7	Harvey Postlethwaite	Cosworth DFV (V8)	Hewland FGA 400 (5)	FM	2642	F 1778 R 1626	Goodyear	592
Fittipaldi F 8	Harvey Postlethwaite	Cosworth DFV (V8)	Hewland FGA 400 (5)	FM	2616	F 1727 R 1626	Goodyear	586
Ligier JS 11/15	Paul Carillo	Cosworth DFV (V8)	Hewland FGA 400 (5)	FM	2800	F 1778 R 1608	Goodyear	575
Lotus 81	Martin Ogilvie Peter Wright	Cosworth DFV (V8)	Lotus-Hewland FGA 400 (5)	FM	2678	F 1727 R 1626	Goodyear	590
McLaren M 29	Gordon Coppuck	Cosworth DFV (V8)	McLaren-Hewland FG 400 (6)	FM	2705	F 1740 R 1590	Goodyear	586
McLaren M 30	Gordon Coppuck	Cosworth DFV (V8)	McLaren-Hewland FG 400 (6)	FM	2731	F 1753 R 1626	Goodyear	600
Osella FA 1	Giorgio Stirano	Cosworth DFV (V8)	Hewland FGA 400 (5)	FM	2710	F 1720 R 1620	Goodyear	600
Renault RE 20	Michel Têtu	Renault-Gordini (EF 1 V6 Turbo)	Hewland FGA 400 (5)	FM	2860	F 1720 R 1570	Michelin	615
Shadow DN 12	Vic Morris Chuck Graemiger	Cosworth DFV (V8)	Hewland FGA 400 (5)	FM	2578	F 1575 R 1600	Goodyear	607
Tyrrell 010	Maurice Phillippe	Cosworth DFV (V8)	Hewland FGA 400 (5)	FM	2692	F 1702 R 1588	Goodyear	581
Williams FW 07 B	Patrick Head	Cosworth DFV (V8)	Hewland FGA 400 (5)	FM	2692	F 1727 R 1626	Goodyear	585

Chassis construction: FM = full monocoque; TS = tubular frame with stressed skins.

Year of the Expensive Car

Politics diminish the prestige of Formula One. Teams circumvent the ban on skirts. After an exciting season Piquet in a Brabham wins his first World Championship.

The 1980 season was hardly over before the dispute between FISA and FOCA flared up again. The established British teams decided the way around the seemingly insurmountable problems was to set up a new body independent of either existing organization, and at the beginning of November 1980 the World Federation of Motor Sport was duly announced. A press conference was called, at which Bernie Ecclestone explained that the WFMS would promote its own international series of races, which would be known as the World Professional Championship, and that contracts to this effect had been drawn up with 15 Grand Prix circuits.

But this was a short-lived proposal. Within a week FISA had countered with a declaration accusing FOCA of disseminating false information, and saying that few national automobile clubs would sanction WFMS races in their countries. There was by no means unanimous support from the constructors either, for Ferrari, Alfa Romeo and Renault continued to support FISA throughout the dispute, and were joined by three other teams, Ligier, Osella and the British Toleman team, which was just entering Formula One. The Grand Prix organisers threw their support behind the national clubs in backing the

FISA viewpoint, and then the sponsors too indicated they would not support an "outlaw" series. On December 4th 1980 the Goodyear tyre company in Akron expressed its views on the state of affairs by announcing that it was withdrawing from Formula One, leaving the majority of Grand Prix teams with no source of tyres.

As the international standing of Formula One sank to new depths, the WFMS collapsed. It had lasted just one month.

By this time the teams should have been preparing for the first round of the 1981 Championship, for the Argentine Grand Prix was scheduled to take place on January 25th 1981. But with the arguments between FISA and FOCA still raging, there was no option but to cancel the race. Clearly the situation could not be allowed to continue.

On January 19th 1981 representatives of all the racing teams met at Ferrari's headquarters at Maranello. The talking lasted for 13 hours, during which time a common approach to FISA was hammered out. The points agreed formed the basis of what was later to be known as the Concorde Agreement, named after the Place de la Concorde in Paris where FIA and FISA have their headquarters, and Formula One was saved. In February a peaceful conclusion was finally reached

between FISA and FOCA and, on March 4th, the parties agreed to a common calendar of events. Amongst other things the new Concorde Agreement reaffirmed the FIA's sovereignty over the sport and FISA's status as its executive arm, but stated that FOCA could negotiate with organizers and with the television companies on FISA's behalf and subject to FISA confirmation.

Six-wheeled cars were banned and so was four-wheel-drive. The vexed question of skirts was dealt with by a compromise: sliding skirts were banned, but fixed skirts, at least 60mm above the track surface, were permitted.

FISA had finally passed its skirt ban, but it was not long before designers found ways to circumvent the requirement.

In the meantime the South African Grand Prix had been run on February 7th, but with only FOCA teams participating, their cars complying with the old skirt regulations. FISA accordingly withdrew this race's World Championship status so that the Championship proper did not begin until

Nelson Piquet

Above
Nelson Piquet in a Brabham was winner of the 1981 Argentine Grand Prix, delayed until April because of the argument between FISA and FOCA. Carlos Reutemann (left) in a Williams was second and took over the World Championship lead. Alain Prost was third for Renault.

Left
Brazilian Nelson Piquet, here in the Brabham-Ford BT49C at Hockenheim, was 1981 World Champion. The Brabham's side-skirts are actually scraping the track surface.

March 15th with the United States Grand Prix West at Long Beach. After Goodyear had announced its decision to withdraw from Formula One, Michelin declared itself ready to supply all the teams with tyres, at least for the first race of the season.

In the meantime some reorganisation had taken place in the various racing teams. As has already been mentioned, Ferrari took on Didier Pironi to replace Jody Scheckter, who was retiring, Gilles Villeneuve remaining with the team. Andretti left Lotus and went to partner Bruno Giacomelli at Alfa Romeo. His place at Lotus was taken by Nigel Mansell, with de Angelis also staying. Williams began the new season with Jones and Reutemann, while at Brabham Nelson Piquet was joined by the Mexican Hector Rebaque. René Arnoux remained in the Renault camp but Jean-Pierre Jabouille, who had been seriously injured in a practice crash in Canada at the end of 1980, was replaced by the talented Alain Prost. Jabouille meanwhile joined Jacques Laffite at Ligier, who were mounting a large-scale campaign this year with the backing of the French passenger-car manufacturer Talbot. For their new JS17 model, officially called a Talbot-Ligier, the team switched back to the high-revving 2993cc (79.7 x 50mm) V12 Matra engine. Since Ligier had last used this engine with such success in the seventies, it had been completely revised and brought up to date. Jabouille's leg injuries in fact took longer to heal than had been expected, and his countrymen Jean-Pierre Jarier and Patrick Tambay filled in during his enforced absence.

Emerson Fittipaldi, World Champion in 1972 and 1974, hung up his crash helmet this year in order to devote himself entirely to directing his increasingly successful British-based Brazilian team, with Finnish driver Keke Rosberg and the Brazilian Chico Serra as drivers. McLaren International, now under the sole direction of Ron Dennis and chief engineer John Barnard, kept John Watson but replaced Jochen Mass with the young Italian star Andrea de Cesaris, who came from Formula Two. Arrows retained Riccardo Patrese, and hired another Italian, Siegfried Stohr, to be his No 2.

Gunter Schmid hired first the Dutchman Jan Lammers and later pop drummer Slim Borgudd from Sweden to drive his ATS cars while Tyrrell had an all-new line-up, Jarier and Daly being replaced by the American Eddie Cheever and European Formula Three Champion Michele Alboreto. Ensign began the season with Marc Surer but later replaced him with the Chilean Eliseo Salazar, who had been able to bring healthy sponsorship to the team; Surer then transferred to Theodore.

Toleman, a familiar name in Formula Two, made its Grand Prix debut in the first European Formula One race of the year, the San Marino Grand Prix at Imola. For drivers, Ted Toleman, owner of a big British transport company, hired Derek Warwick and 1980 European Formula Two Champion Brian Henton. The Toleman team were to be the first users of Pirelli tyres, the Milanese company making their comeback in Grand Prix racing this year after an absence since 1957. Pirelli followed Michelin's example in using radial tyres. At the same time the British tyre manufacturer Avon also returned to Grand Prix racing, after a long absence. At the start of the season Goodyear reconsidered its decision and did in fact take part in the European World Championship races, though they limited

Above
The Lotus they wouldn't let race. The twin-chassis Lotus 88 had a primary chassis (left) to which the front and rear wings were rigidly fixed, and a secondary chassis (right) which carried the engine and a conventional suspension system. The softly-sprung primary chassis could be lowered to achieve greater downforce.

Left
The Lotus 87 was a basically conventional design except that the monocoque was made of honeycombed carbon fibre. Lotus and McLaren were the first makes to use carbon fibre for chassis construction.

Right
Canadian Gilles Villeneuve in a Ferrari 126CK with turbocharged 120° V6 engine at the 1981 Monaco Grand Prix, where the marque achieved its first Formula One turbo engine victory.

CERAMICHE
RAGNO
CERAMICHE
RAGNO
Marlbo
MICHELIN
MICHELIN
Agip
27
27
olivetti

Derek Warwick

themselves to supplying just three teams, Williams, Brabham and Lotus.

The new regulations prescribed a continuous ground clearance of 60mm, and as the rigid skirts could no longer be adjusted vertically, they were rendered useless. But it did not take long for the designers, led by the British, to find a way around this. The distance of the flexible skirts from the track could of course be measured only when the car was motionless, so the designers devised suspension systems which lowered the car once it was moving, so the skirts scraped the track surface as before, and the area between skirt and surface was again sealed off to guarantee perfect ground effect.

Progress had also been made in chassis construction methods, with exotic materials being used more and more frequently to improve the torsional rigidity of chassis still further. Instead of the traditional aluminium plates most of the teams were now using carbon fibre plates for the critical parts of the monocoque. But Lotus and McLaren went a step further, beginning a new era of chassis technology by constructing the entire monocoque from carbon fibre laminates, with Kevlar or graphite fibres incorporated into the construction. These carbon/Kevlar plates were partly covered with Nomex honeycomb which increased the torsional rigidity even more.

At the beginning of the season Michelin came up with a tyre designed to work with the downforce pressures of the classic skirt car. Because downforce had been reduced the tyres now had to bear less weight and consequently no longer attained their optimum operating temperature, resulting in a reduction in road adhesion. For example, Patrick Head believed that the new sidepods of the Williams FW07, as run in the first World Championship race of the season at Long Beach, produced only about a quarter of the previous year's downforce at maximum speed. In the short term the cars had to be refitted with front and tail wings and, although these compensated to some degree for the loss of fully-aerodynamic sidepods, one consequence was increased wind resistance.

The fact that the ground clearance had to be continuous for at least 60mm increased designers' ingenuity, and in the spring Colin Chapman unveiled his Lotus 88, which was a stroke of pure genius. It had two chassis, each completely separate from the other. The rigid primary chassis carried the front, side and rear aerodynamic devices, its task being to transfer the forces produced by the wings to the wheels, which were mounted to it by coil spring/damper units. The secondary chassis was a more or less traditional monocoque containing the driver and mechanicals, and the rest of the suspension system. Like the chassis of the McLaren MP4 this monocoque was made of carbon fibre laminates partly covered with honeycomb. The basic idea of the Lotus 88 was to achieve a skirt effect by means of progressively springing the primary chassis as it (and its wings) sank

Millions of television viewers were able to watch this exciting finish, perhaps the most breathtaking in history, on their screens. In the Spanish Grand Prix at Jarama no fewer than five cars shot past the flag within 1.24 seconds: Gilles Villeneuve's Ferrari 126CK, Jacques Laffite's Talbot-Ligier-Matra JS17, John Watson's McLaren-Ford MP4, Carlos Reutemann's Williams-Ford FW07C and Elio de Angelis's Lotus-Ford 87. The Ferrari's chassis was inferior but the power of its turbo engine meant the 126CK could not be passed on the straights.

Alain Prost

Right
The diminutive Frenchman Alain Prost stands on the Formula One winners' podium for the first time at Dijon.

Below
René Arnoux in the Renault RE30.

Above
Mysterious levers, such as seen in the cockpit of this Osella, were needed for the hydropneumatic jacking system. Out on the circuit the car could run low to the ground, but before going into the pits the driver had to pump it up again.

Right
Mario Andretti at the wheel of the V12 Alfa Romeo 179C at Long Beach in 1981. Between 1979 and 1982 Alfa Romeo ran its own team in Formula One but did not win a single race, and thereafter transferred its support to the Euroracing team.

Brian Hart

to the ground under the influence of the aerodynamic forces.

It was a revolutionary concept, but one whose legality was disputed from its first appearance, at Long Beach. Indeed after only a few laps of practice it was wheeled away, pending the outcome of the inevitable protests.

In the meantime it had become clear to everyone that by lowering the sidepods it was possible to recover some of the downforce which had been lost when the skirts were removed. Hydro-pneumatic or hydraulic units were developed so that the chassis could be lowered while the car was being driven, Brabham designer Gordon Murray being the first to find this solution. At the beginning of the season Murray installed a hydraulic unit in the Brabham BT49C, which raised the car to the required minimum height when it was standing still, but, once moving, it was forced down so that its ground clearance was practically nil. The Brabham system worked on the principle of the hydraulics varying the distance between the suspension arms and the springing medium.

Initially, protests were lodged against the team, especially after Nelson Piquet qualified the BT49C on pole position in Argentina in only its second race. But after the San Marino Grand Prix FISA ruled that the system was not illegal, and by the Belgian Grand Prix discussion of the topic had died away. By this time the

Brabham system, or other methods of lowering the car, had been copied by most of the other teams.

Although Renault had been using a turbocharged 1.5-litre V6 engine in Formula One since 1977, it was not until the end of 1980 that another turbo engine had appeared, when Villeneuve had tried Ferrari's 120° V6 in qualifying for the Italian Grand Prix at Imola. With the Maranello team committed to the new engine for 1981, the question on everyone's lips was, were they going to have to wait as long for their first turbo victory as Renault had?

British engine designer Brian Hart had been working on his own turbocharged four-cylinder unit since 1980, based on a design which had proved successful and reliable in normally-aspirated form in Formula Two. The 1496cc (81 x 72.6mm) Hart Type 415T turbo made its first appearance at Imola in 1981 in the Pirelli-shod Toleman. Using an American Garrett turbocharger it developed a modest 490bhp, but even so proved particularly fragile in its first races, and it was in fact Monza before the Toleman-Hart finished a race. Its questionable potential tended to hinder Pirelli's ability to assess the performance of their tyres.

Ferrari used twin KKK turbochargers on its engines, and although experiments were carried out with BBC's Comprex units, they were only ever used occasionally in practice, and were soon discarded

The 1981 Williams-Ford FW07C, another winning Patrick Head design. The large side-pods, which contained the oil radiators, gave excellent downforce. Even the front wings had small skirts.

in favour of the German components.

As the "hydro-pneumatic jacks" became more efficient during the season, and the chassis lay only a few millimetres above the track surface, a new problem emerged. Because suspension travel had been reduced springing was now unbelievably stiff, and this made the drivers' task almost unbearable, as they were now being subjected to a bone-shaking ordeal. They complained continually of neck, back and spinal pains, and Alan Jones even threatened to give up the whole crazy business before he landed in a wheelchair. The Grand Prix cars were fast becoming glorified versions of unsprung karts.

In spite of these developments the 1981 World Championship was fiercely contested and was all the more exciting as the competitors were so evenly matched. It began at Long Beach and reached its peak with the crowning of the victor at Las Vegas.

The ingenious Ford-powered Williams FW07C took the first two places at both Long Beach and Brazil, Jones beating Reutemann on both occasions. Piquet in the Brabham BT49C was hoisted into first place in Argentina, and again in the first San Marino Grand Prix at Imola where, after lengthy discussions, the new hydraulics were finally declared legal. In Belgium, Reutemann was the victor, from Jacques Laffite in the V12 Matra-engined Talbot-Ligier JS17. The Ferrari 126CK with V6 turbo engine, driven by Gilles Villeneuve, had its first win at Monaco, though only by profiting from the misfortune of two other drivers: Piquet in the Brabham had been a clear leader in the opening stages until he had an accident, and then Jones in the

Williams had to withdraw because his fuel supply had become aerated.

The excitement was electric at the Spanish Grand Prix which followed. From the 14th lap on, Villeneuve held a narrow lead in a five-car train, in spite of the fact that his Ferrari had inferior roadholding to that enjoyed by his rivals. The imposing power of the Italian car's turbo was however sufficient to keep it ahead on the straights, and by making no mistakes on the corners he was able to stay in front. This went on for almost the whole distance, and in a finish unprecedented in racing history, the first five drivers — Villeneuve in the Ferrari 126CK, Laffite in the Talbot-Ligier-Matra JS17, Watson in the McLaren-Ford MP4, Reutemann in the Williams-Ford FW07C and de Angelis in the Lotus-Ford 87 — crossed the line within 1.24 seconds.

Ferrari had to be content with Villeneuve's two victories in 1981. After a long period of rough going Renault finally had a win with the RE30 at the

Important characteristics of Formula One cars of 1981

Make	Alfa Romeo	Cosworth	Ferrari	Hart	Matra	Renault
Model	312	DFV	126 C	415 T	MS 81	EF 1
Cylinder configuration	V12 60°	V8 90°	V6 120° Turbo	4 R, Turbo	V12 60°	V6 90° Turbo
Bore & stroke	78,5 × 51,5	85,7 × 64,8	81 × 48,4	81 × 72,6	79,7 × 50	86 × 42,8
Capacity	2991	2990	1496	1496	2993	1492
Main bearings	7	5	4	5	7	4
Fuel injection	Lucas	Lucas	Lucas	Lucas	Lucas	Kugelfischer
Turbocharger	—	—	2 × KKK	1 × Holset	—	2 × KKK
Ignition	Marelli	Lucas	Marelli	Lucas	Marelli	Marelli
Power (bhp) at (rpm)	520 12 000	490 10 750	550 11 500	490 9500	520 12 000	550 11 500

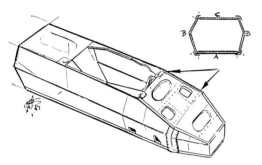

French Grand Prix at Dijon. The race was interrupted by rain, but was then restarted from the point where it had broken off. This race was young Alain Prost's first Grand Prix victory.

McLaren was finally able to put an end to the years of continual crisis when John Watson in the carbon-monocoque MP4-Ford was winner of the British Grand Prix on the fast Silverstone circuit. This was the first victory for the new generation of chassis, of which John Barnard's MP4 was considered to be one of the most advanced. The monocoque of carbon/Kevlar fibres had been constructed by the American firm of Hercules who were specialists in space technology. It was obviously a very strong chassis, for the hotheaded Andrea de Cesaris spun off at least 24 times in 1981 but survived unscathed.

Piquet in the Brabham BT49C won in Germany, then in Austria Laffite drove his Talbot-Ligier JS17 into first place, and in both the Dutch and Italian Grands Prix it was Prost in the Renault turbo who was first across the line. Rain spoilt the Canadian Grand Prix on Notre Dame Island near Montreal but the wiry Laffite notched up his second win of the season in the 12-cylinder Ligier-Matra.

The final Grand Prix was held at Las Vegas, in the World Championship for the first time. The race took place in the giant Caesar's Palace parking area, on a circuit which was very unpopular, being described as little more than a kart track. Piquet, Reutemann and Laffite were all in the running for the World Championship before the race but the winner, after an exhausting race, was Jones in the Williams from Prost, with third going to Bruno Giacomelli in the V12 Alfa Romeo 179C, which now seemed fated never to win a race.

Piquet was World Champion, defeating his Argentinian rival, the Williams driver Carlos Reutemann by just one point. Jones's Las Vegas victory meanwhile enabled him to snatch third place from right under the nose of the Frenchman Laffite.

The World Championship had been extremely exciting but had also aroused a lot of controversy. As the season progressed however a degree of peace and order returned to Formula One, thanks almost entirely to the Concorde Agreement. As well as having served as a peace treaty between the racing teams and FISA, the agreement was also a constitution, prescribing the duties and responsibilities of both parties. Thanks entirely to this piece of paper, Formula One had risen like a phoenix from the ashes during the 1981 season.

The normally-aspirated Ford-Cosworth DFV was again the most successful Formula One engine of the year. Now producing more than 500bhp, the DFV won eight races this year. Renault finished the season with three victories, while Ferrari scored twice in its first turbo year. The 12-cylinder normally-aspirated Matra also won two first places.

During 1981 Renault, Ferrari and Hart had been joined by another turbo engine, the four-cylinder BMW. Produced under the direction of engineer Paul Roche at BMW Motorsport GmbH in Munich, this unit was based on years of experience in Formula Two, the same block having also

Paul Rosche

been thoroughly tested in Group Five Special GT racing in the 1.4-litre BMW 320 saloon. In its Formula One configuration however the engine had 16 valves and KKK turbochargers.

FOCA and Brabham boss Bernie Ecclestone secured exclusive rights to the BMW turbo four, and the Brabham-BMW BT50, with Piquet driving, appeared for the first time during practice for the British Grand Prix at Silverstone. The Brazilian qualified the new car for the second row of the grid, but drove a BT49C-Ford in the race itself. The actual racing debut of the new engine was set for the Italian Grand Prix but it did not race here either, its actual competition debut coming in the South African Grand Prix at Kyalami at the beginning of 1982.

Tyrrell had another unsuccessful season — their fourth in a row — in 1981, and neither Alfa Romeo nor Lotus made it into the first placings either. After the 88 debacle Lotus went back to the more conventional 87 but de Angelis and Mansell played no part in the battle for victory. The Alfa Romeo, despite the potential of its 12-cylinder engine, was plagued by problems and Andretti, too, remained excluded from the top placings.

Renault and Ferrari were gradually notching up more and more turbo victories, indicating that the new engine concept was at last beginning to make a breakthrough. Although still beset with cooling problems it was obvious that success was close at hand, and that the era of the normally-aspirated engine was slowly coming to an end. As far as power was concerned the turbo was clearly superior, as the six-cylinder Renault and Ferrari could achieve at least 560bhp while the best normally-aspirated engines could not produce more than 490 to 530. In 1981 turbo cars started from pole position seven times but in actual races the 3-litre normally-aspirated engines proved to be more reliable.

In October 1981 tests began in Liechtenstein on another new 1.5-litre turbo engine intended for Formula One use. The tuner and engine specialist Max Heidegger, in conjunction with the

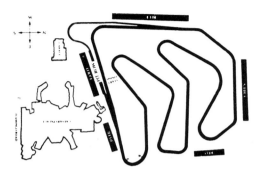

John Watson

Left
At great expense the giant Caesar's Palace parking area in Las Vegas was turned into a 3.64km Grand Prix circuit in 1981.

Centre
John Watson at Buenos Aires in the McLaren-Ford MP4, John Barnard's first carbon fibre monocoque.

Below
Fighting for position shortly after the start of the 1981 French Grand Prix at Dijon. Marc Surer's Theodore TY01 and the McLaren MP4 of Andrea de Cesaris share the lead, with Riccardo Patrese in an Arrows A3, Alan Jones in a Williams FW07C and Eddie Cheever in a Tyrrell 011 close behind.

German engineer Rolf-Peter Marlow, had built a light-alloy engine of unconventional design, in that its six cylinders were angled in the block; two KKK turbochargers were used. Heidegger and Marlow completed this highly expensive project in secret, with a great deal of enthusiasm, on the strength of a verbal understanding Heidegger thought he had with McLaren manager Ron Dennis to the effect that this team would use the in-line six in Grand Prix racing. But as the first prototype of this unusual engine was turning over on the Triesen test-bench, McLaren made it known that they had just reached an agreement with Porsche for the German firm to carry out the design and development of a new V6 turbo engine, to which McLaren would have exclusive rights. This was the TAG-Porsche engine, which would enjoy considerable success. Nothing came of Heidegger's project.

Formula One cars of 1981

Make/model	Chief designer(s)	Engine	Gearbox (speeds)	Chassis	Wheelbase	Track	Tyre make	Dry weight
Alfa Romeo 179 C	Carlo Chiti	Alfa Romeo (V12 60°)	Alfa Romeo (6)	FM	2740	F 1700 R 1500	Michelin	595
Arrows A 3 B	Tony Southgate Dave Wass	Cosworth DFV (V8)	Hewland FGA 400 (5)	FM	2629	F 1854 R 1626	Pirelli	585
ATS HGS (D 5)	Hervé Guilpin	Cosworth DFV (V8)	Hewland FGA 400 (5)	FM	2700	F 1820 R 1690	Avon	585
Brabham BT 49 C	Gordon Murray	Cosworth DFV (V8)	Hewland FGA 400 (5)	FM	2718	F 1702 R 1588	Goodyear	586
Ensign MN 15	Ralph Bellamy Nigel Bennett	Cosworth DFV (V8)	Hewland FGA 400 (5)	FM	2642	F 1753 R 1626	Avon	610
Ferrari 126 CK	Mauro Forghieri Antonio Tomaini	Ferrari 126 (V6 Turbo)	Ferrari (5)	TS	2700—2850	F 1760—1780 R 1680—1650	Michelin	620
Fittipaldi F 8 C	Harvey Postlethwaite	Cosworth DFV (V8)	Hewland FGA 400 (5)	FM	2637	F 1762 R 1829	Michelin	590
Lotus 81 B	Martin Ogilvie Peter Wright	Cosworth DFV (V8)	Hewland FGA 400 (5)	FM	2819	F 1803 R 1676	Michelin	588
Lotus 87	Martin Ogilvie Peter Wright	Cosworth DFV (V8)	Hewland FGA 400 (5)	FM	2705	F 1778 R 1600	Goodyear	587
March 811 RM	Robin Herd	Cosworth DFV (V8)	Hewland FGA 400 (5)	FM	2692	F 1727 R 1575	Avon	590
McLaren MP 4	John Barnard	Cosworth DFV (V8)	Hewland FGA 400 (5/6)	FM	2642	F 1727 R 1676	Michelin	585
Osella FA 1 B	Enzo Osella Giorgio Stirano	Cosworth DFV (V8)	Hewland FGA 400 (5)	FM	2700	F 1715 R 1650	Michelin	600
Renault RE 20 B	Michel Têtu	Renault-Gordini EF 1 (V6 Turbo)	Hewland FGA 400 (5)	FM	2860	F 1720 R 1630	Michelin	615
Renault RE 30	Michel Têtu	Renault-Gordini EF 1 (V6 Turbo)	Hewland FGA 400 (5)	FM	2730	F 1740 R 1630	Michelin	600
Talbot-Ligier JS 17	Michel Beaujon	Matra MS 81 (V12)	Hewland FGB 400 (5)	FM	2780	F 1710 R 1678	Michelin	585
Theodore TY 01	Tony Southgate	Cosworth DFV (V8)	Hewland FGA 400 (5)	FM	2743	F 1753 R 1600	Avon	589
Toleman TG 181	Rory Byrne John Gentry	Hart 415 T (4 cyl Turbo)	Hewland FGB 400 (5)	FM	2692	F 1715 R 1676	Pirelli	592
Tyrrell 010	Maurice Phillippe	Cosworth DFV (V8)	Hewland FGA 400 (5)	FM	2692	F 1702 R 1588	Avon	590
Tyrrell 011	Maurice Phillippe	Cosworth DFV (V8)	Hewland FGA 400 (5)	FM	2692	F 1727 R 1575	Avon	589
Williams FW 07 C	Patrick Head	Cosworth DFV (V8)	Hewland FGA 400 (5)	FM	2692	F 1727 R 1600	Goodyear	587

Chassis construction: FM = full monocoque; TS = tubular frame with stressed skins.

A Bumpy Ride for the Drivers

Huge amounts of downforce and rock-hard suspensions present the drivers with even more problems. Keke Rosberg is World Champion after winning only one race.

Quarrelling, deception and boycotts were the trademarks of 1982, particularly for the first few races. It was only after the Belgian Grand Prix that FISA was able to lay down clear lines acceptable to all parties, and a degree of stability returned.

The other ongoing talking-point of the season was the increased downforce built into the latest "ground effects" designs. The infamous hydraulic jacks were abandoned but new sidepod designs incorporating the latest skirt regulations brought a further escalation in downforce, and horrendous cornering forces of up to 4g were registered during the season. Virtually every team now designed its sidepods in conjunction with research programmes in the wind-tunnel, which accelerated progress towards optimum aerodynamic efficiency.

Although FISA permitted skirts to be used their size was limited, and they had to be fixed firmly onto vertical side plates. No vertical movement was now permitted. The skirts now scraped the track surface and were made primarily of polyurethane, and the portion that actually scraped the ground was manufactured from strips of high-grade hardwood. But experience showed that the more efficient the ground effects incorporated in a design became, the more it was at the mercy of disturbing influences as, for example, when a skirt temporarily lifted from the ground. Even when everything was going according to plan the drivers' task became a scarcely endurable ordeal as suspension systems were modified to reduce ground clearance to around 25mm. The Formula One cars of 1982 were screwed down so hard that virtually the only vertical movement was that which could be provided by the tyres. It was no surprise that drivers complained increasingly of back and neck pains from the tremendous forces they were expected to subject their bodies to. As the centrifugal force on corners climbed closer to the limits of human endurance, the clamour for a drastic reduction in ground effects became correspondingly louder.

As a means of assisting those teams which were still relying on normally-aspirated engines, now clearly inferior in terms of power output, FISA reduced the minimum weight for Formula One cars in 1982 by about five kilograms, so that a car now had to weigh at least 580kg with oil and water but without fuel. It was possible to build a normally aspirated

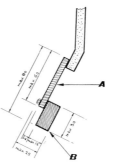

Below
The Williams water ruse. Before the weight check a mechanic fills the car with "brake water" to bring the car up to the prescribed limit.

Left
This was how skirts had to be built after 1982. A flexible piece (A) had to be fixed to the side of the body (dotted area), with a sliding plate (B) attached below.

Below
Nelson Piquet collapsed from exhaustion on the podium after the 1982 Brazilian Grand Prix. Keke Rosberg (second) appears to be giving him some friendly encouragement. Third man Alain Prost is on the right.

car down to this limit, but the turbo designs, with the extra weight required for the turbochargers themselves as well as intercoolers, could not approach the minimum. The weight limit was introduced to prolong the life of the 3-litre engines in the face of the increasing turbo threat.

The weight limit became a preoccupation of the British designers, who came up with a novel means of circumventing the rules. In 1981 Williams, Brabham and Lotus had all adopted the practice of "soaking the car in oil" before the weigh-in: the engine and gearbox were overfilled with oil, far beyond the levels of driveability, but enough to bring them up to the weight limit.

The ploy adopted in 1982 by the same three teams, and by Arrows and McLaren as well, was "water-cooled brakes". The 1982 regulations allowed for any cooling liquid used during a race to be topped up before the weight was checked. The British teams rigged up water containers, with plastic tubes leading to the brakes — which of course did not benefit in the slightest from being cooled by water. During practice or the race the water reservoirs were empty, and the cars were thus lighter; before the weigh-in they were refilled so that even a car that was

actually under weight now equalled the prescribed limit of 580kg.

It didn't take FISA long to react to this ruse. Nelson Piquet in a Brabham and Keke Rosberg in a Williams, first and second across the line in the Brazilian Grand Prix, were disqualified as a result of protests from Ferrari and Renault, who claimed the British cars were in fact under weight. In protest at the FISA ruling the FOCA teams boycotted the San Marino Grand Prix, and it was only at the next race, in Belgium, that the rules were clarified and the practice of water-cooling brakes outlawed.

In the late autumn of 1981 Niki Lauda had made the sensational announcement that, after a break of two years, he was returning to Grand Prix racing. Lauda Air, which the double World Champion had founded some years earlier, was in difficulties and the climate was right for Lauda to reconsider an offer of millions of dollars from his sponsor, Marlboro, for his comeback. The Austrian signed a contract with McLaren, replacing Andrea de Cesaris who had left at the end of 1981 with a couple of dozen spins and a corresponding number of dented cars in his wake. The young Roman was taken on by Alfa, leaving Lauda to drive the McLaren MP4 alongside John Watson.

Alan Jones had meanwhile announced his decision to quit Formula One in favour of returning to Australia, and to replace him Frank Williams took on Keke Rosberg from Fittipaldi. Then, after taking part in the South African and Brazilian Grands Prix, Carlos Reutemann packed his bags and went home to Argentina. His place was taken by Mario Andretti at Long Beach, and later by Derek Daly. After a disappointing season with Alfa Romeo in 1981 Andretti, the 1978 World Champion, had found himself without the possibility of joining a leading team and decided as a consequence to take his leave of Formula One so he could devote his energies to the American CART Indycar series. Despite this decision Andretti continued to deputise on various Formula One teams and actually took part in three Grands Prix in 1982.

Ferrari changed only its brand of tyres: after four Michelin seasons they transferred back to Goodyear. The Maranello team retained both Gilles Villeneuve and Didier Pironi in 1982, while Lotus kept Elio de Angelis and Nigel Mansell, and the Renault team of René Arnoux and Alain Prost was also unchanged. Brabham however placed the former Arrows driver Riccardo Patrese alongside Nelson Piquet, while at Talbot-Ligier the American Eddie Cheever, who had actually grown up in Rome, became Jacques Laffite's new team-mate.

Alfa Romeo re-hired Bruno Giacomelli to drive their V12, while work proceeded at Autodelta in Milan on the new turbocharged V8 engine. Although introduced in 1980, this motor had yet to be raced, and it was now being developed by former Ligier engineer Gérard Ducarouge.

Jean-Pierre Jarier and Formula Two graduate Riccardo Paletti were the drivers at the Turin-based Osella team, while Teddy Yip's Theodore organisation at first took on Derek Daly and then, after the Irishman went to Williams when Reutemann retired, the little Dutchman

Enzo Osella

Jan Lammers; later in the season Geoff Lees and finally Formula Three driver Tommy Byrne were lured into the Theodore seat. Derek Warwick remained with the Toleman team, which was again using the Hart turbo engine, but Brian Henton was replaced by Italian Formula Two driver Teo Fabi. Michele Alboreto remained at Tyrrell while the second car was shared by Henton and the Swedish driver Slim Borgudd. Emerson Fittipaldi's team was going through a bad patch and he cut back to campaigning only one car, which was driven by his countryman

Chico Serra. The Arrows team went into the new season with the Swiss driver Marc Surer and Italian Formula Three driver Mauro Baldi, while Englishman Mo Nunn's little Ensign team took on the

Teo Fabi

Colombian Roberto Guerrero. Jochen Mass returned to Formula One to drive for March, together with the Brazilian Raul Boesel, while the German ATS team, now based in England, took on the Chilean Eliseo Salazar and the German touring-car and Formula Three driver Manfred Winkelhock.

On the engine front, turbocharged units played more and more part in 1982, but although their performance remained superior they continued to be very prone to faults, particularly temperature problems. Renault and Hart were most susceptible in this area, though the six-cylinder Ferrari engine had made excellent progress and was now very reliable.

After remaining a secret for months, it leaked out in the middle of 1982 that Ferrari was using water-injection on the V6. This idea, well-known in the aviation industry, had been developed over the

Riccardo Patrese in a Brabham-Ford BT49C, Didier Pironi in a Ferrari 126C2 and Andrea de Cesaris in an Alfa Romeo 182 dispute the lead in the 1982 Monaco Grand Prix. After a turbulent finale Riccardo Patrese was the surprise winner.

Manfred Winkelhock

second half of 1981 in conjunction with the Agip fuel company. In the new system, water was taken from a 20-litre water container built into the Ferrari's monocoque chassis, mixed with the fuel in a special device and then injected into the exhaust. This absorbed heat from the environment and slightly reduced the exhaust temperatures, which increased the life of the materials. Following Ferrari's lead, Renault also adopted a water-injection system later in the year. While these engine developments were continuing, Ferrari hired the Englishman Harvey Postlethwaite to attend to improvements in chassis design.

The performance of the turbo engines continued to improve, with Ferrari and Renault now achieving 600bhp and Hart about 40bhp less. The normally-aspirated engines on the other hand remained at a maximum of 490 to 530bhp.

In the meantime intensive work was being done by BMW Motorsport GmbH on their turbocharged four-cylinder engine, which made its first racing appearance at the South African Grand Prix in the new Brabham BT50 driven by Piquet and Patrese. The 1499cc (89.2 x 60mm) engine used a KKK turbocharger and a fully electronic Bosch-Motronic fuel-injection system.

The FOCA teams continued to oppose the advance of the turbo motors, which represented a considerable escalation of costs. Again and again the British designers, with Cosworth in the forefront, tried to fight the turbo. And although Brabham had access to turbo power they were reluctant to make the commitment, and Ecclestone delayed making the switch. The Brabham-BMW was entered at Kyalami but DFV-powered cars were run in the following races, which allowed no further development of the BMW engine. Eventually BMW laid down an ultimatum at the Belgian Grand Prix — either Brabham changed over to the BMW engines completely, or the contract would be dissolved.

The turbo cars were clearly superior on the straights but their advantage was reduced on stretches of circuit with a lot of corners because, in spite of the fact that

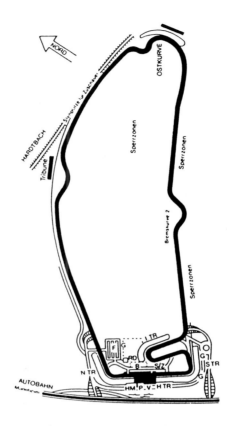

a great deal of progress had been made towards reducing turbo lag, the handicap had still not been completely eliminated.

Even lighter materials were used in the construction of Grand Prix cars this year, particularly when water-cooled brakes were being used. Using conventional materials such as steel, aluminium, titanium or magnesium, a well-designed car with a normally-aspirated engine (Ford-Cosworth, Alfa Romeo or Matra) could be built very close to the 580kg limit, but by the use of more exotic materials in those parts of the car which had to bear light to medium loads the weight could be reduced to 520kg. Such materials had been used for decades in the construction of aircraft and spacecraft, but their application to racing cars as a substitute for the more traditional aluminium was new — but fast increasing.

The new construction method consisted principally of a honeycomb structure of Nomex or aluminium, enclosed in a sandwich of aluminium or, more often, composite materials made from carbon or Kevlar fibres, or a combination of both. These were distributed in an irregular pattern on the surface and then glued together with a resin binder.

The classic aluminium sheet monocoque, which had been used for two decades, had in fact been abandoned by all Formula One teams by 1982. Most designers were working on the aluminium sandwich form, a type of construction pioneered in Formula One by the Wolf WR9 designed by Dr Harvey Postlethwaite. A chassis built of honeycomb plates consisted basically of about seven transverse laminates on top of which longitudinal plates were riveted, with additional strengthening around the cockpit area, where the monocoque tended to distort. This strengthening was achieved with the help of carbon laminates which were also used for strengthening other critical parts. A monocoque built in this way was both lighter than the traditional aluminium structure and had greater torsional rigidity.

Several teams went one step further in the search for a material for chassis construction and used a carbon fibre laminate enriched with Kevlar fibres, the teams in question being McLaren, Lotus, Alfa Romeo and, at the end of the season, Toleman. On the Lotus the honeycomb was made of Nomex, on the Alfa Romeo and Toleman of aluminium. Monocoques constructed in this way could be up to 40% lighter than a chassis made from an aluminium sandwich: a composite tub weighed about 20kg while an aluminium sandwich tipped the scales at 35kg. But these modern constructions were extremely expensive: Lotus for example had to pay about $1700 per monocoque for materials, and the manufacturing costs were very high too. Expensive new edging machines were required for bending the honeycomb structures, and a special refrigerator was needed during manufacture of the laminates as the carbon fibre mats had to be stored at minus 20 degrees. Then after the carbon fibre parts had been shaped, with the help of a mould, the product had to be baked in an oven for about five hours. All this

meant monocoques could no longer be produced in a firm's own workshops; the work had to be done by firms specialising in aircraft construction, and this in turn meant a lengthening of supply times.

Carbon fibre was also being used for components other than the chassis. The material was adapted for use on wings, which had previously been made of aluminium ribs with aluminium plates on top. In another trend modern Kevlar fibres were used for the manufacture of bodies, and by 1982 fibreglass had been entirely superseded for this application. The Kevlar fibre laminates were produced in very thin sheets, strengthened at critical points with one-directional laminates but with all the fibres laid parallel to the direction of force for maximum strength.

Since the late seventies Brabham, in collaboration with Dunlop, AP-Lockheed and Ferodo, had been experimenting with carbon fibre brake discs, and in 1982 other firms also attempted this form of construction. One was the Italian Brembo company, who worked in conjunction with Ferrari. The advantage of carbon fibre discs was the gain in mass of more than 20kg per braking system. In their early stages of development carbon fibre brakes would last for only 20 minutes' racing, so their use was restricted to qualifying. But within a few years, in spite of the incredible expense, they were being used in actual races.

A new tactic introduced into Formula

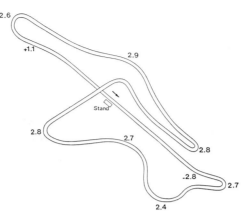

One racing in 1982 was to start a race with the fuel tanks only half-filled, knowing that a refuelling stop would be needed but also that the car would be faster until then. The idea was initiated at the British Grand Prix by Brabham designer Gordon Murray, though in fact the Brabham-BMW retired from the Silverstone race before its planned stop, so it was at the German Grand Prix that the system was first used, and its advantages properly determined. By starting a race with only about 120 litres of fuel, instead of the normal amount of about 250 litres, a car not only had the advantage of carrying less weight, but as a consequence of this could use softer-compound tyres. The fact that these would not last more than half of the race did not matter, as the car had to stop for its fuel anyway. At about half-distance in

the race the car stopped at the pits, the tyres were changed and it was refuelled for the remainder of the race, using pressurised systems familiar from Indianapolis. All this took a crew of 13, eight of them being responsible for changing the tyres (two per wheel).

Two additional aerodynamic refinements were introduced into Formula One racing in 1982. Gearboxes were made smaller to minimise the affect on airflow through the sidepods, and a new concept in suspension design was developed. This was the "pullrod" system, first used by Gordon Murray on the front of the Brabham BT44 in 1974. In this system the upper eye of the damper unit was connected to the chassis, with the lower eye linked by two tubes, on one side to the monocoque and on the other to the extreme end of the steering arm. The geometry of these tubes produced a progressive suspension effect. The first time Murray used the pullrod system on the rear as well as the front was for the Brabham BT49, and a number of other designers soon started using the same idea.

The pattern for this divisive Formula One season was set on the eve of the

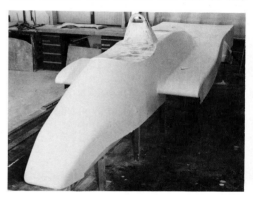

Above
The bare plastic bodyshell of the Talbot-Ligier JS19.

Left
A Talbot-Ligier JS19, with Matra V12 engine, under construction. From left, Eddie Cheever, Jean-Pierre Jabouille and Jacques Laffite, with the technicians J-P Paoli and J-C Guanard.

Top
At the height of the "ground effects" era a team of French doctors carried out a scientific experiment on the 3km Ferrari test track at Fiorano near Maranello to discover the effects of centrifugal force on the human body. This sketch shows the centrifugal forces obtained on each corner, given in g. On the fastest curve they reached a maximum of 2.9g.

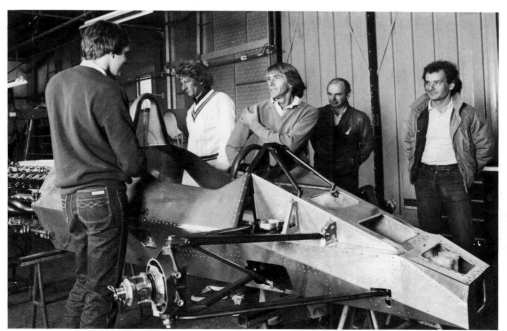

South African Grand Prix when the drivers suddenly went on strike. At issue was FISA's newly-created "super-licence" system. Before being issued with this licence, which they needed to compete in Grands Prix, drivers were expected to sign a declaration which they saw as an unacceptable limitation of their personal freedom. FISA promised to reconsider the matter, but in the meantime the drivers were heavily fined for refusing to go out to practice. The fines were ultimately paid by the teams.

Kyalami's altitude of almost 1800 metres meant the turbo cars dominated practice, for they were at less of a disadvantage in the thin air than were the cars with normally-aspirated engines. The new Brabham BT50s with four-cylinder BMW turbo engines made their debut in this race but it was René Arnoux in the Renault who made the early running, from Nelson Piquet in one of the Brabham-BMWs, Gilles Villeneuve in a Ferrari, Riccardo Patrese in the other Brabham-BMW, Alain Prost in the second Renault, Didier Pironi in the second Ferrari and Keke Rosberg in the Williams-Ford; the six leading positions were held by turbo cars. Mechanical problems however meant that most of the turbo competitors did not last out the race, though one of them was winner, Prost's Renault RE30 leading Carlos Reutemann in the Williams-Ford FW07C and Arnoux in the other Renault across the line.

The turbos also filled the front row of the Brazilian Grand Prix grid, and Nelson Piquet won the race. This time however he was driving the Brabham-Ford BT49D rather than the Brabham-BMW turbo, as the German engine had proved so troublesome that the Brabham team had decided to enter the normally-aspirated machine in its place. But after the race Renault and Ferrari lodged protests against the brake water-cooling of the first two cars, Piquet's Brabham and Rosberg's Williams, and following a meeting of the stewards they were both disqualified and the race awarded to Prost.

The Brazilian Grand Prix was also Carlos Reutemann's last race. He had competed in his first Formula One race in 1971, and after his retirement occasionally took part in rallies in Argentina.

Long Beach was another circuit which suited the normally-aspirated cars better, and Niki Lauda, driving the carbon-fibre McLaren-Ford MP4 in what was only his third race since his comeback, was a surprise winner.

But before the next race, the San Marino Grand Prix at Imola, the arguments between the predominantly British FOCA teams and the other entrants flared up again, with the FOCA teams announcing that they would boycott the Italian race as a protest against the disqualification of Piquet and Rosberg in Brazil. FOCA wanted to have water-cooled brakes admitted to bring the Ford-Cosworth-powered cars closer to competitiveness with the turbocharged opposition. Tyrrell, although a member of FOCA, competed in the race in deference to the wishes of their Italian sponsor.

The Finn Keke Rosberg (left) drove a Williams-Ford FW08 (below) to victory in the 1982 World Championship, though he won only one Grand Prix.

Keke Rosberg

In spite of having only 14 starters, it was an exciting race in front of 70,000 spectators. The public went wild with excitement when the Ferrari 126C2s took the first two places, Pironi winning from Villeneuve. But there was bitterness between the Ferrari team-mates, as Villeneuve claimed that although it had been agreed beforehand that he should win, Pironi prevented him from doing so.

Between the San Marino and Belgian Grands Prix FISA held a meeting, at which it was agreed that water-cooled brakes should be banned. Brabham originally entered the Brabham BT49 with Ford engine for the Zolder race, but then came the BMW ultimatum and they ran the turbo-powered BT50 instead. Another indication of the general British opposition to the use of the turbos came from Ken Tyrrell, who lodged an official protest questioning their legality, but the authorities did not take it seriously and nothing came of it.

A degree of stability finally returned with the Belgian Grand Prix but the event was overshadowed by a tragic practice accident. During the second qualifying session Gilles Villeneuve in the Ferrari 126C crested a rise to find the slow-moving March 821 of Jochen Mass, on its slowing-down lap, in his path. Villeneuve spotted the March too late to

The turbocharged 120° V6 Ferrari 126C2 was the last alloy semi-monocoque design produced at Maranello. With it Ferrari won the 1982 Formula One World Manufacturers' Championship.

take any avoiding action and an accident was unavoidable. The Ferrari cartwheeled over the March and on down the track, and the young Canadian died in the early hours of the evening. Ferrari consequently withdrew Pironi's entry.

The race was dominated by the cars with normally-aspirated engines, John Watson in a McLaren-Ford MP4B winning from Rosberg in a Williams-Ford FW08, which was making its debut, and Lauda in the other McLaren. After the race however Lauda's car was found to be 1.4kg under weight and was excluded from the placings.

The Monaco Grand Prix was particularly exciting. It started to rain during the final laps which created confusion until, finally, Riccardo Patrese in the Brabham-Ford BT49 emerged victor. It was the Padua man's first World Championship race win.

The next Grand Prix, held on a street circuit in the centre of Detroit, the automobile capital of America, was a departure from the norm, for the entire circuit was lined with concrete walls and catchfencing. The course, which was normally used by daily traffic, was not only very twisty, but both bumpy and

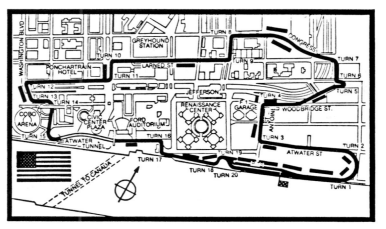

A Formula One Grand Prix was held on a 4.023km-course around the Renaissance Centre in Detroit, the American automobile capital, for the first time in 1982.

Riccardo Patrese

slippery as well. The turbo cars had no success here either, and Nelson Piquet in the Brabham-BMW turbo didn't even qualify, after various technical problems, and was forced to watch the race as a spectator. Watson in the McLaren-Ford MP4 won again with Eddie Cheever in the V12 Matra-powered Talbot-Ligier JS17B second and Pironi in the first turbo car, the Ferrari 126C2, third.

Piquet had full compensation for his sensational Detroit setback in the Canadian Grand Prix a week later when he took the Brabham-BMW to its first victory. His team-mate Riccardo Patrese, who was still driving the normally-aspirated Brabham-Ford at this stage, was second. Unfortunately however this race, too, was overshadowed by tragedy. At the

start, pole man Didier Pironi in the Ferrari failed to get away and although most of the field safely avoided him, Riccardo Paletti in the V12 Alfa Romeo-powered Osella FA1C, starting from the second to last row, did not see the stationary Ferrari until it was too late and drove at full speed straight into Pironi's rear wing. Pironi was unhurt but Paletti was killed instantly.

The turbo cars were back on top in the Dutch Grand Prix when Pironi came in ahead of Piquet, but they suffered another reversal in the British Grand Prix at Brands Hatch when Niki Lauda in the McLaren-Ford was winner once again. Pironi was second with his countryman Patrick Tambay, who had been brought onto the Ferrari team as replacement for

Most of the British FOCA teams boycotted the 1982 San Marino Grand Prix at Imola as a protest against the disqualification of Piquet and Rosberg from the Brazilian Grand Prix. The race was still held, though with only 14 starters. The spectators, sensing a Ferrari victory, came in their hordes and saw the Ferrari 126C2s dominate, with Pironi (behind in this picture) winning from Villeneuve.

Elio De Angelis

Michele Alboreto

René Arnoux and his Renault on their way to winning the 1982 Italian Grand Prix at Monza, relegating the Ferraris of Tambay and Andretti to second and third places. This photograph illustrates how the skirts ''seal'' the car against the racetrack.

Gilles Villeneuve, third.

Renault finally achieved a 1-2 result, with Arnoux in first place and Prost second, in the French Grand Prix at Le Castellet, but their success was clouded by internal politics: Prost, who was much better placed in the World Championship, was meant to win but Arnoux did not keep to team orders. As a result of his actions here Arnoux fell out of favour with the Renault management.

By this point in the season Didier Pironi had taken the lead in the World Championship, by nine points from Watson. In qualifying for the next race, the German Grand Prix at Hockenheim, the Ferrari driver was fastest on the Friday and, when it rained on the Saturday, was assured of retaining pole position for the race. But during a late practice session he was involved in a collision with Prost's Renault which sent the Ferrari rolling end over end. Pironi was trapped in the wreckage and had to be cut free before he could be rushed to hospital. There it was found that he had complicated leg injuries, serious enough in fact to bring his Formula One career to an abrupt end, for it took years for his injuries to heal. The Championship had been within his grasp at Hockenheim, his chances of success the more probable in view of the reliability the Ferrari 126C2 had been showing throughout the season.

In spite of these events Ferrari did win the German Grand Prix when Tambay, who had been unable to find a Formula One drive at the beginning of the season, had his first Grand Prix success. This was the first race in which the Brabham team started with half-full tanks but both Piquet and Patrese were forced to retire before any conclusion could be reached, Piquet in a collision with Salazar and Patrese with engine trouble.

Patrick Tambay

There was another change of fortunes in Austria, where the turbos had to accept defeat once more, being smitten with a variety of problems on the fast Osterreichring. But it was an exciting finish nevertheless. Elio de Angelis in the Lotus-Ford 91 crossed the line ahead of the Finn Keke Rosberg in the Williams-Ford FW08 who, over the last laps, had surged powerfully through the field. This was de Angelis's first visit to the Formula One winner's podium, and Rosberg had his turn in the next race, the Swiss Grand Prix at Dijon. This Burgundy win put the Finn into the Championship lead. The race was another bad one for the turbo cars, the single Ferrari entry failing to start as Tambay was suffering from severe back pains caused by the rock-hard suspension systems of the modern wing cars.

Before the Italian Grand Prix, Ferrari invited Mario Andretti back onto the team as a replacement for the badly injured Pironi and he promptly qualified the 126C2 on pole position — to the intense delight of the *tifosi,* who sensed another success for their favourite marque. But it was not to be, for Arnoux was winner for Renault, relegating Tambay and Andretti in the Ferraris to second and third.

The season ended once again in Nevada, with the Las Vegas Grand Prix on its controversial circuit laid out in the giant parking area and rimmed with concrete walls. The many hairpin bends on the circuit did not suit the turbo cars,

and winner was the Milanese driver Michele Alboreto, at the wheel of a Ford-powered Tyrrell 011. This was not only the first Grand Prix success for the talented Alboreto, but also the first for the Tyrrell team since 1978.

Keke Rosberg was now confirmed as the 1982 World Champion. Although he had won just one race this was not an unprecedented achievement, for Mike Hawthorn's 1958 Championship had also been taken with just one race win. Didier Pironi was second in the World Championship, just five points behind the winner, and John Watson picked up the same number of points.

The Championship had eluded the Ferrari drivers but the Maranello constructor could console itself with victory in the World Manufacturers' Championship, even though the team had missed both the Belgian and Swiss rounds. It was the first time that a team with turbo engines had been successful in this Championship. But in spite of winning the Manufacturers' title, Ferrari had had a catastrophic season in 1982, which saw both Gilles Villeneuve and Didier Pironi ending their careers.

The turbocharged engines had won eight Grands Prix in 1982, but the normally-aspirated engines had achieved the same score.

During the 1982 season calls for improved safety had become increasingly insistent. The tremendous downforce of the wing cars had increased the g forces at maximum speed by more than two tonnes and had enabled cornering speeds to reach prohibitive rates, while the solid suspension systems were subjecting drivers to a bone-shaking torture that was almost unbearable. The drivers were also vulnerable to more serious injuries in the event of an accident because the cockpits had been pushed so far forward that the pedals were ahead of the front axle. During practice in South Africa Marc Surer had had a serious accident in his Arrows and fractured several bones in his legs and feet. FISA had to act to control these dangerous trends, and they listened carefully to pleas for the banning of wing cars by means of requiring that undersides be flat.

At the end of the year, when the teams were already busy at Le Castellet testing the new models for 1983, the sad news arrived from England that Anthony Colin Bruce Chapman, one of the most brilliant designers in racing history, had died suddenly of a heart attack on December 16th, at the age of 54. Again and again over the years the founder and boss of Lotus had come up with ingenious inventions which had revolutionized racing car construction.

Formula One cars of 1982

Make/model	Chief designer(s)	Engine	Gearbox (speeds)	Chassis	Wheelbase	Track	Tyre make	Dry weight
Alfa Romeo 182	Gérard Ducarouge	Alfa Romeo (V12 60°)	Alfa Romeo (5/6)	C	2720	F 1800 R 1670	Michelin	585
Arrows A 4	Dave Wass	Cosworth DFV (V8)	Hewland FGA 400 (5)	A	2705	F 1778 R 1626	Pirelli	580
ATS D 5	Hervé Guilpin Tim Wardrop	Cosworth DFV (V8)	Hewland FGA 400 (5)	A	2718	F 1826 R 1727	Michelin	585
Brabham BT 49 D	Gordon Murray	Cosworth DFV (V8)	Hewland FGA 400 (5)	A	2718	F 1727 R 1600	Goodyear	580
Brabham BT 50	Gordon Murray	BMW M 12/13 (4 cyl Turbo)	Brabham-Hewland (5)	A	2769	F 1753 R 1600	Goodyear	585
Ensign N 181	Nigel Bennett	Cosworth DFV (V8)	Hewland FGA 400 (5)	CA	2692	F 1727 R 1600	Michelin	580
Ferrari 126 C2	Harvey Postlethwaite	Ferrari 126 (V6 Turbo)	Ferrari (5)	A	Trans. 2650 Long. 2800	F 1750 R 1650	Goodyear	582
Fittipaldi F 8 D	Richard Divila	Cosworth DFV (V8)	Hewland FGA 400 (5)	A	2637	F 1880 R 1727	Pirelli	585
Lotus 87 B	Martin Ogilvie Peter Wright	Cosworth DFV (V8)	Hewland FGA 400 (5)	CK	2705	F 1778 R 1600	Goodyear	587
Lotus 91	Martin Ogilvie Colin Chapman	Cosworth DFV (V8)	Lotus-Hewland (5)	CK	2748—2849	F 1883 R 1701	Goodyear	580
March 821	Adrian Reynard	Cosworth DFV (V8)	Hewland FGA 400 (5)	A	2781	F 1734 R 1581	Avon	585
McLaren MP 4 B	John Barnard	Cosworth DFV (V8)	McLaren-Hewland (5/6)	C	2692	F 1816 R 1626	Michelin	580
Osella FA 1 C	Enzo Osella Hervé Guilpin	Cosworth DFV (V8)	Hewland FGA 400 (5)	A	2720	F 1850 R 1705	Pirelli	580
Renault RE 30 B	Michel Têtu	Renault-Gordini EF 1 (V6 Turbo)	Renault-Hewland (5)	A	2730	F 1740 R 1630	Michelin	585
Talbot-Ligier JS 17 B	Michel Beaujon	Matra MS 81 (V12 60°)	Hewland FGB 400 (5)	A	2780	F 1710 R 1678	Michelin	585
Talbot-Ligier JS 19	Michel Beaujon Jean-Pierre Jabouille	Matra MS 81 (V12 60°)	Talbot-Ligier/Hewland (5)	A	2700	F 1800 R 1600	Michelin	590
Theodore TY 01/02	Tony Southgate	Cosworth DFV (V8)	Hewland FGA 400 (5)	A	2667	F 1778 R 1600	Goodyear	585
Toleman TG 181	Rory Byrne	Hart 415 T (4 cyl Turbo)	Hewland FGB 400 (5)	A	2692	F 1765 R 1708	Pirelli	590
Tyrrell 011	Maurice Phillippe	Cosworth DFV (V8)	Hewland FGA 400 (5)	A	2769	F 1727 R 1626	Goodyear	580
Williams FW 07 C	Patrick Head	Cosworth DFV (V8)	Hewland FGA 400 (5)	A	2692	F 1727 R 1600	Goodyear	589
Williams FW 08	Patrick Head	Cosworth DFV (V8)	Hewland FGA 400 (5)	A	2591	F 1803 R 1613	Goodyear	580

Chassis construction: A = alloy monocoque; C = carbon-fibre monocoque; CA = carbon-fibre alloy monocoque; CK = Kevlar/carbon-fibre monocoque

Everyone Goes Turbo

Piquet in the Brabham-BMW becomes the first driver of a turbo car to win the World Championship. Even more turbo engines appear — Honda and TAG-Porsche. The Ford-Cosworth V8's 155th, and last, Grand Prix victory.

After the arguments, boycotts and deception of the 1980–82 period, and the power struggles between FISA and FOCA, 1983 was at last a year free of controversy. FOCA had finally given up its fight against the turbo engines and the escalation of costs that would accompany their development, and the turbos were able to continue their triumphal march unimpeded. The 1983 season was also spared any serious accidents.

There were also major rule changes for 1983, designed to bring to an end the era of the ground effects wing cars. The new regulations required the underside of Grand Prix cars between the outer extremities of the front and rear tyres to be flat, which resulted in a dramatic decrease in downforce, in spite of a return to larger front and rear wings. But the large sidepods which, by the end of 1982, had increased the g force by a good two tonnes at maximum speed, disappeared. Gone too were the rock-hard suspension systems, so that the cars became much more "user friendly". The drivers' back and neck pains were a thing of the past.

The reduction of downforce meant that corners were no longer taken at such high speeds, which required earlier braking to get the speed down to the reduced figures now required. Drivers had become little more than helpless "passengers" in their cockpits in the ground effects era, but now had to use all their driving skills once again.

In another important decision made before the 1983 season the minimum weight of Formula One cars was further reduced, from 575 to 540kg. Now that carbon was being used in chassis construction designers could attain this limit without having to sacrifice any of the car's strength.

In the second half of 1982 the Brabham team had demonstrated the benefits to be gained in a race by making lightning fuel and tyre stops. All going well, these could take between nine and 15 seconds, and sufficient time could frequently be saved to win the race. But in 1983 every other team followed suit and with the fuel stops no longer providing any advantage they would be banned in 1984.

More turbo engines made their appearance this year. Alfa Romeo's 1497cc (74 x 43.5mm) 90° V8 unit with Avio turbochargers had appeared briefly during practice for the 1982 Italian Grand Prix, and was raced from the beginning of the 1983 season. At the Geneva Motor

Show in March 1983 TAG (Techniques d'Avant Garde), a firm owned by Saudi Arabian financier Mansour Ojjeh,

Mansour Ojjeh

unveiled its V6 turbo engine which it had commissioned Porsche to develop and build for the exclusive use of the McLaren team. The 1498cc (82 x 47.3mm) engine, an 80° V6, was built at Porsche's Weissach engineering facility under the direction of Hans Mezger. The McLaren-TAG-Porsche raced for the first time in Niki Lauda's hands in the Dutch Grand Prix.

Hans Mezger

Also on view at the Geneva Show was a second 80° turbo V6 engine, developed by Honda from their successful Formula Two unit. The Honda used Ihi turbochargers, though its cylinder dimensions were kept secret. This engine was raced in a World Championship event for the first time in the British Grand Prix, fitted to the Spirit 201 driven by the young Swede Stefan Johansson. This was only a temporary arrangement however, the Japanese firm later coming to an arrangement for the supply of its engines to Williams only.

Since Renault had first used the V6 turbo in 1977 they had continually developed and improved it but until now had always retained it for use in their own cars. In 1983 however they made their engines available to Lotus as well. The Ford-Cosworth DFV, so successful since 1967, was now struggling, and even those teams which had remained loyal to it for years — such as McLaren, Lotus, Williams and ATS — took the turbo option in 1983. The Ligier team, on the other hand, had

now split with Talbot and returned to the Ford engine.

At the end of 1982 the Alfa Romeo factory withdrew from Formula One, handing all its cars and equipment over to the Formula Three racing stable which Gianpaolo Pavanello ran from a base at Senago near Milan. The private team was renamed Euroracing, and in fact enjoyed support from Alfa Romeo in its Formula One endeavours, and operations continued to be directed by the Frenchman Gérard Ducarouge. The Alfas ran with the new V8 turbo engines originally devised by Autodelta's Carlo Chiti, while from the middle of the season Alfa made their normally-aspirated V12 engines available to the Turin team of Enzo Osella.

BMW continued to run their research programme in close collaboration with Brabham, but the ATS team also acquired the four-cylinder Munich engines — at that time costing 153,000DM apiece — this year. The 1.5-litre turbocharged engines made Formula One racing an even more expensive business than before, for they required a great deal of expenditure on maintenance. Indeed, ATS were told their BMW engines would need to be completely rebuilt every 300 to 500km. When the maximum size of fuel tanks was reduced from 250 to 220 litres in 1984, requiring much better consumption, even greater attention had to be paid to the engines and their associated turbochargers and intercoolers.

The power produced by the turbo engines continued to increase: they were now developing between 700 and 800bhp while the Ford opposition had to make do with 200 to 300bhp less. But Cosworth had not been idle. A short-stroke version of the DFV was built at the works by Swiss engineer Mario Illien. He then produced a new engine, the 2991cc DFY, with short-stroke (90 x 58.8mm) block and new cylinder-heads. This latest version of the successful eight-cylinder

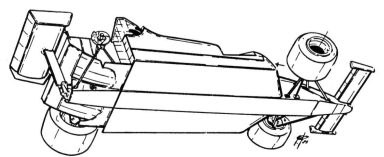

The "wing car" era came to an end in 1983, after which the underside of Grand Prix cars had to be flat.

motor peaked at 11,000rpm and gave 15 to 20bhp more than the DFV. Michele Alboreto was using the DFY in his Tyrrell when he won the Detroit Grand Prix, the 155th and last of the Cosworth Grand Prix victories. This was a unique success story when it is considered that Jim Clark had driven the Cosworth V8, financed by Ford, to a debut victory in his Lotus 49 in the 1967 Dutch Grand Prix. Now, after 16 years, the British V8 was coming to the end of its triumphal march through Formula One.

Hart's four-cylinder turbo engine, built on the monobloc principle, had its only respectable success in the second half of the season, though on several occasions Derek Warwick, driver of the Toleman-Hart, was unable to reach the finishing line. According to the engine's designer Brian Hart, the improved performance was due mainly to a switch to the British Holset turbocharger.

The Ford competitors were declining in number but, in the first half of the season, they kept up with the turbos most of the time, with victories at Long Beach, Monaco and Detroit. But from the British Grand Prix onwards the World Championship was exclusively the realm of the turbocharged engines which could

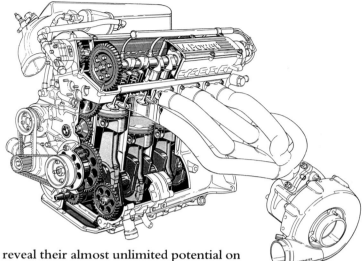

reveal their almost unlimited potential on the faster circuits.

Williams retained Keke Rosberg for 1983 and took on Jacques Laffite, the long-time Ligier driver. Nelson Piquet stayed with Brabham but Riccardo Patrese left to join Arrows. Renault held on to Alain Prost but got rid of René Arnoux, who had been in disgrace since the previous year's French Grand Prix. The American Eddie Cheever became Alain Prost's new team-mate while Arnoux was able to sign with Ferrari, alongside Patrick Tambay.

Andrea de Cesaris and Mauro Baldi formed the new Euroracing Alfa Romeo team while Lotus retained their pairing of Elio de Angelis and Nigel Mansell unchanged, and Niki Lauda and John Watson remained with McLaren. Jackie Oliver's Arrows team took on the new Belgian Thierry Boutsen, who came from Formula Two, to partner Marc Surer, while Tyrrell was represented by Michele Alboreto and the American Danny Sullivan, who was to go on to win the 1985 Indianapolis 500. Jarier and the Brazilian Raul Boesel drove for Ligier, Warwick and Giacomelli for Toleman, and Ghinzani and Corrado Fabi, Teo Fabi's brother, for Osella. Finally ATS was represented by Winkelhock, March-RAM by Acheson and Salazar, Theodore by Guerrero and former World Motorcycle Champion Johnny Cecotto, and Spirit, which appeared only sporadically, by Stefan Johansson.

On the tyre front, Pirelli signed a contract with Lotus which meant that, for the first time, they were supplying a top-notch team, particularly now that Lotus had a turbo engine.

In conjunction with the new "flat bottom" regulations in 1983, FISA set new maximum dimensions for rear wings. These were now permitted to be higher than before, the uppermost permissible point being 100cm against the previously allowed maximum of 90cm, though at the same time maximum width of the wing was reduced from 110 to 100cm and the permissible rear overhang from 80cm above the rear axle to 60cm, so that overall the aerodynamic effect was slightly reduced. The reduction in overhang and width did reduce downforce but the fact that the wings

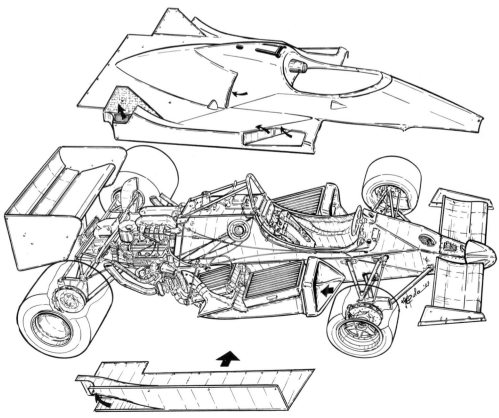

were now allowed to be 10cm higher compensated to some extent as, in the higher position, they were in less turbulent air and thus functioned better.

The combined effect of the various regulation changes was a considerable decrease in downforce, with a corresponding increase in the effectiveness of the front and rear wings.

The amount of downforce produced by the rear wing was more crucial on a turbo car than on one with a normally-aspirated engine due to the still-present turbo lag, which caused a delay of between half a second and a second (depending on the engine) between application of pedal pressure and the actual effect of the turbocharger. On the

exit to a corner this delay caused the car to slide until the benefit of increased power could be transmitted to the track. This made the car very difficult to control, but the problem was eased by increasing downforce on the rear wheels; aerodynamic balance could then be restored by a corresponding enlargement of the front wing. Thus although turbo cars had more wind resistance than cars with normally-aspirated engines they also had more downforce. A great deal of time and money was meanwhile invested in improving throttle response in turbo engines, research which had a direct application to improving the performance of road cars.

During the season more and more rear wings were being used with vertical side-plates extending down to the bodywork. As far as the regulations were concerned, these side-plates were judged to be part of the body, rather than the wings, and were therefore allowed to be as wide as the car body, 140cm. This combined wing section consisted of a normal 100cm rear wing with end-pieces which extended about 50cm above the rear axle. The effect of these new wing designs was to increase downforce by approximately 80kg.

The weight of the car, which now had to be at least 540kg, was rigorously controlled. As the cars entered the pits during practice they had to roll onto portable scales which were made up of four units. The car with driver on board was then quickly weighed, and the driver's weight — recorded at the beginning and in the middle of the season — deducted. As cars could no longer fill up with water after the race it was impossible to cheat on weight, though some teams were caught running underweight cars during the season. Two or three laps before the finish, they would make a hasty pit stop and take on 50 or 60 litres of fuel so they would be over the weight limit as the car finished the race. This was only of use to those competitors still using Ford engines, for the turbo competitors would have taken on more fuel during their tyre stops midway through the race.

The 35kg reduction in the weight limit had given the turbo teams the impetus to be even less compromising in their designs and to adopt lightweight-composite technology for constructing their chassis of carbon and Kevlar.

The latest carbon fibre monocoques had an additional advantage to the

Above
Nelson Piquet, 1983 World Champion, in his Brabham-BMW BT52.

Right
The Brabham-BMW BT52 was shown to the press in Munich at the beginning of March 1983 and then immediately despatched to the first Grand Prix in Brazil, where Piquet drove it to victory. BT52 characteristics were its arrow shape and the location of the cockpit further to the rear. The vertical radiator and the heat exchanger were located around the engine. On the right is the rubber bag-tank which was inserted into the monocoque.

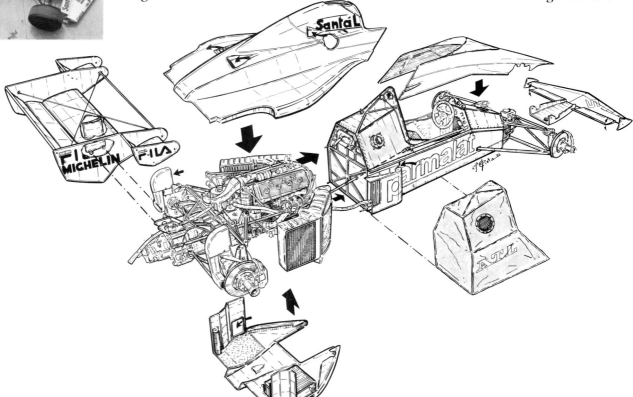

Right
The radiator elements in the Ligier JS21, which reverted once more to Ford-Cosworth power, were placed in front of and behind the rear axle. The aerodynamic shape of the tail section was particularly ingenious. In the lower picture Guy Ligier tells chassis specialist Guilpin what he should do.

Left
The Tyrrell-Ford 011 of American driver Danny Sullivan is lead car in this quintet filing into Sainte-Devote corner at Monte Carlo in 1983. He is followed by his countryman Eddie Cheever in a Renault RE40, Jean-Pierre Jarier in a Ligier-Ford JS12, Keke Rosberg in a Williams-Ford FW08D and Riccardo Patrese in a Brabham-BMW BT52. Sullivan won the Indianapolis 500 two years later.

Right
The radiator elements in the Ligier JS21, which reverted once more to Ford-Cosworth power, were placed in front of and behind the rear axle. The aerodynamic shape of the tail section was particularly ingenious. In the lower picture Guy Ligier tells chassis specialist Guilpin what he should do.

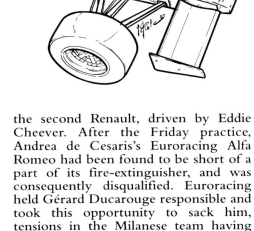

increased torsional rigidity they gave for a given weight: they did not require a separate fibreglass body, for the required outer surface could be built into the outer skin during construction. The first carbon monocoque of this kind was the chassis designed in 1982 by Gustav Brunner for the ATS D7 and built in Switzerland by Segar and Hoffmann, a company which specialized in the production of carbon/Kevlar parts for high-performance cars. But such chassis were unbelievably expensive to produce, the first 18kg ATS unit costing about 200,000DM, including models and moulds.

Monocoques of this kind were practically rigid, but this had a major drawback because additional steps had to be taken to meet the regulations requiring the provision of a deformable zone which would crumple in the event of an accident, thus absorbing the impact. Unlike an aluminium chassis, the deformable sections could not be cut into the composite layer, so had to be incorporated into the first stages of design, and plates embedded in the carbon fibre structure.

Carbon fibre was also used for the construction of brake discs, particularly ones used in practice, for there were still problems of overheating to be solved. The carbon fibre did not dissipate the heat from braking, which resulted in very high caliper temperatures and resultant

sealing problems in the wheel cylinders. Attempts were made to counter this by using pistons made of titanium alloy, but the brake fluid still heated up too much, causing a loss of hydraulic pressure. So the next step was to re-route the brake pipes onto the surface. Carbon fibre brakes had in fact been successfully used on aircraft for two decades, but the technology did not translate. When an aeroplane lands it applies full braking power but the system has time to cool down before it is required again; in a racing car, full-power braking is repeated constantly. But in spite of all the difficulties, and their expense, carbon fibre brake discs were worth persevering with, for they reduced weight by about 15kg over a conventional steel-disc system. Brabham had been experimenting with them since 1976, and was now using them regularly, as were McLaren, and in the following years every other constructor adopted the new technology too.

The 1983 World Championship season began in Brazil where Piquet won in Gordon Murray's latest Brabham-BMW design, the BT52, from Rosberg's Williams-Ford FW08D, but the Finn was disqualified afterwards because his car had been push-started after its pit stop. This promoted Lauda in the McLaren-Ford MP4 into second place ahead of Laffite in the second Williams.

In the United States Grand Prix West John Watson had a seemingly hopeless starting position on the 11th row but nevertheless took his McLaren-Ford across the line in first place, ahead of team-mate Lauda, with the Ferrari 126C2 of René Arnoux third.

The French Grand Prix at Le Castellet was run this year for the first time in the spring rather than later in the year and here Renault were able to take full advantage of the intensive testing they had done on this circuit. Alain Prost in the RE40 was the winner from Piquet and

the second Renault, driven by Eddie Cheever. After the Friday practice, Andrea de Cesaris's Euroracing Alfa Romeo had been found to be short of a part of its fire-extinguisher, and was consequently disqualified. Euroracing held Gérard Ducarouge responsible and took this opportunity to sack him, tensions in the Milanese team having been building up over some time. But this was in fact a tactical blunder on Alfa's part, for in dismissing Ducarouge they were allowing a top-notch engineer to fall into the arms of the opposition. The Frenchman was immediately snapped up by Lotus and, in only five weeks, had the Lotus-Renault 94T on its wheels, giving the team a much-needed boost.

At Imola Ferrari repeated their previous year's success in the San Marino Grand Prix, Patrick Tambay winning and René Arnoux in the other 126C2B placing third behind Alain Prost's Renault.

In the next race, in spite of the inferior Cosworth-Ford engine in the back of Patrick Head's Williams FW0B design, the impetuous Keke Rosberg fought his way to a magnificent win at Monte Carlo. The 520bhp of the best Cosworth engines proved sufficient on this winding street circuit to demote the turbo cars of Piquet and Prost to second and third places. Incredibly, the McLaren-Fords of Watson and Lauda, which had finished in first and second places at Long Beach, were not able to qualify at this, the most prestigious of all Grands Prix where the number of spectators counted in millions, thanks to the vast TV audience.

For the first time since 1971 the Belgian Grand Prix was run on the fast Ardennes circuit at Spa-Francorchamps, the course having been brought up to date in the interim and shortened from 14.1 to 6.94km. Anyone not driving a turbo car here was just a statistic. Andrea de Cesaris in the turbo V8 Euroracing Alfa Romeo 183T shot into the lead from the second row at the start and held it for 18 laps; then his engine gave up the ghost and allowed Alain Prost to win the race.

But at Detroit misfortune befell all the favoured turbo runners and talented young Michele Alboreto, winner at Las Vegas in 1982, was able to profit from this and gain his second North American street-race victory. Alboreto was driving the Tyrrell 012 fitted with the latest short-stroke Cosworth-Ford DFY engine: this was the 155th Grand Prix victory gained by the normally-aspirated Ford-Cosworth engine, and also the last.

From now on the turbos won every Formula One race. Ferrari won in Canada with Arnoux, and the Ferraris both started from the front row in the next race, the British Grand Prix. This time however it was Prost who emerged the winner ahead of Piquet and Tambay.

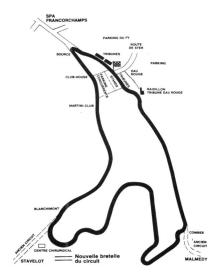

The McLaren team had been slow to adopt the practice of running on half-filled tanks but did so here, for the first time.

The net time gain from a perfectly executed refuelling stop could amount to more than a minute during a Grand Prix. A pit stop cost about 25 seconds: five seconds were needed to drive into the pits, ten seconds for work on the car, and a further ten seconds for driving out of the pits. But the gain amounted to about

Left
In the seventies the circuit at Spa-Francorchamps, which had been in existence since 1925, was shortened from the original 14.2 to 6.949km and brought up to date, and the Belgian Grand Prix was held here again from 1983. The continuation of the circuit is visible on the lower edge of the picture.

Below
Presentation of the six-cylinder TAG-Porsche engine at the 1983 Geneva Motor Show. From left are designer Hans Mezger, Porsche chairman Peter W. Schutz, McLaren team manager Ron Dennis and TAG owner Mansour Ojjeh.

Bottom
World Champion Nelson Piquet in the Brabham-BMW BT52.

Below
FIA prizegiving in Paris at the end of 1983. World Champion Nelson Piquet (centre) with runner-up Alain Prost (right) and René Arnoux (third).

Left
Alain Prost in the Renault RE40 probably lost his chance to become 1983 World Champion at the Tarzan Bend at Zandvoort when he rammed Piquet's Brabham BT53, which was in the lead at the time.

Overleaf
The shot by Italian photographer Franco Villani which won the special Dino Ferrari prize for the season's best Formula One picture. It shows René Arnoux's fuel stop during the San Marino Grand Prix at Imola.

two seconds in an average two-minute lap.

The Honda V6 turbo engine made its first appearance in a World Championship race in this race, in the Spirit driven by the Swedish driver Johansson. Honda wanted to use the Spirit team to collect data with a view to playing a fuller part in the following year; as the Spirit team did not meet the Japanese expectations, their future association would be with Williams.

Ferrari won the German Grand Prix at Hockenheim, René Arnoux in the 126C2C leading home Andrea de Cesaris at the wheel of the Alfa Romeo 183T, the Italian eight-cylinder engine finally attaining a placing.

It was Renault's turn again in the fast Austrian Grand Prix when Alain Prost came in ahead of Arnoux's Ferrari. But this was to be the last victory for the Renault team, as they were unable to repeat their earlier successes in 1984 or 1985 and at the end of the latter year withdrew from Formula One, though they continued to supply Lotus, Ligier and Tyrrell with the V6 engines.

The Dutch Grand Prix was a 1-2 result for Ferrari with Arnoux taking first place

and Tambay coming second. Prost had taken a gamble during the race and it lost him any chance of becoming 1983 World Champion when, braking for the Tarzan Hairpin, he tried to force the leading Brabham, driven by Piquet, off line. The two cars collided and both had to retire; at the end of the season Prost missed out on the title by two points.

During qualifying at Zandvoort, BMW had more than 800bhp at its disposal for the first time. Paul Rosche had done a lot more work on the four-cylinder German engine and, from now on, they would enjoy success after success, Piquet winning two more races before the season was over.

It was also in this race that the Porsche-built TAG V6 turbo engine made its debut, but it was the brand-new McLaren, the MP4/1, which it was mounted in that attracted most attention. The new car's shape was much admired and ultimately copied by all the teams. In an attempt to reduce turbulence around the rear wheels the body was narrowed at the waist, which sucked the air backwards out of this turbulent pressure zone between the wheels and body. In the interests of safety, the TAG engine was run at low turbo boost, but the car developed brake problems and Lauda had to retire. Watson in the McLaren-Ford took third place.

There was now no stopping the BMW engine, and Piquet was winner of the two next races, the Italian Grand Prix at Monza and the European Grand Prix at Brands Hatch.

Going into the last race of the year in South Africa Piquet was one of two likely contenders for the World Championship crown, Prost being the other, as Arnoux

had only a purely mathematical chance of winning the title. Piquet was calm about his prospects beforehand, but in the Renault camp the atmosphere was quite different, as the industrial giant expected its team to win the Championship at any cost. But after 35 of the 77 laps Prost withdrew with turbocharger trouble and it was all over bar the shouting. Piquet had led for much of the distance but could now afford to curb his speed, and towards the end of the race his team-mate Patrese went past and carried on to win. De Cesaris was second and Piquet third.

Lauda drove an amazing race in the still-new McLaren-TAG-Porsche, and was in second place for a few laps near the end, the new machine already displaying outstanding qualities. Shortly before the finish however Lauda was forced out of the race by an electrical fault.

The new Williams FW09 made its debut at Kyalami with Honda power and immediately made a good impression.

For the second time since 1981 Nelson Piquet was World Champion, by just two points from Alain Prost. René Arnoux was third for Ferrari. This was the first time the World Champion's crown had gone to the driver of a turbo car. Ferrari found some solace in winning the Manufacturers' Championship for the second time in succession, with Renault also finishing ahead of Brabham.

Two days after his Kyalami misfortune Prost, fed up with the tensions within Renault, left the French team and, with the help of his sponsor, Marlboro, immediately found a position at McLaren. As would become evident over the next few years this was a particularly happy solution for the little hook-nosed Frenchman.

Forumla One cars of 1983

Make/model	Chief designer(s)	Engine	Gearbox (speeds)	Chassis	Wheelbase	Track	Tyre make	Dry weight
Arrows A 6	Dave Wass	Cosworth DFV (V8)	Hewland FGA (5)	A	2692	F 1791 R 1670	Goodyear	540
ATS D 6	Gustav Brunner	BMW M 12/13 (4 cyl. Turbo)	ATS-Hewland (5)	C	2615	F 1727 R 1626	Goodyear	540
Brabham BT 52	Gordon Murray	BMW M 12/13 (4 cyl. Turbo)	Brabham-Hewland (5)	C	2845	F 1753 R 1651	Michelin	540
Euroracing 183 T/B	Gérard Ducarouge	Alfa Romeo 158 (V8 Turbo)	Alfa Romeo-Hewland (5/6)	C	2720	F 1680 R 1820	Michelin	558
Ferrari 126 C2/B	Harvey Postlethwaite	Ferrari 126 C (V6 Turbo)	Ferrari (5)	A	2660	F 1770 R 1660	Goodyear	578
Ferrari 126 C3	Harvey Postlethwaite	Ferrari 126 C (V6 Turbo)	Ferrari (5)	C	2600	F 1770 R 1660	Goodyear	552
Ligier JS 21	Michel Beaujon	Cosworth DFV (V8)	Hewland FGB (5)	A	2630	F 1800 R 1652	Michelin	540
Lotus 92	Martin Ogilvie	Cosworth DFV (V8)	Lotus-Hewland (5)	CK	2799	F 1786 R 1672	Pirelli	580
Lotus 93 T	Martin Ogilvie	Renault EF 1 (V6 Turbo)	Lotus-Hewland (5)	CK	2667	F 1816 R 1664	Pirelli	560
Lotus 94 T	Martin Ogilvie Gérard Ducarouge	Renault EF 1 (V6 Turbo)	Lotus-Hewland (5)	CK	2654	F 1816 R 1664	Pirelli	545
McLaren MP 4/1C	John Barnard	Cosworth DFV (V8)	McLaren-Hewland (5/6)	C	2682	F 1810 R 1683	Michelin	540
McLaren MP 4/1E	John Barnard	TAG/Porsche TTE-PO 1 (V6 Turbo)	McLaren-Hewland (5/6)	C	2682	F 1810 R 1683	Michelin	562
Osella FA 1 D	Hervé Guilpin Tony Southgate	Cosworth DFV (V8)	Hewland FGA (5)	A	2700	F 1780 R 1695	Michelin	557
Osella FA 1 E	Tony Southgate	Alfa Romeo (V12 60°)	Hewland FGA (5)	CA	2750	F 1750 R 1670	Michelin	565
RAM 01	Dave Kelly	Cosworth DFV (V8)	Hewland FGA (5)	A	2692	F 1791 R 1670	Pirelli	540
Renault RE 30 C	Michel Têtu	Renault EF 1 (V6 Turbo)	Renault-Hewland (5)	A	2730	F 1740 R 1630	Michelin	545
Renault RE 40	Michel Têtu	Renault EF 1 (V6 Turbo)	Renault-Hewland (5)	C	2730	F 1740 R 1630	Michelin	545
Spirit 201 C	Gordon Coppuck	Honda B 7 LE (V6 Turbo)	Hewland FGB (5)	A	2654	F 1753 R 1651	Goodyear	580
Theodore N 183	Nigel Bennett	Cosworth DFV (V8)	Hewland FGA (5)	CA	2692	F 1753 R 1575	Goodyear	550
Toleman TG 183 B	Rory Byrne	Hart 415 T (4 cyl. Turbo)	Hewland FGB (5)	C	2692	F 1848 R 1683	Pirelli	540
Tyrrell 011	Maurice Phillippe	Cosworth DFV/DFY (V8)	Hewland FGA (5)	A	2718	F 1803 R 1626	Goodyear	540
Tyrrell 012	Maurice Phillippe	Cosworth DFV/DFY (V8)	Hewland FGA (5)	CA	2642	F 1727 R 1473	Goodyear	540
Williams FW 08 C	Patrick Head	Cosworth DFV/DFY (V8)	Hewland FGA (5)	A	2604	F 1803 R 1575	Goodyear	540

Chassis construction: A = alloy monocoque; C = carbon-fibre monocoque; CA = carbon-fibre alloy monocoque; CK = Kevlar/carbon-fibre monocoque

Competitors have to make do with 220 litres of fuel. McLaren has a uniquely successful series with the TAG-Porsche V6 turbo engine and Lauda is World Champion — by half a point from Prost.

uel consumption was a major talking point in this 35th year of the World Championship because in 1984 teams would have to achieve with 220 litres what they had until now done with 250. Furthermore, refuelling stops were no longer permitted. The new restriction gave all sides plenty to think about. Engineers had to try, by means of modifying the electronic ignition and injection systems, to obtain the maximum possible performance while at the same time ensuring it was used as sparingly as possible. Meanwhile the rule-makers were worried about how fuel quantity was to be controlled, because it would be possible to hide small reservoirs in the monocoque. By the beginning of the season they were well aware that the teams would chill the fuel, whose density of course varied according to temperature. The teams also prepared special fuel blends, as the regulations did not rule this out, merely laying down the maximum octane rating (at 102 ROZ).

FISA's aim in reducing fuel quantities was to curb the horsepower escalation, as more miles per gallon (or fewer litres per kilometre) inevitably means less power.

With McLaren and Williams both having changed over to turbo cars in the second half of the 1983 season, and Arrows coming to an agreement with BMW at the end of the year for the use of their four-cylinder engine (after the first race of the new season), only Tyrrell remained loyal to the normally-aspirated Cosworth-Ford engine this year.

Between seasons Gordon Murray developed the arrow-shaped Brabham BT52 into the BT53 by relocating the turbocharger and intercoolers to special side pontoons fitted at the rear. New World Champion Nelson Piquet, competing in his sixth season with Brabham, was joined this year by Teo Fabi, who was also planning to contest some races in the CART series in North America; the previous year he had finished in an outstanding second placing in the Indycar Championship. Fabi's performance in qualifying at Indianapolis in 1983 had resulted in a sensational pole position. When he was away doing the CART races his place at Brabham would be taken by his brother, Corrado. The Brabham BT53 was again equipped with Michelin tyres.

At Tyrrell, Maurice Phillippe further developed the 012, using an alloy chassis reinforced with carbon fibre. Ken Tyrrell brought two talented young drivers into his team, the successful English Formula Three driver Martin Brundle and Germany's latest hope, Formula Two star Stefan Bellof.

Patrick Head's new Williams FW09, built for the Honda V6 turbo engine, had been ready (and racing) before the end of 1983, but as the team was not heavily financed at this time it employed an alloy monocoque.

Over the winter McLaren introduced the MP4/2, which looked very similar to the previous MP4/1. The wheelbase had however been extended in the interests of improved weight distribution, and this allowed John Barnard to modify the

Martin Brundle

Right
At the Austrian Grand Prix the McLaren pit team signals their man Lauda, who is in the lead. The message means he is in first place, with five laps to go, and with 10.5 seconds' lead over the driver in second place.

Below
Piaggio always presented the winner of pole position with a Vespa scooter. Here, it's Alain Prost's turn (Zandvoort 1984).

Below right
Alain Prost, in his McLaren-TAG-Porsche MP4/2, won the 1984 Monaco Grand Prix which was stopped early because of rain. Note the additional pieces on the sides of the wing. Any such devices extending in front of the rear-axle line were banned in 1985.

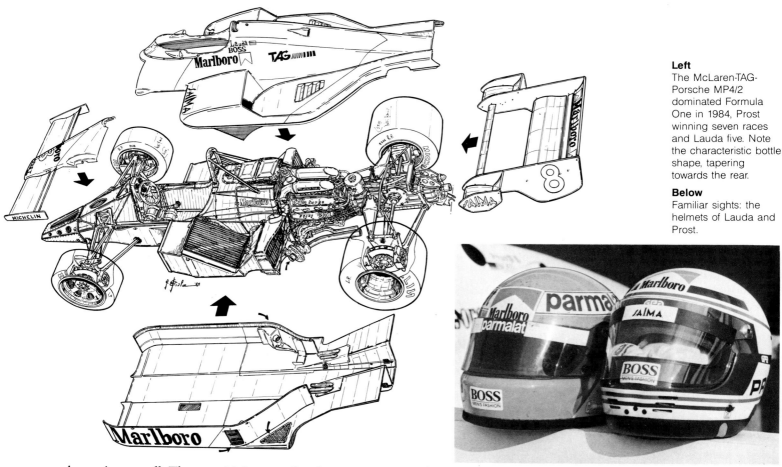

aerodynamics as well. The new McLaren had an even narrower "waist" in front of the rear wheels to draw the air through more efficiently, and correspondingly improve the effectiveness of the rear wing. The carbon fibre/Kevlar monocoque was again produced by the firm of Hercules in the United States, though unlike some of its rivals the chassis was still encased in a body. Renault driver Alain Prost's arrival on the team meant that, incredible as it seemed, John Watson, still counted among the élite, was without a drive for the year. Naturally, Niki Lauda continued to drive for McLaren which was still under contract to Michelin. At Porsche in Weissach meanwhile further work was being carried out on the TAG engine, especially on the electronics, with Bosch making a significant contribution in this area.

Ferrari modified its V6 engine with KKK turbocharger and gave it a new fully electronic Weber-Marelli fuel-injection system, though this was not fully ready for use until the middle of the season. In the interim there were hints that Ferrari, who continued to run on

Goodyear tyres, were also working on a new four-cylinder engine. Patrick Tambay was replaced on the Maranello driving strength by former Tyrrell driver Michele Alboreto, who following his victories at Las Vegas and Detroit was counted as one of Italy's great hopes. Alboreto's arrival marked the first time an Italian had driven for the team since Arturo Merzario in 1973. René Arnoux also remained with the Maranello factory whose new single-cell carbon fibre/Kevlar car, the 126C4, was being developed under the joint direction of Mauro Forghieri and Harvey Postlethwaite.

Renault also adopted single-cell carbon fibre/Kevlar construction for their new RE50 model, and the V6 engine was remodelled too, the old cast-iron block being replaced by an alloy unit. At the same time, experiments were carried out with a fully electronic Renox injection system, and with both the German KKK and American Garrett turbochargers. Having lost both Prost and Cheever to other teams, Renault's drivers this year were Patrick Tambay (from Ferrari) and

Derek Warwick (Toleman).

Both Lotus and Ligier now used Renault's engines. The new JS23 from Vichy was developed under the direction of Michel Beaujon and entrusted to Andrea de Cesaris (who came from Euroracing Alfa Romeo) and French Formula Three driver Francois Hesnault, but the Ligiers were a disappointment this year.

Lotus changed from Pirelli to Goodyear tyres, and Gérard Ducarouge came up with the V6 Renault-engined 95T model, which would be driven by Elio de Angelis and Nigel Mansell.

Over at Toleman, Rory Byrne was working on his TG184, which had a

Andrea De Cesaris

Rory Byrne

Gustav Brunner

Thierry Boutsen

Heini Mader

Eddie Cheever

These four sketches of the 1984 Ferrari 126C4 illustrate how expensive it is to operate in Formula One. Constant aerodynamic modifications meant the sidepods, the wing and the gearbox-level air extractors also had to be continuously redesigned.

The top drawing depicts the 126C4 as it was used at the French Grand Prix; the next two below show the versions used at the German and Italian Grands Prix, and finally a design which was tested at Fiorano at the end of the season. In the last design the exhausts lead directly from the air extractors into the air.

carbon fibre/Kevlar monocoque with separate bodywork. The four-cylinder Hart motor, which had not been designed to bear weight, was fixed onto a subframe at the rear. For drivers Toleman took on two South Americans, former World Motorcycle Champion Johnny Cecotto from Venezuela and a very talented Brazilian called Ayrton Senna. The previous year Senna had dominated the British Formula Three Championship.

Pavanello's Euroracing team sold their Alfa Romeo 183Ts to Osella and under the direction of Luigi Marmiroli developed the new 184T with a single-cell carbon fibre/Kevlar chassis built by a British firm, Advanced Composites, and the V8 Alfa Romeo turbo engine. The Milanese team's drivers this year were Riccardo Patrese (from Brabham) and Eddie Cheever (Renault). Enzo Osella, from Volpiano near Turin, started with the ex-Euroracing Alfa Romeo 183Ts, then built the Osella FA1F which used the Alfa Romeo turbo engine. The monocoque was developed at the Turin firm of CMA (Composite Material Aeronautic) which also did work for Renault and Ligier. Osella drivers were Piercarlo Ghinzani, who had a Lancia agency in Bergamo, and the Austrian Jo Gartner.

In the Arrows factory at Milton Keynes Dave Wass was preparing the new A7 turbo to take the four-cylinder BMW engine, the new car making its debut at the Belgian Grand Prix. The Arrows engines were not serviced by BMW Motorsport GmbH in Munich but at Heini Mader Racing Components in Switzerland where Mader, a former racing mechanic, had a new and very modern workshop for rebuilding high performance engines. The Swiss driver Marc Surer and the Belgian Thierry Boutsen continued to drive for Arrows in 1984.

The German ATS team was plagued by personnel changes, designer Gustav Brunner leaving to go to Euroracing before the season started, but pressed on with work on the new BMW-powered D7 with single-cell carbon fibre/Kevlar chassis. Manfred Winkelhock was once again the driver, but towards the end of the year the team hired the young Austrian Formula Three driver Gerhard Berger.

The Spirit team, which had used the Honda V6 engine in 1983, had to transfer to the four-cylinder Hart this year, and that meant inferior performance. The smallest and also the least affluent of 1984 Formula One teams, Spirit was headed on the technical side by former McLaren designer Gordon Coppuck, with Mauro Baldi as the only driver initially, though the Dutchman Huub Rothengatter later took over.

The RAM team, named after its founders Mick Ralph and John

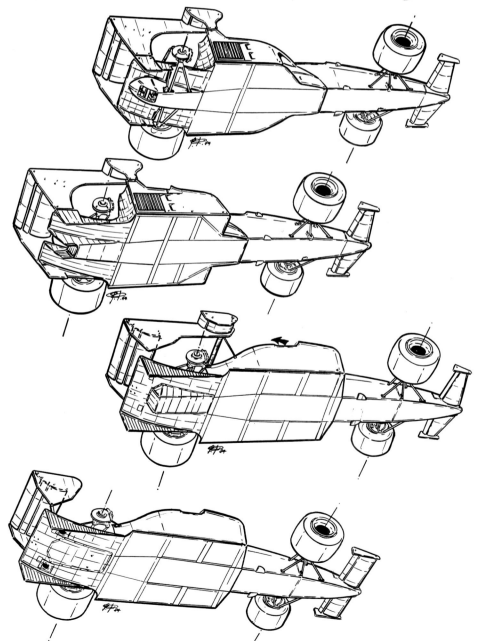

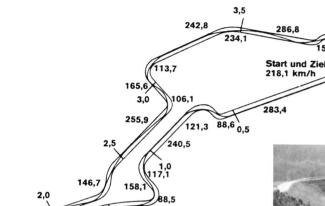

The new 4.542km Nürburgring was opened in 1984. This diagram shows the speed at the different points on the track worked out in advance by computer (based on Porsche 935 times).

Safety has a high priority at the very modern Nürburgring but the track has lost all appeal for spectators. They now have to sit in large sterile concrete grandstands and are forced to watch the race from a distance.

Below
Manfred Winkelhock in the ATS-BMW D7 at the 1984 Dutch Grand Prix at Zandvoort.

Macdonald, fielded the RAM02, designed by Dave Kelly. This car had a chassis formed from one plastic cell with an alloy underlay. The RAMs, which used Hart engines, were driven by Frenchman Philippe Alliot and European Formula Two Champion Jonathan Palmer.

Missing this year was the Theodore team, Asian businessman Teddy Yip no longer being prepared to keep digging into his pocket to keep the unsuccessful team going.

Goodyear, who until now had used radial-ply construction only for its rain tyres, finally changed over from cross-ply designs for all its racing rubber in 1984. Their move meant that all three Formula One tyre manufacturers — Goodyear, Michelin and Pirelli — were now producing exclusively radial tyres for

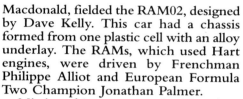

Jonathan Palmer

Formula One. Brabham, McLaren, Renault and Ligier were under contract to Michelin this year, while Goodyear supplied Tyrrell, Williams, Lotus, Arrows, Euroracing and Ferrari. The smaller teams — RAM, ATS, Toleman, Osella and Spirit — used the Italian tyres.

The problem of fuel consumption was now of prime concern, forcing the specialists to expend large sums in trying to find a solution. In modern engine technology a computer controlled the various functions, determining ignition timing, fuel injection timing, length of injection time and the quantity injected, on the basis of the engine's performance.

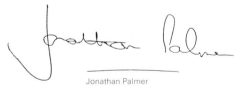

Because the chemists were left plenty of room to manoeuvre within the framework of the fuel regulations, special — and therefore expensive — blends were concocted with high anti-knock properties. The 220-litre fuel-tank limitation was actually aimed at improving engine design, for although it severely limited power during a race it forced steps to be taken to increase the specific weight of the fuel. Because the effects of the 220-litre rule could be minimised by chilling the fuel prior to the start, the teams gradually acquired refrigerator units which were set up in the pits so that advantage could be taken of the variation in density caused by temperature changes: a 1° drop in fuel temperature gives a 1% increase in density. In most cases the fuel was chilled to about minus 30°, but in some cases to

beyond minus 50°. Such increases in density meant that, for example, 235 litres of fuel could be "shrunk" to the legal volume of 220 litres by chilling it to minus 53°, and 15 litres of additional fuel would add about five laps on a medium-length circuit. In a race, that could easily be the difference between crossing the finish line and running out of fuel.

At the first Grand Prix of the year, in Brazil, those teams which had filled their cars with pre-chilled fuel had some anxious moments because the start was delayed by about half an hour. They feared that the hot sun would gradually expand the fuel and the tanks would burst. Their fears were groundless though, as petroleum fuel tends to warm up slowly.

The McLaren-TAG-Porsche MP4/2 provided instant proof that it was going to be hard to beat in the 1984 season, for although the six-cylinder Weissach-built engine was still very much in its infancy, Prost won in Brazil and Lauda in South Africa. Bosch had invested a considerable sum in the engine's development.

In Brazil, the fuel in Tambay's Renault ran out before the finish and other competitors had to lift their feet off the accelerator pedals during the last laps to ensure they had enough fuel to cross the finish line. Grands Prix were showing every sign of turning in economy runs, in which drivers had to resist the temptation to become involved in duels among themselves. This restraint was naturally not welcomed by the fans, the majority of whom were not enthusiastic about the "consumption formula" for they feared that Grand Prix racing would become boring. In fact however their fears were not realised.

In the Belgian Grand Prix at Zolder everything was in Ferrari's favour and Michele Alboreto in the 126C4 finished well ahead of the opposition. It was to be the only Ferrari success of the season. The Arrows A7 with BMW turbo engine made its debut here, driven by Thierry Boutsen, while Marc Surer had to be content with the Ford-powered A6 model.

Shortly before the finish of the San Marino Grand Prix at Imola de Angelis (Lotus), de Cesaris (Ligier) and Cheever (Euroracing) all ran out of fuel. Once again McLaren, whose refined engine electronics provided optimum consumption, were successful, and Alain Prost was a clear winner, ahead of René Arnoux's Ferrari. De Angelis just made it to the finish line with an empty tank to take third place.

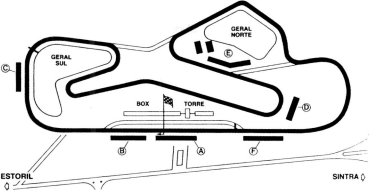

The 1984 World Championship Portuguese Grand Prix, the first since the 1960 race at Oporto, was held on the 4.350km Estoril circuit.

Renault put up a fight in the French Grand Prix at Dijon, and Tambay in the RE50 led for several laps. But at the end Niki Lauda was the winner for McLaren.

It rained the whole time at Monaco and the race organizer, Jacky Ickx, had to end the Grand Prix prematurely with the result that only half the World Championship points could be awarded. Prost was in the lead in the final laps, though, as the rain became heavier, the talented Ayrton Senna in a Toleman-Hart had drawn closer and closer to the leader. If the race had been stopped one lap later it would have been a sensational first victory for the newcomer, obviously a wet-weather specialist. Prost was saved by the chequered flag, but the press subsequently turned on Ickx. A member of Porsche's endurance-racing team for many years, the Belgian was accused of trying to use his position of power to ensure victory for the TAG-Porsche-engined McLaren.

The Brabham BT53 had shown itself to be very fast, but the reliability of the four-cylinder BMW engine left a lot to be desired. Thanks to additional turbo boost it could now deliver around 1000bhp in short bursts, such as in qualifying, and even in race trim still had some 800bhp on tap, but this seemed too highly stressed, and Piquet finished but rarely.

Cracks developed in the engine blocks, so that BMW were forced to cast new ones in which the walls were reinforced at critical places.

Another newcomer to distinguish himself in the rain at Monaco was the German Stefan Bellof, who brought his Ford-engined Tyrrell 012 into third place behind Prost and Senna.

Toleman had been embroiled in a financial dispute with Pirelli and after the French Grand Prix changed to Michelin tyres, which, thanks to development work carried out during the season, the drivers reckoned were worth a second a lap.

The fast but unreliable Piquet/Brabham combination showed its best side in the North American races, achieving victory at both Montreal and Detroit. Dallas in Texas staged a Grand Prix for the first time in 1984, on a circuit with plenty of bends laid out through the streets of the city. Huge blocks of concrete were massed along the route to protect spectators and property but the track surface was very bad and in fact had to be renewed in several places between qualifying and the race. The Grand Prix turned out to be a tough one and many cars ended their race in the concrete walls. For a long time Nigel Mansell in a Lotus led but victory finally went to

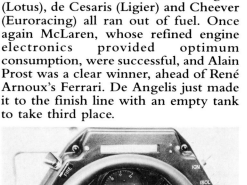

Above
Controls of the Williams-Honda FW09. The two knobs on the steering wheel have been labelled "drink" and "radio".

Right
Keke Rosberg's Williams-Honda FW09 being hounded by the Lotus-Renault 95Ts of Elio de Angelis and Nigel Mansell at the 1984 Dutch Grand Prix.

Keke Rosberg in his Williams FW09, the first success for the Honda motor. The six-cylinder Japanese engine had displayed plenty of power before now but its reliability, in general, had left something to be desired. The chassis of the FW09 did not hold the road well, and the unexpected Williams-Honda victory was due solely to Keke Rosberg's skill, his ability to improvise, and his willingness to take risks. His driving was spectacularly uninhibited.

The second half of the season belonged almost exclusively to Niki Lauda and Alain Prost who, in their McLaren-TAG-Porsches, dominated events as they pleased. Lauda won at Brands Hatch, at the Osterreichring (the first home victory for the double World Champion) and at Monza, while his team-mate was first at Hockenheim, Zandvoort and the new Nürburgring, scene of this year's European Grand Prix.

Going into the final round, the Portuguese Grand Prix, Lauda had accumulated 66 World Championship points and Prost had 62.5. The race, held at Estoril for the first time, would decide which of the McLaren drivers would be 1984 World Champion. Even if Prost won, Lauda had only to finish second to make sure of the title, so the odds were in the Austrian's favour.

In the race however Prost raced into a comfortable lead while Lauda was held up at the start and had to fight his way through to the front, passing car after car. For a long time Stefan Johansson in the Toleman-Hart put up fierce resistance but Lauda increased the turbo pressure of his

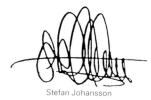
Stefan Johansson

TAG-Porsche engine and finally got past. Profiting from several withdrawals, Lauda duly finished second.

This was sufficient to confirm him as World Champion for the third time,

following his successes in 1975 and 1977, albeit by a margin of only half a point over the despondent Prost. The little Frenchman had won an unbelievable seven Grands Prix in one season, a new record. Lauda's tally on the other hand showed "only" five wins, but the Austrian had more placings.

Another record was McLaren's 12 victories in the 16 World Championship races of 1984, and they — naturally — won the Manufacturers' Championship, by a comfortable margin from Ferrari. In

Important characteristics of Formula One cars of 1981

Make	Alfa Romeo	BMW	Cosworth	Cosworth	Ferrari	Hart	Honda	Renault	TAG-Porsche
Model	890 T	M 12/13	DFV	DFY	126 C	415 T	RA 163 E	EF 4	TTE-PO1
Cylinder configuration	V8 90° Turbo	4 R Turbo	V8 90°	V8 90°	V6 120° Turbo	4 R Turbo	V6 80° Turbo	V6 90° Turbo	V6 80° Turbo
Bore & stroke	74 × 43,5	89,2 × 60	85,7 × 64,8	90 × 58,8	81 × 48,4	88 × 61,5	?	86 × 42,8	82 × 47,3
Capacity	1497	1499	2990	2991	1496	1496	?	1492	1498
Main bearings	5	5	5	5	4	5	5	4	5
Fuel injection	Bosch	Bosch	Lucas	Lucas	Lucas/Weber-Marelli	Lucas	Honda	Bosch	Bosch
Turbocharger	2 × Alfa Avio	1 × KKK	—	—	2 × KKK	1 × Holset	2 × IHI	2 × KKK/2 × Garrett	2 × KKK
Ignition	Marelli	Bosch	Lucas	Lucas	Marelli	Marelli	Honda	Marelli	Bosch
Power (bhp) at (rpm)	620 11 000	640 10 500	510 10 800	530 11 000	660 11 000	560 9800	650 11 000	650 11 500	650 11 500

the drivers' placings, third place went to the consistent Lotus driver Elio de Angelis, who had finished most of the Grands Prix and was in the points on most occasions: he even led the German Grand Prix for several laps before the McLaren steamroller swept past. The Renaults' performance in 1984, on the other hand, was not sufficient to win races.

The season clearly belonged to the combination of McLaren design and management, the TAG-Porsche engine, Michelin tyres and two top-notch drivers — an almost unbeatable combination. Prost had proved to be the faster driver during the season but Lauda was able to call on his outstanding experience and unrivalled tactical ability.

Fuel-consumption problems had however continued to plague the season. Electronic management systems, which controlled the operation of the super-powerful engines and ensured maximum use was made of each drop of fuel, assumed paramount importance. Those teams whose management systems were not as well developed as, say, the McLaren's, had to reduce turbocharger boost — and thus power — earlier in the race in order to ensure a finish. The Alfa Romeo V8 was a real gas guzzler, which meant that the Euroracing duo of Riccardo Patrese and Eddie Cheever were rarely prominent.

The Brazilian Ayrton Senna developed into the great new talent of the year. As early as Zandvoort he announced that he would be driving for Lotus in 1985, even though this meant buying his way out of his Toleman contract. In reaction to Senna's breach of loyalty, Toleman refused to supply him with a car at Monza.

The Tyrrell team, still using the normally-aspirated Ford-Cosworth engine, found themselves in an embarrassing situation in the middle of the season, when it was discovered that their cars were not filling up with fuel during pit stops, but were instead filling the tanks with a thicker liquid. This liquid was found to contain small ball bearings, and Tyrrell was accused of weight deception. The team was stripped of its World Championship points and in spite of Tyrrell's vehement protests the team was banned from racing for the rest of the season, from the Italian Grand Prix. The Tyrrells did not manage to qualify at the Austrian Grand Prix, which meant that race was the first Grand Prix in

Left
Stefan Bellof in the Tyrrell-Ford 012 during practice for the 1984 Monaco Grand Prix, with Swiss driver Marc Surer in an Arrows close behind.

Below
Lauda, the 1984 World Champion, in his McLaren-TAG-Porsche MP4/2 leads Patrese in a Euroracing Alfa Romeo 184T and Arnoux in a Ferrari 126C4 during the Monaco Grand Prix.

Overleaf
Nelson Piquet in his Brabham-BMW BT53 during heavy braking. The lighter carbon brake discs, which had replaced the traditional steel discs, are glowing bright red.

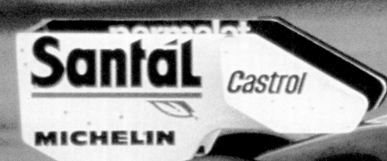

history in which all the competitors were driving turbo cars. For 1985, in spite of his continued opposition to turbo engines, Tyrrell finally rejoined the mainstream, having managed to secure access to the V6 Renault.

At the end of the season the British-based German ATS team withdrew from Formula One, team owner Gunter Schmid no longer being prepared to keep up with the escalating costs. Its place in Grand Prix racing was taken by another German team, Zakspeed. After years of success in touring-car and endurance racing, principally with Ford products, the Niederzissen company had developed their own Formula One car during 1984, targetted for a 1985 debut in conjunction with Zakspeed's own four-cylinder turbo engine.

During 1984 the new Nürburgring was opened in the midst of a blaze of publicity. No Grand Prix had been held on the famous old circuit since 1976, but a huge modern autodrome, surrounded by concrete grandstands, had now been built on the site, at a cost of more than 80 million Deutschmarks. The new Ring conformed to all the latest safety standards but its modern, sterile setting meant that the spectators were some distance away from the racing. The universal feeling was that the new Nürburgring had lost its magnetic appeal for the public.

At the end of the season the teams that had used Michelin tyres received a shock when the Clermont-Ferrand firm, at the height of its Formula One success, announced that it was withdrawing from Grand Prix racing.

Shortly before this Brabham boss Bernie Ecclestone had signed a contract with Pirelli, and over the winter months Nelson Piquet in the Brabham-BMW undertook an intensive test programme with the Italian tyres in preparation for the coming season.

Gérard Larrousse

There were significant personnel changes at Ferrari, too. Engineer Mauro Forghieri, who had accompanied the Ferrari Grand Prix cars to virtually every race since 1961, retired from the racing department, where he had had total responsibility. Forghieri subsequently worked on the Ferrari four-wheel-drive road-car project, while the racing department was relocated at a new site at Fiorano, near Maranello, where Piero

Lardi, the venerable Commendatore's illegitimate son, took over the position of racing director, held for several years before by Marco Piccinini.

There was another surprise in northern Italy in the autumn of 1984 when engineer Carlo Chiti, after some 20 years with Alfa Romeo, left the Milanese company. Former Lancia engineer Gianni Tonti, one of the people responsible for the unsuccessful Alfa Romeo V8 Grand Prix engine, now started work on the design of a new four-cylinder engine for Formula One. The firm of Autodelta, for many years the racing arm of Alfa Romeo, was now absorbed into the parent company, and staff numbers were drastically reduced as a consequence. The Formula One engines did however continue to be overhauled in the Autodelta workshops.

After leaving Alfa, Chiti was appointed director of a new firm founded by Tuscan businessman Piero Mancini and some friends. At the Novara headquarters of this company, Motori-Moderni, Chiti got straight to work designing a new V6 Formula One turbo engine which was to be ready, after a few months of intensive work, in February 1985. The new Motori-Moderni Formula One engine was intended for the new Grand Prix cars of

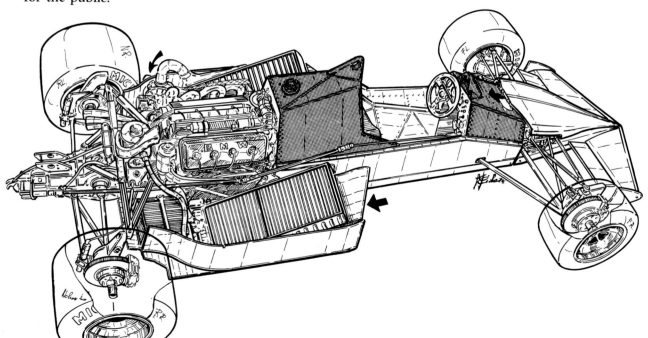

The Brabham-BMW BT53 was an improved version of its outwardly-similar predecessor with which Piquet had become World Champion in 1983. On the BT53 the sidepods were extended because the cooling elements had to be arranged almost horizontally., Piquet won at Montreal and Detroit in the BT53 but had to withdraw on several other occasions.

the Faenza-based Minardi team, who had until now been participating, with some success, in the Formula Two category. The engineer responsible for the design of the Formula One Minardi was Giacomo Caliri, a Sicilian who, after some years working for Ferrari in Modena, had opened his own design office, working as a consultant to various racing teams. On February 21st 1985 the Minardi M185, with V6 Motori-Moderni engine, was introduced to the press.

Giacomo Caliri

Giacomo Caliri

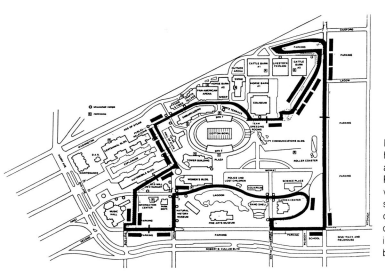

In 1984 Dallas also had its Formula One attraction. Keke Rosberg was the winner on the 3.9km street circuit, but many of the other competitors crashed into the concrete barriers.

Formula One cars of 1984

Make/model	Chief designer(s)	Engine	Gearbox (speeds)	Chassis	Wheelbase	Track	Tyre make	Dry weight
Arrows A 7	Dave Wass	BMW M 12/13 (4 cyl. Turbo)	Hewland (5)	CA	2667	F 1727 R 1600	Goodyear	543
ATS D 7	Gustav Brunner	BMW M 12/13 (4 cyl. Turbo)	Hewland-ATS (5)	C	2735	F 1795 R 1700	Pirelli	548
Brabham BT 53	Gordon Murray	BMW M 12/13 (4 cyl. Turbo)	Brabham-Hewland (6)	C	2946	F 1702 R 1626	Michelin	545
Euroracing 184 T	Luigi Marmiroli	Alfa Romeo 890 T (V8 Turbo)	Alfa Romeo-Hewland (5/6)	C	2720	F 1810 R 1680	Goodyear	546
Ferrari 126 C4	Harvey Postlethwaite Mauro Forghieri	Ferrari 126 C (V6 Turbo)	Ferrari (5)	C	2743	F 1816 R 1664	Goodyear	542
Ligier JS 23	Michel Beaujon	Renault EF 4 (V6 Turbo)	Hewland (5)	C	2810	F 1800 R 1652	Michelin	580
Lotus 95 T	Gérard Ducarouge	Renault EF 4 (V6 Turbo)	Lotus-Hewland (5)	CK	2775	F 1800 R 1700	Goodyear	540
McLaren MP 4/2	John Barnard	TAG/Porsche TTE-PO 1 (V6 Turbo)	McLaren-Hewland (5)	C	2794	F 1803 R 1651	Michelin	540
Osella FA 1 F	Enzo Osella	Alfa Romeo 890 T (V8 Turbo)	Hewland (5)	C	2830	F 1750 R 1600	Pirelli	557
RAM 02	Dave Kelly	Hart 415 T (4 cyl. Turbo)	RAM-Hewland (6)	C	2769	F 1753 R 1607	Pirelli	550
Renault RE 30	Michel Têtu	Renault EF 4 (V6 Turbo)	Renault-Hewland (5)	C	2680	F 1802 R 1670	Michelin	540
Spirit 101 B	Gordon Coppuck	Hart 415 T (4 cyl. Turbo)	Hewland (5)	A	2730	F 1829 R 1626	Pirelli	550
Toleman TG 184	Rory Byrne John Gentry	Hart 415 T (4 cyl. Turbo)	Hewland (5)	C	2800	F 1765 R 1676	Michelin	540
Tyrrell 012	Maurice Phillippe	Cosworth DFV (V8)	Hewland (5)	A	2642	F 1651 R 1473	Goodyear	540
Williams FW 09/09 B	Patrick Head	Honda RA 163-E (V6 Turbo)	Williams-Hewland (5)	A	2769	F 1778 R 1676	Goodyear	558

Chassis construction: A = alloy monocoque; C = carbon-fibre monocoque; CA = carbon-fibre alloy monocoque; CK = Kevlar/carbon-fibre monocoque

Cost and Horsepower Escalation

Stormy development of the turbo engines: up to 1100bhp for qualifying and 900bhp in races. Prost is outstanding for McLaren and becomes France's first World Champion.

Over the winter months of 1984–85 the teams continued their usual preparations for the next season, carrying out intensive test programmes at Le Castellet, on the Jacarepagua track near Rio de Janeiro, and at Estoril, Kyalami and Imola.

The huge Italian Pirelli company, anxious to further their involvement in Formula One, had signed a contract with Brabham for 1985 and this association with a top-notch team gave them the yardstick with which they could evaluate their own technological position. Before the season began, Brabham and Pirelli covered more than 12,000 kilometres in a rigorous test programme, mainly at Kyalami, where Nelson Piquet, working with Gordon Murray and Pirelli engineer Mario Mezzanotte, tested a variety of possible combinations of tyres and suspension settings.

Brabham was not the only team looking to a new partnership with a tyre company, for in the wake of Michelin's withdrawal from Formula One at the end of 1984, McLaren, who had been so successful the year before, was in the same position, as were Renault and Ligier. Ligier followed Brabham's lead in signing with Pirelli, who also this year had on their books RAM, Osella, the new Minardi team and — ultimately — Toleman. McLaren and Renault meanwhile changed over to Goodyear, the other company continuing to support Formula One. The Americans also supplied Williams, Lotus, Arrows, Tyrrell, Ferrari, Euroracing and Zakspeed, as well as Lola-Beatrice later in the season.

Of these teams, Toleman was in a very difficult situation. Having changed from Pirelli to Michelin rubber midway through the 1984 season, the British team was left without tyres after Michelin's withdrawal, Pirelli advising that they were unable to supply more than six teams. With no tyres and no sponsor either, it appeared as if Toleman would have to pull out of Grand Prix racing.

But another team's misfortune led to their eventual fortune. The tiny Spirit team had been included on the lists at the beginning of the season but, with no worthwhile sponsor, saw no possibility of getting through the season on their budget. Matters were finally resolved in May when the Italian fashion chain Benetton, which was also helping to finance Euroracing, came to Toleman's aid with a substantial injection of finance, enabling them to take over Spirit's lapsed Pirelli contract. Toleman were thus able to take part in the Monaco race with Pirelli tyres while Spirit withdrew from Formula One.

Those teams who had changed tyre brands — McLaren, Renault, Brabham, Ligier and Toleman — all had to redesign their cars around the new tyres, and there was a large question mark over McLaren, in particular, as it seemed they might not be able to adapt their cars to Goodyear tyres in time.

There were again small adjustments in the Formula One regulations for 1985. To reduce cornering speeds, even if only slightly, extensions on the ends of the rear wings were banned, which meant designers had to manage with less downforce. They compensated by making the wings more upright, which led to the old dilemma of more wind resistance on the straights being the price asked for more downforce on corners.

Another new rule required the front part of the chassis to meet specific structural specifications in the interests of protecting drivers' legs in the event of an accident. Fuel use was again restricted to 220 litres per race, though agreement was reached on a further reduction to 195 litres in 1986. Also as before, the race duration had to be shorter than two hours and the distance no more than 320km. Because of the Tyrrell team's actions in 1984 of restoring liquid to the tanks just before the end of the race, in order to bring the car's weight up to the prescribed 540kg minimum, a ban was placed this year on the addition of any liquid during the race. There was also a restriction on the specific components allowed to be replaced during pit stops, while the practice of chilling fuel just before the start was also outlawed. In practice, this had the effect of reducing fuel available for each race by a further 10 to 15 litres.

FISA had also been looking further ahead, and in the autumn of 1984, after lengthy discussions with the teams, announced a series of changes aimed at controlling the escalating horsepower race. Fuel-tank capacity would be reduced, in stages, from 195 litres in 1986 and 1987 to 180 litres in 1988; with a small fuel allowance, engines would have to be more economical, and thus less powerful. But to obviate the necessity for brand-new engines to be built in compliance with these new regulations, it was also agreed that, from 1988, the maximum permitted size of turbo engines would be reduced to 1200cc. In fact this latter requirement was subsequently overturned, and the fuel-consumption requirement modified: whilst still requiring a limit of 195 litres in 1986 and 1987, the allowance for the ensuing three years would be 185 litres. It was confirmed at that point that the existing 1.5-litre turbo formula would remain in force until the end of 1990, but 3-litre normally-aspirated engines would not be admitted after 1986.

Fuel consumption was again an engine specialists' headache in 1985, but they were able to refine the electronic fuel-injection systems to ensure that optimum use was made of the allowance of 220 litres per race, and engine performance figures in fact continued to climb; in 1985 between 820 and 900bhp was available in race trim from the most powerful Formula One engines. Furthermore, drivers could obtain even more horsepower from their apparently bottomless reservoirs by the simple expedient of operating a knob in the cockpit, which increased turbo boost for short spells, long enough to pass another

Thanks to outstanding placings Ferrari 156/85 driver Michele Alboreto was in the World Championship lead at the halfway point in the season. He had won in Canada and Germany and finished second in Brazil, at Monaco and in Britain. But he then had a spate of retirements which lasted into the 1986 season. He was nevertheless runner-up to Prost in the 1985 points.

car. In this way boost could be increased to more than four bar, but it had to be done sparingly, not only in the interests of preserving the engine, but also of ensuring that fuel did not run out before the finish of the race.

There was not much changing of drivers from one team to another this year. McLaren, naturally, retained their successful duo of Lauda and Prost. Rosberg remained at Williams but Laffite had gone back to Ligier and was replaced at Williams by the former Lotus driver Nigel Mansell. At Brabham, where Nelson Piquet was starting his seventh season, they took on the former Ligier driver François Hesnault as No 2. The Frenchman however drove only in the first races, up to Monaco, impressing so little that he was replaced by Marc Surer, who had been without a drive since the beginning of the year. Tyrrell, after its

enforced layoff at the end of 1984, reappeared with Martin Brundle and Stefan Bellof, while the RAM team entrusted their new car, designed by the Austrian Gustav Brunner, to Manfred Winkelhock (formerly of ATS) and Philippe Alliot. At Lotus the faithful Elio de Angelis, in his sixth season with the team founded by Colin Chapman, was given as his team-mate the talented young Brazilian Ayrton Senna da Silva, who had shown such promise in the Toleman in 1984. Patrick Tambay and Derek Warwick went into their second season with Renault but at Arrows, although Thierry Boutsen remained on the team, Marc Surer stood down: the Swiss driver wanted to concentrate on his second great passion, rally driving. Jackie Oliver replaced him with the promising young Austrian Gerhard Berger.

The uncertainties surrounding the Toleman team at the beginning of the season meant they could not pursue their intention of providing a car for Stefan Johansson, and by the time of Benetton's life-saving intercession before the Monaco Grand Prix the Swedish driver had gone elsewhere. Toleman thus started their 1985 campaign with former Brabham driver Teo Fabi, and later took on the Osella driver Piercarlo Ghinzani as well. Euroracing-Alfa Romeo retained both Eddie Cheever and Riccardo Patrese but while Osella began the season with Ghinzani he was replaced, after his

departure for Toleman, by the Dutchman Huub Rothengatter. Ligier's line-up this year was Jacques Laffite and Andrea de Cesaris, while Ferrari renewed contracts with Michele Alboreto and René Arnoux. That situation did not remain for long however, for after the first race of the new season, the Brazilian Grand Prix, Arnoux was released from his contract, the Ferrari management considering he was not giving of his best. His place in the second race of the season, in Portugal, was taken by Stefan Johansson.

Minardi and Zakspeed, both entering Formula One for the first time, concentrated on only one car each per race. The Minardi, with its V6 Motori-Moderni motor, was driven by 1983 European Formula Three Champion Pierluigi Martini, and the Zakspeed by former RAM driver Dr Jonathan Palmer.

There was one other team on the grids in 1985, though it did not appear until late in the season. In January 1985 the American consumer goods giant Beatrice announced plans to enter Formula One, starting with the Italian Grand Prix, with former World Champion Alan Jones as their driver. Since retiring from Grand Prix racing in 1981 Jones had competed

Teddy Mayer

Top
Alain Prost and Michele Alboreto took first and second places in the 1985 Monaco Grand Prix.

Above
John Barnard, the highly successful McLaren designer.

Right
Niki Lauda won the last victory in his successful career at the Dutch Grand Prix.

in long-distance touring car races in Australia and was waging a constant battle with a weight problem. Beatrice set up a new company called Formula One Race Car Engineering, or FORCE, and built a modern new factory at Poyle, near London airport. Directors of the new operation were former McLaren board members Teddy Mayer and Tyler Alexander, and American Lola importer Carl Haas, well known in the United States as a CanAm and CART entrant, also played a leading part.

In the meantime the first Formula One Beatrice was being penned at Lola by a team comprising John Baldwin, Neil Oatley and long-time Lola boss Eric Broadley himself. Beatrice had supplied the Anglo-American racing company with a generous budget but even this had not enabled them to obtain the TAG-Porsche engines they wanted. Instead they had to use the unloved four-cylinder Hart engine while waiting for an engine of their own in 1986. This was the new V6 turbo announced by Ford of America in December 1983, and being built under contract by Cosworth in Britain. Development on this motor was a collaborative effort between Cosworth and the Ford research centre in Detroit, and the first trials were held in both in Britain and the United States in the summer of 1985. Beatrice-FORCE had managed to negotiate exclusive rights to the use of this new engine.

Renault's Formula One department at Viry-Chatillon, south of Paris, was completely restructured this year in the wake of the departure for Ligier of team manager Gérard Larrousse and chassis and aerodynamics specialist Michel Tétu. Renault president Georges Besse appointed Gérard Toth as new manager of the various sporting activities though he had not, in his previous positions within the Renault organisation, had any involvement with motor racing. Jean Sage, whose hobby was vintage racing cars (especially Ferraris), remained as racing director, while Patrice Ratti and Jean-Marc d'Adda were made responsible for the new cars and Bernard Dudot continued to be in charge of the engine section.

For this year's racing Renault developed the new single-cell monocoque RE60 which was given the 90° V6 engine and a completely new six-speed gearbox. The EF4 engine was replaced by the interim EF4*bis* model, which retained the familiar cylinder

Carl Haas

Below
The Lola THL1 with Hart 415T engine was developed in Britain in the first half of 1985. From left: team manager Teddy Mayer with engineers Neil Oatley and John Baldwin.

Right
Nigel Mansell celebrated his first Grand Prix victories in 1985 at Brands Hatch and Kyalami, both in the Williams-Honda FW10B. Here, though, Mansell and Frank Williams seem to have a problem.

dimensions (86 x 42.8mm, 1492cc), until the introduction after the first few races of the season of the completely new EF15 engine. This also had a capacity of 1492cc, but bore and stroke were 80.1 x 49.4mm, and it had a fully electronic fuel-injection system made by a Renault subsidiary, Renix. The EF15 revved to 12,000rpm-and had better torque characteristics than its predecessor.

The Ferrari racing department had also undergone a restructuring process, long-time chief engineer Mauro Forghieri, who was actually the son of a former Ferrari employee, having been transferred to a new position outside the racing department in the autumn of 1984. Under the direction of Piero Lardi Ferrari, Dr Harvey Postlethwaite was now in charge of chassis design and aerodynamics, while engineers Ildo Renzetti and Luciano Caruso were given specific responsibility for engines and transmissions. Antonio Tomaini took over the technical direction of the team at the track, but Marco Piccinini, who had shown himself to be a skilled and hard-headed negotiator during discussions with FISA and who knew the rulebook like the back of his hand, was kept on as

Piero Lardi-Ferrari

Jean Sage

Marco Piccinini

racing director and was also appointed to the Ferrari board.

In the summer of 1985 it gradually became known that Ferrari was interested in building an Indianapolis car. This had been one of the Commendatore's long-time dreams and, as early as 1952, he had made a tentative foray into this specialised arena with Alberto Ascari. Ferrari now let it be known that they were working on a 2.65-litre V8 turbo engine for use in the American CART racing series, based on a Ferrari design which had been used by Lancia in endurance racing since 1983.

For Formula One the Maranello organisation was working on a four-cylinder engine, though this concept was abandoned before it saw the light of day, and the team continued to use the 120° V6 in 1985. This had however been completely revised, the two KKK turbochargers being moved from their previous position within the V to the outside of the engine. This enabled a flatter engine to be used, which in turn increased the effectiveness of the rear wing, though the transverse gearbox continued to be used. When the new 1985 model was unveiled on February 16th, Enzo Ferrari — two days before his 87th birthday — announced that his revised six-cylinder engine developed 789bhp at 11,000rpm at a turbo boost pressure of 3.5 bar. For qualifying boost could be increased so that the engine could deliver about 1000bhp. Naturally, the new engine used Weber-Marelli fully electronic fuel injection and the water injection which had been used by Ferrari since 1982. As early as the 1984 Italian Grand Prix Ferrari had displayed McLaren's bottleneck body shape on their 156/85 model, though this was used only in practice.

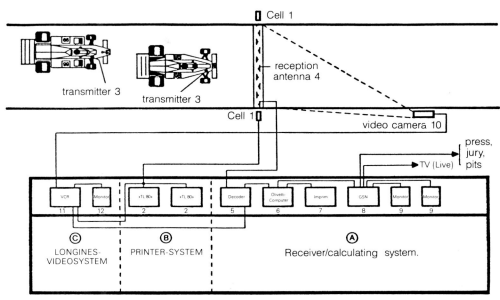

This is how the Longines timing system works. As the cars pass through the photo cells (1) the time is registered. It is then sent to "TL 80" (2) for identification. At the same time the transmitter (3) resolves the magnetic tape at the finish (4) and sends this impulse on for identification (5). The time from "TL 80" (2) is processed further. It continues via the Olivetti computer P6066 (6) where both times are compared/transmitted and at (7) Imprim, the printed results are compiled. At GSN (8) the data is distributed by monitor to the press/officials/pits or to the "live" television transmission. Monitors (9) relay the control to the timekeepers. The internal video unit consists of the camera (10) which has a view over the whole of the track, relaying a hundred pictures per second to the video recorder (11) and the control monitor (12).

The programme for the construction of the newest Ferrari chassis was worked out by Aermacchi on their computer, while the calculations for the aerodynamics were carried out in collaboration with the American computer firm of Gould. Enzo Ferrari's opinion, expressed at the launching of the new 156/85, was that the computer "accelerates the whole calculation process and saves a great deal of time. In the past it could take three months before a new crankshaft was worked out and correctly balanced; today, with the appropriate computer programme, the same task can be completed in nine hours. But it is still the engineer's creative thinking which remains the basis of the whole process."

John Barnard's new McLaren MP4/2B relied on what was familiar and did not look very different from its successful predecessor, the major work having been the adaptation to the Michelin tyres they were using. In the Porsche research centre at Weissach meanwhile the engine specialists under the direction of Hans Mezger were continuing work on the six-cylinder TAG engine which had been so successful in 1984, and which was both reliable and economical. At the Geneva Motor Show in March, McLaren announced that the team would in future be owned by the TAG group, and that they were thinking of founding a centre for research and development in Britain as soon as possible. This lavish undertaking was to be called TAG/McLaren Research and Development.

The Williams weapon for this year was the FW10, but apart from making the switch for the first time to carbon/Kevlar monocoque construction, Patrick Head had applied conventional solutions to his problems. In Japan a great deal of work was being done on the Honda V6 engine which was rumoured to have ceramic components. In the middle of the season, at the French Grand Prix, the Williams appeared with a new longer-stroke Honda engine which proved to be very powerful indeed. Considerable progress had been made on reliability as well, and the six-cylinder engine, which had won only once in 1984 — at Dallas, and then thanks only to Keke Rosberg's driving — was able to carry off four victories in 1985.

Also appearing for the first time at the French Grand Prix at Le Castellet was Maurice Phillippe's Tyrrell 014, with the turbocharged V6 Renault engine. In the earlier 1985 races team drivers Stefan Bellof and Martin Brundle had had to rely on the old faithful normally-aspirated Cosworth-Ford engine; the French race marked the end of the era of normally-aspirated engines. The slow but sure transition of the 3-litre formula, in force since 1966, into a 1.5-litre turbo formula was now complete.

It will do no harm to recall the unique career of the eight-cylinder Ford-Cosworth DFV engine, for it had not only been by far the most successful engine of its time but had also experienced a tremendous growth in popularity during its Grand Prix life. The DFV — Double Four Valves — had made its debut in the 1967 Dutch Grand Prix in Jim Clark's Lotus 49, and achieved instant victory in that Zandvoort race.

Over the years, although the basic layout was never altered, the engine had been continually improved and the performance increased. From 1967 to 1983 the Ford motor won a total of 155 Grands Prix and took drivers to no fewer than 12 World Championship titles, and constructors to ten World Manufacturers' Championships. Outside Formula One, the Cosworth creation was victorious at Le Mans in 1975 and 1980 and also in the CART racing series for Indianapolis cars, the turbocharged 2.65-litre DFX version having actually made its debut at Indianapolis in 1976. A total of 382 DFVs were built, including 40 DFL (3.3 and 3.9 litres) versions which were built for long-distance sportscar races, the DFX turbo models for use in the USA, and the short-stroke DFYs. Production was not actually closed down however, as the less powerful Formula 3000 version followed, and was in use from 1985.

The new Brabham model for 1985 Formula One was called the BT54 and was a further development of its predecessors, the suspension of which Gordon Murray had had to redesign to handle the Pirelli tyres. But there was a surprise for journalists when the car was first shown to them at the BMW headquarters in Munich on March 25th 1985, for the name of the Italian dairy company Parmalat, main sponsor of Bernie Ecclestone's team since 1978, was not in evidence. Instead the new Brabham carried in large letters on its side the name of the Italian computer firm of Olivetti. This was a surprise, although Olivetti had for years worked in close collaboration with Longines in evaluating Grand Prix timing and thus was closely connected with the sport.

On the subject of timing, it should be mentioned that considerable progress had been made in this area over the past few years, thanks to developments in the area of electronics. It had started in 1978 when, as an experiment, Longines had fitted small coded transmitters to six of the Formula One cars competing in the United States Grand Prix West at Long Beach. An aluminium strip at the finish line served as an antenna, receiving signals transmitted by each of the six cars as they crossed the line. Each of the six transmitters operated at a different frequency, so the times for each car could be automatically identified. The signals were then transferred through a decoder to the chronographs which printed them in thousandths of a second, then sent them on to the Olivetti computer which automatically supplied times and placings. The system of coded transmitters allowed for timing to be automatic and represented an important step forward in providing information not only for officials but also for the teams and, ultimately, for television. The next step after the Long Beach experiment was for every car in the field to carry timing decoders. In 1981 ten Grands Prix were officially timed by this method and the following year the remaining Formula One races were brought into line.

Cost and horsepower escalation were the topics of discussion in 1985. It became very clear that in qualifying teams were using maximum turbo boost in their efforts to earn the best possible grid positions, and running on ultra-soft "qualifying" tyres which lasted for only one or two laps. The most powerful engines, the four-cylinder BMW and the Honda V6, produced up to 1150bhp for qualifying, with Ferrari and Renault attaining about 1000bhp. McLaren did not use special qualifying engines which explains the fact that although Prost won five races during the year, and was World Champion, he qualified on pole position only twice. Questions were being asked about the sense of such high power outputs, and there was a feeling that funds were being senselessly squandered. Certainly no attention at all was paid to fuel consumption during qualifying.

Even in race trim the best engines developed between 820 and 900bhp this

year, which gave rise to calls for limits to be set on turbo boost. Renault were in favour of a reduction, but Ferrari and BMW were very much against any such move. There was also discussion on the subject of possible new approaches to qualifying, with suggestions being made that grid positions should be determined by a string of five or even ten laps, rather than the traditional one-lap blind. This would eliminate the usage of fast-wearing qualifying tyres and also of special high-power qualifying engines. In the end however the status quo remained, and no changes were made.

The three new teams in Formula One in 1985 — Minardi, Zakspeed and Beatrice — all took different approaches, Giancarlo Minardi's Faenza-based team using the Motori-Moderni V6 engine, Zakspeed its own four-cylinder unit, and Beatrice the Hart engine in a Lola chassis. Chiti's 90° V6 Motori-Moderni engine developed 720bhp at 11,000rpm from its 1499cc (80 x 49.7mm), using electronically controlled Bosch-Kugelfischer mechanical fuel injection; this system was however later replaced by the system originally developed by Lucas for the Ferrari V6. During Minardi's first season they had to make do with KKK turbochargers with a rather moderate boost pressure of 3.2bar, in the interests of keeping the engines in one piece, which meant the car and driver Martini were rarely more than also-rans.

Although Erich Zakowski's Zakspeed firm at Niederzissen had almost completed its new Formula One car with four-cylinder Zakspeed engine by the

Gianni Marelli

Giancarlo Minardi

Top
At the beginning of the season Frenchman François Hesnault was the second Brabham driver but he was replaced after only a few races by Marc Surer, pictured in a BT54 at Spa.

Erich Zakowski

summer of 1984, the car did not make its racing debut until the 1985 Portuguese Grand Prix. The carbon fibre/Kevlar monocoque chassis was developed under the direction of Englishman Paul Brown, who had formally worked for Chevron and March, and then for Maurer in Formula Two. Zakspeed engineer Norbert Kreyer was responsible for the engine design, with Italian Gianni Marelli, formerly a top engineer with Ferrari and Alfa Romeo, acting as adviser. The light-alloy four-cylinder 1495cc (90.4 x 58.25mm) Zakspeed engine used an American Garrett turbocharger and, initially, mechanical fuel-injection. The car was the first completely German Formula One car to be raced since 1962, when Porsche were running under the 1.5-litre formula. Jonathan Palmer was the team driver until he was injured in practice for the Spa 1000km sportscar race at the end of August, after which Munich driver Christian Danner, on his way to winning the 1985 European Formula 3000 Championship, was installed in Palmer's place.

At Brazil at the beginning of the season it seemed as if everything was as it had always been. Rosberg in the Williams-Honda FW10 led briefly at the start but Alain Prost in the McLaren-TAG-Porsche MP4/2B was the winner with Michele Alboreto in the Ferrari 156/85 second. At the Portuguese Grand Prix at Estoril heavy rain caused great confusion and Ayrton Senna, who had demonstrated his outstanding wet-weather abilities as early as the 1984 Monaco race, outclassed his rivals and led from start to finish. This was the first Grand Prix success for the talented Senna and also the first victory for the Renault engine in any chassis other than its own, in this case the Lotus 97T designed by Gérard Ducarouge. Alain Prost had an unpleasant experience in this race when his McLaren suddenly swerved going through a puddle on the straight and crashed into the barriers. Alboreto again took second place for Ferrari ahead of de Angelis in the second Lotus. This race marked Stefan Johansson's first drive in the second Ferrari, as a replacement for Arnoux.

The outcome of the San Marino Grand Prix at Imola was turned upside down by fuel consumption problems. Senna was in the lead again when he ran out of fuel after 56 laps. Johansson's Ferrari went into the lead, much to the delight of the patriotic Italian spectators, but was there for just one lap before his tank, too, was empty. Prost's McLaren took over first place from de Angelis in the Lotus, and kept going to win. However, when his MP4/2B was weighed after the race it registered only 538kg, instead of the regulation minimum 540kg, and he was disqualified, which gave de Angelis his second Formula One victory. Prost took his revenge at Monaco where he was the victor — but ran out of fuel on his lap of honour. Alboreto, whose Ferrari had proved the most powerful on this circuit round the streets, was second.

Next race on the schedule was the Belgian Grand Prix at Spa-Francorchamps on June 2nd, but the Ardennes circuit had just been resurfaced and, during practice, had started to lift on some of the fast corners. The teams considered there was great danger of cars losing control on the loose stones and, after a lot of discussion, the race was postponed until September 15th. The World Championship thus resumed with the Canadian Grand Prix at Montreal where the Ferrari 156/85s confirmed the excellent form they had shown in the first half of the season by taking Alboreto and Johansson to first and second places, ahead of Prost's McLaren. In the following Grand Prix however, at Detroit, Johansson and Alboreto had to be content with second and third positions, for here Rosberg in the Williams-Honda FW10 celebrated a triumph about which there was no doubt.

In the French Grand Prix at Le Castellet, Nelson Piquet in the BMW-powered Brabham BT54 proved himself to be unbeatable. It was high summer and the high speeds at Le Castellet suited the Brabham's Pirelli rubber perfectly, the

Italian tyre manufacturer scoring its first victory since withdrawing from Formula One after the Maserati and Vanwall successes of 1957.

The British Grand Prix held at Silverstone was flagged a lap early, but this did not affect Prost, who was a convincing winner yet again. Second man Alboreto had forfeited more than a lap to his rival in the World Championship during the race. The Italian had gone into the Championship lead at the halfway stage, after the

Below
Zakspeed built their own four-cylinder turbo engine as well as the Type 841 chassis designed by the Englishman Paul Brown.

Overleaf
Characteristic turbo flames are produced when changing down. By 1985 several teams had made the change to the extremely expensive turbo engines. The picture shows a Ferrari 156/85 at Monaco.

Canadian Grand Prix, but since Le Castellet the Ferraris had been showing very poor form, especially on fast circuits. The chassis of the 156/85 did not hold the road well, and the 120° engine was continually being forced to increase its performance to compensate, which meant it was no longer displaying the reliability which was normally a characteristic of Ferrari engines. Be that as it may, at the German Grand Prix on the Nürburgring Alboreto fought back and emerged victor over Prost in the McLaren and Jacques Laffite in the Ligier-Renault JS25. This Ferrari success on the Nürburgring was of particular significance, for it was 50 years previously, at the 1935 German Grand Prix, that a Ferrari entry had first won this race, when Tazio Nuvolari in a P3 Alfa Romeo entered by Scuderia Ferrari had scored his historic defeat of the "invincible" Auto-Union and Mercedes-Benz teams.

Proceedings at the Nürburgring in 1985 had begun with almost as much of a surprise. During qualifying on the Friday the little Milanese driver Teo Fabi in the Toleman TG185 had set fastest time, and as it rained in the second qualifying day, Fabi retained his pole position for the race. Rory Byrne's Toleman TG185 chassis was considered one of the best designs of the season, but its four-cylinder Hart engine had now been given an increase in power by a change to Holset turbochargers and an electronic fuel-injection system devised by former Lucas employees. The effort all came to nought however when the Toleman's clutch went at the start. Notwithstanding the disappointment, Pirelli viewed Fabi's qualifying effort as further confirmation of the progress they had made, for all other pole positions as well as race victories had gone to Goodyear.

Prior to his home Grand Prix in Austria, Niki Lauda surprised the press — as he had done in Canada at the end of 1979 — by announcing that he was going to retire from Formula One again at the end of the season. Bernie Ecclestone later tried to tempt the triple World Champion to drive for Brabham in 1986 with a princely offer — there was talk of an annual fee of around 6.5 million dollars — but although Lauda gave the offer serious consideration for weeks, he finally confirmed his second retirement before the last World Championship race in Adelaide, in order to devote himself to Lauda Air. At the same time it was made

public that Lauda's place at McLaren would be taken in 1986 by Keke Rosberg, after four years with Williams. Then at the following race, in Holland, Nelson Piquet announced that he was going to transfer to Williams-Honda in 1986.

Yet another team personnel change followed the Austrian race. During the event Andrea de Cesaris had a spectacular somersault in his Ligier-Renault, and although he was not injured the crash was the last straw for Guy Ligier, who dispensed with the Roman's services for the remainder of the season; at Monza he was replaced by up-and-coming French

Formula 3000 driver Philippe Streiff. In Lauda's last Austrian Grand Prix he actually led for a while but once more technology left him in the lurch, as it had so often done in the 1985 season. Prost won again and thus brought his points score equal with Alboreto's.

Two tragic accidents overshadowed international racing events in the summer of 1985. On August 11th the German RAM driver Manfred Winkelhock suffered a fatal accident driving a Porsche 956 for the Kremer team in the 1000km sportscar race at Mosport in Canada. And then during another long-distance

sportscar race, the Spa 1000km on September 1st, a second German Grand Prix driver lost his life when Stefan Bellof crashed the Porsche 962 he was driving for the Brun team. Bellof had been considered to be the great hope of German motor racing. A factory Porsche driver in 1984, he had emerged as World Endurance Champion after a number of successes in 1000km races. Although these fatalities had come in quick succession, they were in fact the first involving Formula One drivers since Riccardo Paletti's death in the start-line accident in Canada in 1982.

Niki Lauda and his McLaren finally clicked in the Dutch Grand Prix at Zandvoort, when the Austrian won, albeit by only 0.23-second from his team-mate Alain Prost. Lauda gave Prost no special treatment at Zandvoort: each drove his own race. But Prost's second place allowed the Frenchman to overtake Alboreto for the World Championship lead. The 1985 Dutch result was the 25th Grand Prix win in Niki Lauda's Formula One career, which had begun in 1973, and elevated him to second place on the all-time list of winners. Jackie Stewart still topped the list with 27 Grand Prix victories, with Jim Clark having also scored 25. Five-times World Champion Juan-Manuel Fangio, who had actually started in only 51 Grands Prix, remained in fourth position with 24 victories.

On August 27th the Formula One world was shaken by a news bulletin from Paris announcing that, as from the end of the season, Renault would be withdrawing its team. The company had been in the red for years and president Georges Besse was now making drastic cutbacks. Renault had entered Formula One in 1977 and were the first to use the 1.5-litre turbo engine against the 3-litre normally-aspirated engines. Between 1979 and 1983 the yellow, white and black Renaults had won a total of 15 Grands

Prix, nine courtesy of Prost, four by Arnoux and two by Jabouille. But 1984 and 1985 had been particularly disappointing years, the Renaults failing to take a single Formula One victory, though Renault engines did manage three World Championship races in 1985 in other cars, the Lotuses of Senna and de Angelis. Renault would however honour its contracts to supply engines to other constructors, Lotus until the end of 1987 and Tyrrell through 1986. At the beginning of November the contract with Ligier was also extended.

The season carried on with the Italian Grand Prix at Monza where Keke Rosberg demonstrated the capabilities of the 80° V6 Honda engine for much of the way, but in the end it was Prost in the reliable McLaren who won. The Anglo-American Beatrice FORCE team made its debut in this race with the Lola-built THL1, but Alan Jones disappeared from the race very early with chronic defects in his Hart engine.

The deferred Belgian Grand Prix at Spa-Francorchamps now took place. It rained at the start but this suited Lotus-Renault driver Ayrton Senna, who was in complete control throughout. Mansell in the Williams-Honda was second. In the European Grand Prix at Brands Hatch Nigel Mansell drove to the first victory of his Formula One career, ahead of Senna and Rosberg. Prost in his McLaren finished fourth, which assured him of taking the Championship. He was the first Frenchman to win the World Drivers' Championship since its inception in 1950 and was a thoroughly deserving winner, having narrowly missed the title in both 1983 and 1984.

But there was great disappointment at Ferrari for Alboreto had had to retire three times in a row since the Italian Grand Prix, and had now lost any hope of winning the Championship.

Events in the two remaining races

followed the same pattern.

The South African Grand Prix did not take place without considerable debate, for there was considerable international pressure for a total boycott of the race because of the South African government's apartheid policies. The French government suggested that Renault and Ligier should not participate and the teams accordingly withdrew their entries. Some of the sponsors covered over their advertising logos at Kyalami in deference to their public.

When the race finally took place, the Williams-Hondas could not be restrained, and Mansell won again, with Rosberg second, having lost the lead to his team-mate when an oil leak from another car caused him to spin off onto the grass. Prost crossed the line in third place with a stuttering engine caused by faulty electrics. The Ligier withdrawal enabled Philippe Streiff to drive a Tyrrell-Renault at Kyalami; the second Tyrrell had been driven for the first time in the European Grand Prix by Ivan Capelli, a newcomer to Formula One but one of the top men in Formula 3000.

The World Championship season came to an end with the Australian Grand Prix, a new fixture on the Formula One calendar. The race at Adelaide, a very well organized event, was held on a 3.8km street circuit. The grandstands were filled to capacity and the enthusiastic public were treated to a tension-filled World Championship finale. Senna led for Lotus but then made several errors and finally retired. Lauda also had a turn in front but his carbon brakes were his undoing, pulling him to one side and causing him to crash into the barriers. Keke Rosberg was in excellent form and drove at his spectacular best, delighting the crowd with his attacking style. In spite of three pit stops for tyre changes, the Finn drove back through the field and won the race. The Ligier-Renaults of Jacques Laffite and Philippe Streiff crossed the finish line side by side to take second and third placings. Newcomer Ivan Capelli, driving for Tyrrell in only his second Grand Prix, was fourth after an excellent race. For the first time in the 1985 season, Alain Prost had to retire because of a mechanical fault; it was usually Lauda's McLaren that had suffered problems.

To add to Ferrari's disappointments, the World Manufacturers' Championship went to McLaren. Renault had not had a successful season either, and Gérard Toth had handed in his resignation even before

1985

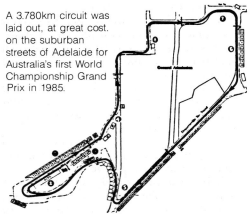

A 3.780km circuit was laid out, at great cost. on the suburban streets of Adelaide for Australia's first World Championship Grand Prix in 1985.

the Australian Grand Prix. Euroracing, with the V8 Alfa Romeo-powered cars driven by Eddie Cheever and Riccardo Patrese, had done even worse, and had not won a single World Championship point. A particularly hard time was suffered by Toleman, RAM and Beatrice-Lola, because the four-cylinder Hart engine was continually breaking down, both in practice and in the races. In October, Benetton succeeded in securing BMW engines for Toleman for 1986.

The following month Alfa Romeo announced they would no longer be supplying engines to Euroracing and Osella, and at the same time stopped any further development work on the eight-

cylinder engine, first used in 1983. Alfa Romeo engineers had been working on a new four-cylinder 1499.7cc (92 x 56.4mm) engine for the past year at the newly formed Alfa Corse operation in the former premises of Autodelta. At the time of Alfa Romeo's withdrawal they announced their intention of returning to Formula One with the new engine in 1987. Like Renault, Alfa Romeo was also very much in the red, mainly because of the Arna production car project.

In spite of the great popularity which Grand Prix racing enjoyed worldwide, it was being threatened by the huge escalation in its costs.

Formula One cars of 1985

Make/model	Chief designer(s)	Engine	Gearbox (speeds)	Chassis	Wheelbase	Track	Tyre make	Dry weight
Arrows A 8	Dave Wass	BMW M 12/13 (4 cyl. Turbo)	Hewland (5)	CA	2794	F 1778 R 1651	Goodyear	545
Brabham BT 54	Gordon Murray	BMW M 12/13 (4 cyl. Turbo)	Brabham-Hewland (6)	CK	2962	F 1682 R 1606	Pirelli	540
Euroracing 185 T	Luigi Marmiroli	Alfa Romeo 890 T (V8 Turbo)	Alfa Romeo-Hewland (5/6)	CK	2720	F 1810 R 1680	Goodyear	546
Ferrari 156/85	Harvey Postlethwaite Antonio Tomaini Ildo Renzetti	Ferrari 126 C (V6 Turbo)	Ferrari (5)	CK	2762	F 1797 R 1664	Goodyear	558
Ligier JS 25	Michel Têtu	Renault EF 4 B (EF 15) (V6 Turbo)	Hewland (5)	CK	2835	F 1790 R 1662	Goodyear	540
Lola-FORCE THL-1	Neil Oatley John Baldwin	Hart 415 T (4 cyl. Turbo)	FORCE-Hewland (6)	CK	2794	F 1803 R 1626	Goodyear	557
Lotus 97 T	Gérard Ducarouge	Renault EF 4 B (EF 15) (V6 Turbo)	Lotus-Hewland (5)	CK	2720	F 1816 R 1620	Goodyear	540
McLaren MP 4/2 B	John Barnard	TAG/Porsche TTE-PO 1 (V6 Turbo)	McLaren-Hewland (5)	CK	2794	F 1803 R 1651	Goodyear	540
Minardi M 185	Giacomo Caliri	Motori Moderni (V6 Turbo)	Minardi-Hewland (5)	CK	2607	F 1813 R 1661	Pirelli	550
Osella FA 1 G	Giuseppe Petrotta	Alfa Romeo 890 T (V8 Turbo)	Hewland (5)	CK	2830	F 1750 R 1600	Pirelli	557
RAM 03	Gustav Brunner	Hart 415 T (4 cyl. Turbo)	RAM-Hewland (6)	CK	2794	F 1778 R 1626	Pirelli	550
Renault RE 60/60 B	Bernard Touret	Renault EF 4 B (EF 15) (V6 Turbo)	Renault-Hewland (6)	CK	2800	F 1800 R 1650	Goodyear	540
Toleman TG 185	Rory Byrne	Hart 415 T (4 cyl. Turbo)	Toleman (5)	CK	2692	F 1816 R 1683	Pirelli	545
Tyrrell 014	Maurice Phillippe	Renault EF 4 B (EF 15) (V6 Turbo)	Tyrrell-Hewland (6)	CK	2756	F 1765 R 1638	Goodyear	550
Williams FW 10/FW 10 B	Patrick Head	Honda RA 166 E (V6 Turbo)	Williams-Hewland (6)	CK	2794	F 1803 R 1651	Goodyear	545
Zakspeed 841	Paul Brown	Zakspeed (4 cyl. Turbo)	Hewland (6)	CK	2820	F 1800 R 1600	Goodyear	565

Chassis construction: CA = carbon-fibre alloy monocoque; CK = Kevlar-carbon-fibre monocoque

The Honda V6 Dominates 1986

Only 195 litres fuel per Grand Prix. Nigel Mansell and Nelson Piquet in the Williams-Honda win nine World Championship races between them, but Alain Prost in the McLaren-TAG-Porsche is the Champion.

The 1986 season belonged firmly to the V6 Honda-engined Williams FW11, which was almost invincible. The superiority this combination had demonstrated at the end of 1985 was even more evident in 1986. In Japan a great deal had been invested in the further development of the six-cylinder engine, and it was suspected that components subject to the greatest heat were made entirely of ceramics, or at least had ceramic coatings. In races the 80° Honda engine proved not only to have considerable power, but was economical as well and this gave the Williams-Honda drivers, Piquet and Mansell, greater reserves of power than their rivals had available to them.

The further limitations of fuel use — only 195 litres of fuel was available for each race in 1986 instead of 220 — forced the engine and electronics specialists to carry out further research so that they could make the utmost use of their fuel allowances. But the ban on 3-litre normally-aspirated engines passed virtually unnoticed as none of the teams had used these configurations since the beginning of 1985.

The year 1986 started with the celebration of the 100th birthday of the motor car, for it was on January 29th 1886 that Karl Benz had applied for a patent for a vehicle powered by an engine which ran on fuel "produced by an apparatus which was carried along with it to convert substances to gas". In the same year, Gottlieb Daimler had built a motor coach with benzine engine. Naturally, the firm of Daimler-Benz played a leading part in the centennial celebrations held in honour of these two great automobile pioneers.

The Formula One world played only a peripheral part in the festivities, for they were well into preparations for the new season at this time of year, and the first tests were already being run on the Jacarepagua circuit at Rio de Janeiro.

The departure of Keke Rosberg for McLaren, where he would be team-mate

Carl Benz

Gottlieb Daimler

to World Champion Alain Prost, and his replacement at Williams by Nelson Piquet — after seven years with Bernie Ecclestone's Brabham team — were only two of several changes in the make-up of the leading teams before the start of the new season.

Alfa Romeo's announcement that they were halting further development on the V8 engine, and would return after a 12-month absence with a four-cylinder design, left Euroracing boss Pavanello with no option but to disband his team, leaving his drivers, Eddie Cheever and Riccardo Patrese, to look around for new teams. Patrese went to Brabham, where his partner was Elio de Angelis. The Roman driver had now left Lotus — where he had been for six years — as he felt the team had discriminated against him in favour of Ayrton Senna. Cheever however was unable to find a Formula One drive and was forced to sign up with the Jaguar team for endurance racing instead. He had been under consideration at Tyrrell, but eventually it was the Frenchman Phillippe Streiff, who was able to bring sponsorship with him, who got the second Tyrrell, alongside Martin Brundle. When Renault announced the dissolution of its Formula One team in August 1985, Patrick Tambay had been able to find himself a place in the Lola Haas team, while Derek Warwick was widely tipped as the logical candidate for the second place at Lotus. But Ayrton Senna was against having a driver of Warwick's calibre on the same team, preferring a younger and less experienced team-mate who would not deflect team effort away from him, and the drive was eventually given to the young Scottish

nobleman, Johnny Dumfries.

The future of Carl Haas's Lola-FORCE team, with which Tambay had come to an arrangement, as again had 1980 World Champion Alan Jones, was somewhat up in the air as the season began. From the beginning of the season the name of Beatrice, the team's backers, was written in much smaller script on the Lolas, for the American conglomerate had been sold and the new management were not interested in pursuing their involvement in Formula One. Ford and Cosworth were however happy to continue work on the Ford V6 turbo engine in conjunction with the Haas team. The new unit should have been ready for the Brazilian Grand Prix, first race of the season, but its debut was in fact postponed until the San Marino Grand Prix, and the team started the year still with the four-cylinder Hart motor, which they had used in the last races of the 1985 season, in their Lola THL1s.

The talented Austrian Gerhard Berger left Arrows for the Toleman team, which was wholly owned by the Benetton clothing company and was now known as Benetton Formula Ltd. But although the British team was now under Italian control, the personnel remained largely unchanged, with Rory Byrne still in charge of design. One significant change however was that the Benettons — as they were now known — were finally able to abandon their Hart engines, as an agreement had been reached with BMW

Gerhard Berger

1986 was the 100th birthday of the automobile. Karl Benz and Gottlieb Daimler were among the greatest of the pioneers, building respectively a motor coach with petrol engine and a three-wheeled gas-powered vehicle, both in 1886.

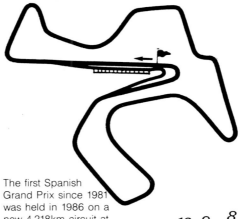

Bernard Dudot

for the supply of the German engines instead. These were not however maintained by BMW Motorsport GmbH in Munich, as were the Brabham team's engines, but instead by Swiss engine-builder Heini Mader, who was also responsible for the BMW engines used by the Arrows team.

The unsuccessful association of Lola, Toleman and RAM with the Hart motor in 1985 led to the final disappearance from Formula One of the British four-cylinder turbo engine in 1986. John Macdonald's RAM team also disappeared from the scene, nothing having come of suggestions that an Australian syndicate would ensure its survival.

Ford started testing its new V6 turbo engine in the Lola THL2 on Ford's own test track at Boreham in England in February, though it would be April 27th before the engine made its racing debut, at Imola. In the development and construction of the new 130° V6, Ford used the EEC-IV series module developed from the unit already in use on their Scorpio and Sierra production cars. It was naturally given a more complex task in controlling the fuel injection, ignition and turbocharger boost. Cylinder dimensions of the Anglo-American engine were not made public but, fitted with twin Garrett turbo-chargers, it was known to run at 11,000rpm.

In the spring of 1986 Alfa Romeo, as an image-boosting exercise, announced the formation of a new racing department called Alfa Corse. This was little more than the old Autodelta company renamed, occupying the same premises as a division of the main factory. But the establishment of Alfa Corse seemed to confirm the company's intention of continuing development of the new four-cylinder Formula One engine for a top Formula One team in 1987.

Renault produced a surprise during the pre-season tests in Brazil, when they announced a new version of their EF-15 engine in which the valve springs were replaced by a pneumatic pressure system. The heart of this system was a half-litre tank of pressurised nitrogen, mounted in the vee between the banks of cylinders. This fed through a system of pipes to an arrangement of coaxial control pistons, one for each of the 24 valves. This system ensured that each valve was in constant pressure contact with the camshaft and reduced operating delay. According to

Renault's chief Formula One engine development engineer Bernard Dudot, the pneumatic system increased maximum possible engine speed from 11,500 to 12,500rpm. Having dissolved their own Formula One team, the Renault base at Viry-Chatillon was concentrating on supplying engines for

The first Spanish Grand Prix since 1981 was held in 1986 on a new 4.218km circuit at Jerez in the southern part of the country.

the Lotus, Tyrrell and Ligier teams in 1986, former Renault Formula One racing director Jean Sage acting as liaison between the teams and Renault.

For some drivers, plans for the 1986 season were finalised only at the very last minute, for the last cockpits were not filled until just before the Brazilian Grand Prix. The Minardi team released Pierluigi Martini and took on Andrea de Cesaris and Alessandro Nannini in his place. At the last moment Marc Surer found a seat at Arrows, taking the place of Berger, who had gone to Benetton. Zakspeed also expanded its team to two cars and entrusted these to Jonathan Palmer and Huub Rothengatter. Ligier renewed their contract with Jacques Laffite and also took on René Arnoux, who returned to Formula One after his year's break after leaving Ferrari. Jones and Tambay had to compete in the first two races still using the old Hart engine. Jones received the

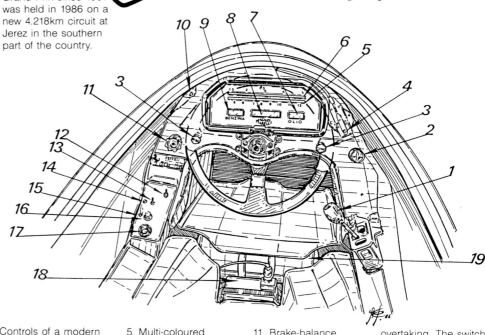

Controls of a modern Formula One racing car (Ferrari F1-86)
1. Gear lever (5 forward gears and reverse). A locking device has to be released before reverse is selected.
2. Turbo boost knob: turn to the right to increase pressure.
3. Outlets for the on-board extinguisher.
4. Electrical circuit breaker.

5. Multi-coloured horizontal rev counter.
6. Turbo boost gauge.
7. Oil pressure gauge.
8. Digital display which gives the fuel available, and also indicates how many laps can still be covered at the same speed.
9. Fuel pressure gauge.
10. Switch for consumption gauge (8).

11. Brake-balance adjustment: turn to the right for increased braking at the front.
12. Selector for the computer data which can be read on the dashboard.
13. Switch for tail lights (have to be switched on in the rain).
14. Switch which turns the rev-limiter off. Is used only for short bursts, such as

overtaking. The switch is sealed by a thin wire so that the pits know immediately if the engine is being over-revved.
15. Switch for the fire extinguisher.
16. Gauge for the fire extinguisher unit.
17. Red emergency switch for fire extinguisher unit.
18. On-board fire extinguisher.

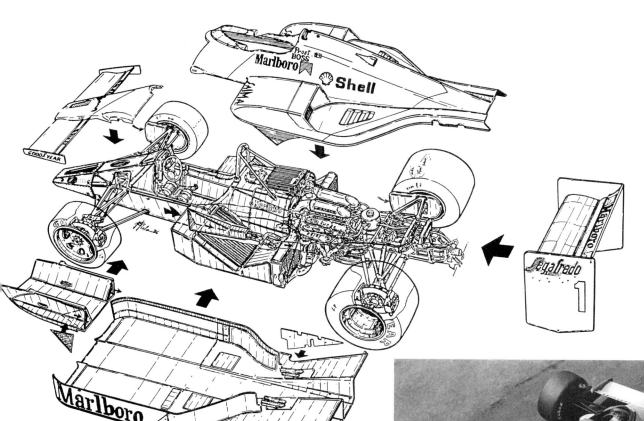

new six-cylinder at the San Marino Grand Prix at Imola, despite the fact that Tambay had, in the meantime, proved himself to be the faster driver.

With the exception of Brabham, all teams produced basically conventional new designs for 1986, in each case a logical development of the team's previous year's model. But Brabham designer Gordon Murray, in close collaboration with BMW, produced an ultra-low car in which the four-cylinder BMW engine was laid almost flat. The car also had an extremely long wheelbase of no less than 2040mm. The Brabham-BMW BT55 was hailed as a revolutionary solution, and even before it turned a wheel there was a feeling that all cars would follow the BT55 concept in the future. In order to meet the new car's design requirements BMW racing engineer Paul Roche had had to redesign the four-cylinder engine completely. Installing the engine in the chassis at an angle of 72° meant the crankshaft lay to one side of the longitudinal central axis. The position of the engine and the low design of the chassis also meant a new gearbox had to be designed and built; the American firm of Weismann came up with a seven-speed unit, which was mounted transversely. In the official

Right
At the end of 1985 Keke Rosberg transferred from Williams to McLaren, but was rarely able to achieve the same performance as teammate Alain Prost.

release of the BT55 the car's sponsor, Olivetti, made special mention of the unusually high expense involved in the project: some 732 sketches had been made, 117,000 man/hours spent, and a total of £6.8 million invested.

After failing to lure Niki Lauda back into racing, and with the other leading drivers — Senna, Rosberg, Piquet and Prost — all committed elsewhere, Bernie Ecclestone took on the Italians Elio de Angelis and Riccardo Patrese to drive the new car. The BT55, nicknamed "The Flounder", was so low that the driver had virtually to lie down in the cockpit, but right from the very first tests there were indications that there might be more serious problems. The car had tremendous cooling and gearbox problems, and the drivers later

complained of poor traction. The BT55 was in fact a flop, never moving from midfield positions.

Another make entering Formula One this year — though its debut was not scheduled until the Italian Grand Prix — was *Automobiles Gonfaronaises Sportives*, or AGS, a small French outfit led by Henri Julien. Over the years, from his base at Gonfaron in the south of France, Julien had been very successful with his own designs from Formule Renault to Formula Two and even Formula 3000. Now, with the support of the Italian Jolly Club, he wanted to take the step into the upper echelon, using the Motori-Moderni engine. The Belgian Christian Vanderpleyn, who had worked for Julien at AGS for several years, designed a carbon monocoque chassis which was

Important characteristics of the new Formula One cars in 1985 and 1986

Make	Alfa Romeo	Ford	Motori Moderni	Renault	Zakspeed
Model	415.85.T	GB	F.1 Turbo	EF 15 (C)	841
Cylinder configuration	4 R Turbo	V6 120°	V6 90° Turbo	V6 90° Turbo	4 R Turbo
Bore & stroke	92 × 56,4	?	80 × 49,7	80,1 × 49,4	90,4 × 58,25
Capacity	1499,7	?	1499	1492	1495
Main bearings	5	4	4	4	5
Fuel injection	Bosch	Ford	Weber/Marelli	Renault	Bosch
Turbocharger	1 × Garrett/ 1 × KKK	2 × Garrett	2 × KKK	2 × Garrett	1 Garrett
Ignition	Bosch	Ford	Marelli	Marelli	Zakspeed
Power (bhp) at (rpm)	860 10 500	?	720—750 11 300	780—850 12 000	700—750 10 000

built at the specialist French firm of MOC. Julien had bought up several gearbox and suspension parts at a very reasonable price from Renault, after that team retired from Formula One, and these were incorporated into the AGS JH21C. For his driver Julien took on the Italian Ivan Capelli who, after taking part in a handful of Formula One races at the end of 1985 had gone back to Formula 3000.

After the Williams successes at the end of 1985 there was a great deal of interest

Henri Julien

in their new design for 1986, particularly as they had exclusive rights over the powerful 80° V6 Honda V6 engine for another year. Patrick Head settled for a straightforward design for his FW11 which, in the hands of Mansell and Piquet, proved to be the best Formula One car of the season. Its superiority was enhanced by continuing intensive work on the Type RA163E engine by the Honda engineers, and their success in adapting to the new 195-litre fuel limit.

McLaren's contender was the MP4/2C, which was barely distinguishable from its predecessor externally, for John Barnard was not the sort for sudden revolutionary breakthroughs and preferred instead to improve on a known quantity. At Lotus, Gérard Ducarouge developed the Renault-powered 98T which was rumoured to have rather high fuel

consumption so that superstar Ayrton Senna had to use its power sparingly in races. The Ferrari F1-86 was developed under the direction of Dr Harvey Postlethwaite, but Alboreto and Johansson could never quite keep up with the race leaders. Ferrari seemed to have simply lost the knack of producing an outstanding car, even though Maranello had constant proof that the V6 engine did have an outstanding performance potential: on the Mistral Straight at Le Castellet, for example, the F1-86 reached a top speed of 342.2km/h. But the roadholding and traction left something to be desired, as did the aerodynamics.

Prior to the start of the 1986 season FOCA boss Bernie Ecclestone had brought off a real coup when he managed the seemingly impossible task of launching a Grand Prix in an Eastern European country. After long and tiring discussions with the representatives of the Hungarian Automobile Club and the Budapest authorities he had succeeded in getting agreement, and on October 15th

Above
Marc Surer returned to Arrows in 1986 and drove the BMW-powered A8. During practice at Spa a small fire broke out in his car, as shown here. Just one week later, on May 31st 1986, he had a serious accident in the Hessen Rally.

Right
The Monaco course was modified yet again, the famous chicane on the harbour being reshaped. On the day of the 1986 Monaco Grand Prix the Milanese *Gazzetta Sportiva* published this drawing of the Principality's famous circuit.

Below right
The brilliant South African designer Gordon Murray was responsible for all Brabham designs since 1973. Several times his ideas revolutionized Formula One car design and the knowledgeable viewed him as Colin Chapman's successor. His innovative BT55 was not a success however.

Right
On paper the Brabham BT55 seemed to be a revolutionary step forward in racing car construction, but the results were anything but encouraging.

Below
Riccardo Patrese tells BMW engineer Paul Rosche exactly what his impressions are during practice for the 1986 German Grand Prix. The four-cylinder BMW turbo engines were developed for Formula One under Rosche's direction.

1985 work started on a large and modern autodrome on a hilly piece of land about 20 kilometres from the centre of Budapest. This circuit, the Hungaroring, was 4.014 kilometres long and was opened with a small race meeting on June 15th 1986, in preparation for the World Championship Hungarian Grand Prix on August 10th. The Hungarians mobilized a giant crowd of spectators, thanks to huge spending on advertising.

There was a new circuit in Spain as well, a 4.191km course near Jerez de la Frontera in the southern part of the country where, after a five-year break, the Spanish Grand Prix resumed its long tradition in 1986. Another new date on the World Championship calendar this year was the Mexican Grand Prix, reviving a race last held in 1970. The Mexicans had not had a Grand Prix driver since the death of Pedro Rodriguez, but now the Magdalena Mixhuca circuit in Mexico City, where races were held in the sixties, was modernized and shortened from five to 4.421km, two parts of the old circuit being eliminated. Particular attention had been paid to bringing the circuit up to modern safety requirements.

Shortly before the World Championship season started the Williams team suffered a heavy blow. On March 8th Frank Williams had a serious accident driving a rental car back to his hotel from Le Castellet, where he had been attending Formula One testing. Williams lost control of his car on a corner and it overturned, inflicting serious injuries on the unfortunate driver. He was taken to hospital in Marseilles where the diagnosis was devastating. He was paralyzed from the waist down and

has been confined to a wheelchair ever since.

The 1986 season was to bring even worse events. On May 13th Elio de Angelis had a serious accident during a test session with the Brabham BT55 at Le Castellet, and died two days later. Apparently the accident was caused by part of the rear wing breaking away. The Le Castellet organisation came under close scrutiny following this accident, for precious time was lost before fire on the burning car was extinguished and the unfortunate driver extricated.

Then on May 31st there were two more tragic accidents. Jo Gartner, who had competed for Osella in several Grands Prix in 1984, went off the track at the beginning of the Hunaudières straight at Le Mans during the 24-hour race and was killed instantly. Only hours before Marc Surer, who had made a commitment to rallying and had in fact signed a contract with Ford, left the road during the Hessen Rally and was severely injured. His co-driver, Michel Wyder, was killed in the blazing wreck and Surer was taken to hospital with several broken bones and internal injuries. It took several months for him to recover, his Formula One season over after five races. Surer was replaced at Arrows by Christian Danner, while Derek Warwick took de Angelis's place at Brabham. After de Angelis's accident a decision was made to shorten the Le Castellet circuit from 5.8 to 3.318km, by cutting out the infamous S bend at La Verrerie where de Angelis had had his accident.

The season belonged to three cars, the Williams-Honda FW11, the Lotus-Renault 98T and the McLaren-TAG-

Christian Danner

Porsche MP4/2C, and from that small circle of favourites the Williams-Honda soon emerged as leader. During qualifying, when there seemed to be no limits to the power escalation, Ayrton Senna in the Lotus 98T stood out as the leading driver, but in every race he had to give precedence to the Williams-Hondas to avoid running out of fuel. Prost and the McLaren-TAG-Porsche were still the fast, well-balanced combination which was always good for a victory. But the superiority which the Porsche-designed engine had demonstrated in 1984 and 1985 was gone, for Honda had made up a great deal of ground and had now established a clear superiority.

Piquet in a Williams-Honda won the Championship opener, the Brazilian Grand Prix, but then Senna in the Lotus-Renault won the Spanish Grand Prix at Jerez — by half a car's length from Mansell's Williams-Honda.

In the San Marino Grand Prix at Imola World Champion Alain Prost won the victor's laurels once again, but used up his very last drop of petrol as he rolled stutteringly over the finish line. This was the first time that the TAG engine had had consumption problems. But there were no consumption problems for anyone in the Monaco Grand Prix, because of its relatively short distance, and Prost won his third victory in the Principality in a row.

Then it was Nigel Mansell's turn for a string of successes, the Englishman proving invincible and winning one race after another. The Isle of Man resident won the Belgian Grand Prix at Spa, the Canadian at Montreal, the French on the shortened course at Le Castellet, and the British Grand Prix at Brands Hatch.

By the middle of the season his team-mate Nelson Piquet had been forced into Mansell's shadow, but in the German Grand Prix the Brazilian was victorious while Mansell fell back into third place with a chassis problem. Two weeks after his success at Hockenheim, Piquet was winner again, in the Hungarian Grand Prix on the Hungaroring, with Senna again finishing in second place and Mansell in third. Although Senna usually started from pole position, the talented Brazilian managed only two wins in the first half of the season, in Spain and at Detroit.

The driving skill of the Williams team's rivals could not fully compensate for the superiority of the Honda six-cylinder.

Although consumption had been reduced to 195 litres, it was generally agreed that the Honda was still producing between 900 and 920bhp in race trim in 1986, though these figures could only be guessed at; Honda never confirmed them. The Japanese were very noncommittal about technical data, even the cylinder dimensions of the 80° engine remaining secret. During qualifying, when consumption did not matter, they were said to have 1200bhp available, at maximum turbo boost of 4.5bar absolute. The teams used special qualifying engines as well as qualifying tyres; of the leading teams only McLaren-TAG still refused to use either qualifying engines or qualifying tyres.

The Pirelli racing department which, under the direction of development engineer Mario Mezzanotte, had developed special tyres for the Brabham BT55, hoped that 1986 would see them finally making some headway in competition with the cars using Goodyear tyres, but they had to be content with average results. The best Pirelli team proved initially to be Ligier, who used the Renault-powered JS27 designed by Michel Tétu. Both Jacques Laffite and René Arnoux won Championship points with this car, and at Detroit Laffite actually made it into second place.

In the British Grand Prix at Brands Hatch Laffite, who was now 43 years old, equalled the record of 178 World Championship Grand Prix starts held by Graham Hill for more than a decade. But exactly 200 metres after his last start in a World Championship race Laffite was

Above
Gérard Ducarouge talking to Brazilian superstar Ayrton Senna. Ducarouge was originally a designer for Matra, Ligier and Alfa Romeo, but from 1983 was responsible for the design of Lotus's Formula One cars. When Honda agreed to collaborate with Lotus from 1987 they stipulated that both Ducarouge and Senna had to remain.

Above
The 1986 Lotus 98T with Renault V6 turbo engine was the fourth Lotus Formula One design by the Frenchman Gérard Ducarouge.

Right
The extremely fast combination of Ayrton Senna and Lotus-Renault 98T was on pole position numerous times during 1986.

Ayrton Senna

After Elio de Angelis's fatal accident in May 1986 it was decided that although the French Grand Prix would still be held at Le Castellet the course would be shortened from 5.81 to 3.318km.

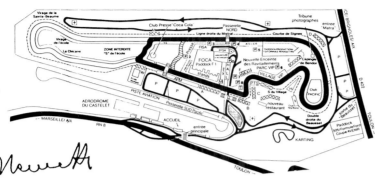

Mario Mezzanotte

Derek Ongaro

involved in a multiple collision triggered by Arrows driver Thierry Boutsen. It took half an hour before rescuers could free the Frenchman from his cockpit. He had broken several bones when the Ligier crashed into the barriers at full speed.

At the French Grand Prix, just two weeks before, an even worse disaster was narrowly missed. The engine in Alboreto's Ferrari died just before the starting signal was given, and the Milanese driver could only sit there helplessly, waving his arms in the air. In

such a case Derek Ongaro, FISA's man in charge of circuit safety and the person responsible for starting every Grand Prix since 1980, should have signalled a false start but unfortunately he was unaware of Alboreto's plight and switched the signal to green. The field shot past the stationary Ferrari and it was a miracle Alboreto wasn't hurt.

The 1986 French Grand Prix was, incidentally, the 400th World Championship race Ferrari had contested since the series began in 1950 but they

were not under a lucky star for at the start of the German Grand Prix at Hockenheim there was another start-line collision. About 150 metres from the start Ferrari driver Johansson and Alliot, who had taken Laffite's place in the Ligier team, bumped into each other; the Ferrari was thrown across the track into Fabi's Benetton which, in turn, came to a halt in the barriers. Johansson and Alliot, on the other hand, were able to continue the race after hasty repairs in the pits. This spate of start-line pile-ups was an indication that the enormous performances of which the 1.5-litre turbo engines were capable were very difficult to control. A small irregularity in the starting procedure could result in a mass collision.

FISA president Jean-Marie Balestre —

In the British Grand Prix at Brands Hatch Nelson Piquet in the Williams-Honda FW11 leads the field after one lap from Gerhard Berger in the Benetton-BMW B186 and Nigel Mansell in the second Williams-Honda. The leader's car has just hit a bump, causing sparks to fly from the undertray.

who since the autumn of 1985 had, in addition to being president of FISA and of the French national association, FFSA, become president of the FIA as successor to Prince Paul-Alfons von Metternich — was very worried about the shocking speed with which costs were escalating.

On June 26th 1986 FISA drew up new regulations to come into effect in 1987. The amount of fuel would be further reduced from its existing limit of 195 litres per race, and in addition the familiar qualifying system would be abolished. Seventy percent of the grid places would be taken from the results of the previous race, also taking Championship standings into account; the remaining places would be determined by a qualifying race on the

Fürst Paul-Alfons von Metternich

afternoon before the race, over 25% of the Grand Prix distance. FISA's intention was to limit teams' reliance on super-powerful qualifying engines though, by having two starts per weekend, they were increasing the risk of damage to the engine or car. This would make it impossible for the ordinary racegoer to calculate the starting positions: a powerful computer would now be needed.

Most of the teams did not support the proposed new qualifying system, and

FISA was ultimately forced to reconsider. The International Sporting Commission also determined that engine output should be reduced to around 600bhp for 1987. This could be achieved either by reducing engine size to 1100 or 1200cc, or by abandoning turbocharged engines altogether, and running Grands Prix for cars with normally-aspirated engines under 3500cc. So many new regulations had been put forward and rejected in the previous few years, to be replaced by other proposals, that few teams took the latest recommendations seriously.

On June 27th the BMW board of directors surprised the Grand Prix world by announcing that their Formula One activities would cease from the end of 1986, and development of the four-cylinder turbo engine would stop. The Brabham BT55-BMW's unsuccessful season was most likely behind this decision, though Nelson Piquet had used this engine to win the World Championship with the Brabham BT52 in 1982.

Shortly after the BMW announcement, on July 6th, Alfa Romeo and Ligier reached a surprising agreement by which Alfa Romeo would supply Ligier exclusively with Grand Prix engines for three seasons from 1987. In addition, the Milan company would provide financial support for the team's running; this was in spite of the fact that Alfa Romeo were in a critical financial state, and were talking with Ford about the possibility of a takeover.

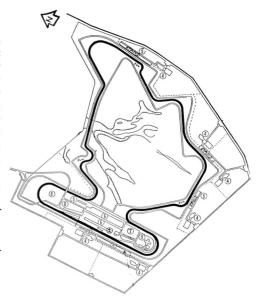

In October 1985 work had started on the construction of the 4.014km Hungaroring.

The course was ready by the middle of June 1986.

More surprises followed. During practice for the German Grand Prix at Hockenheim, Keke Rosberg announced he would be stepping down from Formula One at the end of the year. He had been somewhat in Alain Prost's shadow at McLaren and, without realizing it, had slipped into a No 2 position. On the following day, July 26th, Honda also had important news, announcing that they would be increasing their support for the Williams team, and extending their arrangement to include Lotus, whose contract with Renault was due to expire. As part of the deal, Lotus agreed to take on a Japanese driver as their No 2 and Satoru Nakajima, who had competed in Japanese Formula 3000 races with a Ralt-Honda in 1986, and had also done all the testing for Williams-Honda in Japan, was chosen. Until this time Williams had been negotiating with Renault and the two parties had practically reached agreement, but then Honda came up with a better deal for Williams and the two partners decided to continue working together for a further two years.

McLaren had also had negotiations with Honda as the TAG owner, Mansour Ojjeh, did not appear to be willing to pump more of his millions into the Porsche-built McLaren-TAG engine project, for the German company was prepared to continue development only if someone else was paying. But Honda's decision to go with Lotus as well as

Alain Prost's McLaren-TAG-Porsche MP4/2C ran out of fuel about a hundred metres from the finish line in the German Grand Prix at Hockenheim. Although it was against the rules, the World Champion, in desperation, got out and pushed his car. At Imola he had won but only by rolling over the line with a stuttering engine, the TAG-Porsche engine experiencing consumption problems for the first time.

Below right
Bernie Ecclestone, English head of FOCA, may be small in stature but, in 1986, he pulled off the coup of having an East European race included in the World Championship calendar.

Below
The Hungarian Grand Prix opened a new era in spectator numbers. On race day 200,000 fans streamed into the Hungaroring, and by including the numbers attending practice days the figure rises to 380,000.

Right
The Hungaroring was a highly modern design which astonished even visitors from the West. The organization of this Grand Prix was also exemplary.

Williams left McLaren without any hope of obtaining the coveted Japanese engine for 1987. Until 1986 the TAG engine had been considered one of the most economical, having not had any consumption problems, but at Hockenheim the engines failed to go the distance, for the first time. Both Rosberg and Prost were left stranded with empty tanks, the Frenchman only about 100 metres from the finish.

During 1986 Ferrari moved heaven and earth to entice a top-notch designer to Maranello. Since August 1985 the Austrian Gustav Brunner had been there, working on an Indianapolis model for the CART series with V8 turbo engine. Ferrari also sent out feelers to Lotus designer Gerard Ducarouge — who, after much consideration, decided to stay at Lotus — and McLaren man John Barnard, who was unwilling to tear himself away from England. For over a year Ferrari had been in a very tight spot.

The Hungarian Grand Prix on the new Hungaroring was a great success. More than 200,000 entrance tickets found curious takers for race day, and a vast crowd of people lined the Grand Prix track. Such numbers had probably never

Above
British designer Rory Byrne (left), who was so successful at Toleman and Benetton. He is pictured here with the talented Austrian driver Gerhard Berger.

Right
From the middle of the 1986 season the Benetton B186 had a BMW engine and Pirelli tyres. In Mexico, Berger secured the first Grand Prix victory both for himself and his make.

before been seen at a World Championship race. The Hungaroring was exemplary in every way and motor sport could look back on a day of immense historical significance. Not only was it the first World Championship race to be held in an Eastern European country but other East European delegations had made the pilgrimage there as observers. There is a great deal of enthusiasm for motor racing in the Eastern bloc countries. Shortly after the race the Hungarian Ministry of the Interior confirmed that 200,000 spectators attended the race but, by including practice and qualifying sessions, the total was nearer 380,000.

Nelson Piquet in the Williams-Honda and Ayrton Senna in the Lotus-Renault fought out an exciting duel in the historic Hungarian race, which the Williams driver finally won.

In the meantime, the general impression was that the career of the TAG-Porsche engine would come to an abrupt stop at the end of the season, and McLaren opened discussions with Renault with a view to possibly joining up with the French company in 1987.

At the Austrian Grand Prix the Benetton B186s, with four-cylinder BMW engines and Pirelli tyres, suddenly found themselves not only in the front row at the start but, for the first time in their careers, both their drivers, Gerhard Berger and Teo Fabi, led the race — though Fabi's moment of glory lasted for only about 100 metres. The Benettons both struck trouble however, leaving Alain Prost in the McLaren to take his third Grand Prix of the season. This was his 24th Formula One victory, which meant he had equalled five-times World

Champion Juan Manuel Fangio in the list of Grand Prix winners. Both Williams cars withdrew at the Osterreichring.

Alfa Romeo had meanwhile begun the first tests of its new four-cylinder turbo engine, the Type 415/85T, designed under the direction of Gianni Tonti at Alfa Corse and intended for Ligier, though its first trials were carried out in an old Euroracing chassis.

In the Italian Grand Prix at Monza and at Estoril in Portugal the Williams-Honda FW11 with Goodyear tyres continued its string of victories, Piquet securing his fourth win of the season at Monza (with Frank Dernie, as usual, looking after his car) and Nigel Mansell taking his fifth 1986 victory in Portugal (where Patrick Head was in charge of his Williams). At Estoril, Ayrton Senna ran out of fuel during the last lap, which left only three drivers — Mansell, Piquet and Prost — in the running for the World Championship. After Estoril, Mansell's position was greatly consolidated, for he was leading Piquet by ten points. But Williams-Honda was already confirmed as Manufacturers' Champions for 1987 by Portugal, a great honour not only for the small English operation but also for Honda, who had invested a great deal in the development of the 80° engine in the three years they had been competing in Grands Prix.

Progress in turbo engine development had been made in leaps and bounds in this time and the resulting escalation in costs was reflected in horrendous top speeds. During qualifying for the Italian Grand Prix, for example, an unofficial "world record" was registered when the Benetton-BMW B186 driven by Gerhard Berger was timed at a speed of 351km/h. Considering that modern racing cars, with their wide tyres and wings, have very poor wind resistance, this speed is all the more impressive.

The escalation in costs was too much for some. At the beginning of September Pirelli announced its withdrawal from Formula One, for the rewards did not compensate for the high costs of development. In 1985 and 1986 Pirelli had relied completely on Brabham and had assumed they would win the World Championship with Gordon Murray's design, even though Nelson Piquet had been victorious only in France in 1985. In 1986 the BT55, originally thought to be such a revolutionary concept, proved in practice to be quite mediocre and did not produce the expected results.

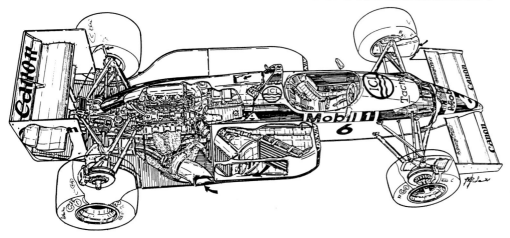

The Ford-engined Lola THL2 finally gained points in Austria and Italy.

With McLaren, TAG and Porsche having reached agreement on future cooperation, Renault seemed to have lost its last chance to work with a top-notch team in 1987. At the end of September BMW changed its mind about the decision it had reached in June to withdraw from Formula One, and committed itself to supplying Brabham and possibly Benetton as well with engines in 1987. The original contract with Brabham did not in fact expire until the end of 1987.

But the horrendous escalation in costs meant the whole Grand Prix situation had to be rethought. Gradually there were louder and louder calls for a future formula catering exclusively for normally-aspirated engines, with a limit of 3.5 litres seeming to be the most popular choice. But it was still necessary to find a compromise to enable both the existing turbo engines and the normally-aspirated engines to compete on more or less equal terms during an interim period.

In the summer of 1986 FISA president Balestre discussed proposed changes to the Grand Prix formula with the teams, most of whom wanted to have less power and less expensive materials in the future. There was a plea to do away with the turbo engines which had resulted in such a frightening escalation in costs.

The new regulations, to remain in force until the end of 1989, were published in Paris on October 3rd 1986. The normally-aspirated engine, banned in 1986, would be readmitted in 1987, but with a capacity of 3500cc rather than the 3000cc which had been in force until the end of 1985. Minimum weight for these cars would be 500kg, though for cars powered by turbo engines the limit remained 540kg, and turbo boost would be limited — by means of a pressure release valve — to 4bar. The fuel limit of 195 litres per Grand Prix remained in force for 1987, for both turbocharged and non-turbocharged cars. Regulations governing both the chassis and the external dimensions were further altered, which meant that, from 1988, the pedals had to be positioned behind the front axle so that the driver was better protected.

It was envisaged that turbo engines would have a chance of winning against the 3.5-litre normally-aspirated engines in 1987, but that the next step, to come into force in 1988, would rob them of any advantage. For the second "phase-out" year turbo engines would be forced to run at a maximum boost to 2.5bar, which would considerably reduce performance, and in addition their fuel allowance was reduced to 150 litres per Grand Prix, whereas no limit was set on the amount of fuel for cars with normally-aspirated engines. This was seen as leaving turbo engines completely in the cold in 1988, but the following year they would be banned altogether from Formula One.

Most of the designers reacted positively to the decisions published on October 3rd 1986, because the new 3.5-litre normally-aspirated engines did not threaten to swallow up the immense sums of money that the former 1.5-litre turbo engines had, and this would have immediate effect as qualifying engines would be dispensed with from 1987. Honda was however disappointed about the ban on turbo engines, as they had invested immense sums of money in the development of their six-cylinder engine, which had become almost invincible. The British teams were disappointed at the new regulations' limiting of the maximum number of cylinders to 12. They would have preferred a maximum of eight cylinders so they could use the Cosworth-Ford again and argued that, by stipulating 12 cylinders, FISA seemed to be favouring Ferrari.

There had meanwhile been other developments at Maranello. Even before the World Championship season had finished 88-year-old Commendatore Enzo Ferrari called a press conference at which he confirmed what had been common knowledge for weeks: the team had hired John Barnard, the successful McLaren designer. At the same time Ferrari announced that in 1987 — their 40th continuous season in Grand Prix racing — their drivers would be Michele Alboreto and Gerhard Berger.

In October there was sensational news from England: Gordon Murray, who had worked for Brabham since 1970 and had been responsible for designing all the team's Formula One cars since 1973, had left Bernie Ecclestone's company.

The 1986 World Championship could have been decided in the second to last race, held on the circuit dedicated to Pedro and Ricardo Rodriguez in Magdalena Mixhuca Park, Mexico City, but neither of the two Williams-Hondas was able to win at this altitude (more than 2200 metres) and the winner was Austrian Gerhard Berger in the Benetton B186 equipped with four-cylinder BMW engine and Pirelli tyres, with Prost second and Senna third. This was the first success of Berger's Formula One career which had begun in 1984, and was also the first

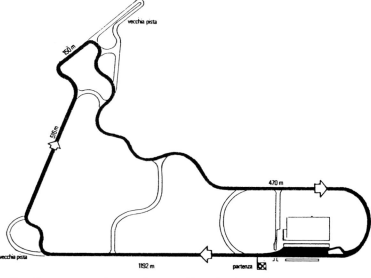

Top
After a gap of 16 years a World Championship race was held once again on the Autodrome in the Magdalena Mixhuca Park in Mexico City. The course had been shortened from 5km to 4.421km and renamed the "Circuito Hermanos Ricardo y Pedro Rodriguez" and was of a very modern design.

Grand Prix victory for Benetton, the huge Italian clothing firm which had taken over the Toleman racing team. Its chief designer was Rory Byrne and his cars had been in exceptional form for over two years. Both BMW and Pirelli also had their first success since Nelson Piquet's victory in the 1985 French Grand Prix. Berger, Benetton, and BMW had the Pirelli tyres to thank for the victory in Mexico for they were able to cover the whole distance without having to change tyres, while their rivals had to put on new tyres not just once but as many as three times, in some cases. Yet Pirelli had already announced its withdrawal from Formula One.

Going into the Australian Grand Prix at Adelaide, the 16th and last Grand Prix of the season, three drivers — Nigel Mansell, Alain Prost and Nelson Piquet — were in contention for the 1986 World Championship title. An incredible number of spectators had gathered at the Adelaide street circuit and they were witnesses to a dramatic World Championship finale. Initially Keke Rosberg, who had just announced his retirement, dominated with his McLaren-TAG-Porsche MP4/2C, and was clear leader from the seventh lap on. If he could stay ahead of Prost and Piquet, Nigel Mansell did not need to be particularly worried about his title chances, for as long as he finished in the points one of his two rivals had to win if they were to snatch away his crown. The race covered 82 laps and after 41 the order was Rosberg, Piquet, Mansell and Prost. If it had remained so Mansell would have been World Champion. On the 62nd lap Rosberg, who had not made a tyre change, was eliminated from the equation

when, still in the lead, his McLaren burst a tyre.

Now Piquet was in the lead from Mansell and Prost. Mansell could still win the World Championship if he came in in second, or even third position. But then in the last quarter of the race, to his great disappointment, the Englishman was forced out when a tyre burst to ribbons on the straight.

Suddenly Piquet, the new race leader, was favourite for the World Championship. But now he had to stop for new tyres and Prost, who had made his pit stop long before, swept past. The Frenchman carried on to win his 25th World Championship race victory and, with 72 points, his second World Championship title. Mansell was second in the table and Piquet third. Only Ascari (in 1953), Fangio (1955, 1956 and 1957) and Brabham (1960) before him had managed to win a second successive World Championship. Jackie Stewart still led the list of all-time Championship Grand Prix winners, with 27 first placings, but Prost with 25 now shared second position with Clark and Lauda.

Williams-Honda were clear winners of the Manufacturers' Championship with Mansell's five victories plus Piquet's four. Prost's four wins placed McLaren-TAG second, followed by Lotus-Renault, from Ayrton Senna's four first placings. But a McLaren-TAG-Porsche driver had now won the World Drivers' Championship three times in a row, a result no team had ever achieved previously.

Formula One cars of 1986

Make/model	Chief designer(s)	Engine	Gearbox (speeds)	Chassis	Wheelbase	Track	Tyre make	Dry weight
AGS JH21C	Christian Vanderpleyn	Motori Moderni (V6 Turbo)	Renault-Hewland DGR (5/6)	C	2830	F 1810 R 1654	Pirelli	560
Arrows A 8	Dave Wass	BMW M 12/13 (4 cyl. Turbo)	Arrows-Hewland (6)	CA	2794	F 1778 R 1650	Goodyear	540
Arrows A 9	Dave Wass	BMW M 12/13 (4 cyl. Turbo)	Arrows-Hewland (6)	C	2921	F 1854 R 1676	Goodyear	540
Benetton B 186	Rory Byrne	BMW M 12/13 (4 cyl. Turbo)	Benetton-Hewland (5/6)	C	2690	F 1816 R 1682	Pirelli	540
Brabham BT 55	Gordon Murray	BMW M 12/13/1 (4 cyl. Turbo)	Weismann (6/7)	C	3048	F 1778 R 1675	Pirelli	555
Ferrari F1-86	Harvey Postlethwaite	Ferrari 126 C	Ferrari (5/6)	C	2766	F 1807 R 1663	Goodyear	548
Lola-FORCE THL-1	Neil Oatley	Hart 415 T (4 cyl. Turbo)	FORCE-Hewland (6)	CA	2794	F 1803 R 1625	Goodyear	555
Lola-FORCE THL-2	Neil Oatley	Ford (V6 Turbo)	FORCE-Hewland (6)	CA	2794	F 1803 R 1625	Goodyear	545
Ligier JS 27	Michel Têtu	Renault EF 4 B (EF 15) (V6 Turbo)	Ligier-Hewland (6)	CA	2835	F 1790 R 1662	Pirelli	555
Lotus 98 T	Gérard Ducarouge	Renault EF 4 B (EF 15) (V6 Turbo)	Lotus-Hewland (5)	CK	2600	F 1816 R 1620	Goodyear	540
McLaren MP 4/2 B	John Barnard	TAG-Porsche TTE-PO 1 (V6 Turbo)	McLaren (5)	CK	2794	F 1816 R 1676	Goodyear	540
McLaren MP 4/2 C	John Barnard	TAG-Porsche V6 Turbo	McLaren (5)	CK	—	F — R —	Goodyear	540
Minardi 185	Giacomo Caliri	Motori Moderni (V6 Turbo)	Minardi M 101 (5)	C	2605	F 1800 R 1661	Pirelli	550
Osella FA 1 G	Giuseppe Petrotta	Alfa Romeo 890 T (V8 Turbo)	Hewland DGR (5)	C	2830	F 1800 R 1670	Pirelli	560
Osella FA 1 H	Giuseppe Petrotta	Alfa Romeo 890 T (Turbo)	Hewland DGR (5)	C	2860	F 1800 R 1670	Pirelli	560
Tyrrell 015	Maurice Phillippe	Renault EF 4 B (EF 15) (V6 Turbo)	Tyrrell-Hewland (5)	C	2756	F 1765 R 1651	Goodyear	560
Williams FW 011	Patrick Head Frank Dernie	Honda RA 166 E (V6 Turbo)	Williams-Hewland (6)	CK	2794	F 1803 R 1651	Goodyear	540
Zakspeed 841 (861)	Paul Brown	Zakspeed (4 cyl. Turbo)	Zakspeed-Hewland (5)	C	2820	F 1800 R 1600	Goodyear	565

Chassis construction: C = carbon-fibre monocoque; CA = carbon-fibre alloy monocoque; CK = Kevlar/carbon-fibre monocoque

Pop-off Valves and Active Suspension Systems

The FIA curbs the performance of turbo units and re-admits normally aspirated engines. Mansell in a Williams-Honda wins six races, but teammate Piquet is World Champion.

The winter break was unusually long, for the 38th World Championship did not begin until the Brazilian Grand Prix on April 28th. During the lay-off the cards in the Formula One pack were redistributed once again, and nearly all the teams started the season with at least one new member. A total of 17 teams were competing and 27 drivers registered with the FIA for the 16-race series.

The most striking change in regulations was the limiting of turbo boost pressure by means of a pressure-release or "pop-off" valve and the consequent disappearance of qualifying engines. Unfortunately however the pop-off valves were initially unreliable, opening at between 3.5 and 3.9bar pressure instead of the regulation 4.0. Moreover the boost restriction had a greater effect on the four-cylinder engines than the faster-revving V6s. During the season it was believed in some quarters that the engineers had discovered a legal way to outwit the pop-off valve, apparently by utilizing the force of gravity to raise boost to an equivalent of 4.3bar.

After being excluded for a year, normally-aspirated engines were readmitted in 1987, but this time with a limit of 3500cc. Cars using these engines had a clear weight advantage as their maximum weight was 500kg, while the turbocars' limit remained 540kg. As far as power was concerned however the turbo engines retained their supremacy. To encourage participation by teams in the normally-aspirated category the FIA offered two special awards: constructors would compete for the Colin Chapman Cup and drivers for the Jim Clark Cup.

One of the major changes in 1987 was that, with Pirelli's withdrawal from Formula One, Goodyear was now the sole tyre supplier. They dispensed with qualifying tyres, which joined qualifying engines as a relic of the past, and decided to supply all teams with the same type of tyre. But the end of the tyre war meant that further development at Formula One level was virtually put on ice.

Lotus had announced as early as the summer of 1986 that it was about to enter into negotiations with Honda for the supply of engines, following the announced withdrawal of Renault.

Meanwhile Alfa Romeo had come to an agreement with Ligier to supply the French team with their new four-cylinder turbo engine, but on January 1st 1987 the Milan company became part of the Fiat

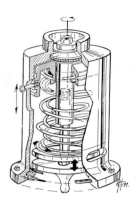

Pop-off valve mounted (left) on TAG engine and (right) in action.

Below
Ayrton Senna in the Lotus 99T-Honda winning the 1987 Monaco Grand Prix.

empire, and the Turin giant, who were also part owners of Ferrari, did not want a rival to their established Grand Prix make. Using negative statements made by Arnoux about the new Alfa engine as an excuse, the Italians cancelled the contract with Ligier, leaving the French team once again without engines, just a few weeks before the beginning of the World Championship. They found a temporary solution in the form of the four-cylinder BMW engine which was inserted almost horizontally in their ultra-low chassis.

The American USF&G company, sponsors of the Arrows team, had meanwhile bought the rights to the original upright version of the Munich four, which they developed in co-operation with the Swiss engine specialist Heini Mader, under the name of Megatron.

BMW themselves had, in the summer of 1986, expressed their intention of withdrawing from Formula One at the end of the season, but had a change of heart, apparently after having been

reminded by Brabham boss Bernie Ecclestone of their contractual obligations.

In 1987 the Anglo-Italian Benetton team changed over to the Ford V6 engine, previously used by the Beatrice team in their Lola cars. Beatrice team owner Carl Haas wanted to concentrate solely on the American CART races and sold his English firm of FORCE, which had provided the base for his Formula One team, to Bernie Ecclestone.

The teams that withdrew were constantly being replaced by new ones. As early as November 1986 Gérard Larrousse, formerly team manager at Renault and then Ligier, announced that he was forming a new Formula One team with his friend Didier Calmels to be called Larrousse-Calmels. Their cars were built by Lola and used the Ford-Cosworth DFZ engine, the 3.5-litre version of the DFV. These were supplied by Heini Mader Racing Components, who also provided Cosworth engines for AGS and the reorganized March team.

In preparation for the new Formula One season two of the leading racing designers had changed teams. John Barnard, the highly successful McLaren designer, had been appointed technical director of Ferrari's racing department on November 1st 1986, a position which placed him above such specialists as Gustav Brunner and Harvey Postlethwaite. Barnard signed a three-year contract with Ferrari, apparently for a fabulous salary, on the understanding that he would work not at Maranello but from England, where he had a new research and development centre built at Guildford. This gave rise to a great deal of controversy in Italy as it was seen as indicating that Barnard was not particularly well disposed towards the Italians. The Fiat company were very critical of the fact that both racing director Marco Piccinini and Enzo Ferrari himself, who was now 89 years old, had wanted to engage Barnard, but this was apparently kept from the old man. He had in the meantime appointed his son Piero Lardi Ferrari as the actual director of the racing department, which ensured that Enzo Ferrari in fact retained complete control.

Barnard was replaced at the McLaren stable by Gordon Murray, previously chief designer at Brabham.

At the end of 1986 some of the leading drivers withdrew from Formula One. These included 1980 World Champion

Alan Jones, whose comeback had been so disillusioning, and 1982 World Champion Keke Rosberg, who had been somewhat in the shadow of Alain Prost in 1986. While Jones preferred to withdraw quietly to Australia to devote himself to his business interests there, Rosberg remained a part of the sporting scene as a businessman and made occasional appearances on German television as a co-commentator for Formula One racing.

Newcomers to full-time Grand Prix racing in 1987 included the Frenchman Pascal Fabre (AGS), Spaniard Adrian Campos (Minardi) and Italians Alex Caffi (Osella) and Ivan Capelli (March), along

with the Japanese driver Satoru Nakajima, part of the package demanded by Honda for supplying its engines to Lotus. After a ten-year gap the FIA readmitted the Japanese Grand Prix to the World Championship calendar, but instead of being held at Fuji, as in the seventies, it would now be run on Honda's 5.85km Suzuka circuit.

Even though the Ford-Cosworth DFZ engines were producing between 560 and 580bhp, no-one was in any doubt that the turbo-powered cars retained a margin of power advantage. However, they all had to make do with 195 litres of fuel and although this was not expected to present any problems to the normally-aspirated

Left
The presentation ceremony at Monte Carlo. From left: Lotus team boss Peter Warr, Prince Rainier, Ayrton Senna, FIA president Jean-Marie Balestre, Michele Alboreto and Nelson Piquet.

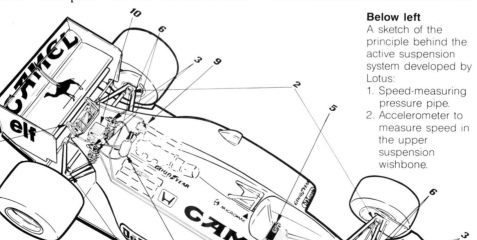

Above
Satoru Nakajima was the first Japanese Formula One driver to complete a whole season.

Below left
A sketch of the principle behind the active suspension system developed by Lotus:
1. Speed-measuring pressure pipe.
2. Accelerometer to measure speed in the upper suspension wishbone.

3. Electromagnetic control valves to guide the suspension damper units.
4. Two acceleration sensors to measure the transverse and longitudinal acceleration of the chassis.
5. Central computer.
6. Springs, which if the active suspension fails, keep the car off the ground.
7. Oil reservoir, which supplies oil as required to the suspension damper units.
8. Oil cooler for hydraulic system.
9. Oil pump to increase the storage pressure.
10. Storage tank for hydraulic system.

Left
In 1987 Nelson
Piquet was World
Champion driver for
the third time. This
time he was driving a
Williams FW11B with
Honda V6
turbocharged engine.
The Brazilian won the
German, Hungarian
and Italian Grands
Prix and was placed
in Brazil, Monaco, the
USA, France, Britain,
Austria and Mexico.

Right
The sketches illustrate
the tail wing profiles
of the Lotus 99T-
Honda (left) at the
British Grand Prix
and (right) at the
French Grand Prix.

cars, it would not be sufficient for the turbo runners.

In March 1987 those parties who were directly concerned with Formula One signed a new Concorde Agreement, a 110-page document which was to be binding until December 31st 1991. Its details remained secret, only the sporting associations and the teams being privy to its contents. In addition to Grand Prix regulations it also covered the television rights under which 30% of the total takings would now go to the FIA and 24% would be for the FOCA, managed by Bernie Ecclestone, whom Jean-Marie Balestre had appointed vice-president of the FIA. The teams received a 46% slice of the TV cake. The former distribution ratio had been 10%, 30% and 60% so that the FIA was actually now receiving a great deal more than previously.

From now on the ten best-placed teams in the World Championship each year would travel free of charge to the following season's Grands Prix, their transport costs paid out of the pool. The new Concorde Agreement also stipulated that all the important technical regulations were to remain unchanged up

till the end of 1991. Five-year contracts were signed with individual circuits, which meant that Grands Prix could no longer alternate. This regulation affected in particular the French Grand Prix (which had alternated between Le Castellet and Dijon), the British (Silverstone and Brands Hatch) and the German (Hockenheim and Nürburgring). Le Castellet, Silverstone and Hockenheim got the contracts; Dijon, Brands Hatch and the Nürburgring were left out in the cold and would have to concentrate on second-class events for the next five years.

Satoru Nakajima

As usual the teams were thoroughly prepared for the new season. The successful McLaren team, which had provided the 1984 World Champion in Niki Lauda and the 1985 and 1986 Champion Alain Prost, also included the reigning World Champion in 1987; Stefan Johansson meanwhile replaced the retired Keke Rosberg. The new model was the MP4/3, developed while John Barnard was still in charge and fitted with the TAG-Porsche engine which was now entering its fifth season.

At Williams the FW11B was developed under the direction of Patrick Head who, as always, could rely on the specialized aerodynamic knowledge of Frank Dernie. This model was an improved version of the previous year's car, and was powered by the powerful RA167E version of the V6 Honda engine. In the second half of the season Williams used a car with a hydraulic level-regulator for the first time. This was guided by a computer that maintained a constant distance between the chassis and the track regardless of the weight of the car which became lighter during the race as the tank was emptied. Nelson Piquet and Nigel

Mansell continued to drive for Williams but this was not a harmonious combination, as the two leading drivers had become fiercely competitive rivals.

At Ferrari Gustav Brunner had taken over the design of the new Type F187 immediately after the previous year's Italian Grand Prix, so that when John Barnard transferred to Ferrari in November he was met by a project that was nearing completion. Work had also continued up till the end of 1986 on the 2650cc V8 Indianapolis engine project, but these plans were now put on ice once again, as Barnard wanted to concentrate solely on Formula One. But although the Indy Ferrari project was stillborn the work had not been in vain, for the V8 engine provided a useful basis for Alfa Romeo's later entry in CART events.

With an eye to the 1987 Formula One season Ferrari designed not only a new chassis for the Type F187 but an all-new

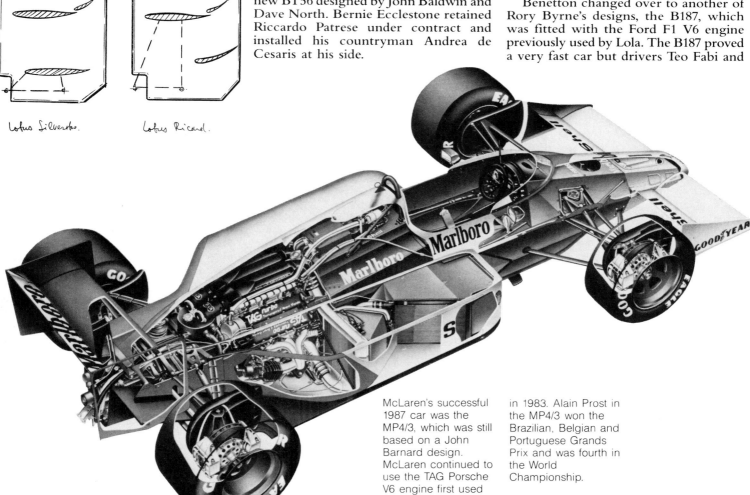

Lotus Silverstone.   Lotus Ricard.

V6 turbo engine was also built, by former Renault engineer Jean-Jacques His, together with Ildo Renzetti. The cylinder dimensions (81 x 48.4mm, 1496.4cc) remained unchanged but the angle between the banks was narrowed from 120° which had been used since 1980 to 90°. A Weber-Marelli digital electronic injection unit was again used and American-made Garrett turbochargers fitted. The gearbox was however completely remodelled. Instead of the traditional transverse gearbox which had been used since 1975 the new car had a longitudinal gearbox with ZF differential. During the season Ferrari was not able to fully match the power of the six-cylinder Honda, but achieved two victories at the end of the season, in Japan and Australia. Drivers of the F187 were Gerhard Berger, who had just transferred from Benetton, and Michele Alboreto.

The Brabham team had gradually sunk into mediocrity, but they hoped to retrieve some honour this year with the new BT56 designed by John Baldwin and Dave North. Bernie Ecclestone retained Riccardo Patrese under contract and installed his countryman Andrea de Cesaris at his side.

Yet again this year Lotus displayed its innovative streak. Right at the beginning of the season they made use of what came to be known as "active" suspension. This system, on which Lotus had been working for years, was controlled by a computer via hydraulics. Through numerous sensors the computer was continually fed with information, and the electronic brain gave the corresponding orders to the hydraulics. This was Frenchman Gérard Ducarouge's fifth season with Lotus and he had designed the Lotus 99T for the new season. With this car its No 1 driver, Senna, was ranked as one of the leading favourites for the World Championship. The second Lotus 99T was driven by the former Japanese Formula Two driver, Satoru Nakajima. Lotus also had a completely new sponsor in the R.J. Reynolds Tobacco Company which advertised its Camel cigarettes on the now-yellow British cars. Marlboro finally had a worthy rival on the Formula One promotion scene.

Benetton changed over to another of Rory Byrne's designs, the B187, which was fitted with the Ford F1 V6 engine previously used by Lola. The B187 proved a very fast car but drivers Teo Fabi and

McLaren's successful 1987 car was the MP4/3, which was still based on a John Barnard design. McLaren continued to use the TAG Porsche V6 engine first used in 1983. Alain Prost in the MP4/3 won the Brazilian, Belgian and Portuguese Grands Prix and was fourth in the World Championship.

407

Thierry Boutsen were initially let down by the engine's high fuel consumption. Towards the middle of the season however it started to make headway after the specialists at Ford and Cosworth had thoroughly revised the turbo system.

The Arrows team led by Jackie Oliver and Alan Rees had taken on a new designer in Ross Brawn who was responsible for the A10 model driven this year by Eddie Cheever and Derek Warwick.

After Alfa Romeo had cancelled their contract, Ligier's designer Michel Tétu had to redesign the Type 29B to take the Megatron engine. Piercarlo Ghinzani remained the sole link with Alfa Romeo and competed as René Arnoux's team-mate. The new Ligier was not ready to start at the beginning of the season at Rio de Janeiro but made its first appearance, untested, in the next World Championship race, at Imola.

After a gap of several years March reappeared in Formula One in 1987, with substantial sponsorship by the Japanese firm of Leyton House. Gordon Coppuck and Andy Brown produced the March 781 which used a Mader-supplied Ford-Cosworth DFZ engine and was driven by Ivan Capelli, who had previously competed for both Tyrrell and AGS on a one-off basis. Capelli, a former winner of the Italian Formula Three and European Formula 3000 titles, was considered to have a great future in Formula One.

At Tyrrell meanwhile Maurice Phillippe and Brian Lisles designed the Cosworth-powered 016 model for drivers Jonathan Palmer, who had just transferred from Zakspeed, and the tall Frenchman Philippe Streiff; they were later joined by the young Frenchman Yannick Dalmas.

The newly founded firm of Larrousse-Calmels had taken on the Frenchman Philippe Alliot to drive the LC87 which had been developed at Lola under Ralph Bellamy.

The Minardi team from Faenza remained with the V6 Motori-Moderni turbo engine, even though it was considered to be particularly unreliable. The Spaniard Adrian Campos brought welcome funds with him from his sponsor, Lois, to drive one of the cars, the other being driven by Alessandro Nannini.

The team of Osella, suffering from a chronic lack of funds, further improved the FA1I with turbocharged Alfa Romeo V8 engine and now entrusted it to the young Alex Caffi, though Gabriele Tarquini and later Franco Forini also drove the cars during the year.

For the small AGS concern, Christian Vanderpleyn designed the JH22 with Ford-Cosworth engine. The car was driven for most of the year by Pascal Fabre but at the end of the season the Brazilian Roberto Moreno was also given a drive.

A new make, the Coloni, appeared during practice for the Italian Grand Prix. Designed for Enzo Coloni by Roberto Ori, it was a conventional car with Cosworth engine, but Nicola Larini did not succeed in qualifying it and its debut had to be postponed to Jerez.

At Niederzissen in the Eifel Chris Murphy and Heinz Zällner built the new Type 871 for Zakspeed, powered again by Zakspeed's own four-cylinder turbo motor. Christian Danner from Munich and the Englishman Martin Brundle were engaged as drivers but the car continued to perform very poorly.

Piercarlo Ghinzani

Theirry Boutsen

With the eighties, telemetry had made its appearance in Formula One. By this computer controlled system for gathering and processing data, the most important functions on the car — relating to suspension, chassis, bodywork, tyres, engine and engine peripherals — can be continually monitored. Data on temperatures, pressures, forces, speeds, movement and acceleration can be gathered while the car is being driven around the circuit, then either stored in an on-board computer or transmitted to another computer in the pits. Naturally only those teams with very solid financial backing could afford a sophisticated telemetry system. In 1987 Honda were the biggest investor in this area. At the opening race in Rio there were no fewer than 39 Honda technicians. Bosch on the other hand had delegated only three men in Brazil to look after the TAG-Porsche cars.

The 1987 World Championship belonged to the Williams-Honda team and Prost's McLaren-TAG-Porsche, though occasionally Ayrton Senna in the active-suspension Lotus-Honda got a look in, and towards the end of the season there was a crescendo from Ferrari.

At the first World Championship race in Rio, Prost in the McLaren-TAG-Porsche clearly dominated. Mansell in the Williams-Honda was the victim of tyre damage but his team-mate Piquet crossed the line in second place. Gerhard Berger, making his debut for Ferrari, came fourth.

Piquet had an accident during practice at Imola and on doctor's orders was forbidden to start. He had to watch the race from the commentator's box of Italian RAI and co-commentate for the enthusiastic TV viewers as Mansell in the Williams-Honda won from Senna in the Lotus-Honda with electronically controlled suspension followed by Alboreto in a Ferrari.

There was a surprise during practice for the Belgian Grand Prix at Spa when the news spread that the famous Mauro Forghieri, who had been head engineer at Ferrari since the early sixties but had recently fallen from grace, had suddenly left to design a new V12 engine for Lamborghini, which had been taken over by Chrysler. They established a new research and development centre at Modena and it was here that Forghieri worked on the design of the Formula One engine and gearbox.

Philippe Alliot

Garbriele Tarquini

At the Belgian Grand Prix Prost gained an easy victory after Mansell and Senna collided. At Monte Carlo Mansell looked set for another convincing win but a fault suddenly developed in the Honda's exhaust system and he had to resign himself to letting his powerless car coast off the track. The race turned into an historic victory for the Lotus 99T with active suspension, driven by Ayrton Senna.

It was known that Williams were also working on a controlled supension system, though theirs was a simpler design. During 1987 and 1988 other teams became interested in electronically controlled suspension systems, for after the Lotus victory at Monte Carlo it was generally believed that a new era was

Enzo Coloni

beginning. However experience showed that this was not quite the case. This type of suspension was both highly complicated and very expensive and its advantages were not wholly convincing.

After their Monaco success, Ayrton Senna and his Lotus were also victors on the Detroit circuit. Mansell was hampered by cramp in his leg and his team-mate Piquet came in in second place. In the French Grand Prix at Le Castellet on the other hand Mansell had a great day and was the clear winner. Piquet and Prost were relegated to the placings, the Lotus seemingly disadvantaged on this fast track.

In the summer it was suddenly reported from Italy that Gustav Brunner was leaving Ferrari. The Austrian did not see eye to eye with his new boss, John Barnard, particularly after the Englishman took him off the F187 project.

The British Grand Prix at Silverstone turned into a marvellous Honda demonstration. Once again Mansell was the clear winner, followed by Piquet, Senna and Nakajima, to give Honda the first four places.

The restructuring at Ferrari, together with the constant modification of suspension and aerodynamics, now began to bear fruit. At the Hungarian Grand Prix Berger was suddenly on the front

row next to the fastest qualifier, Nigel Mansell. Mansell lost the race because a wheel nut on his Williams-Honda came off, leaving Berger in second position behind Piquet, until he had to withdraw when his transmission developed a fault. Piquet was the victor but the general impression was that the Brazilian was only successful when his strongest rivals, namely Mansell, Prost and Senna, were plagued by some kind of technical problem.

The Austrian Grand Prix had to be started three times because of two mass collisions. Piquet had to be content with second place here, behind Mansell. A fierce rivalry had developed between the two, and at the Osterreichring it was known that the marriage between Williams and Honda was doomed to end in divorce at the end of the season. Benetton-Ford came into the limelight once again in this race when Fabi was third and Boutsen fourth.

But it was here that Alain Prost finally lost his chance of becoming 1987 World Champion for, after many technical problems, he made it only into sixth place. At this stage of the World Championship Piquet was in the lead with 54 points, from Senna with 43 and Mansell with 39, while Prost had managed to accumulate only 31 points. Piquet, Senna and Mansell were all contenders for the title.

Right
In 1987, Benetton changed from the four-cylinder BMW engine to the Ford V6. The new engine, developed jointly by Ford and Cosworth, did not prove very reliable and consumed a great deal of fuel. In the photograph, the Benetton B187- Ford is being driven by Theirry Boutsen at the Monaco Grand Prix.

Left
Former Renault and Ligier team manager Gerard Larrousse and his friend Didier Calmels entered the World Championship in 1987 with a new team. Their driver, Philippe Alliot, piloted a Lola LC87-Cosworth.

The World Championship continued with the Italian Grand Prix at Monza, where Mansell had temperature problems with his Honda engine and Piquet was again winner, followed by Senna, Mansell and Berger. Piquet was driving a Williams with electronically controlled suspension in this race, the system proving its worth the very first time it was used. Mansell however used a conventional set-up on his car as he was not very impressed by active suspensions, with which he was well acquainted from his time with Lotus, when he had carried out a great deal of test work.

The day before the Italian Grand Prix at Monza Honda chief engineer Sakurai announced that from 1988 Honda would no longer be supplying Williams with engines but would instead sign a new contract with McLaren. At the same time it was announced that from 1988 Ayrton Senna would represent the McLaren-Honda colours alongside Alain Prost.

Shortly after the announcement of the imminent separation Frank Williams declared that his team would be using normally-aspirated British-built Judd V8 engines in the coming season. John Judd and his tuning firm of Engine Developments at Rugby had specialised in the servicing of racing engines for

Above left
The Ferrari F1-87 with V6 turbo engine, originally designed by Gustav Brunner and then developed further by John Barnard, came good in the second half of the season. At the end of the year, Gerhard Berger won both the Japanese and Australian Grands Prix.

Above
Ferrari celebrated its 40th anniversary in 1987. The 89-year-old Enzo Ferrari presents a memento to his two drives, Michele Alboreto (left) and Gerhard Berger.

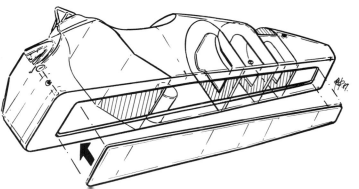

A sketch of the Ferrari monocoque. This illustrates the parts made of carbon fibre and Kevlar which are then bonded under pressure and baked in an autoclave.

years, and were now building their own 3.5-litre V8 Formula One engine, based on the Honda block used for Formula 3000. Judd had already signed up both March and Ligier by the time Williams turned to them in September 1987, and the 40-man Derby operation was actually already working to capacity.

Ferrari's efforts in the summer came good at the Portuguese Grand Prix at Estoril when Alboreto qualified on pole, the first time a Ferrari had done that since April 5th 1985 when Alboreto achieved a similar honour in Brazil. In the race Berger led until just before the finish when his car started to give trouble and Prost, who was just behind, went past to win. This was the Frenchman's 28th victory and he had finally overtaken Jackie Stewart's total. Mansell in the Williams-Honda had to withdraw because of electrical problems; Berger gained second place and Piquet third followed by Fabi in a Benetton whose turbocharged V6 engine was still consuming too much fuel.

Mansell was superb in both the Spanish and Mexican Grands Prix so that just before the second to last race, the Japanese Grand Prix at Suzuka, the top positions in the World Championship were held by Piquet with 73 points, Mansell with 61 and Senna with 51. Mansell had started from pole eight times and had won six races while Piquet had managed only three victories; the Brazilian had however finished second on no fewer than seven occasions. There was great excitement at the anticipated clash at Suzuka for this could well be decisive.

The decision was made, though in a rather unexpected way: Mansell had an accident during practice and was not able to start. Although he did not have any visible injuries he had hurt his back when

Since his road accident, team boss Frank Williams has been confined to a wheelchair. In spite of this he retains firm control of his racing stable. Nelson Piquet won the World Championship for Williams in 1987, but at the end of the season he left to drive for Lotus.

he crashed against the barriers with such tremendous force. This left Piquet as the 1987 World Champion, even though he had to withdraw from the race because of engine damage. The race turned into a Ferrari triumph as Berger was in the lead for the whole of the race except when he had to make a tyre change. It was Ferrari's first Grand Prix win since

Below left
The collaboration between McLaren and Honda was announced at a press conference at Monza, as was Senna's transfer to the team. From the left: Ayrton Senna, Alain Prost, McLaren team director Ron Dennis and chief engineer for Honda, Yoshitoshi Sakurai.

Below right
Alain Prost in the McLaren-TAG Porsche drove to his 28th World Championship Grand Prix victory in Portugal in 1987. The Frenchman thus surpassed Jackie Stewart's previous record of 27 wins.

August 1985, when Alboreto was the victor at the German Grand Prix on the Nürburgring.

Ferrari continued its triumphal procession at the final Grand Prix in Adelaide. Berger in the F187 was in pole position once again and then led from the front for the whole of the race, with Alboreto backing him up with second place. This was Ferrari's 93rd World Championship Grand Prix victory, and also Goodyear's 200th.

In the final 1987 World Championship placings Nelson Piquet in the Williams-Honda headed the list with 73 points followed by his team-mate Nigel Mansell with 61, Ayrton Senna in the Lotus-Honda with 57, Alain Prost in the McLaren-TAG-Porsche with 46 and Gerhard Berger in the Ferrari with 36 points. Williams-Honda won the Formula One Manufacturers' Championship with 137 points, leaving them well ahead of their competitors; McLaren-TAG-Porsche

were second with 76, Lotus-Honda next with 64 and Ferrari fourth with 51 points. The Jim Clark Trophy for drivers of cars with normally-aspirated engines was won by Jonathan Palmer in a Tyrrell-Cosworth and Tyrrell-Cosworth easily won the Colin Chapman Cup for cars with normally-aspirated engines.

At the end of the season, Bernie Ecclestone quietly withdrew his Brabham team, without making any official communique, though it was said that, after a break of a year, they would re-enter Formula One.

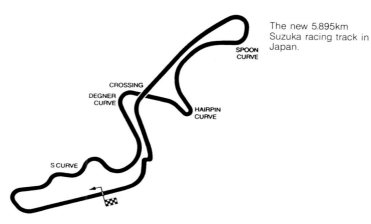

The new 5.895km Suzuka racing track in Japan.

Formula One Cars of 1987

Make/Model	Designer(s)	Engine	Gearbox (number of gears)	Front Track	Rear Track	Dry Weight (kg)
AGS JH22	Christian Vanderpleyn	Ford-Cosworth DFZ (V8 SM)	Hewland-Renault (5/6)	2870	F 1700 R 1560	520
Arrows A 10	Ross Brawn	Megatron M 12/13 (4 cyl Turbo)	Arrows-Hewland (6)	2743	F 1803 R 1625	540
Benetton B 187	Rory Byrne	Ford TEC F1 (V6 Turbo)	Benetton-Hewland (5/6)	2690	F 1816 R 1682	540
Brabham BT 56	Dave North John Baldwin	BMW M 12/13-1 (4 cyl Turbo)	Brabham-Weismann (6)	2794	F 1803 R 1676	540
Coloni FC	Roberto Ori	Ford-Cosworth DFZ (V8 SM)	Hewland-Coloni (6)	2800	F 1750 R 1550	510
Ferrari F1-87	John Barnard Gustav Brunner	Ferrari (V6 Turbo)	Ferrari (6)	2800	F 1791 R 1673	542
Lola LC-87	Ralph Bellamy	Ford-Cosworth DFZ (V8 SM)	Lola-Hewland (6)	2603	F 1714 R 1600	500
Ligier JS 29 C	Michel Têtu	Megatron M 12/13 (4 cyl Turbo)	Ligier-Hewland (6)	2835	F 1790 R 1665	550
Lotus T 99	Gérard Ducarouge	Honda RA 167 E (V6 Turbo)	Lotus (6)	2720	F 1800 R 1650	540
March M 871	Gordon Coppuck Andy Brawn	Ford-Cosworth DFZ (V8 SM)	March (6)	2742	F 1798 R 1669	500
McLaren MP 4/3	Gordon Murray	TAG-Porsche TTE-PO 1 (V6 Turbo)	McLaren (6)	2768	F 1816 R 1676	540
Minardi M 186	Giacomo Caliri	Motori-Modemi MM F1 T (V6 Turbo)	Minardi-Hewland (5)	2690	F 1812 R 1661	550
Osella FA 1 L	Giuseppe Petrotta	Alfa Romeo T 890 (V6 Turbo)	Hewland DGB (5)	2830	F 1800 R 1670	570
Tyrrell 016	Maurice Phillippe Brian Lisles	Ford-Cosworth DFZ (V8 SM)	Tyrrell-Hewland (5/6)	—	F — R —	500
Williams FW 011 B	Patrick Head Frank Dernie	Honda RA 167 E (V6 Turbo)	Williams-Hewland (6)	2794	F 1803 R 1651	540
Zakspeed 871	Chris Murphy Heinz Zöllner	Zakspeed (4 cyl Turbo)	Zakspeed (6)	2840	F 1800 R 1600	550

Monocoques: All monocoques are made up of a combination of Kevlar with carbon fibre, some with a honeycomb alloy inner layer.
A: Atmospheric engine
Cubic capacity: 3.5 litres; turbocharged engines: 1.5 litres
Tyres: All cars were fitted with Goodyears.

The turbo engines' last season — Ayrton Senna (McLaren-Honda) is
World Champion. Enzo Ferrari dies in Modena.

If one excludes the early fifties, when fields were smaller and more evenly matched, there was never a World Championship year dominated by one team as much as in 1988, when the McLaren MP4/4 with Honda V6 turbo engine won 15 of the 16 qualifying races, and in ten of them took second place as well. In their last year, the turbocharged engines were restricted to a maximum boost pressure of 2.5bar, which restricted power to between 630 and 700bhp, but with the best of the normally-aspirated engines still rarely capable of 600bhp in 1988 the turbo motors remained superior.

Weight restrictions remained the same as in 1987, but the turbo motors faced a further limitation in the amount of fuel they were allowed for each race, from 195 litres in 1987 to 150; there was no limit on the amount cars with normally-aspirated engines could use, but the 20-30kg of additional fuel they carried virtually wiped out the advantage given them by the weight regulations.

In preparation for 1988 Honda had not only angled for the best racing team, namely McLaren, but in Ayrton Senna and Alain Prost had also obtained the two drivers who were generally considered to be the best available.

The TAG-Porsche and BMW turbo engines had officially been withdrawn from Formula One at the end of 1987, though BMW still participated indirectly in Grand Prix racing as the older version of their four-cylinder engine continued under the Megatron name, again powering the Arrows cars.

Two leading teams, Williams and Benetton, had made early changes to normally-aspirated engines, Williams using the new Judd V8 while Benetton, which had an exclusive contract with Ford, equipped its new cars with a considerably revised engine, the DFR, which had been developed by Cosworth and Ford. In the spring of 1988 Ford announced they had made an agreement with Yamaha for the use of the Japanese five-valve cylinder heads, but nothing came of this agreement and the DFR retained the traditional four-valve heads.

In its first Grand Prix season Judd, a major shareholder of which was former World Champion Sir Jack Brabham, equipped three teams, Williams, Ligier and March.

Three new teams entered Formula One this season. In Germany former ATS team owner Gunter Schmid set up a new operation which was given the name of

A successful trio in discussion. From the left: McLaren chassis engineer Steve Nichols, Ayrton Senna and Alain Prost. The McLaren MP4/4 which Nichols developed proved to be invincible right from the start.

A new Formula One team was formed in Brescia, too. This was Scuderia Italia, which entered the Dallara 188-Cosworth for Alex Caffi.

Rial, another of Schmid's wheel brands. In Brescia the industrialist Giuseppe Lucchini, a passionate collector of vintage racing and sports cars, founded Scuderia Italia which used cars constructed by Dallara. And the third newcomer was EuroBrun, founded by sportscar entrant Walter Brun from Lucerne in Switzerland and the Italian Gianpaolo Pavanello and actually based on the former Euroracing team.

The new list of Grand Prix contenders comprised 18 teams though some of them fielded only one car. There were 31 drivers competing for a maximum of 26 starting places and, as the regulations permitted only 30 cars to take part in qualifying, a pre-qualifying session was required in the run-up to each race, to eliminate the slowest runner from the new teams. This was the procedure over the first half of the season; from then on the slowest teams from the first eight races had to compete in the pre-qualifying session.

Twelve of the 31 competing cars used engines built by Heini Mader in Switzerland, Arrows with their four-cylinder Megatron turbos and, with V8 Cosworth-Fords, AGS, Rial, Minardi, Larrousse-Calmels, EuroBrun and Scuderia Italia.

Mader recommended its Cosworths should be overhauled every 1000 kilometres but the Megatron, which was subjected to greater stresses, required servicing every 650 kilometres.

Before the beginning of the season most observers were agreed that in spite of the restrictions the turbo competition would continue to dominate, though the normally-aspirated engines would have a chance on street circuits with no long straights, such as at Monaco, Detroit and Adelaide, and also at Budapest.

The turbo engines had to be revised and adjusted to the new formula. Engine revolutions, the bore/stroke ratio and electronic management systems all had to be adjusted to the changed demands. In order to achieve higher revolutions, it was not sufficient just to shorten the piston stroke; weight also had to be removed from the movable parts within the engine. The "second generation" normally-aspirated engines, ten- and 12-cylinder designs constructed at great cost, would not appear until 1989.

A new regulation applying to all Grand Prix cars was a requirement to locate the pedals behind the line of the front axle, to give greater protection for the driver's legs and feet in the event of an accident. Those makes which were competing with turbo engines could however still use their 1987 chassis without altering the total structure of the car. Ferrari, Zakspeed and Arrows thus drove improved versions of their previous year's chassis. Only McLaren and Lotus, of the turbo runners, in fact fielded all-new cars, McLaren because of the enforced changeover to the Honda engine, and Lotus because they were not happy with the handling of the 1987 active suspension design. The teams which changed from turbo to normally-aspirated engines all had to build new cars: Williams (from Honda V6 to Judd V8), Ligier (from Megatron four to Judd V8) and Benetton (from Ford V6 to Ford V8).

McLaren and Ferrari were considered joint favourites for the 1988 World Championship. The British team was a well-organized one with outstanding engineers, on top of which they now had the engine which had dominated the 1987 series. For the first time in many years their new car did not owe its basis to the departed John Barnard, design in this instance having been the responsibility of Steve Nichols and Neil Oatley, under the direction of Gordon Murray. The new McLaren-Honda MP4/4, which had a low and very slender monocoque, did not make its appearance until the last minute, about two weeks before the beginning of

Below
Thierry Boutsen in the Benetton B188-Ford leads Grand Prix newcomer Yannick Dalmas in the Lola LC88-Cosworth at Monaco. Benetton had already changed over to a 3.5-litre atmospheric engine.

Right
The founder of the Rial team was the former ATS owner Gunter Schmid, who took on Andrea de Cesaris for 1988.

Above
Walter Brun (centre) and Giancarlo Pavanello founded the new EuroBrun team for the 1988 season. Their drivers were the Argentinian Oscar Larrauri (left) and the Italian Stefano Modena (right).

Right
In 1988 a new British engine make — Judd — appeared in Formula One.

Below
The March 881, which was designed under the guidance of Adrian Newey. Its efficient aerodynamics featured a very small "concorde beak", which was later copied by other designers.

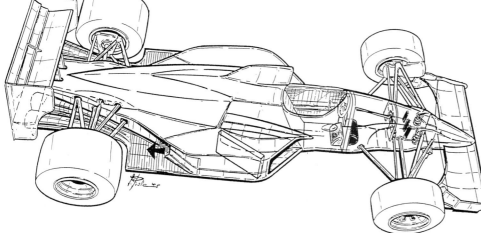

A view into the March cockpit with its ultra small (25cm) footroom. Because of the narrow width, it was not possible to insert both feet into the available space at the same time.

Alex Caffi

the World Championship in Brazil. Most of the other teams had completed their tests at Imola in March but when Senna and Prost began their tests with the MP4/4 they pulverized the times achieved in the previous weeks, and suddenly McLaren had become the sole World Championship favourite.

Ferrari's 1987 chassis, originally designed by Gustav Brunner before he went to Rial, had been developed over the winter by John Barnard and Harvey Postlethwaite while Jacques His, the engineer responsible for engine development, had adapted the turbocharged V6 to the new regulations. During the season however it became apparent that the Ferrari engine developed its power too brutally and also consumed too much fuel.

On February 20th an event of great significance took place when Enzo Ferrari celebrated his 90th birthday. The event was given worldwide press coverage as the now venerable hero had been in the centre of racing for nearly six decades.

Gérard Ducarouge's Honda-powered Lotus 100T design no longer had the complicated and very expensive suspension of the 99T as they had decided to return to conventional suspension. The racing team was, it should be said, run as a separate entity from the production-car company which had been taken over by General Motors in January 1986. Ayrton Senna had been the ideal working partner for Ducarouge, but his replacement, reigning World Champion Nelson Piquet, did not get on well with the French engineer. The Japanese driver Satoru Nakajima, whose first Formula One season had been rather colourless, remained in the team.

A feature of the Judd-powered Williams FW12, designed by Patrick Head and Frank Dernie, was the six-speed gearbox which was mounted transversely in front of the back axle-line, which improved weight distribution. As early as the winter tests it became apparent that the Williams-Judd, the March-Judd and the Benetton-Ford were the fastest of the normally-aspirated engine cars.

The new Benetton B188 was once again a creation of the South African-born Rory Byrne, and he had produced yet another outstanding design. Its drivers were the Belgian Thierry Boutsen and former Minardi driver Alessandro Nannini.

The new March 881 designed by

415

John Judd

Adrian Newey was considered to be a very progressive design. The front of the monocoque was so tight that the drivers had practically no room to move their feet and both Ivan Capelli and the Brazilian Mauricio Gugelmin, a new signing this year, initially found it difficult to cope in the narrow cockpit. As far as aerodynamics were concerned however, Newey and March boss Robin Herd had succeeded in creating a masterpiece of modern racing car construction.

At Arrows, Ross Brawn revised the Type A10's chassis and produced the A10B, while Heini Mader Racing Components continued development on the four-cylinder Garrett-turbocharged Megatron engine. Drivers were again Eddie Cheever and Derek Warwick.

The partnership of Gérard Larrousse and Didier Calmels ran two new Lola-built LC85 cars with Cosworth-Ford DFZ engines and took on the talented new driver Yannick Dalmas to join Philippe Alliot. Minardi finally discarded the Motori-Moderni V6 turbo in favour of a Ford V8 and, under the direction of Giacomo Caliri, developed the M188 for Spanish drivers Adrian Campos and Luis Perez Sala. After a few races however Campos realized that he was not destined to have a great Grand Prix career and retired, his place being taken by Pierluigi Martini. Scuderia Italia's new BMS-Dallara-Ford was designed by the Argentinian Sergio Rinland and its driving was entrusted to former Osella driver Alex Caffi.

Tyrrell must have thought it had been a long time since the glorious days of Jackie Stewart and Jody Scheckter. For the new season Maurice Phillippe and Brian Lisles produced the 017, whose principal driver would be Jonathan Palmer; he was joined at the last moment by Julian Bailey, a newcomer to Formula One. In Germany the Austrian Gustav Brunner designed the ARC01 for Gunter Schmid's new Rial team, the car looking rather similar to the Ferrari F187 which Brunner had designed a year before. Rial took on the Roman daredevil Andrea de Cesaris as driver.

Michel Tétu's Ligier JS31 was an unusual design, with an additional monocoque carrying fuel between the Judd engine and the rear axle. By dividing the chassis in two, Tétu was aiming for improved weight distribution. The race plan was for the additional tank to empty first, thus further improving distribution. In practice however the JS31 proved to be a total flop, continually plagued by chassis and aerodynamic problems. Drivers were René Arnoux and Stefan Johansson.

The Zakspeed 187, which in 1988 was driven both by Piercarlo Ghinzani and German Formula One newcomer Bernd Schneider, was actually the previous year's car whose turbocharged four-cylinder engine was drastically affected by the boost limit. It never achieved its optimal performance and was continually confronted by qualifying problems.

The small AGS team from southern France produced an astounding new car, the JH23, which was another of Christian Vanderpleyn's designs. Henri Julien had succeeded in capturing a wealthy sponsor but he was not available for the whole season and although Philippe Streiff achieved some excellent performances with the JH23 in the early races the limited financial backing meant there could be no systematic development and Streiff gradually slipped into the background.

Sergio Rinland

The EuroBrun ER188, designed by Mario Tolentino, was similar to the old Euroracing Alfa Romeo, but after a promising start to the season the cars had more and more trouble qualifying. The EuroBruns were driven by 1987 European Formula 3000 Champion Stefano Modena and the Argentinian Oscar Larrauri, who was already driving for Brun Motorsport in long-distance races.

Enzo Osella's team modified their turbocharged Alfa Romeo V8 engines to such an extent that they should no longer be described as Alfa Romeos. Former Ferrari engineer Antonio Tomaini devised the FA1L for former Italian Formula Three Champion Nicola Larini, who had made his Grand Prix debut with Coloni the previous year.

Luciano Pavanello

Antonio Tomaini

Philippe Streiff

Christian Vanderpleyn

Coloni themselves were competing in their first full season this year, and to drive the CF188, designed by Roberto Ori, Enzo Coloni took on the former Formula 3000 driver Gabriele Tarquini, but the operation was sadly underfinanced.

In spite of all the changes the turbo-cars again dominated and in only one of the 16 races, the Japanese Grand Prix at Suzuka, did a car with a normally-aspirated engine lead the field. This was the March-Judd driven by Ivan Capelli, and he was in the lead for only about 200 or 300 metres. Otherwise all the races, with a few exceptions, were led by the superior McLaren-Honda MP4/4s. Gerhard Berger in a Ferrari was winner at Monza but was able to take the lead in only two other races, at Silverstone and Adelaide. In the Italian Grand Prix the McLarens for once had bad luck and Ferrari was unexpectedly able to achieve its only victory of the season.

Ten times the McLaren-Hondas took first and second places. They were in pole position at 15 Grands Prix, in 13 of which Senna was the driver in question, and a McLaren set the fastest lap in 12 races. Ayrton Senna clinched the title at the second to last Grand Prix, in Japan, and became the third Brazilian — after Emerson Fittipaldi and Nelson Piquet —

to win the crown. At the concluding Grand Prix in Australia Senna had gearbox problems but Alain Prost's victory there (the 35th of his career) was no use to him. Even though the Frenchman had accumulated more World Championship points than Senna, only the 11 best results counted towards the World Championship. Prost was the first

Left
Gerhard Berger in the Ferrari F1-87/88C.

Right
Everything went well for McLaren in 1988. They had an outstanding chassis; the Honda V6 turbo engines were powerful and reliable, and they also had the best drivers in Ayrton Senna and Alain Prost. Their organization was also one of their great strengths. Here Senna's car is given a tyre change at the Brazilian Grand Prix.

Left
Ivan Capelli in a March-Judd and the Williams-Judd of Nigel Mansell at La Source hairpin during the Belgian Grand Prix at Spa-Francorchamps.

driver in Grand Prix history to gain more than 100 points in one season; but of these only 87 counted for the final placings.

There was no doubt that in Ayrton Senna the fastest driver of the 1988 season had become World Champion. Senna's driving had not always been perfect though. At the Monaco Grand Prix for example he ran into the barriers when in the lead, allowing Prost to win at Monaco yet again. At the Italian Grand Prix victory was in the young Brazilian's grasp when, shortly before the finish, he decided to overtake the Williams-Judd being driven a lap behind by the Frenchman Jean-Louis Schlesser (standing in for Mansell, who was ill). The result was a collision and Senna had to retire. He had been the clear leader until then but after both Nakajima and Prost had trouble with their engines the Honda technicians advised him to use a richer fuel mixture. This increased consumption so much that over the last laps Senna was forced to throttle back to make sure of finishing. The two Ferraris crept closer and closer to the leading McLaren and when the collision occurred, Berger won the race with Alboreto a close second. Thus, one month after the death of Enzo Ferrari, Monza was the scene of a Ferrari 1-2.

During the summer Ferrari had equipped its F187/88 with electonically controlled shock absorbers which enabled the height of the car to be adjusted during a race.

With Enzo Ferrari's death on August 14th the most revered figure in the history of motor racing disappeared from the scene. He died on a Sunday morning in his house in Modena surrounded by members of his immediate family; Piero Lardi Ferrari was amongst those present. The news of the death was not announced until the following day, August 15th, the Ferragosto (an Italian holiday). By this time Enzo Ferrari had already been laid to rest for some hours;

On February 18th 1988 the Commendatore Engineer Enzo Ferrari celebrated his 90th birthday in Modena, but on August 14th that year the great figure of modern motor racing died.

Below
Ayrton Senna, soon to be World Champion for 1988, talking to Honda chief engineer Osamu Goto.

Right
Ayrton Senna in the McLaren MP4/4 with Honda turbocharged V6 engine at Monaco. This combination won eight Grands Prix and Senna emerged as World Champion.

only his closest relatives had attended the burial service.

Before Ferrari's death personnel at Ferrari had already begun trying to fill the vacuum that would be created. Piero Lardi Ferrari had moved out of the racing department to take over the newly created function of vice president of Ferrari SpA, while Fiat boss Vittorio Ghidella continued as president (until resigning at the end of the year). The engineer Piergiorgio Cappelli was appointed head of the racing department with John Barnard under him as director of the racing department.

After Ferrari's death 90% of Ferrari was taken over by Fiat; this action had been agreed upon as early as 1969 when the giant firm had regained 50% of Ferrari's shares. Piero Lardi Ferrari had been named Enzo's sole heir and according to the agreement he retained 10% of Ferrari's shares.

1988 was an unusually turbulent year for Ferrari. In the summer some of the leading technicians left. Harvey Postlethwaite went to Tyrrell, engine designer Jacques His rejoined Renault who were working on a new Formula One engine and Jean-Claude Migeaud, who had been in charge of wind-tunnel research at Maranello, followed Postlethwaite's example and went to England. In light of all these changes it was understandable that Ferrari was plagued by a host of problems. The engines in particular were not proving

satisfactory, fuel consumption being too high. However, in terms of overall performance, the Ferraris were second only to the McLarens.

The McLaren series of successes in the eighties was very impressive, and their association with Honda ensured that every detail harmonized perfectly, from the chassis through the aerodynamics to the total organization of the team where each member had his precise task. In 1988 Honda entered two versions of its then invincible six-cylinder engine, the choice between the XE2 and the XE3 being made according to the characteristics of the track.

The six-speed gearbox was in fact the one weak point in the McLaren-Honda MP4/4, both drivers having problems in several races. The unit had been developed at McLaren under the direction of Dave North in collaboration with the American gearbox specialist Pete Weismann, who had designed a special gearbox for Brabham some years before. In spite of their occasional gearbox problems however the McLarens were still unbeatable. Whether on fast circuits or ones with plenty of corners, Senna and

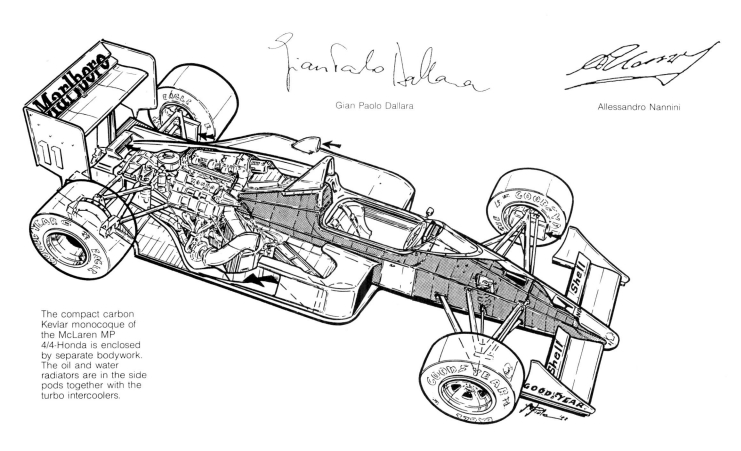

Gian Paolo Dallara

Allessandro Nannini

The compact carbon Kevlar monocoque of the McLaren MP 4/4-Honda is enclosed by separate bodywork. The oil and water radiators are in the side pods together with the turbo intercoolers.

Osamu Goto

Prost were always in the front. In the rain Senna was able to demonstrate his skill even more impressively, as he did at both Silverstone and Hockenheim. At the end of the season Prost had to resign himself to the fact that he had now passed the zenith of his career. Senna regularly drove faster than the little Frenchman and most of the time Senna was also able to start from pole position.

Many fans were disappointed with Prost's performance at Silverstone when the double World Champion not only dropped back because of the torrential rain but finally threw in the towel and left his undamaged McLaren standing in the pits. Clay Regazzoni commented bitingly, "that was an unforgiveable *faux pas* for a World Champion".

The Benetton-Ford B188 confirmed its position as one of the best Formula One cars of 1988. In it Thierry Boutsen was placed third no fewer than six times, while his team-mate Nannini proved to be a great find.

The Williams-Judd FW12 also performed extraordinarily well in the hands of Nigel Mansell and Riccardo Patrese. In the rain at Silverstone Mansell

gained a convincing second place, after having finally convinced chief designer Patrick Head that they should give up the active suspension and change back to a conventional system.

The March-Judd 881 made great progress, particularly from the middle of the season. The fiery Ivan Capelli from Milan proved himself to be an absolutely top-notch driver who was definitely in the running for a victory, and Mauricio Gugelmin turned out to be a very skillful team-mate who, in his first Formula One season, proved that he knew how to put up a good fight.

Lotus, as much because of the animosity between lead driver Nelson Piquet and designer Gérard Ducarouge as anything else, did not enjoy a good season.

Among the others, Arrows occasionally produced good individual performances, such as at the Italian Grand Prix where Cheever and Warwick took third and fourth placings behind the two Ferraris. Jonathan Palmer in the Tyrrell also did very well as did Alex Caffi for Dallara. De Cesaris in the Rial once again had a whole series of crashes, while

Minardi gained its very first World Championship points with Martini's sixth placing in Detroit. Lola, Dallara, AGS, Coloni, Ligier, EuroBrun, Zakspeed and Osella all failed to score any points. The first worry of the Coloni, Ligier, Euro-Brun, Osella and Zakspeed drivers was qualifying, and Bailey in the second Tyrrell had the same problem, as 31 competitors continued to compete for 26 starting places.

McLaren won the coveted Manufacturers' Championship, well ahead of Ferrari. The British team missed out on the 200 mark by a hair's breadth, the MP4/4 having won a record 199 points; Ferrari followed with 65; then Benetton with 46, though the Benetton's points were later reduced.

With the Australian Grand Prix on November 13th 1988 the era of the turbo engines in Formula One came to an end. It had begun on July 16th 1977 with the appearance of the Renault RS01 with 1.5-litre V6 turbocharged engine driven by Jean-Pierre Jabouille at Silverstone. Over 12 Grand Prix seasons the turbo engine had had a stormy career. Astronomical sums must have been invested in the units while temperature, materials and other problems were solved. The performance per litre increased from 400bhp in 1977 to about 900 in 1986, which was the last year in which no limits were set on turbo boost.

Formula One Cars of 1988

Make/Model	Designer(s)	Engine	Gearbox (number of gears)	Front Track	Rear Track	Dry Weight (kg)
AGS JH23	Christian Vanderpleyn	Ford-Cosworth DFZ (V8 SM)	AGS (5/6)	2680	F 1710 R 1640	500
Arrows A 10 B	Ross Brawn	Megatron M12/13 (4 cyl Turbo)	Arrows (6)	2743	F 1803 R 1625	540
Benetton B 188	Rory Byrne	Ford DFR (V8 SM)	Benetton (6)	2690	F 1816 R 1682	500
Coloni FC 188	Roberto Ori	Ford-Cosworth DFZ (V8 SM)	Coloni-Hewland (6)	2820	F 1790 R 1650	520
BMS Dallara 188	Sergio Rinland	Ford-Cosworth DFZ (V8 SM)	BMS-Hewland (6)	2880	F 1792 R 1672	500
EuroBrun ER 188	Mario Tolentino	Ford-Cosworth DFZ (V8 SM)	EuroBrun-Hewland (6)	2740	F 1820 R 1670	500
Ferrari F1-87/88 C	John Barnard Harvey Postlethwaite	Ferrari (V6 Turbo)	Ferrari (6)	2800	F 1791 R 1673	540
Lola LC-88	Ralph Bellamy	Ford-Cosworth DFZ (V8 SM)	Lola-Hewland FGB (5)	2700	F 1714 R 1600	515
Ligier JS 31	Michel Têtu	Judd CV (V8 SM)	Ligier (6)	2865	F 1790 R 1662	525
Lotus T 100	Gérard Ducarouge	Honda RA 168 E (V6 Turbo)	Lotus (6)	2770	F 1800 R 1650	540
March M 881	Adrian Newey	Judd CV (V8 SM)	March (6)	2850	F 1770 R 1670	500
McLaren MP 4/4	Gordon Murray Steve Nichols	Honda RA 168 E (V6 Turbo)	McLaren/Weismann (6)	—	F — R —	—
Minardi M 188	Giacomo Caliri	Ford-Cosworth DFZ (V8 SM)	Minardi (5)	2670	F 1787 R 1651	506
Osella FA 1 L	Antonio Tomaini	Alfa Romeo/Osella T 890 (V8 Turbo)	Osella-Hewland (6)	2776	F 1800 R 1672	560
Rial ARC 01	Gustav Brunner	Ford-Cosworth DFZ (V8 SM)	Rial (5/6)	2800	F 1800 R 1600	500
Tyrrell 017	Maurice Phillippe Brian Lisles	Ford-Cosworth DFZ (V8 SM)	Tyrrell (5/6)	—	F — R —	500
Williams FW 012 B	Patrick Head Frank Dernie	Judd CV (V8 SM)	Williams-Hewland (6)	2743	F 1803 R 1676	500
Zakspeed ZK 871 B	David Kelly	Zakspeed (4 cyl Turbo)	Zakspeed (6)	2830	F 1810 R 1617	550

Monocoques: All monocoques are made up of a combination of Kevlar with carbon fibre, some with a honeycomb alloy inner layer.
A: Atmospheric engine
Cubic capacity: 3.5 litres; turbocharged engines: 1.5 litres
Tyres: All cars were fitted with Goodyears.

The year 1989 saw the beginning of a new era, for the turbocharged engines which had dominated the earlier 1980s were no longer allowed. From now on only "atmospheric" or non-turbocharged engines of 3.5 litres maximum capacity could participate in Formula One.

The McLarens proved superior once again, though the MP4/5 with V10 Honda engine was not as successful as its turbocharged V6 predecessor had been, and won "only" ten races in 1989. Ferrari won three times, Williams-Renault twice and Benetton-Ford once. McLaren did however win the Formula One Constructors' Cup by a considerable margin.

The battle for the Drivers' World Championship remained in balance right up to the final race, even though Alain Prost had built up a comfortable lead over his team-mate Ayrton Senna by mid-season. Senna lagged behind as a result of several retirements, but because of the points system's requirement that worst performances should be dropped, he was able to make up some ground towards the end of the season.

This was the 40th Drivers' World Championship, and had the greatest number of participants ever. A total of 20 teams, and 39 drivers, registered with FISA for the contest, and eight more drivers joined in during the season.

This number of competitors meant that for the first time elimination trials had to be held before qualifying at each Grand Prix. Between 8am and 9am on the Friday before each race, 13 runners were reduced to four who would be allowed to take part in qualifying itself. That left 30 drivers to compete on the Friday and Saturday for the 26 starting places in the race. Those teams competing in Formula One for the first time, and those with the poorest results from the second half of the 1988 season, were required to take part in the pre-qualifying trials.

With Goodyear supplying all the teams in 1987 and 1988, the tyre scene had been relatively peaceful for once. This year though, after withdrawing for a year, Pirelli re-entered Formula One, and this meant the reappearance of super-soft qualifying tyres and a new tyre war. Goodyear supplied five contract teams (McLaren, Ferrari, Benetton, Williams and Lotus) free, and also sold tyres to Tyrrell, Arrows, March, Ligier, Onyx, Rial and AGS. Pirelli likewise supplied a contract service to Minardi, BMS-Dallara, Zakspeed and Brabham, while Osella, Coloni and EuroBrun had to pay for their own tyres.

Each Formula One team was required to participate in all 16 World Championship races. If they did not, they had to pay FISA a hefty fine. These

Ferrari and Nigel Mansell (centre) won a completely unexpected victory in the season's first Grand Prix at Rio de Janeiro. Mansell's face is screwed up with pain because he had just injured himself on a sharp edge of the giant trophy during the victory presentation. Alain Prost (left) was placed second, followed by Mauricio Gugelmin. After this surprise victory at Rio, Ferrari suffered a series of retirements.

conditions were particularly hard on those teams without strong financial backing; some competitors did not succeed in qualifying for a Grand Prix all year, but still had to turn up for every round.

The new regulations also stated that for safety reasons the pedals had to be placed behind the front axle-line. This meant that cockpits were again moved further back, which in turn reduced the space available for the fuel tank and engine. These restrictions influenced the configuration of the engines themselves: should it be an eight, or the maximum allowable 12 cylinders? The reduction in available space suggested a V8 would be the most favourable solution, but these would be unable to match the performance expected from the high-revving V12s. But a V12 is longer than a V8 of the same capacity, and any car using one of these would have to make use of side-mounted fuel tanks in order to accommodate the required capacity of 200 to 220 litres.

What was needed was a compromise between the high-performance but longer and heavier, and probably less economical, V12, and the more traditional V8 with its opposite characteristics. That compromise was found in the V10, a configuration never hitherto used.

Although limitations on consumption had been abolished, fuel economy continued to play an important part in designers' thinking. The better the fuel economy, the less fuel it would be necessary to carry. And a saving of ten litres represented 7.5kg less weight at the start. The 102-ROZ limit for fuel was still in force, but the emphasis was no longer

on the so-called heavy fuels that had been used with the turbo engines; the chemists were now preparing other mixtures.

After devoting considerable time and effort throughout the 1980s to developing turbo engines, engine designers now had to do a complete turnaround and concentrate on atmospheric engines, on which no advanced development work had been done for years. All the know-how accumulated in the turbo era was virtually useless. No longer would engineers have to contend with the astronomically high performance figures produced by the turbo engines, which had peaked at 1400bhp (in qualifying trim) in 1986. The new atmospheric engines would not however be significantly cheaper to develop.

No fewer than nine different 3.5-litre atmospheric engines were registered for use in the 1989 Championship, an unheard-of number. Renault and Honda pioneered the V10 concept, but Cosworth remained faithful to the V8 configuration, DFZ and DFR versions of which had appeared in 1988. Ford also chose a V8 (built by Cosworth) as did Judd, whose 1988 CV design was superseded by the EV, and Yamaha. Lamborghini, entering Formula One for the first time, decided the V12 variation suited their image better, and so did Ferrari, while other 12-cylinder projects were planned by Neotech in Austria, the new firm of Life in Modena and Motori Moderni in Novaro, where Carlo Chiti was developing a 180° design under contract to Subaru.

The new 75° unit developed by Ford was undoubtedly the leading design among the V8s, and 25 examples were built by Cosworth in Northampton.

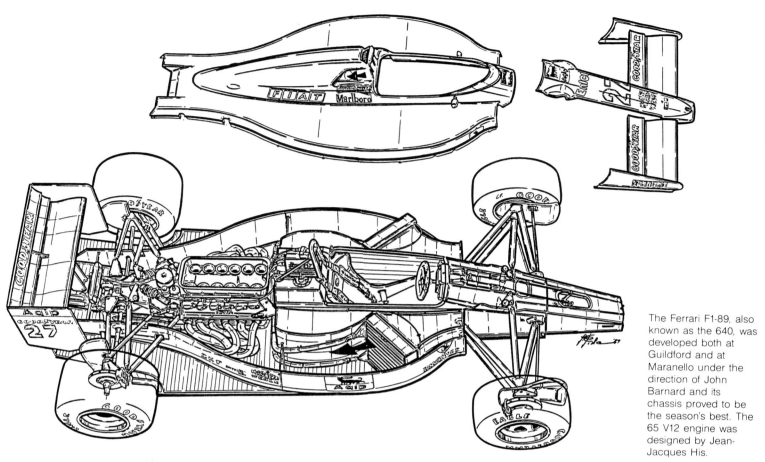

The Ferrari F1-89, also known as the 640, was developed both at Guildford and at Maranello under the direction of John Barnard and its chassis proved to be the season's best. The 65 V12 engine was designed by Jean-Jacques His.

Compared to the earlier 90° Ford-Cosworth DFV, the new unit was smaller, which gave it aerodynamic advantages. Its main characteristics were a light-alloy block, four valves per cylinder and a specially developed electronic management system. Ford did not release specifications of the engine, which was intended for the exclusive use of the Benetton team, but insiders estimated the performance at between 615 and 630bhp at 11,500rpm.

With this new engine, Alessandro Nannini's Benetton won the Japanese Grand Prix at Suzuka after the McLarens and Ferraris had all been eliminated.

Ford meanwhile put the DFZ engine, which Benetton had used in 1988, up for sale. Cosworth provided a modification which repositioned the crankshaft, thus bringing its design closer to the DFR. While Cosworth themselves then concentrated on the new 75° Ford motor, the DFR was further developed by the tuning firms of Langford and Peck, Brian Hart and Heini Mader Components.

The conventional 90° V8 Judd engine had already been used in 1988 by Williams, Ligier and March, but in preparation for 1989 the 76° EV version was developed. This was intended for the sole use of March, now backed by the Japanese firm of Leyton House. The new four-valve Judd V8 was a more compact unit than its predecessor, and used a Marelli electronic management system in place of the CV's Lucas components.

Although both Williams and Ligier abandoned Judd engines in 1989, Lotus reached agreement with the tuning firm of Tickford for the use of Judd engines with specially-developed cylinder heads. These had three camshafts, and five valves per cylinder. But although the Judd-Tickford "five-valver" was tested during the year, it did not prove a success, and was not in fact raced.

The Japanese motorcycle manufacturer Yamaha entered Formula One for the first time in 1989. They also decided on a 75° V8 but used five valves per cylinder, developed from an engine used in national events in Japan, and this was the only V8 in which the camshafts were driven by belt rather than gears. These OX88 engines, which were used exclusively by Zakspeed, proved very unreliable in their first year, and

were also underpowered — the talk was of only 570 or 590bhp being available. Bernd Schneider, the principal Zakspeed-Yamaha driver, managed to qualify for only two races all year.

News of the advent of ten-cylinder racing engines was greeted with some scepticism, for the knowledgeable maintain these have vibration problems which are difficult to control. Whatever vibration problems there were in 1989, they made little difference to the performance of either the Honda or the Renault engine.

Honda's RA109E, with its two banks of cylinders angled at 72°, was shown as early as the Tokyo Motor Show in November 1987 — proof that the Japanese had been working on solutions to the problem for a long time — and first track tests were carried out in conjunction with McLaren the following August. Honda chose a thin-walled engine-block of cast steel, which allowed increased engine speeds without additional weight. The first version had belt-driven camshafts but by the time the 1989 season began, gear drive had been adopted. Both the engine management

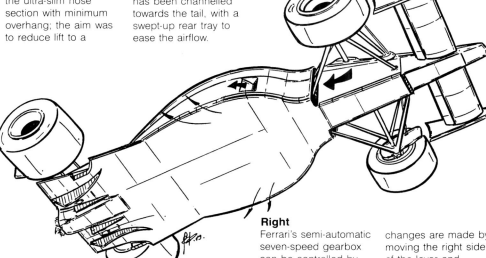

A view of the Ferrari F1-89 from below. Note the ultra-slim nose section with minimum overhang; the aim was to reduce lift to a minimum. Of interest here is the way the air has been channelled towards the tail, with a swept-up rear tray to ease the airflow.

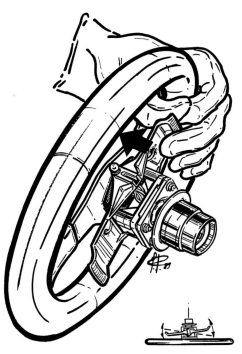

Right
Ferrari's semi-automatic seven-speed gearbox can be controlled by the finger tips through a small lever installed behind the steering wheel. Upward changes are made by moving the right side of the lever and downward changes by the left side. The driver need never take his hands off the wheel.

and fuel-injection systems were produced by Honda.

Honda did not reveal the cylinder measurements or performance of their new engine, but it is believed that power was 640bhp at the beginning of the season, increasing to 670bhp at 12,800rpm by the end of the year. The engines were tended at the circuits by a team of Japanese engineers under the direction of Osamu Goto.

While Senna and Prost were taking the V10 Honda engine to victory after victory in 1989, the same team of engine specialists was already working on a V12, which was displayed at the Tokyo Motor Show in November 1989.

Renault returned to Formula One in 1989 after only a brief absence, though on this occasion they restricted themselves to supplying engines rather than racing their own complete cars. Their new ten-cylinder engine was developed under the direction of Bernard Dudot, while Jean-Jacques His returned to the fold to assist with the project, after working on the design of Ferrari's V6 turbo and the new V12 atmospheric engine.

The French manufacturer opted for a light-alloy 67° block, with camshafts driven by belts. Applying the technology learned on the last generation of six-cylinder turbos, they did without valve-springs, each cylinder's four valves being closed pneumatically. The Renault V10, which weighed only 141kg, used Marelli electronics. Its performance was initially estimated to be about 610bhp at 12,500rpm, but probably increased during the season by 50bhp and 1000rpm.

The Renault V10s were used exclusively by Williams, for whom the Belgian Thierry Boutsen won the Canadian and Australian Grands Prix, both run in wet conditions.

The V12 Ferrari Type 3500 had been designed as early as 1987 by the former Renault engineer Jean-Jacques His, though there had been delays with its actual construction. Like Honda, Ferrari also chose a thin-walled cast-steel block and, using the construction technique in use since the 180° Type 312 of 1969, incorporated only four main bearings. The first version, tested in 1988, had four valves per cylinder but by the start of the 1989 season five-valve heads with gear-driven camshafts were fitted.

Ferrari was the only constructor to make public the cylinder dimensions of its 1989 engine: 84 × 52.6mm (3498cc). A later version used a shorter piston stroke. As with the turbocharged V6, Ferrari used Marelli engine management and Weber-Marelli fuel-injection on its new design. Ferrari's V12 proved to be the second most powerful of the 1989 engines, after the ten-cylinder Honda. It was estimated that at the beginning of the season, running on a compression ratio of 11.5:1, the "3500" produced between 615 and 630bhp, but it probably improved to 640/650bhp at 12,500rpm before the season was over. The automatic rev-limiter did not cut in until 13,600rpm.

Lamborghini, for its first involvement in motor racing, set up a new firm at Modena where former Ferrari engineer Mauro Forghieri, as technical director of the project, designed an 80° light-alloy engine with four main bearings, gear-driven camshafts and four valves per cylinder. Initially the Type 3512 engine used Marelli electronics but was switched to Bosch equipment after just one race. The Lamborghini engines, used only in Gerard Larrousse's Calmels-Lola cars, proved unreliable, and the small company did not have the resources to develop its output beyond 615/630bhp at 12,800rpm.

In terms of power output per litre, the ten- and 12-cylinder designs produced between 180 and 188bhp/litre, and the V8s between 171 and 178. It must be repeated however that little data was officially released, and these are figures estimated by "insiders".

Anyone who believed the changeover to atmospheric engines would see a reduction in development costs compared with turbocharged designs was deluded. When Honda showed their new V12 engine in November 1989, their chief engineer Nabuhiko Kawamoto said the development of the new engines for

Formula One had already cost between 10 and 15% more than the amount spent on the turbos.

Gearbox design was also going through a new development phase in 1989. From the end of the fifties, longitudinal gearboxes had been in general use, mounted almost without exception behind the rear axle. In the 1970s Ferrari with its 312T series had started using transverse gearboxes placed forward of the axle line, and in 1988 Williams had also used transverse mounting. The trend continued in 1989, with Arrows, Lola-Lamborghini, Onyx and, from mid-season, McLaren, all using transverse-mounted six-speed units, the McLaren box being developed by Weismann.

This arrangement had two advantages. First, because the gearbox was placed between the axles, it had a positive effect on weight distribution. And the positioning meant that the rear end could be redesigned to be aerodynamically more effective. As the gearbox was placed in front of the rear axle, the underbody could be sited higher.

March and Benetton did not change over to transverse gearbox designs but instead placed their longitudinal gearboxes in front of the rear axle-line.

With the exception of Ferrari, all other teams used conventional six-speed longitudinal gearboxes behind the axle line. The Ferrari gearbox, although longitudual, was hardly conventional, as will shortly be seen.

Right from pre-season testing, the McLaren-Honda was firm favourite among the 20 teams which took part in the 1989 World Championship, for the V10 produced the sort of power no-one could hope to match. First tests had been carried out in an adapted MP4/4 chassis, but the new MP4/5, designed by Neil Oatley and Steve Nichols, appeared in time for the first Grand Prix of the new season.

Ferrari had tested their F1-89 as early as July 1988 in a first version, the type 639. This led to the 640, which differed from the prototype only in detail. The new car, the first (and only) Ferrari developed entirely under the direction of John Barnard, had a carbon fibre/Kevlar monocoque chassis built at GTO (Guildford Technical Operations), the English Ferrari design centre in Surrey. The car was then completed at Maranello, where the mechanical components were added.

The most interesting aspect of the new Ferrari was its seven-speed semi-automatic gearbox. This was extremely fast and easy to operate, gears being changed by means of a small toggle-switch behind the steering wheel. Pushed to the right, it selected a higher gear, to the left, it changed down. The clutch pedal was needed only at the start: once the car was moving, the clutch was operated automatically by the same switch. The new system gave a lot of trouble in the early part of the season, but this was under control by mid-year.

It had been announced as early as the summer of 1988 that Nigel Mansell would be driving for Ferrari in the coming season, and Gerhard Berger's contract did not expire until the end of 1989. Marco Piccinini meanwhile retired

Above
Ayrton Senna and the McLaren-Honda MP4/5 proved to be the fastest combination of 1989. Senna was in pole position 13 times and won six Grands Prix. However, he had to retire so many times that in the end he was only second in the World Championship behind his team rival Alain Prost.

Nigel Mansell won both the Brazilian and Hungarian Grands Prix in the Ferrari F1-89. After a long run of bad luck, Gerhard Berger scored a victory in the Portuguese Grand Prix.

from the position of team manager after nearly a decade at Maranello, his place being taken by Cesare Fiorio, who was also well known, after 25 years with Lancia's competition department.

Benetton, the Italian clothing giant which had taken over Toleman's works at Witney in England, did not have its new model ready for the beginning of the season, and had initially to use the previous year's car, the B188 with Cosworth DFR engine. The new 75° Ford engine, which Cosworth had developed for Benetton, could not however be fitted to the older car, and the new model's debut suffered continual delays. There were problems with the suspension, and then Cosworth had to carry out further work on the crankshaft to stop vibration.

Benetton's Number One driver, Alessandro Nannini, was joined by the young English Formula 3000 driver Johnny Herbert, but he was on crutches as the season began, as a result of a serious accident at Brands Hatch the previous August. Despite a promising fourth place in his Formula One debut race in Brazil Herbert was replaced before the French Grand Prix by Emanuele Pirro, who until then had been acting as test driver for McLaren-Honda.

At Williams Patrick Head adapted the FW12, which had run with Judd engines in 1988, to take the V10 Renault engine, and the interim FW12C in fact worked so well that the FW13 did not make its debut until the Portuguese Grand Prix. In the

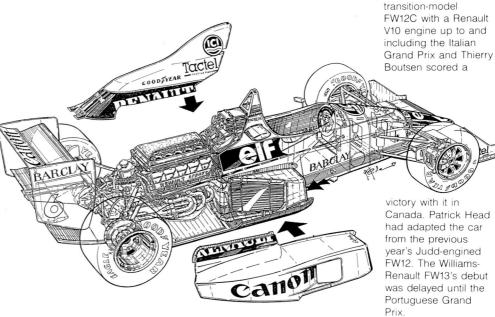

Williams entered the transition-model FW12C with a Renault V10 engine up to and including the Italian Grand Prix and Thierry Boutsen scored a victory with it in Canada. Patrick Head had adapted the car from the previous year's Judd-engined FW12. The Williams-Renault FW13's debut was delayed until the Portuguese Grand Prix.

late summer the team lost Argentine-born engineer Enrique Scalabroni, who transferred to Ferrari as John Barnard's three-year contract with the Italians expired on 31st October. Williams retained Riccardo Partrese on the driving strength, and also took on Thierry Boutsen to replace Nigel Mansell.

Judd had given exclusive rights to its new V8 engine to March, whose CG891 model was developed under the direction of Adrian Newey. The car was designated CG in honour of the team's Italian supporter Cesare Gariboldi, who had had a fatal accident a short time before. The revised design was aerodynamically very promising, but when it made its debut in the Monaco Grand Prix it was disappointing, and Ivan Capelli and Mauricio Gugelmin were not able to achieve the same excellent results that they had the previous year.

Lotus's weapon for 1989 was the 101, designed by former Williams aerodynamicist Frank Dernie. Still owned by the Chapman family, Lotus was going through a difficult phase and neither Nelson Piquet nor Satoru Nakajima was able to contest the lead. In the middle of the year team manager Peter Warr was released and engineer Tony Rudd, who had designed the successful V8 BRM in the 1960s, took over as chief executive and appointed Rupart Manwaring as a team manager. The five-valve Judd-Tickford engine project was dropped at the same time.

Brabham returned to Formula One this year after its one-year absence. At the end of 1987 Bernie Ecclestone had secretly sold the firm to the Fiat group, who used its resources to develop the V10 Alfa Romeo 164. This was intended for a Pro-Car saloon series which never got off the ground, and in the autumn of 1988 the Brabham organisation changed hands again. Walter Brun played a role in this transaction but control soon passed to Swiss financier Joachim Lüthi. However, late in 1989 Lüthi was taken into custody in relation to various financial dealings,

Left
At the Monaco Grand Prix the Brabham-Judd BT58s of Brundle (pictured) and Modena performed outstandingly, as did the AGS-Cosworth JH23 driven by Tarquini. Modena finished third and Brundle was sixth despite a long pitstop. Note the small television camera mounted on the Brabham (behind the driver's helmet).

Right
The British Onyx team made its first appearance in Formula One during the 1989 season. The Ford Cosworth-powered Onyx ORE1 driven by Stefan Johansson and Bertrand Gachot (later replaced by JJ Lehto) had to pre-qualify before every race and during the first half of the season in particular they found it very difficult to clear the first hurdle.

Theirry Boutsen sprays both his teammate Riccardo Patrese and Bernard Cassin, the director of Renault Sport, with champagne after their unexpected success in the Canadian Grand Prix, when they celebrated a 1-2 victory.

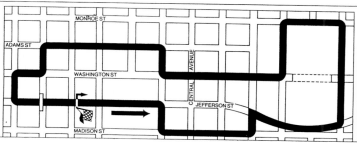

In 1989 the United States Grand Prix was held for the first time on a 3.62km long street circuit in Phoenix, Arizona. The circuit is made up almost entirely of right-angled corners.

and the ownership question came up again. The Brabham factory buildings and land remained in Ecclestone's hands throughout all this, as did the team's collection of every model of Formula One Brabham.

The new Brabham BT58 was designed to run with Judd power and Pirelli tyres by former Dallara engineer Sergio Rinland, who provided Martin Brundle and Stefano Modena with an efficient design.

The 1989 season started well for Tyrrell, whose new 018 model was designed by Englishman Harvey Postlethwaite, the former Ferrari employee, in conjunction with French aerodynamics specialist Jean-Claude Migeod, who had also been at Ferrari. Michele Alboreto and Jonathan Palmer took the car into battle, but early in the summer the Italian driver left the team in a dispute over money and went to Larrousse. He was replaced by Frenchman Jean Alesi, who continued to contest the Formula 3000 Championship and in fact won the 1989 title in that category. Alesi, daredevil son of Sicilian parents, caused a sensation in his first season in Formula One.

Eddie Cheever and Derek Warwick

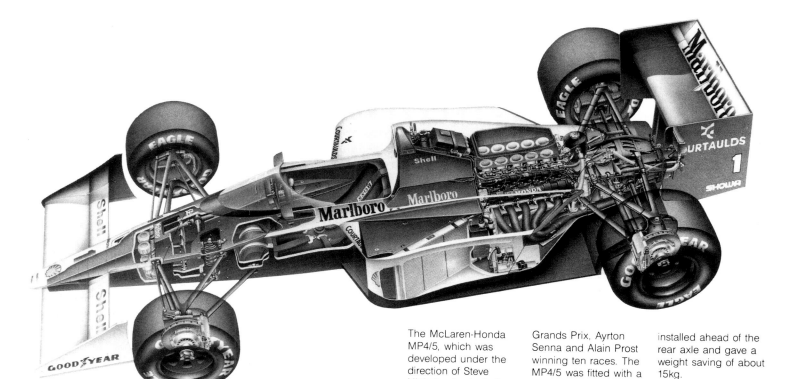

The McLaren-Honda MP4/5, which was developed under the direction of Steve Nichols, dominated most of the 1989 Grands Prix, Ayrton Senna and Alain Prost winning ten races. The MP4/5 was fitted with a transverse gearbox in mid-season, which was installed ahead of the rear axle and gave a weight saving of about 15kg.

continued to drive for Arrows, where Ross Brawn devised the AII model with Cosworth DFR engine and a new transverse gearbox. The Formula One family gained a new member in Onyx, a British team managed by Mike Earle but backed by the Moneytron concern of Jean-Pierre Van Rossem, the Belgian mathematician and shares wizard. Onyx's Cosworth-powered ORE1, the work of Alan Jenkins, was driven by Stefan Johansson and Belgian newcomer Bertrand Gachot, though towards the end of the season Finnish driver J J Lehto was taken on in place of Gachot.

In Italy, Giampaolo Dallara also used Cosworth engines in his BMS189 designed for Scuderia Italia, whose drivers were Alex Caffi and Andrea de Cesaris. At Osella, Antonio Tomaini produced the Cosworth-powered FAIM89, undertaking many wind-tunnel tests in their first serious experimentation with aerodynamics. Piercarlo Ghinzani and Nicola Larini were the drivers. The Minardi design office had seen considerable change: Aldo Costa and Tommaso Carletti, together with former Lotus man Nigel Copperthwaite, were responsible for the M189-Cosworth, which was driven during the year by Pierluigi Martini and the Spaniard Luis Perez Sala. Both drivers, but particularly Martini, became increasingly competitive as the season wore on, confounding the opposition with sensational qualifying times which reflected the quality of Pirelli's tyres.

The Ligier team, which had moved from Vichy to Magny-Cours, engaged the Brazilian Richard Divila who, together with Michel Beaujon, designed the JS33 with Cosworth DFR engine, but neither René Arnoux nor Formula One newcomer Olivier Grouillard was ever in contention for victory. Lola meanwhile developed the LC89 for the Larrousse-Calmels team run by Gérard Larrousse. The V12 Lamborghini-powered cars were handled initially by Philippe Alliot and young Yannick Dalmas, though Dalmas was later replaced by Alboreto.

The new combination of Zakspeed and Yamaha was awaited with interest but Gustav Brunner's ZK189 suffered from an acute lack of horsepower. There was talk of considerably less than 600bhp, which meant that Bernd Schneider and his Japanese team-mate Aguri Suzuki practically never managed to pre-qualify.

Both the Coloni and EuroBrun teams slipped hopelessly into oblivion in 1989,

and were joined by Rial, though the last-named team did manage to score some points in the first half of the season. EuroBrun started by entering a revised version of their 1988 car but their driver, Gregor Foitek from Zurich, never made it past pre-qualifying. The situation did not improve when Foitek was replaced by the Argentinian long-distance expert Oscar Larrauri. In July George Ryton's new ER189 model, with Judd engine and Pirelli tyres, made its appearance, but this too was a disappointment.

The small AGS team from southern France changed hands, though businessman Cyril de Rouvre, the owner, retained the services of founder Henri Julien as an adviser. AGS fielded an interim Cosworth-powered model, the JH23B, for drivers Philippe Streiff and the

The type RA 109E Honda V10 was clearly the top-performing engine of 1989. Between the Brazilian Grand Prix and the final round of the World Championship in Adelaide its power output increased by 30bhp. The first version of the engine, used only in tests, had its camshafts driven by a toothed belt (picture), but in the later version used throughout the season the camshafts were gear-driven.

During the 1989 season the Lotus team was badly off form and the type 101 with its Judd engine could not match the pace of the leaders. Lotus also tested a special Tickford version of the Judd V8 engine with five valves per cylinder, but proved to be disappointing. Three fourth places by Nelson Piquet and one by Satoru Nakajima were the best results for the 101.

In 1989, Nelson Piquet, the three times World Champion, usually viewed the world with a worried expression. For once, the former victor of many Grands Prix was not to play a leading role in the World Championship. Beside him stands the Lotus designer Frank Dernie, who is an oustanding aerodynamicist.

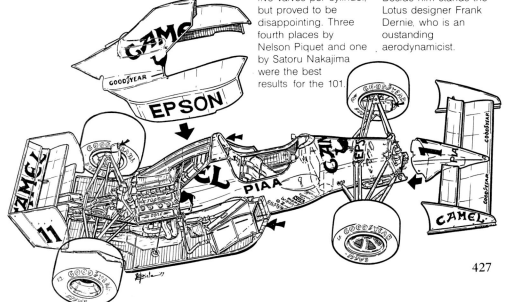

Lamborghini made its first appearance in Formula One in the 1989 season. The V12 engines from, Modena were installed in the Lola LC89 of the Larrousse team, who suffered numerous retirements and a lot of engine problems. However at the Spanish Grand Prix in Jerez, Philippe Alliot in the LC89 came in sixth to claim the first World Championship points for Lamborghini.

up-and-coming German Joachim Winkelhock, brother of the late Manfred Winkelhock. Unfortunately however Streiff had a dreadful accident during testing at Rio de Janeiro, and although he survived, it was as a paraplegic. He was replaced by the Italian Gabriele Tarquini who achieved some good results before AGS slipped further and further into the background.

The 1989 season was unusually hard on the weaker teams because of their requirement to take part in pre-qualifying. Those required to do so because of poor (or no) results in the second half of 1988 were Brundle and Modena (Brabham), Ghinzani and Larini (Osella), Caffi (Dallara), Raphanel (Coloni), Foitek (EuroBrun), Schneider and Suzuki (Zakspeed), Johansson and Gachot (Onyx), Weidler (Rial) and Winkelhock (AGS).

Against most predictions, the 1989 cars with 3.5-litre atmospheric engines proved capable of similar lap times to those achieved by the 1.5-litre turbocars. This was due not only to the progress made in chassis design and aerodynamics, but also to the characteristics of the normally-aspirated units. They did not have the "turbo lag" of their predecessors, which meant the cars could be driven around corners more efficiently, and acceleration was equally impressive. A 1989 Grand Prix car could accelerate from a standing start to 200km/h in 5.2 or 5.3 seconds. Thanks to their light construction, some designs even had to use ballast to bring them up to the 500kg minimum weight limit.

When devising the aerodynamics of their new cars, many designers were

inspired by the March 881, and the small "Concorde beak" became an accepted feature. Its main advantage was in the reduction of "lift" because its small size meant wider — and therefore more effective — nose-fins could be used. At the same time air was drawn more efficiently into the side-mounted radiator air-intakes.

The continual quest for perfection and the increasing time spent testing meant that several teams employed a test driver in addition to their two regular race drivers. J J Lehto performed this task for Ferrari and Emanuele Pirro for McLaren, while Benetton used Johnny Dumfries and Formula 3000 ace Martin Donnelly occasionally drove for Lotus.

The 40th World Drivers' Championship began on 26th March with the Brazilian Grand Prix on the Nelson Piquet circuit at Rio de Janeiro, with McLaren and Honda the favoured combination. Ferrari was also expected to do well, though in testing the new gearbox had shown a worrying tendency to develop faults.

This prognosis held throughout the season, though the McLaren MP4/5s

Above left
In 1989 Benetton retained Alessandro Nannini (right) and took on the English Formula 3000 driver Johnny Herbert for the second car. However Herbert's serious leg injuries sustained the previous year in Formula 3000 were not properly healed and he was replaced by Emanuele Pirro in the middle of the season. Nannini won the Japanese Grand Prix.

Above
The great discovery of the season was young Jean Alesi, from southern France. Born of Sicilian parents, Alesi joined the Tyrrell team for the French Grand Prix and after finishing fourth on his Formula One debut this talented driver was soon competing regularly for points. Alesi also won the European Formula 3000 Championship.

were not as dominant as the MP4/4s had been in 1988.

By far the fastest driver was McLaren's Ayrton Senna. He proved particularly dominant in qualifying, earning pole position for 13 of the Grands Prix. His pole position in the Australian Grand Prix, last World Championship race of the season, was the 43rd of his career, and he would have retained his World Championship title too but for mechanical and other faults. He won six

Jean Alesi

Right

Alain Prost in the McLaren MP4/5-Honda became World Champion for the third time in 1989. This photo was taken at the Ascari Curve, where he is being tailed by Gerhard Berger's Ferrari. After Senna had engine problems at Monza, Prost took the lead and was the eventual winner. A few days earlier Prost had announced that he would be transferring to Ferrari for the 1990 season.

Below

Pierluigi Martini in his Minardi M189 with Ford Cosworth-DFR engine impressed the racing world with his excellent qualifying performances which were aided by Pirelli's excellent qualifying tyres. Here the Minardi is being followed by a Tyrrell 018 and a Lola LC189.

Grands Prix, those of San Marino, Monaco, Mexico, Germany, Belgium and Spain, and was in the lead for a total of 2295 racing kilometres.

His team-mate Alain Prost, who wrested the World Championship from him, led 1217km, but this was well clear of the next best: Patrese (Williams-Renault) led 428km, Mansell (Ferrari) 333, Berger (Ferrari) 236, Boutsen (Williams-Renault) 227, Warwick (Arrows-Cosworth) and Nannini (Benetton-Ford) both 18 and Martini (Minardi-Cosworth) 4.4km.

At the season's premiere in Brazil Senna collided with Berger on the very first bend. For a long time Patrese held the lead but his ten-cylinder Renault engine finally gave up. This gave Nigel Mansell a surprise debut win in the Ferrari, a car whose semi-automatic gearbox not even team insiders had expected to last.

Senna had his revenge when he took clear victory in the San Marino Grand Prix at Imola and again at Monaco, and also won in Mexico, where few believed the McLaren-Hondas would retain their superiority.

At Ferrari, the new gearbox remained a source of anxiety for weeks, and Mansell was unable to score a single point in any of the five races which followed his Rio success. Team-mate Berger meanwhile had a huge accident at Imola when a front wing broke. He was driving into the Tamburello curve at high speed and crashed head-on into the barriers. Within seconds, the wrecked Ferrari was in flames, but Berger was rescued by the track marshals, whose courage deserves nothing but praise. The Austrian was taken to hospital with severe burns to his hands, but although he had to miss the Monaco Grand Prix, he had recovered in time for Mexico.

Alain Prost started the season well, with second in each of the first three Grands Prix, and was thus early leader in the World Championship contest. Then in the United States Grand Prix, moved from Detroit to Phoenix in Arizona, Senna had to withdraw with an ignition fault and Prost won his first victory of the season. This race was run in unbearable heat on a 3.8km street circuit comprising mainly right-angled corners.

Incessant rain caused confusion in the Canadian race. Senna again demonstrated his superior abilities until his engine packed up just before the end, which enabled Williams driver Thierry Boutsen to give the V10 Renault engine a deserved victory.

In the French Grand Prix at Le Castellet Mauricio Gugelmin was involved in a mass collision just after the green light, and the race had to be restarted. Jean Alesi made his Formula One debut here in a Tyrrell after Michele Alboreto and Ken Tyrrell had parted company, and the young man from the south of France held second place for a short time, finally finishing fourth. Senna was eliminated by differential damage right at the start, and Prost won with Mansell second in his first finish since Brazil.

Senna had to withdraw again from the British Grand Prix at Silverstone, sliding off on a corner with gearbox trouble, and Prost was able to take his third victory of the season. The McLaren-Hondas appeared here for the first time with their new transverse gearboxes, which were about 15kg lighter than the old longitudinal units. Mansell underlined the new-found Ferrari reliability with another placing.

Senna's run of bad luck ended at the German Grand Prix at Hockenheim, which he won in pouring rain from Prost, though the Frenchman remained well ahead in the Championship. Mansell took third place but Berger was again out of the running, this time after an accident.

The new rankings for pre-qualifying took effect from this race. The two Brabham drivers and Dallara man Caffi no longer had to take part in the elimination trials, but the two Lola-Lamborghini drivers, Alliot and Alboreto, slipped down into the unlucky 13.

The Hungarian Grand Prix proved to be the most fascinating and exciting race of the year. Riccardo Patrese in the "old" Williams-Renault FW12C set the pace at first but, from the middle of the field, Nigel Mansell was soon overtaking one rival after another. Patrese's engine then started to overheat as a result of a punctured radiator and, after a thrilling duel with Senna, Mansell wrested the lead from the McLaren. Ferrari thus took their second win of the year, on a circuit which did not allow the McLaren-Hondas to utilise to the full their amazing acceleration out of slow corners, or their superior straight-line speed. Senna for once was only placed, followed by the ever reliable Boutsen.

The Belgian Grand Prix at Spa-Francorchamps was an amazing battle fought in the rain. Senna proved his wet-weather superiority and won from Prost and Mansell. Yet again Berger had to retire, for the tenth time this year.

Senna seemed certain to add another win to his tally in the Italian Grand Prix but then went out with engine problems and on the 44th lap Prost was able to take over the lead and win once more. Berger finally managed to keep going to take second place, but Mansell had to pull out of the race with gearbox trouble. Prost's win was the 39th of his career and for once the Monza crowds were enthusiastic, for shortly before the race the Frenchman had signed to drive for Ferrari in 1990. It had been known since early July that he would be leaving McLaren, and that his place would be taken by Berger.

Ferrari had been steadily gaining ground on McLaren all season and the Italian cars' improvement was confirmed in the Portuguese Grand Prix at Estoril where, for the first time, they were dominant, and Berger took his first win of the season. He was followed over the line by Prost, who thus increased his World Championship lead even further, as Senna had retired after a dramatic incident in which he collided with Mansell.

Some laps previously Mansell, well in the lead, had overshot his pit by a few metres when coming in for a tyre change, and then reversed into place. Driving in reverse is not allowed however, and the Englishman was shown the black flag. Apparently he did not see the signal, and continued for the four more laps. On the 48th lap the Ferrari and Senna's McLaren collided on a corner, both cars coming to rest off the track. For ignoring the black flag, Mansell was banned from the next Grand Prix, in Spain. Ferrari lodged an appeal, but to no avail.

Meanwhile tension had been building up in the McLaren team, and the drivers had hardly exchanged a word since Imola. Prost accused his team-mate of failing to keep to an agreement in the race, and pushing him out of the lead. Each attacked the other in newspaper interviews, and Prost accused Honda and McLaren of providing Senna with better equipment. Neither Honda nor McLaren accepted such allegations, which Prost subsequently withdrew.

If Ayrton Senna was to be World Champion in 1989 he would have to win

One of the most tense moments in 1989: at Suzuka, Ayrton Senna in his McLaren MP4/5-Honda (No 1) tried to force his way past teammate Alain Prost, who was in the lead, at the entrance to the chicane. The result was a collision, both McLarens coming to rest at the edge of the track. Prost climbed out, but Senna was pushed-started back into the race and despite a pitstop crossed the line in first position, only to be disqualified for taking a short-cut back into the race and subsequently to be even more heavily penalised for alleged dangerous driving.

the three remaining Grands Prix, in Spain, Japan and Australia. In the first of these races he had no competition, and won from Berger and Prost. Before this race it was announced that John Barnard had Been unable to reach agreement with Ferrari president Piero Fusaro about his future, and that he would be moving to Benetton.

The Japanese Grand Prix at Suzuka was another dramatic race. A highly motivated Prost held the lead ahead of Senna until the Brazilian attempted a risky overtaking manoeuvre into the chicane. Prost held his line and the two McLarens collided and slid off the track. Prost, believing he was now World Champion, got out of his car, but Senna had the marshals push him out of the danger zone, then push-start him, after which he rolled through the back of the chicane and rejoined the race. After stopping at the pits for a new nose-cone he retook the lead from Nannini just before the finish, and was first over the line.

But the race officials promptly disqualified him for missing out part of the course in the aftermath to the incident with Prost, and although McLaren protested the decision, Alessandro Nannini in the Benetton-Ford was confirmed as winner.

McLaren then mobilised its lawyers for an appeal, but FISA simply took the opportunity to review Senna's case. reproaching the Brazilian for his previous sins. His collisions in earlier races were mentioned, and he was given a six-month suspended ban and fined $100,000.

But the upshot of all this was that Prost had won his third World Championship, for even victory in the final race would not give Senna the title.

Continuing torrential rain caused headaches in Adelaide, and serious questions were asked as to whether the race should be delayed. The slippery city streets were particularly dangerous because of inadequate drainage, and aquaplaning was the rule of the day. The race was duly started, but had to be stopped after just one lap because of collisions. Prost, a strong advocate of stopping the race, got out of his car at this point and returned to his hotel.

The restarted Australian Grand Prix was an eventful one, with no fewer than 13 cars involved in accidents. The long straight was particularly treacherous, as the spray thrown up by the cars created an impenetrable wall. Following drivers simply could not see, and both Senna and Piquet crashed into the tails of cars they were lapping. Both Ferraris withdrew because of accidents.

But Thierry Boutsen in the Williams-Renault performed impeccably. He did not make a single mistake, and won his second victory of the season. Nannini, victor at Suzuka, was placed second for he too was spared an accident. Riccardo Patrese completed a fine result for the Williams FW13 with third place. This was the Padua driver's 192nd Grand Prix.

The Adelaide race brought the 40th World Championship to a close. Alain Prost won his third title with 76 points after wins in France, Britain and Italy and numerous second and third placings, Senna remained on 60 points, while Patrese pipped Mansell for third in the last race, with 40 points. McLaren-Honda again dominated the Constructors' Championship, gaining 141 points. Williams-Renault were second with 77 followed by Ferrari with 59 and Benetton-Ford with 39.

During the summer Prost had again and again led journalists to believe that Honda were not supporting him with good equipment, and in November his accusations were answered by the Japanese company. Osamu Goto, the engineer responsible for Honda's Formula One engines, maintained that engines of the same specification had been supplied to both Prost and Senna. Honda also suggested that in 1988, when the turbo engines were restricted to 150 litres per race, Prost proved better able to cope with the fuel limitations simply because of the way he drove. But the company also released data showing that in 1989 Senna was usually the faster driver. During qualifying at Monza, for example, telemetry showed Senna to be about two seconds faster than Prost. The Frenchman maintained his rival had been given a more powerful engine, but the telemetry showed the two cars to be equally fast on the straights, though Senna was usually faster on the corners. On the Parabolica curve just before the finishing straight, for example, Senna was 1000rpm faster than Prost, and as a result was 24km/h faster into the straight.

Honda also countered accusations that a car's performance could be influenced during a race by telemetry from the pits. "This is absolutely not true," Osamu Goto said. "Even if we had the technology to carry out this procedure we would not do so."

Behind the four main protagonists in the 1989 World Championship — McLaren-Honda, Ferrari, Williams-Renault and Benetton-Ford — there was a considerable gap to "the rest". March had lost considerable ground, and Capelli did not succeed in gaining a single World Championship point. The Lotus-Judd was also disappointing and Nelson Piquet, a three-times World Champion, seemed to lack motivation. The Minardi-Cosworth moved into the limelight in the last races of the season when Pierluigi Martini demonstrated the superiority of Pirelli tyres in qualifying, though the race rubber was not up to Goodyear standards. All in all it had been a promising start to a new era of Grand Prix racing.

The Australian Grand Prix on the city circuit at Adelaide was run in continuous rain. The track was unusually smooth and there were numerous spins. However Thierry Boutsen in the new Williams FW13-Renault came through unscathed to claim his second win of the season.

Formula One Cars of 1989

Make/model	Chief designer Other engineers	Engine	Gearbox (number of gears)	Wheelbase	Track	Tyre make
AGS JH24	Claude Galopin	Cosworth DFR V8 90°	AGS (6)	2794	F 1803 R 1695	G
Arrows A 11	Ross Brawn James Robinson	Cosworth DFR V8 90°	Arrows (6) Q	2844	F 1803 R 1676	G
Benetton B 189	Rory Byrne	Ford V8 75°	Benetton VH (6)	2690	F 1816 R 1622	G
Brabham BT 58	Sergio Rinland John Baldwin	Judd CV V8 90°	Brabham (6)	2794	F 1803 R 1676	P
Coloni C 3	Christian Vanderpleyn Michel Costa	Cosworth DFR V8 90°	Coloni (6)	2800	F 1810 R 1660	P
Dallara BMS 189	Gianpaolo Dallara Mario Tolentino Alessandro Mariani	Cosworth DFR V8 90°	Dallara (6)	2858	F 1792 R 1676	P
EuroBrun ER 189	George Rayton Roberto Ori	Judd CV V8 90°	EuroBrun (6)	2905	F 1810 R 1688	P
Ferrari F1-89	John Barnard Giorgio Ascanelli Fabrizio Nardon	Ferrari 3500 V12 65°	Ferrari (7)	2880	F 1800 R 1600	G
Ligier JS 33	Ricardo Divila Michel Beaujon	Cosworth DFR V8 90°	Ligier-Hewland (6)	2850	F 1810 R 1698	G
Lola LC89	Gérard Ducarouge Chris Murphy	Lamborghini 3512 V12 80°	Lamborghini (6) Q	2850	F 1810 R 1620	G
Lotus 101	Frank Dernie Mike Coghlan	Judd CV V8 90°	Lotus (6)	2900	F 1800 R 1650	G
March CG 891	Adrian Newey Tim Holloway	Judd EV V8 76°	March (6) VH	2794	F 1778 R 1651	G
McLaren MP 4/5	Gordon Murray Steve Nichols Neil Oatley	Honda RA109E V10 72°	McLaren (6) Q	2896	F 1820 R 1670	G
Minardi M 189	Aldo Costa Nigel Copperthwaite Tommaso Carletti	Cosworth DFR V8 90°	Minardi (6)	2927	F 1800 R 1640	P
Onyx ORE1	Alan Jenkins Bernie Marcus	Cosworth DFR V8 90°	Onyx (6) Q	2819	F 1816 R 1676	G
Osella FA1-M89	Ántonio Tomaini Ignazio Lunetta	Cosworth DFR V8 90°	Osella-Hewland (6)	2850	F 1800 R 1680	P
Rial ARC 02	Bob Bell Stefan Faber	Cosworth DFR V8 90°	Rial (6)	2800	F 1800 R 1600	G
Tyrrell 018	Harvey Postlethwaite Jean-Claude Migeod	Cosworth DFR V8 90°	Tyrrell (6)	2920	F 1808 R 1670	G
Williams FW 12 C	Patrick Head Enrique Scalabroni	Renault RS1 V10 67°	Williams (6) Q	2997	F 1803 R 1600	G
Williams FW 13	Patrick Head Enrique Scalabroni	Renault RS 1 V10 67°	Williams (6) Q	2921	F 1803 R 1676	G
Zakspeed 891	Gustav Brunner Peter F. Wyss Nino Frison	Yamaha OX 88 V8 75°	Zakspeed (6)	2820	F 1800 R 1650	P

Monocoques: All cars were carbon/Kevlar constructions
Tyres: G = Goodyear; P = Pirelli
Dry Weight: The exact dry weight was not made public, but it was probably between 500 and 515kg for most of the cars.

Vanwall

ferrari

MASERATI

BENETTON FORMULA F1 TEAM

ALFA-ROMEO MILANO

BALLOT EB PARIS

osella

march

Ford

DUESENBERG

RAM AUTOMOTIVE

AUTO UNION

Cooper

FIAT

PIC

AUSTIN

STEYR

LIGIER

TAG turbo engines

minardi

TECNO

CHEVROLET

ZAKSPEED

uop shadow

HOTCHKISS · PARIS

LANCIA

Buick

ALFA ANONIMA LOMBARDA FABBRICA AUTOMOBILI TIPO N° MILANO

BRABHAM

SPA

OWEN ORGANISATION B.R.M

BMW

ASTON MARTIN

AUTOMOBILES TALBOT PARIS

ALTA